CATULLUS
Edited with a
Textual and Interpretative
Commentary by
D.F.S. Thomson

This work contains a major revision of Douglas Thomson's *Catullus: A Critical Edition* (1978), with the addition of a full commentary and a wholly new introduction. For the introduction and for each of the poems there is an extensive and current bibliography.

In the introduction, apart from sections on the life of Catullus, on the arrangement of the poems, and on their literary background, there is a lengthy discussion of the history of the text, as well as a review of the progress of Catullan studies from the *editio princeps* to the present day.

There are about seventy changes from the previous edition in the text of the poems. The critical apparatus has also been extensively revised. In addition, the Table of Manuscripts, which has come to be regarded as standard, has been updated without alteration to the numbering sequence.

Though this is not primarily intended as a 'school edition,' the commentary includes, in addition to critical judgments, translations and interpretations of words and phrases that may help to illuminate readings in the text.

Catullus offers readers a new text of the poems, with a commentary, a codicology of the manuscript tradition, and a thorough review of Catullus scholarship.

DOUGLAS F.S. THOMSON is Professor Emeritus of Classics, University of Toronto, and author of *Catullus: A Critical Edition.*

PHOENIX

Journal of the Classical Association of Canada
Revue de la Société canadienne des études classiques
Supplementary Volume XXXIV
Tome supplémentaire XXXIV

CATULLUS

Edited with a
Textual and Interpretative
Commentary by
D.F.S. Thomson

UNIVERSITY OF TORONTO PRESS

Toronto Buffalo London

National Library of Canada Cataloguing in Publication

Thomson, D.F.S. (Douglas Ferguson Scott), 1919–

Catullus / edited with a textual and interpretative commentary
by D.F.S. Thomson.

(Phoenix. Supplementary volume ; 34)
Includes bibliographical references and indexes.
ISBN 0-8020-0676-0 (bound).—ISBN 0-8020-8592-X (pbk.)

1. Catullus, Gaius Valerius – Criticism, Textual.
I. Catullus, Gaius Valerius   II. Title.
III. Series: Phoenix. Supplementary volume (Toronto, Ont.) ; 34.

PA6276.T5 1997   874'.01   C96-931284-9

University of Toronto Press acknowledges the financial assistance to its publishing
program of the Canada Council and the Ontario Arts Council.

This book has been published with the help of a grant from the Humanities and Social
Sciences Federation of Canada, using funds provided by the Social Sciences and
Humanities Research Council of Canada.

To my wife
ELEANOR

CONTENTS

Preface ix

INTRODUCTION 3
General: The Poet's Life, Works, and Literary Environment 3
Life and Chronology 3
The Arrangement of the Poems 6
The New Poets and the Alexandrians: Parallels and Influences 11
The History of the Text 22
Chronology of the Text 23
Excursus. Variant Readings in the Hand of R²: Suggested Origins 38
The Progress of Catullan Studies from the *Editio Princeps*
to the Present Day 43

BIBLIOGRAPHY 61
General 61
On the History of the Text 65

CHANGES FROM THE TEXT OF THE CRITICAL EDITION OF 1978 69

TABLE OF MANUSCRIPTS 72
Supplementary List (Short Fragments or Extracts) 89
'Ghost' Manuscripts 91

STEMMA CODICUM 93

SOURCES OF EMENDATIONS CITED IN THE *APPARATUS* 94

SIGLA 97

CATULLI VERONENSIS LIBER 99

COMMENTARY 195

INDEXES 557
Metres 559
First Lines 560
Names in the Text of Catullus 563
Renaissance and Modern Scholars and Writers 569

PREFACE

The text of Catullus offered here replaces my University of North Carolina Press edition of 1978, with the addition of a Commentary devoted in part to textual, in part to interpretative matters. In more than a few places, the object of the Commentary is to make clear the reasoning that lies behind the constitution of the text; it is, at all events, directed in some degree to those who are seriously interested in the textual side of Catullan studies. Especially in the Introduction and Apparatus Criticus, I have also sought to identify and discuss the readings of the fourteenth-century manuscripts and to ascertain the relations among them.

From what I have just written it will be clear that this book is not in the first place intended for the use of beginners, as a 'school edition.' Nevertheless, I have included in the commentary a certain number of observations, and renderings into English of words and phrases, that may appear rather too elementary for more advanced scholars. I have done this for two reasons. First, a translation of a word, or a comment on the meaning of a line or a phrase in the text, is sometimes a valuable instrument for the defence of the text itself. In the second place, for practical purposes it can scarcely be doubted that the graduate readers, at whom the work is primarily aimed, will themselves have students who may seek guidance of this sort; and to these students I hope the commentary may prove at least indirectly useful. Such notes, again, will often (perhaps usually) indicate my disagreement with versions or interpretations commonly adopted and presumed to be correct.

In the commentary, I have tried to do two things especially: first, to take account of all the more recent contributions of scholarship to Catullan studies, and secondly to notice points that are not made in the editions generally available in classical libraries, in particular those of Fordyce and Quinn. Where I found that a particular problem was most helpfully illuminated in editions long out of print, I have tried as a rule to give the gist of what they say. In general, I have not sought to reproduce the kind of detailed information – e.g., on the history of individual Latin words, or on Greek literary parallels – that was readily to be found elsewhere, except in cases where such information served the purpose of immediate understanding. On such topics as the two just mentioned, the editions of Kroll and Fordyce provide a great deal of information in an admirably concise form. Both of these, however, are out of date in textual matters, and my hope is that the present edition will in this respect, as well as by virtue of its more comprehensive and up-to-date bibliography, be held to fill a gap. Where manuscripts are concerned, recent codicological research has made it imperative to revise, in several places, what I published in 1978. In the interim, a number of emendations, suggested or revived by scholars of the present day, have found at least some degree of favour; and information has accumulated concerning some of the manuscripts in my Table. Full descriptions of forty-two manuscripts containing Catullus have been published in James L. Butrica, *The Manuscript Tradition of Propertius* (*Phoenix*, Supplementary Volume xvii, Toronto 1984); I have listed these in a new column in the Table. Above all, Dr David S. McKie of Cambridge has written a doctoral dissertation (*The Manuscripts of Catullus: Recension in a Closed Tradition*, Cambridge University dissertation, 1977) that supersedes a part of the introduction to my earlier edition; I am indebted to this fundamental study for correcting at many points the account I previously gave of the history and internal relationships of the cardinal Mss. Where – occasionally – I find myself unable to accept its conclusions, I have noted the fact in the Commentary.

One further function of the new commentary is to explain and defend, not only readings in the text (as I have suggested above) but also remarks made – in a necessarily abbreviated form – in the Apparatus Criticus. In this connection, the readings of m (the first manuscript to be copied from R) are no longer cited in full; to publish them once, in my 1978 edition, was an inescapable duty, since a proper collation was wanting, but m is after all a *codex descriptus* (see the Introduction, p. 35). Accordingly I have for the present edition decided not to give the readings of m except where these tell us something of interest or importance about m's exemplar, namely R as modified by R^2; in such cases, a note will usually be found in the Commentary. The readings of the second hand in G (G^2), which were imported into G from m, and scrupulously follow those of their parent manuscript, have been eliminated for a like reason.

Throughout the Introduction and Commentary, in writing of the poet I use the abbreviation C. unless this seems to involve possible ambiguity. To certain standard editions of Catullus I refer by initial:

B. = Baehrens
E. = Ellis
F. = Fordyce
Fr. = Friedrich
Kr. = Kroll
Q. = Quinn

For Fe. = Fedeli, see the intr. n. to poem 61.

The initial L., occasionally found in the Commentary, refers to my former tutor, R.G.C. Levens, to whose lectures I owe a great many suggestions, particularly on the subject of metre. The classification of metrical variations in poem 63, which appears in my introductory note, was devised by him.

The abbreviation *CE* refers to my critical edition of 1978. The name 'McKie' should be taken to refer to D.S. McKie's 1977 thesis (see above), unless another date is added. The names of journals are given, wherever possible, in the abbreviated forms employed in *L'Année Philologique*. Other abbreviations include the following:

OLD = Oxford Latin Dictionary
RE = Pauly-Wissowa, Real-Encyclopädie der kl. Altertumswissenschaft
TLL = Thesaurus Linguae Latinae
FLP = E. Courtney, Fragmentary Latin Poets

In the Table of Manuscripts, under the heading 'Designations,' I have removed the column allotted to Hale in *CE* and substituted the name of Butrica, since many of the manuscripts that contain Catullus are fully described in J.L. Butrica's *The Manuscript Tradition of Propertius*.

In order that the bibliographies to the poems, taken singly, may act as guides to the progress of research, with few exceptions their contents are limited to the books or articles devoted to the poem itself in each instance. They are arranged chronologically. The main Bibliography, on the other hand, is arranged alphabetically by authors' names. Readers of the Commentary who find a reference in short form may find it amplified in the bibliography to their poem; if not, it will be found in the main Bibliography.

Where a standard edition of Catullus, or of another author, is referred to, the editor's name is given without indication of date. So far as Catullus is concerned these dates may be found on pp. 43–60 of the Introduction. Again, wherever the Apparatus Criticus is referred to and an emendator's name is cited, the place and date of first publication will appear under 'Sources of Emendations' on pp. 94–6. Thirty-four bibliographical references to books or articles cited only once in the present edition have been left on its pages in order to avoid adding to the bulk (already too great) of the Bibliography.

Classical scholars are, one hopes, sufficiently familiar with this procedure to find these few interruptions to their reading not too troublesome in a work of some length.

Since the labours devoted to the present edition, and especially to the Commentary, have extended over many otherwise busy years, I am well aware of my cumulative debt, for advice and assistance, to persons and institutions over and above those named in my 1978 Preface, some of whom have continued to help me (and I beg them to accept this renewal of my thanks). Among newer obligations, I owe to Daphne Levens in particular two generous gifts: that of the volume in which Ellis inscribed his successive collations of *R*, and that consisting in two series of notes on which her late husband (and my tutor) R.G.C. Levens based his lectures on Catullus to undergraduates. I should also like to thank Professor Julia Haig Gaisser for advice on Catullan matters, and in particular for the privilege of early access to her major work *Catullus and His Renaissance Readers* (1993). Since the publication of *CE*, the Department of Classics of the University of North Carolina at Chapel Hill has kindly continued to allow me to consult, for checking purposes, the collations and other materials in its possession. In Canada, my work has been supported both by the Social Sciences and Humanities Research Council and by the University of Toronto. The Department of Classics at this University granted me sabbatical leave to continue it.

My thanks are due also to the Fondation Hardt, the Institute of Classical Studies of the University of London, the Nuffield Foundation, the Warden and Fellows of Merton College, the Warden and Fellows of Wadham College, and Professor George Forrest, for providing my studies with a base and for many acts of kindness.

Finally, on a more personal level, I wish to thank my son James for invaluable advice and assistance of a practical sort in matters connected with the operation of a computer; and, in the same field, I would record my thanks to Philippa M.W. Matheson for her judicious and outstandingly accurate work, and for dealing with some unusual problems in a spirit of unflagging helpfulness. To the editors of the University of Toronto Press I should like to say how much I appreciate their patience.

And once again to my wife I declare my gratitude for her never-failing support and encouragement.

D.F.S.T.
Toronto

Catullus

INTRODUCTION

General: The Poet's Life, Works, and Literary Environment

Life and Chronology

The external evidence we possess for the life of Catullus can be summarized in a very few words. Jerome, in his supplement to Eusebius' *Chronica*, offers in effect three pieces of information:

(i) C. was born at Verona in 87 BC (*Abr. ann.* 1930; Ol. 173.2; 150 H);

(ii) C. died aged 30; see (iii);

(iii) C. died in Rome aged 30 (or in his thirtieth year, if we take Jerome's 'XXX aetatis anno' [*Abr. ann.* 1959; Ol. 180.3; 154 H] literally; but see Sumner 1971: 261, on 'the common tendency (*sc.* of Romans) to blur the difference' between 'the 30th year' and '30 years old.' As he remarks, 'there can be no precision.'

Not more than one of these three can be correct. We know from internal references in C.'s poems that he was still alive in 55 (poem 113, the second consulship of Pompey; 55.6, the *porticus Pompei*), and fairly certainly in 54 (references to Britain and Syria in poems 11, 45, 84); as for poem 29, Rambaud 1980 has shown that this could not have been written before the end of 53. Jerome derived his information from Suetonius, *De poetis*. 'To judge by the surviving life of Terence (in that work), it is quite possible that Suetonius gave C.'s age when he died, but not the dates of either birth or death; in that case, Jerome will probably have put the death notice at what seemed to him an appropriate place, and counted back for the date of birth' (Wiseman 1985: 190; he adds in a footnote: 'Cf. Helm . . . following B. Schmidt . . . for the suggestion that Suetonius' notice of C.'s death immediately followed that of his reconciliation with Caesar in Gaul [Suet.

Iul. 73], and that Jerome therefore chose the first year of Caesar's Gallic command as the peg on which to hang C.'s dates'). Since C.'s death need not, and perhaps should not, be supposed to have occurred immediately after the last datable reference in his poems, and yet obviously some weight must be attached to his failure to mention any events after 53 or so, it would be reasonable to adopt the dates (82–52) first proposed by B. Schmidt 1914: 267–8 (though with a faulty argument, as noted by Granarolo 1982: 27–8, who himself adopts the same dates), and later, by Plessis 1909 and subsequently by Herzog 1936 – at least for the date of death – and by Marmorale 1952.

There is at least one more good reason to choose these dates. From the poems it is clear that, of all the friends of his youth, C. was closest to his fellow-poet Calvus; he speaks of him in all respects as an equal, and (we may fairly say) an age-fellow, without awe or patronage; later writers link their names together, and Ovid (*Amores* 3.9.62) implies that both died young, thus tending to confirm Jerome's point (iii) above. It is extremely unlikely that there was more than a year or so between them in difference of age, if indeed there was as much as that. Now, we know from the elder Pliny (*NH* 7.165) that Calvus was born on 28 May, 82 BC; the birth-date of Catullus must surely be sought at no great distance from this year at any rate.

Further, the manuscripts tell us (see, however, my text and apparatus criticus) that at 12.9 Asinius Pollio is called *puer*. Even if we doubt the reliability of the two principal witnesses to the birth-date of Pollio (traditionally 76), namely Tacitus and Jerome, we can still add the testimony of the elder Seneca and Quintilian and 'rest content' (Sumner 1971: 261) with 77/76/75. If we accept 76 *exempli gratia*, Catullus must be old enough at the time of writing poem 12 to refer to Pollio a little condescendingly as *puer*, but still not old enough to sit at the tables of much older persons instead; so far as this slight argument goes, we may guess that six years of seniority in age would not be too disparate.

There is only one further externally attested fact: the reconciliation between Julius Caesar and C.'s family, mentioned above (on the first page of this Introduction) and recorded by Suetonius in the following words (*Iulius* 73): *Valerium Catullum, a quo sibi versiculis de Mamurra perpetua stigmata imposita non dissimulaverat, satis facientem eadem die adhibuit cenae hospitioque patris eius, sicut consuerat, uti perseveravit.* The phrasing implies a certain interval between the time of composition of the offending verses and the day of forgiveness. Mamurra must at the time have been in Caesar's service (and occupying high rank there) for some years, while Caesar himself must have been sojourning, or wintering, in Cisalpine Gaul. This narrows the possible dates to late 55 – early 52 BC.

Although, as we have seen, Jerome's birth-date for C. is wrong, the *place* of the poet's birth, given in the same statement – see (i) above – is independently attested by Ovid (*Amores* 3.15.7) and Martial (14.195), quite apart from the evidence of the poems of C. themselves (poems 35, 68, 100, and especially *Veronae ... meae* at 67.34). Although the gentile name Valerius occurs frequently in Veronese inscriptions (it is not in itself Transpadane but originates rather in south-central Italy), it is interesting to observe that it is not there found in combination with the cognomen Catullus; at Brixia, however (which C., uniquely, claims in poem 67 as the 'mother city' of his native Verona), there are a number of inscriptions recording Valerii Catulli, who seem to have been domiciled there. Since Verona possessed only the *ius Latii* until 49 BC, those who in the time of C.'s boyhood exercised the rights of Roman citizens there – as did C. and his father, who must have been *equites* (C. required both citizenship and equestrian status in order to serve as he did on the staff of a provincial governor; see below) – will have acquired Roman citizenship either (a) by individual grant, or (b) elsewhere before settling in Verona.

It is possible to say with confidence that C. served in Bithynia, during the year 57–6, under Memmius as propraetor; but this is really no more than an inference from C. himself (28.7-9, where he refers to ill-usage under Memmius as *meus praetor*, taken together with poems 10, 31, and 46, where he speaks of having been in Bithynia), added to the known fact that Memmius was praetor in 58, from which we may guess that he probably went on to govern some province in the office of propraetor – Bithynia would be suitable – though in fact the records do not inform us either that he did so, or (if he did) where his province was.

One other *testimonium* is generally included, and rightly so, among the external evidence for C.'s life: the real name of 'Lesbia,' the woman addressed or mentioned in about twenty-six poems (listed in the Introduction to Quinn's edition, p. xvi) was Clodia, according to Apuleius (*Apol.* 10). If this is correct – and there is no reason to doubt it – then the most likely candidate for identification as 'Lesbia' will be one or another of the three sisters, all known as Clodia (or Claudia), of P. Clodius Pulcher, especially since in poem 79 (*Lesbius est pulcer ...*) C. accuses 'Lesbius' (that is, on this identification, Clodius) implicitly of incest with his sister, playing on the word *pulcer* as he does so; cf. Cicero, *Pro Caelio* for the accusation, and certain passages of the letters (*Ad Att.* 1.16.10 *surgit pulcellus puer*; 2.1.4; 2.22.1) for the word-play. Historically, it may be that the charge of incest attached itself in particular to the youngest of the three sisters and was by Cicero transferred by insinuation to the second sister Clodia Metelli, as one of a battery of arguments directed towards representing Cicero's client Caelius as the victim of a wicked and scheming woman. The case for the traditionally preferred identification of 'Lesbia' with Clodia Metelli is certainly not proved; scholars now admit that the youngest sister will fit the few known facts just as well, provided that the spelling *Clodia*, for *Claudia*, can properly be applied to both of them (and here too there is disagreement). It must be said, however, that since the *Pro Caelio* was a famous and familiar speech the simple mention of 'Clodia' in later literary circles is more likely to have conjured up Clodia Metelli than any other. Moreover, it is clear from 68.145–6 (cf. 83.1–2) that C. paid court to Lesbia when she was still married (to translate *vir* as *amant en titre* makes the story of C.'s courtship improbable). Here chronology enters: the wife of Lucullus was divorced in 66, the wife of Metellus widowed in 59; this makes the wife of Metellus the better candidate unless we suppose (as Professor Wiseman does) that the word *vir* is to be understood as signifying the husband in a second marriage, of which in neither case is there the slightest evidence. For both of these reasons the traditional identification of 'Lesbia' as Clodia Metelli, though it is entirely right that it should be questioned rigorously, as Wiseman has done, should still be held to possess, on its merits, a little extra weight.

The Arrangement of the Poems

In recent times, and particularly in the last two decades or so, the question whether C. himself arranged the collection in the order in which we have it has become one of the liveliest issues in Catullan studies, particularly since (in *Catullan Questions* [1969]) Professor T.P. Wiseman espoused, and defended in subsequent books and articles, the view that C. did so, and (further) that the placing of the poems, and cross-references between them, were intended by the poet to be perceived by the reader as having, throughout the corpus, additional poetic significance beyond that conveyed by the poems themselves taken singly. It would take too much space to rehearse the debate here, but in a carefully selected bibliography (below, pp. 61–5) I have tried to indicate where it can best be followed. Perhaps the first thoroughgoing exposition of the theory of an intentionally integrated pattern of this kind was made in B. Heck's Tübingen dissertation of 1951, 'Die Anordnung der Gedichte des C. Valerius Catullus.' To those who have studied this ninety-two-page dissertation, with its diagrams, it has often seemed that the argument for a planned order, confidently expressed in the section dealing with the first part of the collection, faltered more and more as it approached the end of the *liber Catulli*. Modern arguments, of the same general sort, have tended to induce in those who follow them a similar feeling of *decrescendo*. All the same, who has not been struck, independently, by the tight coherence and pleasing balance of the first few poems when they are read together? This surely must be C.'s doing.

In the book referred to above, which gained wide attention, Professor Wiseman argued for a three-part division of the collection as published by Catullus, originally in three rolls, *tribus cartis* (= *voluminibus*), like Nepos' work alluded to in poem 1, though he frankly admitted that the parts (poems 1–60, 61–8, 69–116) would be very unequal in numbers of lines per *volumen*. Ten years later, in *Clio's Cosmetics* (1979b), chapter 12 (see especially p. 175 n. 3), he revised this opinion, substituting a division as follows (as suggested by Quinn): poems 1–60 (total, 848 lines), 61–4 (total, 795 lines), and 65–116 (total, 646 lines). He is to some extent influenced here by Macleod 1973, an article with a cyclic view of 65–116 and emphasis on the references to *Battiades* in poems 65 and 116 as a link between the beginning and the end of the last section (assuming the inclusion of poem 116 as an integral part of the collection; in 1969 he had regarded it as an extraneous addition). His argument that the appearance of the Muses in poems 1, 61, and 65 makes all three poems programmatic seems to me of little weight (see Wiseman 1979b: 177), but there are much stronger arguments in favour of his 1979 position (which he adopts also in *Catullus and His World* [1985]). These arguments, which I do not remember him using at all in defence of that position, are two in number, and they are both drawn from another area altogether, namely the history of manuscripts.

It was B.L. Ullman (1955: 103 n. 2) who first drew attention to the fact that '<Ms> O begins poem 65 and all subsequent poems with an illuminated initial and capitalized second letter in line with the initial letters of the following verses. This distinctive form may reflect a separate manuscript tradition for poems 65–116.' (Hubbard 1983: 220 n. 8, quotes this observation with approval.) An analogous change in style is noted by McKie (see Preface) at the beginning of poem 61. In his discussion of the titles in the manuscripts, he observes that in spite of the fact that in *O* the last of the short poems, poem 60, ends five lines above the bottom of folio 14ᵛ, the scribe begins poem 61 at the top of the next page, contrary to his usual practice; he, too, cites Ullman 1955: 99 in support of the view that this represents 'a survival perhaps of the ancient division of Catullus' work into *libelli*.' More recently, Giuseppe Billanovich has pointed out (1988: 38) that in an annotated manuscript of Terence, British Library Harl. 2525, on fol. 11ʳ, a line from Catullus (52.1), is quoted as being *prope finem primi operis*. The note in question is linked by Billanovich with Petrarch. This too would then imply that by the first half of the fourteenth century, and perhaps for very long before that, the codices of Catullus showed the results of descent in three parts; and some of the evidence points to the possibility that these parts were originally published separately and for a time travelled in separate streams. The words *prope finem primi operis* would most naturally be taken to confirm the idea, already reached on different grounds, that the first section contained poems 1–60. Since, as many scholars have noted, the final group of these 'polymetric' poems contains several short effusions that are clearly unfinished, experimental, or rejected drafts (see for example poem 58[b], in comparison with poem 55), or even (as some suggest) short scraps found among the poet's papers, all this evidence, taken together, seems to point away from the conclusion that C. himself deliberately assembled or planned a *Gesamtausgabe* in the form in which we have it.

A question which Wiseman does not raise is why, if C. himself carefully isolated the short epigrams in elegiac metre at the end of the collection (poems 69–116), neither Martial (that close follower and imitator of Catullus' shorter poems) nor Statius in his *Silvae*, nor (so far as we are aware) the author of any similarly varied corpus of verse, seems to have thought of doing the same. Another kind of reservation, which I at least entertain, applies to the arguments used by Professor Wiseman to show that the first section (poems 1–60) is divided into subsections (poems 15–26, 28–60) of differing character, clearly announced and described in advance by the 'programmatic' poems 14[b] and 27. Others have objected to the supposition that the poems in these subsections exhibit a peculiar or consistent character; my doubt concerns Wiseman's interpretation of the poems that are said to introduce them. Let us examine poem 14[b] first. Wiseman 1969: 7 writes: 'Why should C.'s readers *shrink* [his italics] from touching his book? The language seems too strong for mere modest deprecation. However, when we consider that the cycle of poems on Aurelius, Furius and Juventius begins immediately afterwards, it becomes intelligible as part of a warning to the reader that poems of an avowedly homosexual nature follow.' But surely this is to dismiss too lightly a much less colourful meaning of *horrere* – amounting to little more than 'hesitate' or 'be unwilling' – attested in passages such as the following:

Plin. *NH.* 8.169 asinae horrent vel pedes ... tinguere

Livy 10.10.11 imminui agrum ... accolas sibi quisque adiungere ... homines horrebat

Iuvenc. 4. 809 sacri sibi nominis horret imponi pondus Constantinus.
For *abhorrere* we may cite Plin. *Ep.* 1.2.5 *ab editione non abhorrere*, which .has been translated, quite properly, 'not averse to publishing' (see the reference in the n. on 14[b].3). On an impartial view of the evidence, is it not more in line with the probable intention of this admittedly fragmentary poem to vote for 'modest deprecation' after all? In any event, the suggestion

that the poet utters a warning of something dire to follow appears to fall short of proof.

As for poem 27, Wiseman finds this poem 'apparently pointless' if it relates to a drinking party. He goes on to add: 'It also contains a difficulty which has never been satisfactorily explained: why should the slave pour out bitterer wine?' Consequently, he maintains, the poem is really about *invective*. Now, it cannot be denied that of the following group of poems, if group it be (28–60), a substantial number – a bare majority, perhaps – contain serious invective; but is the percentage sufficient to justify a programmatic announcement of a change to 'the real savage stuff,' as Wiseman puts it? A rapid calculation may find here about seventeen poems, at most, which can truly be described as consisting of 'savage' invective, against sixteen or so which do not seem to fit this description. But the preceding group (15–26) consists entirely, unless I am mistaken, of what would appear to be invective by the same definition; thus the reader can hardly be said to have to face a new group of a startlingly different kind. Finally, if we look at the elegiac epigrams (69–116) placed at the end of the collection, we find that there the proportion of invective to non-invective is about thirty-four to fourteen or fifteen. The character of poems 28 to 60 seems, in this respect, hardly unique.

At this point let us look back at the poem itself, and see what it says. Clearly Catullus uses *amariores* at any rate *as though* it meant *meraciores* (which, by the way, is the actual reading proposed by Sabellicus in his *Ex Catullo*, a set of notes added to his *Annotationes in Plinium et alios auctores*, 1497, p. 10, where it is printed as *meratiores*; for the text see Gaisser 1993: 300 n. 95). Scaliger, for his part, glossed *amariores* as *meraciores* – perhaps independently, rather than following Sabellicus. From the drift of our poem it is reasonable to conclude that the point lies in the strength of the wine, in some sense, rather than its sweetness or bitterness – unless one has already made up one's mind that 'bitterness' *must* be what the poet intends. But there is nothing to force this conclusion, and much to the contrary, especially in view of the fact that the exclusion of water, desiderated in the second and concluding part of the poem, also points in the direction of 'strength.' Much more remains to be said on this point; for a longer discussion, see the note on 27.3 below.

To sum up: the debate on the question whether C. arranged and published the collection of poems as we have it is still open; but the general conclusion that there are three sections, divided at 61.1 and 65.1, is reasonable. Originally these may have been issued in three rolls; their length would be suitable for this. They may even have borne the labels *hendecasyllabi*, *epithalamium* (referring in the first instance to poem 61, where the heading *epithalamus* appears in the Mss), and *epigrammata*, after the first-occurring metre in each: we never hear of 'Catullus, Book 1' in antiquity, but we do hear of *Catullus in hendecasyllabis, Catullus in epithalamio* (though in relation to a poem, 62, which is itself *not* an epithalamium, so that the support of a certain kind of proof is wanting). What is hard to believe is that Catullus, who clearly intended to plan his book (as suggested above), ever came to the end of laying it out; poem 58[b], for instance, looks very like the pieces of a rough unfinished draft – discontinued perhaps – especially when we see it in the company of poem 55. As all are agreed, our poet died very young; and as most agree, his poetic career was extremely brief. Whether at the end of it he had time enough to put together a *Gesamtausgabe*, is an open question, of an essentially historical, rather than literary, kind.

The social, literary, and economic background of the poet's life, taking especial note of his Veronese origin, requires at least some brief comments before we proceed further.

From the third century BC onwards, the writers of Latin verse – even those who were not Greeks, or Greek-speaking Italians, themselves – were deeply aware of what was going on in the world of Greek letters under Alexander the Great and in the kingdoms of his successors. Those cultural contacts were reinforced by commercial relations, especially with the richest of the lands and cities of the eastern Mediterranean: Antioch, Pergamum, and above all Egypt, which under the first three Ptolemies, and with the absorption of Cyrene, emerged as by far the wealthiest and most settled realm of them all. But the attraction felt in many parts of Italy, particularly those accessible to trade, for this apparatus of prosperity, was not merely cultural but reflected their own new wealth and aspirations. It was not surprising if the enterprising inhabitants of Cisalpine Gaul acquired the habit of making business arrangements with – roughly speaking – the whole Eastern world that many centuries later was to become virtually the private domain of Venice.[1] Their prosperity and self-assurance were based securely on the produce of their own highly fertile plains, linked together by a navigable river and easy land communications, while for the exporting of that produce they had at hand the Adriatic shipping route: short of harbours, indeed, but possessing at least a few useful ports, such as Ancona and Brundisium, on the Italian side. In return, it was easy for citizens of the Greek east – now politically unified and delivered from the internecine war of city against city – to make their way, often in the role of teachers who bore their literary culture with them, to the flourishing towns of Cispadane and Transpadane

---

1 Wiseman 1985: 110: 'The *Transpadani* had wide horizons'; see pages 107–11 for an expansion of this remark, and especially for the economic background.

Gaul. Among these last Verona stood out as easily the leader by the time of Catullus; this was partly because of its geographical situation, since it lay at the point of intersection of one trade route from the north with another (and the most important of all) that ran from west to east and vice versa. Citizen rights, beginning with the *ius Latii* in 89, were granted, by stages, to all these places during the first century BC. As a result, and because of the highly visible prosperity enjoyed by the inhabitants of the Province, Roman citizens from more southerly parts (C.'s family among them, in all likelihood) settled in Verona and neighbouring cities, in pursuit of trade as well as of military or administrative careers. Naturally, such immigrant families[2] looked in two ways at once: to the north, for the vast opportunities of wealth and comfort it offered, but also to their roots in the south, and particularly to Rome, as the source of coveted honours, of *nobilitas*, and of a more varied and sophisticated social life – especially for young people who craved to be 'in the fashion' – than could be secured in what must inevitably have been regarded, by those with an eye to the glitter of a metropolis, as still essentially a 'provincial' sphere of existence despite the excellence of its schools under Greek teachers. Thus the potent literary culture, originating within the Hellenistic sphere, approached the capital city not only from the south, that is to say from the direction of the Greek settlements of Magna Graecia – as in the time of Ennius – but also from Gallia Cisalpina, where an abundance of natural talent (if we may judge from the numbers of distinguished authors produced there) lay ready for awakening stimuli from the East.

The New Poets and the Alexandrians: Parallels and Influences

Alexandrianism: The Original Impetus

The poetic movement designated by the name of Alexandrianism is centred on the city of Alexandria during the reign of the first three rulers belonging to the Ptolemaic dynasty, and on the famous Library, which was a university in all important respects. Both the library and the service of the royal court were nurseries of poets. If we concentrate attention on those poets who were destined to influence Catullus and his contemporaries, the movement itself may be said to have begun with Philetas of Cos. Philetas (the spelling Philitas seems to be favoured at Cos itself, where it appears on inscriptions) may, indeed, be regarded as the father of an Alexandrian drive towards a more subtle kind of poetry. His dates are earlier, by a generation or so, than those of his successor Callimachus. He flourished as poet and educator

2 Wiseman 1985: 108–9.

in the reign of Ptolemy I, and became the tutor of the future Ptolemy II. His pupils included Theocritus, as well as the Librarian (and renowned literary critic) Zenodotus, and also the poet Hermesianax. He himself was described as ποιητὴς ἅμα καὶ κριτικός. It seems that Callimachus had an immense respect for his forerunner Philetas; at any rate, he appears to praise him warmly in the fragmentary prologue to the second edition of the *Aetia* (lines 9–10, with the *Scholia Florentina*). Propertius places him on a pedestal, together with Callimachus, as a founder of elegy (2.34.31; 3.1.1; 3.9.43–4), and Catullus himself surely draws an idea from him at 3.12 (where see the note in the Commentary). In language, Philetas was distinguished for his frequent use of rare vocabulary taken from old poems. His desire to avoid the obvious and the familiar led him to introduce a certain amount of rococo ornamentation in his narratives, and made his compositions obscure, yet highly interesting. These characteristics were passed down to the next generation of Alexandrian poets, along with two other important traits: a taste for mythology, especially that which was clothed in unusual versions of a story, and the ceaseless quest for stylistic and metrical variety. His oeuvre included a hexameter 'epyllion' or short epic,[3] entitled *Hermes*; also a short narrative elegy on Demeter, and a collection of παίγνια (the equivalent Latin term would be *lusus*) which Stobaeus seems to distinguish from his ἐπιγράμματα, though both were evidently written in the same elegiac metre, so far as we may judge from the few surviving fragments.

Callimachus, in a later reign, exhibits the same dominant interests. In him, as in Philetas, the search for perfect artistry, based on minute attention to detail and the total rejection of the 'thunderous' effects that went with attempts – still made by some in his day, Apollonius Rhodius for example – to rival Homer, were the foundations of a new kind of poetry that was destined to revive the capacity for genuinely original creation. Callimachus had a strong preference for shorter as opposed to more extended literary forms. He did not, however, avoid altogether the art of mythological narrative; but (and here too he trod on new ground) he treated myths as vehicles for the depiction of emotional subtleties, and for the display of recondite learning, especially in offering unfamiliar and entertaining versions of the myths themselves. Because of the latter tendency he has often been rebuked as a 'poet of the study,' a description which in its very nature appeared to deprive his work of all force and freshness. This was especially so in the nineteenth century and for a short time afterwards, when a romantic view of the poet's function prevailed. Yet it remains true that it was this same poetry,

---

3 The term 'epyllion,' in this sense, is modern; but the genre itself was greatly favoured by the Alexandrians, who first brought it to prominence.

rooted in learning, that revivified the entire literary art. The excitement generated by a feeling of altogether new possibilities, in that place and at that particular time in history, is palpable. Its rejections, as well as its assertions, were to be faithfully echoed, much later, in a Roman setting. When we read Callimachus' declaration βροντᾶν οὐκ ἐμόν, ἀλλὰ Διός (*Aetia* 1. 20) we think of Propertius 2.1.39–40 *sed neque Phlegraeos Iovis Enceladique tumultus / intonet augusto pectore Callimachus* and 2.34.32 *non inflati somnia Callimachi*. If Propertius later went so far as to refer to himself as the 'Roman Callimachus' (4.1.64), Catullus, who never does so, at the very least is thoroughly permeated with Callimachean influence; this I hope to show, both in the Introduction and also in the Commentary.

A third figure of the movement, who also made a strong impression on the Italian poets, was Euphorion of Chalcis, a follower of Callimachus in most (though, as we shall see, not all) respects. He had a reputation, which was to be inherited by his Latin imitators, for excessive obscurity. His most frequently discussed work was an epyllion called *Thrax*; here, the poet's attitude to the art of narrative seems to have been overtly anti-Homeric. Unlike Callimachus, Euphorion evidently rejected the entire Homeric tradition, whereas Callimachus had condemned, not Homer himself – whose supremacy in his own domain he recognized – but the feebleness of Homer's imitators, above all Antimachus, in attempting something that no reasonable author could any longer contemplate. On page xx of the introduction to Fordyce's Catullus, it is pronounced that 'the poetry of Alexandria … was a literature of exhaustion.' Presently it will be clear that I find this verdict overstated; still, few would deny the justice of its application to Antimachus. In Catullus, poem 95, Antimachus stands for the whole class of writers of dull and lengthy conventional epics; regrettably – from C.'s point of view – these still found readers in his own time.

The Reincarnation of Alexandrianism in Italy
Roman literature – or at least the literature of the central tradition, which continued to develop from generation to generation – was almost from its beginnings thoroughly impregnated with Greek influence. This was true to some extent even in prose; notwithstanding the fact that prose was the medium of indigenous Roman institutions – of the law, of the forum, of administration and all public and indeed private business – in its more artistic forms it looked to Greek writers on rhetoric for guidance. Much more was this true of poetry (including drama, which hardly concerns us here). For poets in search of a genre (so to speak), the prestige of Homer, enhanced as it was by the scholarly activities of the Alexandrian commentators based on the Library, ensured that down the centuries the mythical epic maintained

a grip that was never quite loosened. (Conversely, the feeling that one must break away from this is what underlies poetic 'revolutions' in both literatures.) At the same time, the Greek verse forms themselves – not only the Homeric hexameter but its offshoot, the universal and omnipresent elegiac couplet, to take only two examples – swept native Italian metres into deep obscurity. Ennius, as a pioneer in the use of Latin 'heroic' hexameters and also of the elegiac, had a considerable effect on his successors, in both metre and style, however much they rejected his typically 'Homeric' choice of subject. And Ennius was, of course, perfectly aware of the work of Greek fellow-poets, such as Callimachus, whose outlook differed widely from his own.[4] After him, however, there was a great hiatus in the making of poetry at Rome. In the latter part of the second century BC, we become aware of a very different phenomenon. Amateur poets, of indifferent levels of talent (Lutatius Catulus, for instance), set themselves to imitate – not, strictly speaking, to translate – Hellenistic poetry. But the originals on which they focused were not the best. They consisted, for the most part, of a body of decadent erotic epigram in a late and weak stage of the development of that genre, composed in their own time or shortly before it. They regarded their own activities in this field as an elegant accomplishment for their hours of leisure, with no passionate commitment to any search for literary fame or eagerness to express some kind of poetic truth. Cicero in due course inherited their mantle of amateurism: though his metrical technique was respectable, and his translations often deft enough, none of his poems rises above the level of the merely decorative at best. (Still later, the younger Pliny and his friends indulged in poetic composition in just the same spirit.)

About the beginning of the first century, Laevius and a few others wrote attractive Latin verses in a great variety of metres, including the hendecasyllable (named 'Phalaecian' after a minor Greek poet who in his turn had adopted the metre from older lyric and developed its use). These short compositions were written in a Hellenistic vein, but they altogether lack the power of the school of Alexandria. So far as Italy was concerned it was only with the arrival of a Greek, Parthenius of Nicaea, that the situation altered from one of desultory interest to one of excitement. The motive of these fresh stirrings lay in emulating the best creations of those among the Alexandrian poets who were already recognized as masters of the art, Callimachus above all. What Parthenius had to offer this generation of Roman youth no longer consisted in the effusions of Callimachus' followers at one or two removes, but in the works of Callimachus himself, together with those of his predecessor Philetas, and (a less worthy model for imitation,

4 For Ennius and Callimachus, see the references given in Crowther 1971: n. 3.

it must be admitted) of his pupil Euphorion. It was, apparently, Parthenius'
influence on Catullus' friend Cinna that was decisive, as I hope to show;
and Cinna, in due course, emerged clearly as the leader of the 'neoteric,' or
modern, movement in Rome.

From various passages in Cicero (especially *Ad Att.* 7.2.1) we hear of a
group (to use the word in a broad sense) of poets in Rome: not, strictly
speaking, Roman poets, since many of them, including Catullus himself,
originally came from Cisalpine Gaul. Reasons for this have already been
suggested (see above, pp. 10–11). All of them were apparently younger
than Cicero. In a literary, if not a political, context they were considered
as having somewhat revolutionary tendencies; so much is implied in the
way Cicero uses the expression οἱ νεώτεροι in referring to them. They were
enthusiastic followers of the Hellenistic Greek, or (in a wider, as well as a
narrower, sense) 'Alexandrian,' poets and epigrammatists, and particularly
of Callimachus. Euphorion, whom Cicero elsewhere mentions in connection
with the same kind of literary manifestation at a slightly later date, and
Rhianus (about whom very little is at present known) also seem to have
been favourites of the 'neoterics' or 'poetae novi' as they were variously
called. (For a full discussion of these terms, see Crowther 1970.)

It is universally agreed (and agreement reaches back to Ovid's time) that
both Catullus and his age-fellow and close friend Calvus (they are always
linked together) were among the most distinguished leaders of this 'neoteric'
movement. But there were others, more than a handful of whom would
have had to be reckoned with if their works had survived (Calvus himself
has come down to us in no more than a few short fragments). From our
standpoint, most of these poets are shadowy indeed.[5] It is nevertheless
important for us to try to ascertain who among them exercised the kind of
influence that determined the way in which Catullus himself would develop
his genius. In this light, two names are usually considered to be especially
prominent: Publius Valerius Cato and Gaius Helvius Cinna. Both were born
about 90 BC: that is, they were some nine years older than Catullus, if the
birth-date suggested for him above is accepted. In view of C.'s evidently
short literary life it is somewhat interesting (but it may be no more than
a coincidence) that in poem 95 he hails the emergence of Cinna's poem
Zmyrna after exactly nine years of labour. If Cinna had been in Bithynia in
66–5, as the *Suda* (s.v. *Parthenius*) relates, then it is legitimate to speculate
that he might have provided Catullus both with the notion of going to that
province in particular, and with 'contacts' there once he had been appointed
to the staff of its governor.

5 See Bardon 1952: passim.

The name of Valerius Cato, the grammarian and critic, is often linked with the neoteric movement, of which he is claimed to have been in some sense the founder. This view has been attacked, on grounds of date, by Professor Wiseman, who seeks to undermine Cato's alleged priority by the following argument:[6]

It always used to be assumed that Valerius Cato was the leader of the new 'neoteric school,' and the idea has unfortunately survived despite refutation. It rests on Furius Bibaculus' reference to Cato 'making' poets, with the anachronistic idea that he did so as an influential critic ... But according to Suetonius, who quotes Furius' lines, Cato had a high reputation as a *teacher*, especially of boys with poetic talent. . . He 'made' poets in the schoolroom, and ... the boys he steered to poetry were younger than the generation of Cinna and Catullus.

Hence Professor Wiseman draws the inference that the actual influence of Cato came too late for him to be fittingly named as the pioneer of the neoteric movement.

While I would agree that he did not fill the leading role, it is not for this reason. The words of Bibaculus are these:

> Cato grammaticus, Latina siren,
> Qui solus legit ac facit poetas.[7]

My reservation concerns the verbs in the second line. Terzaghi has suggested[8] (and I am inclined to agree with him) that they ought to be taken very closely together, *solus* being applied to both of them at once; the corollary is that the *poetae* who are the object of *legit* are the same persons as the *poetae* who are the object of *facit*. It is awkward to suppose that what Bibaculus meant to say was this: 'He, and he alone, reads [pedagogically, we must suppose] some poets – i.e., the texts used in the classroom; and he alone (likewise) 'makes' some poets – i.e., the boys.' Rather, if we bring *legit-ac-facit* together, we may find it easier to interpret *facit* in the less usual sense (much less common, admittedly, where there is no 'genitive of value' in the context) of 'judges, evaluates.' (In the Bobiensian scholia on Cicero, *Pro Sestio* 124, the phrase *cuius et originem et causam nominis ... me fecisse commemini* seems to yield this meaning: see Terzaghi 1938 for

---

6 Wiseman 1974: 53.
7 Fragment 6 *FLP* = 17 M (dubium); Wiseman 1974: 53 n. 53.
8 See Terzaghi 1938.

this and other illustrative passages.) Cato will then not have to be said to 'make' poets but rather to be esteemed for his sagacity in making literary assessments, such as those we may find, at about the same period of history, in a letter of Cicero's (*Ad Quint. Fratrem* 2.9.3) concerning Lucretius, and of course in poem 35, where a friend of Catullus has some criticisms to offer, by way of Catullus himself, to another aspiring poet. If this is so, the recipients of Cato's advice need not be mere boys in the classroom, and can instead be regarded as age-fellows of Cinna, or of Catullus, after all. In any case, even if one hesitates to attribute a rarer sense to *facere* here, it must be further observed that, in another epigram on Cato, Bibaculus remarks:

> Mirati sumus optimum magistrum,
> summum grammaticum, optimum poetam,
> omnes solvere posse quaestiones,
> unum deficere expedire nomen.
> En cor Zenodoti, en iecur Cratetis!

Here we have an apparent distinction and division between three separate functions: *magister*, *grammaticus*, and finally *poeta*. Moreover, the name of Cato, with which the poem begins, is placed on the level of the famous Greek literary critics, with whom the poem ends. And the tone throughout, as in a third epigram on Cato (fr. 2 M, *FLP*) beginning *Si quis forte mei domum Catonis* . . . , is that of a friend and associate, rather than a pupil.

We have, then, a picture of Cato – not as 'trail-breaker,' perhaps, but as an esteemed literary critic and a popular member of the neoteric coterie to which Catullus belonged; poem 56 is most likely to have been addressed to him. Both Cinna and Cato wrote miniature epics ('Epyllia,' as we have come to call them). If these two men were slightly older members of Catullus' circle, whom he particularly admired, we may guess that some prompting or desire to emulate his friends' success in that genre may have come to him from one or both of them, inspiring him to venture on a long poem, the *Peleus and Thetis* (poem 64).

To Cinna we may now turn; he was not only an extremely close friend and associate of Catullus, but also – and this was of the greatest importance – a fellow-Transpadane, hailing from Brixia, a neighbouring city to Catullus' Verona. What is particularly noticeable is the prominence especially bestowed by Catullus on a single poem by Cinna, the *Zmyrna*, an epyllion based on a bizarre theme of incestuous love. (It is possible, indeed likely, that the subject was suggested to Cinna by Parthenius, who actually dedicated to another pupil – Gallus – his ἐρωτικὰ παθήματα, a collection of unusual love-stories from myth.)[9] Catullus appears to hold this work up for the admiration of his friends, as a model of all that poetry should be. If we look at his own masterwork, for it is probable that he so regarded it, namely poem 64, the *Peleus and Thetis*, it is significant that this itself belongs to the genre of the epyllion (and, as such, was destined to be closely studied and sometimes echoed by Virgil among others). Cinna's *Zmyrna*, then, inspired the whole circle of the 'New Poets' by example, just as Cinna himself inspired them by the counsel which he, as a doyen of letters, must be supposed to have offered to his younger fellow-artists; counsel which he had in turn received from Parthenius. The essence of the Callimachean (and Euphorionic) doctrine which both Parthenius and Cinna preached lay in the emphasis they placed on novelty, on variety of forms ($\pi o\lambda\upsilon\epsilon\acute{\iota}\delta\epsilon\iota\alpha$) as well as of metres, and on attention to wit and artistic finish. In the light of the last-named principle, Catullus makes much of the fact that the completion of the *Zmyrna*, to its author's satisfaction, took no less than nine years, in contrast to the facile annual production of works *de longue haleine*, which at least in the Rome of his day were all second-rate narratives destined to speedy and inglorious oblivion. He goes so far as to pronounce that literary immortality, based on perfection of artistic polish, awaits this short piece of work, which had been generated in a notably restricted sphere. In Cinna's person, he evidently felt, Rome had at last placed her name on the poetic map of the world; and she had done so through a younger generation who nourished a spirit of defiance analogous to that in which Callimachus had avoided the easy way of Antimachus – who thought it appropriate for a poet to follow tamely in the footsteps, and so in a sense trade on the long-established reputation, of the old Homeric school. It must nevertheless be added that the $\check{\epsilon}\pi o s$ $\tau\upsilon\tau\theta\acute{o}\nu$ – as Parthenius regarded it – was still an *epos*; it did not throw overboard the whole idea of writing narrative verse, nor did it abandon mythological subject-matter, and to that extent it was not in the strict sense 'revolutionary.' Rather, it emulated the greatest poetry by finding new kinds of interest within the traditional fields of that poetry, and by writing about those subjects in a brilliant new way. The fact that the epyllion could do all this only made it extremely popular among the Romans of an age of expansion, from Valerius Cato to Catullus and his friend Caecilius (unknown to us except from poem 35, where he is encouraged to improve his poem on the Magna Mater), and also to Cornificius and – eventually – the poet of the *Ciris* in the *Appendix Vergiliana*. Even poem 63 of Catullus, for all its novelty of metre, exhibits many of the traits of what was usually a genre of hexameter poetry. In Gallus, who 'was, after Cinna,

9 Crowther 1976: 68.

the chief disciple of Parthenius,' as Brooks Otis remarks,[10] we attend the birth of something which, while it clearly follows Callimachean norms (to which, later, Propertius and Ovid bear witness), achieved, so far as we know, a new direction in literature, namely Roman subjective love-elegy.

The fact that the *Zmyrna* almost from its publication stood in need of scholarly interpreters[11] testifies to its obscurity, a trait which is attached most frequently to the name of Euphorion among the members of the Callimachean school. As we have seen, it was Parthenius who commended Euphorion's work, for imitation, to his Roman friends and pupils. Among these, Gallus translated some of Euphorion's poems into Latin,[12] while from Macrobius (5.17.18) we discover that *Georgics* 1.437 is based on a line composed by Parthenius himself. If Virgil learned Greek, or Greek criticism, from Parthenius, as Macrobius (or his source) also tells us,[13] then he will have been urged to pay attention to Euphorion as well as to Callimachus, his respect for whose work is plain to see. Euphorion, then, enjoyed a wide popularity in the literary circles of the late Republic, largely because of the influence that Parthenius exerted over Cinna, and hence over Cinna's colleagues and successors. It is not surprising to find that Cicero (who disliked their ways) seems to say, in his often-quoted phrase *hi cantores Euphorionis* (*Tusculan Disputations* 3.45), that they were forever 'going on about' Euphorion; the expression *cantores* may, however, point to that concern for verbal 'music' which was such a prominent feature of Euphorion's style.[14] As we find with many of the Callimacheans, Euphorion's most often-discussed work was an epyllion, the *Thrax*; we have already sketched its characteristics. Parthenius was in some way connected with this piece.

As for Catullus himself, in recent years critical investigation has led to a sharpened appreciation of his literary technique, and to the simultaneous acceptance of two propositions which might seem to be contradictory yet are not: C. adapts his material to his own artistic needs and to a Roman cast of mind, but at the same time he draws deeply from Greek wells and emerges as a supreme imitator of Greek literary technique. The second of these has long been perceived as an ideal consciously entertained by him; but its application has often been considered as limited to a very few poems. The prominence accorded by the poet to his own translations from Callimachus, in particular, is manifest: see poems 65 (line 16), 66, and 116, and compare

10 Otis 1963: 32.

11 Charisius, *GLK* I.134.12.

12 Servius, *ap.* Virgil, *Ecl.* 6.74.

13 5.17.18 *versus est Parthenii, quo grammatico in Graecis Vergilius usus est.*

14 On the disputed meaning of *cantores* and *cantare*, see Allen 1972, Crowther 1970, and Tuplin 1977 and 1979.

poem 95 for his general attitude to Callimachus. And in such poems as 61, 62, 63, 68, there is a deeply Hellenistic (always to some extent Callimachean) feeling, not explicitly paraded but taken for granted. As for another, shorter, poem, until quite lately almost universally assumed to be mainly or entirely autobiographical in reference – the powerful but puzzling fourth poem, *Phaselus ille* – it may be legitimate to suggest, though there can at present be no conclusive proof, that this is perhaps most easily understood as an adaptation of a Callimachean original (Βερενίκης φάσηλος).[15] Catullus is, then, profoundly influenced by Callimachus in both literary impetus and technique. Where he differs from Callimachus and goes far beyond him is in the note of personal passion, as opposed to mere sympathy, which he contrives to infuse into so many of his compositions. To take an example, the *Attis* (63) – a poem which it is hard not to think of as having had some kind of Alexandrian prototype – becomes in his hands the expression of a quite private emotion, made explicit in the three concluding lines. As for the translation from Sappho in poem 51, this clearly has a peculiar kind of personal importance for Catullus, though the precise nature of that importance is still debated.

Some further observations under this head. Catullus prefaces his work, exactly as Callimachus had done in the prologue to the second edition of the *Aetia*, with a programmatic poem in which he sets out his philosophy of truly artistic literary composition. In that poem, the Callimachean themes of smallness (*libellus*), lightness (*nugae*), and metrical variety are successively indicated – the last of these by example rather than by precept (the precept is implied in poem 50, together with a privileged view of that Callimachean excitement of which we have already spoken). Looking towards the end of the book, we notice at once that the elegiac section (metrically considered), from poems 65 and 66 to poem 116, begins and ends with an overt Callimachean reference (and, in the former instance at least, with an imitation). Other poems throughout the collection also echo Callimachus: see, for example, the notes on poems 90 and 95, and especially the introductory note to poem 64, which takes up the argument of R.F. Thomas that the *Peleus and Thetis* is partly at least designed to express Catullus' commitment to Callimachean doctrine in the light of the *Victoria Berenices*. Poem 95 clearly contains a second manifesto in favour of Callimachus' Μοῦσα λεπταλέη and against the 'Homeric' opponents of that approach to poetic art. And with the ninety-fifth poem we come, of course, to Cinna, who may fairly be called the leader of the 'neoteric' movement, and to Cinna's relation to Catullus, of which we have already spoken.

15 See the introductory note to poem 4.

Some final remarks about Catullus as an adherent of the Callimachean doctrine: it is noticeable that Catullus fails to name any Greek predecessors, with the sole exception of Callimachus (unless Bergk is right with his suggestion of *Philetae* to fill the gap at 95.9; but the very fact that this would be an isolated instance may itself tell against the reading). Certainly he does not mention Parthenius; and this may be a further piece of evidence in favour of the proposition that Parthenius' influence reached the New Poets only through the medium of Cinna. Catullus is a Callimachean through and through; and no more so than in his longer compositions.[16] We nowadays recognize in him a much greater element of careful technique, and of conscious refinement of language, than our predecessors detected; we have come to accept the verdict of many critics that if he is the unique poet of a personal love, he is also to be relished for his wit. *Doctus poeta*: the phrase does not merely translate as 'skilful poet,' which indeed is one of several meanings it bears, but implies also the possession of rare and valuable insights, acquired by toil and even research. For many passages in Catullus it might be claimed, as it has been claimed in general terms for his forerunner and sometimes model Callimachus, that 'the poet always succeeds in harmonizing, with the charm of his verse, what the scholar cannot forbear putting in.'[17] And the notion of reaping poetic benefits from this kind of preparation applies as much (we are now aware) to short poems as to long. The very simplest effusion, thrown off with apparently nonchalant ease, is recognized as depending for its immortal qualities on knowledge, as well as on highly developed artistic skill.

Perhaps the chief among Callimachus' gifts to Catullus is the principle of variety. For example, the extremely rare and difficult metre in which poem 63 is written was a novelty employed, and possibly first attempted, by Callimachus. Again, one and the same theme might be tossed about, experimentally, between elegiac and polymetric treatment (poem 50 again). The quest for the unusual, including the paradoxical, theme, and the equally urgent quest for lightness and conciseness in treatment – these, too, are Callimachean. So also is the ironical and often humorous tone that enables the poet to glance with affection at his subject even when he is distancing himself from it: often a single touch, in such a context, will serve to bring the essence of a situation unexpectedly into view. To achieve all of these results, scholarship had to go hand in hand with art. Poetry which had its roots in learning was a new departure, as we noted above; and it was precisely this fresh approach that revivified the long-dormant art, both in a

---

16 See Lyne 1978; notice also the argument of Thomas 1983 on poem 64.

17 A. Lesky, *A History of Greek Literature*, English translation (London, 1966): 705.

Greek-speaking and (much later) in a Roman context. Moreover, for Rome at least, this reinvigoration lasted for generations, beginning with that of Catullus and his circle.

Since this part of the Introduction does not claim to be in any way a comprehensive history of the neoteric movement, I have omitted many names that might have been expected to occur here (Ticida, for example, and also Furius Bibaculus, except for his lines on Cato), on the grounds that the persons concerned were not of central importance to the artistic tradition we have discussed. To compensate to some extent for this omission, the selective Bibliography has been given a wider range than might otherwise have been thought sufficient, in order to guide the reader's search for full information. In any case, an excellent general survey of the subject, well argued, can easily be found in Lyne's 1978 article. A very few points, however, may be added to supplement the foregoing pages. The *Garland* of Meleager receives no mention here, although not so long ago its reception in the Roman world was believed to have had a profound effect in bringing the New Poets to an appreciation of Hellenistic and Alexandrian verse. In fact it was one among many similar anthologies known at this time in the west, and there is little evidence that it caused any particular stirring of interest. The long-established tradition of the Roman (as opposed to the purely Greek, though still Greek-influenced) elegiac epigram had an effect on Catullus and his contemporaries, particularly in the matter of linguistic style; here, Professor Ross (1969) has carefully established a distinction between poems 69–116 and the rest of Catullus. I have not touched on this aspect of the poet's art. Finally, the peculiar nature of two contiguous pieces, 67 and 68[a], seems to defy any kind of Callimachean classification; poem 67, in particular, could be regarded as merely an extended epigram, of a disparaging sort, were it not that there is in it a kind of internal character development which hardly belongs to the conventional definition of epigram, with its customary stress on unity. For both of these poems the reader is referred to the Commentary.

The History of the Text

(In this section, 'GB' refers to Giuseppe Billanovich, 'Il Catullo della Cattedrale di Verona,' *Scire Litteras* = Bayerische Akad. d. Wiss, Phil.-Hist. Klasse, Abhandlungen NF 99 [Munich, 1988]: 35–57. I take this article as my starting-point, though I am obliged to disagree with it in several particulars.)

As every modern editor makes clear, our present text of Catullus rests on three late-fourteenth-century manuscripts known as *OGR*, all extremely faulty. These derive from a common source in the lost manuscript *V*, so called because it is usually believed, partly on the strength of Benvenuto Campesani's accompanying verses (see below, p. 194), to have turned up in Verona at some (recently much debated) date. The only other pre-fifteenth-century witness – and it is confined to poem 62 – is *T*, so called because it is an item in an anthology, the *codex Thuaneus*, to which we shall presently refer. *T* is of Carolingian date, and shows by its errors that it belongs to the same branch of the tradition as *V*. The secondary manuscript *m*, to be mentioned later, is a close and early copy of *R*.

Chronology of the Text

(a) Fourth to Sixth Century: Archetype.

The script of the archetype is not certain. Some errors in *V* are overwhelmingly likely to date from the use of capital letters: e.g., 68.41 quam fallius *V*, where QVAMFALLIVS was corrupted from QVAMEALLIVS (as Scaliger, with his methodical interest in recovering antique scripts, was the first to see). On the other hand, a half-uncial style of writing is suggested by certain kinds of error, transmitted ultimately to *T* and *V*. For example, at 62.7 the correct reading is obviously *ignes* (imbres *T*, imber *V*); the letter ȝ (g) may have been mistaken for ƀ by the scribe of a later age, especially if the parent manuscript was written in northern France, 'where the peculiarity of ȝ standing on the line and not coming below it certainly appears in manuscripts.'[18] In 1900, E. Maunde Thompson (see the Bibliography below) suggested for similar reasons that *V* itself might have been a sixth-century manuscript written in half-uncials, while in 1896 W.M. Lindsay had tentatively suggested, in a letter to Hale, 'Anglo-Saxon' half-uncials.[19]

(b) Mid-Ninth Century: GB's 'v,' predecessor of *V* (see below), is in the Cathedral Library at Verona. Hildemar, a Brescian monk, seems to quote from it in 845 (GB). Bishop Rather saw it there in 966.

See GB 35–6. For the sermon in which Rather mentions his acquaintance with Catullus, GB (n. 7) cites B.R. Reece, *Sermones Ratherii episcopi Veronensis* (Worcester, Mass., 1969), pp. 86$^{10-12}$ and 35^{10}.

(c) Ninth Century (third quarter): *T* (poem 62 only; Table of Mss, No. 80) turns up in an anthology, in French script. Perhaps copied from 't' (GB), an

18 E.W.B. Nicholson (Bodley's Librarian) to W.G. Hale, 26 February 1897, Hale-Ullman Papers, Department of Classics, University of North Carolina at Chapel Hill.

19 2 October 1896. Hale-Ullman Papers (see n. 18 above).

extract from 'v' sent from Verona to France. So far as it goes, *T* 'allows us to see the outlines of a pre-C9th archetype' (McKie: 97).

T is included in the *Codex Thuaneus* – i.e., the anthology belonging, in the sixteenth century, to Jacques-Auguste de Thou (Paris, B.N. 8071). B.L. Ullman (1960b: 1028–9) believed that all of *T*, except the Juvenal extracts, was copied from the Vienna Ms 277 (VIIIC–IXC), now lacking Catullus, which corresponds exactly to a description of materials (two manuscripts) brought by Sannazaro to Naples from France ('ex Heduorum usque finibus atque e Turonibus') about 1504, according to Pietro Summonte (see Richardson 1976: 285–6, and Gaisser 1993: 282 n. 62), though there is no mention of a Catullus in Summonte's description. Ullman went on to suggest that both *T* and Vienna 277 emanated from Tours; this is more than likely (both are French in style of writing, and we have just seen an attribution of the Vienna manuscript to an origin among the *Turones*). Because of the Tours connection, Ullman was tempted to go further and to link this origin with the fact that Venantius Fortunatus 'describes a book of verse loaned him by Gregory of Tours between 573 and 576,' and speculated that this book might have been the archetype of Sannazaro's two manuscripts. (Ullman also found that in Venantius 6.10.6 the word *hiulco* is used with *agros*, as it is in Catullus 68.62, while the only other time the verb occurs in Latin literature – in pseudo-Augustine – the context is different.) But the derivation of *T* from Vienna 277 has itself been challenged, and is now virtually disproved: see Zwierlein 1983: 15–23. (*T* and Vienna 277 are regarded by Zwierlein as two copies of the same parent manuscript.) As for *hiulcare* in Catullus, Ullman himself admitted that this does not occur in poem 62 (the only Catullan poem in *T*), so that Fortunatus must have derived any knowledge of Catullus he had from some manuscript other than the source of *T*. Moreover, the 'book of verse' sent by Gregory, in Ullman's account, turns out to be, rather, a metrical treatise with specimens of different metres. (On these points see now Gaisser 1992: 202, and 1993: 16–17.)

Ellis, in his 1878 edition of Catullus, published (in a plate facing p. 100) a careful transcription of the recto of the first folio of *T* (22 lines). The writer of *T*, though he is even less competent in Latin than the scribe of *O* (see below), has the advantage of standing closer to the archetype by perhaps about five centuries, and this fact does not go unreflected in his readings. At line 63, for example, where *T* correctly gives *pars est*, *O* (following his exemplar *A*; see below) has dropped the word *pars*. Presumably because this leads to a metrical fault, *X*, the parent of *G* and *R*, supplied *data* before *pars*.

(d) 1290–1310: Humanists, chiefly Paduan, show knowledge of a Ms apparently at Verona (*V*). This now lost Ms, in late Gothic script, may be tentatively dated ca. 1280. It was seen and used by various Paduan and Veronese humanists in the two decades ca. 1290–1310. GB suggests that it was written to replace 'the now worn-out v,' which seems reasonable.

The practitioners of rhetoric, and to some extent of law, in the region of Padua and Verona, some of whom enjoyed access to the treasures of the Cathedral Library at Verona, created a 'springtime' (GB) of (pre)-humanism; see the articles referred to in his notes, esp. n. 9. They included Benzo of Alessandria, Geremia (Hieremias) da Montagnone, and (according to Ellis and though Ullman 1960b: 1038 n. 25, doubts it) the poet Albertino Mussato. Lovato Lovati's involvement with Catullus is asserted by GB but denied by Walter Ludwig ('Kannte Lovato [1241–1309] Catull?,' *RhM* 129 [1986], 329–57). A slightly later figure – friend to Petrarch – is Guglielmo da Pastrengo of Verona (GB, n. 11). On the question of *V*'s Gothic script, see Ullman 1960b: 1037, who lists eleven errors characteristic of Gothic script; but W. Clausen 1976: 42–3 finds ten of them to be 'common' in Carolingian script, and explains away the eleventh. There is however another argument for a later date for *V*.

First be it noted that the humanists just named, who quote and echo Catullus, have one important thing in common: their readings are earlier than those of *A* (see [e] below), and must provisionally (at least) be supposed to be those of *V*. Among them is Geremia (Hieremias) da Montagnone, as we have already noted. At 64.145, where the first hands of *OGR* all read *postgestit*, Hieremias reads *praegessit*. Because *OGR* all endorse the obvious error in *post-*, the error itself cannot be later than their common source *A* or its immediate predecessor. Since *V*, as read by Hieremias, had the correct *prae-*, we must suppose that *post-* came in with *A*. The cause of the error is this: in Mss of later date, but not in Carolingian Mss, we find compendia for *pre* or *pri* (p̄) on the one hand, and for *post* (p̄) on the other, which are easily confused. *A* has, it appears, misread *V*'s *p̄gestit* as *p̄gestit*. This implies that *A*'s exemplar, *V*, belonged to a period when the compendium in question had come into use, and was therefore of humanistic date, or at any rate later than the ninth century. (We may compare 62.21 and 22, where the word *matris*, spelled out in full in the ninth-century manuscript *T*, is given by *R*, for instance, in the abbreviated form *mat's*). Similarly, at 64.153 *O* miscopies what must have been *p̄da* in *A* (preda *GR*) as *postea*. Even more strikingly, in the much-debated line 11 of the same poem, where *GR* give the correct *primam*, using a compendium (*p's mam*), *O* diverges into the reading *p̄eam* (*posteam*; in the margin, he changed it into *proram* – see the note in the Commentary).

(e) ca. 1300: A scholar, conjecturally identified (by GB) with Albertino Mussato, copies from *V* a Ms, also in late Gothic script, which I propose to call *A* (= GB's 'x'), and enters marginal and other corrections. The scribe of *A* is probably the author of the *Tu lector* addition (see below); if so, he has no second Ms available to correct the deficiencies of which he complains in his exemplar; consequently, it must be supposed that the changes he makes are his own. In a penetrating account of the history of the titles in Catullus (chapter 2 of his 1977 dissertation) Dr McKie has securely established the fact that a manuscript must have intervened between *V* and *OX* (it is nowadays agreed that the surviving Mss *G* and *R* derive from a lost parent Ms, designated *X*) so that the once-prevalent view that *OX* came directly from *V* has to be given up. *A* contained a number of marginal and interlinear variants that must go back beyond *X*, since a few of them have slipped into *O*; for these variants in *A* (so far as they were inherited by R^2 through *X*) see below, pp. 40–1. It may be observed that GB (see his stemma and notes, pp. 53–4) concurs with McKie, whose work he does not appear to have studied, on this point of a manuscript intervening between *V* and *OX*. The account given by GB (to anticipate slightly) allots to Mussato a role in 'improving' his Ms with corrections, metrical notes, and so forth, which consorts well with Mussato's known talents; whereas that same account, if we accept it, leaves little scope for scholarly activity on the part of *X*, which emerges as little more than an apograph of *A*. This too happens to agree with McKie, who in his final chapter assigns to *X* a quite minor role in contributing to the corpus of variants and corrections bequeathed to us by R^2. Examining the text of poem 64, where he finds some 180 divergences between *O* and *X*, McKie identifies only a very few as due to emendatory activity on *X*'s part, though some certainly are (p. 265): for one possible instance to be added to his list, see (c) above (*sub fin.*).

(f) ca. 1315: Benvenuto Campesani (d. 1323) records in an epigram the 'recovery from afar' of Catullus by (?) the notary Francesco (*a calamis, tribuit cui Francia nomen*).

The meaning of Campesani's epigram, and the facts underlying it, are the greatest puzzles in this whole question of the *resurrectio Catulli*. I give the text below, following that of the poems. GB (pp. 48–9) believes *X* to be the Ms mentioned in the epigram: he opines that it was written for political reasons with a dedication to Cangrande of Verona by Campesani, in a bid for protection (*A* having been lent for the purpose by the former pro-Paduan activist Mussato, who also longed for peace and personal liberty); the statement in the first line that Catullus was returning *longis a finibus* was meant to disguise the (to Cangrande, displeasing) fact that it came from exile in Padua, a Guelph city hostile to Verona, under the pretence that the place from which it returned was some 'remote Cathay.' Whether Cangrande would have been deceived by this fantastic invention of a 'distant' origin, as GB claims that scholars and editors for centuries past have been, is a moot point; but if one wishes, as GB does, to assert that Catullus had never left Verona since late antiquity (the time of the archetype), then one must find some plausible explanation for those awkward words at the beginning of the epigram. It appears to be still an open question whether *V*'s ninth-century parent (GB's 'v') really remained always at Verona, as GB insists, or was brought (from France, where its exemplar had gone? Cf. *T*) by the notary Francesco, and destroyed when *V* was made.

(g) 1345–8: Petrarch, at Verona, sees and (possibly) copies and annotates, a Ms which may have been *A*. See (x?) in the Stemma on p. 93.

As I have suggested above, one difficulty in the acceptance of GB's view that the Ms accompanying Campesani's epigram is to be identified with *X* lies in the reasonable assumption that Petrarch, who takes his readings of Catullus invariably from what we may call the *AX* tradition, but at a stage before *X* itself (yet nowhere agreeing with *O* against *X*), must be thought of as somehow close to *A*;[20] and the date allotted to *X* by GB is more than thirty years before Petrarch either came to stay in Verona or shows any knowledge of Catullus (his quotations of Catullus begin in 1347). For Petrarch's adherence to the readings we trace to *AX*, as opposed to the readings of *O*, three passages will suffice as evidence. At 65.5, he quotes *lethei gurgitis* (not *loethi*, as in *O*); at 39.16, he gives *risu*, not *O*'s *risti*; and at 35.4, *menia*, where *O* has *veniam*. It is generally thought likely that Petrarch possessed a (complete) Catullus of his own, though its fate is uncertain. U. Bosco, in what Ullman 1955: 181 described as a 'valuable article' (it has been strangely neglected by scholars since Ullman's book appeared), maintained that Petrarch's quotations of Catullus show that he did not own a complete text of the poet, but drew all of them from an anthology containing poem 64 and a few other poems. (See *Giornale storico della letteratura italiana* 120 [1942]: 65–119, esp. 108–16). Ullman himself (1955: 195–200) answered Bosco, conceding that some of Petrarch's Catullan quotations were at second hand but showing that 'six or seven quotations prove that <Petrarch> saw a complete Catullus' (199), even if 'it cannot be proved' (195) that he owned one. That the text he used was complete is strongly suggested by the fact that his citation of the opening of poem 49 in his Ambrosian Library copy of Virgil (on Servius *ad Aen.* 1.110) adds *et rel<iqua>*, 'indicating that he had the whole poem before him' (Ullman 1955: 197). The same conclusion is drawn by Ullman (197–8)

20 See McKie's thesis, p. 289.

from the general remark on poem 64 in the Virgil (fol. 52ʳ), which shows
that Petrarch was familiar with the structure of the poem as a whole. Hale,
who had originally suggested (*CR* 20 [1906]: 164) that Petrarch's text was
similar to that of *O*, withdrew this opinion in *CP* 3 (1908): 243–4. For
external evidence, chiefly from the letters of Coluccio Salutati, making it
virtually certain that Petrarch was not the owner of *X*, see McKie 1977: 88
and 175–86. For another argument to the same effect ('P. used the word
peplon for poem 64; it is similarly used by G. da Pastrengo, but does not
penetrate to *X*'), see GB, p. 42. Some slight evidence that Petrarch himself
may possibly have contributed emendatory suggestions to the margins of *A*
in a few places is afforded by at least the following two passages:

35.4 menia *Petrarca*, veniam *O*, meniam *GR*: ? veniam (menia) *A*, meniam al.
menia *X* (hence menia *R* ²).

39.11 etruscus *Petrarca*, et truscus *OGR*: ? et truscus, *i.m.* etruscus *A*, et
truscus al. etruscus *X* (hence al. etruscus *R* ²)

Petrarch's practice of annotating Mss in his possession, and influencing
thereby their later destiny, is of course well known; GB ('Dal Livio ...')
and McKie: 170 ('<his> seminal influence on so many texts') have drawn
attention to this in connection with his Livy and Propertius.

(h) ?ca. 1360: Two sister Mss, *X* (now lost) and *O* (Table of Mss, No. 72),
are copied (*O* apparently directly; for *X* see 64.139 n.) from *A*.

(Here I diverge widely from GB, who believes that *X* was copied in 1314 by
Francesco under Campesani's direction. But McKie has shown conclusively
that Petrarch's text predates *X*.) GB also dates *O* in 1375; nothing absolutely
forbids this, but *O* (unfinished in execution, the work of a good calligrapher
but abysmally poor Latinist) may well have been set aside in favour of the
more faithful rendering which *X* gives of *A*'s text. In other words, *X* may
have been written expressly to replace the faulty *O*.

The date I have suggested above can only be approximate. It should be
noted that the scribe of *X* carefully checks his copy against *A*, adding what
appear to be a set of variant readings, generally prefixed by 'al<iter>.' Often
these are really corrections, *A*'s readings being given after *X*'s initial faulty
transcription; since the text was already written, they had to be added, rather
than inserted, so that the Ms would not be disfigured by overwriting. (Later
scribes, such as that of *m*, do the same thing.)

With rare exceptions, *O*, unlike *X*, has little concern for his text: he is a
trained calligrapher, and his principal interest lies in the appearance of his
page. This explains why in his work, which was laid aside before receiving
the decoration for which it was designed, he leaves spaces for the titles which
were to be added later (they are part of the décor), but does not bother

to reproduce either the variants and marginalia, or Campesani's epigram, or the *Tu lector* addition (see below), which were certainly in *X*. For this reason, it is unnecessary to regard *O*'s omission of these last-mentioned elements as making it doubtful that the *Tu lector* addition was generated by *A* rather than *X* – *pace* McKie (288), who argues: 'It [i.e., the *Tu lector*, etc.] could of course go back further <than *X*,> to the parent of *X* and *O*, but the subscription has not been copied by *O*, who ends without any indication that he has seen it (unlike the titles, for which he made provision by leaving interstices).' *O* is useful because, though he makes many mistakes in transcription, in principle he doggedly adheres to what he sees, or thinks he sees, in *A*. At some places, where *X* either slips or does not adequately check his reading with that of *A*, *O* can help in restoring the text of *A* (and hence, probably, of *V*): such are, in poem 64, lines 139, where *O* alone has *blanda*; 273, where *X* apparently omitted *-que*; and 381, where *X* had *sub tegmina ducite*. But in general, as McKie (chapter 6) has shown, the reputation long enjoyed among scholars by *O* as a far more accurate reproducer of the common parent shared by *OX* (my *A*) must be called in question: most of the time, for *A*-stream readings, we should consult *X* rather than *O*. It may be repeated that it is to this stream that the citations and allusions in Petrarch always adhere, never to the readings of *O* where these diverge from it. Indeed, *O* had rather a small influence on the later tradition as well.[21]

The chronicle of *O*'s physical movements is still obscure. It was copied from *A* (see above) – there is no need to suppose that another Ms intervened – at Verona, most probably, or at any rate in northeast Italy (the hand is certainly north Italian, and the scribe's habit of doubling intervocalic consonants where they should be single and *vice versa* smacks of the practice of scribes in the Veneto at that period). Zicàri dealt with the vexed question of readings similar to those of *O* that appear in various groups of Mss, the earliest of which is dated 1423 (Parisinus 7989 = Table of Mss, No. 78).[22] He pointed out that in the year 1390 a copy of Catullus, in which the name is spelled Catulus (as in *O*, but not in *G* or in *R*), turns up in an inventory of the books belonging to a Genoese humanist in the service of the Visconti. Marked similarities to the Parma Ms (Table of Mss, No. 88) copied (in 1471) in the Visconti castle at Pavia suggest that this humanist's library, with the Catullus, went to the Pavia library when he died; yet by 1426, when the books in the library were catalogued, it was not there. On the other hand, the decoration on fol. 1ʳ implies that it was

21 See Zicàri 1958: 79–99 = *Scritti*, 1978, 79–104, for a detailed study of that influence.
22 See n. 21 above.

in Lombardy ca. 1430; so it may by then have come back to Pavia from wherever it was sent (could it have gone to Florence, in 1423, as the result of an effort by the scholarly scribe of Parisinus 7989 to 'improve' the readings of that *R*-derived Ms?). At all events the Pavia Ms agrees with *O* in (for example) the reading *blanda* at 64.139, which is unknown to *GR* and is otherwise shared only with a few late Mss. How *O* could have reached Pavia by 1390 is still uncertain. Zicàri, following a suggestion by É. Pellegrin 1955: 46, thought it might have been included in the loot brought from Verona and Padua in 1387 by Gian Galeazzo Visconti; but see GB ('Dal Livio ...,' 163–4); he dismisses this notion, claiming that almost all the classical Mss at Verona disappeared and were destroyed at the time of the fall of the Scaligers. The subsequent history of *O* may have unrolled in northeast Italy; it is not altogether without interest that it made its way to Oxford from a *Venetian* collection. As Ullman (1960b: 1040) noted:

O is in a collection bought in 1817 from the large library of Matteo Canonici of Venice. He had been in such cities as Parma, Bologna, and Ferrara, where we may suppose that he acquired some of his books. Some he obtained from Mantua. Thus northern Italy is again indicated as the original home of *O*.

GB traces *O* directly from *V*, without the intervention of *A* or any other Ms; this represents a second major difference between his stemma and the views of McKie and myself.

(i) 1375: *G* (Table of Mss, No. 87) is copied from *X*, at Verona, by Antonio da Legnago.

19 October 1375 is the date inscribed in *G* by Antonio da Legnago, who finished writing it while Cansignorio della Scala (the ruler of Verona, whose chancellor Antonio was) *laborabat in extremis*. The same year, according to GB, saw the copying of *R* (see below, however) from *X* (at Verona, he believes); he also conjectures that *O* may have been made in that year, at Verona and directly from *V*, possibly by Giacomo dalle Eredità.

In 1877 Max Bonnet made for the first time a serious effort to determine which of the changes and insertions in *G* are due to the original scribe and which are in a second hand. As to the second hand itself, Schwabe erroneously supposed the date of this to be only slightly later than that of *G*; see the first page of the *Praefatio* to his Berlin edition of 1886 ('paullo recentiori'). At least two editors of considerable repute, who were permitted to make use of Bonnet's collation (now at Chapel Hill), relied to a great extent on the accuracy of his findings. It must be said, however, that his attempt to disentangle the two important hands in *G* was only partially successful.

This will be evident to anyone who takes the trouble to examine the minute studies of the hands and inks in G made by Hale's pupils (especially Susan Ballou and O.M. Washburn) under Hale's direction. The hands and inks of G^1 and G^2 are indeed so similar that many distinctions escape the eye of a camera. Hale and his students, Ullman among them, in the end had to leave some questions unresolved, even after using a very powerful lens and re-examining difficult places repeatedly on widely separated dates and in different lights. In these matters I have tried to build on their work, and to use the same methods. After each examination in Paris, I have checked my own decisions with the voluminous notes that Hale left to Ullman. Where I have finally rejected the verdict of either or both of them, it is for reasons that seemed to me palaeographically sound. Decisions related to G which appear in the Apparatus Criticus are those that have exacted by far the greatest amount of time and care; my aim has been to render them accurate, in terms of palaeography, as far as is humanly possible.

After copying out his basic text from X, G's scribe went back to the beginning and began to add the variants, and a few explanatory scholia, which he had observed in his exemplar. (These we call the 'G^1' additions.) For some reason, however, he soon stopped doing this. (Did the political situation, immediately after the death of Cansignorio, impose more urgent tasks? As McKie: 178 points out, two days previously Antonio had been appointed one of the regents to Cansignorio's designated successors, who were still minors.) There are times when he adopts in his text – not retrospectively, but at the first stage of transcription, or so it would appear – what must have appeared as a variant reading in X.[23] At some later date, probably around 1400, G turns up in Florence, where it was to receive, after 1397/8 (see below), a second stream of corrections in a different hand (G^2) which were drawn entirely from m, an apograph of R/R^2. These corrections include the m^2 changes and additions (which I now attribute to a different scribe) as well as the original work of m^1. Since both of the scribes who contributed to m are concerned only to reproduce or correct what they see in R/R^2, it follows that the G^2 changes and additions, like those in m/m^2 which they copy, are entirely dependent on R/R^2, and have nothing of their own to contribute to the search for what must have been in A or in V.

We must now address the problem of the *subscriptio*. Since a very thorough account of this has been given by McKie: 168–78, a few remarks will suffice. The *subscriptio* is in three parts (see the instructive facsimile in McKie: 176 for their layout); all are in the hand of G. The second part, which is indented – as the others are not – and lacks the notarial flourishes which

---

23 See below, pp. 39–40, for examples.

adorn the other two entries, seems to have been squeezed into an interstice (it has hardly three short lines); this part contains Antonio's name and the date of writing. The third part (a gloss from Papias on the name Lesbia) is only of importance because, being the only one of the three to be found in another Ms (*R*), it clearly was present in *X*. Was the first, and by far the longest, entry also copied from *X*? É. Chatelain thought so, a century ago (*Paléographie des classiques latins*, Part I, pl. XV, n.). It should perhaps be given in full:

Tu lector quicumque ad cuius manus hic libellus obvenerit Scriptori da veniam si tibi coruptus videbitur. Quoniam a corruptissimo exemplari transcripsit. Non enim quodpiam aliud extabat, unde posset libelli huius habere copiam exemplandi. Et ut ex ipso salebroso aliquid tamen suggeret decrevit pocius tamen coruptum habere quam omnino carere. Sperans adhuc ab alliquo alio fortuito emergente hunc posse corigere. Valebis si ei imprecatus non fueris.

This complaint by the scribe that there was only one Ms extant that he could lay his hands on, and a bad one at that, seems much more suitable to the first quarter of the fourteenth century than to the last quarter. Moreover, as McKie: 173 has pointed out, its despair over improving the text until another Ms might emerge argues a serious concern which hardly fits the character of *G*'s first scribe (*G*¹), who from *A* took only a very few titles, and a round dozen of variants – and these only at or near the beginning of his text – and who evidently failed completely to take the elementary step of checking his readings against those of his exemplar. This does not seem to be a scholarly scribe, distressed at the lack of means to correct the corrupted text before him. Contrast, in every respect, what we have seen to be the character and procedures of *A*, who may well have been someone like Mussato (GB's nominee). *A* (whoever he was), and also *R*² (who was certainly Coluccio Salutati) both set about revising the text extensively; *G* does not dream of this, for all that he adds in the margin those few early variants taken from *X*. If, then, the *Tu lector* complaint suits *A* and does not suit *G*, we have every reason to suppose that the complaint was merely inherited by *G* and was copied by the latter in the same uncritical spirit as that in which he reproduced the handful of variants and the gloss on *Lesbia* (which, as already remarked, we know to have been at least in *X*). *Per contra*, Salutati, who presided over and directed the writing – at his own scriptorium in Florence – of *R*, eminently possessed a critical sense; hence the rearrangement by which Campesani's epigram is in *R* transferred to the head of the Ms, while the *Tu lector* complaint, being no longer relevant, is omitted; the Lesbia-gloss, not too obviously irrelevant, is added after the *Deo gratias* at the end, in very small letters in Coluccio's own hand (therefore, the scribe was originally told to leave it out, and its inclusion was an afterthought).

It is, then, reasonable to attribute the *Tu lector* complaint to *A*. McKie more than once considers this possibility (against *X*): the only thing that deters him is the fact that *O* does not have it, but we have seen (above, p. 29) reasons to discount this. The irregularities of spelling (*coruptus* in two places, *corr*- elsewhere; *alliquo*; *corigere*) with their double for single consonants and vice versa, suggest an origin in the Veneto (and this would not clash with Mussato's authorship, though it is not admissible as evidence (*O* shows the same phenomenon). The inconsistencies in spelling also indicate that *G* copied, rather than originated, the complaint. Finally, the substitution of *suggeret* for *suggereret* was 'a strange mistake to make, if the note was his (i.e., *G*'s) own <work>' (McKie: 169).

G had, as might be expected from its proximity to *R* and to *m*, a family of its own; but it was not nearly so large a family as many scholars have supposed. Even if we include the now lost manuscript from which the first part of Riccardianus 606 (Table of Mss, No. 31 – the parent of Lachmann's *D*, No. 4 [see *CE*, 35–40]) was copied, and also the mere influence, rather than *patria potestas*, which *G* seems to have exerted over the San Daniele Ms (No. 93), its offspring and descendants can be easily counted on the fingers of one hand. And those '*G*' manuscripts we do possess (e.g., Nos. 18 and 65) are descendants, probably several generations removed and 'contaminated' from other sources; there are not in the case of *G* such manuscripts as we find in the immediate family of *R*, namely those that in one way or other betray a first-hand acquaintance with the face of the parent Ms. A test of descent from *G* rather than *R* is the reading *colitis* at 66.83.

(j) ?1391: *X*, which had finally reached Florence, is copied there to the order of Coluccio Salutati; the copy is *R* (Table of Mss, No. 101). Coluccio (*R*²) makes changes and adds variants, some taken from *X* – and thus largely inherited from *A* – and some of his own creating. (GB believes that *X* was copied at Verona by *R*, and never went to Florence at all. For several reasons, including a consideration of the editing and checking procedures of *R*², especially where lines were omitted by *R*¹, this is unacceptable.)

I do not see that we are compelled to subscribe to McKie's view that the removal to Florence of *X* certainly took place in 1375, immediately after Coluccio had requested it, or that (even if it did) there was not a considerable delay before it could be satisfactorily copied in *littera grossa* (see Ullman 1960a: 12–15; see also Novati II. 386, on Coluccio's failing eyesight at this period). It is also important to bear in mind that Coluccio has not a single quotation of Catullus in his surviving correspondence before 1391–2 at the earliest; the very few quotations we do have suddenly begin at that date. One of them is in Novati III. 36; that letter dates from 1392–4. The other is claimed by McKie to date from '1383–91,' but the claim requires examination. It is given near the *end* of Coluccio's *De Laboribus Herculis* – in the last ten per cent of the completed text – a work *contemplated* within the years 1383–91 (*inter annos 1383 et 1391 nova operis ratione inita*, Praefatio p. vii), but mentioned as actively being proceeded with only during the years after 1391. It looks, on this evidence, as if the actual words of Catullus began to be a new and exciting discovery for Coluccio either in the years 1391–2, or a trifle later. If there was a delay in carrying out Coluccio's wish to bring X to Florence for copying, it could possibly have been due to the very troubled state of Verona in those years. In any event, 1375 or 1376 seems too early for the copying of R from X.

We do not know the name of the writer of R, but he was obviously a professional scribe (see for example the flourishes on *Deo gratias* at the end), working to the order of Coluccio in the latter's scriptorium. Coluccio instructed his scribe to produce only the bare text, reserving most of the task of correcting for himself. Evidently he told the scribe to leave spaces for the titles, marginal variants, and notes (on metre, for example) which he had observed to exist in X. Later on, he addresses himself to R, making (apparently in a first rapid 'run-through') many corrections out of his own head, and also taking – a few at first, but more in a second, more careful recension – a number of variants from X, some of which originate with X itself but more go back to A. Thus these R^2 contributions ('R^2' here denoting everything written in R in the hand of Coluccio) represent three strata in the early textual history of Catullus. See the tables on pp. 38–43 below for the assignment of individual readings to one or other of these strata. In those pages, I have made it my aim to refrain from taking any given variant further back in the tradition than the evidence positively demands; sometimes, where that evidence is susceptible of more than one explanation, I have been reluctantly compelled to add a question-mark to the attribution.

In his attempts at original emendation 'ope ingenii' (as the humanists used to express it), Coluccio Salutati was often remarkably successful, though of course not always. For a vivid illustration of his procedures and weaknesses in this domain, let us glance at 44.11, where plainly the reading of V and also that of A must have been that which we find in OGR, namely *oratione minantium petitorem*. As the editor Achilles Statius discerningly saw in 1566, this is the correct reading, if we allow for the false word division that attaches the first m to the following instead of the preceding word, and also allow for the failure of scribes to realize that *Antium* is a proper name. Not guessing at the second of these two facts, but correctly divining that the syntax demanded that *orationem* should be in the accusative case, Coluccio first placed a virgula over the *e* of *oratione*, producing the required case (-*nē*), and then proceeded to change the case of *petitorem* to the genitive plural *petitorum* (by a dot of expunction and a superscript *u*) in agreement with the still-remaining participle *minantium*. The correction, such as it is, has an ingredient of truth in it, for *orationem* is after all the correct reading; and thus, even in this context, Coluccio has earned a measure of literary immortality as the author of a permanent emendation.

Together with a number of Coluccio Salutati's other manuscripts, *R* seems to have come into the possession or keeping of the Medici family in Florence. It was there, and because of this fact, that in the year 1457 the splendid Codex Laurentianus 33.12 (Table of Mss, No. 21) was copied, apparently from *R* itself, by Gherardo del Ciriagio for Giovanni Cosimo de' Medici. Then again we find it in Florence about 1475, when the R^3 additions were made to it by the person who, at that period, was secretary to Donato Acciaiuoli.[24] No doubt Donato owed his access to, and perhaps at least temporary custodianship of, the manuscript to his stalwart championship of the Medici. After the decade of the 1470s there is a gap in which it is hard to follow the movements of *R*. We know, however, that it was in Rome by a time certainly no later than 1566, and possibly a good deal earlier; for it, or a close copy of it, became the Codex Maffeianus – i.e., belonging to Achilles Maffei – which was used by Statius in 1566, together with other Mss, for his edition of Catullus (Ullman 1908: 10–17). Probably *R* stayed in Rome from that time onwards, until in due course it passed into the collection of Cardinal Ottoboni, and thence ultimately into the library of the Vatican, where it slumbered (under a false inventory number) until its rediscovery by William Gardner Hale in 1896; see the accounts of this discovery in *CE* 6–9 and Thomson 1973: 121–6.

(k) ca. 1399: In Florence, *m* (Table of Mss, No. 115), a copy of *R*, is made on paper for Coluccio Salutati. *m* follows R/R^2 even in minute details, but does so in a rather slapdash fashion, hurrying especially towards the end (see the textual notes in the Commentary). A little later, the anonymous scribe I now call m^2 (in *CE* I identified him as Poggio himself, and hence referred to him as *m'*) compares *m*'s work with *R* and finds that it needs to be 'up-dated' to conform more closely with *R* (one suspects that Salutati

---

24 Thomson 1970. The identification of the R^3 hand was first suggested by A. C. de la
Mare. If my collation is compared with the present edition it will be seen that the R^3
readings are seldom, if ever, original.

himself directed this revision to be undertaken; see below). Still later, G (which has only a few variants in the first hand, taken directly from X at the time of original copying, and virtually limited to the first few folios) is given very many additions and corrections (G^2) to make it conform exactly to m/m^2. G^2 certainly knew no other Ms than m as a source of alternative readings; clearly he had no acquaintance with either X or R.

After R had been at least partially revised by Coluccio (R^2), a copy was made on paper in what appear to be three successive phases of an attempt to shape a new style of writing that strives to imitate the *lettera antica* as a replacement (of a more easily legible sort) for the currently used Gothic hands.[25] From our point of view, accordingly, it foreshadows the 'humanistic' script as practised by Poggio. If it is indeed written by him,[26] it may be worth recalling that at this time (1397/8) Poggio worked as a tyro in Coluccio's scriptorium, and further that he shows, even at this time in his eighteenth year or so, the same inclination to disagree rather violently with his master on minor issues such as spelling which in practice we observe to be shown by the writer of m towards R/R^2 – that is, towards Coluccio's habits.[27]

So much for the intentions of $m(^1)$. As for m^2, he for his part is so far from taking issue with Coluccio on any matter that his sole concern, as already suggested, is to correct, and supplement, m in such a way that the copy will finally conform in the minutest details to its exemplar R/R^2. It is m^2 who, in the parent Ms R itself, contributes the marginal or interlinear additions we find at 55.16 (fol. 14^r) and 64.276 (fol. 25^r). In the first of these, m by a slip replaces the obviously correct *crede* with the nonsensical *crude*; m^2 replaces this with *crede* from R, but expresses it as a variant: 'al. crede'; he then writes, in the margin of R itself, *al. crude*, as though m's error had the status of a true variant! At the other place, 64.276, where R gives the unmetrical *tamen* (arising from confusion, in the Gothic script of V or of

25 de la Mare 1977: 89.

26 See de la Mare and Thomson 1973. Their view has however been vigorously· challenged by McKie (1989); he attributes to Niccolò Niccoli the hand which inserted the marginal spelling correction *phrygium* in R at 61.18. As for m^1 and m^2, he assigns them to two different scribes, as I have come to do, and reasonably finds the Poggiesque features in m^1 to be attributable not to P. himself but to the *example* of Poggio, working in the Florentine milieu where Niccoli also was influential in the development of a new script; see page 76 of his article.

27 Since our article was published, GB has claimed the discovery of a slightly earlier manuscript written by Poggio in the same general style: 'Alle origini della scrittura umanistica,' *Miscellanea Augusto Campana, Medioevo e Umanesimo* 44–5 (Padua 1981): 125–40. See also the illustration of fol. 1^r of m in de la Mare 1973 I. i, frontispiece.

A, between *tū* and *tñ*), *m* had substituted the word *tibi* – no doubt in an endeavour to heal the metrical fault. In his turn, *m*[2], who unlike *m*[1] does not have the independence to try this kind of emendation himself, nevertheless thinks it necessary to add the *R*-reading *tñ* (= *tamen*) in the margin of *R*, and to alter *R* itself by adding *al. tibi* above the line, simply because he has found *tibi* in *m*. (It will be clear enough from his former effort at 55.16 that he does not do so out of an intelligent concern for the metre.)

If *m*[2]'s scribe is now to be seen as a different person from *m*[1], there will no longer be any need to posit a considerable gap of years between the original writing of *m* (together with those readings in *R*/*R*[2] that are closely followed by *m*/*m*[1]) and the revisions in the *m*[2] hand, simply in order to conform with the known movements of Poggio, including his absence in Rome. (It was because in 1978 I identified both *m* and *m*[2] with Poggio himself that I then gave the latter the siglum *m'*.)

Some categories of *m* or *m*[2] reading attach themselves entirely or pre-dominantly to some kinds of *R*[2] contribution, others to other kinds. This suggests that they reflect two separate recensions of *R* by Coluccio, perhaps a few (but not many) years apart. It is clear that Coluccio must have had at least a brief look over *X* almost as soon as it was prepared for him; the lines omitted by *R* at 61.142–6 and 64.353–6 could not otherwise have been supplied by Coluccio. (The marginal restoration at 42.12 could easily have been prompted by a glance at line 20.)

In *CE* (App. Crit.), as in the present edition, and also in my collation of *R* (published in 1970), no distinction whatever is made between 'earlier' and 'later' contributions by *R*[2] to *R*. In an article written over twenty-five years ago[28] I sought to evolve a method of separating two recensions in *R*[2] by noting whether a given *R*[2] correction or variant was picked up by *m* or only (later) by *m*[2]. Now that the entire time-span for Coluccio's critical activity in respect to *R* can be reduced to no more than five or six years (that is, between 1391/2 and 1397/8), this theory is of less significance, and I am willing to urge it only in a modified way. I still believe that there were two *R*[2] recensions which may be approximately distinguished by being reflected either in *m*[1] or in *m*[2], according to whether they were earlier or later. Some of the evidence for this will be given in the notes in the Commentary. To the earlier recension, for instance, should be attributed the few passages – three only, as the lists on pp. 38–40 of the Excursus will show – where inherited variants, of a striking sort, derived by *R*[2] from X, or else from *A* by way of X, are reflected in *m*[1]. (The contrast, in the proportion of these included in *m*[1], with the many

28 Thomson 1973.

variants invented by R^2 himself which are so included, is arresting: see the lists in the Excursus below.) As for R^2's corrections (as opposed to variants), these are overwhelmingly original to R^2 himself, and all but a very few of these are taken up by m^1. We may say, then, that Coluccio at first ran rather quickly through R, with an eye on X for obvious slips and omissions, and later (at the time he had reserved for finally entering the titles and metrical notes) made a careful second recension based on the readings of X. After all, Coluccio must have grappled with X at least twice: once in order to see what it contained and to reserve certain critical functions (the necessity for which he must have gauged at this earlier encounter) for himself; and at a later time, once the whole of the text had been laid out and carefully copied by his scribe in accordance with his instructions, in order to set about fulfilling the functions he had chosen, and carefully to discharge them. To sum up: we should, I think, still reckon with two separate recensions by Coluccio, in the former of which he must be supposed to have consulted X to some extent, but more spasmodically – that is, less rigorously and systematically – than in the latter. But it is of importance more for the purposes of codicology than for the primary purpose of reconstituting the text, to know for sure whether there were two R^2 recensions or only one.

These, then, are the Mss of Catullus up to 1400. They are listed in the Table of Manuscripts, as are the secondary Mss of later date (only two of them earlier than 1425), almost all of which derive from R either directly or indirectly.[29] Nothing should obscure the fact that, as Hale and Ullman (see below) insisted, R is the foundation of the later tradition.

Excursus.
Variant Readings in the Hand of R^2: Suggested Origins

(The following lists, numbered 1 to 3 and embracing variant readings attributed to A, to X, and to R^2 himself, must of necessity contain a number of speculative attributions. Possibly X copied A indirectly: see 64.139 n.)

1. Variants originating in self-correction by X, and usually revealing A's readings. (The *first* reading given – i.e., that of X's probable text – is normally *corrected* by the variant reading, following 'al.' The latter is taken

---

29 See, however, Zicàri 1958 for a certain amount of cross-influence, chiefly found in manuscripts of northeast Italian origin, of readings apparently deriving from O or from a copy of O.

to represent *A*'s text.) Observe that all of these, except those at 15.13 and 39.4, are first taken from R^2 by m^2, not by m^1. Notice how often, when *X* 'emends' by a variant, *G* adopts the variant as his text.

3.9 al. vacat hoc verbum [The word *movebat*, from line 8, is not added in *O*]

7.4 feris al. fretis (not in G^1) See the Commentary

9.4 suam al. sanam (*O*) (al. sanam G^1)

10.13 non al. nec (*O*) (al. nec G^1)

12.2 ioco al. loco (*O*) [*X* was right, but *A* plausible] (al. loco G^1)

14.16 false (*OR*) al. salse (*G*) (false *A*, false al. salse *X*) [*G* took the variant; cf. 23.7, 100.2]

?15.13 pudenter al. prudenter (m^1) [Wrong correction by *X*, without Ms authority: an attempt by *X* to emend? *X*, like *G*, did not recognize, or did not understand, *pudenter*]

16.12 vos al. hos [*X* was right, but text corrupt]

23.7 ne al. nec [ne *A*, ne al. nec *X*; *X* attempts to emend (*G* took the variant)]

24.5 neque 1°] nec al. neque [*X* emends in a variant (*G* took the variant)]

25.7 sathabum al. setha (= *G*) [săthabum *A*, sathabum al. setha- *X* (*G* took the variant)]

28.11 parum al. pari (*O*) (al. pari G^1)

28.12 verba al. verpa <ve>l urpa (urpa *O*)

30.9 inde al. idem

35.4 meniam al. menia [vēniam *A*?] But see the Commentary

39.2 seu al. sei

39.4 (m^1) pii al. impii (*O*) [*X* was right, but text corrupt (*regum filii*)]

50.13 omnem al. essem (*O*)

?53.4 manus al. inanius (= *G*) [? manus *A*; but *X* thought it *looked* like inanus, yet saw *inanus tollens* would be unintelligible; hence wrote *manus al. inanius*?]

59.1 fallat al. fellat

61.225 bolnei al. bonei [? boňei *A*; bolnei al. bonei *X*; i.e., *A* tried to 'modernize' the spelling of *bonei*, but his superscript *i* was taken for an *l* by *X*]

63.49 miseritus al. miseriter [Did *A* have an unclear abbreviation for the final syllable?]

63.49 maiestas al. maiestates [Both wrong, but text very corrupt]

64.55 tui se al. terni [*X* misread *A*; at all events, there must sometime have been a supralinear abbreviation for *re*, intended to be placed over *se* – which would bring us close to Voss' restored text – but taken (by *X*, perhaps) as meant to stand over *tui*, read as *tni*]

64.89 mirtus al. -tos (mirtos *O*) [mirtus al. -tos *X*]

64.109 omnia al. obvia

64.344 tenen al. teuen (teuen *O*) [Both wrong, but text very corrupt]

65.1 confectum al. defectum (defectu *O*)

66.5 sublimia al. sublamia (sublamina *O*) vel sublīmina [i.e., *X* has difficulty in reading *A*; cf. 53.4, 61.225] See the Commentary

66.24 nunc al. tunc

66.45 atque al. cumque

66.54 asineos al. arsinoes

66.56 advolat al. collocat [advolat from line 55 avolat]

66.86 indigetis al. indignatis [Prof. Courtney suggests that *indignatis* may derive from *indignis* with *al. eis* added above]. See the Commentary

68.46 certa al. carta (cerata *O*) [cer̃ta *A*? Here again, *A*'s supralinear correction seems to have been ambiguously placed]

68.119 nec causa <carum> al. neque tam <carum>

74.1 lelius al. Gellius

80.6 tanta al. tenta

83.4 samia al. sana [? sanna *A*, as in *O*]

100.2 treron- *O*, trenor- *R*, veron- *G* [Attempt to improve sense and metre, on the part of *X*, whose al. veron- here emends, in the guise of a variant reading]

?100.6 est igitur est al. exigitur [Attempt at emendation by *X*; *G* took the variant]

2. Variants that may possibly have stood *as such* in *A*. (All of these were transmitted to R^2 by way of *X*.) Observe that all, except 15.11, are first taken from R^2 by m^2, not by m^1.

1.8 al. mei [A marginal note, which does not attempt to replace *libelli*, but 'explains' it]

2.3 al. cui (O^1)

2.3 petenti al. patenti (petenti *V*) (al. patenti G^1)

4.27 al. castorum (castrum *V*)

6.9 al. hic (hec *V*) (hic *s.s.* G^1; al. *add.* G^2)

7.6 al. beari (beati *V*) (al. beari G^1)

7.9 al. basia (basiei *V*) (al. basia G^1)

10.8 al. quonam (quoniam *V*) (al. quonam G^1)

10.9 al. neque ipsis (neque nec in ipsis *V*) (al. neque ipsis G^1)

12.4 al. salsum (falsum al. salsum *O*)

12.15 al. muneri (numeri *V*) (al. muneri G^1) [Metrical emendation?]

15.11 (m^1) al. ut iubet (cf. ut al. iubet *O*) [ut iubet *A*? ut al. iubet *O*, mistaking *l* for *l.* = al.; ut lubet al. ut iubet *X*?]

16.12 al. hos (= *O*) (cited by *X* from *A*, though *vos* is better)

22.15 vel neque nec (*O*)

?23.7 al. nec (nec *G*) (ne *V*) [Emendation picked up by *G*; cf. 6.9]

?25.5 al. aries (*O*) vl. alios (*G*) [No obvious 'error' corrected by *X*]

25.7 (?s$\overset{e}{a}$tha *A*) [satha- *OR*, saetha- *G*, al. setha (= R^2)*X*]

34.21 al. placet (*O*)

39.11 al. etruscus (= Petrarch)

63.28 ?thiasus al. iis *A* (= *Rm*^{1}), ?th$\overset{y}{\imath}$as$\overset{u}{\imath}$is *X* (thiasiis R^2, thiasis *O*, thysiis *G*, thyasiis *G*^{1})

?64.324 (see Section 3)

66.86 al. indignatis

?68.11 al. mauli [Possibly an emendation by *X*, based on *A*'s (?: see *O*) *maulio* at 61.215]

101.1 multas [Correction by *A*, not by *X*; otherwise either *G* or *R* would show signs of it]

2a. Other possible variants by *A* (not in R^2):

2.9 luderem *O*, *corr.* *O*^{1}, al. luderem *G*^{1} (ludere al. luderem *AX*?) [Unmetrical]

3.14 al. quae *G*^{1} (-que *V*). [No vestige in *R*/*R*^{2}]

3.14 .i. pulcra *OG*^{1}

3. Variants originating with R^2 himself. Though variants in form, these are in fact intended as corrections (some *ope ingenii*, some from other classical authors). Observe that about 30 per cent of these are taken from R^2 by the 'first hand' (m^1) in *m*; contrast, in this respect, Sections 1 and 2. The 'al.' preceding each of the readings in this section is omitted.[30]

6.9 ille

10.27 deferri

12.16 hoc

13.10 quod

14.15 optimo

30 Arguing against a former view based on an identification of m^2 which I have since
   abandoned (see pp. 35–9), McKie 1989: 69 cites four lines (17.17, 44.20, 64.28, 78^b.4)
   where R^2's corrections are false or ineffective and therefore, he suggests, due to *X*, not
   to R^2. Three of them present *cruces* only solved generations or centuries later; in all,
   R^2 – a sensitive critic short of time for reflection – did his hurried best with what he
   saw. There are other places where R^2 offers a variant which is faulty either metrically
   or otherwise; e.g., 12.16, 17.23, 34.15, 36.18, 45.13, 64.11, 64.23, 66.48, 68.81.

15.17 tum (suggested by Pliny's *tunc*?) [quoted by Coluccio, 1391+, with *tum*)

16.12 quod

17.17 vim (*m*¹)

17.23 hunc eum

23.1 servus est (*m*¹)

28.14 vobis (*m*¹)

32.1 ipsicilla

?33.4 volantiore But see the Commentary

34.15 noto es

36.12 ydalium (*m*¹; from Virgil, *Aeneid* 1.681, 693?)

36.18 venire

39.14 puriter (*m*¹)

39.20 expolitior (*m*¹)

42.3 iocum (*m*¹)

44.20 sertio (*m*¹)

45.13 septinuelle

51.5 quod

53.5 salapputium (from Seneca, *Contr.* 7.4.7?)

55.4 in (*m*¹)

55.22 no- (*m*¹) [observe *V*'s reading, *sis*)

58^{b}.3 pinnipes (*m*¹)

61.38 in modum (*m*¹)

62.37 quid tum

63.18 ere citatis (*m*¹)

?64.3 phasidos See the Commentary

64.11 amphitrionem *R*² *bis*

64.23 matre

64.28 neptine (*m*¹)
  neutūne *R*² *bis*

64.132 avectam

64.285 os

64.288 nonacrios

?64.324 tu tñ opis [Possibly, however, 'the only surviving trace of the correct *tutamen*' (McKie: 126)]

65.7 Troia

66.21 at

66.35 si (*m*¹)

66.48 celorum
  celtum *R*² *bis*

66.74 quin

66.79 quam
66.86 indignis (*m*)
?68.11 mauli But see Section 2
68.29 factat
68.81 vo-
68.91 fratri (*m*^{1})
71.1 quo
77.4 mi
78^{b}.4 -e- (*m*)
92.4 amat [Justifiable correction by R^{2}, given the omission of two lines by
  R; R^{2} saw only X, who *omitted* the lines – so he corrected *amo* to *amat* in
  order to make sense. *A*, which R^{2} did *not* see, had the lines]
97.1 quicquam
100.2 -ant
103.3 numi

The Progress of Catullan Studies from the *Editio Princeps* to the Present Day

(For a full account of the fifteenth- and sixteenth-century editions, the reader should consult Gaisser 1993: xii–xiii and 24–192. To Professor Gaisser's research on this period I am greatly indebted, particularly in the first part of the following section.)

The text of Catullus was first printed in 1472, at Venice, by Vindelinus de Spira (Wendelin von Speyer), in a volume that also contained the poems of Tibullus and Propertius, in addition to the *Silvae* of Statius. For the *Silvae*, as well as for Catullus, it was the *editio princeps*; but for Propertius[31] priority must be conceded to the edition printed at Venice in February of the same year by Federicus de Comitibus. Nevertheless, even in the case of Propertius all editions before 1500 can be shown to be derived from de Spira's slightly later edition – except, of course, for the *princeps* itself.[32] From this moment, the works of the *tresviri amoris* – Catullus, Tibullus, Propertius – tended to be published together in a single volume, sometimes with the addition of a part of Statius or Ovid, or of both, and sometimes with that of Avantius' *Emendationes in Catullum* (see below, p. 48). By the date of the first edition, scores of manuscripts of Catullus were in circulation, all

31 Also, apparently, for Tibullus; see D. Coppini, *Annali della Scuola Normale Superiore di Pisa* IX (1979): 1162 n. 3.
32 See Butrica 1984: 160.

of them exhibiting a deeply corrupted text based on *V*, the desperate state
of which is noted in the subscription to *G*, inherited from a predecessor, as
McKie (170–7) has shown. There were no manuscripts in existence which
were good enough, or differed sufficiently from *V*, to have afforded a more
intelligible version of the poet's text, for the purpose of correction or even
of comparison. In 1472, de Spira simply took up the first manuscript that
lay to hand (one that was close in its origins to No. 46 in my Table),[33] just
as he did for Propertius (in the latter case, either Vat. Barb. lat. 34 – which
about 1493–5 acquired an anonymous marginal commentary – or a similar
'commonplace conflation of readings of F and g.')[34] There was virtually
no attempt at editing, though a 'Life' of Catullus – adapted from that of
Sicco Polentonus[35] – has been added. As was the fashion in the Humanistic
period, the *editio princeps* became the basis of the received text for the time
being; so it was a copy of de Spira's edition, extremely faulty as it was,
that had to carry the annotations of Angelus Politianus, together with two
separate subscriptions, written twelve years apart.[36] Similarly annotated
copies include one belonging to A. Colotius.[37] Consequently, when we
come to the Parma edition of the following year, we are not surprised
to find that *1473* (which did in fact receive some editing at the hands of
Franciscus Puteolanus) is merely a revised version of *1472*, corrected to
some extent from a member of the *O*-influenced group of manuscripts to
which No. 122 in my Table belongs.[38] Since the reading *iuventi* at 48.1 is
present in *Sen.* (No. 95 in the Table), and also in γ-class manuscripts, but
not in those influenced by *O*, it seems just possible that Puteolanus also
saw a second manuscript. In the colophon to the Statius part he is credited
by his printer with the intention of correcting the Venice edition of 1472,
and moreover with no fewer than 3000 emendations to Catullus and Statius
alone, generated in the process of doing so.

An edition nowadays ascribed to Milan – previously, to Venice – and
dated 1475, simply repeats the text of de Spira 1472, with the same 'Life'
of Catullus. Its direct descendant is the Reggio (Calabria) edition of 1481,
which sets out simply to correct it. At least for Catullus, however, a much
more important and influential text-edition was that published, in this same
year 1481, at Vicenza, and edited by Joannes Calphurnius. His work likewise

33 See Zicàri 1958 = *Scritti*, 1978: 106.
34 Butrica 1984: 145, 160.
35 *Scriptores illustres latinae linguae*, ed. B.L. Ullman (Rome, 1928), II: 63–4.
36 Rome, Biblioteca Corsiniana Inc. 50 F 37; the subscriptions mentioned are on fols. 37[r]
   and 127[v].
37 See the illustration in Gaisser 1993: 27.
38 Zicàri 1958: 95–6 = *Scritti*, 1978: 99. For *O*-type changes in *1473* see Gaisser 1993: 33.

treats *1472* as a *textus receptus* and – as the dedicatory epistle to Hermolaus Barbarus makes abundantly clear – its raison d'être lay in his discovery of the corrupt state of the Venice edition and a desire to print a version that made sense. He did not (like Puteolanus in *1473*) compare the *editio princeps* with a manuscript. Indeed, it is not at all certain that he had access to any manuscript; for him, printed editions alone were the source of the text.[39] What he did was to examine *1473* against *1472*, sometimes combining their readings, and frequently advancing his own suggestions. It is clear, however, that textual improvement, rather than a commentary of any kind, is what he had in mind throughout.

When we turn to Politianus' notes, made in the margins of the *editio princeps* (as we noted above), we find on the contrary that, although a desire to improve the text is still the dominant motive, there is at least an element of commentary as well. In the subscription to Propertius in the same book, written in 1485, he uses the expression *vel corrigere vel interpretari*, though elsewhere he explicitly declines to compose a full commentary. Politianus' notes are concerned with points of metre and of grammar; linguistic *notabilia*, including difficult words; and illustrative parallels in Greek as well as in Latin. (These last were sometimes adduced as being helpful in restoring the text.) In the same year, 1485, in which Politianus composed the subscription (to Propertius) just mentioned, a full commentary on Catullus was at last published, under the name of Antonius Parthenius of Verona; the publication reflects the intense pride of that city in its native poet. Not only this; it draws attention to the interpretations of Tibullus by Bernardinus Cyllenius on Tibullus, of Domitius Calderinus on Statius, Juvenal, and Martial – and both of these scholars were Veronese. Parthenius' edition contains a 'Life' of Catullus, a history of lyric poetry, and a commentary that begins with a discussion of the identity of 'Cornelius' in poem 1, and ends with a metrical note on elided *s* in poem 116; finally there is an epistle to the reader, promising more studies on Catullus, in the form of *Quaestiones* (which in fact were never published). There is however a defensive note in Parthenius' dedication; he 'has rushed his work into print to forestall someone else, and now he is afraid of the consequences.'[40] The person referred to was Baptista Guarinus, who seems to have been engaged at this time on an edition of his own. But Parthenius in the end established his claim to have produced the first Catullan commentary (and Guarinus' notes were suppressed until 1521, when Baptista's son Alexander Guarinus incorporated them in his own edition). The work of Parthenius

39 Gaisser 1993: 42.
40 Gaisser 1993: 82.

is designed to clear up the kinds of difficulties in reading Catullus that would be encountered by pupils in school, rather than mature scholars. Its creator regarded it, in all modesty, as provisional. Nevertheless it is, unlike Politianus' contributions (to which we shall return in a moment), a *complete* commentary, not just an examination of selected problems. At the very outset, Parthenius is the first to realize that 'Cornelius' in poem 1 cannot be Cornelius Gallus the poet (despite the heading 'Ad Cornelium Gallum' in *1472* and subsequent editions), but must be the historian; even Politianus had been misled into identifying 'Cornelius' with the poet. Parthenius, whose learning was distinctly limited, naturally came to many wrong conclusions; among them some false poem divisions, which he passed down to the early sixteenth-century editors, and a totally wrong interpretation of poem 35 as being concerned with love, not literature.[41] Generally, however, Parthenius confines his commentary to minor points; he will explain what figure of speech is used, or describe the tone of a certain passage. His discussion of poem 63, however, goes beyond this and offers genuine literary criticism, as his successors recognize.[42] The text he used was that of Calphurnius, but with corrections out of his own head (fifteen of which have endured to the present). Lacking the brilliance of Politianus, he nevertheless established a comparatively intelligible text – for its time – and, profiting by his schoolroom experience, initiated as early as 1485 the procedures and practice applicable to a full line-by-line commentary on his author. In comparison, Propertius had to wait a couple of years longer, until in 1487 the elder Philippus Beroaldus produced his Bologna commentary (which derived its text from Calphurnius' Vicenza edition of 1481).[43] What may be termed the spasmodic mode of commentary, ignoring the claims of continuous exposition and concentrating on individual problems selected for their interest, was practised by Beroaldus himself, in relation to Catullus, in his *Annotationes Centum* of 1488. This mode, which suited the epideictic tendency of brilliant scholars who were averse to drudgery, could be said to be a fashion of the times, beginning from about 1475, when Domitius Calderinus added his *Elucubratio in quaedam Propertii loca quae difficiliora videbantur* to a commentary on Statius' *Silvae* and the pseudo-Ovidian *Epistula Sapphonis* (Rome); this work should by no means be described as a commentary on Propertius, especially for the later books, where it is very thin indeed. Similar essays in this fashionable mode were published by Hermolaus Barbarus in *Castigationes Plinianae* of 1492, and by Politianus

41 Gaisser 1993: 91–2.
42 Gaisser 1993: 94–5.
43 See Butrica 1984: 164.

in the first series of his *Miscellanea*, dated 1489. In the last-named work there are no more than seven discussions of passages in Catullus.[44] Most of these are developed from the marginal notes, already referred to, which had been written between 1473 and 1485. All of them were prompted by the annotations of Parthenius, whose commentary had already been republished more than once and was now accepted as the 'standard' edition of Catullus.

The next editor of a thoroughgoing commentary on Catullus (it was published at Venice in 1496) was Palladius Fuscus, or Niger. Although he was born in Padua, he spent most of his working life in Dalmatia, where he held various educational and legal appointments after unsuccessfully seeking a teaching post in Udine. He, too, had to take as his basis for revision the now established commentary of Parthenius. The corrections he made to it were sometimes, but not always, his own; he depends on the work of Hermolaus Barbarus (consisting of a number of Catullan observations in the *Castigationes Plinianae*) as well as those of Beroaldus in the *Annotationes Centum* (referred to above) and also those of Avantius in his *Emendationes in Catullum* (published in 1495), which we shall presently discuss. In other words, Palladius had a second-rate talent, and his work was in large part derivative. But he did in fact expand the basis of knowledge on which future commentators would draw. Where he had nothing to add, he would merely reproduce Parthenius' note. Essentially, then, by the end of the century there was in the field a school edition – that of Parthenius – with some modifications by others; it served the needs of a rapidly growing public of young readers, and for the next few decades all interpretation tended to focus on the wording of Parthenius' notes, rather than on the text of the poet himself so far as that was accessible. In the last decade we should also mention, as being similarly based on Parthenius, the brief contribution of Sabellicus (whose real name was Marcus Antonius Coccius), contained in twenty annotations 'Ex Catullo' appended to a volume consisting of notes on Pliny the Elder; these annotations were published in 1497, though they had been composed apparently between 1485 and 1493. Sabellicus' intention was to correct the *text* of Parthenius, *ope ingenii*; at 27.2, for example, instead of the accepted reading *amariores* he urges the claims of *meraciores* (later reintroduced as a gloss by Scaliger), but does not press the correction.[45] Again, poem 29 is divided by Sabellicus into two separate poems;[46] and he, for the first time, separates poems 2 and 3.

---

44 They are listed in Gaisser 1993: 70.

45 Gaisser 1993: 300 n. 95; on p. 49 she draws attention to his modesty and diffidence.

46 As it was to be again, much later, by P.R. Young <Forsyth> in *Classical Journal* LXIX (1969): 327–8.

For a greater figure than Sabellicus, however, we must go back a year or two. Hieronymus Avantius (Girolamo Avanzi) initially created his *Emendationes in Catullum* in the years 1492–3, then privately circulated them among his friends, and finally published them at Venice in 1495; there was a second edition, considerably enlarged and altered, which appeared, also at Venice, in 1500. Both of these editions are concerned with problems of text and metre; Avantius' interest in interpretative commentary is minimal, and (unlike Politianus) he seldom quotes illustrative passages from other authors, Greek or Latin (and if he does, his quotations are not on a lavish scale). As to textual readings, however, he made a careful study of two manuscripts that came his way, as well as the previous editions; all of which sources of information he collated and compared. The second edition, unlike the first, accompanies a text of Catullus (and of Tibullus and Propertius); ·but the text itself is practically the same as that of Parthenius (whose pupil Avantius had been), although Avantius is given credit for it. On this second edition was based the epoch-making first Aldine text-edition of 1502, and also the second Aldine of 1515, for both of which he functioned as Aldus' editor; and he was also largely responsible for the *editio Tricavelliana* of about 1535. To anticipate a little: the Aldine editions displaced all others and became the rocklike foundation of the very many texts in circulation – including a stream of counterfeit Alduses, printed in Lyons (by Gryphius) and elsewhere, during the entire first half of the sixteenth century.

It may be remarked in passing that Avantius' *Emendationes*, like the work of Parthenius, originated as a manifestation of loyalty to his native Verona, particularly directed against Politianus for the latter's attacks on another Veronese scholar, Domitius Calderinus (though the note of hostility to Politianus was removed from the 1500 edition). Avantius still starts from Parthenius; but unlike Sabellicus, who corrects Parthenius only by his own wits, Avantius uses external information in order to do so. In the event, it was Avantius who produced the new *textus receptus*, in the shape of the first Aldine edition and its successors. Aldus' bold step in turning out no fewer than 3000 copies – a quite remarkable number, for that age – of his handily sized 1502 edition, contributed not a little to its triumphant success. Another point in its favour was Avantius' application to the study of Catullan metres, which he placed on a sound footing, based on Catullus' own practice, and giving a historical context for metrical developments; an imperfect knowledge of the laws of metre had, in fact, caused recent editors of Catullus' text to print a succession of false readings.

About the time (1493–5) when Avantius was bringing his *Emendationes* to birth, a still extant manuscript (Vat. Barb. lat. 34) shows marginal annotations, quoting Politianus, Hermolaus Barbarus, Beroaldus, and Sabellicus, as well as the basic source, Parthenius.[47] It is evident also that Pontanus, who died in 1503, was interested in Catullus; he possessed a manuscript of the poet's works, and imitated him in his own compositions, and we are told that he wrote some kind of commentary (perhaps no more than annotations in the margins of a text); it was never published, and is now lost. In any case, its direction seems to have been neither text-critical nor interpretative, but rather concerned with the substitution of his own words where the text of Catullus appeared to be unintelligible as it stood: the outstanding example of this procedure is, of course, his marginal suggestion of the line *qualecumque quod* (or *quidem*) *ora per virorum* at 1.9, which was mentioned and discussed by Avantius, Palladius, and Hermolaus Barbarus.[48] These notes by Pontanus were later regarded by him as youthful *lusus*; and despite their author's great reputation they had very little influence on the future course of Catullan scholarship. Just before Pontanus' death, notes on Catullus were written by his friend (and Politianus' former pupil) Franciscus Puccius, who lectured both in Florence and later in Naples, in the course of a highly distinguished public, as well as academic, career. Puccius – who seems to have had only a partial acquaintance with Pontanus' notes – is concerned with the text, with poem divisions, with metre, and with general interpretation. Besides Pontanus, he mentions Politianus, Hermolaus Barbarus, and Beroaldus. Puccius' notes circulated in many versions during the next few decades,[49] though the original version has not been identified. The Neapolitan connection includes Aulus Janus Parrhasius, who (like Puccius) seems to have taken his inspiration from Pontanus. An unfinished commentary (on the first few poems only) in Parrhasius' own hand survives, together with his transcription of Puccius' annotations; this commentary, which comprehends both text and interpretation, has been dated between 1512 and 1519.[50]

In 1521, Alexander Guarinus published *Expositiones in Catullum*, with the double purpose of preserving the textual corrections entered long before, in a manuscript, by his father Baptista (who had died in 1505), and of advancing his own textual and interpretative contributions. The commentary has a great deal to offer, but for some reason commanded little influence. In 1521–2, Pierius Valerianus delivered a successful course of lectures on Catullus at the University of Rome; but they were never

47 Butrica 1984: 299–300; Gaisser 1992: 209.
48 Gaisser 1992: 210–11.
49 Eighteen copies are described in Gaisser 1992: 243–8.
50 B. Richardson, 'Pucci, Parrasio and Catullus,' *Italia medioevale e umanistica* XIX (1976): 277–89, esp. 288.

published, and the manuscript was partly destroyed, five years later, in the Sack of Rome.[51] In 1535, an undistinguished edition of the text was produced by Melchior Sessa, whose principal aim (apparently) was to rival Aldus in profitability.

After about 1535, not much was done in the field of criticism for the poet's works as a whole, though two commentaries on individual poems may be mentioned: Franciscus Robortellus, *Explicatio in Catulli Epithalamium* (poem 61), printed at Florence in 1548, and Bernardinus Realinus, *In Nuptias Pelei et Thetidis* (poem 64), printed at Bologna in 1551. Neither of these two commentaries had much influence on later studies.[52] In 1553, Petrus Victorius devoted twelve of the chapters of his *Variae lectiones* to Catullus. (He added further chapters in later editions.) Sometimes he explains passages, often from the idiom of Greek and Roman Comedy. Clearly he owes a debt to Puccius, whose notes he had copied out in 1521.

With Marcus Antonius Muretus, whose commentary on Catullus first appeared at Venice in 1554, we enter a new age (indeed, Doering in 1788 was to style it the *aetas Muretiana*). Yet, as Ellis correctly noted, Muretus' commentary was distinctly slighter than that of Alexander Guarinus, and 'less minute in the explanation of particular words,' but reinforced by a greater knowledge of Greek; nevertheless still disappointing inasmuch as there is 'very little for the elucidation of passages where the allusion is really recondite.'[53] What is above all interesting in Muretus is the union, characteristic of French Humanism in that period, of poetry and scholarship. The scholarship itself, however, was directed towards poetic explication and away from textual emendation and indeed all study of the text as such, the text being taken as something virtually established. As one of Ronsard's circle, Muret had been a prominent member of a youthful – almost revolutionary – movement, later to be known as the Pléiade. For the purposes of literary creation, Catullan attitudes, and style, and even metre, were recommended for imitation to young practitioners by Muretus in his lectures. So far, so good. But even as he was completing his commentary on the poems of Ronsard, Muretus suddenly found himself forced into exile on accusations of pederasty, to which a charge of heresy was added. Paulus Manutius – Aldus' successor – made a place for him in Venice, assigning to him the editorship of a series of classical texts, beginning with Catullus. While he was studying this poet, he acquired by good fortune the notes on various authors made by Petrus Victorius in 1553, containing twenty-four

---

51 See Gaisser 1993: chapter 3, 109–45; also 1992: 255–9.
52 Gaisser 1992: 283–4 and 286–8.
53 Ellis, *Commentary*[2]: viii.

chapters specifically devoted to Catullus himself. Muretus accordingly used Victorius (and sometimes acknowledged the fact), but also abused him, and disparaged his scholarship wherever he could.

In estimating Muretus' success, it must be borne in mind that no commentary on the whole of Catullus had been published since that of Alexander Guarinus thirty-three years before, though – as we have seen – many editions and reprints of the text alone had appeared, including pirated reproductions of the first and second Aldines. Muretus himself based his text largely on the second Aldine (or possibly a reproduction thereof), but he incorporated with this the suggestions of earlier editors. Though in the matter of textual accuracy his is by no means a thoroughgoing or systematic revision, his sheer talent enabled him on several occasions to make a material contribution to the improvement of the text. Of course he inherited a more purified *textus receptus* than his predecessors had possessed; but he also ventured emendations of his own, not from any appeal to manuscript evidence but out of clear-headed personal judgment. It should be repeated, however, that he considered his business to lie with the content – that is to say, with the poetry of Catullus. Hence his reluctance to tamper unduly with the given text, and his extreme conservatism in admitting 'modern conjectures and supplements, no matter how apposite.'[54] On the other hand, Muretus' pronounced interest in Catullan metre, for reasons already given, is reflected in the fact that he is the first editor of a published commentary to observe that poem 4 is in the pure iambic, which is, as he notes, so hard to bring off in Latin (Pierius Valerianus had caught this point in his unpublished lectures). He is especially interested in the longer poems, on which his literary observations are outstanding for their acuteness. In general, however, his commentary as a whole shows, from the point of view of detailed scholarship, the effects of the haste with which it was produced. A second edition in 1558 merely added Tibullus and Propertius to Catullus.

A far more significant edition, if scholarly ends are considered, was that of Achilles Statius (Aquiles Estaço, a member of a well-established Portuguese family), who began to study the Roman poets as a preparation for the pious enterprise of translating the Psalms of David into a variety of Latin metres (one wonders if he was aware of the version of these same Psalms made in 1551 by the Scottish humanist, George Buchanan, when he was detained in Portugal by the Inquisition).[55] When with this end in view he

---

54 Gaisser 1993: 261.
55 The text of Buchanan's paraphrase of the Psalms is given in *Opera Omnia* (Edinburgh, 1715), II: 1–100. See Ian D. McFarlane, *Buchanan* (London, 1981): 247–86, for an account of this work and its composition.

had composed a body of notes on Tibullus, Virgil, Lucretius, the Odes of Horace, and Catullus, those to whom he showed this work pressed him to publish it. He decided to begin with Catullus (in 1566) and followed this with Tibullus (in 1567); but the notes on Virgil even today remain in manuscript, and those on Lucretius seem to be lost, as do those on Horace (though an unconnected commentary on the *Ars Poetica* had appeared in 1553). As for the Psalms in Latin, these too remain in manuscript, along with sacred and profane lyrics (*carmina*, showing very little influence from Catullus). There is a copy of the first Aldine, containing his marginal notes, in the Bibliothèque Nationale (Rés. p. Yc. 375); but here the annotations are infrequent and very brief.[56] In his published commentary, Statius is — by contrast with Muretus — interested primarily in textual problems. His literary observations are not very numerous, and they are more limited in scope than Muretus'; under this head, his topics include such matters as the effectiveness of particular words or phrases in their context. In one department, however, his range is wider than that of Muretus: many parallels are adduced to explain Catullan linguistic usage, not only from Latin and Greek authors, but also – a notable departure – from inscriptions. In this field, even Scaliger sometimes does little more than merely repeat him.[57] He was interested in comparing the readings of a group of manuscripts, to which he often refers;[58] and he cites emendations offered by other Humanists, many of them contemporary with himself – but he never mentions the work of Muretus. Apart from a difference in aims and methods (he is 'factual and historical where Muretus is uncritical and literary' [Gaisser 1993: 175]), factions were clearly involved. The party in Rome to which Statius belonged was that of Petrus Victorius, Gabriel Faernus, and Fulvius Orsinus, none of whom was friendly to Muretus. For all its good qualities, Statius' commentary was much less influential than Muretus'; it never had a second edition of its own, and was not reprinted until the seventeenth century brought in a fashion for variorum editions. Above all, in his use of multiple manuscripts he strikes out on a new and hitherto unmapped path. Even if he did not 'weigh' his manuscripts (Victorius and Faernus had done this better), cited them unevenly, and did not provide full collations, yet 'not since <Avantius> had anyone studied the text so thoroughly and in such detail.'[59] It is the more surprising, given this interest in text rather than in content, that Statius did not produce a critical edition arising directly

56 I rely on Gaisser 1992: 265, not having seen the volume myself.
57 Ellis, *Commentary*[2]: viii.
58 See Ullman 1908: passim.
59 Gaisser 1993: 177.

from his own research but was content to rest on the second Aldine as the basis of his studies. Nevertheless what Statius had to say in textual matters had a powerful influence on Joseph Justus Scaliger, the author (in 1577) of the next notable edition. Although Scaliger professed to despise the work of Statius, still he used it repeatedly and often followed it closely.

On the other hand, Scaliger had at least initially a high regard for Muretus, whose influence is no less evident in his work than that of Statius; but because of a literary trick by Muretus,[60] he approached him in a spirit of rivalry and 'getting even.' Yet Scaliger was in any case a great individualist in many respects. For the first time, so far as editors of Catullus were concerned, he attempted systematically to reconstruct the history of the text and to explain the genesis of false readings; in what may be called a partial anticipation of the 'method of Lachmann,' he even went so far as to seek to reconstruct an archetype, pronouncing on the script in which it must have been written, and also where it was written. The collations he made with this end in view are to be found in the margins of his copy of the 1569 Plantin Catullus.[61] Consequently Scaliger's 1577 edition is a landmark in textual studies. Though it was attacked by several distinguished scholars, including Petrus Victorius, it ran into several reprintings, the series of which extended throughout the seventeenth century if we include variorum editions. In effect, this challenging edition became the *textus receptus* for the philological epoch to come (Doering's *aetas Scaligerana*). Its great leap forward was to amass readings methodically from manuscript evidence, thus modifying the practice, established now for over a century, of altering the base text by simply examining and comparing the printed editions. Unfortunately, the manuscript he chiefly collated for the purpose – the present British Library MS Egerton 3027 – is virtually worthless, as Ellis, who first identified it, pointed out.[62] But Scaliger reinforced his new method by looking for, and finding, resemblances between his chosen Ms and the seven manuscripts of which the readings are given (though somewhat erratically) by Statius; and he saw that 'such close agreement could come about only if all the manuscripts were descended from a common exemplar.'[63] In other words, he formed an impression – supported by Benvenuto Campesani's epigram, which accompanied the text in his collated manuscript – that a single Verona codex (our *V*) underlay the entire body of extant manuscripts. He also concluded from the nature of the common

60 Gaisser 1993: 179.
61 Now at Leiden: Bibliotheek der Rijksuniversiteit, 755 H 23.
62 Ellis, *Commentary*[2]: viii.
63 Gaisser 1993: 185.

errors that this codex was in 'Lombardic' (a term then used to include Carolingian) script. Scaliger's method would have yielded outstandingly successful results if it had been applied to really good manuscripts. As it was, his advancement of Catullan studies resulted substantially from innate intelligence as much as from his use of the body of collations made partly by himself, partly by Statius.[64] Presented in a controversial way, his conclusions naturally provoked opposition; but the remarkable fact is that the work of Scaliger remained quite unchallenged, as the newly established 'standard' text-plus-commentary, at least until Passerat's posthumous Catullus appeared in 1608, and continued to dominate the field for some time thereafter. There are certain 'cultural' reasons for this: if Statius, with his versification of sacred literature, emerged as a characteristic figure of the counter-reformation period in Rome, Scaliger, on his part, marks the transfer of Catullan studies to the now somewhat puritanical North, a geographical region where Catullus (who unlike his follower Martial was not a satirist and could teach no moral lessons) was out of favour.[65] When in the 1580s the elder Janus Dousa extolled Catullus to his Dutch compatriots, it was as a model of style; a similar, purely literary, end was served by the collection of parodies and notes on poem 4, published in 1579.

If, at this period, the influence of Scaliger's Catullus was profound, especially in the Low Countries, there were nevertheless some stirrings in Paris, where Jean Passerat was studying Catullus intensively. He did not particularly relish emerging as a rival to Scaliger, and possibly refrained for this reason from completing his annotations.[66] But his commentary is – as Ellis notes – particularly good on the wedding poems, 61 and 62; it is also rich in the accumulation of passages cited to illustrate the meaning of individual words. The *praelectiones* (as he called his commentary) are somewhat unequal, and most of the short poems are omitted from them. What we have, therefore, scarcely amounts to a regular commentary on Catullus as a whole. Though it was published after his death (he died in 1602), Passerat's work really belongs to the sixteenth century – as clearly do the four lectures, ostensibly on poem 63,[67] by Robertus Titius, an outspoken critic and rival of Scaliger's, which were published at Bologna in 1599.

The seventeenth century was an age of consolidation, marked by variorum editions and compendia, such as Janus Gruterus' *Lampas, sive fax*

---

64 Gaisser 1993: 186–7.
65 Gaisser 1993: 192.
66 Ellis, *Commentary*[2]: ix.
67 See, however, Gaisser 1992: 216.

artium liberalium (Frankfurt, 1602), which embraced the commentaries of Sabellicus, Robortellus (on poem 61), and Realinus (on poem 64), and the Paris variorum edition of 1604, which was to be followed by less ample versions in 1659 and 1680. The rather brief annotations of Johannes Livineius (d. 1599) came out posthumously in 1521 when they were added to the second (Frankfurt) impression of an edition by Janus Gebhardus; Livineius frequently finds occasion to disagree with Scaliger's commentary, and with that of Muretus. Of the *Asterismi* of Marcilius, little need be said; a slight work, several times reprinted but in no way influential, these 'Asterisms' first appeared as a part of the 1604 edition already mentioned, but may have been composed before that date. Towards the end of the century we encounter the considerable figure of Isaac Vossius, whose edition (bearing the date 1684) was published in London from sheets apparently printed in Leiden. Vossius industriously collected manuscripts, which he compared with some effect, and was moreover an accomplished scholar in several different fields; in editing Catullus, as Ellis remarks, he supplemented his knowledge in one department of philology by his experience in another.[68] To quote Ellis further: '<Vossius>, unlike Passerat, throws light on corrupt or hitherto unexplained passages ... Of all commentaries on Catullus, his is the most erudite.' This goes far to explain why the work achieved such a wide circulation, inaugurating Doering's *aetas Vossiana*. At about the same time, the reviving interest in Catullus in France was shown by the appearance of the first *editio in usum Delphini* (Paris, 1685). Finally, it should be added that the seventeenth century also saw the publication of no fewer than seven commentaries exclusively devoted to poem 64.

The earlier part, at least, of the eighteenth century was not a fertile period in the history of Catullan scholarship. It is dominated – if the word can be used – by the two Paduan editions of Johannes Antonius Vulpius (Volpi), published respectively in 1710 and 1737. Although it was voluminous, and professed to be all-embracing, it contained very little that was new, though conscientiously repeating the material of previous commentaries. Sober, pedantic, and clerically decorous, it relied on multiple quotations of parallel passages, rather than helping the reader who sought an understanding of Catullus; and even the quotations themselves are of a commonplace and uninteresting sort. If there was an *aetas Vulpiana* (Doering's term again), it was marked by a somewhat cautious dullness. Johannes Franciscus Corradinus, whose edition, marred by fraudulent claims,[69] appeared in 1738,

---

68 Ellis, *Commentary*[2]: ix.
69 On these, see Gaisser 1992: 217.

has at least the merit, noted by Ellis, of seeing Catullus as his own best expositor; and modern texts credit him with one good emendation, at 39.17.

Much later in the century, the *editio Bipontina* (Zweibrücken, 1783) includes a useful check-list (*notitia literaria*) of earlier editions. Five years later, F.W. Doering published at Leiden his edition (reprinted in 1792 and subsequently), which exerted a surprising amount of influence in view of its very sparse commentary; it furnished the text for several nineteenth-century Catulluses, including the London *editio Delphina* of 1822. Also in 1788, Laurens van Santen, whose interests lay primarily in the text, published a short but important study of poem 68 as a sample of an intended commentary on the whole of Catullus; but this was the year when Doering's work emerged, and (regrettably) Santen's commentary was discontinued. In the preface to his sample, Santen reveals that he had sought far and wide for readings in manuscripts:

No fewer than twelve scholars are named who had contributed MS readings, and one of these had excerpted ... seven MSS with his own hand. He complains, however, that many codices still remained of whose readings he could procure no information; and by an accident which has preserved the sheets of paper on which the variants had been written out for Santen but not sent, we know that among these was the celebrated Canonici codex (O) ... Santen's *apparatus criticus*, therefore, though large, was not complete. It comprised, however, the Datanus. When Santen's library was sold in 1800, it was purchased by H.F. von Dietz, by whom it was subsequently transferred to the Royal Library of Berlin. On this collection, partly of actual MSS, partly of the collations supplied to Santen by his friends, Lachmann ... based his epoch-making edition of 1829, laconically informing his readers that he had selected two MSS, the Datanus (*D*) and another which he called *L* (for Laurens van Santen) as representing all the rest. '*Codices D et L, cum quorum alterutro ceteri non interpolati ubique consentiunt, hac editione totos exhibemus.*'[70]

With the name of Lachmann, we enter the realm of nineteenth-century scientific – in large measure, German – philology. The two manuscripts just indicated (Nos. 3 and 4 in the Table) lay close to Lachmann's hand in Berlin, but were regrettably inadequate for his purpose. *D* had a long career in critical apparatuses as a 'good' manuscript, thanks to Lachmann's commendation and the prestige of his name; its expulsion from this undeserved place, largely due to B.L. Ullman, has now been accepted.[71] I. Sillig, who in 1823 had

70 Ellis, *Commentary*[2]: xvi–xvii.
71 See *CE*, Introduction: 35–40.

collated the Dresden manuscript (No. 15 in the Table), correctly assigning it a place among the poorer Mss, announced in 1830 his discovery of *G*, one of the three 'cardinal' fourteenth-century manuscripts, though its great importance was not adequately recognized until 1862, when L. Schwabe published his *Quaestiones Catullianae*.[72] Sillig's work on the text was followed closely by Moritz Haupt, with *Quaestiones Catullianae* in 1837 and *Observationes Criticae* in 1841, resulting in some successful emendations (a field in which the harvest had, naturally, now become increasingly meagre). Haupt's edition of Catullus, however, was not to appear until 1853. General descriptions of Catullus' poetry were written by O. Ribbeck, in 1863,[73] and later by A. Couat,[74] who discussed the topic of Catullus' relationship to the Alexandrian poets.

Schwabe followed up his 1862 *Quaestiones* with a full text-edition (Giessen, 1866) – the first, be it noted, to offer a collation of the readings of *G* – which twenty years later he was to expand into a notable second edition (Berlin, 1886) that gave in its apparatus criticus a painstakingly accurate record of the readings of *O* and *T* as well as of *G*, and also contained two extremely useful lists of *testimonia* (comprehensive, to 1375, with a selective supplement to 1500), and an *index verborum*. To return to the 1860s: A. Rossbach's edition (1867), and that of Lucian Müller (published in 1870) need not detain us here. Looking for a moment into the next decade, we notice a useful little Jena dissertation of forty-three pages, entitled *De Catullo Graecorum imitatore*, by K.P. Schulze, of whom we shall hear more presently. Robinson Ellis' first text-edition appeared in 1867; it called attention to *O*'s importance, but failed to exploit it fully. Meanwhile, from 1859 to 1867, he had been working on a commentary, accumulating a vast quantity of illustrative references and parallel passages in Greek and Latin. This was first published in 1876, and followed two years later by a second text-edition. At the same time, Emil Baehrens – who in 1874 had published his *Analecta Catulliana* on textual questions – brought out his text-edition (1876), in which the text was for the first time based on the authority of *G* and *O* alone. Baehrens' commentary, in Latin, followed in 1885; it was ample in bulk, but marred by waywardness in its readings:

72 This work also embodied – though not, as is usually supposed, for the first time; W.T. Jungclaussen had essayed the task in 1857 – an attempt to establish a firm chronology for the events in Catullus' life, mainly based, as was inevitable, on references in the poems.

73 *Geschichte der römische Dichtung* I: 312.

74 *Étude sur Catulle*, Paris, 1874.

Baehrens was handicapped by a literal and prosaic mind which led him to insist that a poet should express himself in terms of standard literary usage; consequently much of his space is taken up with the manufacture of difficulties which would trouble no one nowadays, and the tendency of his solutions is towards re-writing Catullus in a manner which, if he had so written, would have been fatal to his survival as a poet.[75]

Ellis' commentary achieved a second edition in 1889; disorganized in method, it still compels admiration for its sheer wealth of marginal reference. The year 1879 saw the appearance of H.A.J. Munro's *Criticisms and Elucidations of Catullus*, an examination of selected poems and passages.[76]

In the 1880s some notable additions were made to the critical literature on Catullus. After Baehrens' commentary (1885), Ellis produced (in 1889) the second edition of his own. Of E. Benoist's Paris commentary, where textual and interpretative notes were separated, the first volume appeared in 1882 (the work was completed by E. Thomas in 1890). A. Riese's edition of 1884, with a commentary, was unambitious but sound. B. Schmidt's *editio maior*, with prolegomena but no commentary, came out in 1887. J.P. Postgate's Catullus text in the *Corpus Poetarum Latinorum* is dated 1889. The year 1893 saw the publication both of E.T. Merrill's Boston Catullus, with a commentary directed to students (and a facsimile reproduction of one folio of *O*), and also of K.P. Schulze's revision of Baehrens, which sought to exalt the manuscript known as *m* (No. 115 in the Table) to a position of equal importance with *G*. Unfortunately, Schulze (whose reports of *m*'s readings were far from accurate) was half right, in a sense, since *m* was later shown to be a close copy of the still-to-be-discovered *R*. Naturally, Schulze defended *m*, and regarded *R*, on its unveiling three years later, as an upstart – which led to infinite trouble.[77] In 1896, apart from W.G. Hale's momentous discovery of *R* in the Vatican library, there appeared an unpretentious but sensible (and most attractively produced) Catullus – taking of course no account of *R* itself – edited by A. Palmer.

For our present purpose the twentieth century may be said to have begun with Ellis' two Catulluses (1904, in the Oxford Classical Texts series; London, 1911). Ellis had made two separate visits to Rome, in 1897 and 1902, in order to collate *R* for himself; but his eyesight was failing, and

75 R.G.C. Levens, in *Fifty Years (and Twelve) of Classical Scholarship* (Oxford, 1958): 358. The comparison between Ellis' and Baehrens' rival commentaries, on the same page, is worth reading *in extenso*.
76 Ellis regarded this book, not quite fairly, as an extended review of his 1876 Catullus.
77 See, for the whole story, Thomson 1973: 121–6.

he did not wish to encroach on Hale's territory. In 1908, G. Friedrich published an outstandingly rich commentary – where it existed, that is; for its author annotated only those passages and those questions that engaged his keen interest. Although it lacks an apparatus criticus, it well repays consultation. C. Pascal's Catullus (1916) and that of G. Lafaye (1922; often reprinted) show no great originality. Merrill's text-edition of 1923 failed to make an impression on scholars and was withdrawn. But, also in 1923, W. Kroll brought out an edition with notes, which (augmented in 1929 and subsequently) has remained a favourite to this day. It is particularly well informed on the subject of Greek influences and parallels, and amounts to a major commentary despite its compact format. M. Lenchantin's Italian edition of 1928 is clear and helpful in comment, though conservative in text. I. Cazzaniga's text-edition (first published in 1941) is judicious in its readings, which bear comparison with those of Mynors (see below). M. Schuster's Teubner edition of 1949 was revised and improved by H. Eisenhut in 1958, the year when R.A.B. Mynors' Oxford Classical Text appeared. This important Catullus, which conveniently grouped the secondary manuscripts under Greek letters, showed taste and discretion; it could however have profited from a closer study of the later hands in *R*, for example.[78] In 1961 a commentary was provided for it (with the exception of thirty-two poems 'which do not lend themselves to comment in English')[79] by C.J. Fordyce. Fordyce's notes are the repository of decades of close study of Roman literary usage, and are supremely informative about Latin syntax, grammar, and style. In poetical analysis, and literary criticism in general, they are uneven: sometimes excellent (on poem 45, for example), sometimes dismissive and inadequate (e.g., on poem 85). G.B. Pighi's handsomely printed and illustrated three-volume edition of 1961 was a work of Veronese *pietas*, financed as a public service by a local bank, and was not produced for sale.

In 1970 Kenneth Quinn's commentary, intended for the use of students, brought in a fresh (and primarily literary-critical) interpretation of the

78 The searching review-article by G.P. Goold ('A New Text of Catullus,' *Phoenix* XII [1958]: 93–116) still deserves to be consulted. Inter alia, it clothes with statistics the observation first made (as far as I am aware) by Ellis in the preface to his commentary, that the contributions made to the improvement of the text of Catullus in the period of Italian Humanism immeasurably outweigh the contributions of all other periods combined.

79 The editor was not responsible for this omission; the proof lies in the fact that, in the first printing, there are references to notes that do not appear in the commentary. He told me himself that the publishers, hopeful of a school market, consulted thirty headmasters and headmistresses, and that it was on the advice thus canvassed that the poems in question were not included.

poems. In the same year, Henry Bardon published his first Catullus, which was followed by a second version, for Teubner, in 1973. My own critical edition (*CE*) appeared in the United States in 1978; in it, I sought inter alia to give for the first time an accurate account of the readings of *m*. W. Eisenhut produced his own Teubner edition in 1983; G. P. Goold brought out in the same year a briefly annotated text with an English translation. Among recent articles, editions, and commentaries, published after 1981–2 and hence not included in J. P. Holoka's bibliography, are the following:

R.J. Tarrant, 'Catullus,' in *Texts and Transmission*, ed. L.D. Reynolds, 1983, 43–5.
H.P. Syndikus, *Catull: Eine Interpretation* (vol. 1, 1984; vol. 2, 1990; vol. 3, 1987).
P.Y. Forsyth, *The Poems of Catullus: A Teaching Text* (addressed to the needs of undergraduates), 1986.
P. Fedeli, *Introduzione a Catullo*, 1990.
A.G. Lee, *Catullus, Edited with a Translation and Brief Notes*, 1990.
G. Lafaye, *Catulle* (12th edition, revised and corrected by S. Viarre), 1993.

A notable contribution, falling just before this last period, was the collection of Marcello Zicàri's extremely important and previously scattered articles (many of which had appeared in Italian journals that were difficult of access) by Piergiorgio Parroni into the volume *Scritti Catulliani* (Urbino, 1978). Of Professor Wiseman's many Catullan studies, the latest, *Catullus and His World: A Reappraisal* (1985), contains a very useful appendix on references to Catullus in ancient authors. Two works by Professor Julia Haig Gaisser (the article on Catullus in the series *Corpus Translationum et Commentariorum*, volume VII, of 1992, and the monograph of almost 450 pages on *Catullus and his Renaissance Readers*, published in 1993) are mentioned in the Introduction and elsewhere in this book. Lastly, mention should be made of V.P. McCarren's *A Critical Concordance to Catullus* (Leiden, 1977), which fills the need for a convenient index verborum.

BIBLIOGRAPHY

General

Alfonsi, L. 1945. *Poetae novi*. Como.

– 1960. 'Cicerone e i "Lirici,"' *RFIC* 88: 170–7.

Allen, W. 1972. 'On "cantare" and "cantores Euphorionis,"' *TAPA* 103: 1–14.

Bardon, H. 1943. *L'art de la composition chez Catulle*. Paris.

– 1948. 'Réflexions sur les "Poètes Nouveaux,"' *RBPh* 36: 947–60.

– 1952. *La littérature latine inconnue* t. 1. Paris.

Buchheit, V. 1975. 'C.s Literarkritik und Kallimachos,' *GB* 4: 21–50.

Campbell, D.A. 1982. *Greek Lyric* (Loeb Classical Library), Vol. 1. Cambridge, Mass., and London.

Carilli, M. 1975. 'Le Nugae di Catullo e l'epigramma greco,' *ASNP* 5: 925–53.

Castorina, E. 1965. 'Il neoterismo nella poesia latina,' *Convivium* 33: 113–51.

Clausen, W. 1964. 'Callimachus and Latin Poetry,' *GRBS* 5: 181–96.

– 1970. 'Catullus and Callimachus,' *HSCP* 74: 85–94.

– 1986. 'Cicero and the New Poetry,' *HSCP* 90: 159–70.

Courtney, E. 1982. 'A Miscellany on Latin Poetry,' *BICS* 29: 49–50.

Crowther, N.B. 1970. 'οἱ νεώτεροι, *poetae novi*, and *cantores Euphorionis*,' *CQ* 20: 322–7.

– 1971. 'C. and the Traditions of Latin Poetry,' *CP* 66: 246–9.

– 1976. 'Parthenius and Roman Poetry,' *Mnemosyne* 29: 65–71.

Daly, L.W. 1952. 'Callimachus and Catullus,' *CP* 47: 97–9.

Della Corte, F. 1951. *Due studi catulliani*. Genoa.

– 1989. 'I carmi veronese di C.,' *Maia* 41: 229–34.

Deroux, C. 1973. 'L'identité de Lesbie,' *ANRW* I. 3: 390–416. [L. = Clodia Metelli; new arguments in defence of this identification. Propertius 2.32 offers good evidence.] (But see Wiseman 1979a: 167.)

Dettmer, H. 1988. 'Design in the Catullan Corpus: A Preliminary Study,' *CW* 81: 371–81.

Drachmann, A.B. 1887. *Catuls Digtning*. Copenhagen.

Ehlers, W. 'Die Ciris und ihr Original,' *MH* 11: 65–88.

Ferguson, J. 1970. 'The Epigrams of Callimachus,' *G&R* 17: 64–80.

– 1986. 'The Arrangement of C.'s poems,' *LCM* 11. 2–6 and 11. 18–20.

Fletcher, G.B.A. 1967. 'Catulliana,' *Latomus* 26: 104–6.

– 1991. 'Further Catulliana,' *Latomus* 50: 92–3.

Frank, T. 1919. 'Cicero and the Poetae Novi,' *AJP* 40: 396–415.

Giardina, G.C. 1974. 'La composizione del *Liber* e l'itinerario poetico di C.,' *Philologus* 118: 224–35.

Gigante, M. 1952. 'Catullo, Cicerone e Antimaco,' *RFIC* 32: 67–74.

Giri, G. 1922. 'Se Lesbia di C. sia Clodia, la sorella di P. Clodio,' *RIGI* 6: 161–77. [Rejects the identification of L. with *any* of the 3 sisters of P. Plodius Pulcher.]

Granarolo, J. 1958. 'C. et César,' *AFLA* 32: 53–73. [Date of reconciliation: 55 or 54.]

– 1975. 'L' époque néotérique ou la poésie romaine d'avant-garde au dernier siècle de la République (Catulle excepté),' *ANRW* I. 3: 278–360.

– 1982. *Catulle, ce vivant*. Paris. [Chapter I, 'Biographie,' is valuable: it takes account of Rambaud 1980.]

Green, E.H. 1940. 'Furius Bibaculus,' *CJ* 35: 348–56.

Guillemin, A.M. 1934. 'Le public et la vie littéraire à Rome,' *REL* 12: 52–71 and 329–43, esp. 330–1.

Hartman, J.J. 1915. 'De Cantoribus Euphorionis et de quibusdam aliis,' *Mnemosyne* 43: 245–67.

Heidel. W.A. 1901. 'C. and Furius Bibaculus,' *CR* 15: 215–17.

Hendrickson, G.L. 1917. 'Horace and Valerius Cato: III. The Neoteric Poets and the Latin Purists,' *CP* 12: 329–50.

Herzog, R. 1936. 'Catulliana,' *Hermes* 71: 338–50, esp. 350. [C. died not earlier than Jan. 52.]

Hillard, T.W. 1973. 'The Sisters of Clodius Again,' *Latomus* 32: 505–14. [L. = Clodia Metelli.] (See however Wiseman 1977: 167.)

– 1981. 'In triclinio Coam, in cubiculo Nolam: Lesbia and the Other Clodia,' *LCM* 6: 149–54. [Arguments for the identification of L. with Clodia Metelli are doubted.]

Holoka, J.P. 1985. *Gaius Valerius Catullus: A Systematic Bibliography*. New York and London.

Horváth, I.K. 1960. 'Chronologica Catulliana,' *AAntHung* 3: 335–68. [Pp. 361ff., on the chronology of the Lesbia-poems: conclusion, p. 368: 'All we can say with confidence from the historical references in the poems is that the poems complaining of L.'s faithlessness were without exception written after autumn 55 BC.']

Hubbard, T.K. 1983. 'The Catullan Libellus,' *Philologus* 127: 218–37.

Irwin, M.E. 1974. *Colour Terms in Greek Poetry*. Toronto.

King, J.K. 1988. 'C.'s Callimachean *Carmina*,' *CW* 81: 383–92.

Lindsay, R.J.M. 1948. 'The Chronology of C.'s Life,' *CP* 43: 42–4. [Dates: 85–55 or 88–55. Against Maas 1942, only *one* Eastern journey.]

Loomis, J.W. 1969. 'M. Furius Bibaculus and Catullus,' *CW* 62: 112–14.

Lyne, R.O.A.M. 1978. 'The Neoteric Poets,' *CQ* 28: 167–87. [Bibliography at the opening and in the notes.]

Maas, P. 1942. 'The chronology of the poems of C.,' *CQ* 36: 79–82. [We may assume that C.'s literary life began 56 BC ... *Two* voyages to the East ... C. may have lived until 50 BC. Accepts L. = Clodia Luculli.]

Macleod, C.W. 1973. 'Catullus 116,' *CQ* 23: 304–9.

Marmorale, E.V. 1952. *L'ultimo Catullo*. Naples. [82–52: see pp. 11, n. 1, and 168.]

Messer, W.S. 1917. 'Ad Cic. Tusc. Disp. 3.19.45,' *Mnemosyne* 45: 78–92. [On 'cantores Euphorionis' in Cicero.]

Minyard, J.D. 1988. 'The Source of the *Catulli Veronensis Liber*,' *CW* 81: 343–53.

Most, G.W. 1981. 'On the Arrangement of C.'s *carmina maiora*,' *Philologus* 125: 109–25. [Not '*minora*' as given in J.P. Holoka's bibliography, item 2625.]

Munro, H.A.J. 1905. *Criticisms and Elucidations of Catullus*. 2nd ed. London.

Nisbet, R.G.M. 1978. 'Notes on the Text of C.,' *PCPS* 24: 91–115.

– 1991. 'How Textual Conjectures Are Made,' *MD* 26: 65–91.

Novati, F. 1890. *Epistolario di Coluccio Salutati*. Rome.

Offerman, H. 1977. 'Zu C.s Gedichtcorpus,' *RhM* 120: 269–302.

– 1978. 'Einige Gedanke zum Aufbau des Catull-corpus,' *Eranos* 76: 35–64.

Otis, B. 1963. *Virgil: A Study in Civilized Poetry*. Oxford. [Index, *s.v.* Parthenius.]

Pepe, L. 1960. 'Lesbia madre, suocera e pompeiana,' *GIF* 13: 97–105. [Only the second of Clodius' sisters changed the spelling of her name to Clodia; see p. 97, n. 2.] (For this point, cf. Della Corte 1951: 207ff.)

– 1963. 'I Valerii Catulli di Verona,' *GIF* 16: 1–63. [Useful citation of sources.]

Plessis, F. 1909. *La poésie latine* (Paris): 145ff. [Dates: 82–52 BC.]

Powell, J.U. 1925. *Collectanea Alexandrina*. Oxford. (Reprinted 1970.)

Rambaud, M. 1980. 'César et Catulle,' *Actes du colloque 'L'Élégie romaine: enracinement – thèmes – diffusion* (mars 1979) = Bulletin de la faculté des lettres de Mulhouse, fasc. X (Paris): 37–50.

Rankin, H.D. 1969. 'Clodia II,' *AC* 38: 501–6. [L. = Clodia Metelli.]

Reitzenstein, E. 1931. 'Zur Stiltheorie des Kallimachos,' *Festschrift Richard Reitzenstein* (Leipzig): 23–69.

Robinson, R.P. 1923. 'Valerius Cato,' *TAPA* 54: 98–116.

Ross, D.O. 1969. *Style and Tradition in Catullus*. Cambridge, Mass.

Rothstein, M. 1923. 'C. und Lesbia,' *Philologus* 78: 1–34. [Improbable that C. went East after a breach with L.; poems 46, 101, 4, and 31 show no sign of that kind of heartbreak. Cf. also poem 10, written shortly after return. And (p. 19) L. could as well be Clodia Luculli as Clodia Metelli.]

Schmidt, B. 1914. 'Die Lebenszeit C.s und die Herausgabe seine Gedichte,' *RhM* 69: 267–83. [82–52 BC.]

Schmidt, E.A. 1973. 'C.s Anordnung seiner Gedichte,' *Philologus* 117: 215–42.

– 1979. 'Das Problem des Catullbuches,' *Philologus* 123: 216–31.

Scivoletto, N. 1974. 'Ticida, "poeta novus,"' *Poesia latina in frammenti: Miscellanea filologica* (= Univ. di Genova, Facoltà di Lettere, Istituto di filologia classica e medioevale, pubblicazioni, 39: 201-11).

Skinner, M.B. 1982. 'Pretty Lesbius,' *TAPA* 112: 197-208. [See n. 1 for a response to Wiseman 1969: 'His objections <to equating L. with Clodia Metelli>, which rest entirely on a tenuous supposition about the date of composition of the Lesbia poems, have not convinced me. C. Deroux (1973: see above) adduces strong circumstantial grounds for keeping the old identification.']

– 1983. 'Clodia Metelli,' *TAPA* 113: 273–82. [The 'Clodia' of the *Pro Caelio* <is to be regarded as> a literary construct similar to 'Lesbia'; Cicero's *letters* are the best source for the activities of Clodia Metelli. See p. 282, nn. 23 and 25, for the question whether all three sisters of P. Clodius used the spelling Clodia: esp. n. 23, 'Use of the plebeian spelling is his (Cicero's) standard way of specifying a connection with Clodius himself.']

Skutsch, O. 1969. 'Metrical Variations and Some Textual Problems in C.,' *BICS* 16: 38–43.

Solodow, J.B. 1989. 'Forms of Literary Criticism in C.: Polymetric vs. Epigram,' *CP* 84: 314–9.

Sumner, G.V. 1971. 'The Lex Annalis under Caesar,' *Phoenix* 25: 246–71.

Suolahti, J. 1954. 'The Origin of the Poet Catullus,' *Arctos* 1: 159–71. [To which branch of the *gens Valeria* did C. belong, and how did he come to belong to it?]

Syndikus, H.P. 1984. *Catull: Eine Interpretation*. I. Darmstadt. (II, 1990; III, 1987.)

Terzaghi, N. 1938. 'Facit poetas (À propos de l'épigramme sur Valerius Cato attribuée à Furius Bibaculus,' *Latomus* 2: 84–91. [*facere* = 'expliquer.']

Thomas, R.F. 1981. 'Cinna, Calvus, and the *Ciris*,' *CQ* 31: 371–4.

– 1983. 'Callimachus, the *Victoria Berenices*, and Roman Poetry,' *CQ* 33. 92–113, esp. 112–13. [Poem 62 as a profession of its author's Callimachean allegiance.]

Tränkle, H. 1967. 'Neoterische Kleinigkeiten,' *MH* 24: 87–103.

Traill, D. 1988. 'Ring Composition in C. 63, 64 and 68b,' *CW* 81: 365–9.

Tuplin, C.J. 1977. 'Cantores Euphorionis,' *Papers of the Liverpool Latin Seminar* 1 (= *Arca* 2): 1–23.

– 1979. 'Cantores Euphorionis Again,' *CQ* 29: 358–60.

Ullman, B.L. 1955. *Studies in the Italian Renaissance*. Rome.

Watson, L.C. 1982. 'Cinna and Euphorion,' *SIFC* 54: 93–110.

Wheeler, A.L. 1934. *C. and the Traditions of Ancient Poetry*. (Berkeley): ch. 3, esp. 77–86.

Williams, G. 1968. *Tradition and Originality in Roman Poetry*. Oxford.

Wimmel, W. 1960. *Kallimachos in Rom*. Wiesbaden. [= *Hermes*, Einzelschr. 16.]

Wiseman, T.P. 1965. 'The Last of the Metelli,' *Latomus* 25: 60–1.

– 1969. *Catullan Questions*. Leicester. [Of fundamental importance; see esp. chs. 4–6, and review by J. Briscoe, *JRS* 61 (1971): 303–4.]

– 1974. *Cinna the Poet and other Roman essays*. Leicester.

– 1975. 'Clodia, Some Imaginary Lives,' *Arion* n.s. 2: 96–115.

– 1979a. 'C., His Life and Times' (a review of F. Stoessl, *C. Valerius Catullus: Mensch, Leben, Dichtung*, 1977), *JRS* 69: 161–8.

– 1979b. *Clio's Cosmetics*. Leicester. [See esp. ch. 12, 'The Collection,' pp. 175–82.]

– 1985. *Catullus and His World: A Reappraisal*. Cambridge.

– 1987. *Roman Studies*. Liverpool.

On the History of the Text

Bartoniek, E. (ed.). 1940. *Catalogus Bibliothecae Musei Nationalis Hungarici*, vol. 12, *Codices Latini Medii Aevi*. Budapest.

Beldame, C. 1882. 'Scolies inédites de Juvénal,' *RPh* 6: 76–103.

Billanovich, Giuseppe. 1959. 'Dal Livio di Raterio al Livio di Petrarca,' *IMU* 2: 103–78.

– 1974. 'Terenzio, Ildemaro, Petrarca,' *IMU* 17: 1–60.

– 1988. 'Il Catullo della Cattedrale di Verona,' *Scire litteras* = Bayerische Akad. d. Wiss., Phil.-Hist. Klasse, Abh. NF 99: 35–57. Munich.

Bonnet, M. 1877. Review of Baehrens' edition. *Revue critique d'histoire et de littérature*, No. 4 (27 January): 57–65.

Butrica, J. 1984. *The Manuscript Tradition of Propertius* (*Phoenix*, supplementary volume 17). Toronto.

Carter, J.W. 1960. 'Farewell, Catullus,' *Texas Quarterly* 3: 274–84.

Clausen, W.V. 1976. 'Catulli Veronensis Liber,' *CP* 71: 37–43.

Codrignani, I.C. 1963. *Catulli Codex Bononiensis 2744*. Bologna.

Cremaschi, G. 1955. 'Catullo e Properzio in un codice della Biblioteca civica di Bergamo,' *Aevum* 29: 88–94.

Cremona, V. 1954. *Catulli Codex Brixianus A VII 7*. Bologna.

Csapodi, C., and Csapodi, K. 1969. *The Library of King Matthias Corvinus of Hungary*. New York.

Cunningham, I. 1983. 'An Italian Catullus (Edinburgh, Nat. Libr. of Scotland, Adv. MS 18.5.2),' *Scriptorium* 37: 122–5.

D'Angelo, M. (ed.). 1970. *Alcune notizie inedite su Guarnerio d'Artegna da un antico regesto*. San Daniele del Friuli.

de la Mare, A.C. 1973. *The Handwriting of Italian Humanists*. I. Oxford.

– 1976a. 'The Library of Francesco Sassetti.' In *Cultural Aspects of the Italian Renaissance: Essays in Honour of Paul Oskar Kristeller*, 160–201. Edited by Cecil H. Clough. Manchester.

– 1976b. 'The Return of Petronius to Italy.' In *Medieval Learning and Literature: Essays Presented to Richard William Hunt*, 220–54. Edited by J.J.G. Alexander and M.T. Gibson. Oxford.

– 1977. 'Humanistic Script: The First Ten Years.' In *Das Verhältnis der Humanisten zum Buch*, edited by Fritz Krafft and Dieter Wuttke. Deutsche Forschungsgemeinschaft, Kommission für Humanisten zum Humanismusforschung 4: 89–110. Boppard.

– 1985. 'New Research on Humanistic Scribes in Florence.' In A. Garzelli, *Miniatura fiorentina del Rinascimento 1440–1525*: I. 393–600. Florence.

de la Mare, A.C., and Thomson, D.F.S. 1973. 'Poggio's Earliest Manuscript?' *IMU* 16: 179–95.

Delisle, L. 1868–81. *Le cabinet des manuscrits de la Bibliothèque Nationale*. Paris.

Della Corte, F. 1985. 'Il codice Beriano CF Arm. 6 = D bis 4.3.5 degli elegiaci,' *Umanistica* 3: 235–42.

de Meyier, K.A. 1977. *Codices Vossiani Latini*. Bibliotheca Universitatis Leidensis, Codices Manuscripti vol. 15. Leiden.

de Nolhac, P. 1887. *La bibliothèque de Fulvio Orsini*, Bibliothèque de l'École des Hautes Études, vol. 74. Paris.

Fanfani, Olinto. 1925. *Inventario dei manoscritti della Biblioteca Comunale di Poppi*. Florence.

Ferguson, A.C. 1934. *The Manuscripts of Propertius* (diss. University of Chicago).

Gaisser, J.H. 1981. 'Schlägl 143 and Brussels IV. 711,' *Manuscripta* 25: 176–8.

– 1992. *Catullus, Gaius Valerius*. In *Catalogus Translationum et Commentariorum*, vol. 7: 197–292.

– 1993. *Catullus and His Renaissance Readers*. Oxford.

Ghiselli, A. 1987. *Catullo: Guarnerianus 56, Escorialensis ç IV. 22*. Bologna.

Grafton, A.T. 1975. 'Joseph Scaliger's Edition of Catullus (1577) and the Traditions of Textual Criticism in the Renaissance,' *Journal of the Warburg and Courtauld Institutes* 38: 155–81.

Gutiérrez, D. 1966. 'La Biblioteca di San Giovanni a Carbonara di Napoli,' *Analecta Augustiniana* 29: 59–212.

Hale, W.G. 1908. 'The Manuscripts of Catullus,' *CP* 3: 233–56.

– 1922. 'Stampini and Pascal on the Catullus Manuscripts,' *TAPA* 53: 103–12.

Hand, F.G. 1809. *Observationum criticarum in Catulli carmina specimen*. Leipzig.

Hunt, R.W., et al. 1975. *The Survival of Ancient Literature: Catalogue of an Exhibition of Greek and Latin Manuscripts*. Oxford.

Kellogg, G.W. 1900. 'A New MS of Catullus,' *CR* 14: 127–8.

Kristeller, P.O. 1967. *Iter Italicum*. Vol. 2. London.

Mazzatinti, G. 1896. *Inventari dei manoscritti delle biblioteche d'Italia*. Vol. 6. Forlì.

McKie, D.S. 1977. *The Manuscripts of Catullus: Recension in a Closed Tradition* (diss. Cambridge University).

– 1989. 'Salutati, Poggio, and Codex M of Catullus.' In *Studies in Latin Literature and Its Tradition in Honour of C.O. Brink*, 66–86. Edited by J. Diggle, J.B. Hall, and H.D. Jocelyn (Cambridge Philological Society, supplementary volume 15). Cambridge.

Müller, K. (ed.). 1961. *Petronii Arbitri Satyricon*. Munich.

Muntz, E., and Fabre, P. 1887. *La Bibliothèque du Vatican au XVe siècle*. Bibliothèque des écoles françaises d'Athènes et de Rome, vol. 48. Paris.

Muzzioli, G. 1959. 'Due nuovi codici autografi di Pomponio Leto,' *IMU* 2: 337–52.

Mynors, R.A.B. (ed.). 1966. *Catullus: Carmina, Codex Oxoniensis Bibliothecae Bodleianae Canonicianus Class. Lat. 30*. Codices Graeci et Latini Phototypice Depicti, XXI. Leiden.

Nigra, C. 1893. *Liber Catulli Bibliothecae Marcianae Venetiarum*. Venice.

Pellegrin, É. 1955. *La Bibliothèque des Visconti*. Paris.

– et al. 1975. *Les manuscrits classiques latins de la Bibliothèque Vaticane*. Vol. 1. Documents, Études, et Répertoires ... publiés par l'Institut de Recherche et d'Histoire des Textes, 21. Paris.

– 1982. *Manuscrits latins de la Bodmeriana*. Cologny-Geneva.

Pighi, G.B. (ed.). 1951. *A. Statii lectiones atque emendationes Catullianae*. Humanitas, vol. 3. Coimbra.

– 1954. *Catulli Codex Bononiensis 2621*. Bologna.

Richardson, B. 1976. 'Pucci, Parrasio and Catullus,' *IMU* 19: 277–89.

Ruysschaert, J. 1959. *Codices Vaticani Latini 11414–11709*. Vatican City.

Sabbadini, R. 1905. *Le scoperte dei codici latini e greci ne' secoli XIV e XV.* Vol. 1. Florence.

Schenkl, H. 1883. 'Zur Textgeschichte der Eclogen des Calpurnius und Nemesianus,' *WS* 5: 281–98.

Schulze, K.P. 1888. 'Der Codex M des Catull,' *Hermes* 23: 567–91.

Shailor, B.A. 1984. *Catalogue of the Medieval and Renaissance MSS in the Beinecke Rare Book and MS Library*, vol. 2. Binghamton.

Thompson, E. Maunde. 1900. 'Catulliana: A Letter to Professor Robinson Ellis,' *AJP* 21: 78–9.

Thomson, D.F.S. 1970. 'The Codex Romanus of Catullus: A Collation of the Text,' *RhM* 113: 97–110.

– 1973. 'A New Look at the Manuscript Tradition of Catullus,' *YCS* 23: 113–29.

Ullman, B.L. 1908. *The Identification of the Manuscripts of Catullus Cited in Statius' Edition of 1566* (diss., University of Chicago).

– 1910. 'Hieremias de Montagnone and His Citations from Catullus,' *CP* 5: 66–82.

– 1960a. *The Origin and Development of Humanistic Script.* Rome.

– 1960b. 'The Transmission of the Text of Catullus.' In *Studi in onore di Luigi Castiglione*, 1027–57. Florence.

Vielhaber, G., and Indra, G. 1918. *Catalogus Codicum Plagensium (Cpl.) manuscriptorum.* Linz.

Zazzeri, R. 1887. *Sui codici e libri a stampa di Cesena.* Cesena.

Zicàri, M. 1953. 'Il codice pesarese di Catullo e i suoi affini,' *SOliv* 1: 5–23 = 1978: 43–60.

– 1956. 'Il "Cavrianeus" antaldino e i codici affini al Bononiensis 2621,' *SOliv* 4: 145–62 = 1978: 61–77.

– 1957. 'Calfurnio editore di Catullo,' *A&R* 3: 157–9 = 1978: 105–8.

– 1958. 'Ricerche sulla tradizione manoscritta di Catullo,' *BPEC* 6: 79–104.

– 1959. 'Il Catullo di Guarnerio d'Artegna,' *IMU* 2: 453–65 = 1978: 109–22.

– 1978. *Scritti catulliani*, a cura di Piergiorgio Parroni. Urbino.

Zwierlein, O. 1983. *Prolegomena zu einer kritischen Ausgabe der Tragödien Senecas*, Abhandlungen der Geistes- und Sozialwissenschaftlichen Klasse der Akademie der Wissenschaften und der Literatur, Nr. 3: 15–23. Mainz.

CHANGES FROM THE TEXT OF THE CRITICAL EDITION OF 1978

Reference	Read:
1.8	libelli,
3.17	vestra [line 16 in parentheses]
17.6	Salisubsili
22.6	regiae novae libri,
24.7	'quid?
27.4	ebriosa
29.10	et aleo. [Corr.]
20	Gallicae … Britannicae.
32.1	ipsimilla,
36.15	Dyrrachium
37.17	omnes,
38.2	(*del.* est)
43.4	lingua.
5	Formiani,
45.26	venerem
46.3	auris.
48.3	trecenta;
51.8	<vocis in ore>
54.2	at, mi
55.9	†avelte† (sic usque
11	reduc<ta pectus,>
14	amice.
58^b.6	cursum:
7	dicares,
61.15	taedam;
25	umore:

30	Aganippe,
40	Hymenaee,
154	usque,
170	urit in
215	Manlio, ut facile obviis
62.54	marita,
56	innupta manet
63.39	Sol
54	operta
63	puber
64.3	Aeeteos
73	ferox qua robore
100	quam tum saepe
153	iniecta
175	haec
196	miserae, imis
215	longe
271	Solis,
292	circum [Corr.]
351	putriaque
395	Rhamnusia
65.1	defectum
66.74	nostri
77	fuit,
91	ne
92	effice muneribus
93	cur iterent 'utinam coma regia fiam,'
67.5	nato
20	attigerat,
33	qua molli percurrit
68.23	gaudia [Corr.]
91	quae nunc et
133	Cupido
157	†terram dedit aufert†
71.4	est apte nactus
74.4	Harpocraten.
76.3	in ullo
23	contra ut me
83.6	coquitur.
86.6	veneres.
90.4	relligio,

95^b (heading)	[*Delete* '95^b' and close up]
97.2	utrum os
3	immundior ille est
101.4	cinerem,
6	mihi.
102.3	me aeque esse
107.3	nobis quoque, carius auro
109.1	proponis:
2	perpetuum usque
110.3	quod mentita inimica es,
111.4	ex patruo <parere>.
112.1	<est qui>
2	discumbit:
115.1	†instar†

TABLE OF MANUSCRIPTS

No.	Short Title	Location and Press-Mark		Designation Ellis	Zicàri	Butrica	Date	Contents
1		Austin, Texas: Humanities Research Center	HRC 32				1451	C (to 61.134) T
2		Bergamo: Bibl. civica	Σ 2.33 (3)		p	1	post 1459; XV 3/4?	TPC+
3	Diez.	East Berlin: Deutsche Staatsbibl. Diez. B. Sant.	36	L			1450–60?	C+
4			37	D			1463	C+

Note: In the column headed Contents, C = Catullus, T = Tibullus, P = Propertius, and + = other matter. In the column headed Zicàri, double lower-case letters refer to his 'Ricerche' (1958); single lower-case letters, to his 'Il "Cavrianeus"' (1956) or, in two instances, to 'Il codice pesarese,' where (1953) is added. For bibliographical details see p. 68.

The following Mss have the a-class transpositions (see No. 8 n.): 2, 8, 9, 12, 17, 22, 27, 35, 39, 41, 47, 48, 50, 52, 64, 66, 67, 69, 70, 71, 74, 76 (but see n.), 77, 82, 83, 90, 92, 95, 100, 102 (but see n.), 104, 105, 107, 109, 111, 112, 117, 121, 127 (but see n.).

1 Codex Antenoris Balbi. In Ellis' time it belonged to Walter Ashburner; hence it is also known as Codex Ashburneri. See Carter 1960.

2 Close to No. 41. Written in Italy, probably northeast. See Zicàri 1956: 152–62 = 1978: 68–77. Discussed by Cremaschi 1955: 88–91; and for the date, 94).

3 Codex Laurentianus, or more properly Santenianus (i.e., of Laurens van Santen). The second hand reveals O-influence not mentioned in Zicàri 1958 (M.D. Reeve, *Phoenix* 34 [1980]: 181).

4 Probably, though not certainly, written in northeastern Italy. A copy of No. 31; see Ullman 1960b: 1052–3.

No.	Short Title	Location and Press-Mark	Ellis	Zicàri	Butrica	Date	Contents
5					40	ca. 1460–70	C
6					46	ca. 1600	C
7					56	1481	C
8	*a*	Bologna: Bibl. universitaria	2621	B	b	1412	C
9	Bon.		2744		bn	ca. 1460-80?	C (to 88.6)
10	Brix.	Brescia: Bibl. Queriniana	A vii 7		qu	10	post 1451 (ca. 1455–60?)	PCT+
10a = 94		Brussels: Bibl. Royale	IV. 711					

5 Copy of a copy (slightly corrected, with influence from another manuscript, and with marginal index and notes added) of No. 19.

6 A copy, made by 'M.P.' (fol. 1), of No. 17. In No. 17 the line 44.9 was at first omitted, then added below the last line on the page, which is 44.20. The marks added to indicate displacement are small and faint. In No. 6, 44.9 is written immediately after 44.20 with no hint of anything wrong. The copy, apparently very carefully done, exhibits on fol. 72ᵛ the following date and note of ownership ('additum aliena manu' in the exemplar, according to M.P., who plainly thought of them as a single addition): 'an(n)o 1495 MCCCCLXXXXV. Antoni Seripandi et amicorum.' The last four words are absent from No. 17, at least as it now stands. See Gutiérrez 1966, who gives Seripando's date of birth as 1485. If we accept this, the date 1495, cited above, is not that of the note of ownership, but presumably confirms the date found in a fragmentary state in No. 17. See now Cunningham 1983 (on No. 17): 123.

7 Written at Ferrara. The Propertius (Diez. 57 = Butrica, No. 5) formerly bound with it and written in the same hand is dated 1481 in the *subscriptio*. The Propertius is signed 'G.F.'

8 Codex Bononiensis (*a*). Written, or at least finished, at Venice by Girolamo Donato. Text published (with photographic illustrations) by Pighi 1954. See Zicàri 1956. All the *a*² corrections and variant readings are in the hand of Ermolao Barbaro (Herm. Barbarus, 1454–95), who owned it; Mynors suggested in the preface to his 1958 edition (p. ix, n. 1) that many of these were taken from the 1481 edition by Calphurnius, which was dedicated to Barbaro. The order of the poems ('*a*-class transpositions') is confused: 44.21–62 are placed between 24.2 and 25, and there are certain omissions. (There are slight variations in other manuscripts.)

9 The readings of this manuscript show a family likeness to those of No. 12. The hand is somewhat similar in style to that of *R*³. Text published by Codrignani 1963.

10 Written in Ferrara? Text published by Cremona 1954. Close to Nos. 49 and (less strikingly) 59.

10a See 94 n.

No.	Short Title	Location and Press-Mark		Ellis	Zicàri	Butrica	Date	Contents
11		Budapest: National Museum	137			XV		C
12	Carp.	Carpentras: Bibl. Inguimbertine	361	cr	13		1440–50?	CTP
13	Caes.	Cesena: Bibl. Malatestiana	29 sin. 19	cs			1474	CT+
14		Cologny, Geneva: Bibl. Bodmeriana	Bodmer 47				ca. 1495	C
15	Dres.	Dresden: Sächsische Landesbibl.	Dc 133	dr	16		ante 1479	CPT

11 Written in central Italy, possibly Florence. Not now considered to have belonged to Matthias Corvinus. On fol. <1> (unnumbered) a note of presentation by 'Jacobus Antonius,' 18 May 1528. See Bartoniek 119–20. Unknown to Hale and Ullman.

12 Written in northeastern Italy. Contains 92.3–4 (cf. *O*). At the top of fol. 2, a note of ownership: 'marci donati iuris consulti patricij veneti.' (See also Butrica p. 215.) The annotations in the Propertius may possibly be by him. Donatus was a considerable patron of humanists, and himself composed a number of Latin orations: examples in Codices Vat. lat. 5197 and Marc. 11.59 (4152). Professor Butrica, to whom I am indebted for the above information, also informs me that though there may originally have been two manuscripts (difference in decoration of initials and a blank folio at the end of the last gathering of the Catullus suggest this), the consecutive numbering of the gatherings and early binding show that the two must have been joined at an early date.

13 Written probably in Romagna (Zicàri 1958: 96 = 1978: 100). A direct and very early copy of *1473*. Dated at the end of the Catullus (f. 51ʳ). Most of the notes and corrections seem to be by the first hand, despite a note on the flyleaf at the end which seems to attribute them to Giuseppe Isei, or Isaeus (ca. 1500; see his Lactantius in the same library, 2 *dextr.* 11). See Zazzeri 1887. On the influence of *1473*, see now Gaisser 1993: 32–4 and nn. 36–8.

14 Written by Lodovico Regio of Imola, who also wrote, at about the same time, No. 17 (q.v.). Also close to No. 106. Formerly owned by S.C. Cockerell. See Pellegrin 1982: 92–4.

15 Written in Italy, 'in or near Milan' (Butrica 1984: 64). One hand only. The transcript at Chapel Hill (University of North Carolina, Department of Classics) lacks the following: 107.6 *nobis* ... 113.4 *adulterio*. Collated by Sillig for his edition (1823). Used by Hand (1809; see especially p. 22). Heyne also used it for his Tibullus, Barth for his Propertius. It was purchased in 1479 by the famous jurist Jason de Mayne, who lived at Pavia from 1471 to 1486 (autograph note on fol. 200ᵛ; arms on fol. 1ʳ). The flyleaf contains a note of ownership suggesting that the owner was a certain Paulinus: 'per primam, tertiam et ultimam vocalem et has literas, p. l. n. s., cognosci<tur> meus dominus.' Close to Nos. 37 (with which in the Propertius it shares at least one highly unusual reading) and 57.

No.	Short Title	Location and Press-Mark	Ellis	Zicàri	Butrica	Date	Contents
16		Dublin: Trinity College					
		Library 929			17	XV	PC
16a		1759				XV (2nd)	C+
17	Edin.	Edinburgh: National					
		Library of Scotland					
		Adv. 18.5.2				1495	C
18	Esc(a)	Escorial Ç. IV. 22(a)			18	ca. 1450–60?	TCP+
19		Ç. IV. 22(b)				XV med.	C
20	Laur.	Florence: Bibl.					
		Laurenziana 33.11	(La^4)		21	post 1472	CPT
21		33.12	La^2			1457	CT
22		33.13	La^1			XV 1/4	C Pers.
23		36.23	(La^3)			ca. 1425	Ov. (*Fasti*) C+
24	Ashb.	Ashb. 260				ca. 1500?	C

17 Written by Lodovico Regio of Imola, apparently in 1495 (the date, given in the *subscriptio*, has been partly erased); but No. 6 (on which see my note), apparently a copy of this manuscript, has an addition which seems to confirm the date. The same scribe, at about the same date, wrote No. 14. For a description of No. 17, see now Cunningham 1983. Close to No. 106.

18 Written in northern Italy: see Zicàri 1959: 456, = 1978: 113, n. 13. One of the few manuscripts in the *G* tradition; see the note on No. 65 (of which it is the parent, according to Hale, Ullman, and Butrica). Single Humanistic book-hand; notes in a second hand. See Ghiselli 1987, which has a complete photographic reproduction.

19 Close to γ class. One hand only (humanistic cursive).

20 Written at Florence by Bartolomeo Fonzio (1445–1513); see de la Mare 1976b: plate XXIII. There are some marginal annotations, also by Fonzio. The arms are those of Francesco Sassetti (1420–91), who was closely connected with the Medici as a collector of manuscripts; many of Fonzio's were written for him. See de la Mare 1976a: 178. Noting its 'advanced editing,' Hale records the opinion of Heyse and other scholars that this manuscript is 'the original of the *editio princeps*.' In fact it appears to have been copied *from* the *editio princeps*; Professor Butrica assures me that this is quite certain for the Propertius, and see now de la Mare 1985: I.487 ('copied in part at least' from 1472).

21 Written at Florence by Gherardo del Ciriagio (cf. No. 83) for Giovanni Cosimo de' Medici. Close to No. 95; hence fairly close to *R*, and of good tradition. Many of its readings suggest direct copying from *R*. See de la Mare 1985: I.496.

22 Spells *michi*, not *mihi*; cf. No. 95. Close to No. 8 (cf. No. 109).

23 The writer is identifiable as Bartolomeo di Piero Nerucci of San Gimignano. The arms are possibly those of Mattia Lupi of San Gimignano. This manuscript (note the relatively early date) is very close to *R*: e.g., 2b.3 *erat negatam*, 73.6 *habet habuit*. Cf. No. 95, and see the Stemma Codicum. See also de la Mare 1977: 98–100.

24 A direct copy of No. 44. (Formerly Saibante 324.)

No.	Short Title	Location and Press-Mark	Designation			Date	Contents
			Ellis	Zicàri	Butrica		
25		Ashb. 973				XVI med. (post 1548)	C
26	Magl. Bibl. Nazionale						
		Magl. VII 948				1475	Pers. Juv. C
27		1054				ca. 1480–90	TC
28		1158				1460–70	C
29		Panciatichi 146				1475	*Priap.* TC+
30		Inc. Magl. A.3.39				(nn) 1522	CTP Stat. (*S.*)+
31	Ric.	Bibl. Riccardiana 606				(prob.) 1457	CT+
32		2242 (25)				XVII	C (63.37–93 and poem 64) +
33		2242 (25 *bis*)				XVII	C (poem 64) +
34		Genoa: Bibl. civica					
		Berio Cf. arm. 6				XV	TC (see n.)

---

25 Written (at Florence?) by Braccius Ricasulanus, who also added the variants and marginal notes (signed on fol. 31). Note the references to an Aldine edition: e.g., at 2.8 'Ald. tum gravis acquiescat.' On the date, see further, in the Commentary, 63.77 n.

27 Descended from No. 109 (cf. No. 92); corrected from a manuscript similar to No. 79. Formerly a Strozzi manuscript.

28 Corrected in a sixteenth-century hand; some of the corrections appear to depend ultimately, if not immediately, on the first Aldine edition (e.g., 64.21 *tum*). Formerly a Strozzi manuscript.

29 Written at Pistoia by Francesco Viviano, 'Lambertini F. notarium collensem.' Good textual tradition. Close to *m* (No. 115) rather than to *R* (e.g., 8.5 *amabiliter*).

30 Notes and emendations in the hand of Bernardus Pisanus, written in the margins of a copy of Calphurnius' 1481 edition. The *subscriptio* to the notes on Catullus reads as follows (giving the date): '. . . recognovi ego Ber. pisanus collato emendatissimo F. Puccij exemplari anno MD.xxij.' See Gaisser 1992: 244, and Richardson 1976: 278.

31 Parent of No. 4, q.v. Written by 'two scribes, the first ending at 64.278. The two scribes used entirely different exemplars. The first part is a rather faithful descendant of *G*, with some readings derived from a late manuscript. The second part is based on an exemplar descended from *R*.' (Ullman 1960b: 1053). See further the Introduction, pp. 33 and 56. There are some later additions, such as names in the margin, which in Ullman's view might be attributable to Bartolomeo Fonzio (on whom see note on No. 20).

32 63.37–93 and 64. Marginal and interlinear commentary.

33 Poem 64 only: variant readings.

34 Catullus incomplete, lacking 68.101–50 and 104–16. Formerly contained Propertius also. See Della Corte 1985: 235–42

No.	Short Title	Location and Press-Mark	Designation Ellis	Zicàri	Butrica	Date	Contents
35		Göttingen: Universitäts-bibl. Philol. 111b	g	38		(prob.) 1456	TPC
36		112				XVI	C (64) +
37	Grat.	Grenoble: Bibl. de la ville 549 (858: 117)	gr	39		1472	TCP
38	Hamb.	Hamburg: Stadt-u.-Univ.-Bibl. *scrin.* 139.4	H		41	ca. 1460–70	TPC
39	Voss.	Leiden: Bibl. der Rijksuniversiteit Voss. lat. in oct. 13	le		42	1459+	TPC
40		59				1453	TC+
41		76	l			1451	CT
42		81	ln		44	ca. 1460?	*Priap.* CTP+
43		St Petersburg [formerly Leningrad]: Saltykov-Shchedrin State Public Library cl. lat. Q 6				XV ex.	C+

35 Written at Bologna (Prof. de la Mare). On the group to which it belongs, see Zicàri 1956: 152–3 = 1978: 68. Dated on fol. 1 (Tibullus); see however Butrica 1984: 119 and Zicàri 1956: 149 = 1978: 64–5, for some conflicting indications of date.

37 Written at Pavia. Single Humanistic cursive hand; some additions, and many corrections, in the same or a contemporary hand. Dated at end of Propertius. Close to No. 57, and to No. 15 (where see n.).

38 Written at Ferrara. Not now considered to have belonged to Matthias Corvinus. Marginal variants (fol. 118$^\mathrm{r}$, poem 1, only) in a later hand somewhat resembling that of R^3. *Ad patriam* epigram at end of text.

On Nos. 39–42, see de Meyier, 1977.

39 Related to Nos. 9 and 12. Miscellaneous contents are similar to those of No. 10.

40 Written by 'presbiter petrus Antonides.' Dated on fol. 81$^\mathrm{r}$. Descended from a manuscript that had 23 lines to a page (note the transpositions in poems 63 and 64; cf. Nos. 73 and 103). Close to No. 38.

41 Written by Antonio Beccaria of Verona (b. ca. 1400); the manuscript is identifiable as number 17 in the list of his books. See Zicàri 1956: 152–62 = 1978: 68–77. On the first leaf (originally the cover) is a note of ownership: FEDERICI CERVTI. Cerruti was born in 1541 at Verona; on his library, see the references in Zicàri 1956, n. 30. Close to No. 2.

42 Possibly copied in northeastern Italy (it has η-class affiliations). Close to No. 107, and also (strikingly) to No. 78 (β). See Müller 1961, where the manuscript (including selections from Petronius) is designated as F. See the discussion by de la Mare 1976b: 223–4.

43 Some of its readings are reported in Henry Bardon's Teubner edition, under the siglum λ; see his *praefatio*, p. xvii. Its existence was known to Hale, but I find no

No.	Short Title	Location and Press-Mark	Designation			Date	Contents
			Ellis	Zicàri	Butrica		
44	add.	London: British Library Additional 10386		(51)	(prob.)	1474	C (orig. + P = Add. 10387)
45		11674	c			XV 3/4	TC
46		11915	a	a(1953)		1460	C
47		12005	b			1460–70?	Mart. C (to 64.400 *lugere*)
48		Burney 133	d			1470–80?	C
49	Harl.	Harley 2574	h	ha	58	ca. 1460?	TPC+
50		2778			59	ca. 1450–75	PC
51		4094	h²			XV	C (61; 62; 2; 10; 5–9; 11–17.14)+
52	Cuiac.	Egerton 3027	P	p(1953)	56	1467	PTC *Priap.*

report of its contents in his papers or those of Ullman. See Zicàri 1965: 236 = 1978: 147 n. 12, for a reading shared with No. 52.

44 Written at Verona by Pierfilippo Muronovo, as was also British Library Ms Add. 10387 (a Propertius, dated 1474, in the same hand as the Catullus, and on paper bearing the same watermark), which was originally bound with it (as Saibante 329); it may be noted that No. 24, which is a direct copy of our manuscript, was formerly Saibante 324.

45 Formerly at Siena, where it may have been written. From the Piccolomini manuscripts. At 64.28 it has *neptunine* (cf. No. 60 and the second hand, β², in No. 78). The arms are probably those of Martinozzi, of Siena.

46 Formerly in the library of Mapheus Pinelli, of Venice. Corrected (early) from another manuscript, probably contemporary. Its origins lie close to the parent Ms of *1472* (Zicàri 1957: 157 = 1978: 106).

47 Close to No. 50. Related also to No. 82, the text of which is better if not earlier.

48 A fine Neapolitan manuscript, adorned with the emblems of the Aragonese kings of Naples (no arms). Single Humanistic book-hand. The titles are from the same source as those of No. 52. Copied from a corrected manuscript up to 64.183, then changed, as the scribe's note informs us, to copying from an uncorrected exemplar; hence no variant readings are given from 64.184 onwards.

49 The decoration suggests that the manuscript originated in Rome or Naples. One hand only. See Butrica 1984: 132–43 for its possible derivation from a Ms belonging to Giovanni Aurispa.

50 Ferrarese; Strozzi family arms. Single humanistic book-hand; no corrections. On the page immediately preceding the text: 'ego Alexander Branchaleonus.' Close to No. 47; cf. also No. 82.

51 The contents include letters dated 1442 and 1443.

52 Codex Cuiacianus (Scaligeri), Codex Perusinus. Written by Pacificus Maximus Irenaeus de Asculo ('Asculanus' or da Ascoli), Professor at Perugia. Many corrections, variant readings, glosses, and notes by the first writer, but in different inks. See,

No.	Short Title	Location and Press-Mark	Ellis	Zicàri	Butrica	Date	Contents
53		[formerly] London: Robinson Trust (now in private hands)					
		Phillipps 3400				ca. 1475	C
54	Ambr.	Milan: Bibl. Ambrosiana					
		D 24 *sup.*		am		ca. 1500	C
55		G 10 *sup.*				XV (med.?)	TC (101; 62.39–48; 59–66; 5; 8; 13)+
56		H 46 *sup.*			64	ca. 1460–70	PTC+
57		I 67 *sup.*		as	65	ca. 1470–80?	CPT
58		M 38 *sup.*	A			ca. 1430(+?)	C
59		Bibl. Nazionale di Brera (Braidense) AD xii 37		br		1450?	TC+
60		Mons: Bibl. de la ville					
		218.109		mt	68	XV (2nd)	T[Ov.]*Ep.*15CP

on this manuscript and on Scaliger's use of it, Grafton 1975, especially 158ff. Closely related to No. 85. Apparently removed between 1533 and 1577 from the library of San Salvatore at Bologna. Parent Ms of θ class (Mynors, p. xi)

53 Written in northeastern Italy (Padua?) by Bartolomeo Squara. Has 'munus Francisci Mutatii P.V.' on the flyleaf. The late Alan Thomas (London) included it in his catalogue 41, 1980. It was sold by him to a dealer in the U.S.A., as Mrs Shirley Thomas has kindly informed me.

54 At 4.10 omits *post* (characteristic of δ-class manuscripts).

55 Fols. 75–7 contain parts of Catullus, in this order: 101; 62.39–48; 62.59–66; 5; 8; 13. The style looks early. A note of ownership reads: 'Liber D. Grimani Car[lis] S. Marci ... Nunc Patriarcha Aquileie.' Domenico Grimani became Cardinal 13 September 1493, Patriarch of Aquileia 21 March 1498; he died 27 August 1523. The last three words quoted look like an addition; possibly the book was given to Grimani before he left Rome for Venice.

56 Cf. *Tom.* Closely related to No. 38; possibly written at about the same time. At 68.47, this marginal note: 'Seneca supplevit' (surely derived from the note 'supplevit Seneca' in No. 78).

57 Lacks (1) *Ad patriam* epigram, (2) poem 1. Written by a professional scribe 'in or near Milan' (Butrica, p. 64). 'Early' style. Dotted *y*s. Some of its readings suggest a close relationship to γ and ζ classes. Close to Nos. 15 (see n.) and 37.

58 Clearly early style (heavy strokes; cf. No. 109).

59 Date at the end of the Tibullus (which is in the same hand as the Catullus, but in a different ink). Closely related to No. 10.

60 Copy (direct or at one remove) of No. 78. Written in a non-Italian hand (Zicàri 1958: 90 = 1978: 93), possibly at Padua or Trogir (Butrica 1984: 136). See also A.C. de la Mare (n. on No. 78) for an alternative account. Formerly at Tournai.

No.	Short Title	Location and Press-Mark	Designation Ellis	Zicàri	Butrica	Date	Contents
61		Munich: Bayerische Staatsbibl. lat. 473				XV	C (begins at 4.7 *negare*)
62	Neap.	Naples: Bibl. Brancacciana IV A. 4				XVII	C (frag.) +
63		Bibl. oratoriana dei Gerolamini C. F. III. 15			74	1484	PC Stat. (*S.*) T
64		Bibl. Nazionale IV. F. 19			70	1467+	CTP+
65		IV. F. 21			72	1450–60?	CP
66		IV. F. 61				1505?	C+
67		IV. F. 63				XV (late)?	Stat. (*A.*) Ov. C (1–54.2)
68		New Haven, Connecticut: Beinecke Library, Yale University 186				ca. 1470?	TC
69	Bodl.	Oxford: Bodleian Library lat. class. e. 3			78	ca. 1460–70?	TPC

61 Descendant, but not a direct copy, of No. 124. Has α-class titles. Two folios missing (from 12.11 to 21.1 inclusive).

63 Written at Florence by Antonio Sinibaldi for the Aragonese royal family of Naples (cf. No. 48). Neapolitan decoration. For the writer, see Ullman 1960a: 118–23. Copied from 1472 (de la Mare 1985: I.485).

64 Written at Naples (note the predominantly Neapolitan authorship of the humanistic additions). From the library of Aulus Ianus Parrhasius (Aulo Giano Parrasio, 1470–1522): 'the heir of Valla, Politian and Laetus, who continued their methods' (Sabbadini 1905: 159, 170). Ownership note (fol. 165^v) of Antonio Seripando, who was a pupil of Francesco Pucci and inherited many of Parrhasius' manuscripts. On Antonio Seripando, see note on No. 6. See Richardson 1976, and de Nolhac 1887. Some θ-class readings.

65 Written in Italy. Single Humanistic book-hand. One of the very few manuscripts in the *G* tradition, as contrasted with the numerous direct or indirect descendants of *R*. A copy of No. 18. Cf. also No. 93 for the influence of *G*.

66 At 17.25 has *derelinquere* (the reading of *O*). Date is from a blotted n. on fol. 13^v or 14^r.

68 Copy of a corrected copy of No. 31. One hand throughout. See Shailor 1984

69 Written in Italy. Single humanistic cursive book-hand, except for additions in a more formal script (fols. 130, 133, 134) and notes and additions in another hand. Closely related to Nos. 70 and (probable exemplar) 121. Has 'petrus odus' supplement at 68.47 (cf. No. 82).

No.	Short Title	Location and Press-Mark	Ellis	Zicàri	Butrica	Date	Contents
			Designation				
70		e. 15	Phil. alter			1459+	C+
71		e. 17	Phil.	f		1453	CT
72	*O*	Canon. lat. 30	*O*	*O*		ca. 1370?	C
73	Canon.	33				1450+	TC
74		34				XV ex.	CT *Priap.*
75	Laud.	Laud. lat. 78		ld		ca. 1460–70	TC (to 109.6)
76	Pat.	Padua: Bibl. capitolare C 77			80	ca. 1468–9?	PC+
77		Palermo: Bibl. comunale 2. Q. q. E. 10				1459+	TC+

70 Written, according to Ullman, by the scribe of a Tibullus in the British Library (Ms Add. 11962), which was probably joined to it at first. Dated by the inclusion, among the miscellaneous contents of the volume, of the poem 'Pii Papae 1459' (cf. Nos. 2, 39, and 77). Closely related to Nos. 69 and 121. Has 'petrus odus' supplement (see No. 82).

71 Copied, probably directly, from No. 41. Venetian (Conegliano). The *subscriptio* to the Tibullus part reads: 'Tibulli poetae liber explicit III° Idus sextilis M°CCCC°LIII° Conegl(i)ani mei Francisci Crobati Veneti.' One hand only. At 55.17 has the reading *lacusteolae* (cf. *a*). See Zicàri 1956: 153–6 = 1978: 68–71.

72 Codex Oxoniensis (*O*). See Introduction, pp. 28–30. On the date and certain other matters, see Hunt 1975: 80. The corrections are by the first scribe, not – as many scholars have supposed – by a second. (Professor de la Mare has expressed to me her opinion that there is no reason to attribute anything in *O* to a second hand.)

73 Closely related to No. 38.

74 This manuscript seems to have influenced No. 85, q.v.

75 Written at Padua. Closely related to (descended from?) No. 128. Corrected in a slightly later hand.

76 Close to *a* (No. 8). Written by Pietro Barozzi (1441–1507). The writer, who became bishop of Belluno, was translated to Padua in 1487.

There are now at Padua four manuscripts by Barozzi; two of them are signed. One of these, Ms C.74, is dated thus in the *subscriptio*: 'absolvi ego Petrus Barrocius Patricius Venetus XI Kal Octobres MCCCCLXVIII.' On the relationship of our manuscript to Nos. 48, 52, and 90, see Zicàri 1953, especially 13–17 (1978: 50–4), where some of its readings are given. For a further list of readings, see Pighi 1951: 36ff. Though an *a*-class manuscript, it seems to be independent of the group of *a*-derived manuscripts discussed in Zicàri 1956. There are certain similarities to No. 35 (e.g., 87.2 *amata mea*; and the two verses 87.3–4 are omitted). Much correction, of the first part at least, was done by the original scribe from a manuscript other than his exemplar. Some corrections in poem 62 were added later by a different hand.

77 Written by 'Johannes Asper, alias Scharp.' Markedly similar, especially in the second part of its contents, to No. 70; but it does not exhibit the 'petrus odus' supplement.

No.	Short Title	Location and Press-Mark		Designation			Date	Contents
				Ellis	Zicàri	Butrica		
78	β	Paris: Bibl. Nationale	7989		pa	82	1423	TPC Petron.
79	Par.		7990			83	1475+	TCP
80	*T*		8071	T			IX	Juv. C (poem 62)+
81	Par.		8231				XVII	C (poem 64, nn.)+
82			8232				XV 3/4	C *Priap.* +
83			8233			84	1465	CTP
84			8234	C			ca. 1450?	TC
85			8236			86	ca. 1500	PTC *Priap.*
86			8458			88	1474+	TPC+
87	*G*		14137	G	G		1375	C

78 Codex Traguriensis (β). Written by a scholar for his own use. For the place of writing (probably Florence) and the scribe's place of origin (Venetian territory?), and for a description, history, and bibliography, see de la Mare 1976b: 239–47.

79 Florentine. Arms not identified. Later belonged to Cardinal Ridolfi. Closely connected with No. 111. The Propertius was copied from the edition published at Milan in 1475. Cursive. See de la Mare 1985: I.491.

80 Codex Thuaneus (*T*). Ullman believed it to be a copy of the Vienna florilegium Cod. lat. 277; but see Zwierlein 1983: 15–23; he shows that *T* and Vienna 277 are copied from a common parent. Since Vienna 277 now lacks Catullus, it cannot be demonstrated that *T*'s Catullus extract came from the parent Ms. See Richardson 1976.

82 At 68.47: 'petri odi supplementum' (cf. Nos. 47, 50, 69, and 70); for Petrus Odus supplement see Mynors' edition, p. xi. The manuscript is by several hands: on fols. 91–130 there is a Greek Aratus by 'Joh. Rhosus, presbyter' of Crete (note on flyleaf, which has apparently been displaced), but the whole codex is not, as might be hastily supposed, written by him. The Aratus part is dated 1488.

83 Codex Memmianus. Written at Florence by Gherardo del Ciriagio (cf. No. 21). Copy of a slightly corrected copy of No. 95 (cf. Nos. 105 and 117). All these manuscripts show a close relationship to *R* (see the Stemma Codicum).

84 Codex Colbertinus.

85 Very close to No. 52, with which it shares not only the readings common to the θ class but many that are not present in the other members of that class. May have been written in the vicinity of Padua, and may be linked with a group of four manuscripts of the *Priapea*, two of which are hybrid and contain readings (absent from the two 'purer' manuscripts) which are very close to the readings of the manuscript under review.

86 Written in Rome. Bought at Constantinople in 1672; thought to have been looted from Matthias Corvinus. See Delisle 1868: I.297 n. 3.

87 Codex Sangermanensis (*G*). Written at Verona, probably by Antonio da Legnago. For writer and date, see Billanovich 1959: 160–5.

No.	Short Title	Location and Press-Mark	Designation			Date	Contents
			Ellis	Zicàri	Butrica		
88		Parma: Bibl. Palatina					
		HH5.47 (716)	pm	91		1471	PCT
89		HH3.124 (1092)				1736	C
90		Pesaro: Bibl.					
		Oliveriana					
		1167 (formerly 1217)		92		1470	CTP+
91		Rome: Bibl.					
		Casanatense 15		97		1470–1	TPC (lacking 27.5–61.142 and 108–116)
92	Cors.	Bibl. Corsiniana					
		43.D.20				ca. 1500	TC+
93	Dan.	S. Daniele del Friuli:					
		Bibl. Guarneriana 56		104		ca. 1455	P Ov. (*H.* 15) TC+

88 Written at Pavia by Bernardo Prato of Parma 'in arce papie apud Magistrum Gandulfum de Bononia castellanus' (fol. 110, at end of Catullus, together with date). Close to No. 129a; cf. No. 104. At 64.139 reads (with *O* and a few late manuscripts) *blanda* instead of *nobis*.

89 Apparently the author's manuscript of Vulpius' annotated edition of 1737. Contains two *nihil obstat* certificates, signed by clerics and dated 1736.

90 Written at Siena by Francesco Fucci of Città di Castello. See Zicàri 1953 = 1978: 43–60. Dated in the *subscriptio* to the Catullus; other parts are dated separately.

91 Written by Pomponius Laetus, with rubrication by Bartolomeo Sanvito; see Muzzioli 1959: 337–52 (date, p. 348). British Library Ms Sloane 777 belongs to the same series. Cf. also No. 110.

92 A descendant of No. 109 (cf. No. 27). The note on poem 14b, 'in codice antiquo non leguntur hic,' which appears in No. 86, and a similar observation in the manuscript under review, were first indicated by Mynors; cf. Richardson 1976: 285.

93 Not, as Hale once supposed (though he later changed his mind), a *G*-tradition manuscript, but rather a manuscript in the *R a* tradition prevalent in northeastern Italy, with, however, substantial influence from the tradition of *G*. Compare for example 112.1 *homoque* (= R^2), 112.2 (*est G, es OR, om. SDan.*). For an example of possible *a*-influence cf. 68.38 *ingenuo*. See Zicàri 1959 = 1978: 109–22. For the date, see D'Angelo 1970: 28, item 134 (inventory dated 1461). There are two different hands, the second of which begins on fol. 31 at 64.351. There are few corrections; most of them are in the former hand, identified by Zicàri 1959: 460 = 1978: 117–18, as that of Battista Cingolano. See Ghiselli 1987, which contains photographs of a few folios.

No.	Short Title	Location and Press-Mark	Ellis	Zicàri	Butrica	Date	Contents
94		(formerly) Schlägl (Austria): Prämonstratenserstiftsbibl. 143 Cpl. 59				1465	Aristotle Cic. (*De fato*) Hor. (*Epod.*) C+
95	Sen.	Siena: Bibl. Comunale H.V. 41				ca. 1425	C+
96	Tub.	Tübingen: Universitätsbibl. M^e 104				XV (2nd)	TC+
97		Turin: Bibl. reale *Varia* 54				ante 1466	C (1–61)
98		Vatican: Bibl. Apostolica Vaticana Barberini lat. 34			109	XV (med.?)	TPC+

94 (= 10a). Written at Pavia by Johannes de Rabenstein. One hand only. Dated at end of Catullus (fol. 96ᵛ). A later note on the same page claims that the readings are exactly the same ('*eaedem plane*') as those of No. 57. For the contents, see Vielhaber and Indra 1918: 249–50. Unknown to Hale and Ullman. For the knowledge of this manuscript I am indebted to the director of the Hill Monastic Manuscript Library, Saint John's University, Collegeville, Minnesota. Now in the Bibl. Royale (Albertina), Brussels. See Gaisser 1981.

95 Very close to *R*; a sister of No. 22 (see the Stemma Codicum). Spells *michi, nichil*. Among the contents (fol. 48) there is a dedication to Coluccio Salutati which is not without interest. Corrected in a mid-fifteenth-century hand; No. 117 derives from it *before* correction (see Nos. 83, 105, 112 nn.).

96 Written by a professional scribe: 'scrips. Heinricus Koch de Sch[. . .].' Some of the spellings are old-fashioned (*michi, nichil, capud, velud*), but many of the readings suggest influence of the later tradition from β to η, especially that of the γ class. None of the readings corresponds to those introduced by the 1472 edition, but some to those first found in the edition of 1473. Unknown to Hale and Ullman.

97 Epigram *Ad patriam* at end of the (incomplete) text. Agrees in a few places with γ class; much more frequently, with δ class, to which there is a fairly marked resemblance; but hardly more than once with ε class. Disagrees more often than not with ζ class, and much more often than not with η (about 18 disagreements in 25 readings) and also θ (some 21 disagreements in 30 readings). At the end, a note of ownership, some of it erased or illegible, which reads in part: 'Ego Iohannes baptista clericus parmensis emi hunc catullum a quodam Scriptore b . . . re<giensi?> pro quinquaginta be<zanti?>is anno dñi milesimo sexagesimo sexto die . . .' Not known to Hale or Ullman.

Vatican Library. For the Barberini, Ottoboni, and Chigi collections, including Nos. 98–102 and 107 below, see especially Pellegrin 1975.

98 On the annotations (chiefly based on *Parth.*), see Gaisser 1992: 228; she dates the annotator's work tentatively in 1493–5 (ibid. 209).

No.	Short Title	Location and Press-Mark	Designation Ellis	Zicàri	Butrica	Date	Contents
99	Ottob.	Ottob. lat. 1550			116	XV med.	CP+
100		1799		v		post 1460	C
101	R	1829	R	R		1375+	C
102	Ottob.	1982				XV (2nd)	C (to 63.44)+
103	Pal.	Pal. lat. 910			118	ca. 1475?	T Ov. PC+
104		1652			119	1445–59 (prob. ca. 1455)	TCP+

---

99 Certainly a descendant of No. 23 (both omit the lines 61.125–9, 62.54–5, 62.62; and there are a great many striking agreements besides, even against other manuscripts that correspond very closely with No. 23 in general). Yet it was probably not a direct copy, but a copy of a copy, for the following reasons: at 22.3 (*itemque*) and 40.3 (*advocatus*) it agrees with *m* (No. 115: see Introduction, pp. 35–8) against both No. 23 and *R*; it spells *michi*, *nichil*; and (what is more significant) after 55.10 the scribe missed several lines and began to write line 18, but stopped after three words (detecting his error), erased the words, and replaced them with line 11. This means that the scribe must have been copying from a manuscript that had lines 11 and 18 on the same page – but this is not true of No. 23. (The last observation I owe to an unpublished note by Ullman). At 63.25 it agrees with No. 15 (*sacra cohors*). Written perhaps in northeastern Italy; Ullman suggested the Friuli. See G. Mercati, *Codici latini Pico Grimani* = Studi e Testi 75 (1938): 253.

100 Copy of a corrected manuscript close to *a*. Cf. Nos. 22 and 105. See Zicàri 1956: 153–62 = 1978: 68–77.

101 Codex Romanus (*R*). See Introduction, pp. 33–5. For a collation, with brief introduction, see Thomson 1970.

102 Written in Italy (Humanistic cursive). A miscellany from P. Laetus' circle. See Gaisser 1992: 250–1, for contents and date. There is a fifteenth-century note in a German hand: 'Wolfgangus Gügler clericus Frisingensis diocesis.' Has *a*-class transpositions, with a variation: 24.5–10 are left out; then, after the end of poem 62, we find 24.3–10 (there are two versions of 24.3 and 4). See Kellogg 1900. On fol. 215^V, at the end of the printed text of Aesop, appears the date 1475.

103 Written perhaps in northeastern Italy. Dated 1467 at the end of the Tibullus, and also on fol. 91^V; but Ullman guessed 1475 for the Catullus (on fols. 306–42, in a different hand from the Tibullus, and probably slightly later); in doing so he compared with it 'the Leyden Tibullus.' (By this he presumably meant Voss. o.42, dated 1473).

104 Two parts: fols. 1–28, Tibullus (perhaps not all by one hand); 28^V–129^V, Catullus, Calpurnius, Propertius, written by Giannozzo Manetti ca. 1450 or somewhat later. Both parts have decorated 'vine-stem' initials, in a mid-century style which may be Florentine, but could be Roman, as could the script of the first part. The initials may of course have been added later; but if they are Roman then they, at least, are likely to have been executed in the mid-1450s, when Giannozzo was in exile in Rome and before he went on to Naples. He died in 1459. On fol. 132 there is a poem composed 'a m[agistro] petro o[do] Montipolitano die xii febr. 1460/Pro clar^{mo} viro Dño Jañozio Manetto.' Against Sabbadini (1905: 16, n. 82) Ullman points out that there is no proof

No.	Short Title	Location and Press-Mark	Ellis	Zicàri	Butrica	Date	Contents
105	Urb.	Urb. lat. 641			120	ca. 1465–70	CTP
106		812				1495–1500?	C
107	Chis.	Chigi H.IV.121		ch		ca. 1467	CT
108	Vat.	Vat. lat. 1608		va		1479	C *Priap.*
109		1630	V			ca. 1425+	Plaut. C+
110		3269				ca. 1470	C *Priap.*
111		3272			124	ca. 1465–70	PTC+

that this is the autograph of Petrus Odus, and holds it to be 'almost certain' that it is not. Another version is given by Schenkl 1883: 293. Close to No. 129a; cf. No. 88.

105 A sister of No. 83; probably copy of a copy of No. 95. Written at Florence by C. Sinibaldus (see de la Mare 1985: I.538; on C. Sinibaldus, ibid. 432).

106 Close to Nos. 14 and 17. This must be the 'Vaticanus' of Santen (cf. the reading 68.141 *fas*, with Santen's note). For the writer's name the *subscriptio* gives the following: 'ego Iulius Cesar Ia ... cus sentinatus [i.e. from Sentino in Umbria] scripsi.' Note of ownership on fol. 70ʳ: 'Antˢ Borgˢ.'

107 Written in Rome by Guido Bonatti of Mantua (d. 1494?). See Ms Chigi H. V. 169 (Ovid *Amores*, *Priapea*, etc.), which is by the same hand but in a different ink, and is dated 1467 (inside the back cover; at the end of the *Priapea*, in the same hand, the words 'finit per me Guidonem Bonactium'). Our manuscript, though written relatively late, represents a fairly early state of the text.

108 Written in Rome for Pope Sixtus IV: on the first page, the arms of the della Rovere family, surmounted by the papal insignia, indicate Sixtus as the original owner. See Muntz and Fabre 1887: 155 (account book of Sixtus IV): 'Satisfeci scriptori qui scripsit Catullum poetam et Priapeiam Virgilii simul in bonis litteris ducatis tribus, die ultimo maii 1479.' Professor Reeve informs me that the *Priapea* part derives from a printed edition; but in the Catullus part I find little to suggest that either the readings of the 1472 edition or those of the 1473 edition have been followed, and some positive evidence to the contrary. At 66.11, however, the reading *quare ex* has been emended to *qua rex* (= 1473 edition), which suggests that in one or more passages the latter edition may possibly have been consulted.

109 The Plautine contents (consisting of the following plays only: *Amphitruo, Asinaria, Aulularia, Captivi, Curculio, Casina, Cistellaria, Epidicus*) may point to a date ca. 1425+ – before, that is, manuscript *D* of Plautus arrived in Rome (in 1429), and became known. The parent, or ancestor, of Nos. 27 and 92. Close to No. 8 in character.

110 It is stated on the manuscript that it was written by Pomponius Laetus (1428–98); the statement ends with the name of 'Ful. Ors.' (Fulvio Orsini, 1529–1600). Categorical as it is, the statement about Laetus appears to be based on Orsini's fantasy. Nevertheless, the manuscript clearly originated in Laetus' circle. Cf. No. 91. Part of No. 145 once formed a part of this manuscript.

111 Close to No. 28, according to Hale; cf. also No. 79. On a flyleaf: 'Catullo ... di mano di huomo dotto, Ful. Ors.' (cf. note on No. 110). More than one hand, but the hands

No.	Short Title	Location and Press-Mark	Designation Ellis	Zicàri	Butrica	Date	Contents
112		3291				XV 3/4	Lucr. Pers. *Priap*. CT+
113		7044				1520	C
114		11425				XV (late)	TC
115	*m*	Venice: Bibl. Nazionale Marciana lat.					
		12.80 (4167)	Ven.			1398–1400	C
116	Marc.	12.81 (4649)		mr		ca. 1460–70?	TC
117		12.86 (4170)				ca. 1440–50?	Ov. C
118		12.153 (4453)		mo		ca. 1460–70	TC+

are of about the same date. There are only a few corrections or variant readings; for the most part these were made or added by the first hand in each passage, and immediately after writing.

112 One hand only. See de Nolhac 1887: 359, no. 16. Fairly close to either *R* or *m*. Related to Nos. 83 and 105.

113 The indication 'Catullus, copied by Basilius Zanchus (1581)' in Kristeller 1967: 342, is partly incorrect. The date (MDXX Kal. Mart.) is given on the flyleaf, preceded by the following (heavily overscored but partly legible): 'Catullus Petrei Bergomatis ex antiquissimo exemplari Joviani Pontani diligentissime descriptus.' At the bottom of the page, in a later hand: 'Ego Laurentius Gambara Brixianus fidem facio librum hunc scriptum esse manu Basilii Zanchi Bergomatis, cuius consuetudine et amicitia usus sum per multos annos. 1581.' Here the date 1581 is plainly meant to be understood as that of Gambara's correcting note (observe the punctuation and phrasing). The erasures appear to be Gambara's. Note the references to a manuscript described as that of Pontanus. For Petreius and Pontanus, see further Richardson 1976: 279 and n. 1. Ullman 1908: 10, n. 1, observes that Petreius was the 'Academy' name of Basilius (Zanchi): see his reference to Tiraboschi. Ullman also notes that Zanchi died in Rome in 1558 or 1560.

114 See Ruysschaert 1959: 17. One scribe only. A note inside the cover reads 'Dono di Pio X.'

115 Codex (Venetus) Marcianus (*m*). A very close copy of R/R^2, written at Florence. See the Introduction, pp. 35–8, on the scribe's identity and other matters; for a description see de la Mare and Thomson 1973.

116 Written probably at Padua or Venice; possibly in Rome. Capitals by Bartolomeo Sanvito of Padua (1421–1511/12). At 66.83 reads *colitis* (= *OG*).

117 Very close to No. 95 (e.g., 45.16 *medulis*, 58b.7 *mihic*, 63.25 *diva cohors*, 80.6 *canta vocare*: these and other readings show that it was copied before the exemplar was corrected). It should not be included in the η class; Mynors (pref., p. x) evidently confused it with No. 116.

118 May have been written at Padua. The hand is similar to the early work of Sanvito (see note on No. 116). Has the β titles. See Zicàri 1958: 80–8 = 1978: 80–90.

No.	Short Title	Location and Press-Mark	Ellis	Zicàri	Butrica	Date	Contents
119		(ed. Ald^1, nn)					
		12.127 (4020)				1530	C
120		(ed. Ald^2, nn)					
		12.128 (4021)				XVI (med.?)	C
121		Venice: Museo Civico					
		Correr					
		fondo Cicogna 549		32		XV	T Ov. PC
122	Vic.	Vicenza: Bibl. Berto-					
		liana G. 2.8.12 (216)	Vic. vu	133		1460	TCP
123	Vind.	Vienna: National-					
		bibl. 224		134		1463+	CTP
124		3198				ca. 1460	C Petron. T+

119 A copy of the first Aldine edition (Catullus, Tibullus, Propertius) with notes derived from those of Francesco Pucci, which were made in 1502; copied in 1530 by Donato Giannotti (signed on title page: 'Donati Jannotij.' At the end of the Propertius there is a further note: 'Franciscus Puccius haec annotavit anno Salutis MDII, Augustino Scarpinella comite studiorum, secutus fidem antiquissimi codicis qui primum fuit Berardini Vallae patricij Romani viri doctissimi dein ab eo datus est Alfonso secundo Regi Neap^{no} principi litterarum amantissimo. Consulit Laurentius Benivenius ut omnia in suum exscriberet: ego autem cum ipso Laurentij sic adtuli ut nihil intermissum sit. Absolutum opus An. MDXXX iiij Cal. Augusti. Obsessa urbe. Donatus Jannoctius'). For the diffusion of Pucci's notes, and for a copy of the 1481 Reggio edition, now in Florence, which belonged to Pucci and has virtually the same note down to *amantissimo*, see Brian Richardson, 'Pucci, Parrasio and Catullus,' who also mentions Benivieni on pp. 279–80, and esp. Gaisser 1992: 243–9.

120 Plainly later than No. 119, with the contents of which the annotator appears to be well acquainted. The same abbreviations are used ('p' for Puccius, 'v.c.' for *vetus codex*), but others ('A,' for example) are added.

121 Written in Italy. Two Humanistic cursive hands; originally two separate manuscripts. The Catullus, fols. 127–75, is in a different hand from the rest. Close to Nos. 69 and 70. Cf. also Nos. 47, 50, 82, and 104. The correcting hand in the Catullus may be that of Petrus Odus.

122 Written at Padua by Bartolomeo Sanvito (cf. Nos. 116 and 118) for Marcantonio Morosini of Venice. One hand only, including the addition of many variant readings, and of a small number of corrections; but the manuscript is very carefully written, with few errors. Many of its readings correspond with those of the 1473 edition, the editor of which may possibly have consulted this manuscript as a source of ideas for improving the text. Evidently the parent of the η class, as No. 52 is of the θ class.

123 Direct copy of No. 124. Belonged to Matthias Corvinus. See Csapodi 1969: 71, 302, and pl. CVI; de la Mare 1985: I.496 tentatively attributes the hand to Gabriel de Pistorio.

124 Written by Giorgio Antonio Vespucci (ca. 1434–1514). Described by de la Mare 1976: 230 (see n. 3 for references to other descriptions, and n. 4 on the question of date).

No.	Short Title	Location and Press-Mark	Designation Ellis	Zicàri	Butrica	Date	Contents
125		3243				1499	C (to 54.6)
126		Wolfenbüttel: Herzog August Bibl.					
		65.2 Aug. 8°			136	1486+	CTP
127	Gud.	283 Gud. lat.				ca. 1500	C
128		332 Gud. lat.		gu		ca. 1460	TC+
		Location unknown:					
129		(formerly) Phillipps					
		6433			146	XV?	PTC
		In a private collection:					
129a	Tom.	Codex Tomacellianus			143	XV med.	PCT

Supplementary List (Short Fragments or Extracts)

No.	Location and Press-Mark	Date	Contents (C.)
130	Basle: Universitätsbibl.		
	F.II.35	1534	(f. 19) frag.
131	Cracow: University Library		
	no. 3244, DD.12.15	XVI ex.–XVII in.	(ff. 2^r–9^v) extracts
132	Florence: Bibl. Laurenziana Strozz. 100	ca. 1460–80?	poem 49

125 Written in Germany.

126 Written by Clemens Salernitanus, who worked at Naples in the second half of the fifteenth century. The Propertius was copied from the Brescia edition of 1486. Arms apparently those of Montefeltro. Venetian illumination. There is insufficient proof of its having belonged to Matthias Corvinus.

127 Copy of a copy of No. 100. Order of poems: 1–24; 44.21–62; 30–44.20; 63–116 (that is, in general it has the α-class transpositions).

128 Probably the parent or ancestor of No. 75. Incorporates some ζ-class readings, e.g., 44.19 *gestire cesso* (found also in Nos. 45 and 46).

129 W.G. Hale believed this to be identical with No. 52; see Hale 1908: 238. No. 52, however, contains no indication that it ever was a Phillipps manuscript. I have not discovered what led Hale to identify the two.

129a The designation, which I suggested, was accepted by Professor Butrica; see Butrica 1984: 106–10.

131 'Selecta Phalerciorum Q. Valerii Catuli, Veronensis.'

No.	Location and Press-Mark	Date	Contents (C.)
133	Florence: Bibl. Nazionale (fondo naz.) II. ix. 8	1479(?)	5; 13; 31.6–10; 64.143–4; 49; 39.16
134	London: British Library Additional 21908	XV	(f. 45^v) '*Ad patriam*' epigram
135	Marseilles: Bibl. de la ville 1283	XVII	extracts
136	Munich: Bayerische Staatsbibl. lat. 7471	XV–XVI	poem 49
137	Nice: Bibl. de la ville 85	XV med.	(Juv., *Schol. Sat.* vi.8, f. 23^r): 3.1–5, 8–10, 17–18

———

133 'Excerpta Catulli' on fol. 133^{rv}. Date 1479 in Arabic and Roman numerals appears (among scribbles) on fol. 149, followed by the words 'Hic liber est Caesaris Malvicini Viterbiensis.' Later the book belonged to Iohannes Laurentius Puccius (this, with its further history, is recorded on fol. 146^r).

137 Date probably after 1450. Superb Venetian binding. On fol. 23^r (in margin), scholia to the sixth satire of Juvenal, line 8, including the following excerpts from Catullus (poem 3):

Catullus in primo:	Et subdit	Et paulo post

Lugete o veneres cupidinesque quantum est hominum venus-
  torum passer
mortuus est meaeque puellae
  quem plus
oculis illa suis amat
	Nec sese agremio illius
	  movebat
	Sed circumsiliens modo huc
	  modo illuc
	Ad solam dominam usque
	  papillabat
		Tua nunc opera, meae puellae
		Flendo turgiduli rubent ocelli.

(I have expanded some of the standard abbreviations used.)

See Beldame 1982, where the manuscript is assigned to the twelfth century. Inspection reveals significant errors in Beldame's report of the above-quoted extracts from Catullus. The scholia 'were in the scribe's exemplar,' and are therefore for the most part earlier (not later, as Beldame seems to say, p. 77) than the present text. In this connection I have two observations to make: (1) Though *papillabat* is, so far as I know, a unique reading, it may well be a mistake for *pipillabat*, which would point to a date scarcely before 1460; on the other hand, (2) the inversion *oculis illa* occurs chiefly in manuscripts of the first half of the fifteenth century. The apparent division of Catullus into 'chapters' (*capitula*; hardly 'books') implied by the words *in primo* of the heading is also intensely interesting, since it appears not to be paralleled except (in a different form, where poem 3 is not in the first 'chapter,' and at a prehumanistic date) in the context discussed by Ullman 1910. On the general character of the scholia, Beldame (77, n. 3) remarks that they differ both 'from those known since Pithou, and

No.	Location and Press-Mark		Date	Contents (C.)
138	Paris: Bibl. Nationale			
	nouv. acq. lat. 719		ca. 1476	(f. 49) 78.1–5
139	Rome: Bibl.			
	Casanatense	904	XVI (1st)	*Florilegium Sententiarum*
140	Vatican: Bibl. Apostolica			
	Vaticana			
	Ottob. lat. 1471		XVI (2nd)	55.20
141	Ottob. lat. 1507		XV	(f. 115^{v}) poem 49
142	Regin. lat. 1879		1491	(f. 144^{v}) frag.
143	Vat. lat. 2886		XV	(f. 139) frag.
144		2951	XV	5; 49; 8
145		7192	1527	extracts (ff. 165^{r}–184^{v})

    also from those collected by Cramer (*In D. Junii Juvenalis satiras commentarii vetusti ...*, Hamburg, 1823).' Perhaps they deserve further examination.

138 The first part of the manuscript was written at Modena and dated 1476 (fol. 19); the date 1477 also appears (fol. 30^{v}).

141 Exhibits the late fifteenth-century arms of Bartolomeo Ghisilardi of Bologna.

145 Part of this manuscript was originally part of No. 110, q.v.

'Ghost' Manuscripts

A small number of manuscripts, the existence of which has been recorded or alleged, are not included in the Table of Manuscripts: some of these do not exist at all, while others have been wrongly identified.

Poppi, Biblioteca Rilliana Ms 54 contains no Catullus but only Tibullus and Propertius, despite Mazzatinti 1896: 134, and also Fanfani 1925: 16, where the wording is exactly the same; and despite a printed label inside the front cover: 'Tibullii [sic] Catulli Propertii opera exeunte Saec XIV [sic] cum adnotationibus.' I can detect no sign that a Catullus has been removed; this, I now find, was also Zicàri's opinion (see below). Further, on the flyleaf there is a note of purchase, as follows: 'Hic liber vocatur Tibullus,' etc. At the end of the Tibullus, these words: 'Finis die sabbati hora 3^{a} die decima aprilis 1472 Senis in domo Ludovici Doti. ego Gaspar. et Audivi A ... poeta.' (Several words have dropped out. For the erased name, Professor Butrica suggests 'Maximo Pacifico,' for whom see the note on No. 52 in the Table of Manuscripts.) The writers and compilers of inventories, quoted above, and also Ferguson 1934: 66–7, give the alleged contents in the order Catullus, Tibullus, Propertius. See now Butrica 1984: 287–8.

Other 'ghosts' may be more summarily dealt with. Codex Parisinus 8074, which has been reported to contain Catullus, is a Prudentius. For what is sometimes referred to as 'Hamburg Ms 125' see No. 38 in my table and notes; there is only one Hamburg manuscript of Catullus. The reported fragment at St Andrews University is merely a specimen of the modern calligrapher's art.

In Hale's article 'The Manuscripts of Catullus' (Hale 1908: 233–56) on pages 242 and 243 there is a supplementary list of 'MSS and other material not found (or not identified).' Referring to this list, I make the following observations:

Cavrianeus is now Göttingen Ms Philol. 111b (No. 35 in my table).

The manuscript alluded to in the words 'London: in aedibus Iacobaeis (Mss Angliae, T. ii, p. 247, No. 8236)' is Voss. lat. in oct. 59 (No. 40 in my table). See de Meyier 1977: 105–8. For 8236 read 8636 (Tibullus, Catullus).

STEMMA CODICUM

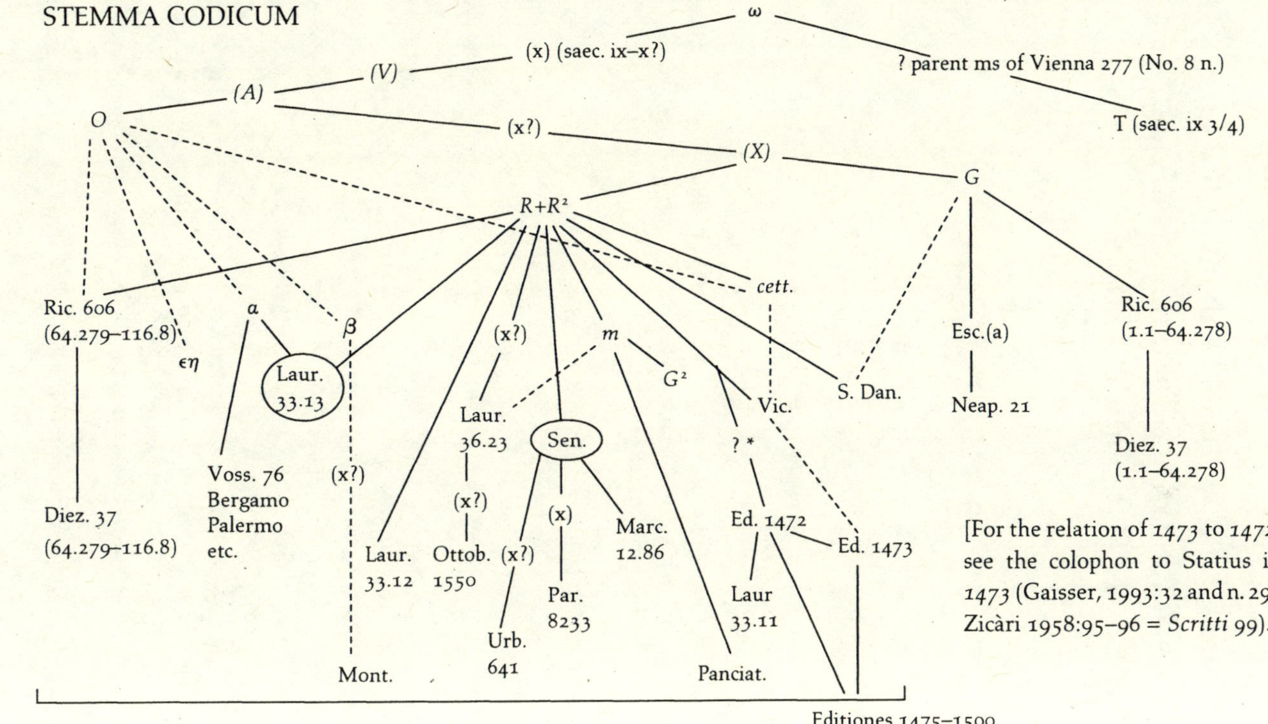

[For the relation of *1473* to *1472*, see the colophon to Statius in *1473* (Gaisser, 1993:32 and n. 29); Zicàri 1958:95–96 = *Scritti* 99).]

* A manuscript (probably destroyed by the printer) similar to Lond. 11915; see Zicàri (1957) 157 = *Scritti* 106

SOURCES (OTHER THAN EDITIONS)
OF MODERN (POST-1600) EMENDATIONS
CITED IN THE *APPARATUS CRITICUS*

E. Badian, *CP* 72 (1977): 320–2: 29.20

– *HSCP* 84 (1980): 81–9: 67.6

E. Baehrens, *Analecta Catulliana* (Jena, 1874): 55–6: 64.395, 402

R. Bentley, *Callimachi fragmenta et notae ad Elegiam Catulli de Coma Berenices* (*editio Graeviana*[1], 1697): 436–8: 63.9, 20, 35, 74, 84, 91; 581–3: 66.23, 53, 54

W.T. Bergk, *ap*. A. Rossbach, ed. (1854): 17.6; 23.27; 64.16, 61, 253, 258, 288, 378; 67.27; 68.29; 95.9; 110.7; 115.5

– *Philologus* 16 (1860): 618–19: 31.13, 61.46–7, 221

– *RhM* 15 (1860): 507–8: 78b (*post* 80.8)

F. Buecheler, *RhM* 18 (1863): 401: 5.13 (*ex Priapeo* 52.12)

P. Burman, *ad Anth. Lat.* vol. 1. (1732): 305, repr. in *Miscellanea* (Amsterdam, 1759): 61.215

W.A. Camps, *AJP* 94 (1973): 131–46: 64.320; 116.7

– *ap*. G. Lee, ed. (1990): 186: 6.13

J. Czwalina, *ap*. E. Baehrens, ed.[1] (1876): 64.148

R. Dawes, *Miscellanea Critica* (Cambridge, 1745[1], 1781[2], etc.): 60 (ed.[2]): 61.215–16

E.H. van Eldik, *ap*. Laur. Santenius, *C. Valerii Catulli Elegia ad Manlium* (Leiden, 1788; see p. 56 above): 42–3: 68.101

R. Ellis, *Philologus* 49 (1890): 170, and *Classical Review* 4 (1890): 311: 64.109

F.B. Eschenburg, *Observationes criticae in Propertium, dissertatio philologica* (Bonn, 1865), *sub fin.* (*Sententiae controversae*, no. 5): 66.77

J. Fleischer, *Jb. des gr.-or. Über-Gymnasiums in Suczawa* (Suceava, Romania) 1898: 10–13: 64.119

J. Fröhlich, *Catulli Liber: Vorschläge zur Berichtigung des Textes* 5.3 (Munich, 1849): 233–75: 21.11; 29.20; 41.8; 64.73; 67.5; 68.39, 102; 97.5; 115.2, 7

L. Fruterius (XVI[c]) in: *Lampas*, ed. J. Gruter, vol. 5 (Frankfurt, 1605), Ep. 4: 389: 64.320

G.P. Goold, *Phoenix* 23 (1969): 186–203: 3.16

A.S. Gratwick, *CP* 87 (1992): 234–40: 45.8

J. Gulielmius, in: *Lampas*, ed. J. Gruter, vol. 3 (Frankfurt, 1604), part 2: 446: 23.21

F. Hand, *Quaestiones Catullianae: Programmschrift Jena* (1848): 40: 17.3

M. Haupt, *Quaestiones Catullianae* (Leipzig, 1837): 19–23 (= *Opusc.* 1.15–18): 29.23, 61.46; 71–3 (= *Opusc.* 1.52–4): 64.28; 79–82 (= *Opusc.* 1.58–60): 66.9

– *Observationes criticae* (Leipzig, 1841): 24–32 (= *Opusc.* 1.97–105): 11.11; 69–70 (= *Opusc.* 1.142): 64.287

N. Heinsius, *Adversariorum libri IV* (Haarlem, 1742): 633–53: 22.5; 61.120, 199; 64.75, 287; 68.91; 107.2

– (elsewhere): *ap.* Schwabe, ed.: 37.11; 66.7; *ap.* Lachmann, ed.: 76.10

W.A.B. Hertzberg (and W.S. Teuffel), trans. of Catullus in *Ausgewählte Gedichte der röm. Elegiker* (Stuttgart, 1843¹, 1862²): 145: 68.139

R. Herzog, *Hermes* 71 (1936): 346: 25.5

J.H. Hoeufft, *Classical Journal* 10 (1815): 169: 64.215

A.E. Housman, *ap.* J.P. Postgate, ed. (1889): 95.3

– *CR* 4 (1890): 340: 64.282

– *CR* 9 (1915): 229–30: 64.324

K. Lachmann, *ad Lucr.* 3.954 (ed. Berlin, 1850): 196: 114.6

G. Lafaye, *RPh* 46 (1922): 56–75: 25.5

W.S. Landor, *Foreign Quarterly Review* 29 (April and July 1842): 361: 68.145

F. Leo, *Hermes* 38 (1903): 305: 95.9

W.M. Lindsay, *CR* 33 (1919): 105–6: 39.11

E. Lobel, *Oxyrynchus Papyri* 20 (London, 1952): 98: 66.78

D.S. McKie, *PCPS* 30 (1984): 74–8: 11.11

J.N. Madvig, ed.³ Cicero, *De Finibus* (Copenhagen, 1876): 721 (*ad* 5.23.5): 64.23–4

J. Maehly, *NJbb.* 103 (1871): 345–57: 15.2; 39.9; 64.402; 66.7; 101.3; 102.1; 113.1

T. Marcilius, *In C. Catullum Asterismi* (Paris, 1604): 5–19: 6.14; 22.5; 68.91, 141

A. Meineke, *Vindiciarum Straboniarum Liber* (Berlin, 1852): 152–3: 64.35

W. Morel, *ap.* R. Pfeiffer, ed. *Callimachus*, vol. 2, Addenda: 116: 66.78

H.A.J. Munro, *Criticisms and Elucidations of Catullus* (Cambridge/London, 1878¹, 1905²): 10.26; 21.11; 27.4; 73.3; 95.3

R.G.M. Nisbet, *PCPS* 24 (1978): 92–115: 22.6; 63.64; 68.39, 49, 60; 84.5

F. Orioli, *Epp. in C. Valerium Catullum* (Bologna, 1822): 18–19: 64.23b

P.H. Peerlkamp, ed. *P. Vergilii Maronis Aeneidos Lib. II* (Leiden, 1843): 110: 64.23b

L.R.S. Peiper, *Q. Valerius Catullus: Beiträge zur Kritike seines Gedichtes* (Breslau, 1875): 25–32: 22. 13; 61.53; 66.11

C. Pleitner, *Des Catulls Hochzeitsgesänge kritisch behandelt* (Dillingen, 1858): 49: 61.216

– *Des Catulls Epigr. an und über J. Caesar und Mamurra* (Prog. Speyer, 1849): 15: 113.2

J.P. Postgate, *Journal of Philology* 17 (1888): 252–3, 257–8: 68.142; 107.7–8

O. Ribbeck, *Jbb. für Philologie und Paedagogik* (ed. P. Jahn) 85 (1862): 378: 107.1

O.L. Richmond, *ap.* F.W. Cornish, Loeb edition, 1912: 179: 114.6

F. Ritschl, *Index lect. Bonn,* Winter 1857: 6: 64.73

F. Ritter, '1828' (Riese): *ap.* Doering, ed. 1834 [*v. CR* 4 (1890): 312] 51.8

<Readings of others in> F. Robortelli, ed. (1604): 169: 61.191; 67.42

A. Riese, *NJbb.* 91 (1865): 298: 55.11

K. Rossberg, *NJbb.* 115 (1877): 845: 116.7

L. van Santen, *ad Terentianum Maurum* (ed., 1788): 278: 63.68

F. Schoell, *NJbb.* 121 (1880): 471–80: 68.30; 100.6

J. Schrader, *Observationum Liber* (Franeker, 1761): 11: 51.11; 68.110, 122

– *Liber Emendationum* (Leeuwarden, 1776): 15: 62.35

– (unpublished): see M. Puelma in *MHelv* 34 (1977): 156 n. 1, where the source is
given as Ms Berlin *Diez. B. Sant. 44,* fols. 55 and 69: 64.14

L. Schwabe, *NJbb.* 91 (1865): 18: 68.143

O. Skutsch, *Philologus* 106 (1962): 281–2: 64.254

– *BICS* 16 (1969): 40: 61.171

D.A. Slater, *CR* 19 (1905): 59: 25.5

L. Spengel, *Archivium philologicum* 3.4 (Munich, 1827): 93–127, esp. 121: 39.9;
62.41a [lacuna].

R. Syme, *ap.* C. Neudling, *A Prosopography to Catullus* (Oxford, 1955): 185: 61.16

D.F.S. Thomson, *RhM* 113 (1970): 87–91: 64.196

– *LCM* 9.8 (1984): 119–20: 109.1–2

– *Phoenix* 47 (1987): 191–2: 112.2

J.A.K. Thomson, *CR* 64 (1950): 90: 4.8

D.A. Traill, *CP* 87 (1992): 326–8: 64.24

B. Venator, "Spicilegium" in Gebhardus/Livineius edition (Frankfurt, 1621): 20: 21,
11

W.S. Watt, *CP* 85 (1990): 129–31: 66.74

H. Weber, *Quaestiones Catullianae* (Gotha, 1890): 73–5: 62.56 (cf. Quint. *ad* 62.45)

U. von Wilamowitz-Moellendorff, *Hermes* 14 (1879): 200 [= *Kl. Schr.* 2 (Berlin,
1971): 7]: 66.77

M. Zicàri, *Rend. Ist. Lomb.* 86 (1953): 377–82 [= *Scritti catulliani* (Urbino, 1978):
134–6]: 67.33.

SIGLA

V	fons communis codicum *OGR* (nunc deperditus)	ca. 1280?
O	Oxoniensis Bodleianus Canonicianus class. lat. 30	s. XIV (ca. 1360?)
G	Parisinus lat. 14137	anni 1375
R	Vaticanus Ottobonianus lat. 1829	ca. 1390?
T	Parisinus lat. 8071 (carmen 62)	s. IX
m	Venetus Marcianus lat. 12.80 (4167)	ca. 1398–1400

$O^1G^1T^1m^1$ codex ab ipso librario vel statim vel brevi correctus; similiter
   $a^1 \beta^1$ (vide sis infra)

$$\left.\begin{array}{l} G^2G^3G^4 \\ R^2R^3R^a \\ m^2 \end{array}\right\} \text{manus recentiores}$$

a	Bononiensis bibl. Universitatis 2621	1412
β	Parisinus lat. 7989 ·	1423

γ–θ Quamquam hisce notis intellegendum est maiorem fere codicum
   partem, immo persaepe omnes, consentire, est ubi lectionem in
   paucis admodum codicibus invenias; si in uno tantum exstat,
   notam sic interclusi: (*θ*)

γ Mediolanensis Ambrosianus H 46 *sup.*
   Oxoniensis Bodleianus Canonicianus class. lat. 33
   Codex Antenoris Balbi sive Ashburneri (= No. 1)

Leidensis Vossianus lat. in oct. 59
Vaticanus Palatinus lat. 910
Hamburgensis scrin. 139.4

δ   Mediolanensis Braidensis (Brerensis) AD xii 37, no. 2
Parisinus lat. 8234
Berolinensis Diezianus B. Sant. 36

ε   Mediolanensis Braidensis (Brerensis) AD xii 37, no. 2
Brixianus bibliothecae Querinianae A vii 7
Londiniensis bibliothecae Britannicae Harleianus 2574

ζ   Florentinus bibliothecae nationalis Magliabechianus VII 1158
Londoniensis bibliothecae Britannicae add. 11915
Londoniensis bibliothecae Britannicae add. 11674

η   Vicentinus bibliothecae Bertolianae G. 2. 8. 12 (216)
Guelferbytanus 332 Gudianus lat.
Leidensis Vossianus lat. in oct. 81
Oxoniensis Bodleianus Laudianus lat. 78
Venetus Marcianus lat. 12.81 (4649)
Venetus Marcianus lat. 12.153 (4453)
Vaticanus Chisianus H.IV.121
Vaticanus Vat. lat. 1608

θ   Londoniensis bibliothecae Britannicae Egertonianus 3027
Londoniensis bibliothecae Britannicae Burneianus 133
Pisaurensis bibliothecae Oliverianae 1167
Parisinus lat. 8236
Neapolitanus bibliothecae nationalis IV. F. 61

Editiones:

1472 ed. Veneta
1473 ed. Parmensis
ed. Rom. (Romae ca. 1475 impressa)
Calph(urnius): ed. Vicentina 1481
Av(antius): Emendationes in Catullum, Venetiis 1495
    (*Av.*², Venetiis 1500)
Pall(adius): ed. Veneta 1496
Ald(ina): ed. Veneta 1502 ⎫
*Ald.*²: ed. Veneta 1515 ⎭ (utramque curavit Avantius)
Trinc.: ed. Veneta apud Trincavellium ca. 1535

CATULLI VERONENSIS LIBER

1

Cui dono lepidum novum libellum
arida modo pumice expolitum?
Corneli, tibi: namque tu solebas
meas esse aliquid putare nugas
iam tum, cum ausus es unus Italorum   5
omne aevum tribus explicare cartis
doctis, Iuppiter, et laboriosis.
quare habe tibi quidquid hoc libelli,
qualecumque quod, <o> patrona virgo,
plus uno maneat perenne saeclo.   10

1 1 *Ausonius, Eclogarum liber 1.1*   1–4 *Schol. Veron. in Vergilium, Ecl 6.1*   1–2 *Plinius, Naturalis historia 36.154*   *Isidorus, Etymologiae (= Origines) 6.12.3*   *Pastrengicus, De orginibus rerum (ed. Veneta) p. 88b*   1, 2, 4 *Grammatici Latini (ed. H. Keil) VI: 148 (Marius Victorinus), 261 (Caesius Bassus), 401 (Terentianus); cf. 298 (Atilius Fortunatianus)*   3–4 *Plinius, Naturalis historia 1 praefatio 1*   4 *Petrarca, Epistolae rerum senilium 11.3*   5–7 *Pastrengicus, De originibus rerum (ed. Veneta) p. 16a*

---

1 2 arida *Servius, Pastrengicus,* V?, arido *OGR*   punice *R, corr.* R²   5 tum ε: tamen *V* es ε: est *V*   6 evum (euū) *O, Pastrengicus:* eum *GR, corr.* R²   8 habe tibi η: tibi habe *V* libelli] al. mei *G¹R²*   9 <o> *add.* θ, est (ē) *Statius*   quidem *1472* (qualecumque quidem est, patroni ut ergo *Bergk*)   10 perire *O*

2

Passer, deliciae meae puellae,
quicum ludere, quem in sinu tenere,
cui primum digitum dare appetenti
et acris solet incitare morsus,
cum desiderio meo nitenti   5
carum nescioquid lubet iocari,
ut solaciolum sui doloris,
credo, ut tum gravis acquiescat ardor;
tecum ludere sicut ipsa possem
et tristis animi levare curas!   10

2^b

*   *   *

tam gratum est mihi quam·ferunt puellae
pernici aureolum fuisse malum,
quod zonam soluit diu ligatam.

3

Lugete, o Veneres Cupidinesque
et quantum est hominum venustiorum:
passer mortuus est meae puellae,
passer, deliciae meae puellae,
quem plus illa oculis suis amabat.   5
nam mellitus erat suamque norat
ipsam tam bene quam puella matrem,

---

2 1 *Grammatici Latini VI: 260 (Caesius Bassus), 293 (Atilius Fortunatianus), 614*
("Censorinus de metris")
2^b 3 *Priscianus, Institutiones grammaticae 1.22; cf. Carmina Epigraphica (ed. F. Buecheler)*
1504.49

---

2 3 qui *V, al.* cui *O*¹   appetenti *γ*: at petenti *V, al.* patenti *G*¹*R*², *al.* parenti *G? (manus*
recentior)   4 ea *V, corr. R*²   6 karum *V, corr. m*   libet *V, al.* iubet *O*¹   7 ut *B. Guarinus:*
et *V*   8 tum ... acquiescat *B. Guarinus:* cum ... acquiescet *V*   9 tecum *V, al.* secum *O*¹
ludere *GR,* luderem *O, corr. O*¹, *al.* luderem *G*¹
2^b 3 negatam *V:* ligatam *Priscianus R*², erat negatam *R*² *in margine*
3 3 motuus *G, corr. G*²

nec sese a gremio illius movebat,
sed circumsiliens modo huc modo illuc
ad solam dominam usque pipiabat;   10
qui nunc it per iter tenebricosum
illuc, unde negant redire quemquam.
at vobis male sit, malae tenebrae
Orci, quae omnia bella devoratis:
tam bellum mihi passerem abstulistis   15
(o factum male! o miselle passer!);
vestra nunc opera meae puellae
flendo turgiduli rubent ocelli.

4

Phaselus ille, quem videtis, hospites,
ait fuisse navium celerrimus,
neque ullius natantis impetum trabis
nequisse praeterire, sive palmulis
opus foret volare sive linteo.   5
et hoc negat minacis Hadriatici
negare litus insulasve Cycladas
Rhodumque nobilem horridamque Thracia
Propontida trucemve Ponticum sinum,
ubi iste post phaselus antea fuit   10

3 12 *[Seneca] Ludus de morte Claudii* 11.6; *cf. Carmina Epigraphica* 1504.11   16 *cf.*
Carmina Epigraphica 1512.4   18 *Petrarca, Epp. Var.* 32.43
4 *Cf. [Vergili] Catalepton* 10   1 *Grammatici Latini VI:* 134 *(Marius Victorinus),* 393
(Terentianus), 612 *("Censorinus de metris"); Scholia Bernensia ad Vergili Georgicon*
4.289; *Scholia ad Lucanum* 5.518; *Augustin., De Musica* 5.5, 11, 16

9 circumsiliens] c. silens *V*, al. siliens *O*¹, *corr. R*²   illuc movebat *GR*, al. vacat hoc verbum
*G*¹*R*²   10 pipiabat γ, pipilabat ζ: piplabat *V*   11 tenebricosum *Parth.*: tenebrosum *V*
12 illud *V*, al. illuc *O*¹   14 orci quae β (al. quae *iam G*¹): orcique *V*   bella *super scripto*
id est pulcra *OG*   15 passarem *R, corr. R*²   16 o (1°) η: bonum *V*   o miselle *1473,*
quod, miselle *Goold:* bonus ille *V* (bellus ille *R*³)   17 vestra *cod. antiquior ap. Av.;* tua *V*
18 turgidoli *R, corr. R*²
4 1 phasellus *V, corr. m*   2 ait *Calph.:* aiunt *V*   celerrimus *Parth.*: celerimum *O*, -rr- *GR*
3 ullius *Calph.:* illius *V*   trabis *Av.* (trabis impetum *iam Calph.*): tardis *V*   4 nequisse θ:
neque esse *V*   4–5 sive ... sive (γ?) ηθ: sine ... sine *V*   6 negant η   minacis ζ: mina ei *V*
7 insulasve cieladas *G* (cicl- *G*²), insula vegeladis *O*   8 Thracia *J.A.K. Thomson* (traciam
iam *a*): tractam *V*   9 siniam *O*   10 ubuste *O*   phasellus *V, corr. m*

comata silva; nam Cytorio in iugo
loquente saepe sibilum edidit coma.
Amastri Pontica et Cytore buxifer,
tibi haec fuisse et esse cognitissima
ait phaselus: ultima ex origine   15
tuo stetisse dicit in cacumine,
tuo imbuisse palmulas in aequore,
et inde tot per impotentia freta
erum tulisse, laeva sive dextera
vocaret aura, sive utrumque Iuppiter   20
simul secundus incidisset in pedem;
neque ulla vota litoralibus deis
sibi esse facta, cum veniret a mari
novissime hunc ad usque limpidum lacum.
sed haec prius fuere: nunc recondita   25
senet quiete seque dedicat tibi,
gemelle Castor et gemelle Castoris.

5

Vivamus, mea Lesbia, atque amemus,
rumoresque senum severiorum
omnes unius aestimemus assis!
soles occidere et redire possunt;
nobis, cum semel occidit brevis lux,   5
nox est perpetua una dormienda.
da mi basia mille, deinde centum,
dein mille altera, dein secunda centum,
deinde usque altera mille, deinde centum;
dein, cum milia multa fecerimus,   10
conturbabimus, illa ne sciamus,

25–7 *Priscianus, Institutiones grammaticae 9.49 (= Grammatici Latini II: 484); Grammatici Latini I: 252 (Charisius), 344 (Diomedes)*

---

11 cytorio η, citherio (γ): citeorio *V*   13 cytore ζη (cithore *iam* γ): citheri *V*
14 cognitissima γ: cognot- *V*   15 phasellus *V, corr. m*   17 tuas *GR*   18 in potentia *R*,
corr. R¹   20 vocaret aura (γ): vocare cura *V*   21 -de- *in rasura R²*   22 literalibus *R*,
corr. m   23 a mari γ (-ei *Lachmann*): amaret *V*   24 novissimo ζη   25 hec α: hoc *V*
recomdita *O*   27 castor γη: castrum *V, al.* castorum *G¹R²*
5 3 estinemus *O*, extimemus *GR*   4 ocidere *O*   5 nobiscum *V*   8 dein mille *Calph.*: deinde
mille *V*, deinde mi *R²*   dein *Puccius*: deinde *V*, da *R²*   10 dein η: deinde *V*   millia *GR*
11 conturbabimus θ: -avimus *V*   nesciamus *V*

aut ne quis malus invidere possit
cum tantum sciat esse basiorum.

6

Flavi, delicias tuas Catullo,
ni sint illepidae atque inelegantes,
velles dicere nec tacere posses.
verum nescioquid febriculosi
scorti diligis: hoc pudet fateri.   5
nam te non viduas iacere noctes
nequiquam tacitum cubile clamat
sertis ac Syrio fragrans olivo,
pulvinusque peraeque et hic et ille
attritus, tremulique quassa lecti   10
argutatio inambulatioque.
nam nil stupra valet, nihil, tacere.
cur? non tam latera effututa pandas,
ni tu quid facias ineptiarum.
quare, quidquid habes boni malique,   15
dic nobis. volo te ac tuos amores
ad caelum lepido vocare versu.

7

Quaeris quot mihi basiationes
tuae, Lesbia, sint satis superque.
quam magnus numerus Libyssae harenae
lasarpiciferis iacet Cyrenis
oraclum Iovis inter aestuosi   5

5 13 cf. Priapea 52.12

13 tantum β¹: tantus V   sciet *Buecheler*
6 2 ni θ: ne V   5 hic (ħ) O   7 nequid quam O   8 ac syrio *Av.*, et syrio *Ald.*: asirio OG, a
sirio R, a syrio m (assirio β)   fragrans ζθ: flagrans V   9 et hec et illo V, hic *supra scr.* G¹
(al. *praescr.* G²), al. hic R², al. ille R²*bis*   12 nil stupra valet *Haupt*, ni stupra valet
Scaliger, nil ista valet *Lachmann, alii alia:* inista prevalet O, ni ista prevalet GR   13 cum
Camps   ecfututa *Lachmann* (exf- *iam* 1472): et futura V   pandas ζη: panda V   14 ni
A. Guarinus (nei *Marcilius*): nec V   15 babes bonique O   17 versum V, corr. R²
7 1 quot a: quod V   4 lasarpici feris GR (al. fretis R²), l. fecis O   iaces O   tyrenis OR,
tyarenis G (a *del.* G²), al. cyrenis R²   5 oraclum γ: oradum V

et Batti veteris sacrum sepulcrum,
aut quam sidera multa, cum tacet nox,
furtivos hominum vident amores;
tam te basia multa basiare
vesano satis et super Catullo est,   10
quae nec pernumerare curiosi
possint nec mala fascinare lingua.

8

Miser Catulle, desinas ineptire,
et quod vides perisse perditum ducas.
fulsere quondam candidi tibi soles,
cum ventitabas quo puella ducebat
amata nobis quantum amabitur nulla.   5
ibi illa multa cum iocosa fiebant,
quae tu volebas nec puella nolebat,
fulsere vere candidi tibi soles.
nunc iam illa non vult; tu quoque inpote<ns noli>,
nec quae fugit sectare, nec miser vive,   10
sed obstinata mente perfer, obdura.
vale, puella. iam Catullus obdurat,
nec te requiret nec rogabit invitam.
at tu dolebis, cum rogaberis nulla.
scelesta, vae te! quae tibi manet vita?   15
quis nunc te adibit? cui videberis bella?
quem nunc amabis? cuius esse diceris?
quem basiabis? cui labella mordebis?
at tu, Catulle, destinatus obdura.

9

Verani, omnibus e meis amicis
antistans mihi milibus trecentis,

<hr>

6 batti *ed. Rom.* (bati *iam* ηθ): beati *V, al.* beari *G¹R²* 9 basiei *V, al.* basia *G¹R²*
10 catulo *O* 11 euriosi *V, corr. R²*

8 3 candida *G, corr. G²* 4 quod *V, corr. R²* 5 amabiliter *m* 6 cum *V,* tum *R²*
  8 candid≡i *G¹* 9 inpotens ε: inpote *O,* impote *GR* noli *om. V: add. Av.* 10 necque *OR*
  (*corr. R²*), nec que *G* 15 ve *Ottob. 1982, Neap. F. 19:* ne *V* teꝗ *O,* teꝗ *GR,* te ꝗ *R²*
  16 adhibit *O* 18 cui] cum *O*

9 1 ver(r)ani ζ, veranni *V* e *om. O:* o *Baehrens* 2 antistans *Av.,* antestans *Pall.,* antistes ζη:
antistas *V*

venistine domum ad tuos penates
fratresque unanimos anumque matrem?
venisti. o mihi nuntii beati!   5
visam te incolumem audiamque Hiberum
narrantem loca, facta, nationes,
ut mos est tuus, applicansque collum
iucundum os oculosque saviabor.
o quantum est hominum beatiorum,   10
quid me laetius est beatiusve?

10

Varus me meus ad suos amores
visum duxerat e foro otiosum,
scortillum, ut mihi tum repente visum est,
non sane illepidum neque invenustum.
huc ut venimus, incidere nobis   5
sermones varii: in quibus, quid esset
iam Bithynia; quo modo se haberet;
ecquonam mihi profuisset aere.
respondi, id quod erat, nihil neque ipsis
nec praetoribus esse nec cohorti,   10
cur quisquam caput unctius referret,
praesertim quibus esset irrumator
praetor, nec faceret pili cohortem.
"at certe tamen," inquiunt "quod illic
natum dicitur esse, comparasti   15
ad lecticam homines." ego, ut puellae
unum me facerem beatiorem,
"non" inquam "mihi tam fuit maligne,
ut, provincia quod mala incidisset,
non possem octo homines parare rectos."   20
at mi nullus erat nec hic neque illic,

4 unanimos η (-es ζ): uno animo V   anumque *Faernus*: sanamque O, suamque GR,
al. sanam G¹R²   8 tuis R, corr. R²   9 suaviabor ζ (suabiabor *iam* β): suabior V
11 lecius G

10 1 var(r)us γ: varius V   mens V, corr. R²G² (meus *supra scr. iam* G¹)   2 ociosum G,
occ- OR, oc- R²   3 tum G, tunc OR (*corr.* R²)   4 inlepidum G, corr. G²   7 iarbithinia O
se η: posse V   8 ecquonam *Statius*: et quoniam V, al. quonam G¹R²   aere (ζ): here V
9 neque nec in ipsis V, corr. (al. *praescr.*) G¹R²   10 nec (1°) *om.* R (al. nec R²): nunc
Westphal   11 referet R   13 nec O, non GR (al. nec G¹R²)   facerent γ   16 lecticam α:
leticam OR, letittam G, leticiam G¹   hominis V

fractum qui veteris pedem grabati
in collo sibi collocare posset.
hic illa, ut decuit cinaediorem,
"quaeso" inquit mihi, "mi Catulle, paulum   25
istos commoda; nam volo ad Serapim
deferri." "mane," inquii puellae,
"istud quod modo dixeram me habere,
fugit me ratio: meus sodalis –
Cinna est Gaius – is sibi paravit.   30
verum, utrum illius an mei, quid ad me?
utor tam bene quam mihi pararim.
sed tu insulsa male et molesta vivis,
per quam non licet esse neglegentem."

11

Furi et Aureli, comites Catulli,
sive in extremos penetrabit Indos,
litus ut longe resonante Eoa
   tunditur unda,

sive in Hyrcanos Arabasve molles,   5
seu Sagas sagittiferosve Parthos,
sive quae septemgeminus colorat
   aequora Nilus,

sive trans altas gradietur Alpes,
Caesaris visens monimenta magni,   10
Gallicum Rhenum horribile aequor ulti-
   mosque Britannos,

22 fractum qui (γ): fractumque V   24 decuit θ: docuit V   sined- O   26 commoda G,
comodam O, comoda R (corr. R²): commodum enim Hand, da; modo Doering, da modo;
Munro   sarapim GR, corr. R²   27 deserti V, al. deferri R²   inquii Scaliger (inquio iam
Ald.): inquid O, inquit GR   28 differam R, corr. R¹   29 mens GR, corr. R²   30 cinna est
Caius 1473: cuma est gravis V   31 ad γ: a V   32 paratis Status   33 tu insulsa η: tulsa O,
tu insula GR   mane G, malle G¹, corr. G²   nivis O
11 2 penetrabit 1473: -avit V   Iindos R, corr. R²   3 ubi R²   resonans Status   coa O
5 hircanos O   arabaesque G, arabesque R   6 seu θ: sive V   sagas a (sacas 1472):
sagax V   sagitiferos ve O   7 siveᴍ O, sive qua η   8 epra O   9 sui O   gratietur R,
corr. R¹   11 horribile aequor Haupt, horribiles vitro McKie: horribilesque V (que del. R²)
11/12 ulti/mosque R²: / ultimosque V (vitimosque O)

omnia haec, quaecumque feret voluntas
caelitum, temptare simul parati,
pauca nuntiate meae puellae   15
    non bona dicta.

cum suis vivat valeatque moechis,
quos simul complexa tenet trecentos,
nullum amans vere, sed identidem omnium
    ilia rumpens;   20

nec meum respectet, ut ante, amorem,
qui illius culpa cecidit velut prati
ultimi flos, praetereunte postquam
    tactus aratro est.

12

Marrucine Asini, manu sinistra
non belle uteris: in ioco atque vino
tollis lintea neglegentiorum.
hoc salsum esse putas? fugit te, inepte;
quamvis sordida res et invenusta est.   5
non credis mihi? crede Pollioni
fratri, qui tua furta vel talento
mutari velit: est enim leporum
differtus puer ac facetiarum.
quare aut hendecasyllabos trecentos   10
exspecta, aut mihi linteum remitte,
quod me non movet aestimatione,
verum est mnemosynum mei sodalis.

---

12 9 *Pastrengicus, De originibus rerum fol.* 18ᵛ

    13 feret η: fere *V*   15 nunciare *O*   22 qui ζη: cui *V*   23, 24 *eodem versu V; adoneum suo loco posuit G², erasa c. 12 tituli parte*

12 1 marrucine *Parth.*: matr- *V,* al. matrutine *G*¹   2 ioco *GR,* loco *O,* al. loco *G*¹*R*²   3 linthea *O*   neglegenciorum *O*   4 salsum *G,* falsum al. salsum *O,* falsum *Rm,* al. salsum *R*²*m*²   7 frater *O*   8 voluit *O*   9 differtus *Pastrengicus:* dissertus *O,* disertus *GR*   pater *Calph. (et "vetus codex," adn. Marc. 12.128) (an diserte pater legendum?)*   faceciarum *O*   10 endeca sillabos *V* (endecas- *m*¹)   11 lintheum *O* remicte *R*   12 monet *O*   estimatione (γ): ext- *V*   13 est mnemosinum (η): nemo est sinum *O,* est nemo sinum *GR*

nam sudaria Saetaba ex Hiberis
miserunt mihi muneri Fabullus 15
et Veranius; haec amem necesse est
ut Veraniolum meum et Fabullum.

13

Cenabis bene, mi Fabulle, apud me
paucis, si tibi di favent, diebus,
si tecum attuleris bonam atque magnam
cenam, non sine candida puella
et vino et sale et omnibus cachinnis. 5
haec si, inquam, attuleris, venuste noster,
cenabis bene – nam tui Catulli
plenus sacculus est aranearum.
sed contra accipies meros amores
seu quid suavius elegantiusve est: 10
nam unguentum dabo quod meae puellae
donarunt Veneres Cupidinesque,
quod tu cum olfacies, deos rogabis
totum ut te faciant, Fabulle, nasum.

14

Ni te plus oculis meis amarem,
iucundissime Calve, munere isto
odissem te odio Vatiniano:
nam quid feci ego quidve sum locutus,
cur me tot male perderes poetis? 5
isti di mala multa dent clienti,
qui tantum tibi misit impiorum.
quod si, ut suspicor, hoc novum ac repertum

17 *Plinius, Naturalis historia 1 praefatio 1*

---

14 settaba *O*, sethaba *GR*   ex hiberis (η), -eis *Lachmann*: exhibere *V*   15 misserunt *G*, corr. *G*²   numeri *V*, al. muneri *G*¹*R*²   16 haec] al. hoc *R*²   amem δ: ameni *OG*, almeni *R* (-l- *exp. R*¹)   17 ut (θ): et *V*

13 6 inquam δ: unquam *V* (um- *R*)   7 bn *R*, bñ *R*²   8 saculus *V*   9 set *R*, sed *R*²   meos *O* 10 quid γδ: qui *V*, al. quod *R*²   elegancius ve *O*   13 olfaties *R, corr. R*²

14 1 ni (δ) (nei *Lachmann*): ne *V*   3 vaciniano *GR*   4 loqutus *R, corr. R*²   5 male 1472 (mali iam β): malis *V*   6 dent ζη: dant *V*   8 si ut] sive *G, corr. G*¹

munus dat tibi Sulla litterator,
non est mi male, sed bene ac beate,   10
quod non dispereunt tui labores.
di magni, horribilem et sacrum libellum!
quem tu scilicet ad tuum Catullum
misti continuo, ut die periret
Saturnalibus optimo dierum!   15
non non hoc tibi, salse, sic abibit.
nam, si luxerit, ad librariorum
curram scrinia; Caesios, Aquinos,
Suffenum, omnia colligam venena,
ac te his suppliciis remunerabor.   20
vos hinc interea valete abite
illuc, unde malum pedem attulistis,
saecli incommoda, pessimi poetae.

14^b

Si qui forte mearum ineptiarum
lectores eritis manusque vestras
non horrebitis admovere nobis,

*   *   *

15

Commendo tibi me ac meos amores,
Aureli. veniam peto pudenter,
ut, si quicquam animo tuo cupisti,
quod castum expeteres et integellum,
conserves puerum mihi pudice,   5

---

14 9 *Martianus Capella 3.229*   15 *Macrobius, Saturnalia 2.1.8*

9 sulla δ (Sylla *Martianus Capella*): si illa *V*   10 mi *η*: michi *V*   14 misti *η*: misisti *V*
15 opimo *GR*, al. optimo *R²*, oppinio *O*   16 hoc *γδ*: hec *V*   salse *G*, false *OR*, al. salse *R²*
sic *γδ*: fit *OG*, sit *R*   adhibit *O*, adbibit *GR*, corr. *R²*   17 luserit *G*, al. -x- *G²*   18 curram δ:
curam *O*, cur tam *GR*   scrinea *R*   19 suffenum *η* (suphenum *iam 1472*): suffenam *V*
20 ac α: hac *V*   tibi hiis supplitus *O*   23 secli *η*: seculi *V*   incomoda *OR*, corr. *R²*
14^b *(a c. 14 seiunxerunt B. Guarinus et Av.)*   3 ammovere *O*
15 1 tibe *G*, corr. *G²*   2 pudenter *Maehly*: -em *V* (pudentem peto *G, transp. G²*)

non dico a populo – nihil veremur
istos, qui in platea modo huc modo illuc
in re praetereunt sua occupati –
verum a te metuo tuoque pene
infesto pueris bonis malisque.   10
quem tu qua lubet, ut lubet, moveto
quantum vis, ubi erit foris paratum;
hunc unum excipio, ut puto, pudenter.
quod si te mala mens furorque vecors
in tantam impulerit, sceleste, culpam,   15
ut nostrum insidiis caput lacessas,
a tum te miserum malique fati!
quem attractis pedibus patente porta
percurrent raphanique mugilesque.

16

Pedicabo ego vos et irrumabo,
Aureli pathice et cinaede Furi,
qui me ex versiculis meis putastis,
quod sunt molliculi, parum pudicum.
nam castum esse decet pium poetam   5
ipsum, versiculos nihil necesse est;
qui tum denique habent salem ac leporem,
si sunt molliculi ac parum pudici,
et quod pruriat incitare possunt,
non dico pueris, sed his pilosis   10
qui duros nequeunt movere lumbos.
vos, quod milia multa basiorum
legistis, male me marem putatis?
pedicabo ego vos et irrumabo.

16 5–8 *Plinius, Epistulae 4.14.5*   5–6 *Apuleius, Apologia 11*

---

8 inre *O*, inte *G*, in re *R*   occupari *OR, corr. R²*   9 me tuo *OR, corr. R²*   10 bonis *η*:
bonisque *V*   11 qualibet *V (corr. R²)*   ut libet *1472*: ut al. iubet *O*, ut iubet *G*, om. *Rm*,
al. ut iubet *R²m¹*   moneto *O*   13 huc *G*, nunc *R (corr. R²)*   pudenter *OR*, prudenter *G*
(al. prudenter *R²*)   16 nostrorum *OR*   capud *R, corr. R²*   17 ha *V*, ah *R²*   tamen *V*, al.
tum *R²*   18 atractis *O*   19 percurent *G, corr. G¹*

16 1, 14 pedicabo *β*: ded- *V*   3 mi *V, corr. R²*   4 quod *G*, q'(?) *G⁴*   moliculli *G, corr. G⁴*
6 reccesse *O*   7 tamen *V*, al. tum *R²*: tunc *Plinius*   ac *V*: et *Plinius*   8 sunt *Plinius*: sint *V*
moliculi *G, corr. G¹*   ac *V*: et *Plinius*   10 hiis pillosis *O*   12 hosque *O*, vosque *GR*, al.
hos al. quod *R²*

17

O Colonia, quae cupis ponte ludere longo,
et salire paratum habes, sed vereris inepta
crura ponticuli axulis stantis in redivivis,
ne supinus eat cavaque in palude recumbat:
sic tibi bonus ex tua pons libidine fiat,   5
in quo vel Salisubsili sacra suscipiantur,
munus hoc mihi maximi da, Colonia, risus.
quendam municipem meum de tuo volo ponte
ire praecipitem in lutum per caputque pedesque,
verum totius ut lacus putidaeque paludis   10
lividissima maximeque est profunda vorago.
insulsissimus est homo, nec sapit pueri instar
bimuli tremula patris dormientis in ulna.
cui cum sit viridissimo nupta flore puella
et puella tenellulo delicatior haedo,   15
adservanda nigerrimis diligentius uvis,
ludere hanc sinit ut lubet, nec pili facit uni,
nec se sublevat ex sua parte; sed velut alnus
in fossa Liguri iacet suppernata securi,
tantundem omnia sentiens quam si nulla sit usquam,   20
talis iste merus stupor nil videt, nihil audit;
ipse qui sit, utrum sit an non sit, id quoque nescit.
nunc eum volo de tuo ponte mittere pronum,
si pote stolidum repente excitare veternum,

17 19 *Festus p. 396 (Lindsay) s.v.* suppernati

---

17 1 o culoniaque δ (o c. quae θ): oculo in aque *V* ludere *ed. Rom.* (loed- *Scaliger*): ledere *V*
3 axulis *Hand* (acsuleis *Ellis*, axuleis *Schwabe*²), assulis *Statius*: ac sulcis *V* stantis
Vossius: tantis *V* inreduivis *O*, in redivinis *R* (*corr. R*¹) 4 canaque *O* pallude *R*,
*corr. R*² 6 salisubsili *Lachmann*, -silis *iam Statius*, salisubsali *Diez. 37*², *Bergk*, salisubsuli
B. Guarinus; sali subsili *OG*, sali subscili *R* suscipiantur *B. Guarinus et Av.*: -iant *V*
7 maximi *om. G, add. G*² 8 quedam *V, corr. R*² 9 capudque *R, corr. R*² 10 tociuṣ *G*,
*corr. G*² putidaeque θ: pudiceque *V* paludis η: -des *V* (pall- *R, corr. R*²) 12 insulsi
simus *O*, insuliissimus *GR* (*nisi forte* -lisissimus *R*), *corr. R*² 13 himuli *O* 14 cui cum
B. Guarinus et Av. (quoi quum *Scaliger*, quoi iam θ): cui iocum *V* 15 et δ: ut *V* edo *V*
16 adservanda *R*, ass- *R*² 17 uni] al. vim *R*² 18 se *1472*: me *V* alvus *V, corr. R*²
19 suppernata *Politianus, teste Av. Emend. a 3*ᵛ, *Puccius* (expernata *Politianus, Misc. cap.*
lxxiii): superata *V* 21 merus *Passerat*: meus *V* nil … nihil (θ), nil … nil (γ): nichil …
nichil *V* 23 nunc cum *GR* (al. hunc eum *R*²), nunc volo *O* 24 pote stolidum *Puccius*:
potest olidum *V* excitare ζη: exitare *V*

et supinum animum in gravi derelinquere caeno,   25
ferream ut soleam tenaci in voragine mula.

21

Aureli, pater esuritionum,
non harum modo, sed quot aut fuerunt
aut sunt aut aliis erunt in annis,
pedicare cupis meos amores.
nec clam: nam simul es, iocaris una,   5
haerens ad latus omnia experiris.
frustra: nam insidias mihi instruentem
tangam te prior irrumatione.
atque id si faceres satur, tacerem;
nunc ipsum id doleo, quod esurire   10
a te mi puer et sitire discet.
quare desine, dum licet pudico,
ne finem facias, sed irrumatus.

22

Suffenus iste, Vare, quem probe nosti,
homo est venustus et dicax et urbanus,
idemque longe plurimos facit versus.
puto esse ego illi milia aut decem aut plura
perscripta, nec sic ut fit in palimpsesto   5
relata: cartae regiae novae libri,

25 delinquere *GRm*   26 mulla *GR*

18–20 *Post 17 propter metri similitudinem at contra librorum auctoritatem inseruerunt editores inde a Mureto tria carmina, quorum primum idem est ac fragmentum 1 Catulli, alterum et tertium in calce Priapeorum (Buecheler 86, 85) invenies; quae omnia eiecit Lachmann*

21 1 exuricionum *OG*, -tionum *R*   4 pedicare δ: ded- *V*   5 nam *om. G, rest. G²*   esiocaris *Diez. 37 primo:* exiocaris *V*   6 haeres *Muretus*   experiris *ed. Rom.:* experibus *OR*, -bus *G*   8 irrumatione ζη: irruminatione *V*   9 id si δ: ipsi *V*   10 esurire *O¹* (esuriere *O*): exurire *GR*   11 a te mei *Munro,* meus iam *1473,* meus mi *B. Venator,* mellitus *Hand,* a temet *Froehlich, alii alia:* me me *V*   12 desine θ: desinat *V*   13 ne *1472* (nei *Baehrens*): nec *V*   facias finem *O, transp. O¹*   irrumatus η: irruminatus sum *V*

22 3 versuum (-sui?) *G, corr. G¹*   4 illi (*altera i in rasura*) *G¹*   5 sic δ: sit *V*   palimpsesto *1473,* -on (*litt. graec.*) *Marcilius,* -um *Heinsius:* palmisepto *V*   6 certe *vel* curte *G,* curte *R, corr. R²*   novi *1473* (novei *Lachmann*)   bibli *Nisbet*

novi umbilici, lora rubra, membranae,
derecta plumbo et pumice omnia aequata.
haec cum legas tu, bellus ille et urbanus
Suffenus unus caprimulgus aut fossor   10
rursus videtur: tantum abhorret ac mutat.
hoc quid putemus esse? qui modo scurra
aut siquid hac re scitius videbatur,
idem inficeto est inficetior rure,
simul poemata attigit, neque idem umquam   15
aeque est beatus ac poema cum scribit:
tam gaudet in se tamque se ipse miratur.
nimirum idem omnes fallimur, neque est quisquam
quem non in aliqua re videre Suffenum
possis. suus cuique attributus est error;   20
sed non videmus manticae quod in tergo est.

23

Furi, cui neque servus est neque arca
nec cimex neque araneus neque ignis,
verum est et pater et noverca, quorum
dentes vel silicem comesse possunt,
est pulcre tibi cum tuo parente   5
et cum coniuge lignea parentis.
nec mirum: bene nam valetis omnes,
pulcre concoquitis, nihil timetis,
non incendia, non graves ruinas,
non facta impia, non dolos veneni,   10

---

22 18 *Hieremias de Montagnone, Compendium moralium notabilium 1.3*   19–21 *Flores moralium auctoritatum (Veronae, 1329) Bibl. cap. clxviii [155] 2.3 (De errore fol. 10ᵛ)* 21 *Porphyrion ad Horati sermones 2.3.299*

———

7 membrane *V*: -na *Av.*   8 derecta *Statius* (directa *iam* η): detecta *OG*, detetta *R* (-cta *R²*) 10 capri mulgus *O*   11 abhoret *O*   13 hac] ac *O*   scitius *L. Mueller*, tritius *Pontanus*, tersius *Peiper*: tristius *V*   14 infacetior θ: infaceto (*bis*) *O*, in f- (*bis*) *GR*   15 neque] vel neque nec *O*   16 ac *β*: ha *V*   17 tamquam *V, corr. R²*   18 nec *O, Hieremias de Montagnone*   21 set *R*, sed *R²*
23 1 servo est *OG*, est servo *R* (est *exp. R²*), al. servus est *R²*   2 neque *1°*] al. neque *O*, animal neque *GR, corr. R²*   nege ignis *G, corr. G²*   7 ne *V* (nec *G*), al. nec *R²*, ni *β* et *G²* 9 ruinas] minas *OR*   10 facta] fata *G³*, furta *Puccius*

non casus alios periculorum.
atqui corpora sicciora cornu
aut siquid magis aridum est habetis
sole et frigore et esuritione.
quare non tibi sit bene ac beate?   15
a te sudor abest, abest saliva,
mucusque et mala pituita nasi.
hanc ad munditiem adde mundiorem,
quod culus tibi purior salillo est,
nec toto decies cacas in anno;   20
atque id durius est faba et lupillis,
quod tu si manibus teras fricesque,
non umquam digitum inquinare posses.
haec tu commoda tam beata, Furi,
noli spernere nec putare parvi,   25
et sestertia quae soles precari
centum desine, nam sat es beatus.

24

O qui flosculus es Iuventiorum,
non horum modo, sed quot aut fuerunt
aut posthac aliis erunt in annis,
mallem divitias Midae dedisses
isti, cui neque servus est neque arca,   5
quam sic te sineres ab illo amari.
"quid? non est homo bellus?" inquies. est:
sed bello huic neque servus est neque arca.
hoc tu quam lubet abice elevaque:
nec servum tamen ille habet neque arcam.   10

12 atqui *η*: aut qui *V* 13 magis aridum *1472*: a.m. *V* 15 si *GR* 16 abest 1°] (*om. O*) abesit *GR, corr. R*² salvia *OR*, saliva *GR*² 17 muc(c)usque *ϛη*: muccusve *V* (-ct- *O*) pictuita *G, corr. G*¹ 19 quod cuius *V*, al. quod culus *R*² sal illo *GR* (*corr. G*³) 21 lupillis *Ianus Gulielmius*: lapillis *V* 22 friesque *Baehrens* 23 possis *ϛη* 24 tu *η*: tua *V* 26 sesterciaque *O*, sextercia que *GR* 27 sat es beatus *Calph.*, satis beatu's *Bergk*: satis beatus *V*

24 1 es *η*: est *V* 2 quot *γδ*: quod *V* 4 midae dedisses *Vossius*: mi dededisses *O*, mi dedisses *GR* 5 qui *V*, al. cui *R*² neque 1°] nec *OR*, neque *G*, al. neque *R*² neque 2°] nec *R*, neque (*supra scr.* al.) *R*² arca *O*, archa *GR* 7 qui *GR* 9 hec *G* quam *V*, al. qua *R*² 10 archam *V*

25

Cinaede Thalle, mollior cuniculi capillo
vel anseris medullula vel imula oricilla
vel pene languido senis situque araneoso,
idemque, Thalle, turbida rapacior procella
cum laeva nummularios offendit oscitantes,   5
remitte pallium mihi meum, quod involasti,
sudariumque Saetabum catagraphosque Thynos,
inepte, quae palam soles habere tamquam avita.
quae nunc tuis ab unguibus reglutina et remitte,
ne laneum latusculum manusque mollicellas   10
inusta turpiter tibi flagella conscribillent,
et insolenter aestues, velut minuta magno
deprensa navis in mari, vesaniente vento.

26

Furi, villula vestra non ad Austri
flatus opposita est neque ad Favoni
nec saevi Boreae aut Apheliotae,
verum ad milia quindecim et ducentos.
o ventum horribilem atque pestilentem!   5

27

Minister vetuli puer Falerni,
inger mi calices amariores,

27 1–4 *Aulus Gellius, Noctes Atticae 6.20.6*

---

25 1 Thalle *Parth.*: talle *V*   2 medulla *GR*   imulla *O*   oricilla *Scaliger*: moricula *V*, al.
moricilla *R*[2]   3 anracoroso *O*, arancoroso *GR*, al. araneoso *R*[2]   4 talle *GR*, tale *O*   5 laeva
Ellis, luna *Heyse*: diva *V*   numularios *Slater*, munerarios *Lachmann*, mulierarios *Haupt*,
balnearios *Riese*, vestiarios *Lafaye*: ml⁵raries *O*, ml⁵r aries *O*[1], mulier alies *G*, mulier alios
s.s. aries *G*[1], mulier aves *R*, al. aries vl. alios *R*[2]   offendit *B. Guarinus*, tetendit *Herzog*:
ostendet *OG*, - it *R*   ossistantes *O*, osscit- *GR, corr. R*[2]   7 -quae *G*   sathabum *OR*,
saetha- *G*, al. setha- *R*[2]   cathagraphosque thinos *OG*, -fosque thinos *R*   8 inepteque *V*,
corr. R[2]   9 remite *O*   10 mollicelas *O*   11 inusta *Calph.*: insula *V*   conscribillent (γ):
-ile- *V*   12 minuta ε: inimica *V*   13 deprehensa *GR*   ve san- *GR, corr. R*[2]
26 1 nostra *GR*   2 *om. O*   favoni *m*, favonii *GR*   5 orribilem (h *exp.*) *G*[1]
27 2 inger mi *Gellius (unde Parth.)*: ingeremi *O*, ingere mi *GR*

ut lex Postumiae iubet magistrae
ebriosa acino ebriosioris.
at vos quo lubet hinc abite, lymphae, 5
vini pernicies, et ad severos
migrate. hic merus est Thyonianus.

28

Pisonis comites, cohors inanis,
aptis sarcinulis et expeditis,
Verani optime tuque mi Fabulle,
quid rerum geritis? satisne cum isto
vappa frigoraque et famem tulistis? 5
ecquidnam in tabulis patet lucelli
expensum, ut mihi, qui meum secutus
praetorem refero datum lucello?
o Memmi, bene me ac diu supinum
tota ista trabe lentus irrumasti. 10
sed, quantum video, pari fuistis
casu: nam nihilo minore verpa
farti estis. pete nobiles amicos!
at vobis mala multa di deaeque
dent, opprobria Romuli Remique. 15

29

Quis hoc potest videre, quis potest pati,
nisi impudicus et vorax et aleo,
Mamurram habere quod Comata Gallia

---

29 1–2 *Quintilianus, Institutio oratoria 9.4.141* 3 *Plinius, Naturalis historia 36.48*

---

4 ebriosa acino *Statius*, ebrioso acino *Munro*, ebria acina *Gellius*, ebriosa acina *Parth.*: ebriose acino *V* 5 quo lubet *ηθ*: quod iubet *V* 7 thionianus *V*
28 3 verā *O* 4 satisve *OR, corr. R²* 6 ecquidnam *ζ*: et quid nam *V* *Post 6 lacunam statuit B. Schmidt* 8 refero *O* 9 o mem mi *a, corr.* (δ): omne mi *O*, omnem mi *GR* suppinum *O* 10 trahe *V*, trabe *R²*, trahe *R²bis* tentus *Vossius* yrruinasti *O*, irr- *GR, corr. R²* 11 pari *O*, parum *GR*, al. pari *G¹R²* fuisti *OG*, fusti *R*, fuisti *R¹, corr. R²* 12 urpa *O*, verba *GR*, al. verpa [ve]l. urpa *R²* 14 nobis *V*, al. vobis *R²* 15 oprobria *O*, obp- *GR* romule *O*, -lei *GR*
29 3 mamurram *θ*: nam murram *V*

habebat ante et ultima Britannia?
cinaede Romule, haec videbis et feres? 5
et ille nunc superbus et superfluens
perambulabit omnium cubilia,
ut albulus columbus aut Adoneus?
cinaede Romule, haec videbis et feres?
es impudicus et vorax et aleo. 10
eone nomine, imperator unice,
fuisti in ultima occidentis insula,
ut ista vestra diffututa mentula
ducenties comesset aut trecenties?
quid est alid sinistra liberalitas? 15
parum expatravit an parum helluatus est?
paterna prima lancinata sunt bona,
secunda praeda Pontica, inde tertia
Hibera, quam scit amnis aurifer Tagus:
nunc Gallicae timetur et Britannicae. 20
quid hunc, malum, fovetis? aut quid hic potest
nisi uncta devorare patrimonia?
eone nomine, urbis o potissimi
socer generque, perdidistis omnia?

30

Alfene immemor atque unanimis false sodalibus,
iam te nil miseret, dure, tui dulcis amiculi?
iam me prodere, iam non dubitas fallere, perfide?

24 [*Vergilius*] *Catalepton* 6.6

---

4 ante *Statius*, uncti *Faernus* (uncta, et *adn. Marc.* 12.127), unctum *Scaliger*: cum te *V*
5 romulle *G, corr. G²*   7 perambulabit (ς): perambulavit *V*   8 adoneus *Statius*: yd- *OG*,
id- *R*   13 vestra ς: nostra *V*   diffututa η: diffutura *V*   14 comerset *O*, comeset *GR*,
corr. *R²*   15 alid *Statius*: alit *V*   16 parum (1°)] partum *O*   17 prima *Puccius*: primum *V*
19 libera *O*, fibera *G*, hybera *R*   scit] sit *GR*   amnis δ: amni *V*   20 nunc γ: hunc *V*
Gallicae … Britannicae *Badian*, eumne Gallia et timet Britannia? *Owen*: -ie … -ie *V*
timetur *Froehlich*, timent, timent (et *om.*) β²: timet *V*   21 hic a: hinc *V*   23 o potissimei
L. Mueller, o piissime *Lachmann* (orbis, o piissimei *Haupt*), o putissimei *Schwabe ad*
102.4: oppulentissime *O*, opulentissime *GR*
30 1 alfene (δ): alphene *V*   false γδ: salse *V*   2 nil 1472: nichil *V*   3 non (γ): non me *V*

nec facta impia fallacum hominum caelicolis placent.
quae tu neglegis ac me miserum deseris in malis.   5
eheu quid faciant, dic, homines cuive habeant fidem?
certe tute iubebas animam tradere, inique, <me>
inducens in amorem, quasi tuta omnia mi forent.
idem nunc retrahis te ac tua dicta omnia factaque
ventos irrita ferre ac nebulas aerias sinis.   10
si tu oblitus es, at di meminerunt, meminit Fides,
quae te ut paeniteat postmodo facti faciet tui.

31

Paene insularum, Sirmio, insularumque
ocelle, quascumque in liquentibus stagnis
marique vasto fert uterque Neptunus,
quam te libenter quamque laetus inviso,
vix mi ipse credens Thyniam atque Bithynos   5
liquisse campos et videre te in tuto.
o quid solutis est beatius curis,
cum mens onus reponit, ac peregrino
labore fessi venimus larem ad nostrum,
desideratoque acquiescimus lecto?   10
hoc est quod unum est pro laboribus tantis.
salve, o venusta Sirmio, atque ero gaude
gaudente, vosque lucidae lacus undae
ridete quidquid est domi cachinnorum.

4 facta *OG*, fata *R* (*corr. R²*)   falla cum *O*   5 quae] quos *A. Guarinus*, quod *L. Mueller*, cum *Munro*   6 eheu *Pall.*: o heu *V*   dic *Puccius*, dice *Ellis*: dico *V*   cuine *OR*, corr. *R²*   7 tu te *G*   me *add. B. Guarinus et Av.*   8 tuta omnia *β*: omnia *O*, omnia tuta *GR*   9 idem *O*, inde *GR*, al. idem *R²*   10 ventos *δ*: vento *V*   11 at *ζη*: ut *V* meminere at *codex (quem adhuc non inveni) a Mureto laudatus*, meminerunt at iam (*ς*)

31 1 sirinio *V, corr. R²*   3 neptūnus *GR*   4 libenter *β*: libente *V*   5 vir *G, corr. G²*   mi *η*: michi *V*   credens *OR*, crederis *G*   bithynos *m*, bithinos *G²* (Bithunos *Schwabe*): bithinios *V*   8 meus *O*   honus *R, corr. R²*   10 acquiesimus *O*   12 sau *G, corr. G¹* hero *V*, al. bero *R²*   13 gaudente *Bergk*: gaude *O*, gaudete *GR*   vosque *vel* vosque o *γδ*: vos quoque *V*   lucidae *B. Guarinus*, limpidae *Av.*, ludiae *Scaliger*: lidie *OR*, ly- *G*

32

Amabo, mea dulcis ipsimilla,
meae deliciae, mei lepores,
iube ad te veniam meridiatum.
et si iusseris, illud adiuvato,
ne quis liminis obseret tabellam,   5
neu tibi lubeat foras abire,
sed domi maneas paresque nobis
novem continuas fututiones.
verum si quid ages, statim iubeto:
nam pransus iaceo et satur supinus   10
pertundo tunicamque palliumque.

33

O furum optime balneariorum
Vibenni pater et cinaede fili
(nam dextra pater inquinatiore,
culo filius est voraciore),
cur non exilium malasque in oras   5
itis? quandoquidem patris rapinae
notae sunt populo, et natis pilosas,
fili, non potes asse venditare.

34

Dianae sumus in fide
puellae et pueri integri:
Dianam pueri integri
puellaeque canamus.

32 1 mea *R*, meas *OG* (*corr. G*¹)   Ipsimilla *Baehrens*: ipsi illa *O*, ipsi thili *G*, ipsi thila *R*,
al. ipsicilla *R*²   2 meae] me *G*, corr. *G*¹   4 adiubeto *adn. Marc. 12.128* (et iubeto *iam*
Puccius)   5 nequis *OG* (*corr. O*¹)   luminis *OR*, corr. *R*²   6 seu *R*, corr. *R*¹   lube *O*,
libeat *R*, corr. *R*²   habire *O*   7 si *R*, corr. *R*¹   meas *R*, corr. *R*²   8 futuciones *OG*
33 3 dextera *R*, corr. *R*¹   inquinatōre *O*   4 voratiore *V*, al. volantiore *R*²   5 oras *β*: horas *V*
8 potes *η*: potest *V*   asse *ε*: ase *V*   venditare *η*: vendicare *V*
34 1 dyane *G*   3 om. *V*: Diane pueri integri *Urb. 812* (*et "vetus codex" teste Pall., fortasse et*
Pontanus), Dianam p. i. *Trinc.* (*et "vetus codex," adn. Marc. 12.128*)

o Latonia, maximi   5
magna progenies Iovis,
quam mater prope Deliam
    deposivit olivam,

montium domina ut fores
silvarumque virentium   10
saltuumque reconditorum
    amniumque sonantum:

tu Lucina dolentibus
Iuno dicta puerperis,
tu potens Trivia et notho es   15
    dicta lumine Luna;

tu cursu, dea, menstruo
metiens iter annuum
rustica agricolae bonis
    tecta frugibus exples.   20

sis quocumque tibi placet
sancta nomine, Romulique,
antique ut solita es, bona
    sospites ope gentem.

35

Poetae tenero, meo sodali,
velim Caecilio, papyre, dicas
Veronam veniat, Novi relinquens

35 2 *Bencius Alexandrinus, Cronica (Cod. Ambros. B 24 inf., fol. 94ʳ)*

5 latōnia *O* 8 deposivit *Carp.*: deposuit *V* 10 virencium *G, corr. G⁴* 11 saltumque *OR, corr. R²* 12 amniumque *θ*: omniumque *O*, omnium *GR* sonantum *Pall.*: sonantium *V* 15 notho es *V*, nothoes *R²*, al. noto es *R² bis* 17 menstruo *B. Guarinus*: menstrua *V* 21 sis quecumque tibi placet *O*, scis q. t. placent *GR*, al. sis quocumque tibi placet *R²* 23 Ancique *Merula*

35 2 occilio *O, Bencius Alexandrinus*: cecilio *GR* papire *V*

Comi moenia Lariumque litus:
nam quasdam volo cogitationes   5
amici accipiat sui meique.
quare, si sapiet, viam vorabit,
quamvis candida milies puella
euntem revocet, manusque collo
ambas iniciens roget morari.   10
quae nunc, si mihi vera nuntiantur,
illum deperit impotente amore:
nam quo tempore legit incohatam
Dindymi dominam, ex eo misellae
ignes interiorem edunt medullam.   15
ignosco tibi, Sapphica puella
musa doctior: est enim venuste
Magna Caecilio incohata Mater.

36

Annales Volusi, cacata carta,
votum solvite pro mea puella.
nam sanctae Veneri Cupidinique
vovit, si sibi restitutus essem
desissemque truces vibrare iambos,   5
electissima pessimi poetae
scripta tardipedi deo daturam
infelicibus ustulanda lignis,
et hoc pessima se puella vidit
iocose lepide vovere divis.   10
nunc, o caeruleo creata ponto,

---

4 *Petrarca, in margine cod. Ambros. Vergili, fol. 28*ᵛ   12 *Grammatici Latini I: 134 (Charisius)*

---

4 veniam *O*, meniam *GR*, menia *Bencius, Petrarca, R*²   5 quasdam *OR*, quosdam *G* (*corr. G*²)   10 inities *O*, -tiens *GR*, corr. *R*²   11 m.s. *R*   12 impotente ζη (*et Charisius*): impotentem *V*   amorem *V, corr. R*²   13 legit *1472*: eligit *O*, elegit *GR*   incohatam *B. Guarinus,* inchoatam *Pall.*: indot- *vel* in dot- *V*   17 docior *O*   18 caecilio *1473*: cecilia *V* incohata *O*, inchoata *GR*

36 1 annales volusi ηθ: an(n)uale suo lusi *V*   5 desissemque *Av.*: dedissemque *V*   vibrate *G,* corr. *G*²   8 ustulanda ζη: ustil- *V*   10 ioco se lepide *Scaliger,* iocosis lepide *Riese*   divis ζη: se divis *V*   11 o *om. O*   ponto α: poncto *O,* punto *GR*

quae sanctum Idalium Uriosque apertos
quaeque Ancona Cnidumque harundinosam
colis quaeque Amathunta quaeque Golgos
quaeque Dyrrachium Hadriae tabernam,   15
acceptum face redditumque votum,
si non illepidum neque invenustum est.
at vos interea venite in ignem,
pleni ruris et inficetiarum   20
annales Volusi, cacata carta.

<h1 style="text-align:center">37</h1>

Salax taberna vosque contubernales,
a pilleatis nona fratribus pila,
solis putatis esse mentulas vobis,
solis licere, quidquid est puellarum,
confutuere et putare ceteros hircos?   5
an, continenter quod sedetis insulsi
centum an ducenti, non putatis ausurum
me una ducentos irrumare sessores?
atqui putate: namque totius vobis
frontem tabernae sopionibus scribam.   10
puella nam mi, quae meo sinu fugit,
amata tantum quantum amabitur nulla,
pro qua mihi sunt magna bella pugnata,
consedit istic. hanc boni beatique
omnes amatis, et quidem, quod indignum est,   15
omnes pusilli et semitarii moechi;

37 1 *Grammatici Latini VI: 293 (Atilius Fortunatianus)*

---

12 adalium *OG*, ad alium *R*, alium *m*, al. ydalium *R*²   uriosque *OR*, utriosque *G*
13 cnidumque *Parth.*: gnidumque *V*   14 colis quaeque ζη: colisque *V*   amathuntā *O*,
–ta *GR*   golgos *Av.*: alcos *V*   15 durachium *V*   17 illipedum *G, corr. G*²   invenestum *G*,
*corr. G*²   18 intereo *O*   venite *V*, al. venire *R*²   19 ruris *Pall.*: turis *V*   20 annales ηθ:
anuale *O*, annuale *GR*   volusi ηθ: suo lusic *O*, suo lusi *O*¹*GR*

37 2 pileatis *R*²   non afr- *O*   3 mentualas *O*   5 confutuere η: confutere *V*   8 irumare *GR*,
*corr. R*²(*R*¹?)   9 at qui *V* (*et m, sed minimo intervallo*), atqui *G*²   tocius *V, corr. R*²
11 nam mi β², *Heinsius* (mei *Schwabe*), namque *Av.*, nam (*spatio relicto*) β: nam me *V*
12 amabiliter *m*   14 comsedit *O*   16 pussilli *O*   semitani *OG*, semithani *R, corr. R*²
mechi *GR*

tu praeter omnes, une de capillatis,
cuniculosae Celtiberiae fili,
Egnati, opaca quem bonum facit barba
et dens Hibera defricatus urina.　　　　　20

38

Malest, Cornifici, tuo Catullo,
malest, me hercule, et laboriose,
et magis magis in dies et horas.
quem tu, quod minimum facillimumque est,
qua solatus es allocutione?　　　　　5
irascor tibi. sic meos amores?
paulum quidlubet allocutionis,
maestius lacrimis Simonideis.

39

Egnatius, quod candidos habet dentes,
renidet usque quaque. si ad rei ventum est
subsellium, cum orator excitat fletum,
renidet ille; si ad pii rogum fili
lugetur, orba cum flet unicum mater,　　　　　5
renidet ille; quidquid est, ubicumque est,
quodcumque agit, renidet: hunc habet morbum,
neque elegantem, ut arbitror, neque urbanum.
quare monendum est <te> mihi, bone Egnati.
si urbanus esses aut Sabinus aut Tiburs　　　　　10

17–18 *Priscianus, Institutiones grammaticae* 5.77, 7.22

---

18 celtiberosae *Priscianus*　celbiberie *O*, celtiberi *GR*　19 opacha *O*　20 e *O*
38 1 male est *Calph.*: male est si *V*　cornifici *Av.*: carnifici *V*　(1a) ale est (male est *R²*) si carnifici tuo catullo *R*　va ... cat (*exp. versu*) *R²*　2 male est me *Calph.*: male sime *O*, male si me *GR*, male est si me *R²*　et est *Sillig*, ei et *Lachmann*　4 facilimumque *O*
5 alocucione *O*, all- *G, corr. R*　8 symonideis *R*
39 1 egnacius *O*　candides *O*　2 si] sei *O*, seu *GR*, al. sei *R²*　3 subselium (γ): subscellum *O*, subsellum *GR*　orator excitat θ: excitat orator *V*　4 ad impii *O*, ad pii *G*, ad (*om.* pii) *R* (pii *add. R²*), al. impii *G¹R²*　rogum a: regum *V*　filii *V*　5 ingetur orbicum *O*
9 monendum est te *Maehly*, monendum te est *Spengel*, monendus es *Calph.*

aut pinguis Umber aut obesus Etruscus
aut Lanuvinus ater atque dentatus
aut Transpadanus, ut meos quoque attingam,
aut quilubet, qui puriter lavit dentes,
tamen renidere usque quaque te nollem: 15
nam risu inepto res ineptior nulla est.
nunc Celtiber <es>; Celtiberia in terra,
quod quisque minxit, hoc sibi solet mane
dentem atque russam defricare gingivam;
. ut, quo iste vester expolitior dens est,   20
hoc te amplius bibisse praedicet loti.

40

Quaenam te mala mens, miselle Raude,
agit praecipitem in meos iambos?
quis deus tibi non bene advocatus
vecordem parat excitare rixam?
an ut pervenias in ora vulgi?   5
quid vis? qualubet esse notus optas?
eris, quandoquidem meos amores
cum longa voluisti amare poena.

41

Ameana puella defututa
tota milia me decem poposcit,

39 11 *Corpus Glossariorum Latinorum 5.233 (Goetz)* 16 *Hieremias de Montagnone, Compendium moralium notabilium 4.4; Petrarca, De remediis utriusque fortunae, praefatio libri 2* 19 *Apuleius, Apologia 6*

---

11 pinguis *ex glossario Lindsay (CR 33.1919.105–06)*: parcus *V* etruscus *Petrarca, et* truscus *V, al.* etruscus *R*² 12 lamivinus *OG,* lamivinus *vel* lanuvinus *R* 13 ut ε: aut *V* 14 pariter *R, al.* puriter *R*² 15 usq͗ q̅ *O* 16 risti *O* 17 es *add. Corradinus de Allio* interra *O* 18 quique *O* nuxit *O,* mixit *GR, corr. R*² inane *V, corr. R*² 19 russam β, *Apuleius:* rusam *V* pumicare *Apuleius* 20 noster *O* expolitor *V, al.* expolitior *R*² deus *O* 21 loti (θ): lotus *V*

40 1 Raude (η), *Faernus:* ravide *V* 3 dens *V, corr. R*² avocatus *V, corr. m* 5 pervenias θ: perveniamus *V* hora *O* 6 quid nis *O* 7 ens *O* 8 amare *OG (et R*² *in rasura)* pena *O,* poema *GR, al.* pęna *R*²

41 1 A me an. a. puella *O,* Ame an apuella *G,* A me an apuella *R* defutura *R,* difututa *B. (A.?) Guarinus* 2 popossit *O*

ista turpiculo puella naso,
decoctoris amica Formiani.
propinqui, quibus est puella curae,
amicos medicosque convocate:
non est sana puella, nec rogare
qualis sit solet aes imaginosum.

42

Adeste, hendecasyllabi, quot estis
omnes undique, quotquot estis omnes.
iocum me putat esse moecha turpis,
et negat mihi nostra reddituram
pugillaria, si pati potestis.
persequamur eam et reflagitemus.
quae sit, quaeritis? illa, quam videtis
turpe incedere, mimice ac moleste
ridentem catuli ore Gallicani.
circumsistite eam et reflagitate:
"moecha putida, redde codicillos,
redde, putida moecha, codicillos!"
non assis facis? o lutum, lupanar,
aut si perditius potest quid esse.
sed non est tamen hoc satis putandum.
quod si non aliud potest, ruborem
ferreo canis exprimamus ore.
conclamate iterum altiore voce
"moecha putida, redde codicillos,
redde, putida moecha, codicillos!"
sed nil proficimus, nihil movetur.

42 5 *Grammatici Latini I: 97 (Charisius)*

---

4 forniani *V, corr. R²*   5 puella δ: puelle *V*   6 convocate *1473*: convocare *V*   8 aes
Froehlich: et *V*
42 1 endecha sillabi *V (coniunx. R²G²)*   3 locum *V, al. iocum R²*   meca *O*   4 nostra *Trinc.*:
vestra *V*   7 illam *GR, corr. R²*   8 mimice *β² (mimicae iam Bodl. e 17)*: mirmice *V*
9 catuli *β*: catulli *V*   11 meca *O*   12 moeca *O*   versum om. R, add. R² in margine
13 facit. *Halbertsma*   olutum *G, corr. G¹*   14 perdicius *O*   potest *Vat. 1630,* γη: potes *V*
15 satis hoc *R*   16 allius *G, corr. G¹ et G²*   17 ferreo canis *Laur. 33.11,* ferre ocanis *V,*
ferre o canis *R²*   18 alciore *O*   19 meca *O*   20 meca *O*   21 nil *1472*: nichil *V*

mutanda est ratio modusque vobis,
siquid proficere amplius potestis:
"pudica et proba, redde codicillos."

43

Salve, nec minimo puella naso
nec bello pede nec nigris ocellis
nec longis digitis nec ore sicco
nec sane nimis elegante lingua.
decoctoris amica Formiani,   5
ten provincia narrat esse bellam?
tecum Lesbia nostra comparatur?
o saeclum insipiens et inficetum!

44

O funde noster seu Sabine seu Tiburs
(nam te esse Tiburtem autumant, quibus non est
cordi Catullum laedere; at quibus cordi est,
quovis Sabinum pignore esse contendunt),
sed seu Sabine sive verius Tiburs,   5
fui libenter in tua suburbana
villa, malamque pectore expuli tussim,
non inmerenti quam mihi meus venter,
dum sumptuosas appeto, dedit, cenas:
nam, Sestianus dum volo esse conviva,   10
orationem in Antium petitorem
plenam veneni et pestilentiae legi.
hic me gravedo frigida et frequens tussis
quassavit usque, dum in tuum sinum fugi,
et me recuravi otioque et urtica.   15

22 vobis θ: nobis V
43 2 ocelis G, *corr. G¹ et G²*   7 comparantur O, *corr. O¹*   8 sedum V, *corr. R²*   in sapiens et in facetum G
44 2 cum quibus G, *corr. G²*   4 pignore δ: pignoris V   7 malamque *Av. et Edin.*: aliamque V expuli tussim *Av.* (expui *Scaliger*): expulsus sim V   8 in merenti O   meus venter *Faernus*: mens vertur V   10 festianus O   convivia GR, *corr. R²*   11 oratione V, -nem R² in Antium *Statius* (in Accium *B. Guarinus et Ald.*): minantium OR, minancium G petitorum R²   13 hoc O   gravedo δ: gravido V   15 ocimoque *Herm. Barbarus (teste Puccio)*

quare refectus maximas tibi grates
ago, meum quod non es ulta peccatum.
nec deprecor iam, si nefaria scripta
Sesti recepso, quin gravedinem et tussim
non mi, sed ipsi Sestio ferat frigus,   20
qui tunc vocat me, cum malum librum legi.

45

Acmen Septimius suos amores
tenens in gremio "mea" inquit "Acme,
ni te perdite amo atque amare porro
omnes sum assidue paratus annos,
quantum qui pote plurimum perire,   5
solus in Libya Indiaque tosta
caesio veniam obvius leoni."
hoc ut dixit, Amor sinistra ut ante
dextra sternuit approbationem.
    at Acme leviter caput reflectens   10
et dulcis pueri ebrios ocellos
illo purpureo ore saviata,
"sic," inquit "mea vita Septimille,
huic uni domino usque serviamus,
ut multo mihi maior acriorque   15
ignis mollibus ardet in medullis."
hoc ut dixit, Amor sinistra ut ante
dextra sternuit approbationem.
    nunc ab auspicio bono profecti
mutuis animis amant amantur.   20
unam Septimius misellus Acmen
mavult quam Syrias Britanniasque:

17 ultu' *Muretus*   18 nepharia *R*   19 Sexti recepso *Pall.* (sexti recepso *iam ed. Rom.*):
sestire cepso *V*   quin ζ: qui *V*   20 mi *Av.*: mihi *V*   sestio θ: sectio *V*, al. sertio *R*²
21 nunc *G, corr. G*¹   mecum *O*   legi *Lachmann*: legit *V*

45 1 Acmen ηθ: ac men *V*   septimius (η): septimios *O*, septimos *GR*   2 inquid *O*   acme η:
ac me *V*   3 perdite (γ): perditi *V*   4 omens *O*   5 pote γ: potest *V*   6 libia *V*   8 ut
ante Amor, sinistra, *Gratwick*   9 approbationem ηθ: -ione *V*   10 at Acme *ed. Rom.* (at
acme *iam* η): ad hac me *V*, ad hanc me *R*²   12 s(u)aviata δ: saniata *V*   13 inquid *O*
septimille α: septinulle *V*, al. septinuelle *R*²   14 uno *G, corr. G*¹ *et G*²   17 sinistra ut ζ:
sinistravit *V*   18 dextra *1472*: dextram *V*   19 auspitio *GR*   21 septimius δ: septumius *V*
(-uus *O*)   acmen η: agmen *V*   22 sirias β¹: siriasque *O*, sy- *GR*   britaniasque *O*

uno in Septimio fidelis Acme
facit delicias libidinesque.
quis ullos homines beatiores   25
vidit, quis venerem auspicatiorem?

46

Iam ver egelidos refert tepores,
iam caeli furor aequinoctialis
iucundis Zephyri silescit auris.
linquantur Phrygii, Catulle, campi
Nicaeaeque ager uber aestuosae: 5
ad claras Asiae volemus urbes.
iam mens praetrepidans avet vagari,
iam laeti studio pedes vigescunt.
o dulces comitum valete coetus,
longe quos simul a domo profectos   10
diversae varie viae reportant.

47

Porci et Socration, duae sinistrae
Pisonis, scabies famesque mundi,
vos Veraniolo meo et Fabullo
verpus praeposuit Priapus ille?
vos convivia lauta sumptuose   5
de die facitis, mei sodales
quaerunt in trivio vocationes?

48

Mellitos oculos tuos, Iuventi,
si quis me sinat usque basiare,

23 Acme *ηθ*: ac me *V*   24 libidinesque *a*: libidinisque *V*
46 1 ver egelidos *θ*: vere gelidos *ORmG²*, gelidos ve *G* (*eras. G²*)   2 equi noctialis *O*
3 cephiri silesit *O*   auris *γ*: aureis *V*   4 liquantur *O*   frigii *V*, phrygii *m*   catule *O*
5 uber *Av.*: ruber *V* (rubet *G*, ruber *G²*)   estuose *γ*: estuore *V*   10 longe *G*, corr. *G¹*
quos *η* (*et R³*): quo *OG(R²?)*, quoque *R*   11 diversae varie *B. Guarinus*, -os variae *Av.*, -e
variae *Scaliger*: diverse varie *V*
47 2 scapies *G*, corr. *G²*   mundae *Buecheler*   4 praeposuit *γ*: proposuit *V*
48 1 iuventi *Sen.*: inventi *OR*, in venti *G*

usque ad milia basiem trecenta;
nec mi umquam videar satur futurus,
non si densior aridis aristis
sit nostrae seges osculationis.

5

49

Disertissime Romuli nepotum,
quot sunt quotque fuere, Marce Tulli,
quotque post aliis erunt in annis,
gratias tibi maximas Catullus
agit pessimus omnium poeta,
tanto pessimus omnium poeta
quanto tu optimus omnium patronus.

5

50

Hesterno, Licini, die otiosi
multum lusimus in meis tabellis,
ut convenerat esse delicatos:
scribens versiculos uterque nostrum
ludebat numero modo hoc modo illoc,
reddens mutua per iocum atque vinum.
atque illinc abii tuo lepore
incensus, Licini, facetiisque,
ut nec me miserum cibus iuvaret
nec somnus tegeret quiete ocellos,
sed toto indomitus furore lecto
versarer, cupiens videre lucem,
ut tecum loquerer simulque ut essem.
at defessa labore membra postquam

5

10

49 1 *Petrarca, Epistolae variae 38.6 (anni 1347)*

---

3 milleia *R, corr. R*² basia *R, corr. R*¹ 4 mi umquam *Statius,* umquam *γ:* numquam *V*
videar satur *B. Guarinus* (satur *iam γδ*): inde corsater *V* 6 sint *V, corr. R*²
49 7 omniums *R, corr. R*¹ patronus *O(γ) R*³ (*et manus recentior in m*): patronum *GR et m
primo*
50 2 luximus *R, corr. R*² 3 dellicatos *R, corr. R*² 5 ludebat *V,* al. le- *R*² illos *O* 7 abii *γ:*
abiit *V* 8 licini (*δ*): lacini *V* facetiisque *ζ:* faceti tuique *V* 10 som(p)nus *γ:* somnos *OG,*
sompnos *R* 11 in domitus *G* 12 versarer *γ:* versaretur *V* 13 simulique omnem *GR,*
corr. *R*² (al. *praescr. R*² *bis*) 14 at *α:* ad *V*

semimortua lectulo iacebant,   15
hoc, iucunde, tibi poema feci,
ex quo perspiceres meum dolorem.
nunc audax cave sis, precesque nostras,
oramus, cave despuas, ocelle,
ne poenas Nemesis reposcat a te.   20
est vemens dea; laedere hanc caveto.

51

Ille mi par esse deo videtur,
ille, si fas est, superare divos,
qui sedens adversus identidem te
    spectat et audit

dulce ridentem, misero quod omnis   5
eripit sensus mihi: nam simul te,
Lesbia, aspexi, nihil est super mi
    <vocis in ore>

lingua sed torpet, tenuis sub artus
flamma demanat, sonitu suopte   10
tintinant aures, gemina teguntur
    lumina nocte.

otium, Catulle, tibi molestum est;
otio exsultas nimiumque gestis;
otium et reges prius et beatas   15
    perdidit urbes.

50 18 *Servius ad Vergili Aeneid. 4.409*
51 15–16 *Hieremias de Montagnone, Compendium moralium notabilium 3.4.8*

———

18 cave sis *Pall.*, caveas γ: caveris *V*   praecepsque *O*   19 ocelle *B. (A.?) Guarinus*: ocello *V*
20 nemesis δε: nemessis *G*, ne mestis *R*, ne messis *OR*² resposcat *O*, reponat *R*   ate *OR*
21 vemens *Statius*: vehemens *V*
51 1 mi *G*²: michi *V*   par θ: impar *V*   3/4 te/spectat *G*²: /te spectat *V*   5 -que *V*, al.
quod *R*²   7 supermi *OG*, super mi *R*   8 <vocis in ore> *Ritter, om. V: varie suppleverunt
editores (quod loquar amens Parth., alii alia)*   10 flamma β, *Laur. 33.13, Sen.*: flamina *V*
demant *G, corr. G*¹   11 tintiāt *O*, tintiñat *GR*   aures geminae, *Schrader*   12 limina *GR*
13–16 *carminis deperditi fragmentum esse censuit Statius*   13 catulle θ: catuli *O*,
catulli *GR*   13, 14, 15 oc- *OG*

52

Quid est, Catulle? quid moraris emori?
sella in curuli struma Nonius sedet;
per consulatum peierat Vatinius;
quid est, Catulle? quid moraris emori?

53

Risi nescio quem modo e corona,
qui, cum mirifice Vatiniana
meus crimina Calvus explicasset,
admirans ait haec manusque tollens:
"di magni, salaputium disertum!"   5

54

Othonis caput oppido est pusillum;
at, mi Rustice, semilauta crura,
subtile et leve peditum, Libonis,
si non omnia, displicere vellem
tibi et Sufficio seni recocto.   5

54$^\mathrm{b}$

Irascere iterum meis iambis
inmerentibus, unice imperator.

52 2 *Grammatici Latini VI: 136 (Marius Victorinus), 257 (Caesius Bassus); cf. Plinium, Naturalis historia 37.81, et Boethium, De consolatione philosophiae 3 prosa 4*
53 5 *Seneca, Controversiae 7.4 (19) 7*

---

52 1, 4 emori η: mori *V*   2 incurulu *O*   scrofa *Marius Victorinus*   nonius *Plinius et ceteri testes vett.*: novius *V*   3 peierat γ: perierat *V*   vacinius *GR*
53 1 nisi *O*   e (ζ): et *V*   2 vaciniana *G* (*adrasa c littera; quid lateat, incertum*) *R*^{1} 3 meus ... calvus (θ): meos ... calvos *V*   explicaset *O*   4 amirans *O*   manus *OR*, inanus *G*, al. inanius *R*^{2} 5 salapantium *V*, al. salapputium *R*^{2}, salaputtium *Sen.*   disertum ζη: desertum *V*
54 1 otonis *V, corr. G*^{2} capud *V, corr. R*^{2} apido *O*   pussillum *O*   *Post* 1 *add. V* hoc ... dolorem (50.16–17)   2 at, mi *scripsi,* Heri *Muretus,* Hirri *Ellis, alii alia:* at en Rustice ... Liboni est *Puccius ap. Ven. Marc. 4020* (at iam *A. Guarinus*): et eri *OG*, et heri *R*   Rustice (*nom. propr.*) *Statius,* rustica *Turnebus:* rustice *V*   cruta *O*, trura *G, corr. G*^{1} 5 Fuffitio *Scaliger*   seni recocto *Calph.*: seniore cocto *OG*, seniore copto *R*

55

Oramus, si forte non molestum est,
demonstres ubi sint tuae tenebrae.
te in Campo quaesivimus minore,
te in Circo, te in omnibus libellis,
te in templo summi Iovis sacrato.   5
in Magni simul ambulatione
femellas omnes, amice, prendi,
quas vultu vidi tamen sereno.
†avelte† (sic usque flagitabam):
"Camerium mihi, pessimae puellae!"   10
quaedam inquit, nudum reduc<ta pectus,>
"en hic in roseis latet papillis."
sed te iam ferre Herculei labos est;
tanto te in fastu negas, amice.
dic nobis ubi sis futurus, ede   15
audacter, committe, crede luci.
nunc te lacteolae tenent puellae?
si linguam clauso tenes in ore,
fructus proicies amoris omnes.
verbosa gaudet Venus loquella.   20
vel, si vis, licet obseres palatum,
dum vestri sim particeps amoris.

56

O rem ridiculam, Cato, et iocosam,
dignamque auribus et tuo cachinno!

55 1 molestum est *β*: molestus es *V*   2 demostres *R, corr. R²*   latebrae *Pall.*   3 te in C. q. m.
Sillig, te q. in m. C. *η,* te C. q. m. *Scaliger:* te C. q. in m. *V*   4 id circo *O,* idcirco *GR,* id
exp. et al. in *supra scr. R²*   libellis] ligellis *B. Guarinus,* tabernis *Edin.,* tabellis *Scaliger*
7 prehendi *GR*   8 sereno *β*: serena *V*   9 avelte] *fortasse* audite en (audite *iam Tom.*),
"aufertis ... 10 puellae?" *Goold*   usque *Munro:* ipse *V*   11 quendam *GR*   inquid *O*
reducta pectus *Ellis:* sinum recludens *Riese* (s. reducens *iam Av.*), reduc *V*   12 en *Laur.*
36.23: em *V,* hem *m*   hic *ς:* hec *V*   13 herculis *η*   14 te in *V:* ten' *Muretus*   15/16 ede
hoc / audacter *Vossius*   16 audacter (-citer *O*) hoc *V*   comitte *R*   hoc co- *secl. R?,* comite
hoc ede *1472*   crede *V,* crude *m,* al. crede *m²* (*apud m*), al. crude *m²* (*apud R*)   luci
(*η*) (-cei *Scaliger*): lucet *V*   17 num *codices aliquot recentiores*   lecteole *G, corr. G²*
18 tenens *V, corr. R²*   19 prohices *O,* proiicies *G,* -ties *R*   22 vestri *V,* al. no- *R²*   sim *θ,*
sim ego *Av.:* sis *V*
56 1 catoet *V, corr. R²*   2 chachinno *GR* (*corr. m*)

ride quidquid amas, Cato, Catullum:
res est ridicula et nimis iocosa.
deprendi modo pupulum puellae 5
trusantem; hunc ego, si placet Dionae,
protelo rigida mea cecidi.

57

Pulcre convenit improbis cinaedis,
Mamurrae pathicoque Caesarique.
nec mirum: maculae pares utrisque,
urbana altera et illa Formiana,
impressae resident nec eluentur: 5
morbosi pariter, gemelli utrique,
uno in lecticulo erudituli ambo,
non hic quam ille magis vorax adulter,
rivales socii et puellularum.
pulcre convenit improbis cinaedis. 10

58

Caeli, Lesbia nostra, Lesbia illa,
illa Lesbia, quam Catullus unam
plus quam se atque suos amavit omnes,
nunc in quadriviis et angiportis
glubit magnanimi Remi nepotes. 5

58[b]

Non custos si fingar ille Cretum, 1
non Ladas ego pinnipesve Perseus, 3

3 nide *O*   5 pupullum *Calph.* (pupulum *Parth.*): populum *V*   6 trusantem *V*: crissantem η
7 pro telo *GR*   ridida *G, corr. G*[2]
57 3 pares θ: paris *V*   5 impse *O*   nec eluentur (θ): nece luentur *V*   7 lectulo *GR*   9 nivales *O*
socii et] socii (et *om.*) *Trinc.* (sociei *Scaliger*)
58 1 nostra *m*: vestra *Vm*[1]   4 quadruviis *G*, -rivis *R* (*corr. m*)   agiportis *R, corr. R*[2]
5 magnanimi Remi *Vossius*, magnanimos Remi ηθ, *Calph.*: magna amiremini *O*, magna
admiremini *GR*
58[b] (*vv. 3 et 2 transp. Muretus*)   3 primipes *V*, al. pinnipes *R*[2]

non si Pegaseo ferar volatu,   2
non Rhesi niveae citaeque bigae;   4
adde huc plumipedas volatilesque,   5
ventorumque simul require cursum:
quos vinctos, Cameri, mihi dicares,
defessus tamen omnibus medullis
et multis languoribus peresus
essem te mihi, amice, quaeritando.   10

59

Bononiensis Rufa Rufulum fellat
uxor Meneni, saepe quam in sepulcretis
vidistis ipso rapere de rogo cenam,
cum devolutum ex igne prosequens panem
ab semiraso tunderetur ustore.   5

60

Num te leaena montibus Libystinis
aut Scylla latrans infima inguinum parte
tam mente dura procreavit ac taetra
ut supplicis vocem in novissimo casu
contemptam haberes, a nimis fero corde?   5

61

Collis o Heliconii
cultor, Uraniae genus,
qui rapis teneram ad virum

58^b *2 Ratherius, episcopus Veronensis, in sermone anno 963 habito (p.624 ed. Ballerini = Migne, Patrologia Latina CXXXVI: col. 736)* pennigero, ut poeticus ille, volatu

---

4 thesi *O* vinee *OR* niveis citisque bigis *Muretus* 5 hunc *R, corr. R*¹ plummipedas *GR*
7 vinctos *GRm*, victos *O*, iunctos *G*²: cunctos *Vat. 1630* 8 deffessus *O* 9 langoribus *R*
praesens *O* 10 esse *O* mihi,], mi *Scaliger* amiceque ritando *O*
59 1 Rufulum *Av.*: rufum *V* fellat *O*, fallat *GR*, al. fellat *R*² 3 capere *β* 5 abse miraso *O*
60 1 libistinis *β*²: libissinis *O*, libisinis *GR*, libysinis *m* 2 scylla *δε*: silla *V* 4 suplicus *O*,
supplicus *G*, supplitiiś *R*, -ciis *m* 5 contemptam *(η)*: contentam *O*, contenptam *O*¹,
contem *G*, conteptam *G*¹*R* animis *R*
61 1 obellicon iei *O*, o Eliconei *GR*

virginem, o Hymenaee Hymen,
   o Hymen Hymenaee;   5

cinge tempora floribus
suave olentis amaraci,
flammeum cape, laetus huc
huc veni, niveo gerens
   luteum pede soccum;   10

excitusque hilari die,
nuptialia concinens
voce carmina tinnula,
pelle humum pedibus, manu
   pineam quate taedam;   15

namque Iunia Manlio,
qualis Idalium colens
venit ad Phrygium Venus
iudicem, bona cum bona
   nubet alite virgo,   20

floridis velut enitens
myrtus Asia ramulis
quos Hamadryades deae
ludicrum sibi roscido
   nutriunt umore: 25

quare age, huc aditum ferens,
perge linquere Thespiae
rupis Aonios specus,
nympha quos super irrigat
   frigerans Aganippe,   30

4 (hymenei *R³*?) hymen *om. OR* (*add. R³*) 5 o hymen hymenee *Ald.*: hymen o
hymenee hymen *OR*, o hymenee hymen *G* 7 amaraci *O¹*, amarici *V* 8 flammeum *Vat.
1630*: flameum *V* 12 nupcialia *R, corr. R²* concinens *β*: continens *V* 13 tinnuula *OG*,
tinnuiula *R, corr. R²* 15 spineam *Parth.* 16 iunia *V*, Junia *G²*: Vibia *Syme* manlio *θ*:
mallio *V* 17 id alium *O* (*et R, sed minimo intervallo*), ad alium *G, corr. mG²*
18 frigium *V*, phrygium *m* 21 vult *O* 23 amadriades *V* 24 ludricum *OG* roscido (*δ*):
rosido *V* 25 nutriunt et *R, corr. R¹* 28 aovios *O*

ac domum dominam voca
coniugis cupidam novi,
mentem amore revinciens,
ut tenax hedera huc et huc
   arborem implicat errans.   35

vosque item simul, integrae
virgines, quibus advenit
par dies, agite in modum
dicite, o Hymenaee Hymen,
   o Hymen Hymenaee,   40

ut lubentius, audiens
se citarier ad suum
munus, huc aditum ferat
dux bonae Veneris, boni
   coniugator amoris.   45

quis deus magis anxiis
est petendus amantibus?
quem colent homines magis
caelitum, o Hymenaee Hymen,
   o Hymen Hymenaee?   50

te suis tremulus parens
invocat, tibi virgines
zonula soluunt sinus,
te timens cupida novus
   captat aure maritus.   55

tu fero iuveni in manus
floridam ipse puellulam

31 ac *V*: ad *1472* (*et R*³)　33 revinciens ε: revincens *V*　34 hac et hac *Itali* (*Pal. 1652, Bodl. e 15, Vat. 3269, alii*)　38 in nodum *V*, al. in modum *R*²　40 o hymenee (hi- *O*) hymenee hymen (hi- *O*) *V*: hymen o hymenee hymen (ζ)　41 lubencius *O*　42 citaries *O*　46/47 anxiis/est *Haupt*, est ama/tis *Bergk*: amatis/est *V*　(49a) conperaries ausit *O*, comperarier ausit *GR*: *del.* (γ)　50 o hymen (hi- *O*) hymenee hymen *V*: hymen o hymenee hymen (ζ)　51 suis tremulus η: sui si remulus *V*　53 zonulla *O*, zonulas *Peiper*　55 maritus *Muretus*: maritos *V*　56 fer o *V* (fer oiuveni *O*)　57 puelullam *O*

dedis a gremio suae
matris, o Hymenaee Hymen,
   o Hymen Hymenaee.   60

nil potest sine te Venus,
fama quod bona comprobet,
commodi capere, at potest
te volente. quis huic deo
   compararier ausit?   65

nulla quit sine te domus
liberos dare, nec parens
stirpe nitier; at potest
te volente. quis huic deo
   compararier ausit?   70

quae tuis careat sacris,
non queat dare praesides
terra finibus; at queat
te volente. quis huic deo
   compararier ausit?   75

claustra pandite ianuae;
virgo, ades. viden ut faces
splendidas quatiunt comas?

  . . . .
    . . . . . .   (80)

  . . . .
    . . . . . .

tardet ingenuus pudor.
quem tamen magis audiens,   80
   flet quod ire necesse est.   (85)

58 dedis agremio sue matris *V*, d. a gremio s. m. *m*   59–60 o hymenee hymen (hi- *O*)
hymenee (matris *hinc om.*) *V*, o hymenee hymen o hymenee *R*²   61 nichil *V*, nil *mG*²*R*³
63 comodi *R, corr. R*²   65 comparier *O*   66 quid *GR, corr. R*²   68 nitier *β*: vities *O*,
vicier *GR*   70 comparies *O*   75 comparier *O*, comparī *G(corr. G*¹)   77 ades *adn. Marc.*
12.128: adest *V*   78 quaciunt *O*   *Post 78 lacunam statuit Ellis, post 79 L. Mueller*

flere desine. non tibi, Aurunculeia, periculum est
ne qua femina pulcrior
clarum ab Oceano diem   85
   viderit venientem.   (90)

talis in vario solet
divitis domini hortulo
stare flos hyacinthinus.
sed moraris, abit dies.   90
   prodeas, nova nupta.   (95)

prodeas, nova nupta, si
iam videtur, et audias
nostra verba. viden? faces
aureas quatiunt comas;   95
   prodeas, nova nupta.   (100)

non tuus levis in mala
deditus vir adultera,
probra turpia persequens,
a tuis teneris volet   100
   secubare papillis,   (105)

lenta sed velut adsitas
vitis implicat arbores,
implicabitur in tuum
complexum. sed abit dies;   105
   prodeas, nova nupta.   (110)

o cubile, quod omnibus

. . . .

. . . .

82/83 Au/runculeia *sic divisit Turnebus*   83 / aurunculeia *O*, / arunculeia *GR*
88 ortullo *OG*, -ulo *G¹ (et G²) R*   89 iactintinus *O*, iacintinus *GR*   90 abit (δ): abiit *V*
91 *om. V: add. Ald.*   94 viden (θ), vide ut *Parth.*: videri ut *O*, viden et *R*, viden ut *GR²*
99 probra turpia *Calph.*: procatur pia *V*   101 se cubare *O*   102 lenta ꝗ *O*, lentaꝗ *GR*:
lenta qui *Av.*, l. quin *Trinc.*   velut] vult *O*   105 abit ηθ: abiit *V*   (107–8) "*o cubile quod
omnibus / candido pede lectulis: post ista duo carmina fenestra in codice antiquo sequitur
et sine dubio tres desunt versus*" *A. Guarinus, qui et* 109–111 *om.*

  .   .   .   .

candido pede lecti,   (115)

quae tuo veniunt ero,
quanta gaudia, quae vaga   110
nocte, quae medio die
gaudeat! sed abit dies;
   prodeas, nova nupta.   (120)

tollite, <o> pueri, faces:
flammeum video venire.   115
ite concinite in modum
"io Hymen Hymenaee io,
   io Hymen Hymenaee."   (125)

ne diu taceat procax
Fescennina iocatio,   120
nec nuces pueris neget
desertum domini audiens
   concubinus amorem.   (130)

da nuces pueris, iners
concubine; satis diu   125
lusisti nucibus; libet
iam servire Talasio.
   concubine, nuces da.   (135)

sordebant tibi vilicae,
concubine, hodie atque heri;   130
nunc tuum cinerarius
tondet os. miser a miser
   concubine, nuces da.   (140)

---

109 hero *V*   110 quae εζ: -que *V*   111 quae δε: -que *V*   112 abit ηθ: abiit *V*   114 o *add. η*
115 flammeum ε: flammineum *O*, flamineum *GR*   vido *O*   117, 118, 116 *hoc ordine GR*;
117, 116 (*om.* 118) *O*   118 io *add. V* (*idem in similibus quae sequuntur*)   119 taceat γ:
taceatis *V*   120 fosceninna *O*   iocatio *Heinsius*: locatio *OR*, lotatio *G*, locutio *R*²
121 ne *R*²   nucen *G, corr. G*¹   125 diu] domini *O*   127 nam *O*   129 villice *GR*
132 misera *O*, miserah *R*, miser ah *GR*²

diceris male te a tuis
unguentate glabris, marite,   135
abstinere, sed abstine.
io Hymen Hymenaee io,
    io Hymen Hymenaee.   (145)

scimus haec tibi quae licent
sola cognita, sed marito   140
ista non eadem licent.
io Hymen Hymenaee io,
    io Hymen Hymenaee.   (150)

nupta, tu quoque quae tuus
vir petet cave ne neges,   145
ni petitum aliunde eat.
io Hymen Hymenaee io,
    io Hymen Hymenaee.   (155)

en tibi domus ut potens
et beata viri tui,   150
quae tibi sine serviat
(io Hymen Hymenaee io,
    io Hymen Hymenaee)   (160)

usque, dum tremulum movens
cana tempus anilitas   155
omnia omnibus annuit.
io Hymen Hymenaee io,
    io Hymen Hymenaee.   (165)

transfer omine cum bono
limen aureolos pedes,   160
rasilemque subi forem.
io Hymen Hymenaee io,
    io Hymen Hymenaee.   (170)

134 diceris *1473*: diceres *V*   male *G*, malle *OR*   tu *R, corr. R*[1]   135 unguenta te *V*
138 *om. V, add.* β   139 simus *O*   quod *R*, -que *OGR*[1], *corr. R*[2]   142–6 *desunt in R,*
add. in margine R[2] *(habet m)*   143 *om. O*   144 quae *R*[2], que *V*   tuis *GR*[2], *corr. R*[2]*bis*
145 patet *G*   146 ne *R*[2]   148 *om. OG*   151 sine serviat *Parth.*, sine fine servit *invitis*
numeris γ: sine servit *V*   153 *om. O*   155 anilitas η: anilis etas *O*, annilis etas *GR*
158 *om. O*   159 homine *R, corr. R*[1]*(R*[2]*?)*   160 aureleos *R*   161 nassilemque *O*,
rassilemque *GR, corr. R*[2]   subi ζη: sibi *V*   163 *om. O*

aspice intus ut accubans
vir tuus Tyrio in toro   165
totus immineat tibi.
io Hymen Hymenaee io,
    io Hymen Hymenaee.   (175)

illi non minus ac tibi
pectore urit in intimo   170
flamma, sed penite magis.
io Hymen Hymenaee io,
    io Hymen Hymenaee.   (180)

mitte brachiolum teres,
praetextate, puellulae: 175
iam cubile adeat viri.
io Hymen Hymenaee io,
    io Hymen Hymenaee.   (185)

<vos> bonae senibus viris
cognitae bene feminae   180
collocate puellulam.
io Hymen Hymenaee io,
    io Hymen Hymenaee.   (190)

iam licet venias, marite:
uxor in thalamo tibi est,   185
ore floridulo nitens,
alba parthenice velut
    luteumve papaver.   (195)

at, marite, ita me iuvent
caelites, nihilo minus   190

164 intus *Statius*: unus *V*   169 ac *R*, hac *OG*   170 urit in *Goold*: uritur *OG*, urimur *R*
171 flama *GR, corr. R²*   penite] perit en *O. Skutsch*   175 praetextare *O*, prectate *R*,
corr. R²   puellulae *η*: puelle *V*   176 adeant *GR*   179 vos *add. Av. (qui et* unis
senibus bonae)   viris (*γ*): unis *V*   180 bene *R³* (beue *ed. Rom.*), breve *α*: berve *V*
181 puellulam *η*: puellam *V*   185 tibi est *β* (*sig. transp. add. β¹*): est tibi *V*   187 vult *GR*,
vultu *R²*   189–93 *post* 198 *V: huc revocavit Scaliger*   189 at, marite, ita me iuvent
Scaliger (at marite *iam B. Pisanus Puccium ut videtur secutus*): ad maritum tamen
iuvenem *V*   190 nichil ominus *O*, nichoilominus *G*, nichilominus *G¹*, nichilhominus *R*,
nichil-ominus *R²*

pulcer es, neque te Venus
neglegit. sed abit dies;
   perge, ne remorare.   (200)

non diu remoratus es:
iam venis. bona te Venus   195
iuverit, quoniam palam
quod cupis cupis, et bonum
   non abscondis amorem.   (205)

ille pulveris Africi
siderumque micantium   200
subducat numerum prius,
qui vestri numerare vult
   multa milia ludi.   (210)

ludite ut lubet, et brevi
liberos date. non decet   205
tam vetus sine liberis
nomen esse, sed indidem
   semper ingenerari.   (215)

Torquatus volo parvulus
matris e gremio suae   210
porrigens teneras manus
dulce rideat ad patrem
   semihiante labello.   (220)

sit suo similis patri
Manlio, ut facile obviis   215
noscitetur ab insciis

191 pulcher es *"alii" apud Robortellum*, pulcher is *Puccius* (?), *adn. Marc. 12.127*:
pulcre res *V* neque *θ*: nec *V* 192 negligit *GR* abit *ηθ*: abiit *V* 193 rememorare *GR*
194 remoratus *Calph.*: remota *O*, remorata *GR* 196 iuverit *θ*: invenerit *V* 197 cupis
capis *R²* 198 abscondis *ζη*: abscondas *V* 199 africi *Heinsius* (africei *Lachmann*): ericei *V*
200 micancium *O* 202 vestri *β*: nostri *V* vult *Calph.*: volunt *V* 203 ludi *ed. Rom.* (ludei
Scaliger): ludere *V* 204 ludite ut *Parth.* (ut *iam Calph.*): et ludite et *V* 205 liberos *G¹*
in rasura 207 nididem *O* 208 ingenerati *O* 209 torcutus *O* 210 egremio *G, et*
gremio *OR, corr. R²* 213 semihiante *Scaliger*: sed michi ante *V* 215 maulio *O*, mallio
Laur. 36.23, δ ut *scripsi*: et *V* facie *Burman* insciis *ζη* (-ieis *Lachmann*): insciens *V*
215/216 omnibus / . . . ab insciis *Dawes* obvieis *Pleitner*: omnibus *V* 216 noscite ab *O*

et pudicitiam suae
   matris indicet ore.   (225)

talis illius a bona
matre laus genus approbet,   220
qualis unica ab optima
matre Telemacho manet
   fama Penelopaeo.   (230)

claudite ostia, virgines:
lusimus satis. at, boni   225
coniuges, bene vivite et
munere assiduo valentem
   exercete iuventam.   (235)

62

Vesper adest; iuvenes, consurgite; Vesper Olympo
exspectata diu vix tandem lumina tollit.
surgere iam tempus, iam pinguis linquere mensas;
iam veniet virgo, iam dicetur hymenaeus.
Hymen o Hymenaee, Hymen ades o Hymenaee!   5

Cernitis, innuptae, iuvenes? consurgite contra;
nimirum Oetaeos ostendit Noctifer ignes.
sic certest; viden ut perniciter exsiluere?
non temere exsiluere; canent quod vincere par est.
Hymen o Hymenaee, Hymen ades o Hymenaee!   10

62 1 *Varro, De lingua latina 7.50*

---

217 suae *Calph.*, suo (ζ): suam *V*   218 iudicet *O*   219/220 bona matre/laus *V*
220 egenus *O* 221 ab om. *O* 222 telemacho ζ: thelamacho *O*, theleamacho *GR*
223 pene lopeo *O*, penolopeo *GR* 224 ostia *Carp.*: hostia *V* 225 at boni ζη: ad bonlei *O*,
ad bolnei *GR*, al. bonei *R*[2] 226 bene vivite ζη: bone vite *V* 227 assiduo ζη: assidue *V*
228 exercere *O*

62 1 olimpo *O* 3 pingues *GR* liquere *O* 4 imeneus *O* 5 hymes ades *R, corr. R*[1]
hymeneae ... Hymenaeae *T* 6 con surgi eretera *T*, consurgere contra γ 7 oeta eos *T*,
oetheos *R*[3], hoc eos *V* ignes *R*[3], imbres *T*, imber *V* 8 sic certe est *Statius* (certest
Haupt): siccer tes ·i· (=id est) *T*, sic certe si *V*, sic certe *R*[2] exiluere *TV* 9 quod *T*, quo *V*
vincere *B. Guarinus*: visere *TV* par est *T*, parent *V* 10 hymene (hymeno *T*[1]) hymeneae
hymeneae ades ·o· hymeneę *T*, hymen ohymenee (o hymene *G*, o hymenee *Rm*) hymen
(hi- *O*) ades o hymenee *V*

Non facilis nobis, aequales, palma parata est;
aspicite, innuptae secum ut meditata requirunt.
non frustra meditantur: habent memorabile quod sit;
nec mirum, penitus quae tota mente laborant.
nos alio mentes, alio divisimus aures;   15
iure igitur vincemur: amat victoria curam.
quare nunc animos saltem convertite vestros;
dicere iam incipient, iam respondere decebit.
Hymen o Hymenaee, Hymen ades o Hymenaee!

Hespere, quis caelo fertur crudelior ignis?   20
qui natam possis complexu avellere matris,
complexu matris retinentem avellere natam,
et iuveni ardenti castam donare puellam.
quid faciunt hostes capta crudelius urbe?
Hymen o Hymenaee, Hymen ades o Hymenaee!   25

Hespere, quis caelo lucet iucundior ignis?
qui desponsa tua firmes conubia flamma,
quae pepigere viri, pepigerunt ante parentes,
nec iunxere prius quam se tuus extulit ardor.
quid datur a divis felici optatius hora?   30
Hymen o Hymenaee, Hymen ades o Hymenaee!

Hesperus e nobis, aequales, abstulit unam.

· · · · · · · · · ·

11 nobis *V*, nobilis *T*   aequales *Lachmann*: (a)equalis *TV*   12 aspice *O*   secum *Tβ*, que secum *O¹GR* (querunt secum *O primo*)   meditata requirunt *T*, meditare querunt *V*: meditata requaerunt *Ric. 606*¹⁽²⁾   13 hunc *O*, habent (hn̄t) *GR*   memora psilequod *T* 14 *versum habet T, om. V: adhuc latente T, rest. (ex codice nunc deperdito) Parrhasius* laborent *Vossius*   15 nos *V*, non *T*   (*supra scr.* al. dividamus *G³*)   17 nunc *T*, non *V* convertite *T*, commictite *R*, committite *OGR²*   18 incipiant *T, corr. T¹*   res pondere *T* 19 hymeneae … hymeneae *T*   20 quis *T*, qui *V*   fertur *TV*: lucet (*γ*)   21 conplexua velere (vellere *T¹*) *T*   amatris *O, corr. O¹*   22 con plexu *T*   avellere *V*, avelle *T* Natam *T*   24 credelius *T*   25 Kymeno hymeneę Kymenades ·o· Kymeneę *T*   26 quis *T*, qui *V*   27 firmes *V*, fines *T*   flama *G*   28 quae *T*, quo *V*, quod *θ Tub. (et R³)*   vir *T* 29 vinxere *O*   30 a *om. T*   optacius *O*   31 Kymeno Kymeneae Kymenades oKymeneę *T* 32 Hesperusę *T*   equales *V*, equalem *R²*, ęqualis *T*   Post 32 *lacunam statuit Av.*

. . . .
namque tuo adventu vigilat custodia semper.
nocte latent fures, quos idem saepe revertens,
Hespere, mutato comprendis nomine Eous   35
at lubet innuptis ficto te carpere questu.
quid tum, si carpunt, tacita quem mente requirunt?
Hymen o Hymenaee, Hymen ades o Hymenaee!

Ut flos in saeptis secretus nascitur hortis,
ignotus pecori, nullo convulsus aratro,   40
quem mulcent aurae, firmat sol, educat imber;

multi illum pueri, multae optavere puellae:
idem cum tenui carptus defloruit ungui,
nulli illum pueri, nullae optavere puellae:
sic virgo, dum intacta manet, dum cara suis est;   45
cum castum amisit polluto corpore florem,
nec pueris iucunda manet, nec cara puellis.
Hymen o Hymenaee, Hymen ades o Hymenaee!

Ut vidua in nudo vitis quae nascitur arvo,
numquam se extollit, numquam mitem educat uvam,   50
sed tenerum prono deflectens pondere corpus
iam iam contingit summum radice flagellum;
hanc nulli agricolae, nulli coluere iuvenci:
at si forte eadem est ulmo coniuncta marita,

45 *Quintilianus, Institutio oratoria 9.3.16*

———

35 comprendis *O*, comprehendis *GR* (*corr. G³*), comperendis *T* eous *Schrader*:
eospem *T*, eosdem *V*   36 at libet *V*, adlucet *T*   in nuptis *GR*   37 quittum *T*, quod
tamen *V*, al. quid tum *R²*   carpiunt *T*   tacita quem δε: tacita quam *V*, tacitaquema *T*
38 Kymeno Kymeneae Kymenales Kymeno Kymeneę *T*   39 secretis *R, corr. R²*   ortis *V*
40 convolsus *T*, conclusus *V*, contusus *R²*   41 quaemulcens aurefirma soleducat *T*   *Post*
41 *lacunam unius versus (<iam iam>...) indicavit Spengel*   42 obtavere *V*   43, 44 *om.*
TO   45 dum cara *a, Quintilianus*: tum c. *TOG*, cum c. *R*, tum c. *R²*   suis sed ηθ, suis
est *T, Quintilianus*: sui sed *V*   46 amixit *R, corr. R²*   48 Kymeneo Kymeneę Kymenades
Kymeneę (o *om.*) *T*   49 ut *V*, et *T*   50 numquam (nun- *G¹*) mitem (vitem *O*) educat
uvam *V*, quam muniteam ducatuvam *T*   51 deflectens *V*, perflectens *T*   52 flacellum *T*
53 agrigcule *T*, agriculle *T¹*   nulli coluere *O*, nulli colluere *GR, corr. R²*, multi acoluere *T*
iuventi *O, corr. O¹*   54 at si *V*, apsi *T*   est ultimo *GR, corr. R²*   marita *T*, marito *V*

multi illam agricolae, multi coluere iuvenci: 55
sic virgo dum innupta manet, dum inculta senescit;
cum par conubium maturo tempore adepta est,
cara viro magis et minus est invisa parenti.
Hymen o Hymenaee, Hymen ades o Hymenaee!   58b

Et tu ne pugna cum tali coniuge, virgo.
non aequum est pugnare, pater cui tradidit ipse,   60
ipse pater cum matre, quibus parere necesse est.
virginitas non tota tua est, ex parte parentum est,
tertia pars patris est, pars est data tertia matri,
tertia sola tua est: noli pugnare duobus,
qui genero sua iura simul cum dote dederunt.   65
Hymen o Hymenaee, Hymen ades o Hymenaee!

63

Super alta vectus Attis celeri rate maria,
Phrygium ut nemus citato cupide pede tetigit
adiitque opaca silvis redimita loca deae,
stimulatus ibi furenti rabie, vagus animis,
devulsit ili acuto sibi pondera silice.   5
itaque ut relicta sensit sibi membra sine viro,
etiam recente terrae sola sanguine maculans,
niveis citata cepit manibus leve typanum,

63 1 *Grammatici Latini VI: 154 (Marius Victorinus), 411 (Terentianus)*   2 *Grammatici Latini VI: 262 (Caesius Bassus)*

55 coluere (γ), acoluere *T*, acc- *V*   iuventi *OG*, *corr.* G²   56 innupta *H. Weber* (cf.
Quint. ad 45): intacta *TV*   dum (2°) *V*, tum *T*   57 connubium *V*   58 cura *TV*, *corr.* R²
viro *TOGβ*¹, virgo *R*   58b *add. Muretus*   59 tu *V*, tua *T*   ne *B. Guarinus* (nei *Baehrens*):
nec *TV*   60 equom *T* (equum *β*), equo *V*   61 ipse *om. R, add. R²*   62 *om. T*   63 pars
patris est *Parrhasius*, pars patrist *Haupt* (pars patri *iam Av.*): patris *T*, pars patri *V*   pars
est *T*, est *O*, data pars *GR*   64 solit tu est noli tuignare *T*   66 Kymeno Kymeneae
kymenades ·o· Kymeneae *T*   . . . hymenee *G*, -ne *G*¹
63 1 vetus *O*   attis *Terentianus, Marius Victorinus*: actis *V*   celeri *testes vett.*, θ: celere *V*
2 (*sim. 20, 71*) frigium *V*, phrygium *m*   3 adutque (?) *O* (*desunt apices*)   4 ibi *Puccius*:
ubi *V*   animis *a*, animi *Parth.*: amnis *V*   5 devolsit *Haupt*: devolvit *V*   ilei *Bergk*: iletas *V*
pondera silice *Av.*: pondere silices *V*   7 et iam *G*   maculas *V*   8 typanum *Scaliger*:
timpanum *O*, tym- *GR*

typanum tuum, Cybebe, tua, mater, initia,
quatiensque terga tauri teneris cava digitis   10
canere haec suis adorta est tremebunda comitibus.
"agite ite ad alta, Gallae, Cybeles nemora simul,
simul ite, Dindymenae dominae vaga pecora,
aliena quae petentes velut exules loca
sectam meam exsecutae duce me mihi comites   15
rapidum salum tulistis truculentaque pelagi,
et corpus evirastis Veneris nimio odio;
hilarate erae citatis erroribus animum.
mora tarda mente cedat: simul ite, sequimini
Phrygiam ad domum Cybebes, Phrygia ad nemora deae,   20
ubi cymbalum sonat vox, ubi tympana reboant,
tibicen ubi canit Phryx curvo grave calamo,
ubi capita Maenades vi iaciunt hederigerae,
ubi sacra sancta acutis ululatibus agitant,
ubi suevit illa divae volitare vaga cohors,   25
quo nos decet citatis celerare tripudiis."
    simul haec comitibus Attis cecinit notha mulier,
thiasus repente linguis trepidantibus ululat,
leve tympanum remugit, cava cymbala recrepant,
viridem citus adit Idam properante pede chorus.   30
furibunda simul anhelans vaga vadit animam agens
comitata tympano Attis per opaca nemora dux,
veluti iuvenca vitans onus indomita iugi;
rapidae ducem sequuntur Gallae properipedem.
itaque, ut domum Cybebes tetigere lassulae,   35
nimio e labore somnum capiunt sine Cerere.

9 typanum *Scaliger*: timpanum *V*, tym- *m*   tuom *Lachmann*: tubam *V*   Cybebe *Sillig*
(-es *iam Bentley ad Lucanum 1.600*): cibeles *V*, cyb- *m*   tua *Grat.* (*primo*): tu *V*   matri *O*
10 quatiensque *a*: quatiens quod *V*   tauri ζ (taurei *Lachmann*): tauri et *V*   12 cibelles *O*,
cibeles *GR*   13 pecora *Av.*: pectora *V*   14 aliena quae *P. Laetus, B. Guarinus*: alienaque *V*
loca *B. Guarinus, Polit.*: loca celeri *V*   15 execute *V*, excute *R²*   17 evitastis *OR*   18 here
citatis *Av.*, aere citatis *Lachmann* (ęrę *vel* aere *iam* εη): erocitatis *O*, crocitatis *GR*, al.
ere citatis *R²*   animum ε: an animum *V*   19 cedat *OR*, cedit *G*   ite] te *O*   20 (*cf.*
35, 84, 91) Cybebes *Bentley*: cibelles *O*, cibeles *GR*   23 menades vi η: menade sui *V*
ederigere *Calph.*: ei derigere *V*   27 actis ζη, athis *Tom.*: atris *V*   mulies notha *O*,
transp. *O¹*   nota *GR*, nova ζ   28 thiasus *R*, thiasiis *R²*, thiasis *O*, thysiis *G*, thyasiis *G¹*
31 anelans *GR*   animam agens *Lachmann*, animagens *OR*, aīa gēs *G*   32 athys β, athis δ:
actis *V*   oppaca *O*   33 iugi *1472*: luci *V*   34 properipedem *B. Venator*: propere pedem *V*
35 domum] pedomum *G*, *corr. G¹*   Cybebes *Bentley*: cibelles *O*, cibeles *GR*   lasulle *O*

piger his labante languore oculos sopor operit;
abit in quiete molli rabidus furor animi.
    sed ubi oris aurei Sol radiantibus oculis
lustravit aethera album, sola dura, mare ferum,   40
pepulitque noctis umbras vegetis sonipedibus,
ibi Somnus excitam Attin fugiens citus abiit;
trepidante eum recepit dea Pasithea sinu.
ita de quiete molli rapida sine rabie
simul ipsa pectore Attis sua facta recoluit,   45
liquidaque mente vidit sine quis ubique foret,
animo aestuante rusum reditum ad vada tetulit.
ibi maria vasta visens lacrimantibus oculis
patriam allocuta maestast ita voce miseriter.
    "patria o mei creatrix, patria o mea genetrix,   50
ego quam miser relinquens, dominos ut erifugae
famuli solent, ad Idae tetuli nemora pedem,
ut apud nivem et ferarum gelida stabula forem,
et earum operta adirem furibunda latibula,
ubinam aut quibus locis te positam, patria, reor?   55
cupit ipsa pupula ad te sibi derigere aciem,
rabie fera carens dum breve tempus animus est.
egone a mea remota haec ferar in nemora domo?
patria, bonis, amicis, genitoribus abero?
abero foro, palaestra, stadio et gyminasiis?   60
miser a miser, querendum est etiam atque etiam, anime.
quod enim genus figurae est, ego non quod obierim?

38 *Festus p. 338 (Lindsay) s.v.* rabidus

---

37 hiis *O*   labente *G, corr. G²*   38 abiit *GR*   molli θ (<mol>li *iam Festus*): (inquiete)
mollis *V*   39 oris aurei θ: horis aureis *V*   40 sol adura *V*   42 sonus *OG, corr. G¹ R*
excitam *Lachmann*: excitum *V*   43 trepidantem ηθ   eum α: cum *V*   pasithea ζ: pasitheo *V*
45 ipsa *Ald. et A. Guarinus (at vide n.)*: ipse *V*   attis *G*, actis *R*, atris *O*   46 sine quis
Parth.: sineque is *O*, sineque his *GR*   47 aestuante (γ) *et* rusum *Victorius*: estuanter
usum *V*   tetulit *Calph.*: retulit *V*   49 alocuta *G*, adl- *G²*   maestast ita voce miseriter
Trinc.: est ita voce miseritus (al. miseriter *R²*) maiestates (magestates *O*, maiestas *GR*, al.
maiestates *R²*) *V*   50 genetrix *G*, genitrix *OR*   51 herifuge *OR*, veri fuge *G* (*corr. G¹*)
52 retuli *GR*   memora *O*   53 apud ε: caput *V* (capud *R*)   stabula *R²* (*ita tamen ut a
stabilla vix distingui possit*), stabilla *mG²*: stabilia *V*   54 opaca *vel* operta *L. Mueller*,
amica *Muretus*: omnia *V*   55 patriam *O, corr. O¹*   56 pupula β¹η: popula *V*   ad te β:
atte *V*   58 ferat *G, corr. G²*   60 guminasiis *Ellis*: gummasiis *O*, ginnasiis *GR*   61 ha *O*,
ah *GR*   queri dum *G, corr. G¹*   aīe *G*, anime *G²*   62 figurae est *Ald.*, figuraest *Lachmann*
(figurest *iam ed. Rom.*): figura est *V*   quod obierim *Statius*: quid abierim *V*

ego puber, ego adulescens, ego ephebus, ego puer,
ego gymnasi fui flos, ego eram decus olei:
mihi ianuae frequentes, mihi limina tepida, 65
mihi floridis corollis redimita domus erat,
linquendum ubi esset orto mihi sole cubiculum.
ego nunc deum ministra et Cybeles famula ferar?
ego Maenas, ego mei pars, ego vir sterilis ero?
ego viridis algida Idae nive amicta loca colam? 70
ego vitam agam sub altis Phrygiae columinibus,
ubi cerva silvicultrix, ubi aper nemorivagus?
iam iam dolet quod egi, iam iamque paenitet."
    roseis ut hinc labellis sonitus <citus> abiit,
geminas deorum ad aures nova nuntia referens, 75
ibi iuncta iuga resolvens Cybele leonibus
saevumque pecoris hostem stimulans ita loquitur.
"agedum," inquit "age ferox <i>, fac ut hunc furor <agitet>,
fac uti furoris ictu reditum in nemora ferat,
mea libere nimis qui fugere imperia cupit. 80
age caede terga cauda, tua verbera patere,
fac cuncta mugienti fremitu loca retonent,
rutilam ferox torosa cervice quate iubam."
ait haec minax Cybebe religatque iuga manu.
ferus ipse sese adhortans rapidum incitat animo, 85
vadit, fremit, refringit virgulta pede vago.
at ubi umida albicantis loca litoris adiit,

63 puber *Scaliger*: muliēs *O*, mulier *GR* 64 gymnasi *γ*, -sei *Voss.* 76, gimnasii *β*:
gimnasti *V* fui *O*, sui *GR*: suus *Nisbet* oley *V* 66 corolis *Calph.*: circulis *V*
67 linquendum *α*: liquendum *V* sole *ς*: solo *V* 68 nunc *Santen*: nec *V* decum *G*,
corr. (c eras.) *G¹(G²?)* ministtra *O* cibellos *O*, cibeles *GR* ferar (*γ*): ferarum *V*
69 pās *G*, pars *G²* 70 Idae nive *Calph.*: idenene *O*, yd- *GR* 71 columinibus (*θ*),
Calph.: columnibus *V* 72 apex *O* nemori vagus *V* 74 hinc] huic *θ* citus *add.*
Bentley abiit (*θ*): adiit *V* 75 adauris *O* 76 ibi *ς*: ubi *V* cibelle *O*, cibele *GR*
77 saevumque *Caes., Puccius, Ashb. 973 (primo, ut videtur)*: levumque *V* (lenumque *O*)
pecoris (*η*): pectoris *V* stimulans *O¹* (-im- *in rasura*), sintmulans *G* (n *priorem*
exp. *G¹, corr. G²*) 78 age dum *V* inquid *OR* (corr. *R²*) i *add. Scaliger* face
ed. Rom. (*idem* 79, 82) agitet *add. ed. Cantabrig. anni 1702* 79 uti *Lachmann*, ut
hunc *ςη*: ut *V* ictu *α*: ictum *V* 81 a cede *G*, al. age cede *G²* tergo *GR* verbera
Calph.: verum vera *V* 82 cunta *G* 84 Cybebe *Bentley*: cibelle *O*, cibele *GR*
regligatque *O* 85 adhortans *Ald.²* (adhortatus *iam Ald.*): adortalis *O*, ad horta la *G*
(lis *G¹*), adhorta lis *R*, adorta lis *R²* rabidum *Schwabe* 87 bumida *O*, humida *GR*
litioris *O*

tenerumque vidit Attin prope marmora pelagi,
facit impetum. ille demens fugit in nemora fera;
ibi semper omne vitae spatium famula fuit.   90
    dea magna, dea Cybebe, dea domina Dindymi,
procul a mea tuus sit furor omnis, era, domo:
alios age incitatos, alios age rapidos.

64

Peliaco quondam prognatae vertice pinus
dicuntur liquidas Neptuni nasse per undas
Phasidos ad fluctus et fines Aeeteos,
cum lecti iuvenes, Argivae robora pubis,
auratam optantes Colchis avertere pellem   5
ausi sunt vada salsa cita decurrere puppi,
caerula verrentes abiegnis aequora palmis.
diva quibus retinens in summis urbibus arces
ipsa levi fecit volitantem flamine currum,
pinea coniungens inflexae texta carinae.   10
illa rudem cursu prima imbuit Amphitriten;
quae simul ac rostro ventosum proscidit aequor
tortaque remigio spumis incanuit unda,
emersere feri candenti e gurgite vultus
aequoreae monstrum Nereides admirantes.   15

64 1 *Grammatici Latini VI: 125 (Marius Victorinus)*

---

88 teneramque *Lachmann*   attin *OG*, actin *R*   marmora pelagi γ: marmorea pelago *V*
89 facit *Calph.*: ficit *O*, fecit *GR*   illa *Lachmann*   90 omne *GR*, esse *O*   spacium *O*
famulla *G, corr. G*¹ *et G*²   91 Cybebe *Bentley*: cibelle *O*, cibele *GR*   dindimei *V*   92 tuos
Ellis (tuus *iam* γδ): tuo *V*   hera *GR*   93 rabidos (θ)
64 1 peliaco αβ, *Marius Victorinus*: pelliaco *V*   pynus *R*   2 neptūni *R*²   3 fasidicos *O*,
fascidicos *GR, al.* phasidos *R*²   Aeetaeos *Ald.* (aeetheios *iam Parth.*), oeteios β¹, -th- *1472*,
oëtaeos (η): ceticos *O* (al. tetidicos *O*¹), oeticos *GR*   4 pubis *Mont.* (*et Ald.*): pupis *O*,
puppis *GR*   5 optantem *G, corr. G*¹   cholchis *O*   6 valda *O, corr. O*¹   decurere pupi *O*
7 verentes *V, corr. R*²   abregnis *G, corr. G*¹   9 voluntantem *O, corr. O*¹   10 testa *GR*
11 prima β: post eam *O* (proram *O*¹), primam *GR*, prora *Richmond*   aphitritem *O*
(aphitrite *O*¹), amphitricem *R*, amphitritem *GR*², *al.* amphitrionem *R*² *bis*   12 procidit *G*
13 tortaque *Trinc.*: totaque *V*   incanuit *Ald.*: incanduit *V*   14 freti *Schrader*   egurgite *V*,
e gurgite *R*²   15 equore *O   al.* monstrorum *O*¹   vereides *O, corr. O*¹   āmirantes *O*

illa, atque <haud> alia, viderunt luce marinas
mortales oculis nudato corpore Nymphas
nutricum tenus exstantes e gurgite cano.
tum Thetidis Peleus incensus fertur amore,
tum Thetis humanos non despexit hymenaeos,   20
tum Thetidi pater ipse iugandum Pelea sensit.
o nimis optato saeclorum tempore nati
heroes, salvete, deum genus! o bona matrum
progenies, salvete! iter<um salvete, bonarum!>   23b
vos ego saepe, meo vos carmine compellabo.
teque adeo eximie taedis felicibus aucte,
Thessaliae columen Peleu, cui Iuppiter ipse,
ipse suos divum genitor concessit amores;
tene Thetis tenuit pulcerrima Nereine?
tene suam Tethys concessit ducere neptem,
Oceanusque, mari totum qui amplectitur orbem?   30
  quae simul optatae finito tempore luces
advenere, domum conventu tota frequentat
Thessalia, oppletur laetanti regia coetu;
dona ferunt prae se, declarant gaudia vultu.
deseritur Cieros; linquunt Phthiotica Tempe   35
Crannonisque domos ac moenia Larisaea;
Pharsalum coeunt, Pharsalia tecta frequentant.
rura colit nemo, mollescunt colla iuvencis,
non humilis curvis purgatur vinea rastris,
non glebam prono convellit vomere taurus,   40
non falx attenuat frondatorum arboris umbram;

23b *Scholia Veronensia ad Vergili Aeneid. 5.80*

---

16 illa atque haud *Bergk* (illaque haud *iam Puccius, teste D. Iannoctio*, illa haudque
Sabellicus), illa si qua *Lachmann*: illa alia *O*, illa atque alia *GR*   viderunt $\zeta\eta$: videre *V*
17 oculi *Pal. 1652*   19 cum *O*   20 tum *m*: cum *Vm*¹   21 tum *β*: cum *V*   sanxit
Pontanus   22 seculorum *V, corr. R*²   23 gens *Madvig*   matrum *scholia Veronensia
ad Verg. Aen. 5.80*: mater *V*, al. matre *R*²   23b om. *V, ex scholiis add. F. Orioli*
iterum salvete bonarum *Peerlkamp*   24 saepe memor, vos *Traill*   25 tedis *O*, thetis *GR*
28 pulcerima *O*   Nereine *Haupt*: nectine *V*, al. neptine *R*², al. neutūne *R*² *bis, m*²
(neptunine *codices aliquot recentiores*)   29 tethys $\gamma\delta$: thetis *V*   31 optate ζ: optato *V*
finite *O*   32 advenere $\zeta\eta$: adlenire *V*   33 oppl'etur (= oppul-) *O*   35 cieros *Meineke*,
schyros *a*, scyros η: siros *O*, syros *GR*   ptiotica *O*, pthy- *GR*   36 Crannonisque *Victorius*:
graumonisque *O*, graiunonisque *GR*   moenia larissea θ, *Calph.*: nicenis alacrissea *O*, n.
alacrisea *GR*   37 Pharsalum *Pontanus*: farsaliam (. . . farsalia) *V*

squalida desertis robigo infertur aratris.
ipsius at sedes, quacumque opulenta recessit
regia, fulgenti splendent auro atque argento:
candet ebur soliis; collucent pocula mensae;   45
tota domus gaudet regali splendida gaza.
pulvinar vero divae geniale locatur
sedibus in mediis, Indo quod dente politum
tincta tegit roseo conchyli purpura fuco.

   haec vestis priscis hominum variata figuris   50
heroum mira virtutes indicat arte.
namque fluentisono prospectans litore Diae
Thesea cedentem celeri cum classe tuetur
indomitos in corde gerens Ariadna furores,
necdum etiam sese quae visit visere credit,   55
utpote fallaci quae tunc primum excita somno
desertam in sola miseram se cernat harena.
immemor at iuvenis fugiens pellit vada remis,
irrita ventosae linquens promissa procellae;
quem procul ex alga maestis Minois ocellis   60
saxea ut effigies bacchantis, prospicit, eheu,
prospicit et magnis curarum fluctuat undis,
non flavo retinens subtilem vertice mitram,
non contecta levi velatum pectus amictu,
non tereti strophio lactentis vincta papillas,   65
omnia quae toto delapsa e corpore passim
ipsius ante pedes fluctus salis alludebant.
sed neque tum mitrae neque tum fluitantis amictus
illa vicem curans toto ex te pectore, Theseu,

65 *Isidorus, Etymologiae (= Origines) 19.33.3*

---

43 at (δ): ad *V*   oppulenta *O*   45 soliis *om. G, add.* G¹   47 pluvinar *O*   52 fluenti
sono *O*, fluentinoso (-noso *exp.* G¹) sono *G*   prospettans *R, corr.* R²   littore *O*, litora *R*
die ε: dia *OR*, dya *G*   53 Tesea *O*   54 indomites *O*   ariadna β¹: adriana *V*   55 nec
dum *GR*   ēt *O*, eciam *G*   quae visit visere *Vossius*: -que sui tui se *V* (al. terni R²)   *in
fine versus* se credit /// (*latet fortasse* ēē a R? *additum et post erasum*) *R* (deficit *add.
supra* R²)   56 fallacique *OG*, fallaci. quae *R*   tunc *O*   60 minoeis (-ies?) *R, corr.* R²
61 saxa *V, corr.* R²   bachantis *V*, baccantis *m*   eheu *Bergk*, euoe *Ald.*: heue *V*   62 et]
con *O*, cum *GR, corr.* R²   64 contenta *O*   65 strophyo *GR*   cincta *Isidorus*   papillis *R,
corr.* R¹   66 omniaque *O*   delapsa e ζη: delapse *O*, delapso *G*, delapso e *R*   67 adl- *O*
68 sed neque ζη: (set n. *Lachmann*, sic n. *Rossbach*): sineque *V*   tum ... tum] tamen ...
tamen *O*   69 te *om. O*

toto animo, tota pendebat perdita mente.   70
a misera, assiduis quam luctibus externavit
spinosas Erycina serens in pectore curas,
illa tempestate, ferox qua robore Theseus
egressus curvis e litoribus Piraei
attigit iniusti regis Gortynia templa.   75
  nam perhibent olim crudeli peste coactam
Androgeoneae poenas exsolvere caedis
electos iuvenes simul et decus innuptarum
Cecropiam solitam esse dapem dare Minotauro.
quis angusta malis cum moenia vexarentur,   80
ipse suum Theseus pro caris corpus Athenis
proicere optavit potius quam talia Cretam
funera Cecropiae nec funera portarentur.
atque ita nave levi nitens ac lenibus auris
magnanimum ad Minoa venit sedesque superbas.   85
hunc simul ac cupido conspexit lumine virgo
regia, quam suavis exspirans castus odores
lectulus in molli complexu matris alebat,
quales Eurotae progignunt flumina myrtus
aurave distinctos educit verna colores,   90
non prius ex illo flagrantia declinavit
lumina, quam cuncto concepit corpore flammam
funditus atque imis exarsit tota medullis.
heu misere exagitans immiti corde furores
sancte puer, curis hominum qui gaudia misces,   95
quaeque regis Golgos quaeque Idalium frondosum,
qualibus incensam iactastis mente puellam
fluctibus, in flavo saepe hospite suspirantem!

71–2 Nonius vol. 1, p. 154 (Lindsay) s.v. externavit

---

70 perd*e*bat perdita *R* 71 a *Nonius:* ha *O,* ah *GR* 72 impectore *O* 73 qua robore
Froehlich (quom r. *Ritschl*) quo ex *"Italus in exemplari Veneto ed. Ald. 1502" teste*
Lachmann (at Marcianis quidem deest lectio), -que ex *Bon. 2744, e Vat. 3269 primo,*
quo ζη: -que et *V* tempore *V* 75 invisi *Heinsius* Gortynia *Pall.:* cortinia *V* templa β¹,
"alibi legitur tecta" *Parth.:* tempta *V* 77 cum androgeonee η (cum *del. Calph.*): cum
androgeane *O,* -nee *GR* exolvere *GR* 79 minothauro *O* 80 incenia *O,* inoenia *G,*
inenia *R,* menia *R²* 82 prohicere *O,* proiicere *GR* pocius *O* 86 conpexit *O* 88 allebat *O*
89 eurotae *1472:* europe *V* progignunt θ, praecingunt *Baehrens:* pergignunt *V* mirtos *O,*
mirtus *GR,* al. -tos *R²* 92 flamam *GR* 96 quaeque (1°) β: quod neque *O,* quique *GR*
golgos *Av.:* cholcos *O,* colchos *GR* id alium *O,* ydalium *GR*

quantos illa tulit languenti corde timores!
quam tum saepe magis fulgore expalluit auri,　　100
cum saevum cupiens contra contendere monstrum
aut mortem appeteret Theseus aut praemia laudis!
non ingrata tamen frustra munuscula divis
promittens tacito succepit vota labello:
nam velut in summo quatientem brachia Tauro　　105
quercum aut conigeram sudanti cortice pinum
indomitus turbo contorquens flamine robur
eruit (illa procul radicitus exturbata
prona cadit, late quaeviscumque obvia frangens),
sic domito saevum prostravit corpore Theseus　　110
nequiquam vanis iactantem cornua ventis.
inde pedem sospes multa cum laude reflexit
errabunda regens tenui vestigia filo,
ne labyrintheis e flexibus egredientem
tecti frustraretur inobservabilis error.　　115
　　sed quid ego a primo digressus carmine plura
commemorem, ut linquens genitoris filia vultum,
ut consanguineae complexum, ut denique matris,
quae misera in gnata deperdita laeta<batur>,
omnibus his Thesei dulcem praeoptarit amorem;　　120
aut ut vecta rati spumosa ad litora Diae
<venerit,> aut ut eam devinctam lumina somno
liquerit immemori discedens pectore coniunx?
saepe illam perhibent ardenti corde furentem
clarisonas imo fudisse e pectore voces,　　125
ac tum praeruptos tristem conscendere montes,

99 tullit G　100 quam tum *Faernus*: quanto V　102 oppeteret GR　104 succepit *Statius* (subscepit *iam P. Laetus*): succendit V　105 vult O　106 conigeram θ: cornigeram V fundanti V, *corr.* R²　108 emit O　109 late quaevis cumque *Ellis*, lateque et cominus *vel similia* ζη: lateque cum eius V　obvia O, omnia GR, al. obvia R²　111 ne qdꝯ O　navis O 112 reflixit R, *corr.* R¹　113 ereabunda O　114 laberinthis O, -theis GR¹ (laberientheis R *primo*)　eflexibus V, e flex- R²　115 frustaretur GR　116 a ζ: cum V　117 liquens G, *corr.* G²　119 ingnata OG, ignata R　laetabatur *Lachmann*, lamentata est *Conington* (miseram gnatam ... lamentata est *J. Fleischer*): leta V　120 hiis O　praeoptarit *Statius* (praeoptaret *iam P. Laetus*, praeoptavit *iam* θ): portaret V　121 ut *om.* O　necta OG, vecta R　rati *Passerat*: ratis V　spummosa R, *corr.* R²　littora O　122 venerit *add. Lachmann*　<placido> devinctam *P. Laetus*, devictam η: devincta V　123 ī memori O, in memori G, īmemori R　125 expectore O, epectore GR, e pectore R²　126 actum V, *corr.* R²　praeruptes O　tristem ζ: tristes V　confendere O

unde aciem <in> pelagi vastos protenderet aestus,
tum tremuli salis adversas procurrere in undas
mollia nudatae tollentem tegmina surae,
atque haec extremis maestam dixisse querellis,   130
frigidulos udo singultus ore cientem:
"sicine me patriis avectam, perfide, ab aris,
perfide, deserto liquisti in litore, Theseu?
sicine discedens neglecto numine divum,
immemor a! devota domum periuria portas?   135
nullane res potuit crudelis flectere mentis
consilium? tibi nulla fuit clementia praesto,
immite ut nostri vellet miserescere pectus?
at non haec quondam blanda promissa dedisti
voce mihi, non haec miseram sperare iubebas,   140
sed conubia laeta, sed optatos hymenaeos,
quae cuncta aerii discerpunt irrita venti.
nunc iam nulla viro iuranti femina credat,
nulla viri speret sermones esse fideles,
quis dum aliquid cupiens animus praegestit apisci,   145
nil metuunt iurare, nihil promittere parcunt;
sed simul ac cupidae mentis satiata libido est,
dicta nihil meminere, nihil periuria curant.
certe ego te in medio versantem turbine leti
eripui, et potius germanum amittere crevi   150
quam tibi fallaci supremo in tempore dessem.

143–8 *Hieremias de Montagnone, Compendium moralium notabilium* 4.5.1

127 in *add.* ζη   protenderet R: pretenderet OG   128 salus O   130 hoc G *(corr.* G¹*)* R
estremis O   dixisse mestam G, *transp.* G²   131 tientem O   132 siccine R   prīs (= patris;
an hic = patriis?) O   avertam V, avectam (*al.* avertam *subscr.*) R²   ad G, *corr.* G¹   133 in
om. O   littore O   134 siccine R   discendens G   negleto O   135 inmemor G   ah G,
ha O, ab R, ah R²   136 nullane res β: nullave res GR, nulla veres O   crudeles …
mentes V, *corr.* R²   137 clemencia OG, -tia R   138 miserescere *Calph.:* mirescere O,
mitescere GR   139 blanda O, nobis GR   140 non β: nec V   miseram 1472: misere V
141 himeneos O   142 discerpunt β: disserpunt GR, desserpunt O   143 nunc B. *(A.?)*
Guarinus: tum V   144 sermonee O, *corr.* O¹   fidelis O   145 quis V (*supra scr. pro*
quibus R²): qui *Pall. et Ald.*   aliquit R, *corr.* R²   praegestit V? postgestit OGR, *corr.* R²
(praegessit *Hieremias de Montagnone*)   adipisci O (*corr.* O¹ *et supra scr. pro* adipisci) G,
corr. R (aspici *Hieremias de Montagnone*)   146 promictere R, *corr.* R²   148 meminere
Iulius Czwalina: metuere V, *Hieremias de Montagnone*   149 lecti O   151 falaci G,
corr. G¹   deessem GR

pro quo dilaceranda feris dabor alitibusque
praeda, neque iniecta tumulabor mortua terra.
quaenam te genuit sola sub rupe leaena,
quod mare conceptum spumantibus exspuit undis,   155
quae Syrtis, quae Scylla rapax, quae vasta Charybdis,
talia qui reddis pro dulci praemia vita?
si tibi non cordi fuerant conubia nostra,
saeva quod horrebas prisci praecepta parentis,
attamen in vestras potuisti ducere sedes,   160
quae tibi iucundo famularer serva labore,
candida permulcens liquidis vestigia lymphis,
purpureave tuum consternens veste cubile.
sed quid ego ignaris nequiquam conqueror auris,
exsternata malo, quae nullis sensibus auctae   165
nec missas audire queunt nec reddere voces?
ille autem prope iam mediis versatur in undis,
nec quisquam apparet vacua mortalis in alga.
sic nimis insultans extremo tempore saeva
fors etiam nostris invidit questibus auris.   170
Iuppiter omnipotens, utinam ne tempore primo
Gnosia Cecropiae tetigissent litora puppes,
indomito nec dira ferens stipendia tauro
perfidus in Creta religasset navita funem,
nec malus haec celans dulci crudelia forma   175
consilia in nostris requiesset sedibus hospes!
nam quo me referam? quali spe perdita nitor?
Idaeosne petam montes? at gurgite lato
discernens ponti truculentum dividit aequor.
an patris auxilium sperem? quemne ipsa reliqui   180

171–2 Macrobius, Saturnalia 6.1.42; Petrarca, in margine cod. Ambros. Vergili, fol. 114[r]

152 altibus *G, corr. G*[2]   153 postea *O*   iniecta *Calph.*: intacta *V* (in tacta *G*)   156 sirtix *O* scilla *O*, silla *GR*   rapax, quae] rapaxꝗ *O*   157 taliaꝗ redis *O*   159 pemtis *O*   160 at tamen *O*   nostras *O*   *Post* 160 *posuit* 163 *O*   163 cubille *O, corr. O*[1]   164 si *V, corr. R*[2] conqueror (*γ*): conquerar *V*   aures *V, corr. R*[2] (aureis *Baehrens*)   165 extenuata *GR* maloque *O*   170 fers *O*   in vidit *G*   171 ne] non *Macrobius, Petrarca*   172 littora *O, Macrobius*   pupes *O*   174 cretam *GR*   175 hic *GR*   176 consilia in *η*: consilium *OG*, conscilium *R*   nostris *om. O*   requiesset *η*: requisisset *V*   177 refferam *O*   nitar *ζη* 178 Idaeosne *Parth., teste. Av.*[2] o 2[v], idoneos ne *V* (yd- *G*), Idmoneos ne *R*[2]   at *Puccius,* ah *B. Guarinus*: a *V*   179 pontum *GR*   ubi dividit *V*: ubi *del. Puccius*   180 impatris *O*, in patris *GR, corr. R*[2]   quem ne] ipsam ne q *G*, quem ne *G*[1], quem ve *R*[2]

respersum iuvenem fraterna caede secuta?
coniugis an fido consoler memet amore?
quine fugit lentos incurvans gurgite remos?
praeterea nullo colitur sola insula tecto,
nec patet egressus pelagi cingentibus undis.   185
nulla fugae ratio, nulla spes: omnia muta,
omnia sunt deserta, ostentant omnia letum.
non tamen ante mihi languescent lumina morte,
nec prius a fesso secedent corpore sensus,
quam iustam a divis exposcam prodita multam   190
caelestumque fidem postrema comprecer hora.
quare facta virum multantes vindice poena
Eumenides, quibus anguino redimita capillo
frons exspirantis praeportat pectoris iras,
huc huc adventate, meas audite querellas,   195
quas ego, vae miserae, imis proferre medullis
cogor inops, ardens, amenti caeca furore.
quae quoniam verae nascuntur pectore ab imo,
vos nolite pati nostrum vanescere luctum,
sed quali solam Theseus me mente reliquit,   200
tali mente, deae, funestet seque suosque."

    has postquam maesto profudit pectore voces,
supplicium saevis exposcens anxia factis,
annuit invicto caelestum numine rector;
quo motu tellus atque horrida contremuerunt   205
aequora concussitque micantia sidera mundus.
ipse autem caeca mentem caligine Theseus
consitus oblito dimisit pectore cuncta
quae mandata prius constanti mente tenebat,

186 *Petrarca, De remediis utriusque fortunae 1.33*

---

182 consoles me manet *O*   183 qui ne *O*, qui ve *GR*   lentos] ventos *GR*
184 colitur *A. Palmer*: litus *V*   185 pater *R*   186 racio *R, corr. R²*   187 deserti *G*,
corr. G¹   189 affesso *O*   190 iusta *O*   adivis *V*, a divis *R²*   muletam *O*, mulctam *GR*
191 comprecer ζη, comprecor *V*   192 mulctantes *V*   193 eumenydes *GR*   194 postportat *O*
(cf. 11)   195 meas] et meas *GR (corr. R²)*   querelas *GR*   196 miserae *Ric. 606, θ:*
misera *V*   imis] alr. imis *Rᵃ*, ex imis *Lond. add. 12005, Par. 8232, Casaubon, Vulpius:*
extremis *V*   198 vere *V*   200 quali solam ζη: qualis sola *V*   reliquid *O*   201 fimestet *G*,
corr. G²   204 invicto a: invito *V*   205 quo motu *Heyse:* quomodo tunc *V*   207 mentem θ,
mentis η: mente *V*   208 cunta *GR*

dulcia nec maesto sustollens signa parenti   210
sospitem Erectheum se ostendit visere portum.
namque ferunt olim, classi cum moenia divae
linquentem gnatum ventis concrederet Aegeus,
talia complexum iuveni mandata dedisse:
"gnate mihi longe iucundior unice vita,   215
gnate, ego quem in dubios cogor dimittere casus,
reddite in extrema nuper mihi fine senectae,
quandoquidem fortuna mea ac tua fervida virtus
eripit invito mihi te, cui languida nondum
lumina sunt gnati cara saturata figura,   220
non ego te gaudens laetanti pectore mittam,
nec te ferre sinam fortunae signa secundae,
sed primum multas expromam mente querellas,
canitiem terra atque infuso pulvere foedans;
inde infecta vago suspendam lintea malo,   225
nostros ut luctus nostraeque incendia mentis
carbasus obscurata dicet ferrugine Hibera.
quod tibi si sancti concesserit incola Itoni,
quae nostrum genus ac sedes defendere Erecthei
annuit, ut tauri respergas sanguine dextram,   230
tum vero facito ut memori tibi condita corde
haec vigeant mandata, nec ulla oblitteret aetas;
ut simul ac nostros invisent lumina collis
funestam antennae deponant undique vestem
candidaque intorti sustollant vela rudentes,   235
quam primum cernens ut laeta gaudia mente
agnoscam, cum te reducem aetas prospera sistet."
haec mandata prius constanti mente tenentem
Thesea ceu pulsae ventorum flamine nubes

210 sustolens *GR, corr. R*² 211 Erechtheum *Vossius:* ereptum *V* viscere *G*
212 classicum *O* moenia *R primo, Ald.:* moenico *OGR*¹ die *R*ᵃ 213 concrederet *Av.:*
cum crederet *V* egens *V, corr. R*² 215 gnati *O* longe *Hoeufft:* longa *V* 216 qm̄
(*proprie* quoniam) *O* dimictere *R, corr. R*² 217 rediite *G, corr. G*¹ extremae
Av. 219 quem *GR, corr. R*² 221 lectanti *O* mictam *R, corr. R*² 223 querelas *GR*
224 caniciem *OG,* -tiem *R* infulso *V, corr. R*² fedans *O,* fe?ans *G (corr. G*¹), fedens *R*
(*corr. R*¹) 227 obscura *R*² 228 itoni *H. Barbarus:* ithomi *Om,* yth- *GR* 229 ac ζη: has *V*
Erechthei *Vossius:* freti *V* 230 annuat *Mont.* (*et Ald.*) 231 tu *GR* 232 oblitteret *O,*
oblitteret *G,* obliterat *R,* obliteret *R*² 233 ac ζη: hec *V* 234 antēnene ne *O,* antennē
ne *G, corr. R* 235 sustolant *OR,* substolant *G, corr. R*² vella *O* 237 aetas] sors *Ald.*
et A. Guarinus sistet *O,* sistens *G,* sistant *R,* sistent *G*¹*R*¹(*V?*) 238 cont- *G, corr. G*¹
239 seu *V, corr. R*²

aerium nivei montis liquere cacumen.   240
at pater, ut summa prospectum ex arce petebat,
anxia in assiduos absumens lumina fletus,
cum primum inflati conspexit lintea veli,
praecipitem sese scopulorum e vertice iecit,
amissum credens immiti Thesea fato.   245
sic, funesta domus ingressus tecta paterna
morte, ferox Theseus, qualem Minoidi luctum
obtulerat mente immemori, talem ipse recepit.
quae tum prospectans cedentem maesta carinam
multiplices animo volvebat saucia curas.   250.
    at parte ex alia florens volitabat Iacchus
cum thiaso Satyrorum et Nysigenis Silenis,
te quaerens, Ariadna, tuoque incensus amore.

 .   .   .   .

quae tum alacres passim lymphata mente furebant
euhoe bacchantes, euhoe capita inflectentes.   255
harum pars tecta quatiebant cuspide thyrsos,
pars e divolso iactabant membra iuvenco,
pars sese tortis serpentibus incingebant,
pars obscura cavis celebrabant orgia cistis,
orgia quae frustra cupiunt audire profani;   260
plangebant aliae proceris tympana palmis,
aut tereti tenuis tinnitus aere ciebant;
multis raucisonos efflabant cornua bombos
barbaraque horribili stridebat tibia cantu.
    talibus amplifice vestis decorata figuris   265
pulvinar complexa suo velabat amictu.
quae postquam cupide spectando Thessala pubes
expleta est, sanctis coepit decedere divis.

---

240 aereum *O*   242 ansia *GR, corr. R²*   243 infecti *Sabellicus et B. Guarinus*   linthea *OR,
corr. R¹*   veli] sueti *G, corr. G¹ et G²*   244 et vertice *G, corr. G²*   245 inmiti *O,*
īmitti *G,* īmiti *G¹R*   facto *O*   247 minoidi δ: minoida *V*   249 quem *G, corr. G²*   tum ϵ:
tamen *V*   aspectans *R²* (al. *praescr. R²bis*)   credentem *O*   251 parte δ: pater *V*   iachus *V*
252 tum *O*   thyaso *G*   sathirorum *O,* satyrorum *GR*   nisi genis *V,* nisigenis *R²*
253 et querens *OR,* et querenus *G, corr. R²*   ariadna *β²*: adriana *V*   *Post* 253 *lacunam
statuit Bergk*   254 quae tum alacres *Bergk,* quicum *a. Baehrens,* cui Thyades *O. Skutsch*
(*fort. recte*): qui tum alacres *V*   linphata *O*   255 euhoe ... euhoe *a* (euoe ... euoe
Parth.): euche ... euche *V*   256 horum ζ   thirsos *OG,* tirsos *R*   257 edivolso *Vm,*
e div- *R²*   259 canis *OR* (*corr. R¹*)   260 orgiacȝ *O*   prophani *O*   261 timpana *O*
262 tenais *O*   tintinitus *GR* (*corr. R²*)   263 multis *Puccius*: multi *V*   efflabant *β*:
efflebant *V*   264 horibili *G*   267 thesala *O,* thesalia *GR,* thesala *R²*

hic, qualis flatu placidum mare matutino
horrificans Zephyrus proclivas incitat undas,   270
Aurora exoriente vagi sub limina Solis,
quae tarde primum clementi flamine pulsae
procedunt leviterque sonant plangore cachinni,
post vento crescente magis magis increbescunt,
purpureaque procul nantes ab luce refulgent: 275
sic tum vestibuli linquentes regia tecta
ad se quisque vago passim pede discedebant.
quorum post abitum princeps e vertice Peli
advenit Chiron portans silvestria dona:
nam quoscumque ferunt campi, quos Thessala magnis   280
montibus ora creat, quos propter fluminis undas
aura parit flores tepidi fecunda Favoni,
hos indistinctis plexos tulit ipse corollis;
quo permulsa domus iucundo risit odore.
confestim Penios adest, viridantia Tempe,   285
Tempe, quae silvae cingunt super impendentes,
Haemonisin linquens claris celebranda choreis,
non vacuus: namque ille tulit radicitus altas
fagos ac recto proceras stipite laurus,
non sine nutanti platano lentaque sorore   290
flammati Phaethontis et aeria cupressu.
haec circum sedes late contexta locavit,
vestibulum ut molli velatum fronde vireret.
post hunc consequitur sollerti corde Prometheus,

274 Petrarca, Epistolae familiares 5.5.11

---

269 hec *O*   270 cephirus *O*   proclivit *O*, -ivis *O*[1]   271 sub limina *β*: sublimia *V*
273 leviterque *O*, leviter *GR*: leni *θ*   resonant *ηθ*   chachini *OG*   275 refulgent *ζ*:
refulgens *V*   276 tum *β*: tamen *V*, tibi *m*, tamen *m*[2], al. tibi *m*[2] *(apud R)*   linquentes *α*:
linquentis *V*   277 ad *θ*: at *V*   278 abitum *OG*[3(+)] *(et β primo)*: habitum *GR (et β bis)*
(post h- *Gm*, posth- *R*)   evertice *V*, e vertice *R*[2]   peley *O*, pelei *GR*   279 chyron *G*
280 quoscunque *Ald.*: quodcumque *V*   campi *ηθ*: campis *V*   thesalia *O*, thesala *GR*
magis *OG*, magnis *R*   282 aurea *V, corr. R*[2]   prit *V*, parit *m*: aperit *Housman*
facunda *R, corr. R*[2]   283 in dist- *G*   corulis *OG*, curulis *R*, al. corollis *R*[2]   284 quo
Diez. 37, quis *Calph.*: quod *O*, quot *GR*   285 penies *V*, (a)l. -os *R*[2]: peneios *(η)*, Peneos
1472   adest *εζ*, adit *Ald.*: adest ut *V*   286 tempeꝗ *OR*, tempeꝗ *G*, tempe q̄ *R*[2], tempe
que *m*   287 Haemonisin *Heinsius*, Naiasin *Haupt*, Dryasin *Lee, alii alia*: minosim *V*
claris *Ald.*: doris *V*   288 non vacuos *Bergk* (-uus *iam B. Guarinus*): non accuos *O*,
non acuos *GR*, al. nonacrios *R*[2]   289 fages *O*   290 mutanti *V, corr. R*[2]   sorore *ζ*:
sororum *V*   291 flamati *O*, flamanti *GR*   phetontis *V*   292 tircum *O*   contesta *V,
corr. R*[2]   293 vellatum *V, corr. R*[2]

extenuata gerens veteris vestigia poenae,   295
quam quondam silici restrictus membra catena
persoluit pendens e verticibus praeruptis.
inde pater divum sancta cum coniuge natisque
advenit caelo, te solum, Phoebe, relinquens
unigenamque simul cultricem montibus Idri: 300
Pelea nam tecum pariter soror aspernata est,
nec Thetidis taedas voluit celebrare iugalis.

  qui postquam niveis flexerunt sedibus artus,
large multiplici constructae sunt dape mensae,
cum interea infirmo quatientes corpora motu   305
veridicos Parcae coeperunt edere cantus.
his corpus tremulum complectens undique vestis
candida purpurea talos incinxerat ora,
at roseae niveo residebant vertice vittae,
aeternumque manus carpebant rite laborem.   310
laeva colum molli lana retinebat amictum,
dextera tum leviter deducens fila supinis
formabat digitis, tum prono in pollice torquens
libratum tereti versabat turbine fusum,
atque ita decerpens aequabat semper opus dens,   315
laneaque aridulis haerebant morsa labellis,
quae prius in levi fuerant exstantia filo;
ante pedes autem candentis mollia lanae
vellera virgati custodibant calathisci.
haec tum clarisona vellentes vellera voce   320
talia divino fuderunt carmine fata,
carmine, perfidiae quod post nulla arguet aetas.

  o decus eximium magnis virtutibus augens,
Emathiae tutamen, Opis carissime nato,
accipe, quod laeta tibi pandunt luce sorores,   325

295 pena *V*, pęnę *R* ²   296 quam ζ: qua *V*   resittus *O*   cathena *O*, chatena *G*   297 evert- *V*
298 divi *V*, divum *m*   natisque *α*: gnatisque *V*   300 ydri *V*: Idae (*η*), ydae *β* ², Iri
Ellis, alii alia   301 palea *OR*   302 thedas *O*   305 metu *G, corr. G* ¹   306 ceperunt *GR*,
teperunt *O*   307 vestis *Parth.*: questus *V*   308 talos *B. Guarinus*: tuos *V*   intinxerat *OR*
309 rosę *Ric. 606 primo*: roseo *V*   niveo (*θ*): nivee *GR*, vinee *O*   311 collum *V, corr. R* ²
312 filia *O*   313 digittis *O*   police *V, corr. R* ²   315 epus *O*   dans (?) *G, corr. G* ²
318 molia *O*   319 velera *GR, corr. R* ²   custodiebant *GR*   calathisci *η*: calathisti *V*
320 vellentes *Fruterius*, pectentes *Statius*, pernentes *Camps*: pellentes *V*   velera *R*,
corr. R ²   324 tutamen, Opis] *ita distinxit Housman*: tutum opus *V*, al. tu tñ opis *R* ²

veridicum oraclum; sed vos, quae fata sequuntur,
    currite ducentes subtegmina, currite, fusi.
adveniet tibi iam portans optata maritis
Hesperus, adveniet fausto cum sidere coniunx,
quae tibi flexanimo mentem perfundat amore,   330
languidulosque paret tecum coniungere somnos,
levia substernens robusto brachia collo.
    currite ducentes subtegmina, currite, fusi.
nulla domus tales umquam contexit amores,
nullus amor tali coniunxit foedere amantes,   335
qualis adest Thetidi, qualis concordia Peleo.
    currite ducentes subtegmina, currite, fusi.
nascetur vobis expers terroris Achilles,
hostibus haud tergo, sed forti pectore notus,
qui persaepe vago victor certamine cursus   340
flammea praevertet celeris vestigia cervae.
    currite ducentes subtegmina, currite, fusi.
non illi quisquam bello se conferet heros,
cum Phrygii Teucro manabunt sanguine <campi,>
Troicaque obsidens longinquo moenia bello   345
periuri Pelopis vastabit tertius heres.
    currite ducentes subtegmina, currite, fusi.
illius egregias virtutes claraque facta
saepe fatebuntur gnatorum in funere matres,
cum incultum cano solvent a vertice crinem   350
putriaque infirmis variabunt pectora palmis.
    currite ducentes subtegmina, currite, fusi.

327 Macrobius, Saturnalia 6.1.41

---

326 oraculum *V*   vosque facta secuntur *O*   327 sub tegmina *GR*, subtegmine *O*, corr. *O*[1]
curite *G*   328 aptata *V, corr. R*[2]   329 Hespeus *O*   considere *O*   330 om. *O*   flexanimo
Muretus: flexo animo *GR*   mentis p. amorem *GR*   331 somnos *β:* sonos *V*   332 venia *O*
334 tales umquam (*η*): u. t. *V*   336 tetidi *O, corr. O*[1]   concordie *R, corr. R*[1]   341 flamea *V*
prevertet *β:* pervertet *O*, prevertit *GR*   342 sub tegmina *V*   344 frigii *O*, phrigii *GR*,
phrygii *m*   teucto *O*, teuero *G, corr. R*   manebunt *O*   campi *Puccius (et β*[2]), rivi *Calph.*,
trunci *β* (teucri *a*): teuen *O*, tenen *GR*, al. teuen *R*[2]   346 tercius *V*   347 subtegmina *O*,
sub tegmine *GR* (-a *m*)   350 *sic Baehrens*   incultum] in civos *O*, incivum *O*[1], incivium *G*,
in civium *R*, in cinerem *εζ*   canos *V*   soleunt *O*   crimen *O*, crines *GR*   351 putriaque
Heinsius: putridaque *V*   in firmis *G*   352 sub tegmine *R*, sub tegmina *GR*[2]

namque velut densas praecerpens messor aristas
sole sub ardenti flaventia demetit arva,
Troiugenum infesto prosternet corpora ferro. 355
    currite ducentes subtegmina, currite, fusi.
testis erit magnis virtutibus unda Scamandri,
quae passim rapido diffunditur Hellesponto,
cuius iter caesis angustans corporum acervis
alta tepefaciet permixta flumina caede. 360
    currite ducentes subtegmina, currite, fusi.
denique testis erit morti quoque reddita praeda,
cum teres excelso coacervatum aggere bustum
excipiet niveos perculsae virginis artus.
    currite ducentes subtegmina, currite, fusi. 365
nam simul ac fessis dederit fors copiam Achivis
urbis Dardaniae Neptunia solvere vincla,
alta Polyxenia madefient caede sepulcra;
quae, velut ancipiti succumbens victima ferro,
proiciet truncum summisso poplite corpus. 370
    currite ducentes subtegmina, currite, fusi.
quare agite optatos animi coniungite amores.
accipiat coniunx felici foedere divam,
dedatur cupido iam dudum nupta marito.
    currite ducentes subtegmina, currite, fusi. 375
non illam nutrix orienti luce revisens
hesterno collum poterit circumdare filo, 377
anxia nec mater discordis maesta puellae 379
secubitu caros mittet sperare nepotes. 380
    currite ducentes subtegmina, currite, fusi.

talia praefantes quondam felicia Pelei
carmina divino cecinerunt pectore Parcae.

353–6 *desunt in R, add. R²* 353 praecerpens *Statius:* praeterriens *G,* praecernens *OR²*
dēpsas *O* cultor *GR* 355 tronigenum *O,* trouigenum *G, corr. R²* prosternens *R²*
ferrum *O* 358 hellesponto *a:* elesponto *V* 359 cessis *O* 360 lumina *G* 361, 365, 371,
375, 378 sub tegmine *R,* sub tegmina *R²* 364 percus
sae *Parth.* 366 ac ζ: hanc *V* fons *O*
368 polixenia *O,* polisenia *GR* madefient η, mitescent ζ: madescent *V* 369 subccubens *G,*
succubens *G¹* 370 proiiciet *G* sumisso *O* 372 agitte *O,* agit *R (corr. R¹)* añ *O*
377 hesterno γ: esterno *O,* externo *GR* 378 (= 375) *ut spurium secl. Bergk, alii*
379–81 *om. O* 380 se cubitu *GR* mictet *R, corr. R²* 381 sub tegmina ducite *GR*
382 peley *O* 383 cecinerunt β, cecinere e *Baehrens:* cecinere *GR,* cernere *O*

praesentes namque ante domos invisere castas
heroum, et sese mortali ostendere coetu,   385
caelicolae nondum spreta pietate solebant.
saepe pater divum templo in fulgente residens,
annua cum festis venissent sacra diebus,
conspexit terra centum procumbere tauros.
saepe vagus Liber Parnasi vertice summo   390
Thyiadas effusis evantis crinibus egit,
cum Delphi tota certatim ex urbe ruentes
acciperent laeti divum fumantibus aris.
saepe in letifero belli certamine Mavors
aut rapidi Tritonis era aut Rhamnusia virgo   395
armatas hominum est praesens hortata catervas.
sed postquam tellus scelere est imbuta nefando
iustitiamque omnes cupida de mente fugarunt,
perfudere manus fraterno sanguine fratres,
destitit extinctos natus lugere parentes,   400
optavit genitor primaevi funera nati,
liber uti nuptae poteretur flore novellae,
ignaro mater substernens se impia nato
impia non verita est divos scelerare penates.
omnia fanda nefanda malo permixta furore   405
iustificam nobis mentem avertere deorum.
quare nec talis dignantur visere coetus,
nec se contingi patiuntur lumine claro.

385 heroum et sese *Io. Bapt. Sigicellus, teste Statio* (et *iam 1472*): nereus se
se *V   Post* 386 languidior tenera cui pedens sicula beta (*cf. 67.21*) *V*: del. *Parth.*
387 in fulgente *G, corr. G²   residens Baehrens*: revisens *V*   388 cum η (qū *1473*):
dum *V*   venissent η: venisset *V*   duobus *O, corr. O¹*   389 terram *O*   cemtum *R,
corr. R¹*   procurrere (currus) β   tauros *Lond. add. 10386*: currus *V*   390 sumo *O*
391 thiadas *O,* thyadas *GR*   ovantis *R²*   esit *O*   392 certatim *a*: certatum *V*   ruentes ζη:
tuentes *V*   393 acciperent ζη: acciperet *V*   lacti *V,* al. leti *R²*   spumantibus η
394 mauros *G*   395 ramnusia *1472,* amarunsia *Baehrens*: ranusia *GR,* ramunsia *O*
396 ortata *O*   397 scelus tellus *O, corr. O¹*   nephando *O*   398 iusticiamque *OG,*
iustitiamque *R*   399 fratres] manus fratres *R, corr. R¹*   400 natus *O,* natos *GR*   402 uti
nuptae *Maehly,* ut hinc nuptae *Baehrens*: ut in nupte *O,* ut inn- *G,* ut inupte *R*
poteretur η: potiretur *V*   novellae *Baehrens*: noverce *V,* -cae *R²*   404 penates (*eras.*)
Bodl. Canon. 33 (penates *1472*): parentes *V*   406 iusticiam *G, corr. G²*   mente
advertere *O*

65

Etsi me assiduo defectum cura dolore
   sevocat a doctis, Hortale, virginibus,
nec potis est dulcis Musarum expromere fetus
   mens animi, tantis fluctuat ipsa malis –
namque mei nuper Lethaeo in gurgite fratris   5
   pallidulum manans alluit unda pedem,
Troia Rhoeteo quem subter litore tellus
   ereptum nostris obterit ex oculis.

. . . .

   numquam ego te, vita frater amabilior,   10
aspiciam posthac? at certe semper amabo,
   semper maesta tua carmina morte canam,
qualia sub densis ramorum concinit umbris
   Daulias, absumpti fata gemens Ityli. –
sed tamen in tantis maeroribus, Hortale, mitto   15
   haec expressa tibi carmina Battiadae,
ne tua dicta vagis nequiquam credita ventis
   effluxisse meo forte putes animo,
ut missum sponsi furtivo munere malum
   procurrit casto virginis e gremio,   20
quod miserae oblitae molli sub veste locatum,
   dum adventu matris prosilit, excutitur,
atque illud prono praeceps agitur decursu,
   huic manat tristi conscius ore rubor.

65 5 *Petrarca, Epistolae familiares 24.5.19*

---

65 1 defectu *O*, confectum *Gm*, –ttum *R*, al. defectum *R*²   2 sevocat ζη: sed vacat *V*
3 dulcis musarum ζη (-ces η): dulcissimus harum *V* (havum *O*)   fretus *O*, fletus ε
5 letheo θ, lethaeo in *Parth.*: loethi *O*, lethei *GR*, *Petrarca*   factis *O*   6 pallidullum *O*
7 Tidia *O*, Tydia *GR*, al. Troia *R*²   retheo *O*, rhaeeteo *G*, rheetheo *R*, rhetheo *R*²
supter *G*, *corr.* *G*¹   littore *O*   9 *om.* *V*   11 aspitiam *R*   at ζ: aut *V*   12 carmina γ:
carmine *V*   canam ζ: tegam *V*   14 Daulias η: Bauilla *O*, Baiula *GR*, al. Dauilas *R*²
assumpta *O*, asumpti *G*, assumpti *R*   facta gemes *O*   ithilei *O*, ythilei *G*, ithiley *R*
15 memroribus *R*, *corr.* *R*¹   16 battiade β²: acciade *G*, actiade *OR*, bactiade (*adscripta*
b *littera perquam minuta*) *R*²   18 efluxisse *O*, effuxisse *G* (*corr.* *G*¹)   20 proccurit
(c *exp.* *O*¹) *O*   21 locataum (a *exp.* *O*¹) *O*   23 illic ... preces *O*   24 orbe *R*,
corr. *R*²

66

Omnia qui magni dispexit lumina mundi,
    qui stellarum ortus comperit atque obitus,
flammeus ut rapidi solis nitor obscuretur,
    ut cedant certis sidera temporibus,
ut Triviam furtim sub Latmia saxa relegans   5
    dulcis amor gyro devocet aerio:
idem me ille Conon caelesti <in> lumine vidit
    e Bereniceo vertice caesariem
fulgentem clare, quam multis illa dearum
    levia protendens brachia pollicita est,   10
qua rex tempestate novo auctus hymenaeo
    vastatum finis iverat Assyrios,
dulcia nocturnae portans vestigia rixae,
    quam de virgineis gesserat exuviis.
estne novis nuptis odio Venus? anne parentum   15
    frustrantur falsis gaudia lacrimulis,
ubertim thalami quas intra limina fundunt?
    non, ita me divi, vera gemunt, iuerint.
id mea me multis docuit regina querellis
    invisente novo proelia torva viro.   20
et tu non orbum luxti deserta cubile,
    sed fratris cari flebile discidium,
cum penitus maestas exedit cura medullas.
    ut tibi tunc toto pectore sollicitae
sensibus ereptis mens excidit! at <te> ego certe   25
    cognoram a parva virgine magnanimam.

66 15 *Hieremias de Montagnone, Compendium moralium notabilium 4.6.3*

------

66 1 dispexit *Calph.*: despexit *V*   2 obitus (ε): habitus *V*   3 flameus *V* obsculetur *O*
4 ceteris *O*   5 sub latmia (η): sublamina *O*, sublimia *GR*, al. sublamia vel subli̯mina
(*sic*) *R*²   relegans η: religans *V*   6 gyro *1472* (guro *Ellis*), clivo ε: guioclero *V*   7 in
lumine *Vossius* (lumine *iam* ς), limine *Heinsius*, in limite *Doering*, in culmine *Maehly*:
numine *V*   8 e beroniceo η: ebore′ niceo *V*   9 dare *G, corr. G*²   cunctis *Haupt (fort.
recte)*   10 policita *O*   11 qua rex *1473*: quare ex *V* avectus (ε), *Peiper* himeneo *O*
12 vastatum ςη: vastum *V* iverat γ: ierat *V* assirios *V*   13 noctume *G, corr. G*²
14 exivius *O*   15 anne θ: atque *V*   17 uberum *O* limina ς: lumina *V*   18 divi β: diu *V*
geniunt *O* iuerint *1472*: iuverint *V*   19 q̄relis *O*   21 et *V*, al. at *R*² non] vero (ūo) *O*
22 fratris] factis *O* dissidium *GR*   23 cum] quam *Bentley*, tum *Lachmann*, ut *Baehrens*
24 ibi *G* tunc *O*, nunc *GR*, al. tunc *R*² sollicitae (η): solicitet *V*   25 ex cidit *R*, exc- *R*²
te *add. Trinc.*   26 magnanimam ςη: magnanima *V*

anne bonum oblita es facinus, quo regium adepta es
    coniugium, quod non fortior ausit alis?
sed tum maesta virum mittens quae verba locuta es!
    Iuppiter, ut tristi lumina saepe manu!   30
quis te mutavit tantus deus? an quod amantes
    non longe a caro corpore abesse volunt?
atque ibi me cunctis pro dulci coniuge divis
    non sine taurino sanguine pollicita es,
si reditum tetulisset. is haud in tempore longo   35
    captam Asiam Aegypti finibus addiderat.
quis ego pro factis caelesti reddita coetu
    pristina vota novo munere dissoluo.
invita, o regina, tuo de vertice cessi,
    invita: adiuro teque tuumque caput,   40
digna ferat quod si quis inaniter adiurarit:
    sed qui se ferro postulet esse parem?
ille quoque eversus mons est, quem maximum in oris
    progenies Thiae clara supervehitur,
cum Medi peperere novum mare, cumque iuventus   45
    per medium classi barbara navit Athon.
quid facient crines, cum ferro talia cedant?
    Iuppiter, ut Chalybon omne genus pereat,
et qui principio sub terra quaerere venas
    institit ac ferri stringere duritiem!   50
abiunctae paulo ante comae mea fata sorores
    lugebant, cum se Memnonis Aethiopis
unigena impellens nutantibus aera pennis
    obtulit Arsinoes Locridos ales equus,

27 quo *Puccius*: quam *V*   adepta es *Calph.*: adeptos *O*, adeptus *GR*   28 quo ζη   forcior *O*: fortius *ed. Iuntina anni 1503*   ausit *Puccius, ex eisdem fortasse codicibus quos citat P. Nucettus apud Robortellum*: aut sit *V*   29 cum *O*   mictens *R, corr. R²*   que *GR*, quae *R²*   30 tersti *Av.*   32 adesse *G*   33 me *Puccius*: pro *V*   cuntis *G*   34 taurino *om. O*   35 sed *V*, al. si *R²*   redditum *O*   tetulisset ζ: te tulisset *V*   haud *Ald.*, haut *Statius*: aut *V*   36 asyam *GR*   38 disoluo *O*   40 capud *OR (corr. R²)*   41 feratque *O*   adiurarit *Av.*: adiuraret *V*   43 quae *O*   maximum *Puccius*: maxima *V*   44 Thiae *Vossius*, Phtiae *iam* η, Phthiae *B. Pisanus, Puccium ut videtur secutus*: phitie *O*, phytie *GR*   sup?vehitur *O, corr. O¹*, super vehitur *G*   45 tum *OG*, cum *R*   peperere η: propere *V*   cumque *O*, atque *GR*, al. cumque *R²*   48 chalybon *vel* chalybum *Politianus*: celerum *O*, celitum *GR*, al. celorum *R²*, al. celtum *R²bis*   49 querrere *O*   50 ferri (*ita iam* ζη) stringere *Heyse*: ferris fingere *O*, ferris fringere *GR*   51 facta *O*   52 menonis ethyopis *GR*   53 mutantibus *R, corr. R²*: nictantibus *Bentley*   aeria *R*   54 arsinoes *O*, asineos *GR*, al. arsinoes *R²*   Locridos *Bentley*, Locricos *Stat.*: elocridicos *V*   ales ζ: alis *V*

isque per aetherias me tollens avolat umbras   55
    et Veneris casto collocat in gremio.
ipsa suum Zephyritis eo famulum legarat,
    Graia Canopeis incola litoribus.
hic, liquidi vario ne solum in lumine caeli
    ex Ariadnaeis aurea temporibus   60
fixa corona foret, sed nos quoque fulgeremus
    devotae flavi verticis exuviae,
uvidulam a fluctu cedentem ad templa deum me
    sidus in antiquis diva novum posuit.
Virginis et saevi contingens namque Leonis   65
    lumina, Callisto iuncta Lycaoniae,
vertor in occasum, tardum dux ante Booten,
    qui vix sero alto mergitur Oceano.
sed quamquam me nocte premunt vestigia divum,
    lux autem canae Tethyi restituit,   70
(pace tua fari hic liceat, Rhamnusia virgo,
    namque ego non ullo vera timore tegam,
nec si me infestis discerpent sidera dictis,
    condita quin nostri pectoris evoluam)
non his tam laetor rebus, quam me afore semper,   75
    afore me a dominae vertice discrucior,
quicum ego, dum virgo quondam fuit, omnibus expers
    unguentis, una vilia multa bibi.

---

55 advolat *GR*   56 collocat *O*, advolat *GR*, al. collocat *R*²   57 cyphiritis *OG*, ciphiritis *R*, zyphyritis *R*²   legarat *OR*, legerat *G*, al. legarat *G*²   58 Graiia *Baehrens* (graia iam *Lachmann*): gracia *O*, gratia *GR*   canopeis *Tub.* (canopieis *ed. Rom.*), canopitis *Statius* (canobitis *iam Ald.*): canopicis *GR*, con- *O*   59 hic liquidi *Friedrich*: hi dii ven ibi *V*   lumine *a*, limine *θ*: numine *V* (mumine *R*)   60 ariadneis *θ*: adrianeis *V* avira *G*, corr. *G*²   61 nos *GR*, vos *O*   62 exuvie *R*, eximie *OG*   63 uvidulam *B. Guarinus*, uvidulum *ζη*: vindulum *V*, viridulum *R*²   afluctu *G*, corr. *G*²   ad flāma *R*, corr. *R*¹   deum me *ζη*: decum̄e *V*   66 Callistoe iuncta Lycaoniae *Parth.*: calixto iuxta licaonia *V*, calisto i.l. *aβ*   67 ocasum *OG* (corr. *G*²)   bootē *O*, boothen *G*, boothem *R*   69 quicquam *O*   70 autem *Diez. 37*: aut *V*   tethyi *B. Guarinus*: theti *V* restituit *Lachmann*: restituem *V*   71 parce *V*, corr. *R*²   Ramnusia *Calph.*: ranunsia *O*, ranusia *GR*   72 ullo] nullo *GR*   73 si me *θ*: sine *V*   discerpent *Ric. 606*, discerpant *θ*: diserpent *V*   74 candita *G*   qui *V*, al. quin *R*²   nostri *Watt*; veri *Ric. 606* (verei *Lachmann*): vere *V*   evoluam *1473*: evolue *V*   75 afore *Statius* (abfore iam *β*²): affore *V*   76 afore *Statius* (abfore iam *β*): affore *V*   discrutior *V*   77 omnibus *suspectum*: hymenis *Eschenburg et Wilamowitz*   78 una] nuptae *Morel*   vilia *Lobel*: milia *O*, millia *GR*

nunc vos, optato quas iunxit lumine taeda,
    non prius unanimis corpora coniugibus   80
tradite nudantes reiecta veste papillas
    quam iucunda mihi munera libet onyx,
vester onyx, casto colitis quae iura cubili.
    sed quae se impuro dedit adulterio,
illius a mala dona levis bibat irrita pulvis: 85
    namque ego ab indignis praemia nulla peto.
sed magis, o nuptae, semper concordia vestras,
    semper amor sedes incolat assiduus.
tu vero, regina, tuens cum sidera divam
    placabis festis luminibus Venerem,   90
unguinis expertem ne siris esse tuam me,
    sed potius largis effice muneribus
sidera cur iterent "utinam coma regia fiam,"
    proximus Hydrochoi fulgeret Oarion!

67

O dulci iucunda viro, iucunda parenti,
    salve, teque bona Iuppiter auctet ope,
ianua, quam Balbo dicunt servisse benigne
    olim, cum sedes ipse senex tenuit,
quamque ferunt rursus nato servisse maligne   5
    postquam es porrecto facta marita sene.
dic agedum nobis, quare mutata feraris
    in dominum veterem deseruisse fidem.
"Non (ita Caecilio placeam, cui tradita nunc sum)
    culpa mea est, quamquam dicitur esse mea,   10

79 quas *Calph.*: quem *V*, al. quam *R²*   80 prius *B. Guarinus*: post *V*   unanimis *θ* (-eis *Baehrens*): uno animus *V*   81 reiecta *η*: retecta *V*   82 quam *V*: quin *Lachmann* (*qui in* 80 non post *legerat*)   83 colitisꝗ *O*, colitis que *G*, queritus que *R*   85 levis b. d. *V*: *ordinem rest.* 1472   inita *G*   86 indignatis *O*, indigetis *GR*, al. indignis *R²*, al. indignatis *R²bis*   87 vestras *θ*: nostras *V*   91 unguinis *Bentley*: sanguinis *V*   ne *Baehrens*: non *V*   siris *Lachmann* (siveris *iam Scaliger*): vestris *V*   tuam *Av.*: tuum *V*   92 affice *θ*   93 cur retinent? *Pontanus*, corruerint *Lachmann*   utina *O*   94 Hydrochoi 1472: id rochoi *V* (idr- *G*)

67 4 senex] senes *O*   5 quamquam *O*   nato *Froehlich*, natae *Baehrens*: voto *V*   maligno *G*, malīgno *R*, *virgulam eras.* *R¹*(*R²*?)   6 es *Ald.*: est *V*   porecto *G*, porretto *R*, corr. *R²*   pacta *Badian*   marita *ς*: marite *V*   7 agedum *Calph.*: age de *V*   nobis *γδ*: vobis *V*   8 venerem *GR*   desseruisse *G, corr. G¹*   9 plateam *R*   10 quaquam *O*

nec peccatum a me quisquam pote dicere quicquam;
  verum †istius populi ianua quit† te facit,
qui, quacumque aliquid reperitur non bene factum,
  ad me omnes clamant: ianua, culpa tua est."
Non istuc satis est uno te dicere verbo,   15
  sed facere ut quivis sentiat et videat.
"Qui possum? nemo quaerit nec scire laborat."
  Nos volumus: nobis dicere ne dubita.
"Primum igitur, virgo quod fertur tradita nobis,
  falsum est. non illam vir prior attigerat,   20
languidior tenera cui pendens sicula beta
  numquam se mediam sustulit ad tunicam;
sed pater illusi gnati violasse cubile
  dicitur et miseram conscelerasse domum,
sive quod impia mens caeco flagrabat amore,   25
  seu quod iners sterili semine natus erat,
ut quaerendum unde <unde> foret nervosius illud
  quod posset zonam solvere virgineam."
Egregium narras, mira pietate, parentem,
  qui ipse sui gnati minxerit in gremium.   30
"Atqui non solum hoc dicit se cognitum habere
  Brixia Cycneae supposita speculae,
flavus qua molli percurrit flumine Mella,
  Brixia Veronae mater amata meae,
sed de Postumio et Corneli narrat amore,   35
  cum quibus illa malum fecit adulterium.
dixerit hic aliquis: quid? tu istaec, ianua, nosti,
  cui numquam domini limine abesse licet,
nec populum auscultare, sed hic suffixa tigillo
  tantum operire soles aut aperire domum?   40

12 istius] isti *R²*, isthaec *Par. 8458, alii* (istoc *β²*)   populo *ε*   qui te] quidque *Statius* (*fortasse* istud populi est "ianua quicque facit,")   16 qui vis *V*   senciat *G*   17 qui *Puccius*: quid *V*   possim *ζ*   18 nobis *δ*: vobis *V*   ve *O*   20 attigerat *η*: attigerit *V*   21 *om., post* 64.386 *habet O*   22 ad *Calph.*: hanc *V*   23 illusi *Baehrens*, ille sui *Scaliger*: illius *V*   27 ut *Bergk*: et *V*   quaerendum unde unde *Statius* (q. aliunde iam *Ald.*), quaerendus is unde *Lachmann*: querendus unde *V*   29 parentum *O*   30 sunt *O*   31 hoc dicit se *O*, se dicit *G*, se dicit hoc *R*   32 Cycneae *Vossius* (cycnea iam *Petreius, Pontanum secutus*): chinea *V* supposita speculae *Pontanus*, supposita in specula *Ald., Petreius*: suppositum specula *V* 33 qua *Zicàri*: quam *V*   moli *O*   praecurrit *Trinc.*   Mel(l)a *η*: melo *O*, mello *GR*   34 tuae *Trinc.*   35 posthumio *V*   narrat] amat *G*   37 dixit *O*   hic *G*, hec *O*, his *R* (*corr. R¹*) quid] qui *Ald.*   iste *V, corr. R²*   38 deum *O*   lumine *O*   39 ascultare *O*   hic *ζ*, hoc *γε*: hec *V*   sufixa *O*

saepe illam audivi furtiva voce loquentem
    solam cum ancillis haec sua flagitia,
nomine dicentem quos diximus, utpote quae mi
    speraret nec linguam esse nec auriculam.
praeterea addebat quendam, quem dicere nolo   45
    nomine, ne tollat rubra supercilia.
longus homo est, magnas cui lites intulit olim
    falsum mendaci ventre puerperium."

68(a)

Quod mihi fortuna casuque oppressus acerbo
    conscriptum hoc lacrimis mittis epistolium,
naufragum ut eiectum spumantibus aequoris undis
    sublevem et a mortis limine restituam,
quem neque sancta Venus molli requiescere somno   5
    desertum in lecto caelibe perpetitur,
nec veterum dulci scriptorum carmine Musae
    oblectant, cum mens anxia pervigilat:
id gratum est mihi, me quoniam tibi dicis amicum,
    muneraque et Musarum hinc petis et Veneris.   10
sed tibi ne mea sint ignota incommoda, Manli,
    neu me odisse putes hospitis officium,
accipe quis merser fortunae fluctibus ipse,
    ne amplius a misero dona beata petas.
tempore quo primum vestis mihi tradita pura est,   15
    iucundum cum aetas florida ver ageret,
multa satis lusi: non est dea nescia nostri,
    quae dulcem curis miscet amaritiem.
sed totum hoc studium luctu fraterna mihi mors
    abstulit. o misero frater adempte mihi,   20

41 audivit *R*   42 solam *ςϑ*: sola *V*   ancillis *quidam Venetus (apud Robortellum)*:
concillis *O*, conciliis *GR*   43 ut pete *O*   44 speraret *Calph.*: sperent *V*, speret *R²*
45 addebant *O*   46 ne *a*: te *V*   collat *GR, corr. R²*   47 cui *B. Guarinus et Pall.* (quoi
Lachmann): qui *V*   littes *O*   intullit *G*   48 mendaci *β*: mendacii *V*
68(a) 1 quo *O*   2 haec *O*   mittit *G*, mictit *R*, -tt- *R²*   3 naufragum *ςη*: naufragium *V*
6 disertum *G*   7 veterm (vet'm) *O*   8 ansia *O*   10 petit *G*   11 incommoda *γ*: commoda *V*
(comoda *R*)   manli *Ric. 606*, malli *a*, Mani *Lachmann*, mi Alli *Diels*: mali *V*, al. mauli *R²*
(*signum vocativi o add. supra G³*)   12 seu *G*   16 *om. O, post* 49 (i. cometas f. ut a.)
repet. V   17 luxi *R, corr. R²*   18 amaritionem *O*, amariritiem *G* (*corr. G¹*)   20 omis- *V*
(*corr. m*)

tu mea tu moriens fregisti commoda, frater,
    tecum una tota est nostra sepulta domus;
omnia tecum una perierunt gaudia nostra
    quae tuus in vita dulcis alebat amor.
cuius ego interitu tota de mente fugavi   25
    haec studia atque omnes delicias animi.
quare, quod scribis Veronae turpe Catullo
    esse, quod hic quisquis de meliore nota
frigida deserto tepefactet membra cubili,
    id, Manli, non est turpe, magis miserum est.   30
ignosces igitur si, quae mihi luctus ademit,
    haec tibi non tribuo munera, cum nequeo.
nam, quod scriptorum non magna est copia apud me,
    hoc fit, quod Romae vivimus: illa domus,
illa mihi sedes, illic mea carpitur aetas;   35
    huc una ex multis capsula me sequitur.
quod cum ita sit, nolim statuas nos mente maligna
    id facere aut animo non satis ingenuo,
quod tibi non utriusque petenti copia posta est:
    ultro ego deferrem, copia siqua foret.   40

68(b)

Non possum reticere, deae, qua me Allius in re
    iuverit aut quantis iuverit officiis,
ne fugiens saeclis obliviscentibus aetas
    illius hoc caeca nocte tegat studium;
sed dicam vobis, vos porro dicite multis   45
    milibus et facite haec carta loquatur anus.

   .   .   .   .

    notescatque magis mortuus atque magis,

21 comoda *OR* (*corr. m*)   24 in vita *a*: invita *V*   26 omnem *O*   delitias *R*   27 vetone *O*,
corr. O[1] catullo *ζ*: -e *V*   29 tepefactet *Bergk*, -fecit *γ*, -faxit *Lachmann*: tepefacit *V*, al.
-factat *R*[2] cubilli *O*   30 manli *ε*, *Ric. 606*, malli *β*, Mani *Lachmann*, mi, Alli *Schoell*:
mali *V*   31 ignoscens *O* siᴂ *R*, *corr. R*[2]   32 tum *O*   34 hec *O*   36 ima *O*   me]
mo *O*, *corr. O*[1]   38 ingenuo *a primo*, ingenio (al. ingenuo *in margine*) *a*[1]: ingenio *V*
39 hucusque *Nisbet*   posta *V*: praesto *Froehlich*, prompta *Baehrens*, parta *Schwabe*
40 deferrem (*η*): differrem *V* (differem *G*)
68(b) 41 qua me Allius *Scaliger*: quam fallius *V*   ire *O*, īre *G*, in re *R*   42 invenit *O*   viverit *O*
43 ne *Calph.* (nei *Baehrens*), non *β*: nec *V*   seclis *β*[1] *in margine*: sedis *V*   45 porto *O*
46 cerata *O*, certa *GR*, al. carta *R*[2]: cera *Statius*   47 *om. V*   48 notescamque *G*

nec tenuem texens sublimis aranea telam
    in deserto Alli nomine opus faciat.   50
nam mihi quam dederit duplex Amathusia curam
    scitis, et in quo me torruerit genere,
cum tantum arderem quantum Trinacria rupes
    lymphaque in Oetaeis Malia Thermopylis,
maesta neque assiduo tabescere lumina fletu   55
    cessarent tristique imbre madere genae,
qualis in aerii perlucens vertice montis
    rivus muscoso prosilit e lapide,
qui cum de prona praeceps est valle volutus,
    per medium densi transit iter populi,   60
dulce viatori lasso in sudore levamen,
    cum gravis exustos aestus hiulcat agros:
hic, velut in nigro iactatis turbine nautis
    lenius aspirans aura secunda venit
iam prece Pollucis, iam Castoris implorata,   65
    tale fuit nobis Allius auxilium.
is clausum lato patefecit limite campum,
    isque domum nobis isque dedit dominam
ad quam communes exerceremus amores.
    quo mea se molli candida diva pede   70
intulit et trito fulgentem in limine plantam
    innixa arguta constituit solea,
coniugis ut quondam flagrans advenit amore
    Protesilaeam Laodamia domum
inceptam frustra, nondum cum sanguine sacro   75
    hostia caelestis pacificasset eros.
nil mihi tam valde placeat, Rhamnusia virgo,
    quod temere invitis suscipiatur eris.

49 subtilis *Nisbet*   *Post* 49 *v.* 16 *iteratum V: del.* γδ   50 alli *O*, ali *GR*   51 nam] non *G*
52 torruerit *Turnebus (Adv.* 16.1*)*: corruerit *V*   54 limphaque *O*   oetaeis η: cetheis *O*,
eetheis *G*, cetheis *G*¹, oetheis *G*¹*bis*, oethis *R*   malia (ζ), maulia *V*   termopilis *O*,
termophilis *G*, termophylis *R*   55 lumina θ: nummula *O*, numula *GR*   56 cessarent θ:
cessare ne *V*   59 valle *Laur.* 36.23: valde *V*   voluptus *O, corr. O*¹   60 densi] properi
Nisbet   61 dulce *P. Laetus*: duce *V*   viatorum *O*, viatori *GR*, al. -rum *R*²   lasso η: basso *V*
levamen *Calph.*: levamus *V*   62 hiultat *O*   63 hic *GR*, hec *O*: ac *Pall.*   velud *R, corr. R*²
64 lenius β: levius *V*   65 implorata η: implorate *V*   66 allius *O*, <ve>l manllius *O*¹ *in
margine*, manlius *GR*: Manius *Lachmann*   67 classum *GR*   68 dominam *V*: dominae
Froehlich   72 inixa *O*   argulta *R, corr. R*¹   73 amorem *V, corr. R*²   74 prothesileam
(-tes- *O*) laudomia *V*   75 inceptam *Turnebus (Adv.* 21.17*)*: incepta *V*   76 heros *O*
77 rāmusia *O*, ranusia *GR*

quam ieiuna pium desiderat ara cruorem
    docta est amisso Laodamia viro,   80
coniugis ante coacta novi dimittere collum,
    quam veniens una atque altera rursus hiems
noctibus in longis avidum saturasset amorem,
    posset ut abrupto vivere coniugio,
quod scibant Parcae non longo tempore abesse,   85
    si miles muros isset ad Iliacos.
nam tum Helenae raptu primores Argivorum
    coeperat ad sese Troia ciere viros,
Troia (nefas!) commune sepulcrum Asiae Europaeque,
    Troia virum et virtutum omnium acerba cinis,   90
quae nunc et nostro letum miserabile fratri
    attulit. ei misero frater adempte mihi,
ei misero fratri iucundum lumen ademptum,
    tecum una tota est nostra sepulta domus;
omnia tecum una perierunt gaudia nostra,   95
    quae tuus in vita dulcis alebat amor.
quem nunc tam longe non inter nota sepulcra
    nec prope cognatos compositum cineres,
sed Troia obscena, Troia infelice sepultum
    detinet extremo terra aliena solo.   100
ad quam tum properans fertur <lecta> undique pubes
    Graeca penetralis deseruisse focos,
ne Paris abducta gavisus libera moecha
    otia pacato degeret in thalamo.
quo tibi tum casu, pulcerrima Laodamia,   105
    ereptum est vita dulcius atque anima
coniugium: tanto te absorbens vertice amoris
    aestus in abruptum detulerat barathrum,

68(b) 90 *Nonius vol. 1, p. 291 (Lindsay)*

---

79 desideret θ (*defideret iam* β¹): deficeret *V* (*et* β *primo, ut videtur*)   80 laudomia *V*
virgo *V, corr. R²G³*   81 novi *Trinc.*, novum β²: novit *OG*, venit novit *R* (venit *exp. R¹*)
al. vo- *R²*   84 abinnupto *O*   85 scirant *L. Mueller*, scibat *Lachmann*
abesse ζη: abisse *V*   86 similes *OR*, similles *G*   87 cum *O*   91 quae nunc et *Marcilius*,
quaene etiam *Heinsius*, quaeve etiam *Calph.*: que vetet id *V*   frater *V, al.* fratri *R²*
92 hei *GR*   frateter *GR, corr. G¹R²*   93 hei *V*   iocundumque limine *O*   ademptum α:
adeptum *V*   97 quem (η): que *V*   sepulcrea *G, corr. G¹*   98 cineris *V*   101 tuum *G*
lecta *add. Eldik,* simul *1472*, cuncta *Froehlich*   pupes *O*   102 foccos *O*   103 ne *G*, nec *OR*
pars *O*   104 octia *O*, ocia *GR*   paccato *O*   105 quo ζ: quod *V*   cum *G*   laodamia ζ:
laudomia *V*   108 arruptum *G, corr. G¹*

quale ferunt Grai Pheneum prope Cyllenaeum
    siccare emulsa pingue palude solum,   110
quod quondam caesis montis fodisse medullis
    audit falsiparens Amphitryoniades,
tempore quo certa Stymphalia monstra sagitta
    perculit imperio deterioris eri,
pluribus ut caeli tereretur ianua divis,   115
    Hebe nec longa virginitate foret.
sed tuus altus amor barathro fuit altior illo,
    qui tamen indomitam ferre iugum docuit.
nam nec tam carum confecto aetate parenti
    una caput seri nata nepotis alit,   120
qui, cum divitiis vix tandem inventus avitis
    nomen testatas intulit in tabulas,
impia derisi gentilis gaudia tollens
    suscitat a cano volturium capiti;
nec tantum niveo gavisa est ulla columbo   125
    compar, quae multo dicitur improbius
oscula mordenti semper decerpere rostro,
    quam quae praecipue multivola est mulier.
sed tu horum magnos vicisti sola furores,
    ut semel es flavo conciliata viro.   130
aut nihil aut paulo cui tum concedere digna
    lux mea se nostrum contulit in gremium,
quam circumcursans hinc illinc saepe Cupido
    fulgebat crocina candidus in tunica.
quae tamen etsi uno non est contenta Catullo,   135
    rara verecundae furta feremus erae,

109 fuerunt *G, corr. G*¹ Pheneum *Av.*: peneum *V* cilleneum *V* 110 siccare *Schrader*: siccari *V* (sicari *O*) 112 audit *Palmerius*: audet *V* falsi parens *R* amphytrioniadis *V* (-phi- *O*) 113 stimphalia *OR* 114 perculit β: pertulit *OR*, pertullit *G* deterrioris *G* heri *V* 115 terreretur *O*, treerretur *G*, tereretur *R*, terretur *G*¹*R*² 116 heb₃(= hebe et?) *O* 117 baratro *V* 118 tamen *Heyse*, tunc *Corradinus de Allio*: tuum *V* indomitam *Statius*: domitum *V* 119 nec tam carum *O*, nec causa carum *GR*, al. neque tam carum *R*² 122 ceratas *Schrader* 124 suscitat a θ (suscitata *iam a*): scuscitata *OR*, scusoitata *G*, scusitata *G*¹ voltarium *V* 126 compₚₒ *O*, comparq̄ *G*, compar q̄ *R* ī probius *G* 128 quam quae *Puccius* (?) *adn. Marc.* 12.127, quantum *Calph.*: quamquam *V* 129 tu horum η: tuorum *V* 130 es flavo ςη: efflavo *O*, eflavo *GR* 131 paulum *Colotius* tum *Trinc.*: tu *V* 132 contullit *G* 133 circum cursans *O*, circumc- *GR* 135 cotēpta catulo *O* (catullo *O*¹) 136 here *V*

ne nimium simus stultorum more molesti;
   saepe etiam Iuno, maxima caelicolum,
coniugis in culpa flagrantém contudit iram,
   noscens omnivoli plurima facta Iovis.   140
atqui nec divis homines componier aequum est

  .   .   .   .

  .   .   .   .

   ingratum tremuli tolle parentis onus.
nec tamen illa mihi dextra deducta paterna
   fragrantem Assyrio venit odore domum,
sed furtiva dedit media munuscula nocte   145
   ipsius ex ipso dempta viri gremio.
quare illud satis est, si nobis is datur unis
   quem lapide illa diem candidiore notat.

hoc tibi, quod potui, confectum carmine munus
   pro multis, Alli, redditur officiis,   150
ne vestrum scabra tangat robigine nomen
   haec atque illa dies atque alia atque alia.
huc addent divi quam plurima, quae Themis olim
   antiquis solita est munera ferre piis.
sitis felices et tu simul et tua vita,   155
   et domus <ipsa> in qua lusimus et domina,
et qui principio nobis †terram dedit aufert†
   a quo sunt primo omnia nata bona,
et longe ante omnes mihi quae me carior ipso est,
   lux mea, qua viva vivere dulce mihi est.   160

137 *Hieremias de Montagnone, Compendium moralium notabilium 2.1.5*

137 scimus *R*   139 contudit iram *Hertzberg*, concoquit iram *Lachmann*: cotidiana *O*, quot- *GR*   140 facta *V*: furta ζ   141 atqui θ, at quia δ: atque *V*   componier *Pal. 1652, Harl. 2778, Vat. 3269* (-iere *Bodl. e 3*): componere *V*   equum] fas *Urb. 812*   Post 141 *lacunam indicavit Marcilius*   142 opus *Postgate*   143 dextra θ: deastra *O*, de astra *GR*   144 fragrantem ηθ: flagrantem *V* (*cf.* 6.8)   145 furtiva *OG*, furtivᵃe *R* (a *supra scr. R¹*) media *Landor* (mĩa?), rara *Haupt*, muta *Heyse*: mira *V*   147 hiis *O*, his *GR*   148 diem 1473: dies *V*   candiore *O*   149 hoc *V* (*nisi* ħ= haec *O*)   quo *Muretus*   150 Alli *Scaliger*: aliis *V*   153 plurimaque *O*   155 sitis ζη: satis *V*   et tua vite *OG*, tua virtute (*om.* et) *R*, et tua vite *R¹, corr. R²*   156 ipsa *add.* ζη, *post* qua *add.* nos *alii*   luximus *R, corr. R²* 157 te trandedit (*sic*) *Scaliger*   auspex *Lipsius*   158 nota *R, corr. R¹*   bona (ζ): bono *V* 159 michiꝗ *O*, michi q̄ *GR*   160 dulce mihi est β, dulce mihi (*om.* est) ζ: m. d. est *V*

69

Noli admirari, quare tibi femina nulla,
    Rufe, velit tenerum supposuisse femur,
non si illam rarae labefactes munere vestis
    aut perluciduli deliciis lapidis.
laedit te quaedam mala fabula, qua tibi fertur   5
    valle sub alarum trux habitare caper.
hunc metuunt omnes, neque mirum: nam mala valde est
    bestia, nec quicum bella puella cubet.
quare aut crudelem nasorum interfice pestem,
    aut admirari desine cur fugiunt.   10

70

Nulli se dicit mulier mea nubere malle
    quam mihi, non si se Iuppiter ipse petat.
dicit; sed mulier cupido quod dicit amanti,
    in vento et rapida scribere oportet aqua.

71

Si cui iure bono sacer alarum obstitit hircus,
    aut si quem merito tarda podagra secat,
aemulus iste tuus, qui vestrum exercet amorem,
    mirifice est apte nactus utrumque malum.
nam quotiens futuit, totiens ulciscitur ambos: 5
    illam affligit odore, ipse perit podagra.

70 4 *Petrarca, Invectiva contra medicum 2; cf. Canzoniere 212.4*

———

69 2 ruffe *V*   3 non si illam rarae *Ald.* (non i. r. *iam Calph.*; carae *Ellis*, coae *Baehrens*):
nos illa mare *V*   4 delitiis *R*   5 qua] que *V, corr. G*$^{3?}$ 6 vale *O*   subalarum *OR* (sub
alarum *O*^{1}), suballarum *G*, -alar- *G*$^{3?}$ 8 qui cum ζη: cui cum *V*   10 frigiunt *O*
70 1 male *O*
71 1 cui *Calph.*: qua *V*, al. quo *R*^{2} iure *Pall.*: viro *V*   sacer alarum *Calph.*: sacratorum *O*,
sacrorum *GR*   obstit *R, corr. R*^{2} hyrcus *GR*   2 quem θ: quam *V*   podraga *GR*   secat ς:
secunt *O*, secum *GR*   3 nostrum β   4 murifice *R, corr. R*^{1} apte *Dres.*^{1}: a te *V*
6 podraga *G*

72

Dicebas quondam solum te nosse Catullum,
   Lesbia, nec prae me velle tenere Iovem.
dilexi tum te non tantum ut vulgus amicam,
   sed pater ut gnatos diligit et generos.
nunc te cognovi; quare, etsi impensius uror,   5
   multo mi tamen es vilior et levior.
qui potis est, inquis? quod amantem iniuria talis
   cogit amare magis, sed bene velle minus.

73

Desine de quoquam quicquam bene velle mereri
   aut aliquem fieri posse putare pium.
omnia sunt ingrata, nihil fecisse benigne <est>;
   immo etiam taedet, <taedet> obestque magis;
ut mihi, quem nemo gravius nec acerbius urget   5
   quam modo qui me unum atque unicum amicum habuit.

74

Gellius audierat patruum obiurgare solere,
   si quis delicias diceret aut faceret.
hoc ne ipsi accideret, patrui perdepsuit ipsam
   uxorem et patruum reddidit Harpocraten.
quod voluit fecit: nam, quamvis irrumet ipsum   5
   nunc patruum, verbum non faciet patruus.

72 8 *Donatus ad Terenti Andriam 718*

---

72 2 pre me *R*, per me *G*, prime *O*   6 mi tamen es *A. Guarinus*: ita me nec *V*   7 quod *Ric. 606 ζη, quia Statius*: quam *V*

73 1 quicquam *ζ*: quisquam *V*   3 est *add. Friedrich*   4 *ita Avantius; initio versus prodest suppl. Puccius, iuverit Baehrens, iam iuvat Munro; alii alia*   imo *G*   obestque *OG*, obstetque *R*, stetque *R²*   magis *Av.*: magisque magis *V*   5 quem *Esc.(b)*: ꝗ *O*, que *GR*   6 habet *GR*, habuit *R² in margine*

74 1 gelius *O(corr. O¹)*, lelius *GR*, *al.* Gellius *R²*   solere *B. Guarinus*: flere *V*   2 delitias *R*   3 hec (ħ) *O*   perdepsuit *"vir eruditus" apud Statium*: perdespuit *V*   4 reddit *O*   harpocratem *O*, -them *GR*

75

Huc est mens deducta tua, mea Lesbia, culpa
    atque ita se officio perdidit ipsa suo,
ut iam nec bene velle queat tibi, si optima fias,
    nec desistere amare, omnia si facias.

76

Si qua recordanti benefacta priora voluptas
    est homini, cum se cogitat esse pium,
nec sanctam violasse fidem, nec foedere in ullo
    divum ad fallendos numine abusum homines,
multa parata manent in longa aetate, Catulle,   5
    ex hoc ingrato gaudia amore tibi.
nam quaecumque homines bene cuiquam aut dicere possunt
    aut facere, haec a te dictaque factaque sunt.
omnia quae ingratae perierunt credita menti.
    quare cur tete iam amplius excrucies?   10
quin tu animo offirmas atque istinc te ipse reducis
    et dis invitis desinis esse miser?
difficile est longum subito deponere amorem,
    difficile est, verum hoc qua lubet efficias;
una salus haec est, hoc est tibi pervincendum,   15
    hoc facias, sive id non pote sive pote.
o di, si vestrum est misereri, aut si quibus umquam
    extremam iam ipsa in morte tulistis opem,
me miserum aspicite et, si vitam puriter egi,
    eripite hanc pestem perniciemque mihi,   20

---

76 13 *Hieremias de Montagnone, Compendium moralium notabilium 4.5.11*

---

75 3 queat *Lachmann* (queam *iam* θ): -que tot *V*   optuma *O*
76 1 sique *O*   3 violase *O*   in ullo θ: nullo *V*   5 manent ζη: manentum *O*, manenti *GR*
catulli *G* (*corr. G¹*)   6 exhaec (ħ= haec) *O*   amore] avicere *O*   8 sint *O*   9 omniaque *V*
ingrate *V* (-tae *G³⁺*)   10 cur te te iam *Baehrens*, iam te cur ζη: cur te iam *V*   11 quin θ:
qui *V*   tui *V, corr. R²*   animum *Stat.*   affirmas *R* istinc te ipse *Ellis* (isthinc te usque
iam G. Buchananus), istinc teque *Heinsius*: instincteque *O*, istinctoque *GR*   12 dis (γ),
deis ε: des *V*   13 amicu *R, corr. R¹*   14 qua libet ζ: quam libet *V*   officias *O*   15,
16 hoc] hec *V*(ħ *O*), *corr. R²*   faties *R* (facies *m*)   17 dii *V*   miseri *O*   18 extremam α:
extremo *V*, extrema *R²*   ipsa in *Ald.*: ipsam *V*   20 pernitiemque *R*

quae mihi subrepens imos ut torpor in artus
    expulit ex omni pectore laetitias.
non iam illud quaero, contra ut me diligat illa,
    aut, quod non potis est, esse pudica velit:
ipse valere opto et taetrum hunc deponere morbum.   25
    o di, reddite mi hoc pro pietate mea.

77

Rufe mihi frustra ac nequiquam credite amice
    (frustra? immo magno cum pretio atque malo),
sicine subrepsti mi atque intestina perurens
    ei misero eripuisti omnia nostra bona?
eripuisti, eheu nostrae crudele venenum   5
    vitae, eheu nostrae pestis amicitiae.

78

Gallus habet fratres, quorum est lepidissima coniunx
    alterius, lepidus filius alterius.
Gallus homo est bellus: nam dulces iungit amores,
    cum puero ut bello bella puella cubet.
Gallus homo est stultus, nec se videt esse maritum,   5
    qui patruus patrui monstret adulterium.

78^b

*   *   *   *   *   *   *

sed nunc id doleo, quod purae pura puellae
    savia comminxit spurca saliva tua.

---

21 quae *Calph.*: seu *V*   torpor β^1: corpore *V*   22 leticias *OG*, delitias *R, corr. R*^{1} 23 ut me ζ, me ut β, me ut me *V*   26 dei *OG*, dii *R*   michi *V, corr. R*^{2} hec *OR, corr. R*^{2} proprietate *V, corr. m*

77 1 ruffe *V*, rufe *m*   amico *GR*   2 imo *GR*   precio *G*   3 surrepsti *Calph.*: subrepti *O*, subrecti *GR*   mi $\zeta\eta$: mei *V*   in testina *G*   4 ei *Lachmann*, sic ζ: si *V*, al mi *R*^{2} 4, 5 Heripuisti *G*   5, 6 heu *OR*, he heu *G, corr. R*^{2}: eheu *Baehrens*   5 crudelle *G, corr. G*^{1} 6 nostro *GR*   pestis *B. Guarinus*: pectus *V*   amicicie *OG*

78 4 puela *O*   cubit *O*

78^b *A praecedentibus seiunxit Statius; post 77.6 collocavit Scaliger, post 80.8 Bergk, post 91.10 Corradinus de Allio*   2 sania *V, corr. R*^{2} conminxit *Scaliger*: connuxit *O*, coniunxit *GR*

verum id non impune feres: nam te omnia saecla
  noscent et, qui sis, fama loquetur anus.

79

Lesbius est pulcer; quid ni? quem Lesbia malit
  quam te cum tota gente, Catulle, tua.
sed tamen hic pulcer vendat cum gente Catullum
  si tria notorum savia reppererit.

80

Quid dicam, Gelli, quare rosea ista labella
  hiberna fiant candidiora nive,
mane domo cum exis et cum te octava quiete
  e molli longo suscitat hora die?
nescioquid certe est: an vere fama susurrat   5
  grandia te medii tenta vorare viri?
sic certe est: clamant Victoris rupta miselli
  ilia, et emulso labra notata sero.

81

Nemone in tanto potuit populo esse, Iuventi,
  bellus homo, quem tu diligere inciperes,
praeterquam iste tuus moribunda ab sede Pisauri
  hospes inaurata pallidior statua,
qui tibi nunc cordi est, quem tu praeponere nobis   5
  audes, et nescis quod facinus facias?

3 verum non id G, id verum non R   seda O   4 noscent Om, nosscent GR   quis scis GR
fama loquetur anus Calph.: famuloque tanus (canus G) V, al. -e- (i.e. tenus) R²
79 1 pulcher GR   -ni quem δε (-ni quod η): inquam V   mallit GR   3 pulcher GR
4 natorum GR   sania O   repererit GR
80 2 ruberna O   3 exis et ζη, exisset V   6 tñta O, tanta GR, al. tenta R²   8 ilia et emulso
B. Guarinus et Pall.: ille te mulso V
81 1 viventi V   3 pisanum O   5 qui Calph.: quid V   nuc G   6 quod ζη: quid V, fortasse
recte

82

Quinti, si tibi vis oculos debere Catullum
   aut aliud si quid carius est oculis,
eripere ei noli, multo quod carius illi
   est oculis, seu quid carius est oculis.

83

Lesbia mi praesente viro mala plurima dicit;
   haec illi fatuo maxima laetitia est.
mule, nihil sentis? si nostri oblita taceret,
   sana esset; nunc quod gannit et obloquitur,
non solum meminit, sed, quae multo acrior est res,   5
   irata est. hoc est, uritur et coquitur.

84

Chommoda dicebat, si quando commoda vellet
   dicere, et insidias Arrius hinsidias,
et tum mirifice sperabat se esse locutum,
   cum quantum poterat dixerat hinsidias.
credo, sic mater, sic liber avunculus eius,   5
   sic maternus avus dixerat atque avia.
hoc misso in Syriam requierant omnibus aures:
   audibant eadem haec leniter et leviter,
nec sibi postilla metuebant talia verba,
   cum subito affertur nuntius horribilis,   10
Ionios fluctus, postquam illuc Arrius isset,
   iam non Ionios esse sed Hionios.

82 2 aud *O*

83 2 leticia *OG*, -tia *R*   3 mulle *GR*   4 sanna *O*, samia *GR*, al. sana R^2 5 q$_3$ *O*   6 hoc *G*, hec *OR*   oritur *O*   coquitur *Lipsius*: loquitur *V*

84 1 chommoda *Pontanus*: commoda *V*   2 arrius *O*, a′rius *GR*   hinsidias *Politianus* (hinsidias arius insidias *Calph.*): insidias hee *O*, insidias he *GR* (he *del.* R^2)   3, 4 *post* 10 *V: huc revocavit vel B. Guarinus vel Politianus*   4 hinsidias *Polit.*: insidias *V*   5 liber] semper *Nisbet* (*fort. recte*)   eius η: eius est *V*   7 hoc ε: hec *O*, hic *GR*, al. hec R^2 ($G^{3?}$) Syriam *Parth.*: siria *O*, sy- *GR*   8 audibant η: audiebant *V*   10 nuncius *OR*, mincius *G*   11 illic *O, corr.* O^1 arrius *Polit.*: arcius *O*, artius *GR*   esset *G*   12 esset *O*   hionios θ: ionios *V*

85

Odi et amo. quare id faciam, fortasse requiris.
    nescio, sed fieri sentio et excrucior.

86

Quintia formosa est multis. mihi candida, longa,
    recta est: haec ego sic singula confiteor,
totum illud "formosa" nego: nam nulla venustas,
    nulla in tam magno est corpore mica salis.
Lesbia formosa est, quae cum pulcerrima tota est,   5
    tum omnibus una omnis surripuit veneres.

87

Nulla potest mulier tantum se dicere amatam
    vere, quantum a me Lesbia amata mea es.
nulla fides ullo fuit umquam in foedere tanta,
    quanta in amore tuo ex parte reperta mea est.

88

Quid facit is, Gelli, qui cum matre atque sorore
    prurit et abiectis pervigilat tunicis?
quid facit is, patruum qui non sinit esse maritum?
    ecquid scis quantum suscipiat sceleris?
suscipit, o Gelli, quantum non ultima Tethys   5
    nec genitor Nympharum abluit Oceanus:
nam nihil est quicquam sceleris, quo prodeat ultra,
    non si demisso se ipse voret capite.

86 4 *Quintilianus, Institutio oratoria 6.3.18*

---

85 1 ama *R, corr. R* ¹ nequiris *O* 2 sed] si *O*
86 1 loga *O* 2 singulla *G, corr. G* ¹ 5 pulcⁱima *O*, pulcherrima *G*, pulcherima *R*, pulcherrima *R* ² 6 omnes *GR* subripuit *O*
87 1 potest] pone *G* 2 es *Scaliger*: est *V* 3 nullo *R, corr. R* ¹ umquam in *Pall.*: umquam (*om.* in) *V* tanta ζη: tanto *V* 4 quantam *O*
88 1 facis *R, corr. R* ² furore *R, corr. R* ¹ 2 prurit β: prorurit *O*, proruit *GR* 3 facis *O* 4 ecquid *1473 et corr. Grat.* ¹: et quid *V* sis *O* tantum *R, corr. R* ¹ 5 thetis *V, corr. m*

89

Gellius est tenuis: quid ni? cui tam bona mater
    tamque valens vivat tamque venusta soror
tamque bonus patruus tamque omnia plena puellis
    cognatis, quare is desinat esse macer?
qui ut nihil attingat, nisi quod fas tangere non est,   5
    quantumvis quare sit macer invenies.

90

Nascatur magus ex Gelli matrisque nefando
    coniugio et discat Persicum aruspicium:
nam magus ex matre et gnato gignatur oportet,
    si vera est Persarum impia relligio,
gratus ut accepto veneretur carmine divos   5
    omentum in flamma pingue liquefaciens.

91

Non ideo, Gelli, sperabam te mihi fidum
    in misero hoc nostro, hoc perdito amore fore,
quod te cognossem bene constantemve putarem
    aut posse a turpi mentem inhibere probro;
sed neque quod matrem nec germanam esse videbam   5
    hanc tibi, cuius me magnus edebat amor.
et quamvis tecum multo coniungerer usu,
    non satis id causae credideram esse tibi.
tu satis id duxti: tantum tibi gaudium in omni
    culpa est, in quacumque est aliquid sceleris.   10

89 1 tellius *O*   4 mater *V, corr. R*²   6 sit (γ), *Carp.*: fit *V*

90 1 magus ζη: magnus *V*   3 magus γ: magnus *V*   gignantur *G*   opportet *O*   5 gratus *L. Mueller*, gnarus *Puccius*: gnatus *V*   6 omentum ε: quintum *O*, omnetum *G*, omne tum *R*   flama *GR, corr. R*²

91 3 non nossem *Av.*   constanterve *R*   4 a ζη: aut *V*   mentem ζ, -te *V*   9 id duxti *Ald.*: induxti *V* (in duxti *G*)

92

Lesbia mi dicit semper male nec tacet umquam
de me: Lesbia me dispeream nisi amat.
quo signo? quia sunt totidem mea: deprecor illam
assidue, verum dispeream nisi amo.

93

Nil nimium studeo, Caesar, tibi velle placere,
nec scire utrum sis albus an ater homo.

94

Mentula moechatur. moechatur mentula? certe
hoc est quod dicunt: ipsa olera olla legit.

95

Zmyrna mei Cinnae nonam post denique messem
quam coepta est nonamque edita post hiemem,
milia cum interea quingenta Hortensius uno

. . . .

Zmyrna cavas Satrachi penitus mittetur ad undas,   5
Zmyrnam cana diu saecula pervoluent.
at Volusi annales Paduam morientur ad ipsam
et laxas scombris saepe dabunt tunicas.

92 1–4 *Aulus Gellius, Noctes Atticae 7.16.2*
93 2 *Quintilianus, Institutio oratoria 11.1.38*

———

92 1 L *add.* O¹   2–4 amat … nisi *om. GR, habent O, Gellius*   3 mea *Vossius:* ea O, *codd.
Gelliani*   4 verum *codd. Gelliani:* vero O   amo] *al.* amat R²
93 2 scire *Parth., teste Av.*² (*et "codex vetustior" teste A. Guarino*): si ore V   sis albus an
ater *Parth., teste Av.*¹, *Beroaldus* (sis *iam Sen.*²): si salvus an alter V
94 1 mentulla G, *corr.* G¹
95 1, 5, 6 zinirna V, zmirna R²   crine O   m̄sem O   3 in terrea G   ort- O   Hatriensis *in
Housman* (Hatrianus *in iam Munro*)   5 cavas ζη: canas V   mictentur R, mictetur R²
6 pervoluent *Calph.:* pervoluit V

parva mei mihi sint cordi monimenta . . .,
　　at populus tumido gaudeat Antimacho.　　　　　　　　　　10

96

Si quicquam mutis gratum acceptumve sepulcris
　　accidere a nostro, Calve, dolore potest,
quo desiderio veteres renovamus amores
　　atque olim missas flemus amicitias,
certe non tanto mors immatura dolori est　　　　　　　　　　5
　　Quintiliae, quantum gaudet amore tuo.

97

Non, ita me di ament, quicquam referre putavi
　　utrum os an culum olfacerem Aemilio.
nilo mundius hoc, nihiloque immundior ille est
　　verum etiam culus mundior et melior;
nam sine dentibus est. hoc dentis sesquipedalis,　　　　　　5
　　gingivas vero ploxeni habet veteris;
praeterea rictum, qualem diffissus in aestu
　　meientis mulae cunnus habere solet.
hic futuit multas et se facit esse venustum;
　　et non pistrino traditur atque asino?　　　　　　　　　　10
quem siqua attingit, non illam posse putemus
　　aegroti culum lingere carnificis?

97 6 *Quintilianus, Institutio oratorio 1.5.8; Festus p. 260 (Lindsay)*

9–10 *a praecedentibus seiunxerunt Statius, alii* 　9 laboris *add.* ζη, *poetae B. Guarinus,
sodalis Ald., Philetae Bergk, Catonis Leo, alii alia* 　10 populus vel tu timido *O* 　antimacho
(η): eutimacho *V*

96 1 gratum ε: et gratum *V* 　acceptum ve *V, coni. m* 　3 que *O* 　renovamur *O* 　5 dolori β:
dolor *V* 　6 quintile *OG,* quintilie *G¹R*

97 1 dii *R* 　quicquid *V, al.* quicquam *R²* 　2 utrumne *Trinc.* 　3 nil omundius (-mm- *G*) *V,*
nichilomundius *R²* (c *del. m¹⁷ ap. R*), nihilo mundius *m* 　nihiloque] nobisque *GR*
immundior ille est *Baehrens,* immundior ille *Lachmann:* īmundius illud (ī mūdius
illud *G*) *V* 　5 hoc (η), os *Froehlich* (dentis os *iam* ζ): hic *OGR¹* (hin *R primo*)
sesquipedalis (ζ): seseque dedalis *V* 　6 ploxini (η), ploxeno *Calph.* (ploxino *iam* β):
ploxnio *O,* ploxonio *GR* 　7 diffissus *Statius:* deffessus *O,* defessus *GR* 　aestu ζη: estum *V*
8 megentis *V, corr. R²* 　mule *O,* mulle *GR* (*corr. R²*) 　cōmis *O,* cūnus *G* 　9 hec *O*
fecit *GR* 　10 pristrino *O* 　11 siq̄ *O*

98

In te, si in quemquam, dici pote, putide Victi,
    id quod verbosis dicitur et fatuis.
ista cum lingua, si usus veniat tibi, possis
    culos et crepidas lingere carpatinas.
si nos omnino vis omnes perdere, Victi,   5
    hiscas: omnino quod cupis efficies.

99

Surripui tibi, dum ludis, mellite Iuventi,
    saviolum dulci dulcius ambrosia.
verum id non impune tuli: namque amplius horam
    suffixum in summa me memini esse cruce,
dum tibi me purgo nec possum fletibus ullis   5
    tantillum vestrae demere saevitiae.
nam simul id factum est, multis diluta labella
    guttis abstersti mollibus articulis,
ne quicquam nostro contractum ex ore maneret,
    tamquam commictae spurca saliva lupae.   10
praeterea infesto miserum me tradere amori
    non cessasti omnique excruciare modo,
ut mi ex ambrosia mutatum iam foret illud
    saviolum tristi tristius elleboro.
quam quoniam poenam misero proponis amori,   15
    numquam iam posthac basia surripiam.

98 1 in quenquam (δ), *Av.*: inquam quam *V*   pote *om. O*   Vetti *Statius*, Vitti *Haupt*
4 carpantians *O*, carpatians *GR*, carpatinas *R*²   5 vos *O*   6 hiscas *Vossius*: discas *V*
99 1 surripui *β*²: surmpuit *O*, surripuit *GR* (*et β primo*)   viventi *O*   2 suaviolum *V*
ambrosia ε: ambrosio *O*, amrosio *G*, ambroxio *R*, ambrosio *R*¹   4 sufixum *O*   6 sevicie *O*
7 id *OR*, ad *G*   8 abstersti *O*, astersi *GR*: abstersi *β*, abstersisti *Trinc.* (abstersi guttis
Calph., abstersti guttis *Av.*)   mollibus *Lee*: omnibus *V*   9 ne ε: nec *V*   manaret *O*
10 comitte *O*, commicte *G*, commincte *R*   salivia *O*, salvie *G* (*corr. G*¹)   12 cesasti *G*
(*corr. G*¹)   13 mi *β*¹: michi *V*   ambrosia ζ: ambrosio *OG*, ambroxio *R*   14 saviolum *O*,
suaviolum *GR*

100

Caelius Aufillenum et Quintius Aufillenam
    flos Veronensum depereunt iuvenum,
hic fratrem, ille sororem. hoc est, quod dicitur, illud
    fraternum vere dulce sodalicium.
cui faveam potius? Caeli, tibi: nam tua nobis   5
    perspecta est igni tum unica amicitia,
cum vesana meas torreret flamma medullas.
    sis felix, Caeli, sis in amore potens.

101

Multas per gentes et multa per aequora vectus
    advenio has miseras, frater, ad inferias,
ut te postremo donarem munere mortis
    et mutam nequiquam alloquerer cinerem,
quandoquidem fortuna mihi tete abstulit ipsum,   5
    heu miser indigne frater adempte mihi.
nunc tamen interea haec, prisco quae more parentum
    tradita sunt tristi munere ad inferias,
accipe fraterno multum manantia fletu,
    atque in perpetuum, frater, ave atque vale.   10

102

Si quicquam tacito commissum est fido ab amico,
    cuius sit penitus nota fides animi,
me aeque esse invenies illorum iure sacratum,
    Corneli, et factum me esse putum Harpocraten.

100 1 gellius *O*, celius *GR*   aufilenum … aufilenam *V*   2 treronensum *O*, veronensum *G*,
trenorensum *R*, al. veronensum *R²*   depereunt *η*: depereret *V*, al. -ant *R²*   3 hoc] hec *O*
4 dulcę *G³*   5 pocius *R*, corr. *R²*   6 perspecta (ς): perfecta *V*   est igni tum *A. Palmer*, ex
igni est *Schoell*, egregie est *Baehrens*: est igitur est (ē g̑ ē) *O*, est exigitur est *G*, est.igitur
est *R*, al. exigitur *R²*   7 correret flama *G*

101 1 ultas *V*, corr. *O¹R²*   3 amoris *Maehly*   4 ne quicquam *R*, coni. *R²*   6 hei misero
Trinc. (misero *iam Puccius*)   7 hec *O*, hoc *GR*   prisco que (= quae) *β*: priscoque *V*
 8 infri^as (= inferias?) *O*   10 valle *O*

102 1 i *O*, corr. *O¹*   quoiquam *Stat.*, quoi quid *Maehly*, quid quoi *Baehrens*   taciti *Heinsius*,
tacite *Ald.²*, tacitum *Stat.*   ab antiquo *V*, corr. *R²*   3 me aeque *Vossius*: meque esse *V*
4 putum *Schwabe*: puta *V*   arpocratem *V* (ac po- *O*, corr. *O¹*)

103

Aut sodes mihi redde decem sestertia, Silo,
    deinde esto quamvis saevus et indomitus;
aut, si te nummi delectant, desine quaeso
    leno esse atque idem saevus et indomitus.

104

Credis me potuisse meae maledicere vitae,
    ambobus mihi quae carior est oculis?
non potui, nec, si possem, tam perdite amarem;
    sed tu cum Tappone omnia monstra facis.

105

Mentula conatur Pipleium scandere montem:
    Musae furcillis praecipitem eiciunt.

106

Cum puero bello praeconem qui videt esse,
    quid credat, nisi se vendere discupere?

107

Si quicquam cupido optantique optigit umquam
    insperanti, hoc est gratum animo proprie.
quare hoc est gratum nobis quoque, carius auro
    quod te restituis, Lesbia, mi cupido.

103 1 sextercia *OG*, sextertia *R*   2 esto *Calph*: est *O*, est o *GR*   3 mīmi *O*, mimi *GR*, al.
numi *R*²   delectavit *O*

104 2 michi ꝗ *O*   3 si *om. O* perdita *O* amarem ζ: amare *V*

105 1 pipileium *OG*, pipleium *R*   scandere ζ: scindere *V*   2 furcilis *OG*, furcillis *R*
eiiciunt *GR*

106 1 bello *Ald.*: obelio *OG*, obellio *G*¹*R*   esse *OG*, ipse *R*

107 1 quicquam γ, quoi quid *Ribbeck*: quid quid *O*, quicquid *GR*   cupidoque *Ald.*   optigit *O*
2 insperati *Heinsius* hec *O*   3 hec *O* nobisque hoc *Statius*, nobisque est *Haupt* (*fortasse*
nobis, quod carius auro est*)

restituis cupido atque insperanti, ipsa refers te   5
   nobis. o lucem candidiore nota!
quis me uno vivit felicior, aut magis hac quid
   optandum vita dicere quis poterit?

108

Si, Comini, populi arbitrio tua cana senectus
   spurcata impuris moribus intereat,
non equidem dubito quin primum inimica bonorum
   lingua exsecta avido sit data vulturio,
effossos oculos voret atro gutture corvus,   5
   intestina canes, cetera membra lupi.

109

Iucundum, mea vita, mihi proponis: amorem
   hunc nostrum inter nos perpetuum usque fore.
di magni, facite ut vere promittere possit,
   atque id sincere dicat et ex animo,
ut liceat nobis tota perducere vita   5
   aeternum hoc sanctae foedus amicitiae.

110

Aufillena, bonae semper laudantur amicae:
   accipiunt pretium, quae facere instituunt.
tu, quod promisti, mihi quod mentita inimica es,
   quod nec das et fers saepe, facis facinus.

5 inspiranti *O*   6 lucem *B. Guarinus*: luce *OG*, luci *R*, luce *R*¹   7/8 hac quid / optandum *A. Guarinus*, hac rem / optandam in *Postgate* (hac re *Kroll*), hac res / optandas *Lachmann*: hac est / optandus *O*, me est / optandus *GR*   8 quid *Statius* (*qui et* optandum in *legit*)

108 1 si, Comini *B. Guarinus*: sic homini *V*   populi *Statius* (arbitrio populi *iam Calph.*): populari *V* (sic populari homini *β*¹)   2 in (im *G*) puris *V*   4 execta (ς): exercta *O*, exerta *GR*   5 guture *G*

109 1 amorem *β*: amore *V*   2 hinc *G, corr. G*¹   usque *scripsi*: -que *V*   3 dii *OR* promictere *R, corr. R*²   6 eterne *O*   amicicie *O*, -tie *GR*, -cie *R*²

110 1 auffilena *V*   2 precium *OG*, -tium *R*   quia *O*   3 promisti *γ*: promisisti *OG*, promixisti *R*   4 et *B. Guarinus*: nec *V*   facis] facinus *O, corr. O*¹

aut facere ingenuae est, aut non promisse pudicae,   5
    Aufillenā, fuit; sed data corripere
fraudando officiis, plus quam meretricis avarae <est>
    quae sese toto corpore prostituit.

111

Aufillena, viro contentam vivere solo,
    nuptarum laus ex laudibus eximiis;
sed cuivis quamvis potius succumbere par est,
    quam matrem fratres ex patruo <parere>.

112

Multus homo es, Naso, neque tecum multus homo <est qui>
    discumbit: Naso, multus es et pathicus.

113

Consule Pompeio primum duo, Cinna, solebant
    Maeciliam; facto consule nunc iterum
manserunt duo, sed creverunt milia in unum
    singula. fecundum semen adulterio.

114

Firmano saltu non falso Mentula dives
    fertur, qui tot res in se habet egregias,

5 promisse *B. Guarinus et Parth.*: promissa *V*   6 aut fillena *O*, auffilena *GR*   7 officiis *Bergk*, officio *Riese* (officium *iam Muretus*), effectis *Ellis*, effecti *β*: efficit *V*   est *add. Calph.* 8 toto *γ*: tota *V*

111 1 auffilena *γ*: aut fillenā *O*, auffilenam *GR* (-lemam *R*)   contemptam *O*   2 ex *Passerat* (e *iam Scaliger*; est laus e *Statius*): est *V*   3 par *ς*: pars *V*   4 ex patruo parere *Doering* (*necnon Itali quidam saec. xv, teste Zicàri, Scritti 141*), efficere ex p. 1472, te parere ex p. *Friedrich*, concipere ex p. *Rossbach, alii alia*: ex patruo *V*

112 1 es *Parth.*: est *V*   homo est qui *Scaliger*, homost quin *Schwabe*: homo *V*, homoque *R*[2]   2 discumbit *scripsi*, te scindat *Schwabe* (te scindit *iam Haupt*): descendit *V*   est *G*

113 1 molebant *Maehly*   2 meciliam *G*, mecilia *OR*: Moecillam *L. Mueller*, Mucillam *Pleitner*   3 mansuerunt *O, corr. O*[1]   4 singula 1472: singulum *V*   ad ulterio *G*

114 1 Firmano saltu *Ald.* (saltus *iam B. Guarinus et Av.*): firmanus salvis *V*   mentula *ε*: mensula *V*

aucupium omne genus, piscis, prata, arva ferasque.
    nequiquam: fructus sumptibus exsuperat.
quare concedo sit dives, dum omnia desint;   5
    saltum laudemus, dum modio ipse egeat.

115

Mentula habet †instar† triginta iugera prati,
    quadraginta arvi: cetera sunt maria.
cur non divitiis Croesum superare potis sit,
    uno qui in saltu tot bona possideat,
prata arva ingentes silvas altasque paludes   5
    usque ad Hyperboreos et mare ad Oceanum?
omnia magna haec sunt, tamen ipsest maximus ultor;
    non homo, sed vere mentula magna minax.

116

Saepe tibi studiose, animo venante, requirens
    carmina uti possem mittere Battiadae,
qui te lenirem nobis, neu conarere
    tela infesta <meum> mittere in usque caput.
hunc video mihi nunc frustra sumptum esse laborem,   5
    Gelli, nec nostras hinc valuisse preces.
contra nos tela ista tua evitabimus acta,
    at fixus nostris tu dabis supplicium.

3 aucupium ζη, aucupia γ: an cupiam O, aucupiam GR   4 exuperat V   6 saltem GR
dum modio *Richmond*, dum tamen β, dum domo *Lachmann*: dum modo V
115 1 istar O, instar GR: iuxta *Scaliger* (*fortasse* lustra et)   2 paria *Froehlich*, varia *Baehrens*
3 diviciis OG, -tiis R   potis sit ζη: potuisset V   4 bona *Av.*: moda V   possiderat O
5 iugentis O   altasque paludes (ζ), salsasque paludes *Bergk*, latasque paludes *Rossbach*:
saltusque paludesque (plaudesque O) V   6 hiperboreos O   7 ipse est ζη, ipsest *Froehlich*:
ipse si V   ultro *1473*   8 vere *B. Guarinus et Parth.*: vero V   mencula O, mentulla G
116 1 studiose *B. Guarinus*: studioso V   requirens *Av.*: requires V   2 mictere R, corr. R²
batiade (η), -dae *1473*: batriade V   4 tela *Muretus*: telis GR, celis O   meum *add. Muretus*
mittere inusque (ζ): mitteremusque (mict- R) V   6 hic ζ, huc *Muretus*   7 evitamus ζ
acta *Baehrens*, icta *Rossberg*, amictu ε (contorto … evitamus amictu *Camps, fortasse
recte*): amitha O, amicta GR   8 at fixus ζ: affixus V

Fragmenta

1

Hunc lucum tibi dedico consecroque, Priape,
qua domus tua Lampsaci est quaque ... Priape.
nam te praecipue in suis urbibus colit ora
Hellespontia, ceteris ostriosior oris.

2

de meo ligurrire libido est.

3

at non effugies meos iambos

1 1–4 *Grammatici Latini VI: 406 (Terentianus); versus 1 ab aliis citatur, ibid. pp. 119, 151,
260, 268, 292, 615*
2 *Nonius vol. 1, p. 195 (Lindsay) s.v. ligurrire*
3 *Porphyrion ad Horati carmen 1.16.22*

1 2 lege Priapi *Buecheler*

Versus domini Benevenuti de Campexanis de Vicencia
de resurrectione Catulli poete Veronensis.

Ad patriam venio longis a finibus exul;
    causa mei reditus compatriota fuit,
scilicet a calamis tribuit cui Francia nomen
    quique notat turbe praetereuntis iter.
quo licet ingenio vestrum celebrate Catullum,
    cuius sub modio clausa papirus erat.

Et titulum et versus textui subscripsit G; titulum omisit, versus libro praefixit R.

COMMENTARY

1

Structure: 2 + 5 (question and answer) + 3 lines, articulated by *namque, quare*.

The poet dedicates his *libellus* to his friend Cornelius Nepos (l. 3 n.). As Zicàri 1965 pointed out, the tone of C.'s dedication, unlike Meleager's Μοῦσα φίλα, τίνι τάνδε φέρεις πάγκαρπον ἀοιδάν; (*AP* 4.1.1) and Martial's *cuius vis fieri, libelle, munus* (3.2.1), is easy and relaxed, not bookish: C. himself occupies the scene from the very start, and hence his book is a concrete thing, an object in his hand. The poem's programmatic quality is obvious; less obvious is the fact that here C. *demonstrates* the qualities, or some of them, which he most admired in Greek, and vindicates for Latin, poetry. For example, he claims – by exercising it – the freedom to write poetry in conversational idiom; notice the introductory question-and-answer, and the repeated use of diminutives, such as *libellus* (which is not merely a metrically convenient substitute for *liber*; see Mart. 10.1.1–2); and again, *esse aliquid*; (l. 3 n.); parenthetical *Iuppiter*, as an exclamation (cf. 66.30); the idiom *quidquid hoc libelli*; *habe tibi*, a legal formula (precise but humdrum); and *lepidum*, 'nice' (to look at, as in Plaut. *Pseud.* 27–8 *lepidis litteris, lepidis tabellis lepida conscriptis manu*). The implication is that 'the lyric can be about ordinary life and in the language of the people; and poetry of this kind deserves serious criticism' (Copley 1951; see also Gordon Williams, *Tradition and Originality in Roman Poetry* [1968]: chapter 2). Furthermore, C. claims for himself a high degree of metrical freedom; take lines 2–4, where the 'basis' of the line (in this metre consisting of the first two syllables) is varied each time: trochee, followed by spondee, followed by iambus. A few Latin writers (including Varro before C.; Martial after him) adhere rigorously to the spondaic basis in hendecasyllables; C. by his practice here draws attention to the principle of free variation, and almost flaunts it by applying it in successive lines at the very outset.

For a change of tone in the last two lines of the poem, see ll. 9–10 nn. It may be that C. at first conceived of his poem as ending with the word *libelli*, which echoes so neatly the *libellum* of l. 1, and which again draws attention to brevity. If so, these eight lines would furnish a good example of the 'cyclic' structure so often used in C.'s short poems; and Bardon (1943: 15) has complained that the final wish in ll. 9–10 spoils the clear effect of the repetition of the leading idea of ll. 1–2. Yet Bardon himself has drawn attention (ibid., 18) to the frequent occurrence in C. of a structure wherein the last two lines of a ten-line poem are in some way sharply distinguished from the rest; this '8 + 2' structure, with some variations, he finds in a great many of the 'polymetric' poems. For an example see M. Zicàri's discussion of poem 2, cited in the Bibliography to that poem; the slight change in tone or direction, adumbrated in the final two lines, more or less, of a short poem, is characteristic of C. Seen in this light, the slightly disconcerting asymmetry and redirection, implicit in the ending of poem 1, will prove acceptable and necessary after all. It is doubtful whether such asymmetry can be taken as a sign of early composition (and on the obvious implication, for dating, of *iam tum*, see l. 3 n.); on the other hand, the nature of the claim made for the book is scarcely such as could have envisaged the collected works as we have them. (For a discussion of the chronology of the *liber Catulli*, see the Introduction, pp. 3–10.) The poet's obvious delight in the outward aspect of his new book suggests a first publication; and the tone of the initial 'movement' of the poem is, as Zicàri remarks, 'juvenile' rather than mature.

1 *cui*: on the question whether C. wrote *quoi* (he probably did) see Fordyce. *V* had *qui* for *cui* at 2.3 (corrected by *O*'s variant), and also at 24.5 and 67.47. At 17.14 *cuiiocum* (cf. *V*) may preserve an original *quoi*; if so, we have here an early error in C.'s text. *Quoi* is possibly also the cause of *V*'s *qua* at 71.1. If at 64.254 *V*'s *qui* points to *quoi* standing for *cui*, then O. Skutsch receives additional support (though he does not use it) for his emendation *cui Thyades* in that line.

   dono: the first two lines pretend to depict C. as having just received the first copy of a small volume (*libellus*) of his own poems. It is the physical appearance of the book that is stressed in line 2, and therefore probably also in line 1. We may reasonably conclude that *dono* conveys 'to whom am I in fact presenting . . . ?', which suits the notion of a little scene in which C. himself is the chief actor, even though parallels can be found for taking the indicative *dono* as equivalent to *donem*. (Kr. cites Plaut. *Most.* 368 *quid ego ago?* and Cicero, *Ad Att.* 16.7.4 *nunc quid respondemus?*).

lepidum novum: cf. Plaut. *Epid.* 222 *vestita, aurata, ornata ut lepide, ut concinne, ut nove!*

2 *arida*: on the feminine form see App. Crit. Petrarch's friend Guglielmo da Pastrengo (Pastrengicus), who died in 1362 (before *GR* and perhaps *O* were written), supports Servius on *Aeneid* 12.587 in spelling *arida*. It is true that for his citation of lines 1–2 Pastrengicus (*De Or. Rerum* 88b) refers not to C. but to Isidore, our manuscripts of whom give *arido*; but he also quotes lines 5–7, and some marginalia, from C. directly, and these further quotations make it clear that he saw a Catullus Ms, probably *V*. Therefore, he either found *arida* in his Isidore Ms, or corrected from Servius (unlikely) or, as Haupt suggested, from the text of C.; see E. (note in the App. Crit. of his text-edition) and also B.L. Ullman, 'The Transmission of the Text of Catullus,' *Studi in onore di Luigi Castiglioni* (Florence, 1980): 1041–2. A third possibility (not entertained by Ullman) is this: arida *V*, aridå *A*, arido *OGR*. If Martial 8.72.2 has *aridi* in the masculine, this is hardly decisive for the gender which, as Servius remarks, is (regularly) masculine in Virgil though (oddly) feminine in Catullus. Friedrich noted that the cacophonic sequence *arido modo* was to be avoided; he comments on the strenuous effort made by Cicero, *Pro Milone* 61, to avoid even the less harsh sequence of sounds *populo modo*. For the fem. *arida* see Scaliger, *Castigationes* 4, in reply to A. Statius (cited by Gaisser 1993: 174 and n. 127); Scaliger rightly says that the explicit testimony of Servius about C.'s irregular usage should outweigh the unannotated readings of medieval Mss, which are all that the 'other sources' amount to.

3 *Corneli*: this is Cornelius Nepos the historian, as we know from Ausonius (see App. Crit.). Like C. himself, and many other men of letters in the Rome of the day, Nepos hailed from Cisalpine Gaul; the elder Pliny, in his *Naturalis Historia*, calls him *conterraneus meus* (in the Preface) as well as *Padi accola* (3.127). His *Chronica* (apparently a prose work) seems to have taken the form of a comparative chronology of Greek and Roman history; Aulus Gellius (17.21.3) says that in Book 1 Nepos dated the poetic contest between Homer and Hesiod 160 years before Rome was founded, and also says that Nepos declared Archilochus to have lived at the same time as the early Roman king Tullus Hostilius. If, then, the chronology was 'universal' in the sense that it sought to place Greek and Roman events and personalities from long ago on a single time-scale, the point of *omne aevum* becomes clear, while the adjective *laboriosis* (l. 7) begins to seem highly appropriate. We do not know when the *Chronica* was published; *iam tum* of course suggests that it was more than a few years before this poem was written.

On Nepos and Catullus, and their literary circle, see Wiseman 1979: 154–66.

4 *esse aliquid*: cf. Cicero, *Ad Fam.* 6.18.4 *si est talis <orator>, ego quoque aliquid sum*; also *Ad Att.* 4.2.2 *si umquam in dicendo fuimus aliquid*, TD 5.104 *eos aliquid putare esse.*

nugas, 'nonsense' – a depreciatory word (Plautus so uses it, and cf. Hor. *Ep.* 1.19.42), and not primarily a description of a recognized poetic genre; C. calls his short poems *nugae* and *ineptiae* in order to stress their playful and witty nature. Martial's literary application of the word probably recalls C. The collection – if indeed it was a collection – of *nugae*, praised some time ago (*iam tum* ..., line 5) by Cornelius Nepos, need not be supposed to include, for example, the grim atmosphere of poem 11, or even the serious introspection of poem 8.

5 There is no thought of numerical opposition between *unus* and *tribus*, which would be pointless; there is however some such contrast between *omne* and *tribus*. This in turn rules out a factitious opposition between *unus* and *omne*; so we must take (as the rhythm of the line also suggests) *unus-Italorum* together, in the sense 'first of Italians to ...' (as opposed to Greeks, e.g., Apollodorus, who had written summaries of world history). Both Horace (*Od.* 3.30) and Propertius (3.1.3) claim to be the first to introduce Greek literary genres into Italy.

   The initial *i* in the noun *Italia* is lengthened, against its natural value (so that the word may appear in hexameters) by Callimachus in Greek, and (after C.) in Latin by Virgil (*Aen.* 6.61; see E. Norden ad loc.).

6 *explicare*, 'unroll'; it is interesting that it is of a *chronicle* (by Atticus) that Cicero (*Brut.* 15) writes *ut explicatis ordinibus temporum uno in conspectu omnia viderem*; see note on 3 above.
   cartis here = 'rolls'; these consisted of *cartae* (sheets of papyrus) glued together in a *volumen*.

7 *laboriosis*, 'involving weary work.' This 'non-personal' use (cf. Ter. *Heaut.* 807, Cicero *De legg.* 3.19) is quite regular, contrary to what is said of Calvus' use of the word by Gellius, 9.12.10 (F.).

8 *Est* is implied after *libelli*; but cf. V. *Aen.* 1.78 *quodcumque hoc regni*. The phrase is slightly disparaging, as is *qualecumque*. For the punctuation see the final para. of the n. on l. 9.

   See App. Crit.: *al. mei* is of course not intended as a variant but as an explanatory note: '*my* book, that is.' In R^2 these words have been erased by a later hand, and what was then left of them has been almost, but not quite, obliterated by a library stamp; but on close inspection traces can be seen. Even had they vanished completely, *m* comes to our rescue (as he often does in matters connected with the text of *R*) by picking up the words, and so proving that they had been inserted by R^2; for although *m* is careless, he never invents.

9–10 Notice the change of tone: shy modesty is replaced by modest confidence.

9 The metrical defect in the line as transmitted caused the Humanists either to restore *o* (later adopted by most editors) or or to substitute *quidem* for *quod*. Presumably the second of these remedies prompted Bergk's rewriting of the line (*qualecumque quidem est, patroni ut ergo*), which however is unconvincing

for several reasons. That *virgo* does not occur elsewhere in poems 1–60 is immaterial; these poems have no place for it except in the context of an address to the Muse. Secondly, the word *virgo* does occur twenty-two times in the more formal poems, 61 to 68, and *virgineus* twice; again, it fails to occur in the short elegiac epigrams 69–116. This only means that it belongs to the 'high' or 'elevated' style, and would therefore be appropriate to apostrophizing a god or goddess in a dedication. Thirdly, the word *ergo* absolutely cannot mean, and nowhere comes close to meaning, 'by the agency of' <a person>, as it would have to do on Bergk's interpretation. On the contrary, in every instance quoted in *TLL* it means 'for the sake of' or 'in consequence of' a thing or an aim (except at *Aeneid* 6.670 where, since Anchises is dead and the meaning 'on his account' is in question, we are close to *genitivus rei*). In other words, the alignment of *ergo* is objective, not subjective. See further Clausen 1976: 38–43 (n. 2: 'The evidence against Bergk is clear and damning'). Again, that 'patron' should be applied to the recipient of a dedication such as this hardly fits either the literary atmosphere of the time – however unsurprising it might be in a later generation – or C.'s utterly independent character. Bergk's whole idea contradicts C.'s modest confidence in his work for its own merits – merits acknowledged, after all, by Nepos himself, as is clear not only from lines 2–6 here but also from Nepos' *Life of Atticus*, written in the later 30s BC, i.e., during the time of Gallus and the young Virgil; in that Life, an obscure C. Iulius Calidus is singled out as the 'most elegant' Roman poet since <those two giants, it is implied> Lucretius and Catullus. Again, the Muse is in fact needed, in order to provide a divine addressee for the optative *maneat*. F. Cairns (1969) has pointed out that 'a writer asking or wishing that immortality or long life be granted to his work traditionally makes his request or wish to a divinity.' C. has conquered his doubts before publishing, but still ventures only a modest aspiration to fame (*plus uno saeculo*, l. 10); yet this claim itself, being so severely limited, seems hardly designed to flatter the ego of a *patronus*, if it was through his support alone that the work was to survive. Finally, for the apostrophe, cf. 36.11 (Venus), and also Horace *Odes* 1.4.14 and 1.26.6. For the Muse as the poet's patron cf. also *Priapea* 2, where perhaps *quidquid id est* recalls C. The apostrophe is structurally in place: it gives the poem force, as an example of an epigrammatic device which we shall see C. employing in several poems that follow, namely the surprise ending or change of direction in the last two lines. On the question of metre, 'the elision of *i* before *u* is extremely rare, the two vowels being of a "timbre très fermé" … Such an elision is totally absent from C.'s dactylic poems, for example' (Monbrun 1976: 31–8). It is rare enough in C.'s non-dactylic poems; in 11.22 it is at the end of a line; in 14.8 and 29.22, it follows *si, nisi*.

The punctuation adopted here meets the difficulty, raised by Zicàri, that in Catullus and Martial there is never a heavy pause after the fourth syllable of a phalaecian hendecasyllabic line; and it divides the clauses with equal balance, instead of overloading the former clause. There is a distinction between *quicquid*, which has 'quantitative,' and *qualecumque*, which has 'qualitative,' implications (see Pasoli 1977–8: 55). The punctuation encounters another difficulty, however: relative *quod* is postponed, in a rare hyperbaton. For hyperbaton of a similar sort, see perhaps Propertius 3.21.16; for other hyperbata in C., see 44.9, 64.101, 66.18 with F.'s n., 64.8 and 66.41 (both involving a relative pronoun, as here); cf. also 51.5, 57.8, 62.13 and 14, 64.66 and 216, 67.21, 110.3. For the order cf. 76.9 (*omnia quae*) and 'a much more drastic example' of postponed connecting relative, 68.131 (Wiseman 1979: 172 n. 40, who adds: 'though there is no precise parallel for its positioning inside a subordinate clause, the word-order is perfectly intelligible, and much less contorted than that of (e.g.) 44.9 or 66.18').

patrona virgo = the poet's Muse. The notion of *clientela*, with the consequent duty of *fides* (cf. 34.1 *in fide*), explains why C. can describe a good poet as *pius* (16.5) and a bad one as *impius* (14.7).

Copley, F.O. 1951. 'Catullus, c. 1,' *TAPA* 82: 200–6.

Pasoli, E. 1959. 'C. e la dedica a Cornelio,' *Quaderni di vita veronese* 11/12: 433–6.

Zicàri, M. 1965. 'Sul primo carme di C.,' *Maia* 17: 232–40.

Elder, J.P. 1966. 'C. 1, His Poetic Creed, and Nepos,' *HSCP* 71: 143–9.

Gigante, M. 1967. 'Catullo, Cornelio e Cicerone,' *GIF* 20: 123–9.

Cairns, F. 1969. 'Catullus 1,' *Mn.* 22: 153–8.

Levine, P. 1969. 'C. c. 1: A Prayerful Dedication,' *CSCA* 2: 209–16.

Singleton, D. 1972. 'A Note on C.'s First Poem,' *CP* 67: 192–95.

Latta, B. 1972. 'Zu C.s Carmen 1,' *MH* 229: 201–13.

Németh, B. 1972. 'How Does C.'s Booklet Begin?,' *ACD* 8: 23–30.

Piernavieja, P. 1974. 'En torno al Carmen 1 de C.,' *EClás* 18: 411–17.

Goold, G.P. 1974. 'O Patrona Virgo,' *Polis and Imperium: Studies in Honour of E.T. Salmon*. Toronto: 253–64.

Clausen, W. 1976. 'Catulli Veronensis Liber,' *CP* 71: 38–43.

Monbrun, M. 1976. 'Quelques remarques sur le c. 1 de C.,' *Pallas* 23: 31–8.

Pasoli, E. 1977–8. 'Sul teste e la funzione del carme 1 di C.,' *RAIB* 66.1: 53–60.

Wiseman, T.P. 1979. *Clio's Cosmetics*. Chapter 11: 'The Dedication Poem.' Leicester: 167–74.

Goold, G.P. 1981. 'Two Notes on C. 1,' *LCM* 6: 233–8. [A reply to Wiseman 1979.]

Van Sickle, J.B. 1981. 'Poetics of Opening and Closure in Meleager, C., and Gallus,' *CW* 75: 65–75.

Mayer, R. 1982. 'On C. 1.9, Again,' *LCM* 7: 73–4.

Arkins, B. 1983. 'Further Thoughts on C. 1,' *LCM* 8: 18–20.

Dettmer, H. 1983. 'A Note on C. 1 and 116,' *CW* 77 (1983): 19. [Refers to Van Sickle 1981.]

Santini, P. 1983–4. 'Spunti per una interpretazione stilistica formale dei testi poetici latini (C. I),' *Anazetesis* 8–9: 1–10.

Dettmer, H. 1984. 'A Fresh Look at C. 1.9,' *LCM* 9: 74–5.

Decreus, F. 1984. 'C., c. 1, Cornelius Nepos et les *Aitia* de Callimaque,' *Latomus* 43: 842–60.

Skinner, M.B. 1987. 'Cornelius Nepos and Xenomedes of Ceos: a Callimachean Allusion in C. 1,' *LCM* 12: 22.

Syndikus, H.P. 1987. 'C. 1,' *SPFB* E 32 (1987): 178–80 Nechatová.

Gratwick, A.S. 1991. 'C. 1.10 and the Title of His *libellus*,' *G&R* 38: 199–202.

2

Structure: 8 + 2 (one sentence only, of ten lines; a slight pause before l. 9). This, the best known perhaps of all C.'s lyrics, presents great difficulties of interpretation, partly because of a corrupt text. Debate reaches back to the early Humanists; the most penetrating account is still that of Zicàri 1963. He effectively defends B. Guarinus' emendations; see App. Crit.

Catullus is deeply in love (almost certainly, with Lesbia); and he chooses the trivial-seeming medium of an address to his beloved's pet bird to declare the depth of his passion (*dolor, ardor, tristes curae*). He is clearly not philandering, and by the same token he does not say that he longs to be in the bird's place; the *curae* are the real subject of the poem, and he finds it impossible to forget them in distraction as she does.

Notice above all the poem's *élan*. The continuity of the utterance can be illustrated by one fact: not until we come to l. 9, with *tecum*, do we discover that *passer* is vocative. The address to the bird is carried down to the end of l. 8 before the poet draws breath, as it were, and even to the end of l. 10 (and of the poem) before he finishes the opening sentence (cf. poems 11, 25, 48, 49). In contrast to poem 1, careful development appears to be replaced by a torrent of words, a rush of feeling, and a progression not circular this time but essentially linear, though with discreet repetition of certain concepts. Here we have a clear 8 + 2 line structure (see intr. n. on poem 1), and once more the final couplet leads us in a direction not wholly foreseen (see below). In the order of exposition, as well as in the thought, poem 2 is an extremely sophisticated piece; its imbalance, though apparently 'natural,' is in fact contrived, and applied with great skill. In language there is a mixture of the colloquial (for which poem 1 paves the way) with occasional touches of strangeness or allusiveness. Engelbrecht 1909 protested, with apparently indignant surprise: 'This is not a lovesick poet's groan'; but he wrote when a still somewhat romantic view of C. prevailed (Fr.'s commentary, to which he often refers, had just been published). Much more to our taste is the assessment, two generations later, by Zicàri: 'The fascination of the little poem consists in an air of morbidity, just barely mannered enough to please a reader of refined tastes, or, if we wish, a *docta puella*, who would also know how to appreciate properly the clever variations on, and amplifications of, a familiar *motif*. If the perfection of a poem consists in the degree to which the poet has succeeded in saying what he meant to say, then this poem is perfect – but a *lusus*.' In other words, poem 2 is an *intellectual* poem even while it remains a profound expression of love.

Both Brink 1956 and Zicàri have drawn attention to the carefully formal arrangement ('law of increasing *cola*') by which each of the subordinate relative clauses is a little longer than the preceding one; Brink notices also the way in which the last two lines summarize the opening eight, since *tecum ludere sicut ipsa possem* (l. 9) takes up *ludere* in the opening statement (l. 2), and the words *et tristis animi levare curas* (l. 10) echo *gravis ardor* (l. 8). The charge that the structure of lines 2–8 is 'slack' has to face these and other indications of careful artistry; even its anacoluthon proceeds within traditional literary rules. Zicàri shows how the whole eight-line sentence is carefully organized into two halves, of contrasting structure. He adds: 'The reality of a poem consists in its language; and here the language is not that of passion. For three verses the poet lingers over describing to himself the play between the little creature and the lady; then he thinks over the scene again and interprets it, and from word to word tries out on himself the credibility of his own interpretation. *Credo* … *nescio quid* … *tum*; these are the moments of an evaluation made by the reason. The tenderness and the warmth irradiated by *desiderium* and *solaciolum* are contained within a structure rich in intellectualized elements; and the vocabulary here is the conventional vocabulary of epigrammatic art.'

I have suggested that the last two lines redirect the thought of the poem and thereby contain a surprise. There are in fact two sentiments, each with a considerable literary history, that might be expected by C.'s readers. One of these, 'Would that I were' <some jewel, say, on my mistress' breast> is found in early *skolia* and in Hellenistic poetry. Another (referred to in Bishop 1966) is found at Meleager, *AP* 7.195.1, where ἀπάτημα πόθων is C.'s *solaciolum doloris*. But C. says neither 'could I but be in your place!' nor yet 'could I but be freed altogether from love'; what he says is, 'could I but play with you as she does, and relieve my passion <for the moment>'. There is thus a double surprise, inasmuch as C. alters the customary sentiment in each of the traditional *topoi* he half-recalls.

An obscene interpretation of the word 'sparrow' in this poem and that which follows, and hence of both poems, has commonly been ascribed to Politianus (*Misc.* 1.6), but was originally aired by Pontanus (*Am.* 1.5.1–31);

see Gaisser 1993: 242–3, who appositely remarks, 'There could hardly be a better example of the Renaissance tendency to read Catullus through Martial … placed in Martial's frame [Mart. 11.6], C.'s picture loses its affective and sentimental elements.' The recent revival of this interpretation can be traced in the bibliography below, under the names of Genovese 1974, Giangrande 1975, Hooper 1985, and – on the other side – Jocelyn 1980 and Adams 1982. My own view agrees with that of Wiseman 1985: 138–9; see especially his observation (139, n. 36): 'One of the arguments cited <in favour of the obscene interpretation>, Festus 410 L on *struthion*, is in fact an *e silentio* argument against.' On the passages of Martial usually quoted by defenders of the interpretation, I should like to observe briefly: (i) at 11.6 itself, M. speaks of the conditions of a festival as spurring to *literary* activity (*versu*, … *poetae*), and it seems a priori probable that here, as in 4.14, the phrase *Passer Catulli* does in fact mean a book; in any case, *Catulli* is not quite the same as *Catullianus*; (ii) in 7.14 the *passer*, and Stella's *columba*, are characterized as *nugae*, in contrast with Aulus' genuine human loss. But the coarser interpretation, revived at the Renaissance, especially in Naples by Pontanus and Panormita (and later upheld by Politianus) had a long run, in vernacular literature (where again the sparrow happened to be proverbial for salacity) as well as in Latin. In Pietro Aretino (20.20) *passero* = *membrum virile*; so also *ucello*, in Italian literature of the fourteenth and fifteenth centuries and also of the modern period.

1 *passer*: picked up by *tecum* in l. 9 (after a succession of subordinate clauses in a single sentence without stops; see introductory n.). F. has a long n. on the identification of the bird's species, in which the candidacy of *Passer domesticus* – which, as F. admits, is what Pliny meant by *passer* – is briskly dismissed with a reference to D'Arcy Thompson's *Glossary of Greek Birds*. See however Kipps 1953 for a true and charming account of a house sparrow which sang in captivity and was deeply affectionate.

3 On the apparently strange variant *al. patenti* (X) I wrote in *CE* as follows: 'The original reading *at petenti* was so hard to interpret that (before *appetenti* was thought of) something plainly had to be done to change it for the better, and *at patenti* looks on the whole like an attempt (unsuccessful … and indeed feeble) in this direction.'

 For *appetere* = 'peck at' Kr. cites Livy 7.26.5 (of a bird) *os oculosque hostis rostro et unguibus appetit*.

5 It is usually supposed that *desiderium meum* = 'the object of my longing' (see *OLD* s.v. *desiderium* 2). But Nisbet 1978: 92 overturns this view, with a reference to Anacreon *PMG* 444 (of Ἔρως παρθένιος) πόθῳ στίλβων, and translates 'shining with longing for me' (abl.). See also Baker 1958. I cannot

easily follow M.J. Edwards, *AC* 60 (1991: 262 n. 15) in his contention that *meo* 'must agree with *nitenti* rather than *desiderio*.'

6 See App. Crit. This is (*pace* Kr.) not the only place where *V* apparently had the spelling *libet*, rather than *lubet*. See 62.36, 76.14. In six places however *V* seems to have had *lub-* (*lubet* at 17.17, 24.9, 38.7, 61.126 and 204, *lubeat* 32.6). Notice *O*'s variant here; this may quite possibly be a misinterpretation of *lubet* with superscript *i* (*lǔbet*) in *A*, the *i* being there intended as a correction of the *u*, not – as *O* may have supposed – of the *l*.
   iocari, with partly erotic overtones. Cf. 21.5 *iocaris una*; also 8.6 *multa* ... *iocosa fiebant*, where see n. and reference to Ov. *AA* 3.796.

7–8 Notice that *credo* and *nescio quid* modify *solaciolum* and *carum* respectively, in the direction of uncertainty and vagueness: 'I suppose ...' (C. does not claim to know the girl's inner thoughts). Regarded in this light, *credo* is by no means ironical. It must also be linked, as we have seen, to *solaciolum*; thus B. was wrong in choosing to read *credo, tum gravis acquiescit ardor*. *Solaciolum* as a vocative is also doubtful; it occurs five lines after the initial vocatives *Passer* and *deliciae*. Contrast poem 11, where the addition of the *seu* ... *seu* clauses forms part of a continuation – amplifying *comites* – and the vocative is clearly recalled at l. 14 (*parati*).

7 *doloris*, 8 *ardor*: figurative expressions with erotic significance. Cf. 50.17 *meum dolorem*; 45.16 *ignis* ... *ardet*, 62.23 *iuveni ardenti*, 68.53 *cum tantum arderem* etc. In 62.27 *flamma* and 29 *ardor*, the literal meaning (Hesperus' light) has erotic overtones. For *acquiescere* in the sense intended here, cf. Cicero, *De off.* 1.19 *agitatio mentis, quae numquam acquiescit*, Plin. *Ep.* 4.21.4 *dolor meus acquiescet*. Notice the combination *gravis acq. ardor*; E. quotes Celsus 3.4.14 *febris gravior* and 2.8. 23 *febris quievit*.

9 *O*[1] wrote *secum* (for *tecum*) in the margin, and also glossed *ipsa* with *passer*; clearly he took the meaning to be 'could I but play with *her* as the bird does.' Marginal *secum* can also be seen in the British Library Ms Burney 133 (No. 48 in my Table of Manuscripts). *G*[1]'s variant *al. luderem* must have been taken from *X*, who saw it in *A*; cf. *O*. It does not appear in *R*[2], who presumably rejected it as both unmetrical and ungrammatical.
   Kr. observes that the line has no caesura, each foot consisting of a word; he does not explain this, but compares 42.2. In both poems, it seems to me, the effect striven for is one of heavy emphasis. Notice how *tecum ludere* picks up *quicum ludere* (l. 2).

Engelbrecht, A. 1909. 'Zu C.s Passer,' *Wiener Eranos*: 150–6.

Fay, E.W. 1913. 'C. Carmen 2,' *CP* 8: 301–9.

Braunlich, A.F. 1923. 'Against Curtailing C.'s Passer,' *AJP* 44: 349–52. [Argues strongly for the unity of poems 2 and 2[b]. See however R.G. Kent's *addendum*, which disagrees.]

Brotherton, B. 1926. 'C.'s Carmen II,' *CP* 21: 361–3.

Oko, J. 1928. 'L'ode de C. sur le passereau (Carm. 2),' *Eos* 31: 79–86.

Kipps, C. 1953. *Sold for a Farthing* [U.S. title, *Clarence, the Life of a Sparrow*]. London.

Brink, C.O. 1956. *Latin Studies and the Humanities* (Inaugural Lecture, Cambridge): 9–13.

Baker, S. 1958. 'C.'s Cum Desiderio Meo,' *CP* 53: 243–4.

Putnam, M.C.J. 1959. *Patterns of Personality and Imagery* (diss. Harvard). Cambridge, Mass.: 143–52.

Zicàri, M. 1963. 'Il secondo carme di C.,' *Studi Urbinati* 37: 205–32.

Bishop, J.D. 1966. 'C. 2 and Its Hellenistic antecedents,' *CP* 61: 158–67.

Gugel, H. 1968. 'Die Einheit von C.s erstem Passergedicht,' *Latomus* 27: 810–22.

Link-Moser, E., and Schmidt, E.A. 1970. 'Gebet eines Liebenden: C.s erstes passer-Gedicht,' *Mitteilungen für Lehrer der alten Sprachen*, 1. Jahrgang, Heft II: 3–8.

Genovese, E.N. 1974. 'Symbolism in the Passer Poems,' *Maia* 26: 121–5.

Giangrande, G. 1975. 'C.'s Lyrics on the Passer,' *MPhL* 1: 137–46.

Offerman, H. 1975. 'Zu C. 2, 7f.,' *Eranos* 73: 55–61.

Jocelyn, H.D. 1980. 'On Some Unnecessarily Indecent Interpretations of C. 2 and 3,' *AJP* 101: 421–4.

Adams, J.N. 1982. *The Latin Sexual Vocabulary*. London.

Senzasono, L. 1983. 'Il c. 2 di C.,' *Liceo-ginnasio E. Q. Visconti (Roma), Annuario 1983*: 67–81.

Nadeau, Y. 1984. 'C.'s Sparrow, Martial, Juvenal and Ovid,' *Latomus* 43: 861–8.

Perotti, P.A. 1984, 'Per una rilettura dei carmi 2–3 di C.,' *GIF* 36: 253–61.

Hooper, R.W. 1985. 'In Defence of C.'s Dirty Sparrow,' *G&R* 32: 162–78.

Lund, A.A. 1986. 'Zur korrekten Restitution des zweiten Gedichtes C.s,' *Maia* 38: 153–8.

Wirth, T. 1986. 'C. c. 2: passer und malum als zeichen der Liebe,' *RhM* 129: 36–53.

Felgentreu, F. 1993. '*Passer* und *malum* in C.s c. 2,' *Philologus* 137: 216–222. [Join 2[b] to 2.]

Thomas, R.F. 1993. 'Sparrows, Hares and Doves: A Catullan Metaphor and Its Tradition,' *Helios* 20: 131–42.

2[b]

There can be no link with poem 2: (i) the structure of poem 2 is complete and self-contained, on the pattern 8 + 2 lines, with the energetic resolution (and statement) in the last two lines; (ii) the syntactical change in the tense and mood of the verbs (*possem ... gratum est*) cannot be properly explained away, despite the efforts of editors to do so; Mart. 2.63.3 (*luxuria est si tanti dives amares*) is not a genuine parallel (see Zicàri on poem 2); (iii) some *sudden* event – such as the dropping of the apple in the story, here alluded to, of Atalanta and Hippomenes – is envisaged in poem 2[b], whereas in poem 2 C. is reflecting on a wholly static situation (see Kr.); (iv) it is probable that a short poem, of which poem 2[b] is a fragment, was inserted between the two *passer* poems, just as poem 6 appears in the collection between the two kiss poems 5 and 7.

1 *ferunt* (cf. 64.2 *dicuntur*), 'the tale is told': here a sign that C. is passing from first-person reference (*gratum mihi*) to the world of myth.

   Atalanta (*pernix* = ποδώκης; Hesiod, *Eoeae* fr. 21 Rz = 73 Merkelbach-West) had many suitors, whom she dismissed by inviting them to run a race with her. To one of them, Hippomenes (or Milanion), Aphrodite had given three golden apples from the garden of the Hesperides; these he threw down as she ran, and she could not resist picking them up, so that he won the race (and her). The scholiast on Theocr. 3.42, who tells us this, also interprets the story as indicating that A. herself desired to be defeated – a characteristically Hellenistic psychological innovation. See Philetas fr. 18 Powell, Ov. *M.* 10.560–80.

2 *aureolum*: probably, as Kr. suggests, the adj. refers to colour only. See 61.160 *aureolos pedes*; V. *Ecl.* 3.71, 8.52 (*aurea mala*).

3 *zonam solvere* = ζώνην λύειν (*Od.* 11.245, if the line is genuine); cf. 61.53, 67.28. *soluit*: trisyllable (the *u* was originally vocalic, as at 61.53 and elsewhere; but poets as early as Ennius found the consonantal alternative useful.

   For the leap into simile at the conclusion of a short personal statement, cf. 65.19–24, where the poet's imagination appears to be absorbed, as here, in the simile for its own sake.

   R[2]'s marginal remark *erat negatam* is of a kind unparalleled in his Catullus at least. There is more than one way to interpret it. McKie (198–9) insists that it must have been written immediately after the erasure of the word *negatam* and the substitution for it of *ligatam* were performed. I should have thought that, if this were so, *R*[2]'s natural mode of expressing the change would have been to write simply *al. negatam*. To me, the use of the imperfect tense ('it used to be *negatam*') has a distancing effect; Coluccio appears to imply something like this: 'the original reading – as I remember (and I should like to record the fact) – was *negatam*, though I previously emended it unhesitatingly to *ligatam*; but now I am not so sure.' (No doubt the basis of Coluccio's obvious initial confidence and therefore unusually violent course in actually erasing the word was his finding or remembering the line as it is given by Priscian.)

Eisenhut, H. 1965. 'Zu C.s c. 2a und der Trennung der Gedichte in den Handschriften,' *Philologus* 109: 301–5.

Baldwin, B. 1982. 'Catullan Interpretations: Some Pointers,' *Corolla Londiniensis* 2: 9–13.

Dettmer, H. 1984. 'C. 2B from a Structural Perspective,' *CW* 78: 107–10.

(See also bibliography on poem 2.)

3

Structure: 5 + 5 + 2 + 4 + 2.

On the death of the *passer*. This poem must of course be read as a companion piece to poem 2, whether or not the three lines we designate as poem 2[b] form part of an intervening poem, now lost (and the vast majority of scholars believe that they do).

We saw in poem 2 how the poet surprises us in the ending, at least if we have had the traditional literary genres in mind and have formed our expectations accordingly. The same thing occurs, somewhat more obviously, in poem 3. (Here, however, the structural formula is not 8 + 2 but rather 16 + 2). The note of lamentation for the bird, which is struck at the outset, is to all appearance preserved up to the exclamations in line 16, after which the thought moves in a quite unexpected direction (see 11–12 n.). It is typical of C.'s wit to produce a *fulmen in clausula* of this kind – not, as we might expect, in the short poems usually styled 'epigrams' for metrical reasons (poems 69–116), but rather in the monostichic poems of the 'polymetric' section of the *liber* (poems 1–60); these in many respects cleave strongly to the epigrammatic formulae of Rhianus or Meleager, notwithstanding the difference in metre. (Latin elegiac epigrams hardly acquired this characteristic before the time of Martial; in C. himself, the elegiac epigrams, poems 69–116, are generally marked by unity of theme and treatment from start to finish.)

As we re-read the poem (which, because of the surprise, we are surely meant to do), it becomes clear that certain expressions had all along pointed to a witty conclusion. *Homines venustiores*, for example, has little to do with love: at 35.17 *venuste* indicates intellectual brilliance, at 36.17 *invenustum* the opposite. Cf. also 13.6, where *venuste noster* closely follows *sale et omnibus cachinnis*. In lines 11 and 12, both the sounds (*it per iter*) and the language, with the off-hand colloquialism of *tenebricosum* and *negant* (continued in *male sit*, and in the use in poetry of *bellus*), render the tone by degrees more and more quasi-comical and almost flippant, so that the threatening shades of Orcus, and of solemnity, are kept at arm's length. But the purpose which this creation of an unlamenting tone actually serves becomes clear only in retrospect, at a second reading, and after the last two lines have made their mark.

Despite the change of direction, there are certain indications of circular structure at the end, where *meae puellae* (l. 17) echoes lines 3–4 and *ocelli* reminds us of *oculis* (l. 5); so too the *flendo* of l. 18 reminds us of the opening word *lugete*. By such means the poem's artistic unity is finally asserted.

1 The plurals have seemed to editors to require explanation. But the Latin habit of mind, which gave to so many abstract nouns (e.g., *fides, Fides*) a divine embodiment, implies that the regular and the personified use of such nouns lie close together and could not always be sharply distinguished. Thus some editors think it necessary to print *Veneres* at 86.6, whereas others do not. Similar doubt attends the Graces (*gratiae, Gratiae*). Consequently it seems quite natural to use plurals even when personification is implied.

For the meaning of *venustiorum* cf. intr. n., para. 2. As Kr. points out, Venus is the patroness of all that can be called *venustus* (he quotes Plaut. *Stich.* 278 *amoenitates omnium venerum et venustatum*); hence, of *homines venusti* in any sense of the adj.

2 'All who feel for loveliness.'
quantum est + gen. is colloquial; cf. e.g., Plaut. *Capt.* 836 *quantum est hominum optumorum optume, Rud.* 706 *quantum est hominum sacrilegissume*. Cf. also 9.10 n. The idiom was metrically useful at the end of a hendecasyllabic line: see 10.24, 12.3, (13.10), 23.18, 27.2, 45.26.

5 *oculis:* a Hellenistic figure (Callim. *H.* 3.211 ἴσον φαέεσσι φιλῆσαι, Mosch. 4.9 τὸν τίεσκον ἴσον φαέεσσιν ἐμοῖσιν); cf. 14.1, 82.2, 104.2, Plaut. *Mil.* 984, Ter. *Ad.* 903.

6 *mellitus:* a slang expression (48.1, 99.1; some eds. would read *mellitus puer* at 21.11). Cf. Cicero, *Ad Att.* 1.18.1, and later examples. Before C. the expression *meum mel* (in a similar sense) occurs in Plautus (*Poen.* 367; *melilla* at *Cas.* 135).

7 *ipsam,* 'his mistress'; cf. *ipsa* 2.9 and *ipse* = 'the master, the owner' 114.6; Plaut. *Aul.* 356 *ipsus, Cas.* 790 *ipsa.* We should take *ipsam* with *suam;* the enjambement will then be similar to that in lines 13–14. To take *ipsam* with *matrem* will not do: *matrem* gains nothing, and *suam* can hardly stand alone. At 32.1 I read *ipsimilla* ('my little mistress'); see App. Crit. and n. there, and cf. Petron. 63.3, 69.3, 75.11, 76.1).
puella here = *any* girl.

8 The second syllable of *illius* is always short in C.; B. expelled *illīus* from 67.23, and I have followed him (see n. there).

9 Agreement of $R^2(m^2)$ with *O* points, as it often does, to a correcting variant (*al. siliens*) in *X*, reproducing a similar variant in *A* (note the unusual occurrence of a variant in *O* here). The superfluous *movebat* has slipped in, as a repetition of the end of line 8, because of the similarity of *illius* and *illuc.* The observation *al. vacat hoc verbum* must have come from *X*, who probably was the first to

make the blunder of introducing the word (*O* does not have it). Notice how *m* omits the word, following *R*²'s observation; but *m*² restores it, simply because it occurs in the text of his exemplar *R*, even though it has already been condemned (by *R*²).

10 *pīpiare* usually of infants' cries, or of the shrill chirping of very young birds (*OLD* s.vv. *pipio, pipito*); *titiare*, it has been claimed (see Birt, as quoted by Fr.), was appropriate to the natural song of birds, especially sparrows (Suet. fr. 161 Reifferscheid, *passerum est titiare*; see also A. Riese, *Anth. Lat.*, 762). The substitution, if such it was, is of course metrically necessary. On *pipiare* and other forms, see Ellis, *ed. maior*² (1878): 350–1.

11–12 A parody of epic style; but *tenebricosum* is a colloquial, even somewhat vulgar form, which lightens the tone and firmly identifies it as mock-heroic. The humorous pseudo-solemnity of the whole passage is greatly deflated in the last two lines of the poem, where the *passer* is (or, if we read *vestra*, the shades of Orcus are) reproached for the trivial crime of reddening Lesbia's eyes. For the general idea, editors quote Greek parallels from *AP* 7 (199.3, 203.4, 211.3, 213.6).

12 *illuc*, not *illud*.

(i) The bird *is now* going *by way of* the road (less probably, 'the journey') <*to the place*> *from* which, they say, no one returns. It makes little sense to say that one returns *from* the road, when the journey is not yet over. The bourne from which no traveller returns is of course a firm literary convention, and it is no road or journey but a *place* – the realm of Acheron – as the long list of allusions in Friedrich's edition will confirm. Hence *illuc*, not *illud*.

(ii) Metrically, *illuc* is a spondee, *illud* a trochee. In a very important and influential article (1969: 38–43), Otto Skutsch showed that, in the group of poems 2–26 to which this belongs (though not in the dedication poem 1, which would naturally have been composed and added later), out of 263 hendecasyllabic lines there is not even one with a trochaic 'basis,' i.e., a trochaic first foot; whereas 260 (and I hope presently to show that the number should be 261) out of the 263 have a spondaic basis. Hence again *illuc* is to be preferred to *illud*.

12 For the sentiment: cf. Philetas fr. 6 (Powell, *Collectanea Alexandrina*) ἄτραπον εἰς Ἀίδαο / ἤνυσα, τὴν οὔπω τις ἐναντίον ἦλθεν ὁδίτης and Theocr. 17.118–20 τὰ δὲ μυρία τῆνα ... ἀέρι πᾳ κέκρυπται, ὅθεν πάλιν οὐκέτι νόστος.

13 *at*, to indicate a transition involving a strong contrast: cf. 36.18 n.
vobis male sit ... To the Hellenistic parallels for ideas in this poem (see 11–12 nn.) we can now add a set of papyrus fragments from Euphorion's *Thrax* (frs. 413–15 *SH*) containing a series of curses called down on an unnamed enemy for the death of some victim, published in *Supplementum Hellenisticum* (ed. Lloyd-Jones and Parsons) 1983. Their tone (as was pointed out by Professor C. Brown, who kindly drew the papyrus to my attention) seems to be mock-heroic,

and the editors suggested that the victim is an animal; Lloyd-Jones (*SIFC* 77, 1984: 72) further suggests that it may be a pet bird; and he compares it with our poem.

male ... malae: cf. κακὸς κακῶς (e.g., Ar. *Eq.* 2) and similar expressions (Plaut. *Aul.* 43 *mala malam aetatem exigas*). Cf. also 61.19, 78.4.

14 At 2.9 (where see n.) G^1 alone preserves (from X) a faulty variant reading; here, G^1 alone preserves a *sound* variant reading, from the same source. (It seems possible that R^2, who saw X, was blind to the merits of the variant because he failed to recognize *orci* as the genitive singular of *Orcus*.) *tenebrae Orci* (Lucr. 1.115) is a solemn expression; here (as at Plaut. *Pseud.* 795) the effect is mock-solemn.

bella, 'pretty' – another slightly colloquial word, which further lightens the tone.

15 The effect of *mihi* is to transfer the girl's feeling for the bird to the poet.

15–17 I find difficulties (later to be specified) in accepting the text as it is given in most editions, and have attempted to deal with these by

(i) removing the period at the end of l. 15;

(ii) placing l. 16 in a parenthesis, with a semicolon at the end of the line;

(iii) reading *vestra* (referring to the shades of Orcus) in place of *tua*.

There is some indication of Ms authority for the change from *tua* to *vestra*. Avantius, in his *Emendationes in Catullum*, published in 1495, attributes four readings, differing from the universally received vulgate of his time, to an *antiquior codex* in which he found them. These are:

(a) at 2.9, for *sicut ipsa possem*, read *sicut ipse possem*;

(b) at 2^b.3, for *habet diu ligatam*, read *habet diu negatam*;

(c) (here), for *tua nunc opera*, read *vestra nunc opera*;

(d) at 3.18, for *timent* [not *tument*] *ocelli*, read *rubent ocelli*.

Two of these readings (b and d) prove, as McKie (5–6) has noted, that Avantius' *antiquior codex* was genuine: they reproduce what we now know to be the original reading of R. So there need be no doubt that the two remaining readings, including *vestra* here, really did appear in the codex that Avantius consulted.

Additional probability is added to the reading *vestra* by the metrical fact, just noted, that *tua*, an iambus, is metrically at odds with the spondaic basis used, not only in the rest of this poem (since we have decided that *illuc* is the better reading in l. 12), but, with only two exceptions (both explicable) in the entire 263 hendecasyllables of the group of poems 2–26. *Vestra*, on the other hand, being a spondee, conforms to the (nearly 100 per cent) rule of the group.

McKie, who of course did not contemplate the parenthesis and repunctuation I now suggest, envisaged the possibility that the reading *vestra* might be 'attractive to some,' as he puts it; but he adds (p. 6 n. 1): 'They must rely heavily, however, on Housman's "Vester=Tuus," *CQ* 3 (1909), 244–248.' But if we do as I have urged, putting the preceding line in a parenthesis and altering the punctuation, there will be no need to rely on Housman. Parentheses in Catullus, often of an exclamatory sort, can be found at 1.7 (Iuppiter!), 29.21 (malum!), 61.152–3 (refrain, and apostrophe to Hymen, in mid-sentence), 64.135 (immemor a!), and 68.89 (nefas!), among other instances. At 68.141, Gordon Williams (1968: 712) suggested putting *atqui ... aequuum est* between brackets and thus removing the need to indicate a lacuna after the line.

Now to translate – with slight omissions – the text I offer: 'Shades of Orcus, you have taken my pretty bird away (A shameful deed! Poor little bird!); it is *your* fault that ...' Some early scribe (it may be suggested), not understanding the implied parenthesis, altered *vestra* to *tua* because he thought it referred to *passer*.

Goold 1969, who would altogether eliminate hiatus in Catullus, has constructed a plausible case for reading *quod, miselle passer*. He finds (p. 196) that *o factum male* cannot be balanced against *o miselle passer* because the first *o* is exclamatory but the second merely indicates the vocative, its real function being to 'explain' the pronoun 'you' (implied in *tua*). 'Transpose the rhetorical situation into English, and the clumsiness of the repetition becomes self-evident: "O calamity, o sparrow, you have made her weep."' This begs the question whether the next line has to be attached to the end of line 16; Goold does not accept the possibility that both *o*'s are exclamatory, but merely remarks that 'vocative *o* after exclamatory *o* is intolerable'; therefore he emends the second *o* to *quod*, on the grounds that *o miselle passer* 'contravenes the stylistic practice of Catullus' (p. 199) by placing vocative *o* before a noun and adjective; but in order to establish this 'stylistic practice' he must alter the manuscript reading accepted by scholarship at both 1.9 (where he chooses Bergk's unacceptable rewriting of the line: see n.), and 31.12. But (i) hiatus with pathetic effect does seem to occur in Catullus (66.11; 68.158; 76.10 if we accept the V reading) and also in Propertius (2.15.1 *o me felicem! o nox*, etc.), and would be particularly effective here before the exclamatory repeated *o* (as for parenthetical exclamation in Catullus, there are in all about a dozen instances of this, some of which I have cited above), and (ii) the *wit* of the poem (and Catullus' love poems rarely lack witty touches) depends partly on the final two lines with their surprise ending: at this point in the poem, Catullus is about to show the reader, in a couplet which surely ought to be self-contained, that the poem is not after all a lament for the bird but a reproach, addressed to some person or persons, for reddening the girl's eyes with tears. To introduce this notion too early, in mid-line (as Goold would do), tends to blunt the point when it comes.

Two final arguments. First, the word *opera* should surely be linked to activity rather than to passivity. Qualified by *tua*, it would refer to the prima facie victim, the bird; by *vestra*, to the subject (plural) of the phrases *omnia bella devoratis* and *bellum passerem abstulistis*. Notice the sequence of active verbs: (i) in a general statement, in the present tense, *omnia bella devoratis*; (ii) in a particular application, in the perfect tense, *mihi passerem abstulistis*; then (iii), in a climax, passing in time (and ascending in degree) from the wrong experienced by C. to that now experienced by the *puella*: *vestra nunc* ... ('and *now* it is your fault, again, that ...'). With the reading *tua* there is no real climax, and – what is extremely unlike C. – the word *nunc* becomes little more than a metrical space-filler. Secondly, the apostrophe *at vobis* (l. 13) is marked by a strongly adversative *at*. This should herald a change of direction that dominates the final (climactic) section of the poem. (Examples of *single* apostrophes that do this will be given in a moment.) Instead, if we transfer our attention at l. 16 to *miselle passer*, we get *two* apostrophes, each of three lines – one apostrophe following upon another – which seems to me much weaker. And I doubt if there are any examples in Catullus' shorter poems of a double apostrophe in any way comparable to this. Single apostrophes that turn the movement of a poem and provide a strong ending may be found at poem 27 (*at vos*), 35 (*ignosco tibi*), 36 (*nunc o ...*), 37 (*tu praeter omnes*), 46 (*o dulces*), and 76 (*o di*). In poem 36 there is a strong mid-poem apostrophe to a goddess, returning however at the end, with adversative *at vos*, to the *Annales Volusi* with which we started.

Line 16 finds an echo in a ten-line inscription in memory of the dog Myia (*CE* 1512 Bücheler: see F., who gives the text).

Skutsch, O. 1969. 'Metrical Variations and Some Textual Problems in C.,' *BICS* 16: 38–40. [Read *illuc.*]

Goold, G.P. 1969. 'C. 3.16,' *Phoenix* 23: 186–203.

Walters, K.R. 1976. 'Catullan Echoes in the Second Century AD, *CEL* 1512,' *CW* 69: 353–9.

Moussy, C. 1977. 'Veneres Cupidinesque (C. 3.1),' *Mélanges offerts à L. Séder Senghor*. Dakar: 305–14.

Dahlén, E. 1977. 'Der tote Sperling der Lesbia: einige Randbemerkungen zu C.s Gedicht 3,' *Eranos* 75: 15–21.

Cassadio, V. 1986–7. 'C. III.1 ss.,' *Museum Criticum* 21/22: 337–8.

Mezzabotta, M.R. 1990. 'Johannes Burman, Catullus 3.11–14 and Virgil, *Aeneid* 1.33,' *LCM* 15: 190–1.

Elerick, C. 1993. 'On Translating Catullus 3,' *Scholia* 2: 90–6.

4

Structure: 12 + 12 + 3.
The *phaselus* was a handy vessel, of varying size, used to convey goods, or passengers, or both, in the Mediterranean sea and on the Nile. At sea, for example, it could serve as a tender to ships which by reason of their

deep draught had to stand off the shore; sometimes it was towed astern by larger ships in order to do their inshore ferrying upon arrival in port, and thus could be said to make long voyages *in statu pupillari*, as it were. Again because of its shallow draught, it was particularly useful for transport 'around the fields' during the Nile floods (V. *Geo.* 4.287–94). An Egyptian setting for the poem should perhaps not be ruled out. It has been subjected to an extensive analysis by Peter Glasgow. In an article, not yet published but which he and I hope to publish in consultation, it will be suggested that the poem may be in essence a version, slightly adapted, of a lost *Phaselus Berenices* (Βερενίκης φάσηλος) by Callimachus, on a vessel owned by the royal heroine of poem 66 (as well as of Callimachus' *Coma* and *Victoria Berenices*). In this interpretation the lake, originally, is Lake Mareotis; Catullus' *Iuppiter secundus* is Ζεὺς Οὔριος; the place names derive from ancient trade routes; and the Dioscuri (line 27) are mentioned in connection with their worship at the λιμὴν λιμναῖος. To see a possible translation here may seem to have some slight advantage over the often-expressed view that the poem has something to do with Catullus' return from abroad, at least for the following reason. The view just mentioned raises a question, which editors have not answered. Poems 46, 31, and 10, commonly believed to be linked with poem 4 in a 'return from Bithynia' cycle, leave no doubt about the identity of both speaker and place. Why should Catullus here – and only here – if he is the speaker or is represented by the intermediary, and if the setting is Sirmio, leave out all the names that could attach the poem to its occasion? In Glasgow's words, 'the modern recognition of the hazards involved in the identification of a poet's *persona* with himself causes us to view this traditional hypothesis with suspicion and explore other paths of interpretation ... It has never been seriously considered whether this poem might be, as others of Catullus certainly are, a translation of a Greek original.' Certainly it is so placed in the collection as to attract the greatest possible attention: not only very early, but also between the two pairs, of sparrow poems and kiss poems, which have always been pre-eminently linked with the poet's fame. It would be hardly surprising if Catullus chose here to exhibit his Callimachean affiliation by example, since in the opening poem he had undoubtedly done so by precept. This interpretation, if it could be incontrovertibly established, would explain much that is Greek, and specifically Hellenistic and Callimachean, about poem 4; these characteristics have been noted by several critics. Mette, for example, was in 1962 the first to show systematically that the poem owes much (directly or indirectly, we should now have to add) to four different, or slightly different, categories of Hellenistic epigram: namely, dedicatory epigrams, whether in the first person (self-dedicatory) or third person, and also sepulchral epigrams, which may similarly be expressed either in the first or third person. Certainly these two kinds of epigram, the dedicatory and the sepulchral, on whose fusion the effect of the poem depends, are represented to an outstanding degree in the epigrams of Callimachus himself. Without prejudice to the question whether poem 4 is a translation, and considering it simply as a creation of C.'s art, we may say this:

The poem is an extremely sophisticated composition, inserted between the two pairs of Lesbia poems (just as 2^b divides one pair, and 6 the other) and having nothing to do with her. It brilliantly exploits the pure iambic line – difficult in Latin – to express a feeling of speed in movement, suitable to the ship. Linguistically, it explores the creation of an impression of remoteness and mystery in a short poem – written in a quite unheroic metre – by the use of epic words and phrases, usually with Greek overtones. In addition to this, the poem – like others of C.'s 'polymetrics' – contains a surprise towards the end. In ll. 1–24, it seems to derive from the fusion of two kinds of funerary epigram. In one of these, the deceased person speaks to the passer-by (ξένος, παροδίτης), giving – according to a formula, and in a certain order – his or her name, accomplishments (ἀρεταί), origin (home, parents, antecedents), or ancestors. In the other, the poet or his persona is made to speak about the dead in the third person; in this category are included several epigrams on 'dead' ships, for example *AP* 9.34 and 36. Within the last three lines, however, and not clearly until the middle of these, it suddenly emerges that the poem is not, after all, composed in the vein of a funerary epigram of this sort but rather in that of the dedicatory poem, 'devoting' some object to a god. Such were, in the first person, Callimachus' *Ep.* 5, on a nautilus shell, and in the third person, *AP* 6.69 and 70. The reader, who was familiar (at least in C.'s circle) with the kinds and conventions of Hellenistic poetry, has after 24 lines made up his mind what he is dealing with, namely a funerary epigram of a certain type; thus the sudden change of direction takes him unawares, when the poem becomes a dedication instead.

Apart from the Hellenism of the language (as *impotentia*, for example, reflects the meaning attached in Greek to ἀκρατής), a remote and legendary atmosphere is sustained by the use of an intensely artificial diction. A ship becomes a 'floating plank,' foliage is 'hair,' and oars are 'little palms.' Here we have a strenuous effort to capture the vision of the *phaselus* as a living thing, one to which strangely anthropomorphic language may be applied in acknowledgment of the rapprochement between animate and inanimate beings that pervades the early world of Greek myth. With this mythopoeic end in view, the language maintains its elevation in other respects also: not only is a forest *comata*, a sail *linteum*, but the sea is *aequor* (an epic substitution), or *freta*; a following wind is *Iuppiter secundus*, and Pollux is

'Castor's twin.' Throughout the poem, Catullus – or perhaps Callimachus – gently insists that the ship is to be regarded as a quasi-human organism, with a personality, a life history, and its own record of achievement; and secondly, that its 'life' is to be seen in an ambience of legend. It is the poet's choice of vocabulary that (helped by the rapidity of his metre) seizes the reader's attention and engages his, or her, sympathy for an object that lies altogether remote from any personal feeling.

There is a celebrated full-length parody of this poem (so close that it can be used for checking C.'s text, e.g., at l. 2, where it restores *celerrimus*) in the *Appendix Vergiliana*, *Catalepton* 10 (*Sabinus ille, quem videtis hospites*; Sabinus had been a *mulio*).

Metre: Pure iambic trimeter (cf. poem 29).

1 *hospites*: the address to the casual visitor (ξεῖνε) belongs to the genre of sepulchral, rather than dedicatory, inscriptions (Kr. and F.).

2 *ait ... celerrimus*, a conspicuous Grecism. Cf. 1.16 *stetisse dicit*.
  navium c.: for the fact that the adj. in the superlative fails to follow, as we should expect, the gender of the partitive gen., editors cite Cicero, *ND* (wrongly '*TD*' in F.) 2.130 *Indus, qui est omnium fluminum maximus*.

3–4 *neque ... nequisse*, 6–7 *negat ... negare*: effective use of the double negative has of course the effect of reducing the boastfulness of a claim; cf. Lucil. 33 M *si me nescire hoc nescis*, Plaut. *Amph.* 345 *faciam ut verum dicas dicere*.

3 *trabis* = anything made of timber (which widens the yacht's boast: she could 'overhaul anything afloat').
  impetus in this limited sense is an epic word (Enn. *Ann.* 376 and 506 Skutsch, V. *Aen.* 5.219).

4 For *palmulis* ('only here,' F., but see V. *Aen.* 5.163 [Fletcher 1991: 92]) cf. 64.7 *palmis*.

6 *minacis*: on account of its violent and unpredictable northeast and southeast gales (metaphor in Hor. *Od.* 1.33.15, 3.3.5 and 9.22–3).

7 *-ve* can stand in a mixed series with *-que* because of *negat negare*, which is double negative in syntax, positive in meaning; see 3–4 n.

8 See App. Crit. The ship's course would naturally follow the south side (*not* 'Thrace') of the Propontis; but it was the cold winds *from* the direction of Thrace that made it rough (*horrida*). The nominative form of the name of the wind in question is *Thracias*. (See however the objections raised to the word by van Dam 1990, n. 6, which do not seem to me conclusive.) For *Thracias* as the name of a wind, cf. 26.3, where *Apheliotes* = *subsolanus*. As D. A. Kidd notes ('Some Problems in C. LXVI,' *Antichthon* 4 [1970]: 38–49), 'Pliny *NH* xviii 278 includes Orion among the *horrida sidera* which are responsible for stormy weather'; what should be observed here is the application of the adjective *horridus* to

rough, choppy *waves*, not to rough country. Cf. 64.270 *horrificans*. As editors have commented (see van Dam 1990: 446 and n. 5), the voyager by water will not *see* Thrace as *horrida*.

9 *Propontida*: C. lengthens a final short open vowel at l. 18 and at 29.4 (both in 'pure' iambics). In his n., F. suggests that C. 'may have had precedent for his use in Greek iambographers.'

10ff. Since Bithynia was pre-eminent as a source of ship timber, no necessary conclusion follows from these lines as to the starting point of a particular voyage.

10 *iste post phaselus*: conferring quasi-adjectival force on the adverb *post* may be intended to be seen as another Grecism (cf. 2 above); but it should be noticed (Kr.) that Ennius (in prose, translating Euhemerus) does the same thing (*Varia*, 113 V² *ceterosque tunc homines*); for examples from Terence, Cicero, Virgil, and Horace, see F.

12 *saepe sib-*: for alliteration based on *s* in the description of wind-noises, cf. 84.5–7, 10–12 (and see notes there).

13 Apostrophe, often used by C. (see ll. 26–7, 64.69, 253, 299), is characteristic of Hellenistic poetry; see A. Gellius 13.27.3 on Virgil's somewhat 'neoteric' use of this device.

Boxwood was proverbially abundant on Cytorus, a mountain just to the south of the famous shipbuilding city of Amastris; to take boxwood to Cytorus was to take coals to Newcastle, or owls to Athens (Kr.); see Eust. 88.3 on *Il*. 1.206. Cytorus was also the name of a seaport; but the adj. *buxifer* more naturally applies to the mountain. Cf. also l. 14, where *tibi* suggests that only one seaport, with its interior, is intended. Boxwood, however, seems to have had nothing in particular to do with shipbuilding; and *buxifer* may well be a purely 'learned' epithet, either translating something in Callimachus, or at any rate suggesting Callimachus; cf. 7.4 *lasarpiciferis* (linked to Cyrene and Battus) and see introductory n. Kr. and F. observe that C. uses such compound adjs. chiefly in his longer poems, and among the short poems only where the tone is elevated (as here and at 11.6–7) or else where a solemn note is parodied (36.7, 58ᵇ.3 and 5). Eust. 362.1 on *Il*. 2.853 πυξοφόρος ἡ Κύτωρος περιᾴδεται.

17 *imbuisse*: cf. 64.11. Perhaps tr. 'initiated' or 'baptized.'

18 *impotentia*, a personification: 'uncontrolled, wild.' Used (by poets) of amorous passion, as at 8.9 and 35.12; of the wind, by Hor. *Od*. 3.30.3.

19 The first *sive* is suppressed, as at Hor. *Od*. 1.3. 16 (also *S*. 2.5.10–11 and 8.16).

20 *vocare*, 'invite.' Ov. *Ep*. 13.9 *qui tua vela vocarat . . . ventus* (other refs. in E. and Kr.).

utrumque = *pedibus aequis* (Ov. *P*. 4.5.3), 'running before a stern-wind.'

23 *sibi* = *a se* ('Dative of agent, not of advantage . . . The yacht speaks throughout *in propria persona*, as one who manages her own affairs,' L.). C. adds these datives only to perfect participle passive forms.

24 *novissime* (*V*'s reading; see App. Crit.) should be retained. The adverb, in the sense 'after all else' (*OLD* 2), is perfectly good Latin of the Republican period (Varro *RR* 1.31.4); it will not scan in hexameters and so lacks the poetic *cachet*. But the word, so taken, does not suit the notion that the poem refers to no more than a single (westbound) voyage, since in that event the ship would abstain from vows only at the last stage, that of river navigation, which would be the *safest* part of the voyage. It is reasonable to take *esse facta* as pluperfect in intention; as Munro puts it, the *oratio recta* would be *neque ulla vota dis litoralibus mihi facta erant tum, cum novissime veni ad hunc lacum*, and the implication: 'I reached the last stage without ever having had to make such vows.' This fits the interpretation by which the ship has made *many* voyages to and fro, through many (*tot*, 18) stormy seas, and has now come to sheltered waters in its old age. For a general interpretation, see the introductory n.
   limpidum: As F. points out, the word occurs only here in verse, and 'appears elsewhere only in the most prosaic and technical contexts,' e.g., of a clean water supply in Vitruvius. This serves (among other considerations) to render unlikely the emendation *limpidae* at 31.13 (see n. there).

25 *prius* here = 'long ago'; *fuere* implies 'past and gone,' as in V. *Aen.* 2.325 *fuimus Troes*.

25–6 *recondita senet quiete*: a poetic compression, expanded by Kr. as = *senectutem per quietem loco recondito degit*.

26 *senet* is archaic in style, and solemn in intonation, but (as Kr. notes) the metre demands it here.

27 Castor and Pollux were the protecting deities of seafarers; cf. 68.65. F., who gives references, also shows that Castor was regarded as the senior in rank or prestige, so that the name of Pollux was sometimes suppressed (the pair being sometimes referred to as *Castores*). Besides this passage, cf. Stat. *S.* 4.6.15–16, where Pollux is simply *alter Castor*, and Cicero, *Verr.* 2.1.129, where *aedes Castoris* = their joint temple in Rome.

Smith, C.L. 1892. 'C. and the Phaselus of His Fourth Poem,' *HSCP* 3: 75–89.

Cichorius, C. 1903. 'Zur Deutung von C.s Phaselusgedicht,' *Festschrift für O. Hirschfeld*. Berlin: 467-83.

Sonnenburg, P.E. 1920. 'De Catulli Phaselo,' *RhM* 73: 129–36.

Mackay, L.A. 1930. 'Phaselus ille iterum (C. c. IV),' *CP* 25: 77–8.

Zimmerman, F. 1932. 'Virgil und C.,' *PhW* 52: 1119–30. [*Catalepton* 10.]

Terzaghi, N. 1938. 'Due interpretazioni: 1. – *Catalepton* 10,' *SIFC* 15: 55–64.

Hoppe, P. 1939. 'C.s Phaselus,' *PhW* 59: 1139–42.

Bongi, V. 1946. 'Il carme 4 di C. e la sua critica,' *RAL* 1: 70–82.

Schmidt, M. 1955. 'Phasellus ille (zu C. 4),' *Gymnasium* 62: 43–9.

Copley, F.O. 1958. 'C. 4: The World of the Poem,' *TAPA* 89: 9–13.

Mette, H.J. 1962. 'C. Carm. 4,' *RhM* 105: 153–7.

Putnam, M.C.J. 1962. 'C.'s Journey (Carm. 4),' *CP* 57: 10–19.

Hornsby, R.A. 1963. 'The Craft of C. (Carm. 4),' *AJP* 84: 256–65.

Seelbach, W. 1963. 'Zu lateinischen Dichtern,' *RhM* 106: 348–9.

Richardson, L., Jr. 1972. 'C. 4 and *Catalepton* 10 Again,' *AJP* 93: 215–22.

Leonotti, E. 1982. 'Osservazioni sulla struttura formale del c. 4 di C.,' *Anazetesis* 6–7: 1–7.

Griffith, J. G. 1983. 'C., Poem 4: A Neglected Interpretation Revived,' *Phoenix* 37: 123–8.

Watson, L.C. 1983. 'Two Nautical Points: (1) Hor. *Epod.* 1.1–2, (2) C. 4.20–1,' *LCM* 8: 66–9.

Väisänen, M. 1984. *La Musa poliedrica. Indagine storica su C. 4.* Helsinki.

Tourlides, G.A. 1989. Ἑρμηνευτικὸν σχόλιον εἰς Κάτουλλον (IV.7) (Athens, 1989).

van Dam, H.-J. 1990. 'A Comma in C. IV,' *Mn.* 43: 446–9.

Papy, J. 1992. 'Une imitation de Catulle 4: la Dedicatio pennae Iusti Lipsi de F. de Montmorency,' *LEC* 60: 253–61

Ax, W. 1993. 'Phaselus ille – Sabinus ille,' *Literatur-parodie in Antike und Mittelalter.* Trier: 95–100.

5

Structure: 6 + 5 + 2 (see below, p. 218–19).

To Lesbia: let us enjoy our brief life and the love that our elders disapprove of and the malicious would destroy.

Critics in the past assumed that this was a spontaneous outburst of emotion, of which poem 7 was a more 'literary' reworking. For a time, critical discussion in the journals bore chiefly on the pragmatic question whether finger-counting or abacus-counting was in C.'s mind. More recently, however, interest has shifted to the poem's structure and to a more thoroughgoing evaluation of C.'s artistry.

To a considerable extent, this poem makes its effect by the manipulation of sounds – especially vowel sounds. These are carefully arranged in such a way as to reinforce the structural organization. It is often claimed that there are two distinct parts: lines 1–6 and 7–13. Certainly, after two self-contained statements of three lines each (marked by the repetition *unius ... una*), we come to an obvious break. At this point the utterance of C.'s passion seems to turn into a game of numbers, the poem's 'second theme.' Does the development of this theme continue to the end of the poem, as some would have it? To me, the *aut* of l. 12 implies a restatement: 'Or rather ...'; the preceding five lines will be taken as a climactic unit, with a fairly heavy pause after *ne sciamus*, and in l. 12 we should see, I think, a re-entry of the shadow of the *senes severiores*: 'ne quis malus ...' The implication is that l. 12 recapitulates the first theme, whereas the final line resumes the second theme: 'tantum ... basiorum.' If this is so, we have in the two concluding lines a sort of capping-piece which, detached by its *aut*, stands a little apart from the rest of the structure. Lines 1–3 employ the language of the account book: *assis facere* (cf. 42.13) and *aestimare* (both expressions are first found in C.) are much more precise than *pili facere* (10.13, 17.17) and still more so than *parvi putare* (23.25) and the like (notice also *aestimatio*, meaning an exactly assessed value, at 12.12). But in 4–6 there is no business language at all. With l. 7, however, we return to accountancy; clearly some method of computation is envisaged as the thousands succeed to hundreds; but in the climax immediately after the technical expression *facio* (in the sense of 'assess,' 'calculate,' or 'make up the number') comes the explosive *conturbabimus*: we shall go bankrupt. C. uses the very vocabulary of the *senes*, to whom the poem bids defiance, in order to confound their malignant calculation. What other end could the use of such language serve in a love poem, or at least in this one?

The final summing-up in 12–13 reminds us of poem 45, in which the third section recapitulates the whole, lines 21–2 referring to 1–8 and 23–4 to 10–16. But there is a further link between these two poems: the use of sounds. In both of them open *a*'s are an index of triumph: see 5.1 and 2; 45.20 and 22 (and the refrain as well). In both, *o* sounds announce a male speaker or speakers: Septimius in 45, here the *senes*, whose grumbling is also voiced in the displeasing *s* and *r* sounds of l. 2. An obvious point is the effect of *occidit brevis lux*, with a decreasing number of syllables in each successive word and the chopped-off monosyllable at the end of the line – a very rare thing in hendecasyllables (it is repeated, significantly, at 7.7) – followed at once (to drive it home) by *nox est*. Notice also the phrase *perpetua una dormienda*, with its repetition of the vowel sounds *u* and *a*, together with the use of extended, 'lingering' words (*perpetua, dormienda*), the (somehow) powerfully soporific elision of *-a* before *una*, and the abrupt challenge of the ensuing *da mi*, announced in faint tones in the antecedent *-mienda* and echoed later in the minor key of *dein mille*. Such are the mechanics of a poem once thought of as a delightful impromptu.

1 *vivamus*, 'let us *really* live.' This extended sense was established before C.: Varro, *Men.* 87 Büch. (other parallels in F.).

  atque, 'that is to say.'

2 *rumores*, not 'gossip' here but rather 'grumbling' or 'muttering' (Kr.: 'malicious comments').

  severus of course = 'strict,' not (in our sense) 'severe'; cf. perhaps *saevus* in poem 103, where see nn. Lucretius uses *noctis signa severa*, thinking above all of the *fixity* of the stars' courses (5.1190). The comp. implies *'unduly* strict'; but, as Kr. points out, metrical considerations also apply; cf. 3.2, 9.10.

3 *assis*: cf. 42.13.

5 The comma inserted in my text after *nobis* seems necessary if *nobis* is to be taken as referring (in idea) both to *lux occidit* and to *nox est dormienda*. (Some editors punctuate *nobis cum* ...)

 nobis (in a general sense) = human beings. As Q. remarks, the frequentative 'aorist' perfect tense of *occidit* confirms this.

6 *una* (not, of course, *una* = 'together') combines with *perpetua* to qualify *nox*. Notice the clever use of sound ('wavering' alternations of *u* and *a*) to suggest endless sleep, in contrast with the brutal cutting-off indicated by monosyllables (*lux*, at the end of the line, followed at once by *nox*).

7 On the history of the word *basium* (first used by C.; possibly an importation from his native province), see F.; later it became part of the colloquial language (hence *bacio*, *baiser*, etc.). See also poem 7, intr. n.

8 Both *deinde mi*, in the first part of the line, and *da*, in the second, result from attempts by R^2 to restore the metre by original conjecture. As in the great majority of such cases, the R^2 corrections are picked up by *m* (not merely by m^2), which shows that they belong to R^2's first diorthosis (see 2^b.3 n.). In a letter of Coluccio's (Novati, III. 36), to which a date between 1392 and 1394 is assigned by the editor, this line is quoted, as McKie (190) notes, in the form given to it in the R^2 corrections: *deinde mi altera da* ... This does not, however, give more than a *terminus ante quem* for the corrections. We simply do not know how soon Coluccio began to correct his codex *R*, or even whether he had the copy made as soon as he received *X* or waited for some years to find a suitable scribe; the large clear lettering of *R* appears to meet the needs of a Coluccio whose eyesight was beginning to fail, towards the end of his life (which hardly suggests the year 1375, thirty-one years before Coluccio's death, to which McKie would implicitly assign it). (On p. 197 and n. 1, McKie refers to the year 1392 – quoting Novati, II. 386 – as the time at which complaints of failing eyesight first occur.) It is possible that *R* itself is to be dated as late as ca. 1392–3, and probable (at least) that Poggio or another copied *m* from *R* in the years 1397–8. Thus, if Coluccio returned to *R* to make a second diorthosis shortly after the scribe of *m* took his copy – therefore, when the readings of *R* were 'in the air,' so to speak, in Coluccio's circle – there could be as little as five years between what I formerly called 'early' and 'late' corrections in R^2.

10 *fecerimus*, fut. perf. indic.: note the archaic quantity of the *i*: in later poets it is always short; in Cicero, however, it is as a rule long. *facio* here = 'count, add up.'

11 *conturbabimus*, 'go bankrupt' (always intransitive, in this sense).

illa, 'how much.' ('What *that* sum is – a kind of demonstrative *ille*.) Cf. line 13 *tantum*.

Some editors punctuate *conturbabimus, illa, ne* ...; but see n. on *conturbabimus* (above).

12 *invidere*, 'cast the evil eye on.' In number magic, to be able to count your adversary's possessions gave you the power to put a spell on them.

13 *cum ... sciat*, 'inasmuch as he knows.'

tantum ... basiorum, 'the sum of ...'

Grummel, W.C. 1954. 'Vivamus, mea Lesbia,' *CB* 31: 19–21.
Pratt, N.T. 1956. 'The Numerical Catullus 5,' *CP* 51: 99–100.
Grimm, R.E. 1963. 'C. 5 Again,' *CJ* 59: 15–21.
Commager, S. 1964. 'The Structure of C. 5,' *CJ* 59: 361–4.
Fredricksmeyer, E.A. 1970. 'Observations on C. 5,' *AJP* 91: 431–45.

6

Structure: 5 + 9 + 3 (see below).
Intercalated between two of the most ardent poems arising out of C.'s own passion for Lesbia, this occasional piece removes us temporarily from all deeper and more personal feeling. Who Flavius was is unimportant: Catullus is – *lepido versu* – rallying a friend, in the hope of finding out the name of his present *innamorata*. That the poem is an early composition may be guessed, not from its position in the collection or the fact that Lesbia fails to appear in it directly or indirectly, but from the touch of rhetorical terminology which, in line 11, it appears to contain: *argutatio* and *inambulatio* both belong to the propaedeutic of the orator's craft (see l. 11 n.), and (as I have suggested in discussing poem 1) the prosaic and logical manner of exposition, articulated by *nam* (line 6) and *quare* (line 15), may well do so too. It may most reasonably be supposed that Flavius was occupied in pursuing the *tirocinium fori*, which Catullus himself, as seems inherently probable, came to Rome in the first instance to undertake, though from various hints he drops we may be pretty sure that he is distinctly half-hearted about it.

The poem exhibits a certain circularity of structure, as Bardon (1943: 15) has noted: in lines 1–3 (according to Bardon; I prefer the division 1–5) the theme is 'let's talk of your love-affair'; in 4–11 (or 6–14, on my interpretation) the evidence for the affair itself is presented; finally (11–17 by Bardon's reckoning, or perhaps 15–17) we return to the theme 'let's talk of your love.'

In the concluding line and a half, as so often (in other, similar, poems it
may be a pair of lines, or slightly more or less), we find an unexpected twist:
the friend, having been urged to share a confidence, finds that what Catullus
intends is to celebrate and publish the entire affair – *te ac tuos amores* –
no doubt to his (imagined) consternation. When in l. 16 Catullus says *dic
nobis*, we should look carefully at poem 67, with its *dic agedum nobis* in l. 7
and *nobis dicere ne dubita*: in that poem the house door, as a participant in
an imagined dialogue, is implicitly being asked to yield to a trusted friend
(and sympathizer) a heavily guarded secret. The same thing surely occurs
here.

1 *delicias*, 'sweetheart' (= *amores* 16, though a little stronger); cf. 45.24.

2–3 Notice the sequence of verb tenses (*sint ... posses*), for which cf. 23.22–3; the
primary tense represents a closer degree of possibility, the secondary tense by
comparison that which is somewhat unreal.

5 *febriculosi*, 'sickly.' Association with ill health (cf. 81.3–4) or with hunger
(cf. 21.1 and 10–11; also 47.2, where see n.) is for C. a conventional weapon of
abuse. Plaut. *Cist.* 406 implies that *febriculosa* was used of common (low-grade)
prostitutes: see Morgan 1977.

6 *viduas*, 'without a mate'; cf. 68.6 *lecto caelibe*. Notice that in both places the
epithet is transferred. Kr. cites Ov. *Ep.* 18.69 *tot viduas exegi frigida noctes*,
Petron. 133.1 *contentus fuit vidua pudicaque nocte*.

7 *tacitum*, equivalent to a *si* clause (*si taceat cubile, nequiquam tacet*): 'it's no use
the couch keeping silence, for it shouts aloud.' Cf. 80.7.

9 *peraeque et hic et ille / attritus*: the pillow is equally depressed (or compressed;
not 'worn') on both sides of the bed. Cf. Ov. *Am.* 3.14.32 *pressus prior est
interiorque torus*.

  The variant *al. hic* in R^2 (m^2) is taken from X, as is clearly shown by the
presence of *hic* in G^1. Where X lies behind an R^2 variant, that variant is picked
up by m^2, not by m. To this rule there are virtually no exceptions. It does
not, of course, follow, either in logic or in fact, that where a correction by R^2
(sometimes expressed as a variant) is original, and not taken from X, it *must*
be reproduced in m, not m^2; even in his later diorthosis, R^2 had some original
ideas. Still, most of R^2's truly original changes are due to his earlier diorthosis,
and identifiable as such by their appearance in m/m^1; an example of this will be
found in l. 17.

10 *quassa*: this adj., really appropriate to the bed (Ov. *Am.* 3.14.26 *sponda ...
tremat*), is transferred to the abstract nouns in l. 11.

11 *inambulatio*, 'walking about,' as a courtroom orator's activity (recommended in
Rhet. Her. 3.27; *contra*, Cic. *Brut.* 158). *argutatio* is not found elsewhere, but it
may be suspected that it, too, is (unless C. invented it in order to use it here) a

kind of technical term of rhetorical education: *argutus* is applied to clever speech (cf. *argutator*, Gell. 17.5. 13), to expressive looks and gestures, and to very shrill sounds (hence it is usual to tr. *argutatio* 'creaking'). Nonius (245.30 M = 69 L) says *argutari = loquacius proloqui*. Is it possible that C. is making play in this line with the notion that the couch is acting as counsel for the prosecution, so to speak – mustering 'circumstantial evidence' (Q.) against Flavius? For another pair of rhetorical technical terms cf. 24.9 n.

13 *tam* with *effututa*; for displaced *tam*, cf. 60.3.
   latus is, as Kr. says, regarded as the seat of strength: *Priap.* 26.11 *defecit latus.* See *OLD*, s.v. *latus* 2a.

14 unemphatic *tu* is colloquial (J.B. Hofmann, *Lat. Umgangssprache*, p. 100). Cf. e.g., 13.13, 23.22.

15 *quidquid habes*: cf. Hor. *Od.* 1.27.17–18 *quidquid habes, age / depone tutis auribus.*

16 *volo*, with 'iambic shortening.' Cf. 17.8, etc. Q. quotes R.G. Austin on V. *Aen.* 2.735; see also F. on 10.27.
   amores = l. 1 *deliciae*. For *amores* in 'concrete' sense, i.e., signifying a person, see 10.1, 15.1, 21.4, 38.6 (and n.), 40.7, 45.1.

17 *ad caelum vocare*, 'pay the highest honours to'; cf. Cicero, *Ad Att.* 6.2.9 *nos in caelum decretis suis sustulerunt.*

Fuchs, H. 1968. 'Zu C.s Gedicht an Flavius,' *MH* 25: 54–6.

Tracy, S.V. 1969. 'Argutatiinambulatioque (C. 6.11),' *CP* 64: 234–5.

Morgan, M. Gwyn. 1977. 'Nescio quid febriculosi scorti. A Note on C. 6,' *CQ* 27: 338–41.

Allen, A. 1982. 'Love Awry in C.,' *Maia* 34: 225–26. [Line 12.]

Skinner, M.B. 1983. 'Semiotics and Poetics in C. 6,' *LCM* 8: 141–2.

Nielsen, R. 1984. 'C. c. 6. On the Significance of Too Much Love,' *Latomus* 43: 104–10.

Forsyth, P.Y. 1989. 'C. 6: Theme and Context,' *SLLRH* 5. Brussels: 94–7.

7

Structure: 2 + (4 + 2) + 4 (see below).

A deferred sequel to poem 5: 'You take me up on the "multitude of kisses" and ask how many I really want'; but the difference in psychological standpoint between this poem and its companion-piece, poem 5, is very great. That had been, for all its sophistication, a record of straightforward courtship, of amorous pursuit; this, on the other hand, is a poem of happy satiety, of love achieved. Echoes of poem 5 in poem 7 only serve to make this contrast more evident.

The touch of pedantry in *quaeris* ('your question is'; today, surely, it has a slightly scholastic flavour) sets the tone of quiet, complacent intellectual inquiry which prevails in the first part of the poem. To such a tone the geographical and historical references are wholly appropriate: they would have been out of place in poem 5, which exists throughout in the sphere of action. This ruminative note agrees with the introduction of several long words, coined apparently by the poet to suit the needs of the occasion: *basiationes* (developed out of *basia*, itself a word to which C. seems to have been the first to give literary status; see F. on 5.7); *lasarpicifer*, another fresh coinage, languid in sound as well as learned and exact in reference; and finally *pernumerare*. In l. 7 the strongly disjunctive *aut* is used, just as we found it to be used in poem 5, in order to introduce a new direction to the poem's imaginative movement. Thus we are presented, not with an unbalanced structure but with a carefully counterpoised 2 + (4 + 2) + 4 lines, where the parts of the poem that lie outside the parenthesis might be perceived as a self-sufficient statement, as if C. had first written:

Q. Quaeris, quot mihi basiationes / tuae, Lesbia, sint satis superque.
A. Tam te basia multa basiare / vesano satis et super Catullo est / quae (= ut ea) nec pernumerare curiosi / possent, nec mala fascinare lingua.

and thereafter, inside this framework of question and answer, had inserted two traditional images of numberlessness, those of the sands and the stars, and had arranged these in such a way that their lengths respectively balance, in reverse order, the length of the question and of the answer.

In *nox*, placed (as monosyllables so rarely are) at the end of a hendecasyllabic line, we must see an echo of poem 5 (see intr. n. on p. 219); and there is a graceful echo of that preceding poem in the final two lines, where the *senes severiores* reappear as merely *curiosi*, and the epithet *malus* is gently transferred from man to tongue. Thus the harsh terms used in poem 5 are to some extent softened. Yet in spite of this milder mood C. is very conscious of his obligation to poem 5 and strives to acknowledge the debt in his language, as we have partly seen. In this respect poem 7 stands to poem 5 as poem 3 to poem 2; though the dependence is manifested not by the unchanged repetition of an entire line, as at 3.4, but by a recall with changes, suitable to the altered atmosphere of the second poem. Throughout most of poem 7, the aspect presented by the phrases repeated from poem 5 is, in comparison, less youthful in spirit, less passionate – until we come to the word *vesano* in l. 10, and to the last two lines which it heralds. Here, in the sudden reference back to the dominant thought of poem 5, lies the significant change of direction, at a penultimate stage of the poem, which we have been forced to recognize in each of the other lyrics so far discussed: Catullus is not, after all, beyond the possibility of anxiety at the hands of the *curiosi*.

1 *basiationes*: Q. has called attention to C.'s love of 'learned' polysyllables ending in *-atio* (cf. 48.6 *osculationis*); they are, of course, particularly suited to hendecasyllabic verse.

2 *tuae*, 'of you' (= *tui*). The personal possessive pronoun (possessive adj.) is often substituted for an obj. gen., as here: cf. 87.4 *in amore tuo*.

3 *Libyssa*, 'Libyan'; a Greek form (cf. 60.1 n.).

4 *lasarpiciferis*: the adjective in *-fer*, attached by C. to the proper noun here, is probably as literary and conventional as *buxifer*, similarly attached at 4.13 (where see n.). The identification of the plant known as lasarpicium, or silphium ($\sigma i\lambda\phi\iota o\nu$) is still uncertain. What is known is that it became the peculiar product, and principal source of wealth, of Cyrene: it appeared on the coinage of that city, and of no other. It was used in cookery, and in fattening sheep, etc. Medically, it appears to have been regarded as a panacea; the fact that *inter alia* it was prized as an aphrodisiac is of no significance for understanding this poem. It may have been over-cropped; by C.'s time it was regarded as an article of luxury, in Rome at least, and within a very few generations it had died out, being replaced, as F. says, by 'an inferior quality … from the East.' Strabo (2.5.37) applies the adj. $\sigma\iota\lambda\phi\iota o\phi\acute{o}\rho o\varsigma$ to Cyrene.

Cyrenis: the short *y* is found, in Latin, only here and at *Catalepton* 9.61. Greek practice varies (see F.); C. may, especially in this context, have adopted from Callimachus the liberty to vary the quantity of the *y*.

The provenance of R^2's *al. fretis* is obscure; but if *A* had *f⁵etis*, easily read as *fetis* (altered to *fecis* by *O*; for example, see 42.14 and 18, 66.29, 68.87, and 84.11), then it would be easy to suppose *feris* to have been the reading in the text of *X*, through a not uncharacteristic error, with *al. f⁵etis* as an emending variant. It is to be remembered that the strange and (to say the least) very rare word *lasarpiciferis* appears as two words in our extant Mss, a fact which intensified the difficulty of restoring it and in itself contained a temptation to emend the second 'word' – a temptation to which *X* may be supposed to have succumbed in this instance.

5 *aestuosi*: transferred epithet. The oracle of Zeus Ammon (= *Iuppiter*) lay in the burning desert of the region which, of all the territory belonging to Cyrene, was furthest from the moderating influence of the sea. To transfer the adj. to Zeus himself may have been Callimachus' idea.

6 *Batti*: Battus was the legendary founder of Cyrene; Callimachus (*H.* 4.175) himself claimed descent from him (as 'Battiades'; see 116.2 n.).

It is interesting that Callimachus seems to have been the first poet to use the figure of the stars of the sky as an image of uncountability (in prose, it is found in Plato, *Euthyd.* 294b, combined with the other image in this passage, that of desert sand). Kr., in a note on 5.7, suggests that the 'many kisses' motif also may go back to Callimachus, though Catullus exaggerates the number in a way that is highly characteristic of him.

Battus' tomb was in the *agora* of Cyrene: see Pindar, *Pyth.* 5.125 (93).

8 *furtivos*: cf. 68.145 *furtiva ... munuscula*, in a similar context.

9 We should take *te* as one obj., and *basia* as the other (internal) obj., of *basiare*. As Kr. and F. point out, this has only one Latin parallel, Cato *De Agr.* 134.2, but a Greek one at Mosch. 3.68–69.

11–12 The last two lines introduce a new idea, and contain the point of the poem. The echo of poem 5 is clear; cf. *mala* with 5.12 *malus*. For *mala lingua* cf. V. *Ecl.* 7.28.

11 *pernumerare*, 'count to the end,' 'count up.'
curiosi = malevoli (Plaut. *Stich.* 208 *curiosus nemost quin sit malevolus*).

Moorhouse, A.C. 1963. 'Two Adjectives in C., 7,' *AJP* 84: 417–18.
Segal, C. 1974. 'More Alexandrianism in C. VII?,' *Mn* 27: 139–43.
Bertram, S. 1978. 'Oral Imagery in C. 7,' *CQ* 28: 477–8.
Arkins, B. 1979. 'C. 7,' *AC* 48: 630–5.
Johnston, P.A. 1993. 'Love and *laserpicium* in C. 7,' *CP* 88: 328–9.

8

Structure: 2 + 9 + 7 + 1, with many repetitions; see Q., p. 115, for a good analysis. See also Schmiel 1990/91.

Modern criticism has usually regarded this moving poem as a serious 'dramatic monologue' (Rebert 1920) on the theme of 'the lover's conflict' (Connor 1974). It has however been categorized by some critics as 'a humorous portrayal <by Catullus> of himself in the character of a lover longing to touch her (i.e., Lesbia's) heart by the vain threat of leaving her.' These words were written in 1909 by Morris, and at least until very recently they have still found a following. Their validity has been hotly contested by Ilse Schnelle, J.P. Elder and others, but they were endorsed in 1934 by the authority of R.L. Wheeler. The two points made originally by Morris (humorous tone, and the attempt to win back Lesbia's love) have since become entirely separate critical propositions: Swanson (1963) entitled an article 'The Humor of Catullus 8' without mentioning the plea to Lesbia, and two years later T.E. Kinsey (1965: 539) adopted the view that 'Catullus seeks to win back Lesbia's love' without mentioning the humour. Schuster (*RE*

2372) describes Morris' view as a *zweifellos in die Irre gehende Auffassung*, without giving reasons for his opinion.

In fact there are some fairly weighty reasons against accepting either of Morris' two contentions. Line 5 is repeated, almost unchanged, in poem 37, and in a context where there can be no question of humour:

> Salax taberna ...
> puella nam mi (me, *codd.*), quae meo sinu fugit,
> amata tantum quantum amabitur nulla,
> pro qua mihi sunt magna bella pugnata,
> consedit istic.

If these lines, with so clear and so resonant an echo of poem 8, are intended to be taken as amusing, at least Lesbia did not share this opinion; she thought of them as *truces iambi* (36.5; see intr. n. to poem 36). If this description was not meant by Lesbia to refer to poem 37, the only possible other candidate, in the appropriate metre, would be poem 8 itself, which defenders of Morris' view put out of court by declaring it to be humorous. Moreover, there is no firm evidence, either (a) that when C. referred to *iambi* he could mean hendecasyllables or any other non-iambic metre (see the intr. n. to poem 36), or (b) that we do not possess, for 'practical purposes,' all the published work of Catullus. It would be strange indeed if such a line as this (l. 5) should make its appearance both in the seriously meant invective of poem 37 and in a humorous context in our present poem.

For the relation of this poem to the seventy-sixth (a more leisurely, elegiac meditation on approximately the same topic) see Dyson 1973, and cf. poem 76 intr. n.

1 *desinas*: for the 'jussive' subjunctive, see S.A. Handford, *The Latin Subjunctive* (London, 1947): 42. Cf. 32.7, 61.91, 76.14 and 16. If this type of subjunctive is comparatively rare in prose, this is simply because only verse dictates its substitution for the imperative, as here, on grounds of metrical necessity.

   Self-address (cf. poems 46, 51, 52, 76, 79) is not merely a rhetorical device, but always (in C., at least) has emotional overtones; see F. on 68.135. Here, as Q. points out (and the same is true of poem 76, and perhaps poem 51), it points to C.'s 'awareness of a conflict within himself.'

2 Plaut. *Trin.* 1026 is not metrically parallel, *pace* Fordyce and Quinn; the line is not a hendecasyllable except by chance (really it is part of a trochaic tetrameter); Lindsay reads *periisse* (the form cited in F.'s n. is *perisse*, with no discussion).

3 *soles* = *dies*; appropriately, after *candidi* ('sunny days'). Cf. 5.4 n.

4 C., like many another man in love, was 'enslaved' to his mistress; but with this
line for evidence the absurd inference has been drawn that he stood on a lower
social plane than she did.

5 Repeated (with a slight variation) at 37.12. See intr. n.
   m's reading (*amabiliter*) well illustrates his carelessness. When such a reading
recurs in one of the *deteriores* (see, in this instance, the Table of Manuscripts,
No. 29 n.), it clearly proclaims the dependence of that Ms, at least in part, on *m*.
It is curious how *m* repeats his own error at 37.12.

6 *iocosa*, of 'lovers' play' (Kr.). Cf. Ov. *AA* 3.796 *nec taceant mediis improba verba
iocis* – which suggests that there is nothing 'verbal' about the *ioci* themselves.
   cum (with comma at the end of 7) gives a tighter, more integrated, syntax than
tum. Otherwise the three lines (7–9), each of them virtually self-contained, have
a jerky effect. See E. Fraenkel, *JRS* 51 (1961) 51 n. 20, who defends *tum*.
   tum is not the reading of *R* (as Mynors and Q.), but of *R*^{2}.

9 *non vult*: in an erotic sense. Cf. Alcaeus, *AP* 12.29 οὐ θέλει, ἀλλὰ θελήσει.
   impotens, 'uncontrolled' (= καίπερ ἀκρατὴς ὤν); i.e., with Avantius' reading,
'violently reject her.' Some eds. fill the lacuna with *ne sis*; but *quoque* seems to
make this unlikely.
   <*noli*> balances l. 7 *nolebat*, and should therefore be preferred to Scaliger's <*ne
sis*>.

10 Before *quae* we must supply *eam*, not *ea*. For *quae fugit sectare*, cf. Theocr.
11.75 τί τὸν φεύγοντα διώκεις;
   vivere practically = *esse*; cf. 10.33, Plaut. *Men.* 908.
   The correction in *R*^{2} (*m*) is metrical in character, and as such – given Coluccio's
interests – fairly obvious; it has of course no connection with *G*.

13 *rogabit*, in an erotic sense. Cf. Ov. *Am.* 1.8.43 (*casta est quam nemo rogavit*),
2.7.25.

14 *nulla* (colloquial) = *non*, 'not at all'; cf. Ov. *Ep.* 10.11–12 *nullus erat!* ('he was
not there at all'); also *M.* 11.579 *viro, qui nullus erat*, and 684 *nulla est Alcyone,
nulla est*.

15 *vae te* (accusative) appears less strong than *vae tibi* (B. says the dative implies
execratio, the acc. merely *miseratio*). Since only dat. or acc. case can follow *vae*,
the reading of *V* at 64.196, *vae misera*, is highly suspect; see the text and notes
there.
   tibi manet differs from *te manet* in implying the notion of fate: Cicero, *Phil.*
2.11 <*P. Clodius*>, *cuius tibi fatum manet*.

17 *diceris*: 'who will call you his own now, as I did?' rather than Kr.'s 'with whom
will you be linked now by gossip?'

19 *destinatus*: probably substituted, *metri gratia*, for *obstinatus*.

Morris, E.P. 1909. 'An Interpretation of C. VIII,' *TransConn* 15: 139–51.
Rebert, H.F. 1920. '*Obdura* – A Dramatic Monologue,' *CJ* 26: 287–92.

Swanson, R.A. 1963. 'The Humor of C. 8,' *CJ* 58: 193–6.

Kinsey, T.E. 1965. 'C. 11,' *Latomus* 24: 537–44. [See p. 539.]

Rowland, R.L. 1966. '*Miser Catulle*: An Interpretation of the Eighth Poem of C.,' *G&R* 13: 15–21.

Moritz, L.A. 1966. 'Miser Catulle: A Postscript,' *G&R* 13: 155–7.

Gugel, H. 1967. 'C., carm. 8,' *Athenaeum* 45: 278–93.

Akbar Khan, H. 1968. 'Style and Meaning in C.'s Eighth Poem,' *Latomus* 27: 555–74.

Granarolo, J. 1968. 'La maturation du naturel dans le lyrisme catullien,' *Euphrosyne* [Lisbon] 2: 59–69.

Skinner, M.B. 1971. 'C. 8: The Comic Amator as Eiron,' *CJ* 66: 298–305.

Dyson, M. 1973. 'C. 8 and 76,' *CQ* 23: 127–43, esp. 127–36.

Connor, P.J. 1974. 'C. 8: The Lover's Conflict,' *Antichthon* 8: 93–6.

Kresic, S. 1981. 'Miser Catulle, … Obdura: Lecture poétique du poème VIII,' *Contemporary Literary Hermeneutics and Interpretation of Classical Texts*. Ottawa: 299–316.

McCormick, P.J. 1981. 'Reading and Interpreting C. 8,' ibid. 317–26.

Gadamer, H.-G. 1981. 'A Classical Text – A Hermeneutic Challenge,' ibid. 327–32.

Thomas, R.F. 1984. 'Menander and C.,' *RhM* 127: 308–16.

Colace, P.R. 1985. 'Il poeta si diverte. Orazio, C., e due esempi di poesia non seria,' *GIF* 37: 53–71.

Ramires, G. 1988 (pub. 1990). '*Fulsere quondam / fulsere vere*: tempo del mito e tempo della realtà nel carme 8 di C.,' *Atti Accad. Peloritana* 64: 161–76.

Lieberg, G. 1989. 'Una nuova interpretazione del carme 8 di C.,' *Orpheus* 10: 1–12.

Arcaz, J.L. 1990. 'Un commentario a Catulo 8, 15–18,' *CFC* 24: 157–62.

Schmiel, R. 1990/91. 'The Structure of C. 8: A History of Interpretation,' *CJ* 86: 158–66.

Decreus, F. 1992. 'Le poème 8 de C. et le conflit de ses codes,' *Euphrosyne* 20: 47–72.

Thom, S. 1992. 'Catullus: Arida … pumice expolitum?,' *Akroterion* 37: 15–22.

9

Structure: 5 + 4 + 2.

A cheerful little poem of friendship, welcoming Veranius back from Spain, where he had gone in company with Fabullus (to whom poem 13 is addressed). But the artistry involved in the working-out of this simple and straightforward theme is a good deal more subtle than appears at first sight. Very likely, as its tone suggests, this is a quite early poem: Syme 1956 tentatively dated it to 60–59 BC, when C. would have been about 21 or 22. If Lachmann's view that C. was born in 77 were correct, the poet would be scarcely 15 at the time of the events in the poem, and Asinius Pollio (born in 76) is *puer* (16, or thereabouts) in poem 12, which is also datable to Veranius' return from Spain (12.14–16). If so, then in poem 12 (a) C. addresses an older man as *inepte*, and (b) he calls *puer* one of his own age, or possibly slightly older. While (b) is not impossible, (a) seems unlikely.

As in some other early poems, a certain liveliness is added by the use of unpoetical language (l. 2 *antistans*, 'set off against'; l. 10 *o quantum est hominum beatiorum*, cf. Plaut. *Capt.* 835–6 *o mihi quantum est hominum optumorum optume*). The order of the composition is straightforward, but there is a great deal of carefully introduced variety within it: first (as we shall see presently) by the use of three different time-levels (perfect, pres., fut.) and secondly by rapid movement of the focus from C. to his friend and back again, thus: *Your* return (my best of friends) to *your* family, gives *me* joy. *You*, safe home, I shall see, and hear your tales: what joy for *me*! (Observe the sequence *meis* 1, *mihi* 2, *tuos* 3; *mihi* 5, *te* 6; *tuus* 8, *me* 11.) Perhaps most important of all is the articulation of the little poem by means of *o*, repeated from l. 5 to l. 10. Thus the second-person first section poses a question (l. 3 *venisti?*) in the perfect tense, and answers it with a repeated *venisti* (l. 5) followed by an exclamation in the implied present tense, preceded by *o*. In the second part (ll. 6–9) we pass to the future, anticipating further delights; but in l. 10 we again recur to the present tense preceded by *o*, in order (once again) to voice the poet's own feelings. C.'s careful attention to balance and variety (avoiding, however, rigid symmetry), and the resulting liveliness, are not sufficiently often recognized as having to do with the ease that comes from art. For poetic addresses of welcome, especially to a friend returning from abroad, see Nisbet and Hubbard on Hor. *Od.* 2.7 (intr. n. on p. 107).

1–2 B.'s substitution of *o* for *e* is still sometimes taken seriously by scholars (it is at least mentioned by F., for example); but its corollary, the subjoining of the remark 'who are three thousand in number,' is absurd. It might be claimed that *milibus trecentis* should be taken as an abl. of measure, 'by 300 miles' (cf. Ar. *Nub.* 430 ἑκατὸν σταδίοισιν ἄριστον). But this would leave *antistare ex* = 'stand out from among'; B. says this is not Latin, and he is probably right. Again, *milibus trecentis* cannot be a mere – rather pointless – addition to *amicis* ('who happen to be 300,000 in number'); it must surely be a dative of the indirect object after *antistans* (cf. *praesto*, etc.), while *mihi* clearly means 'in my eyes' (dative of the person affected). A literal rendering might be: 'who <alone> of all my friends <are such as to> surpass 300,000 <friends>.' For a similar use of *antistare*, cf. Claudius Quadrigarius (ca. 80 BC) *qui omnibus virtute antistabat* (B.). Cf. also Cicero, *Ad Att.* 2.5.1 *Cato ille noster, qui mihi unus est pro centum milibus*.

4 *sanam* is plainly imported into *X* as a variant. *A* must have had something like *uno animo sanŭmque*; to *X*, it must have been obvious (assuming this division

of the words, which he did not question) that *sanam* was unmetrical; and so, either deliberately or instinctively, he substituted the metrically acceptable *suam* for it in his text, relegating the old text to the status of a variant. *anum* (adj.): cf. 68.46, 78^b.4; for *senex* as adj., cf. 67.4 *ipse senex* ('the old master').

5 The question is answered by repeating the verb; cf. 77.4–5. For exclamatory *o* with nom. as well as acc., cf. Prop. 2.15.1 *o me felicem! o nox mihi candida! nuntii beati*: nominative (see F.). C. does not employ the -*ii* genitive of nouns (as opposed to adjectives) in -*ium* or -*ius*. Twice, as Fr. points out, C. somewhat awkwardly substitutes a dative in -*io* for what could more easily have been a genitive in -*ii*, if he had used that form (113.4, where see n., and 97.2). Even in Lucr., -*ii* is rare (5.1006 only; see n. on 113.4); and it seems altogether lacking in Cicero. 'The -*ii* form, originally, it seems, a device suggested by Lucilius for avoiding ambiguities, e.g., *iudici* (dat. of *iudex* or gen. of *iudicium*?), was promoted by Varro. Ignored by Horace and used once by Virgil (*Aen.* 3.702, unless *fluvii* is adj.), it occurs five times in Prop. (three of these are proper names) and thereafter becomes normal' (L.).

6–9 The *hysteron proteron*, by which the story precedes the greeting, is characteristic of C. (cf. 31.8, 50.13), and also of Virgil in particular among the other Latin poets. Kr.: 'The story comes before the greeting as being of greater weight.' See further the n. on 50.13.

6 *Hiberum* is probably from *Hiberus*, as Kr. claims (F. agrees: 'Hiber does not occur in the oblique cases').

8 *tuus*: as often happens with original R^2 corrections, *tuus* is superior both in sense and also metrically.
applicans ... collum ('your neck'): drawing towards one the neck of the person to be greeted. Cf. Nisbet and Hubbard on Hor. *Od.* 1.36.6 for the sentiment.

9 *iucundum*, 'pleasant, delightful': a word often applied by C. to his close friends, such as Calvus.

10 *o quantum est ...*; cf. 3.2 n. The syntax is loose: as F. says, 'the whole *quantum* clause takes the place, as it were, of a partitive genitive <and is> equivalent to *omnium hominum beatiorum*, "of all the happy men there are, who is happier than I?"'

Syme, R. 1956. 'Piso and Veranius in C.,' *C&M* 17: 129–34.

10

Structure: (4 + 4) + 15 + 11. See E. Fraenkel, *Horace* 114ff., for an analysis. A genre-piece, purporting to recount a conversation that resulted from a chance encounter in the Forum. The atmosphere and tone are those of Roman satire – editors refer to Horace, *S.* 1.9 – rather than Greek epigram, with its pointedness and 'literary' language; so far as Hellenistic genres are to be thought of as having any possible influence on the poem, the closest resemblance to its tone might be found, as Kr. suggests, in the mime. Besides the suggestion (by the use of colloquial language, interrupted lines, and other means) of a lively dialogue, there is, as Q. points out, an element of 'wry, detached self-observation.' The date attributed to the event (by implication) is shortly after C. returned from Bithynia, i.e., in the late spring, or the summer, of 56 BC. 'Varus' is probably the Varus who is mentioned in the first line of poem 22; but whether he is Alfenus Varus, the eminent jurist who was to become *consul suffectus* in 39 BC (see nn. on poem 30), or Quintilius Varus, the friend of Virgil and of Horace (*Od.* 1.24, on his death, is addressed to Virgil), cannot be determined on the evidence furnished by this poem; both of them came from Cremona, and either of them might have been included in the circle of C.'s friends, of Transpadane origins, who moved in the legal and literary society of the capital.

1 Note the position of *me*, between *Varus* and *meus* (Kr.: 'an enclitic word … cf. 64.228 *quod tibi si.'*).

    For *meus*, see the note on 9.8; R^2's correction is probably independent. G^1, however, shows that the same word, *meus*, was written above *mens* in X. If R^2 had taken it as a variant from *X*, as McKie suggests, he would have prefixed *al*. No one capable of scanning hendecasyllables could accept *mens*.

2 *visum*: *visere* is often used of visiting the sick, especially with *ad*: F. quotes Ter. *Hec.* 188–9, Lucr. 6.1239, Ov. *Am.* 2.2.21, and later passages. Mention of Serapis (l. 26) confirms the probability that V.'s friend is sick, or pretending to be.

3 *scortillum*: a *hapax eiremenon*.

    Here *m* reads *tunc*, thus following (uncorrected) *R*, and m^2 – unusually – either fails to notice R^2's correction or does not think the change from *tunc* to *tum* worth making. The former alternative is much the more likely: (i) m^2 very rarely, if ever, shows even this limited degree of independence; (ii) the way in which the correction was made (*tūṇc*, the expunging dot under the *c* being extremely faint) leaves the shapes of the four original letters intact. (Even Ullman's eye missed the correction.)

    repente, 'at first glance.'

4 *non sane*: as Kr. remarks, *sane* is apt to follow negations.

    illepidum … invenustum: cf. 36.17.

5 *incidit sermo* (or *mentio*) of a topic 'coming up' in conversation: cf. Plin. Ep. 4.22.5 (*sermo*), Livy 1.57.6 (*mentio*).

6 *quid esset*, 'how it was with,' or (F.) 'what was the news of.'

7 *se haberet*: applied to a Roman province in Cicero, *Ad Fam.* 4.5.6.

8 The emending variant is probably to be attributed to *X*; possibly to *A*.

9 *id quod erat*, parenthetical: 'what in fact was true.'

    ipsis must mean 'the inhabitants'; Kr.'s objection that the Roman administrators could not have cared whether the populace made money or not is beside the mark: the main point is that Bithynia turned out to be a miserably poor province. If *ipsis* modifies *praetoribus*, then (as F. says) *nec* at the beginning of l. 10 must be emended to *nunc*; but *nunc* is meaningless (Kr.). The plural in *praetoribus* is best explained as referring to successive praetors (Kr. and F.), rather than as a generalizing plural (Q.), though Q.'s explanation is not unreasonable.

    m seeks to follow *R*, but carelessly omits *nec*. The first step by *m²* was to reinstate *nec*; the second, to follow *R²*'s new reading (= *G¹*), imported from *X*. This seems simpler than the explanation offered by McKie (136–8).

10 *cohorti*, the governor's retinue (F. has a long n. on the history of the term); 'staff' would suggest too much in the way of official position and duties, though 'aides-de-camp' would partly correspond.

11 *unctius*: to anoint the head with rich unguents was a sign of prosperity and of the kind of luxury appropriate to days of ease; cf. 29.22 *uncta ... patrimonia*.

12 *irrumator*: see 16.1 n.

13 *praetor* = C. Memmius; for his name, and what C. says of him, see 28.9.
    faceret, 'assess, value.' Cf. 42.13 *non assis facis?*

14 *quod* of course refers here to the men, not the litter itself, though the eight-bearer litter was particularly associated with Bithynia (Cicero, *Verr.* 2.5.27; for other places where the *lectica octophorus* was used in C.'s time, see F.'s n.).

16 The employment of *ad* is similar to its use in indicating the duties of officials (e.g., *ad epistulas*).

17 *unum*, 'exceptionally' (added to a colloquial 'absolute' comparative, for which cf. l. 24 *cinaediorem*; F. considers this to be an extension of its use with the superlative).
    facerem, 'represent <myself as>'; at 97.9 *facit*, which Kr. and F. compare with this, surely means something different, namely 'judge.'

18 *mihi fuit maligne*, 'I was hard up' (*maligne* = 'stingily,' opp. to *benigne*, 'generously').

20 *rectos*, 'tall, upright' (cf. 86.2).

21 *hic* = in Rome, *illic* = in Bithynia.

22 *grabati*: a light bed or cot (Gk. κράβ<β>ατος, κραβάτιον, Mod. Gk. κρεβ<β>άτι).

24 *hic*, 'at this point'; Kr. compares 64.269, quoting also V. *Aen.* 9.246 and Hor. *S.* 1.9.7 (in both of which places, speeches follow) and citing 44.13.
    cinaediorem: on this use of the comparative, see l. 17 n.; on the word, cf. 16.2, 57.1 n.

25 Some editors punctuate *inquit*, 'mihi, mi Catulle, ...'

26 Scan *commodă*. For the shortened final syllable, which 'may represent colloquial
pronunciation' (F.), cf. *mane* in the next line (and cf. F. on both). See also
O. Skutsch, *BICS* 23 (1976): 19–20. It is hard to find a satisfactory alternative to
the licence of the shortened final *a* in *commoda* (imperative); see (besides F.)
the commentaries of Ellis and Benoist, and also V. Coulon in *RhM* 99 (1956):
248–9. One is tempted by Nisbet's suggested restoration: following E., he takes
commoda as n. pl., and alters *quaeso* to *quaero* and *istos* to *istaec*. See *PCPS* 22
(1978): 93–4 and *MD* 26 (1991): 82–3.

   R^2's spelling of the name Serapis is probably independent (Coluccio is strong
in this field) and not related to the history of the reading we find in *O*.

   ad, 'to the temple of' (cf. Ov. *Am.* 2.2.25 *ad Isin*). The cult of Serapis, imported
from Egypt shortly before 100 BC, was linked with that of Aesculapius; in both,
cures were sought by incubation and in dreams. In C.'s day it was growing in
popularity, especially with the *demi-monde* (see Kr.), and counter-measures
were taken on three occasions (F.).

27 *mane*, 'hold hard,' 'not so fast.'

28 The syntax is as confused as C. himself is on being 'taken up.'
   istud, as F. puts it, 'serves to point the reference – "as for my statement, to which
you refer"'; and F. is surely right in saying that 'the *quod*-clause is best taken as
adverbial like the *quod scribis* of Cicero's letters (cf. 68.27).'

29 *fugit me ratio*, 'I was mistaken.'
   R^2's independent correction (*meus*) is partially metrical in character (cf. l. 1).

30 On confusion of the syntax as an index of C.'s state of mind see 28 n. Here we
also have inversion (of *Gaius Cinna*) and the repetition of the subject involved in
the use of *is*. Besides being marks of C.'s own embarrassment, these are largely
colloquial touches, and so they reflect the style and atmosphere of the poem as a
whole.
   Cinna: a neoteric poet, friend (poem 95) and fellow-countryman of C. (see the
Introduction).

32 *quam = quam si* (Kr. and F. give parallels from the *Digest* and inscriptions as
well as from Cicero.)

33 *male* here intensifies a disparaging adjective; at 14.5, a verb. Cf. 16.13 n.
   vivis: *vivere* is often virtually equivalent to *esse*, especially where the tone is
colloquial. Cf. 8.10 n.

Sedgwick, W.B. 1947. 'C. X: A Rambling Commentary,' *G&R* 16: 108–14.
Coulon, V. 1956. 'Observations critiques,' *RhM* 99: 245–54, esp. 248–9.
Fraenkel, E. 1957. *Horace*. Oxford: 114–15.
Bellandi, F. 1980. 'Nota a C. 10, 9–13,' *Orpheus* 1: 448–58.
Nielsen, R.M. 1987. 'C. and *Sal* (poem 10),' *AC* 56: 148–61.

11

Structure: 4 stanzas (a single sentence) + 2 stanzas.
In this profoundly moving poem two themes are fused, but not on equal terms; the reader, having been lulled into believing that the genial opening note will dominate the poem, suddenly sees it displaced by a much grimmer conclusion. C. begins by addressing his friends Furius and Aurelius – for friends they surely are, despite the rough and even abusive language to which he subjects them in poems 15, 16, 21, 23, 24, and 26; consider their devotion to him, expressed here in ll. 1–4, and the very fact that C. entrusted to them his final message to Lesbia. C. utters the following proposal: 'The three of us have often talked of going abroad on service together; you have said that you would accompany me even to the ends of the earth. Very well, then; if you are ready for such formidable assignments, here is one you can carry out much nearer home: take a message, not a very pleasant one, to my ex-mistress, to say that I abhor her conduct and have finished with her for good; she is not to look for my love again.' Plainly the structure (see above) is somewhat top-heavy, with four stanzas addressed to the bearers of the message and only two to the message itself. When Horace, imitating the first twelve lines, condenses them into four (*Od.* 2.6.1–4 *Septimi, Gades aditure mecum*), he underlines this imbalance. The key stanza is the fourth, where the bombast of the first twelve lines changes to a tone of bleak simplicity, with an effect of anti-climax before the harsh and brutal entry of the second theme – C.'s final renunciation of Lesbia. Of course, it is a fiction that the message is transmitted to Lesbia by way of Furius and Aurelius; but C. can no longer address her directly, and must do so in a poem ostensibly addressed to another person, or persons. This could hardly be done gracefully without giving those addressed a substantial place in the poem; hence – as well as for the sake of anti-climax – the four preliminary stanzas.

The poem must have been composed not earlier than the autumn of 55 BC (from the references to Julius Caesar's campaigns in ll. 10–12) and certainly not later than the battle of Carrhae in 53 BC (l. 6); those who believe C. to have died in 54 will think the latter date too late, but see the Introduction, p. 4.
Metre: Sapphic. C.'s Sapphics, as exhibited in this poem, are not far off the final formalization of the metre by Horace. As to quantity, the only variation is that in ll. 6 and 15 the fourth syllable is short, the line starting with two trochees instead of a trochee and a spondee. The main difference concerns the caesura. (In Horace the weak caesura is only occasionally found in the 21 Sapphic odes of Books 1–3. Only 3 Sapphic odes occur in Book 4, but they contain twice as many examples of weak caesura as do the 21 of

1–3; and the same is true of the *Carmen Saeculare*.) Out of the eighteen long lines in *his* poem, C. has strong caesura only nine times and weak caesura (after the sixth syllable) five times, three of them in one stanza (13–15). Of the other four, lines 7 and 23 seem to follow the principle that a caesura can be reckoned as occurring between the two parts of a compound word, as in the iambics of 4.4 (where some editors would print *praeter ire*) and several times in the hexameters of Lucretius. This brings the numbers of strong and weak caesura up to ten and six. Unless this principle is extended to *sagittiferos*, which seems difficult, line 6 has no caesura at all, and the disputed line 11 appears to have its caesura overridden by an elision. C. does not leave open vowels between lines; on the contrary he elides at the end of a line if the next line begins with a vowel (see ll. 19 and 22). What happens at the end of l. 11 is another story (L).

1 On the identification of 'Furius' (quite a common name in Roman annals: see H.P. Syndikus, *Catull: eine Interpretation I*, 1984, on poem 15) with the lampoonist Furius Bibaculus (who also may or may not have been the same as the Furius mentioned by Horace at *S.* 1.10.36 and 2.5.41: see the inconclusive remarks of Niall Rudd, *The Satires of Horace*, 1966: 289–90) much has been written, from Muretus – who first suggested it – to the present. Messalla (Suetonius, *De Grammaticis* 4) classed Bibaculus with Valerius Cato and Ticidas, as a poet of 'neoteric' sympathies; yet we do not find these sympathies reflected in any of C.'s fairly numerous references to him, as we might expect them to be. (See Syndikus, loc. cit., n. 3.) What C. and Bibaculus certainly had in common (Tac. *Ann.* 4.34) was *contumeliae Caesarum* (since C. attacked Caesar only, Bibaculus must have made Augustus – possibly as 'Octavian' – at least in part his target; Cremutius Cordus, in Tacitus, says both Caesar and Augustus forgave these lampoons).
comites <futuri>, 'ready and willing to accompany' (cf. Hor. *Od.* 2.6. 1 *Septimi, Gades aditure mecum*).
Indos, the people for the country; cf. V. *Ecl.* 1.64 *sitientes ibimus Afros*.
3 *ut = ubi*, 'where' (a very rare use; this and 17.10 are, as F. remarks, the only certain examples in Latin, except as a Grecism in two passages he cites).
   The double epithets (*longe-resonante* and *Eoa*) are in C.'s manner (e.g., 1.1 *lepidum novum libellum*), and A. Statius' change to *resonans* is unnecessary. For *longe resonante* cf. V. *Geo.* 1.358.
   R^2 can hardly be said to be at home with the Sapphic metre; cf. his failure to mend the colometric error at 23–4 (at 11–12, X has done it for him). Hence he claims the right to replace the unfamiliar *ut*, in the sense of 'where,' with *ubi*, which of course is unmetrical.

4 C. wrote *tunditur unda* deliberately, to suggest by the repetition of the *und* sound the repeated pounding of waves on a shore. Horace's *aestuat unda* (*Od.* 2.6.4) echoes C. only faintly, with characteristic Augustan restraint in the deploying of 'sound effects.'

5 *Hyrcanos*: strictly speaking, they populated the southern shore of the Caspian Sea, but here they are vaguely linked with several oriental nations.

6 *Sagas*: Latin spelling uses *g*; Greek has a kappa. The *Sacae* (or *Sagae*) were often vaguely associated with the *Scythae*, and located in the northeast border region of the Persian realm. Here, they are thought of as mounted archers (ἱπποτοξόται is how Arrian 3.8.3 described them), and hence as Mesopotamians, or at any rate plainsmen, like the Parthians.

sagittiferosque Parthos: cf. V. *Geo.* 3.31, 4.313–14; Hor. *Od.* 2.13.17–18.

7 *m*'s ꝗ is mere carelessness, not linked with O.

8 It is hard to say whether *colorat aequora* refers (a) to the annual 'alluvial deposit' (F.) left by the Nile on the low-lying fields (*aequora* in its literal sense of flat places) or (b) to the 'dyeing' of the sea by the silt brought down at the time of flooding. If the word *septemgeminus* is more than a conventional epithet, perhaps we are to think of the actual mouths of the river, and hence of (b). But as none of the other geographical indications in this stanza has to do with the sea, or a sea – ll. 11–12 are another matter – whereas all refer to people or (by implication) a country, (a) may be right after all.

10 *monimenta*, 'reminders,' almost 'trophies.' *monimenta* 'tell a story,' and (especially in Virgil) 'carry personal associations' (F., who quotes several passages). Cf. esp. Prop. 4.6.17 *Actia Iuleae pelagus monimenta carinae.*

magni: surely no indication of friendship, or of political partisanship, towards Caesar is implied, even if the word is not used ironically as it was in certain derisive anti-Pompeian verses and demonstrations in the theatre. (After Waterloo, the man in the London street could easily have referred to 'the great Duke <of Wellington>' without thereby confessing to Tory sympathies in politics – or even before; in 1814, when Wellington entered Paris, 'Young John Cam Hobhouse, friend of Byron and the Radicals, who was travelling on the Continent, had what he called "an insatiable desire" to see "our great man"' [E. Longford, *Wellington: The Years of the Sword*, 1971 reprint (London): 425].)

11 See App. Crit. McKie's (1984) suggestion was partly anticipated by Palmer, who proposed *horribilesque vitro in / usque Britannos*. Mention should be made of L.P. Wilkinson's (1977) suggestion *horribiles quoque, ulti-*, though this had been anticipated (as to *horribiles quoque*) by E. Maunde Thompson (*AJP* 21 [1900]: 78–9), as McKie remarks.

13 *feret*, roughly speaking, = *sit*; the association of *ferre* with *voluntas* is conventional (*si fert ita forte voluntas*).

14 *caelites*, 'heaven-dwellers,' = *dei* (in epic and archaic language). Cf. 61.49 and 190.

temptare: cf. V. *Geo.* 1.207 *fauces temptantur Abydi*, Hor. *Od.* 3.4.30–1 *Bosphorum temptabo.*

15 *meae puellae*: a conscious, and sad, echo of the way in which C. had formerly referred to Lesbia.

16 *non bona*, 'bitter, unkind.' Cf. V. *Aen.* 12.75–6 *dicta ... haud placitura refer.*

17 *vive vale* was a valedictory formula, sometimes dismissive (as at Plaut. *Trin.* 996; Hor. *Ep.* 1.6.67), sometimes not (Hor. *S.* 2.5.110, where the ghost of Tiresias addresses Ulysses in the underworld).

18 *trecentos*: cf. 9.2, 12.10 (see n.); also Hor. *S.* 1.5.12.

20 *ilia* (symbolizing male sexual potency): cf. 63.5, 80.8.

21 *respectet*, 'look in the direction of' (here probably, despite F., with a notion of retrospect). C. seems to imply that Lesbia had sought to be reconciled with him. Cicero, *Planc.* 45 *ne par ab eis munus respectent.* Kr. says 'mehr.'

22 *ultimi*, 'at the furthest edge of.' V. *Aen.* 9.435–6 are surely written in reminiscence of lines 22–4 here.

Reitzenstein, R. 1922. 'Philologische Kleinigkeiten: Zu Horaz und C.,' *Hermes* 57: 363–5.

Balogh, J. 1930. 'C.s Scheltelied auf Lesbia,' *Philologus* 85: 103–5.

Todd, F.A. 1941. 'C. XI,' *CR* 55: 70–3.

Pennisi, G. 1961. 'C. e il carme dei 'Non bona dicta',' *Helikon* 1: 127–38.

Kinsey, T.E. 1965. 'C. 11,' *Latomus* 24: 537–44.

Putnam, M.C.J. 1974. 'C. 11: The Ironies of Integrity,' *Ramus* 3: 70–86.

Bright, D.F. 1976. 'Non Bona Dicta: C.'s Poetry of Separation,' *QUCC* 21: 105–19.

Wilkinson, L.P. 1977. 'C. 11.11–12,' *PCPS* 23: 133–4.

Evrard-Gillis, J. 1977–8. 'C. 11: Quatre voies d' accès,' *Humanités chrétiennes* 21: 418–27.

Mulroy, D. 1977–8. 'An Interpretation of C. 11,' *CW* 71: 237–47.

Woodman, A.J. 1978. 'C. 11 and 51,' *LCM* 3: 77–9.

Yardley, J.C. 1978. 'C. 11.7–8,' *LCM* 3: 143–4.

– 1981. 'C. 11: The End of a Friendship,' *SOsl* 56: 63–9.

Scott, R. C. 1983. 'On C. 11,' *CP* 78: 39–42.

Mayer, R. 1983. 'C.'s divorce,' *CQ* 33: 297–8.

McKie, D. 1984. 'The Horrible and Ultimate Britons: C. 11.11,' *PCPS* 30: 74–8. [Read *horribiles vitro ulti-*.]

Bellandi, F. 1985. 'Meae puellae. Struttura e destinatario del c. 11 di C.,' *Quaderni del Dipart. di lingue e lettere neolatine, Ist. universario Bergamo* 1: 17–33.

Blodgett, E.D., and Nielsen, R.M. 1986. 'Mask and Figure in C., Carmen 11,' *RBPh* 54: 22–31.

Sweet, D.R. 1987. 'C. 11: A Study in Perspective,' *Latomus* 46: 510–26.

Putnam, M.C.J. 1989. 'C. 11 and Virgil, *Aen.* 6.76–7,' *Vergilius* 35: 28–30.

Biondi, G.G. 1989. 'C. 11 e Orazio, carm. 2, 6: due lezioni di poesia,' *Mnemosynum: Studi in onore di A. Ghiselli*: 19–31.

Heath, J.R. 1989. 'C. 11: Along for the Ride,' *SLLRH* 5. Brussels: 98–116.

Benediktson, D.T. 1990. 'Horribilesque ultimosque Britannos,' *Glotta* 68: 120–3. [Recommends keeping the hiatus, in view of the new Gallus fragment, l. 22: *Fata mihi, Caesar, tum erunt ...*]

Forsyth, P.Y. 1991. 'The Thematic Unity of C. 11,' *CW* 84: 457–64.

Celentano, M.S. 1991. 'Il fiore reciso dall' aratro: ambiguità di una similitudine (C. 11.22–4),' *QUCC* 37: 83–100.

Fredricksmeyer, E.A. 1993. 'Method and Interpretation: Catullus 11,' *Helios* 20: 89–105. [The appendix contains a useful survey of previous articles.]

Fernandez Corte, J.C. 1993. 'Un ejercicio de imitacion de C. por Horacio: C. 11 y *Odas* II. 6,' *Latomus* 52: 596–611.

12

Structure: (5 + 4) + (4 + 4). Notice the articulation by means of *quare* 10, *nam* 14. See Q. for a different analysis.

A good-natured squib against a napkin thief (cf. poems 25, 33); not obscene, or in any way sexual, like many of the truly defamatory lampoons, but concerned merely with a lack of good manners or good taste in social behaviour (notice the vocabulary employed: *non belle, inepte, sordida, invenusta*; the question of morals, even the morals of stealing, does not arise).

In fact, three different themes are combined here:

(a) the light-hearted attack on a guest for his poor idea of a joke;

(b) a compliment – by contrast – to the offender's brother, who has the grace to be embarrassed by such witless conduct;

(c) acknowledgment of a present sent to C. by Fabullus and Veranius, who are in Spain; notice that C. says they 'sent' (not 'brought') the gift, so that it is unlikely that they have recently returned; moreover, the use of the word *mnemosyne* suggests this (as L. put it, 'you don't need a memento of someone you see every day'). For the date of their absence in Spain (together; this is not made clear in poem 9, evidently because they returned separately and Veranius arrived before Fabullus), see poem 28 n. The uncertainty of the reading in line 9 (see App. Crit.) makes it undesirable to point to the word *puer* together with Asinius Pollio's date of birth (76 BC) as presumptive evidence for an approximate dating of the poem.

Marrucinus is best taken as a proper name (despite Kr. and others); it was a common custom of new families, like the Asinii who had come to Rome since the Social War, to add a cognomen to mark a branch of a family within a *gens*, in the hope of establishing the family more widely in the society of the *urbs*.

1 *sinistra*: cf. 47.1 and perhaps 25.5 (where see nn.); the left hand was commonly associated with the act of stealing – it is said, because its movements are less prominent, and more easily escape notice, than those of the right; but observe 33.3 *dextra*. Cf. Plaut. *Pers.* 226 *furtifica laeva*, Ov. *M.* 13.111 *nataeque ad furta sinistrae*.

2 *belle*: cf. 4–5 *salsum*, etc.; see intr. n. Most editors (e.g., B., E., Fr., Kr., Lenchantin, Cazzaniga, Eisenhut, but not Mynors or Bardon²) punctuate *uteris in ioco atque vino*: Fr. alone debates the placing of the colon, arguing that punctuation at the end of the line is necessary out of regard for Pollio, to avoid a misunderstanding, since to punctuate after *uteris* would involve telling Pollio *tout court* 'You are a thief.' Q. for his part has only a pair of commas, before and after *in ioco atque vino*, noting: 'Take equally with 2 *uteris* and 3 *tollis*.' I confess that neither persuades me.

   in ioco atque vino: cf. 50.6 *per iocum atque vinum*. Kr. quotes Thuc. 6.28.1 μετὰ παιδιᾶς καὶ οἴνου.

3 *lintea*: see 11 n.

   neglegentiorum: '<fellow-diners>, when they are off their guard.' Cf. 25.5 *oscitantes*.

4 The variant goes back to *A* (McKie: 146); but *R²*'s correction may well be independent, so obviously does the sense demand it.

5 *quamvis*: in this literal sense ('as much as you like') somewhat archaic and colloquial by C.'s time: Plaut. *Pseud.* 1175, *Men.* 318, Lucil. 392 M, Varro *RR* 2.5. 1, Cicero *TD* 3.73.

6 The question is here almost equivalent to a conditional clause (Kr.).

7 *talento*: a Greek denomination is used, in the absence of a Latin word suitable for expressing the idea of a very large sum of money.

8 *mutari*: here not in a monetary sense = *redimi* (Vossius was the first to express surprise that Pollio should have to pay for his brother's thefts), but = *infectum reddere*. B. cites Ter. *Andr.* 40 *haud muto factum*, Hor. *AP* 168 *commisisse cavet quod mox mutare laboret*, and rightly notes that *talento* is not abl. of price but of instrument.

9 Neither *differtus* nor *disertus* will do in close relationship with the genitive *facetiarum*. *Differtus*, as a participle, would require (unlike *plenus*, to which some editors see an analogy) an instrumental ablative. As for *disertus*, the supposed (Greek) genitive of the 'sphere in which' cannot be attested elsewhere in C. To read *pater <leporum ac facetiarum>*, as I suggest, will produce an example of a familiar idiom. See Juv. 14.45 (ed. Clausen): *pater est* ΡΦΣ, *puer est*

A Paris. 7647 *et* 17903, for the exchange, due to abbreviation. The adv. *diserte* is translated by F. 'explicitly,' 'in so many words' (he cites Cicero and Livy). If we take it with *pater* we should perhaps render it 'he is, quite clearly, . . .' or 'he is the very essence of . . .' A. Guarinus has a note indicating his own preference for *pater* (which he renders as *auctor* and *inventor*): 'pater . . . licet alii puer legant, quod non placet' (although the word *puer* appears in the text, as was remarked by Della Corte 1951: 84).

For the unusual pl. *lepores* cf. Cicero, *Orat.* 96 *omnes sententiarum lepores;* but (as Kr. suggests) it may here be influenced by *facetiarum,* a word used regularly in the plural.

It may interest some readers that Pontanus wrote to Panormita a poem (*Am.* 1.27) in C.'s manner, beginning: 'Antoni, decus elegantiarum / atque idem pater omnium leporum / unus te rogat ex tuis amicis / cras ad se venias ferasque tecum / quantumcumque potes facetiarum . . .' Furthermore, Janus Dousa the Elder, in a letter to Victor Giselinus dated 8 May 1571, wrote 'te disertissimo leporum ac facetiarum patre' (C. Heesakkers, *Praecidanea Dousana* [Amsterdam, 1976]: 109).

10 *aut . . . aut*: cf. 69.9, 103.1 and 3 (with imperatives).

trecentos: in Greek as well as in Latin, multiples of 300 are a traditional way of expressing (roundly or vaguely) large numbers: cf. 9.2 *milibus trecentis,* 11.18 *trecentos.* We say 'hundreds' or 'thousands.'

11 *linteum* = 'napkin' here, 'sail' at 4.5; the cloth standing for the article made of it.

12 *movet*: cf. Petron. 30.10 *non tam iactura me movet . . .*

aestimatione, in a more or less concrete sense, 'value.'

13 *mnemosynum*: Greek (only here in Latin). Tr. 'souvenir.'

sodalis: two friends are mentioned, but of course the use of the singular (for metrical reasons) causes no confusion; the *nam* clause explains everything.

14 *Saetaba*: cf. 25.7. For the fame of the flax, and hence the linen, of Saetabis in Spain, see Plin. *NH* 19.9, Sil. Ital. 3.374–5 (cited by E.).

Hiberis: the correction to *-is* (see App. Crit.) 'is confirmed by Martial, who twice ends a line with the words <*ex hiberis*> (4.55.8, 10.65.3)' (F.).

16 *R*²'s 'variant' is a false correction of his own; *m*'s failure to follow it may be due to dislike of it, or more probably to haste and carelessness.

17 *ut*: *V*'s *et* has almost certainly crept in from the preceding line.

Veraniolum: affectionate diminutive; used for metrical reasons, and not implying that he is (as E. believed) preferred to Fabullus, whose name is already in a diminutive form.

Jones, F. 1984. 'A Note on C. 12.1–3,' *CQ* 34: 486–7.

Clausen, W. 1988. 'Catulliana,' *BICS* Suppl. 51, *Vir Bonus Discendi Peritus* [Festschrift for Otto Skutsch]. London: 13–14.

13

Structure: 8 + 6.

As in poem 11, two themes are united in a single composition: the paradoxical dinner invitation to Fabullus (paradoxical because the invited guest must bring the dinner and find the company), and the praise of Lesbia for her gift of ointment to Catullus – the only thing that he, the host, expects to be able to furnish. The occasion of the feast has given rise to much speculation; had Fabullus invited himself? From Cicero, *De or.* 2.246, it would appear to have been perfectly acceptable conduct to invite oneself to dinner at the house of a familiar friend, using the formula *cenabo apud te*. C.'s joking reply certainly appears to temporize – perhaps until Lesbia can be induced to part with the ointment she has promised (*paucis diebus* may conceivably be intended to allow for this delay). As Q. says, the opening lines 'read more like a procrastination than an invitation.' F. allows himself to imagine that it was written 'to welcome Fabullus home from Spain, as poem 9 was written to welcome Veranius, and that Catullus makes play with his own impecuniosity in contrast to the fortune which he supposes Fabullus has brought back with him,' but adds: 'it is as good a guess that it was written to please Lesbia.' As an example of the genre (a poet's invitation or mock-invitation) editors cite Philodemus, *AP* 11.44 (to Piso), Horace *Od.* 1.20, 3.29, 4.12 (the last a parody and inversion of C.'s poem: Virgil is to bring the ointment, while Horace will supply the feast), and Martial 11.52.1 (where the dinner is a poor one, but the host will make up for this by refraining from reading his own verses). As often, C. treats a traditional *topos* with marked originality. See Horace, *Ep.* 1.5, for a more serious invitation.

1 *cenabis* implies an invitation; *cenabo*, a self-invitation (Cicero, *De or.* 2.246); see intr. n.

   mi Fabulle: this form of address suggests close friendship (cf. Cicero's *mi Attice*).

4 *non sine*: cf. 64.290, 66.34, for this emphatic, as well as metrically convenient, way of saying 'and also.'

   candida, 'bright, dazzling' (not solely of fair skin).

5 *omnibus*, 'every kind of.' See Cicero, *Orat.* 96, quoted above (12.9 n.).

   cachinnis, used of distinctly audible, even loud, laughter (as at 31.14, after *ridete*).

8 In the latter part of the second century BC, Afranius (fr. 410 R) formed this image in almost the words used by C. here: *tanne arcula tua plena est aranearum?* Cf. also Plaut. *Aul.* 83–4 *hic apud nos nihil est aliud quaesti furibus, / ita inaniis sunt oppletae atque araneis.*

9 *contra*, 'in return'; cf. 76.23, Ter. *Eun.* 355, V. *Aen.* 7.267.

   amores: in C. this word may be used either, like 'my love,' in a personal sense (see refs. at 6.16 n. and also poem 40, intr. n.) or in an impersonal sense, as here (observe *seu quid* in l. 10) and possibly at 38.6 (but see n. there); for the transference of the impersonal sense to a *thing*, cf. Mart. 14.206 *collo necte, puer, meros amores, / ceston de Veneris sinu calentem* (imitated from C.). For *meros* cf. 17.21 n.

10 The meaning is this: 'If you can't think of a more laudatory way of referring to a perfume than by calling it *meros amores*, that will fit as well.'

   seu quid = aut si quid at 22.13, 82.2.

11–12 Cf. Servius *ad Aen.* 3.279: <Phaon> ... *cum esset navicularius ... Venerem mutatam in anuis formam gratis travexit; quapropter ab ea donatus unguenti alabastro, cum se ... ungueret, feminas in sui amorem trahebat.* (I owe this reference to Professor R.S. Kilpatrick).

11 *dabo*, 'will provide (as host)'; it is only with the pointed *tu* of 13 that we turn back to Fabullus. (Kr., wrongly I think, describes *tu* as 'without emphasis' and colloquial, comparing 6.14.)

   nam: elision in the first accented syllable of a hendecasyllabic, or decasyllabic, line occurs elsewhere in C. only at 55.4–5 (Kr.).

   olfacies, a kind of continuous future: 'when you are smelling it.'

14 *totum*: probably to be taken with *te*, rather than with *nasum*; cf. Cicero, *Pro Cluentio* 72 *totus ex fraude et mendacio factus*. But either way the meaning is the same.

Wilhelm, F. 1906. 'Zu augusteischen Dichtern,' *RhM* 61: 92–3.

Schuster, M. 1925. 'Zur Auffassung von C.s 13. Gedicht,' *WS* 44: 227–34.

Bongi, V. 1943. 'Note critiche sul c. XIII di C.,' *Aevum* 17: 228–36.

Hiltbrunner, O. 1972. 'Einladung zum epicureischen Freundesmal,' *Kraus*: 175–7.

Arkins, B. 1979. 'Poem 13 of C.,' *SOsl* 54: 71–80.

Gamberale, L. 1979. 'Venuste Noster. Caratterizzazione e ironia in C. 13,' *Traglia* 1: 127–48.

Witke, C. 1980. 'C. 13: A Reexamination,' *CP* 75: 325–31.

Helm, J.J. 1980–1. 'Poetic Structure and Humor: C. 13,' *CW* 74: 213–17.

Fitts, R.L. 1982. 'Reflections on C. 13,' *CW* 76: 41–2.

Bernstein, W.H. 1984. 'A Sense of Taste: C. 13,' *CJ* 80: 127–30.

Dettmer, H. 1986. 'Meros amores. A Note on C. 13.9,' *QUCC* 23: 87–91.

Urso, A.M. 1991. 'Fabullo, l'*unguentum*, la *venustas*: osservazioni su C. 13,' *Atti Acc. Pelorit.* 67: 331–42.

Nielsen, R.M., and Blodgett, E.D. 1991. 'C.'s *Cena*: "I'll Tell You of More, and Lie, So You Will Come,"' *RBPh* 69: 87–100.

14

Structure: 5 + 6 + 4 + 5 + 3 (see Q. for a brief analysis of the structure).
Here again, as in poems 11 and 13, two themes are intertwined: a compliment
to C.'s friend Calvus, and a literary attack on the poetaster Suffenus
(cf. poem 22) and others of his kind. The poem is C.'s response to Calvus'
joke (as it must have been; see l. 16 *salse*) in sending to C., as a present for
the Saturnalia, a collection of extremely bad verses by various hands. One
possible difficulty in interpreting the gift as a joke on Calvus' part·is that
C. appears to be more incensed than he would be if he knew Calvus not to
be in earnest in commending the book. But really, as L. remarked, 'the only
appropriate response to such a gift would be to fall in with the spirit of the
jest by allowing oneself to be drawn, and reacting as one was expected to
react; Calvus had clearly intended to draw Catullus' fire, and it would be
a shame to disappoint him.' F.'s suggestion that Calvus 'perhaps made the
selection of poems himself' encounters the difficulty that C. seems to take
it as certain that the book (before it was passed on to him) had indeed been
given to Calvus by a grateful client, since he speculates (*ut suspicor*) on the
identity of the client (ll. 8–9). A similarly teasing atmosphere prevails in
other poems addressed to Calvus (poems 50, 53), where the tone and style
also are relaxed, easy and natural, as here.

1 See App. Crit. (The corruption of *ni* to *ne* is usually supposed to be due to the
   fact that the form *nei* survived to C.'s time).
   ni (= *nisi*) is archaic; cf. 6.2,·14; 45.3.
   oculis meis: cf. 3.5, 82.2, 104.2.
1–2 imitated by Maecenas (to Horace, fr. 3 M, *FLP*) *ni te visceribus meis, Horati, /
   plus iam diligo.*
2 *iucundissime*: see 9.9 n.
3 Does *Vatiniano* mean (i) 'the dislike felt – by everyone, perhaps – for V.,'
   or (ii) 'V.'s dislike for you'? There are supporting passages for each view:
   (i) 53.2, where *Vatiniana crimina* clearly = 'the charges against V.'; (ii) Livy
   2.58.5 *odisse plebem plus quam paterno odio*, 'disliked them more than his
   father had done.' Our choice may partly depend on the chronology of Calvus'
   successive prosecutions of Vatinius; on this question, and on V. himself, see the
   introductory n. to poem 53.
5 *male* is intensive, with *perderes*; see 10.33 n. It adds no fresh meaning (beyond
   the field of reference of the verb). Cf. Hor. *S.* 2.1.6 *peream male, si* . . .
6–7 *clienti* . . . *qui misit*: C. depicts himself as suspecting that the only reason
   why Calvus should have sent him a book of atrociously bad verses was that

a client, defended successfully by Calvus, had given it to him in token of gratitude, and Calvus in his turn – as a joke – sent this unwanted present on to Catullus.

7 *tantum … impiorum*, 'all this wickedly bad stuff,' in a literary sense, but perhaps with a slight allusion to the ideal of *pietas*, a word well suited to describing the relationship between *cliens* and *patronus* (l. 6 *clienti*); it was a treacherous kind of gift.

8 *repertum*: perhaps (as L. suggested) 'original,' rather than the translations offered by F. ('ingeniously designed, recherché').

9 Was Sulla really a *litterator* (elementary school teacher), or does C. simply attach to him, in somewhat malicious fun, this not greatly complimentary designation? It is impossible to say, since he is otherwise quite unknown.

10 *non est mi male*: for the idiom, cf. 23.15 *tibi sit bene ac beate*.

10–11 'At least you should console yourself by reflecting that this unsatisfactory client gave you *something* for your pains; being the kind of man he is, he might not even have done that!'

12 *di magni*: cf. 53.5; also (not flippantly) at 109.3.

13 *scilicet*, 'no doubt the reason why you sent it was …'

14 Much depends on the punctuation here: should a comma be placed before, or after, the word *continuo*? If after (as in my text), then *continuo* is read as an adverb and implies 'you got rid of it at once.' If before, then *continuo die* are linked as adj. and noun, 'on the very next day' (see the two Ovidian quotations in F.). But why should C. put off reading it for a day? (It is doubtful whether *continuo die* can ever mean 'on the very same day.') The difficulty of the former interpretation lies in the awkward apposition *die Saturnalibus* (Plaut. *Poen.* 497 *die bono, Aphrodisiis*, is much less harsh); or the alternative, which is to take as a self-contained phrase, *die optimo dierum* – if, indeed, this is a permissible expression – with *Saturnalibus* inserted.
misti, syncopated form for *misisti*. Cf. 66.21 *luxti*, 30 *tristi*, 77.3 *subrepsti*, 91.9 *duxti*, 99.8 *abstersti*, 110.3 *promisti*.

15 If *oppinio* (= O) or *opinio* stood in *X*, *optimo* (see App. Crit.) strongly assumes the character of a metrical improvement, perhaps first appearing as a variant in *X*.

The *Saturnalia* (17 December) gradually became an extended holiday, marked by goodwill and the giving of presents.

16 For repeated *non*, cf. Ter. *Phorm.* 303 *non non sic futurumst*.
salse, 'you witty fellow!' (false *OR*; but, as F. remarks, Calvus has not broken his word).
tibi abibit: tr. 'you won't get away with *this*' – 'I won't let you off' (not 'it will not come off like that for you' as F. has it).

See App. Crit. Clearly *X* had *false al. salse*, or *false* with superscript *s* (cf. *G*). *R*²'s *abibit* (followed by *m*) improves both metre and sense.

17 *si* = (of course) 'when,' not 'if'; *luxerit* is fut. perf. indic.

18 *Caesios, Aquinos.* These 'generalizing plurals,' as E. and F. call them, here meaning 'persons like C. and A.,' are paralleled at 45.22 (*Syrias Britanniasque*). Both men are unknown, unless at Cicero, *TD* 5.63 the poet's name *Aquinio* should read *Aquino* and its owner be identified with C.'s victim here. The name Aquinus is rare; for an example from Spain, see T.P. Wiseman, *Roman Studies* (1987): 340.

19 *Suffenum: pace* F. ('The change to the singular in *Suffenum* is a mere matter of metrical convenience ...; there is no need to suppose ... that S. is being given special prominence'), I have always supposed (and now find Fr. to have suggested) that there is a point in this change: S. is uniquely bad; there are no others like him. Cf. poem 22. It has been suggested (by Munro) that *Suffenum* is gen. pl. with *venena*; but then ll. 18–19 become unbalanced, and surely *omnia* is better employed in summing up all three offenders and their works (especially with *his* and *suppliciis* to follow).

20 *his suppliciis*: not so much 'with these punishments' as rather, in effect, 'with these *as* punishments.'

21 *interea* is here adversative, not temporal; for this meaning cf. 36.18. Translate 'as for you, ...'
valete abite: these words constitute a single expression ('be off with you, good luck to you'), though strictly speaking *hinc* can properly refer only to *abite*. For the zeugma, cf. Ter. *Ad.* 917 *tu illas abi et traduce*.

22 *malum pedem*: 'bring one's foot' is an elaborate way of saying simply 'come'; cf. Ter. *Andr.* 808 *si id scissem, numquam huc tetulissem pedem*. The adjective, *malum*, brings in the notion of 'unlucky, ill-omened' (cf. Ov. *Tr.* 2.16 *saxa malum refero rursus ad ista pedem*, Apul. *Met.* 6.26 *pessimo pede*). But there is also a suggestion of incompetence in the art of versification (playing on the literary meaning of *pes*, 'metrical foot'); Verrall 1913 finds in this line a parody of the faulty rhythm presumably encountered in the verses of the collection, though F. somewhat unfairly dismisses this as 'more ingenious than plausible.' Certainly, however, Ovid (*Tr.* 1.1.15–16) plays on the double meaning of *pes*: *vade, liber, verbisque meis loca grata saluta: / contingam certe quo licet illa pede.*

23 *saecli incommoda*, 'pests of our time.'

Verrall, A.W. 1913. 'A Metrical Jest of C.: The Hendecasyllable,' *Collected Studies*. London: 249–67.

Bower, E.W. 1961. 'Some Technical Terms in Roman Education,' *Hermes* 89: 462–77.

14[b]

A fragment of an introductory poem. Whether the poem, which was probably intended to be short, was ever completed, is impossible to say. Originally it may have been intended to stand at the head of a collection of light verse (*ineptiae*; cf. l. 4 *nugae*) made by C. himself, from which position it could have been displaced by the present poem 1 when C. decided to dedicate his new and enlarged collection to Cornelius Nepos in gratitude for the latter's approval of the earlier one. The tone of 'apologetic modesty' (F.) resembles that of poem 1, though it is even more pronounced; and it is difficult to see how this 'address to my readers' could have ended with the note of modest confidence on which poem 1 concludes. It is quite possible that, as Kr. suggests, C. intended it to follow poem 1; but why it should have moved from that position to its present place is hard to explain. Since it is immediately followed by a group of poems mostly devoted to sexual themes (particularly the Furius-Aurelius-Juventius cycle, though not all of those are here), attention must be paid to Wiseman's (1969: 7–10) theory that it was written to open a fresh sub-group on a different kind of topic (poems 15–26); but this theory is developed in the service of the view that C. arranged the collection as we have it, and *inter alia* it encounters the difficulty that 16.12 (see nn.) seems to refer to poem 48 rather than to poems 5 and 7. See 16.4 n.

See App. Crit. A. Guarinus has the following note at 14.23: 'tres vero sequentes versus ... pater meus tamquam transpositos suo loco restituit.'

3 *horrebitis* may mean only 'shrink,' 'be reluctant,' with little if any sense of horror or repugnance; see the passages cited in the Introduction, pp. 8–9. It should be noted that Pliny's expression (*Ep.* 1.2.5) *ab editione non abhorrere* is simply and justly translated by Professor Rudd 'not averse to publishing' (*Author and Audience in Latin Literature*, ed. T. Woodman and J. Powell [Cambridge, 1992: 26]).

Forsyth, P.Y. 1989. 'C. 14B,' *CW* 83: 81–5.

15

Structure: 13 + 6 ('a polite request – a threat,' Q.).
Addressed to Aurelius, whom C. suspects of predatory sexual tendencies that may be directed at corrupting the innocent youth, Juventius: 'to lay traps for him will be treated as infringement of *my* charge over him, and you will be punished in the way traditionally reserved for adulterers.' The

poem should not be taken as either altogether serious (though there is in it an element of real jealousy) or wholly playful (though much of what C. alleges and threatens is picturesque fantasy). To treat it as a ferocious attack on an enemy is surely absurd; however much C. may disparage Aurelius and his companion Furius, in comparison with (say) Veranius and Fabullus, they are clearly members of his circle and are never spoken of elsewhere in inimical terms such as C. applies to Gellius or Mamurra. (The 'slanging' habits that prevailed within that circle are another matter.) As Kr. remarks, 'the half-joking tone by no means excludes friendly relations' (he cites poem 11).

1 *commendo*: not (literally) 'entrust to you' – there is no sense in C. saying 'I entrust to your care' if Aurelius is (as the rest of the poem clearly shows) the worst possible person for the charge. Cf. poem 21, where C. (i) calls Juventius *meos amores*, and (ii) says *insidias mihi struentem* (the implication being that, if A. does seduce J., the wrong will be inflicted on C.). In poem 15 we again find *amores* and (l. 16) *nostrum ... caput*, where one might have expected C. to say 'if you try your tricks on J.' L. interpreted the meaning thus: 'I appeal to you to lay off; J. is mine, and he's innocent, so if you have any respect for innocence see you keep him that way; don't think I'm asking for protection against the general public – it's you I worry about, because I know your weakness, which is all right by me as long as you lay off this particular boy; you have plenty of other opportunities. If you are mad enough to poach on my preserves you'll be punished as you deserve.'

With *me ac meos amores* cf. Ter. *Phorm.* 218 *vobis commendo Phanium et vitam meam*, Hirt. *BG* 8.50.4 *se et honorem suum insequentis anni commendaret*.

2 Aurelius is linked with Furius at 11.1, 16.2. He is accused of pursuing Juventius here, and also at 21.1 and possibly 81.4 (where see n.). These last two poems also make Aurelius the target of an accusation of poverty, a charge directed at Furius in poems 23, 24, and 26.

veniam, 'a favour'; cf. Hor. *AP* 11 *veniam petimus damusque vicissim*. For *pudente petere*, cf. Cicero. *Ad Att.* 16.15.5 *pudentissime hoc Cicero petierat*; closer still, 5.21.12 *dedi veniam impudenter petenti*, quoted by Fletcher 1991: 92. The repetition of *pudenter* at line 13 makes Mähly's emendation still more probable, *pace* Kr. If we were to read *pudentem*, the hypallage alleged here would be a violent one, and unparalleled, quite different from the regular sort of hypallage we find in Ov. *Ep.* 19.59 *motus pudentes*; as B. points out, the *pudor* here lies entirely in the way of asking, not in the thing asked for; consequently an adverb is appropriate. (The notion of *pudor* may also be attached to the person asking the favour, as in Cicero, *Ad Fam.* 2.6. 1 *grave est homini pudenti petere aliquid magnum ab eo, de quo se bene meritum putet.)*

5 *pudice*: cf. Plaut. *Amph.* 349 *bene pudiceque adservatur*, Cicero *Brut.* 330 *tueamur ut adultam virginem caste.*

6 *a*: I take this with *conserves* (cf. Cicero, *Ad Fam.* 13.50.2 *ab omni incommodo conserves*) rather than with *pudice*, as Q. does, quoting Plaut. *Curc.* 51 *tam a me pudicast quasi soror mea sit.*

non dico ... verum; cf. 16.10 *non dico ... sed* (E. gives several examples from Cicero).

7 Perhaps a reminiscence of Callim. *Ep.* 28.1–2 οὐδὲ κελεύθῳ χαίρω, τίς πολλοὺς ὧδε καὶ ὧδε φέρει.

8 The reading of *A* appears to have been ambiguous (for *r-t* confusion see 7.6).

9 *R²* corrects, *suo Marte.*

11 A clear instance of a variant in *A* (cf. 12.4 and 22.15; McKie: 146).

12 *foris*, adv.: 'out there,' 'at large.'

erit paratum, impers. neuter: 'whenever an opportunity occurs.' Cf. Hor. *S.* 1.2.117 *praesto est* (in a similar context).

13 *G²'s prudenter* is not a mere slip, as is evident from its reappearance as a variant in *R²m²* (and hence, we may infer, in *X*).

15 *sceleste*, a word applied to two purposes; cf. σχέτλιος, 'wretch.'

16 *nostrum caput = me* (cf. line 1), not 'the object of my affection' (as Q.).

insidiis, in erotic sense: cf. 21.7, and Plaut. *Curc.* 25.

17 The spelling correction *ah* is due to *R²*. The *R²(m²)* variant *al. tum* is an obvious metrical correction, attributable to *X*.

18–19 Notice the punishment mentioned (ῥαφανίδωσις, Schol. Ar. *Nub.* 1083), and see n. on poem 40.

18 *attractis pedibus*, as in *CIL* IV 1261 (an inscription from Pompeii).

porta = πρωκτός, *podex* (*Priap.* 52.5 *porta te faciet patentiorem*).

19 *percurrent*: a typical Catullan exaggeration, which Mähly's *pertundent* quite misses.

mugiles: cf. Juv. 10.317 *quosdam moechos et mugilis intrat.*

16

Structure: cyclical (first line repeated at end; line 4 repeated at line 8): 4 + (4 + 3) + 3.

C. feels he must reply publicly (see poem 48, intr. n.) to a published squib, or two, by Furius and Aurelius, in which his character had been lampooned on account of a kiss poem (most likely poem 48; see n. on line 4 below). For the tone and language used, cf. poem 15, intr. n. Here, however, a wider topic is raised. 'Art does not mirror life, it embroiders on it. If I write erotic poetry, as I do, this doesn't say anything about my character – only about my regard for the rules of that genre. If everything a poet wrote had to conform to the high standards demanded of him in life, there could not be any erotic poetry worth having' (L).

1 As a word of picturesque abuse, *irrumare* is frequently used by C. (including the verb and its derivatives, seven times in all, not counting separately the repetition at line 14 of this poem); whereas outside this poem *pedicare* appears only once, at 21.4, and then in a literal sense (as Q. has pointed out). Why, then, is it added to *irrumabo* here, in a set of *versiculi* (l. 6; tr. 'light verses')? Because, since Furius and Aurelius had impugned C.'s actual manhood in scoffing at his kiss verses, it was not enough to use in his reply only the figurative language of *irrumabo*; in order to say 'this time I'm really serious,' he had to support it with something that lay outside the regular extravagances of literary obscenity.

2 *pathice et cinaede*: cf. 57.1–2, with n. on 2.

3 The R^2 correction (*mi* to *me*) is obvious.

Notice the indicative mood of *putastis*; the relative clause here does duty for a causal clause (cf. lines 12–13).

4 *parum pudicum* = *impudicum*. The word is usually appropriated to homosexuality; hence it seems likely that the *milia multa basiorum* in l. 12 are those of poem 48, rather than of poems 5 and 7. This would seem to cast doubt on the contention of T.P. Wiseman and others that C. arranged the poems intending them to be read in the order in which we have them.

5 *castum* (in this context) probably 'sexually normal' (not 'chaste'). For the sentiment cf. Ov. *Tr.* 2.354, Mart. 1.4.8. See also App. Crit. for Pliny's endorsement of lines 5–8.

pium poetam: certainly not 'the godly poet' (E.). A *pius poeta* was one who was true to his calling, as a client of the Muse; the opposite, in describing poets or poetry, was *impius* (see 14.7).

7–8 After *tum denique*, the following *si* (or *cum*) clause is regularly in the indicative; cf. Plaut. *Capt.* 142–3, Cicero *De legg.* 2.10, *TD* 3.75 (quoted by E.).

7 *X*'s variant (adopted by R^2m^2) is essentially metrical in character.

Pliny cites this line with *tunc* and also with *et*, obviously quoting from memory; but on the other hand his *sunt* in line 8 is right, against *V*, and conforms to grammatical practice (see the preceding n.).

8 After this repetition of l. 4, we move, without a break, into the first of two three-line sections; see n. on structure (above).

9 *quod pruriat* = *pruritum* (B., Kr.).

10 The pronoun *his* seems to suggest that the poet pictures them in his mind; cf. perhaps Pers. 5.86 *Stoicus hic*.

m^2 wrote *sed his* over an erasure. Nevertheless it would be rash to conclude that he was at some point confronted with *O*'s *hiis* (which of course is metrically tolerable, if the preceding word were dropped), in the absence of supporting evidence of *O*-type readings in m^2.

11 *lumbos*: not exactly = *penes* (as Kr.), but of stiffness (*duros*) in the lower regions, with the *implication* of flagging sexual activity.

12 It may be conjectured that, of the two variants inherited from *X* by $R^2(m^2)$, the former points to *hosque A* (= *O*), whereas the other is the result of a good correction in the *X*-stratum.

13 *male marem*: Q. misleadingly cites, as a parallel, 10.33 *insulsa male*; there, *male* intensifies the adjective, but here it negates it.

Cherniss, H.F. 1962. 'Me ex versiculis parum pudicum,' *Critical Essays on Roman Literature: Elegy and Lyric*. Cambridge, Mass: 15–30.

Kinsey, T.E. 1966. 'C. 16,' *Latomus* 25: 101–6.

Sandy, G.N. 1971. 'C. 16,' *Phoenix* 25: 151–7.

Winter, T.N. 1973. 'C. Purified: A Brief History of Carmen 16,' *Arethusa* 6: 257–65.

Macleod, C.W. 1973. 'Parody and Personalities in C.,' *CQ* 23: 294–303, esp. 300–1.

Fehling, D. 1974. 'De Catulli carmine sexto decimo,' *RhM* 117: 103–8.

Rankin, H.D. 1975. 'C. and the Privacy of Love,' *WS* 9: 67–74, esp. 73–4.

Kinzl, K.H. 1976. 'De Catulli carmine sexto decimo annotatiuncula quaedam,' *RhM* 119: 95. [On Fehling 1974.]

Wiseman, T.P. 1976. 'C. 16,' *LCM* 1: 14–17.

Buchheit, V. 1976. 'Sal et lepos versiculorum (C. c. 16),' *Hermes* 104: 331–47. [Pp. 346–7: *Nachtrag*, criticizing Fehling 1974.]

Rankin, H.D. 1976. 'Poem 16 of C.,' *SOsl* 51: 87–94.

Bannert, H. 1977. ʺΑποραφανίδωσις: der Rettich für den Ehebrecher,' *Mn* 30: 293–5. [On Fehling 1974.]

Adamik, T. 1977/78. 'On the Aesthetics of the Short Poems of C.: Carm. 16,' *AUB* 5/6: 115–27.

17

Structure: 11 + 11 + 4. For a more detailed analysis of the structure, on the same general lines, see Q. Lines 1–11 are further divided by Rudd 1959 into three parts, as follows: in lines 1–4, a description of the town and its (unsafe) bridge; in lines 5–7, a transition ('May you have a new bridge if my wish is fulfilled'); and finally, in lines 8–11, the wish itself. Here we have 4 + 3 + 4; a symmetrical pattern, as Rudd remarks.

On a lethargic and indifferent fellow-citizen of C.'s who (whether at Verona or elsewhere is not clear) neglects, and fails to protect, his lively young wife; C. suggests (l. 17) that she is cuckolding him. Although the topic is sexual, the situation is not one in which C. is personally involved (cf. poem 67, where also C. is the detached observer and commentator), and the expression is correspondingly delicate; contrast the aggressive coarseness that tends to break out in the sexual lampoons where C.'s personal feelings are voiced. As often happens in C.'s poetry, two themes are interwoven by an association of ideas: the sexual history on the one hand, and on the other the frail condition of the town's bridge (parallel to the man's emotional torpor), which causes its citizens to yearn for a new bridge to replace the old. C. thinks a fall from the present bridge, with a consequent ducking in the swamp it crosses, will rouse his fellow-citizen from his indifference and make a new man of him, metaphorically speaking (though not of course literally; here the parallel between man and bridge, *pace* Rudd, is incomplete; nor has Walsh 1985, who has noticed the defect in the argument, succeeded in rescuing it, since it remains evident that a cure is envisaged for the man but only total replacement for the bridge).

On the site of *Colonia* (or *colonia*) see E. and especially Fr. As the latter observes, the fact that C. describes his victim as *municeps meus* (l. 8) need not be intended as a device for distinguishing him from the inhabitants of Colonia; it was the only way to say 'Veronese' in this metre. See however below, nn. 6 and 8.

Metre: Priapean (glyconic + pherecratean). For C.'s use of this type of metre, cf. poem 34 (stanza of three glyconics and one pherecratean) and poem 61 (four glyconics + pherecratean). The Priapean is found in early Greek lyric poetry (Sappho, Anacreon; see F.'s n., p. 140, for examples taken from Pindar and the tragedians), but was first used in the Hellenistic poets (e.g., Euphronios) for 'Priapean' poems and was then named accordingly. The glyconic and pherecratean parts are very closely joined; indeed it is only the fact that elision is used between them that caused the Priapean to be written as one long line rather than a 'stanza' of two short ones. Neither hiatus nor *syllaba anceps* is permitted between the first and second parts. As Kr. remarks, the spondee is permitted only in the first foot of the first part, and twice at the first foot of the second part; here C. returns to the freedom of the archaic and classical Greek writers, whereas Hellenistic technique imposed greater restrictions. Fragments 1 and 2 of Catullus (printed at the end of the text) are also in this metre.

1 *Colonia*: see introductory n.

longo of course does not imply that the new bridge should be longer than the old; it merely indicates which of several existing bridges the poet has in mind ('the long one that crosses the swamp').

2 *paratum habes* (= *parata es*); for the use of this phrase with infinitive, cf. Tac. *A.* 11.1 *turbare ... promptum haberet.* For its much more common use with a noun, cf. 60.4–5 *vocem contemptam haberes.*

inepta should not be translated too literally as *in-apta* ('ill-fitting,' F., who admits that 'the word is not so used elsewhere'), but rather in the (originally transferred, and later usual) sense in which it is applied (e.g., by C. himself: 12.4, 25.8, 39.16) to human beings; perhaps tr. 'crazy.' As Rudd 1959 has pointed out, a certain analogy is drawn between the bridge and the man pilloried by C.; see introductory n.

3 *OGR* read *ac sulcis*, from which E. deduced *acsuleis.* Most editors follow E., adopting however the spelling *axul(e)is* and assuming *axula*, or *acsula* (not otherwise attested), or *assula*, to be the diminutive form of *axis*, 'plank.' Fr. reads *assuleis.* The word *assulae* is certainly found; it means 'chips, shavings,' usually of wood; and this may be accepted if there is gross exaggeration; as L. suggested, we might say 'made of matchsticks.' Palmer conjectured *aesculeis*, 'oaken piles,' taking the adj. as standing for a noun.

redivivis, 'used, second-hand.' Cf. Cic. *Verr.* 2.1.147, 148, Vitruv. 7.1.3, and the definition in Fest. 334.25 Lindsay (*redivivum est ex vetusto renovatum*).

4 *supinus*, literally 'on its back' (normally used of a human being), but here in fact suggesting no more than 'falling flat'; possibly C. has a mental image of the bridge as heeling over sideways, and turning turtle; cf. the table mentioned in Prop. 4.8.44, which (*pace* F., who quotes the line) surely does not turn upside-down.

cava, 'engulfing' (cf. 95.5 n.).

5 *sic*, 'as you hope for.' The imperative in l. 7 picks up this *sic*: 'May you have the bridge you want, provided that you grant me this.' For the construction (*sic ...*, followed by an imperative), Q. quotes V. *Ecl.* 9.30–2. The high-flown language of 5–6 contrasts with the 'modesty' of the poet's request in 8–11 (Carratello 1983).

6 *Salisubsili*: taken with *sacra*, this ought to be the gen. sing. of a cult title pertaining to a god; in the nom., *Salisubsilus.* One thinks of the priestly college of the *Salii*, with their ritual dances. Cf. l. 2 *salire*; but the dancing there is not 'Salic,' otherwise the climax implied by *vel* would lose its effect. Also, the phrase *sacra suscipere* denotes the introduction of a new cult, with unfamiliar rituals (Cicero, *In Vat.* 14, Lucr. 5.1163, Livy 1.7.15, 1.31.4, 2.27.5, Suet. *Nero* 11.2). From this it may possibly be concluded that 'Colonia' is not Verona, where we know that there *were* Salii in C.'s time (*CIL* V[1] 4492). See also line 8 n.

With *sali subsali, m* has apparently blundered into a reading virtually identical with that adopted by some modern editors; *m*[2], however, undoes this by adding as a variant the reading of *R*. The *codex Diezianus* 37 (*D*) cannot have taken *salisubsali* from *m*, since – as B.L. Ullman observed (1960: 1053) – the part of the *liber Catulli* that includes this line was derived by *D*'s parent manuscript from a source depending neither on *R* nor on *m*, but on *G*.

Attribution of the reading *salisubsuli* to Baptista Guarinus is confirmed by his son Alexander (*expositiones*, fol. xvii 'pater meus').

7 *munus*: hardly = 'task' (Q.); rather, 'spectacle' (Kr.). In Cicero, *Sest.* 124, the word is used, as here, with *dare*: <consessus gladiatorius>, *munus Scipionis, dignum ... Metello, cui dabatur.*

8 *municipem meum*: i.e., a Veronese fellow-citizen of Catullus himself, and thus perhaps not an inhabitant of 'Colonia'; observe the juxtaposed and contrasting pronouns (a common device of C.'s) in *meum de tuo* (see also l. 6 n.). There is no reason to suppose this to be the person C. attacks in poem 67.

9 *per*, 'over'; cf. Livy *per.* 22 *ab equo ... per caput devolutus*. The double *que* is Ennian (perhaps mock-epic); later it became a 'neoteric' mannerism. See D.O. Ross 1969: 63–5.

10 *verum*, adding a reservation or special proviso: 'but it must be where ...' Cf. Ter. *Heaut.* 598 *dicam, verum ut aliud ex alio incidit.*
ut = *ubi* (cf. 11.3). Ronconi, quoted by Carratello 1983, points out that this Grecism, and the 'idyllic' tones of lines 13–16, seek to introduce an element of poetic parody into an otherwise generally colloquial piece.

11 *maxime profunda* = *profundissima*; substituted for purely metrical reasons.

12 F. showed that *instar* has always a quantitative, not qualitative, denotation; tr. 'as much as ...'

13 Notice the two diminutives, the use of which underlines the suggestion of rocking and crooning.
patris: not *matris*; perhaps partly for metrical reasons, but C. elsewhere presents haunting images of paternal affection in a variety of contexts: see 61.209–13, 64.214–37, 72.3–4.

14 On *quoi* (= *cui*) as a cause of the reading *cuio(cum)*, see 1.1 n. Scaliger's source for *quoi* was of course the manuscript at the head of the θ class, that written by Pacificus Maximus Asculanus (No. 52 in the Table of Manuscripts: British Library Ms Egerton 3027; see the article quoted in my note in the Table).

15 *et* = 'and, what is more, ...' (esp. with word-repetition, as of *puella* here). Frequent in Cicero; Carratello 1983: n. 84 gives examples.
delicatior: cf. 50.3 *delicatos*. For the sexual content of this term, cf. the introductory n. F. translates 'skittish,' rightly: *delicatus* is explained as *lusui dicatus* by Festus. The word is connected with *deliciae* (2.1 n.). The words *tener, tenellulus* (as here) have similarly erotic overtones (cf. Laevius, fr. 4 M *manu lascivola ac tenellula*, Ov. *M.* 13.791 *tenero lascivior haedo*), and perhaps carry an echo from Theocr. 11.20 ἁπαλωτέρα ἀρνός.

17 *ludere*, in erotic sense (see the introductory n.). Cf. 61.204 *ludite ut lubet.*
nec pili facit uni, 'and doesn't care a straw' (cf. 10.13 for the idiom).

uni = *unius*. On this and other instances of 'pronominal adjectives following the adjectival ... declension,' see F. They are not merely 'vulgar' (as Kr. says of *uni*).

R^2's *vim* – not a genuine variant – is so perverse as to be almost inexplicable. (See however Intr., p. 41). Although *m* blindly accepts *vim*, G^2 exercises – as now and then he does – a certain independence in rejecting an absurd, or unmetrical, reading found by him in *m*. In the next line, however, where the $R^2(m^1)$ correction *alnus* is sound, G^2 does not hesitate to follow. In line 22, the reading *quid*, exhibited by *m* – resulting from an error – is not so manifestly wrong as to be rejected by G^2.

18 *sublevat*; metaphorically, 'bestirs himself <to put things right>'; the literal meaning is continued in the simile that follows.

ex sua parte, simply 'for his part.' The case is not one of sexual impotence on the husband's part (otherwise C.'s complaint of his neglect of the *puella* would be useless, and the cure outlined in ll. 23–6 – which is that prescribed by Celsus, 3.20.104, for lethargy, not for impotence – would be impossible), but rather of sexual indifference.

19 *Liguri*: to be taken with *securi*, not with *fossa*. The alder tree is linked in legend with the plain of the river Po (V. *Ecl.* 6.63, *Geo.* 2.451), where C.'s story is set; Liguria lies westward, towards Genoa. It is true that boats of alder-wood are mentioned by Silius Italicus (4.491) in connection with the river Trebia in Liguria. But there seems little reason why C. should locate his simile at such a distance. Agricultural implements often retained adjectives describing their origin, as we speak of a Dutch hoe or a Swedish saw; cf. Hor. *Od.* 1.31.9 *Calena* (the reading preferred by Nisbet and Hubbard) *falce*, 3.6.38 *Sabellis ... ligonibus*.

suppernata, 'hamstrung'; Ennius (*Ann.* 287 Skutsch *his pernas succidit iniqua superbia Poeni*) seems to have invented the metaphorical application of the idea, though not exactly of the word itself. Notice the doubly figurative statement here: the man is *like* a felled tree (a log, as we should say), and the tree is helpless *like* a hamstrung beast.

See App. Crit. It is not very clear, from Av. *Emend.* (1495) a 3 v, whether Politianus should be credited with both suggestions (*suppernata* and *expernata*, as remedies for *V*'s unmetrical and nonsensical *superata*); see Polit. *Misc.* ch. lxxiii for *expernata*. As a matter of history, noted by Carratello 1983, *superata* is still retained in the text by Muretus and Statius, though they were tempted by the emendation; Scaliger's edition first canonized *suppernata*. The question is discussed in Gaisser 1993: 58–61.

20 This line is part of the *velut*-clause; the subject of *sentiens* is *alnus*, which is referred to in *nulla* (fem.): 'aware of everything just as much as if it (sc. the tree) did not exist at all (lit. anywhere at all).' The simile is answered by *talis*, which

begins the apodosis with l. 21, after the comma at the end of 20 in my text;
Mynors prints a semicolon, but this seems to be an unsatisfactory compromise
with the text of E., who ends a sentence with *usquam*. As L. observed, 'the period
would involve taking *quam si nulla sit usquam* = *quam si illa* (i.e., the wife)
n. s. u. This unexpressed change of subject is surely impossible Latin when there
is a feminine subject already in possession; and by taking *sentiens* as referring to
the husband, it not only requires us to read *iacet* as a kind of ἀπὸ κοινοῦ verb,
i.e., *iacet ut alnus iacet*, but makes the simile redundant by giving it a double
pick-up.'

For *nulla* = 'not at all,' see 8.14 n.

21 Palaeographically, *merus* (*meꝰus*) involves only a slight change from *meus*.
Cf. 13.9, where *meros* is *meos* in *O*; the letter *r* is sometimes indicated by a small
mark (ꝰ) above the word, which easily disappears. *iste* (lit. 'that of yours') does
not go well with *meus* (C. has no parallel, whereas he uses *iste vester* and *iste
tuus* twice each); and unqualified *stupor* (of a person) is much less likely than
merus stupor. A harsh expression of this sort is uncharacteristic of Catullus.

22 *qui sit*: cf. 78ᵇ.4 *qui sis*; *qui* is 'the normal form in this collocation' (F., who
quotes Plaut. *Aul.* 714–15 and *Capt.* 560; add *Trin.* 849 *qui sit homo nescio*).
Cf. 66.42 *qui se*, used for similar reasons of euphony.

23 *O*'s slipshod transcription (*nunc volo volo*) suggests to me that *A* had *nunc eum
volo*. Presumably *X* copied it carelessly from *A*, writing *nunc cum*, and then
added a self-correcting variant which *R*² – rightly or wrongly – read as *al. hunc
eum*. This is partially faulty on linguistic grounds, and therefore *G*² rejects it
when he sees it exactly copied in *m*², in spite of the fact that *eum* represents a
metrical improvement.

24 *si* = *si forte*, 'to see if …'
pote = *pote sit* = *possit*; cf. 45.5, 67.11, 76.16. The subject of this verb, and also
of *excitare*, must be the husband, who is obviously the subject of *derelinquere*.
excitare: this verb is used in the passage of Celsus (3.20) referred to in the n. on
l. 18 above. In that passage, the grammatical object of *excitare* is the patient; but
in Pliny, *NH* 19.155 (quoted by F.), the *torpor* ('lethargy') itself is the object of
excitante.

26 *soleam* ('slipper') denotes a strapped-on (and hence easily removable) leather
shoe, with a metal sole attached to it. Carratello 1983 has a long and informative
note on Roman practices (n. 7). He cites Gargilius Martialis fr. 6 *De persicis* (p. 24
l. 121 Condorelli) *iumentorum soleas in itinere derelictas*; cf. also E. and Kr.

The verb *derelinquit* must of course be supplied in this line.

Birt, T. 1926. '*Pontifex* und *Sexagenarii de ponte* (zu C. c. 17),' *RhM* 75: 115–26.
Rudd, N. 1959. 'Colonia and Her Bridge: A Note on the Structure of C. 17,' *TAPA*
90: 238–42.

Rutter, J. 1967. 'A Further Note on the Structure of C.17,' *CW* 60: 269–70.

Rankin, H.D. 1968. 'A Note on C. 17,' *Latomus* 27: 418–20.

Cèbe, J.-P., and Veyne, P. 1969. 'Remarques sur le poème 17 de C.,' *Renard* 1: 238–49.

Quinn, K. 1969. 'Practical Criticism: A Reading of Propertius i.21 and C. 17,' *G&R* 17: 19–29.

Glenn, J. 1970. '*Fossa* in C.'s Simile of the Cut Tree (17.18–19),' *CP* 65: 256–7.

Alfonsi, L. 1970. 'Sul primo Catullo,' *Festschrift . . . Karl Büchner I–II*. Wiesbaden: 2–9.

Carratello, U. 1983. 'Il c. 17 di C.,' *GIF* 35: 25–51.

Walsh, P.G. 1985. 'C. 17 and the Priapean,' *Arctos*, Suppl. 2: 315–22.

Prete, S. 1986. 'A proposito di un verso di C. (17.6),' *Paideia* 41: 48–50.

Fedeli, P. 1991. 'Il carme 17 di C. e i sacrifici edili,' *Studi di filologia classica in onore di C. Monaco*. Palermo: 707–22.

18–20

See App. Crit. Petrus Victorius (*Variae lectiones* 12.3) seems to suggest adding Bücheler 86 after poem 17. He also mentions, as an afterthought, that C. wrote Frag. 1 (*Hunc lucum*). But he does not seem to mention Bücheler 85, or to seek to impose the order found in Muretus a year later.

21

Structure: (6 + 2) + (3 + 2). Each two-line unit contains a threat of *irrumatio*. A lampoon on Aurelius, clearly part of the cycle of poems on Juventius, even though the *puer* is not named. As editors have noticed, it forms a sequel to poem 15, which records that C. suspected Aurelius of designs on Juventius, who is *mei amores* in both poems. C. now claims to have seen him making advances to the youth, and threatens (as he had done in poem 15 and also in poem 16) to retaliate violently. This squib is also linked to poem 23; notice in both the stress on the notion of *esuritio*. For C., Furius and Aurelius are so closely associated that the same gibe about going short of food and drink can be used indifferently about one or the other (L). The poverty gibe reappears in poem 24, clearly referring to Furius, though he is not actually named (24.5 *isti . . . arca* practically repeats 23.1 *Furi . . . arca*). In poem 24 Juventius is warned not to accept the advances of Furius, who is poor. Quite possibly poem 40 (q.v.), though it is not addressed either to Furius or to Aurelius (unless 'Raude' conceals an allusion to either of them), belongs to the same Juventius cycle; notice, especially, its links with poem 15 (to Aurelius): *mala mens* and *vecors* (neither of which is used by C. outside this pair of poems), *miser / misellus*, and the threat at the end. It should also be observed that the formula *mei amores* (40.7), in the personal sense (38.6 is a doubtful exception), is elsewhere in C. limited to Juventius (15.1, 21.4). Is it conceivable that the name 'Raude' may allude to Aurelius? *Raudus* (neuter) was an old piece of brass coinage; and at 81.4 (another Juventius poem, like poem 24 warning the boy against a rival who is a *bellus homo* but poor) Zicàri has seen a reference to Aurelius in the word *inaurata*; was the superficial gilding of *Aurelius* really brass?

1 C. affects to despise Furius and Aurelius as starvelings, or at least poverty-stricken; cf. poems 23, 24, 26 (and possibly poem 81, where see nn.). *pater*: cf. 12.9 n.

2 *harum*: 'present-day, current.'

2–3 For the idiom, cf. 24.2–3 and 49.2–3.

4 Notice that *amores* is here masculine by implication; cf. 15.1, 38.6.

5–6 See App. Crit. It is better to leave *haerens*; if we do this, the third statement (l. 6) is more coherent in itself and also forms an extended climax in accordance with the 'law of increasing *cola*.' *Haeres ad latus*, detached from the rest, would virtually duplicate *simul es*.

7 *frustra: nam*; cf. Hor. *Od.* 3.7.21.
instruentem = si instruas. For *instruentem* Ribbeck proposed *struentem*, and B. supports this with several examples to show that this was the common idiom. Cf. however Livy 6.23.6 *insidiis instruentem locum* (see Walters and Conway, app. crit., for the reading *instruendis quaerentem locum*); Apul. *M.* 7.25 *Fortuna ... novas instruxit insidias*.

9–11 See line 1 n.

11 The colloquial use of *mi* for *meus*, etc., may be supported by the now universally accepted Humanistic emendation *puella nam mi* at 37.11, where (as here) the Mss read *me*. The use of *mihi* by C. at such passages as 63.15 *mihi comites*, 68.35 *illa mihi sedes, illic mea carpitur aetas*, approaches this idiom fairly closely.

Konstan, D. 1979. 'An Interpretation of C. 21,' *SLLRH* 1. Brussels: 214–16.

22

Structure: (3 + 5 + 3) + 6 + 4. For a more detailed analysis, see Q.
Suffenus, who had already been mentioned as a bad poet (among others) at 14.19, is held up to ridicule for his extreme wordiness, as well as for his egregious vanity, manifested in the sumptuous wrappings in which he clothes his volumes of amateurish scribblings. By Catullan standards, the scorn poured on Suffenus is fairly mild; furthermore, 'this poem is unlike

any other of C.'s in that it ends by moralizing, making Suffenus into a sort of fable and using him as an illustration of human weakness' (L). Here, for once (we may say) C. is a *satirist*.

We do not know who Suffenus was, or whether he existed. In 14.18–19 he is linked with Caesius (also unknown) and Aquinus (who may well be the poet mentioned by Cicero, *TD* 5.63, as an egregious example of a poet who seemed *optimus* to himself – this being exactly how C. sees Suffenus here). If Aquinus was a real person, known to C. and to Calvus under that name, the same is probably true of Suffenus. No one is more likely to remain a mere name than the *worst* poets of a prolific generation. The Varus who is addressed here is perhaps more likely to be Quintilius Varus, the literary man and friend of Virgil and Horace, than the jurist Alfenus Varus; see intr. n. to poem 10. (Kr. thinks the identification with Alfenus more probable, but does not state his reasons for this belief. He is right, however, in pointing out that Varus, mentioned only in the first line, has nothing to do with the situation, and that the disguising of a piece of literary criticism as a letter to a friend is a Hellenistic device of a purely ornamental kind.) For C.'s view of *cacoethes scribendi* in poets, cf. poem 95. Clearly, S. was a poet of the old, or 'Ennian,' tradition, like Hortensius.
Metre: Choliambic (which implies that C. is *serious*, in this instance about the proper attitude of poets to their work: S.'s social polish turns to naïvety when he addresses himself to literary creation).

1 *Suffenus*: see intr. n. and cf. 14.19 n.
   probe, colloq. (esp. with *nosse, scire*, etc.); frequent in Comedy (examples in F.); Cicero, *Ad Fam.* 2.12.2.
2 *venustus* (cf. 3.2, 13.6) implies 'the charm in speech and behaviour which comes of taste and breeding' (F.). *dicax*: scathingly witty (Quint. 6.3.21).
3 *idem*: see 25.4 n.
   G^2's deference towards m is manifest here: m's original reading, *itemque* (no more than a careless slip in the first place), is inserted in G^2 as a variant even though it had been corrected by m^2.
   longe plurimos surely implies comparison with some others (because of the adverb), though Q. simply translates 'a terrific lot.' Kr. cannot make up his mind.
5–8 One of the few pieces of surviving evidence on the subject of books in their physical aspect in the time of C. In Cicero (*Ad Fam.* 7.18.2, partly quoted by F.) we read: 'nam quod in palimpsesto, laudo equidem parsimoniam, sed miror quid in illa cartula fuerit quod delere malueris quam haec <non> scribere.' It is uncertain whether in this passage of Cicero *cartula* means literally papyrus – if so, the 'palimpsest' itself may be papyrus, not parchment, as has usually been supposed.

5 *palimpsesto*: this word is very rare; F. cites the only two instances of it in Greek
(Plut. *Mor.* 779c, 504d, both of them 'figurative'). Latin literature yields only
one further instance (see Cicero's letter, already quoted). Formerly, I read *-on*,
on the grounds that acc. is generally used after *referre in*, in the sense indicated
in *OLD* 8. See Gamberale 1982: n. 18; despite several mistakes (in Cicero, *ND*
1.29, *referre in* = 'include in <a category>' [*OLD* 9], not 'set down' [*OLD* 8], and
Mynors did not 'keep the ablative'), the last sentence of his note argues well for
-to, a reading which is supported against *-ton*, not only by Val. Max. 2.10.1 *in
his relatae*, but also by the form appearing in *V*. See the discussion in F., who
was clearly inclined to favour *-to*. A.S. Pease, on Cicero, *ND* 1.29, notes that
Lambinus altered *numero* to *-um* on the strength of 1.34 *refert in deos*, but
defends the ablative, quoting *Q. Rosc.* 5 *in codice* (Mss; *-cem* Beroaldus) …
relatum, and Hyg. *Fab.* 177, as well as our passage.

6 Most eds. read *novi libri*: see App. Crit. *V* has *nove* (= *novae*, agreeing with
cartae regiae), and this gives good sense (taking *cartae regiae* as virtually a single
noun indicating a particular quality of papyrus, for which see Pliny, *NH* 13.74):
not scrap-paper, written over, but proper rolls (*libri*), made of new papyrus of
the best quality. L. suggested that Suffenus (whose books were on sale – see
14.17–19 – and could be read in this format) was 'rushing into print' by selling
his books in a de luxe edition at a stage where others kept their work 'in the
rough' (palimpsest) in order to revise it. But it may only be that when he first
showed it to a few close friends, as the custom was, his vanity made him present
it in this sumptuous dress. L. was on firmer ground when he suggested deleting
the comma after *regiae* even if *novi* should be read: *novi libri* by itself has little
point, since if the sheets are of high quality and not yet written upon, they must,
when glued together, automatically make a 'new book.' See also Nisbet 1978: 96,
who suggests *novae bibli*, without any stop after *regiae*: 'Catullus is describing
royal sheets of new papyrus (genitive).'

  Probably *X* had *curte*; if *G* originally wrote *certe*, he did so in error. The
correction to *carte* is *R*²'s own idea, and as usual in such cases it is reflected in *m*
rather than *m*².

7 The *umbilicus* was the wooden cylinder around which the papyrus book was
wrapped; in the plural, *umbilici* = the bosses, often decorated, attached to the
ends of the cylinder and projecting from the roll. Cf. Mart. 3.2.9–11 (F. divides
this into three separate quotations): *pictis luxurieris umbilicis / et te purpura
delicata* (= *membrana* in C.) *velet / et cocco* ('scarlet') *rubeat superbus index*
(*index* = *lorum*, in the usual sense of σίλλυβος or title-tag attached to the roll,
though *lora* here is often taken in the sense of ties for the parchment wrapper,
membrana).
membran(a)e (*V*) is nominative. We need a plural; Suffenus is clearly not a man
of a single *libellus* (cf. l. 6 *libri*). The word was forced into the singular (by

Avantius, and later by many others) in order to avoid *membranae* without an epithet – which those editors found in *derecta plumbo* (but who would rule with lines, made by lead, the outer case of the book?).

Munro rightly isolated *membranae*; the other things mentioned are essential to book production, and therefore if they are unusually handsome the fact must be noted, whereas to have *membranae* at all was a luxury. To punctuate as Mynors does (*lora rubra membranae,*) is to vote for the interpretation by which *lora* become the ties securing the cover. But (i) this meaning for *lora* is unparalleled; (ii) if *lora* are plural and *membranae* singular there seem to be *several* ties to each – but why? (iii) *membranae* (gen.) would then be singular where everything else is plural.

8 Take *omnia* as the subject: 'the whole thing (i.e., the book as a whole) lead-ruled and levelled off with pumice-stone' (which was done in order to even up the edges of the pages or sheets, and in general to 'sandpaper' away any faults).

9 *tu* = 'one' (general, not personal); the subjunctive with *cum* or *si* is quite common in this sense, but added *tu* is very rare (as F. remarks; he suggests metrical necessity here, comparing 23.22). For both the construction and the thought, cf. Hor. *Ep.* 2.2. 106–8:

> ridentur mala qui componunt carmina; verum
>
> gaudent scribentes et se venerantur et ultro,
>
> si taceas, laudant quidquid scripsere beati.

10 *unus*, here = 'just any' (contrast 10.17 n.).

11 *abhorret*, not quite the same as *mutat*: 'so strange he appears.' Cf. Cicero, *De or.* 2.85 *plane abhorrebit et erit absurdus*; also Livy 30.44.6 *absurdae atque abhorrentes lacrimae*, and 27.37.13 *carmen ... abhorrens et inconditum*. F. however prefers to translate it as if with <*a se*> (= *OLD* s.v. 6). Both meanings seem to be inherent in the word as used here; cf. 28.1 n.

12 *hoc ... esse?*, 'What are we to make of this?' *scurra*, in C.'s time a complimentary word ('wit'); later disparagingly, of a professional 'diner-out.' See Putnam 1968: esp. 557–8; also Philip Corbett, *The Scurra*, Edinburgh, 1986. Cf. Cicero, *Pro Quinctio, passim*.

13 See App. Crit. The attribution of the reading *tritius* to Pontanus rests on the authority of Statius. It should be noted, however, that Pierius Valerianus, in his unpublished lectures on Catullus, defends *tritius* and says that he found it in a manuscript owned by Hermolaus Barbarus (I owe this statement to Professor Gaisser; see Gaisser 1993: 129). It is probably best to adopt *scitius*; *tⁱtius* (or *tⁱtius*) and *scitius* are not far apart palaeographically. In Latin, *tritus* means either well-worn or 'trite' in our sense; in Cicero, at least, it is not directly applied to people (the nearest approach to this is to be found at *Brut.* 124 and *Ad Fam.* 9.16.4 *tritae aures*). In Greek, on the other hand, τρίβων can mean 'a clever rascal.' Of course *hac re* refers to *scurra* (see F., who considers this use

of *hac re* colloquial, 'though there is no exact parallel'; notice however that Kr. would read *hac re*, not altogether implausibly, at 107.7, interpreting it there as = *hoc*); we should expect *est* to be added, since *videbatur* goes with *scurra*, but cf. 1.8 *quidquid hoc libelli* (without *est*). It will not do to read *est acutius* (B.), since this would remove a caesura which is present in all the other lines of the poem.

14 For the idiom in *inficeto* ... *inficetior*, cf. 9.10–11, 23.18, 27.4, 39.16.

15 *attigit*, 'has got his paws on.'

  The reading of *O* probably reflects that of *A* (McKie: 146), possibly written thus: *neque* (*vl. nec*). *X*, then, seems to have shown some critical spirit in rejecting the variant *vel nec* and retaining *neque*. See the Introduction, p. 40.

17 *gaudet in se*, 'is very pleased with himself.'

18 *nimirum* probably answers the question posed in l. 12 (B. and Kr.).

21 For the fable of the *mantica* (a knapsack with one pocket resting on the back, one on the chest – interpreted as containing our own and others' faults respectively, since what is behind is invisible), see Phaedrus 4.10 (quoted by F.), which ends with this motto: *hac re videre nostra mala non possumus; / alii simul delinquunt, censores sumus.*

  quod manticae, 'the part of the knapsack that ...'

Putnam, M.C.J. 1968. 'C. 22, 13,' *Hermes* 96: 552–8.

Gamberale, L. 1982. 'Libri e letteratura nel carme 22 di C.,' *MD* 8: 143–69.

Watson, L. 1990. 'Rustic Suffenus (C. 22) and Literary Rusticity,' *Papers of the Leeds International Latin Seminar* 6: 13–33.

23

  Structure: (6 + 8) + 1; 8 + 2; 2. Lines 24–5 sum up the 'blessings of poverty' thus far enumerated; lines 26–7 give, in a typically Catullan surprise ending, the real reason for the enumeration: Furius is far too well-advantaged to keep asking C. for a loan! As Kr. remarks, 'The drastic and broadly-extended picture of <Furius'> poverty ... has the strong draughtsmanship of the early iambographers, but outdoes them in heaping up exaggerated traits (cf. Lucilius, and many of Martial's epigrams). The conclusion παρ' ὑπόνοιαν is most skilfully executed.' L. described the poem's content succinctly as 'uproarious banter.'

1 *m²* cites (as a variant) *servo*, the discarded reading of *R*. (*V*'s *servo*, like *Calvos* at 53.3, shows clearly that C. used the older spelling *-uos* which avoided duplication of *u/v*). McKie (195) appears to have misread *R²*, who does not, as he claims, write *servo est* (= *OG*), but merely *servo* (erasing the preceding *est*); notice that

m has *servus est* (following *R*²'s added variant), and *m*² merely adds *al. servo* (not *al. servo est*). I am obliged to draw attention to this because he uses this passage, together with 32.7 (where see n.), to argue against my view that *R*² could have made his first run of corrections without detailed examination of *X*.

The threefold repetition of *neque servus neque arca* in the next poem suggests that the plea of poverty made by Furius when he asked C. for a loan may have been expressed in exactly these terms. The list of things wanting is grotesquely extended in l. 2, which sets the tone for the derisive treatment ending at l. 25 – after which we return to the target, namely Furius' 'begging act.'

2 *animal* is probably *X*'s faulty expansion of the *al.* which *O* has preserved. Once again *R*² corrects, followed by *m*.

4 The relatives are schooled by hunger to eat anything at all (which must be a consolation to Furius, if he is as poor as he claims).

5 *est pulcre tibi*, colloquial; cf. l. 15 (also 14.10 *non est mi male, sed bene ac beate*).

6 *lignea* (of thinness), 'a stick.'

7 *nec mirum*: idiomatic; cf. 57.3, 62.14, 69.7, Cicero *Acad.* 2.63.

nam is postponed, as at 37.11, 64.301 (and *namque* at 64.384 and 66.65); Kr. and F. point out that the postponement of connecting particles is a Hellenistic poetic trick, which C. in those passages is probably imitating (F.'s n. refers to other particles – *atque, nec/neque, sed* – similarly postponed by C.).

*R*²'s suggestion, expressed as a variant, is late (followed by *m*²). Did he derive it from the margins of *X*? I did not think so (Introduction to *CE*, pp. 20 and 26), because nothing seemed to point to this except *G*'s very doubtful first reading *nee*. After re-examining *G* I decided to change this opinion concerning *R*² (though I now think it still more likely that *G* meant to write *nec*).

9 Editors all point to the frequency of fire and structural collapse as a hazard of daily life in Rome.

10 These are dangers *within* the family. For this reason, and because the adj. *impia* would be unsuitable, the emendation *furta* (see App. Crit.: it is Humanistic, not – as Mynors and F. believed – Hauptian) must be rejected (cf. also 68.140 n.).

11 *casus*, 'occurrences' (F.); cf. Cicero, *Ad Fam.* 6.4.3 *omnes casus subitorum periculorum*.

12–17 for ancient medicine, with its doctrine of humours, a dry body (or soul) was best.

12 As Kr. says, *atqui* adduces something positive, in contradistinction to the preceding negatives.

13 *aut siquid*: cf. 22.13 (also 13.10, 42.14, 82.2).

magis aridum = siccius.

14 *frigore et esuritione*: cf. Mart. 12.32.7 *frigore et fame siccus*.

15 recalls 5 *est pulcre tibi*.

quare non: cf. 89.4 *quare ... desinat?* (= 'There's no reason why ...').

16–17 Editors quote Varro ap. Non. Marc. 634 L: *Persae propter exercitationes pueriles modicas eam sunt consecuti corporis siccitatem ut neque spuerent neque emungerentur.*

19 Although *cuius* has been corrected by R^2, m^2 adds it (above the line) out of loyalty to *R*; and G^2, in turn, out of loyalty to m^2.

  salillo: the diminutive is otherwise unknown (except in Plaut. *Trin.* 492, where *A* reads *satillum*); cf. Hor. *Od.* 2.16.13–14 *paternum splendet in mensa tenui salinum*, and for *purum salinum* see Persius 3.25.

21 *id = quod cacas.*

  See App. Crit. The slight change to *lupillis* is easy (*a* and *u* being endlessly confused), and keeps the comparison within the natural order of things to which *faba* belongs. For passages illustrating the conjunction of the two, see E. The expression in the Greek passage quoted by B. in defence of *lapillis* (Ar. *Acharn.* 1168) seems to me quite different.

22–3 *teras ... posses*: cf. 6.2–3 for the sequence: 'suppose you ..., you never could ...'

23 *non umquam*, 'an emphatic colloquialism for *numquam*' (F., who compares Plaut. *Merc.* 288).

25 *nec* for *aut* after *noli* is not strictly grammatical, but it is an understandable colloquialism ('as if *ne spreveris* had been written,' F.). Cf. Plaut. *Poen.* 1129 *mirari noli neque me contemplarier.*

26 *desine*: sc. *precari* ('beg'; the verb C. chooses to employ is studiously contemptuous, like so much else in the language of the poem).

Fraenkel, E. 1966. 'Nam satis beatus,' *MH* 23: 114–17.
Németh, B. 1971. 'Notes on C., c. 23,' *ACD* 7: 33–41.

24

Structure: 6 + (2 + 2). Note the varied repetition of l. 5 at ll. 8 and 10.
For the Juventius cycle of poems, see the intr. n. to poem 21, where it is made clear that in C.'s view both Furius and Aurelius were after the boy (poem 48, where Juventius is named, is probably the source of the reference at 16.12). Here, Juventius is urged to reject Furius' attentions on the grounds of the suitor's poverty. As F. remarks, the Juventii 'were an old and distinguished Roman family, originally from Tusculum (Cic. *Planc.* 19); the name is also found at Verona.' Although Kr. doubts whether Juventius had anything to do with this family, and suggests that he may have come from Verona, where Juventii are found – Kr. refers to inscriptions, citing *CIL* V^1 3316 – it is certain from poem 81 that Juventius was a Roman (both from the phrase *in tanto populo* and because of the sneer at C.'s rival, who comes *moribunda ab*

sede Pisauri, and is described as *hospes*, 'stranger'). Q. sensibly observes, à propos of *amari* in l. 6: 'It is a reasonable supposition that the accusation ... rests on no more damning evidence than that adduced in Poem 21 against Aurelius; 6 *sic*, like 21.5 *nec clam*, by appealing to public knowledge, limits the matter to what can be publicly observed.' The exaggerated language of this poem (in which again it resembles other Juventius poems), and even more that of the immediately preceding and connected poem 23, where the intention is so obviously humorous, both tend to show that there is no bad blood between C. and Furius, though the latter's small means clearly gave rise to constant 'chaffing' on C.'s part; observe that in poem 26 the family villa belonging to Furius is mortgaged for a surprisingly small amount. When C. says he himself is hard up, he says it to *Fabullus* (13.8).

2–3 *horum* represents the present ('the Juventii of today') in the sequence past-present-future; for this formula, cf. 21.2–3 (where notice *harum*, used as above) and 49.2–3.

4 *divitias Midae*: a proverb in Greek (Tyrt. 12 West 5–6 οὐδ᾽ εἰ πλουτοίη ... Μίδεω ... μάλιον and (after C.) in Latin; e.g., Mart. 6.86.4 *qui mavult heres divitis esse Midae*, of one preferring wealth to true blessings. The tale of Midas is told by Ovid, *M.* 11.100–93.

    See App. Crit. O's *mi dededisses* is an outstanding example of his willingness to write nonsense and so, in the end, occasionally produce a better text than that of *X*. No doubt *A* had exactly what we find in *O*, and *X*, whether consciously or not, introduces an 'improvement' resting on false word-division.

5 For the change from *quoi* to *qui*, see 1.1 n.
neque (1°): *G*² feels that he must insert *nec* – not from *G*, who had the true reading already, but from *m*, even though *m*² has offered *neque* after all.

6 *sic* (with *sineres*), 'in that way.' As Kr. observes, *sic* is placed before, and not after, *te*, both for euphony (to avoid the sigmatism of *sic sineres*) and also for emphasis.

7 O's *quid*, it seems to me, reflects the conversational tone.
homo bellus: linked with *urbanus* at 22.9; 'a polished gentleman.' Notice particularly poem 81, addressed to Juventius, with which this poem should be closely compared; *bellus homo* occurs there in the second line, and the person mentioned in the epigram, who may well be Furius' friend Aurelius (cf. line 4 *inaurata*, and see Zicàri ad loc.), is held up to Juventius' obviously *Roman* contempt (see intr. n. above) as a *hospes* from a miserable country town. It follows that, even if there were Juventii at Verona, as the editors tell us there were, the acquaintanceship must have ripened at Rome.

9 *hoc*, 'the fact just established.'
quam lubet, as F. says, normally accompanies an adj., rarely a verb as here and at Phaedr. 1.25.6.

abice (a rhetorical term) = 'dismiss, minimize.' Cicero, *De or.* 3.104 and esp. *Orator* 127 *augendis rebus et contra abiciendis*.

eleva, 'make light of'; cf. Prop. 2.34.58 *hoc ego quo tibi nunc elevor ingenio*.

25

Structure: (5 + 3) + 5. For an analysis of the structure of lines 1–5, see Q.'s illuminating n. on line 1.

An attack on Thallus under two heads: he is soft, and at the same time he is grasping, to the point of ruthlessness; two charges which are in a sense contradictory (cf. l. 4 *idem*), and which are held, as a double theme, in a kind of counterpoint throughout the poem. This interweaving of themes constitutes the principal element in the poem's artistry, together with the rich and exuberant inventiveness of its defamatory language. Notice the effectiveness of the sounds, especially the liquid diminutives conveying *mollitia*. Notice also that C. 'begins with pasquinade and ends with threats of physical violence' (Q.); for this sequence, cf. poems 15, 21, and perhaps 40 (q.v.). For the trait of napkin-stealing, of which Thallus is accused, see poem 12 (cf. also poem 33).

'Thallus' was probably a freedman: the name, in Greek, signifies a young shoot or branch. E. cites seven inscriptions where it appears as a cognomen; it also occurs in Apul. *Apol.* 43 and 44. The first Thallus quoted by E. was *superpositus numulariorum* (his other names, C. Iulius, give some indication of date); it seems not inconceivable that some such office, or occupation, came down as it were in the family; see l. 5 as emended in my text.

Metre: iambic tetrameter catalectic (often employed by Aristophanes). C. in poem 4 succeeded in keeping to pure iambic trimeters, with no spondees at all, and in poem 29 did the same except when what he wanted to say could not be expressed in iambics without recourse to a spondee. The metrical treatment here is similar to that of poem 29: eight of the thirteen lines are free of spondees. There are first-foot spondees in lines 4, 7, 9, and 13, and 13 has one in the fifth foot as well; so has l. 5 in my text. There are no third-foot spondees; and C. always has a diaeresis after the fourth foot, which in Aristophanes is usual but not invariable (L). A glance at the App. Crit. will suffice to show the total unfamiliarity of this poem's metre to the early scribes and correctors.

1 *cinaede*: cf. 16.2, 57.1–2 (n. 2); also 10.24. Thallus, a Greek name, is attached as a cognomen to names belonging to Roman *gentes* in a number of inscriptions, probably referring to freedmen. It is interesting that a later Thallus appears as *superpositus numulariorum* (cf. l. 5 in my text): see intr. n.

2 *anseris medullula*: this has been interpreted as meaning the soft inner down (feathers) of the goose, or its liver, not its marrow, in which sense it is normally plural; see Plin. *NH* 10.53 (interpreted as 'inner feathers' by Vossius). Notice the echo of C. in *Priap.* 64.1 *mollior anseris medulla* (see also – in relation to line 3 – *Priap.* 83.30, ascribed to Tibullus).

imula oricilla: cf. Cicero, *Ad Q. F.* 2.13.4 *auricula infima molliorem*, Amm. Marc. 19.12.5 *ima, quod aiunt, auricula mollior*. It is possible that the phrase was invented by C.; Cicero's letter (of 54 BC) seems to quote his brother Quintus, who may have quoted Catullus; and Q. Cicero more than once, in the correspondence, refers to or discusses living poets: cf. ibid. 2.9.3 (of the same year) on some specimens of Lucretius. But it is not necessary to conclude that C.'s works had already been 'published' in 54; a few poems may have been circulated among friends (see n. on poem 1), just as, in the reference to Lucr. just quoted, the word *poemata* need only mean 'passages'; see C. Bailey's *Lucretius*, vol. 1, p. 4 (quoting F.H. Sandbach) and p. 19.

See App. Crit.; since the form *oricilla* is not clearly given in the tradition, it is possible that this rare diminutive should be restored here as *auricilla*.

3 *situ araneoso* = a spider's web, deserted by the spider, which has gathered dust so as to make a 'cobweb.' *Priap.* 83.30 (see line 2 n.).

4 *idem* often introduces an action contrary to the character of the agent, as we had previously supposed that to be. Cf. 22.14. The ostensible contrast here is between the *mollities* sketched in lines 1–3 and the savage violence of the rapacious action recorded in lines 4–5. C. attacks Thallus both for being *mollis* and for being *rapax* (contrary as these two qualities are here said to be); and it is on the counterpoint between the two themes (see intr. n.) that the entire poem ultimately depends.

turbida rapacior procella; cf. 64.156 *quae Scylla rapax?*

5 The double variant in *R*² is in fact the same as that in *G*¹, but reversed.

laeva: cf. Plaut. *Pers.* 226 *furtifica laeva*. Cf. 12.1 (*sinistra*) and n. there.

6 *involasti*, 'you have pounced on.'

7 *sudarium*: cf. 12.3 and 11.

catagraphos: the meaning of this otherwise unknown word has to be conjectured. There is no particular reason why we must suppose it to denote an article of clothing, or something else made of cloth, simply in order to assimilate it to *pallium* and *sudarium*, if the Greek elements (κατα-γράφειν) seem to point another way, in the direction of 'writing tablets,' which were obviously important to C. (42.5 *pugillaria*, cf. 50.2 *in meis tabellis*). Quite probably it is an equivalent to *pugillares*, made perhaps – as these were – of boxwood, for which Bithynia was famous (4.13). At 50.2, C. has taken his tablets with him to a midday meal away from home (7 *illinc abii*, etc.); the other articles mentioned (cloak, napkins) are also such as would be brought to a house by a guest.

See App. Crit. Notice that the R^2 variant agrees with G and not with OR, which proves that it comes from X and had there the status of a variant on *satha-*. See p. 41.

8 *inepte*: cf. 12.4.

palam habere = 'flaunt, display.'

10 *laneum*, returning to the theme of softness (see l. 4 n.): 'your fleecy flanks.'

11 Cf. Hor. *Epod.* 4.3 *Hibericis peruste funibus latus* (possibly borrowed from C.; see also *Ep.* 1.16.47 *habes pretium, loris non ureris*). Whipping – a slave's punishment – left visible marks.

conscribillent, 'scribble all over.' (For the notion, cf. Plaut. *Pseud.* 543–5: *si de istac re umquam inter nos convenimus, / quasi in libro quom scribitur calamo litterae, / stilis me totum usque ulmeis conscribito*). The shortening of the first *i*, which has given editors pause, may be excusable on the grounds that in this 'diminutive' form of the verb it has a strong following syllable to dominate and weaken the sound (cf. *mamilla*, from *mamma*, and *ofella*, from *offa*).

12–13 *aestuare* = 'toss' (also 'boil'); the verb has both a literal meaning as in Hor. *Od.* 2.6.4 *aestuat unda* (hence the figure of the storm-tossed ship here), and a figurative meaning. (Intermediate between these is the picture of a wind-tossed tree at Lucr. 5.1096–7 *ventis pulsa aestuat arbor*.) Applied to Thallus, *aestuare* has psychological overtones: his usual barefaced insolence will be overcome (*insolenter*) by violent agitation when C. sets about punishing him.

minuta magno: this juxtaposition of opposites of course increases the effect of the foregoing diminutives. With the second of these two adjs. cf. Lucr. 2.1 *mari magno turbantibus aequora ventis*.

13 *deprensa*: for *deprehendere* in this sense cf. Lucr. 6.429 *deprensa tumultu navigia*.

deprehensa (*X*): cf. App. Crit. at 62.35 *comprehendis*, and also 50.21 *vehemens* (*V*); in each instance the familiar – and unmetrical – word is substituted for the less familiar. Notice, once again, how *O*'s virtual ignorance of Latin – so at least it often seems – is sometimes a source of strength to him as a witness to the transmitted text; cf. 24.4 n.

vesaniente, for the more conventional *furente*: cf. Hor. *Od.* 3.4.30 *insanientem navita Bosphorum temptabo*.

Slater, D.A. 1905. 'On C. XXV.5,' *CR* 19: 59.

Colin, J. 1958. 'L'heure des cadeaux pour Thallus le cinède,' *REL* 32: 106–10.

Granarolo, J. 1958. 'L'heure de la vérité pour Tallus le cinède (C., XXV),' *REA* 60: 290–306.

Putnam, M.C.J. 1964. 'C. 25.5,' *CP* 59: 268–70.

MacKay, L.A. 1966. 'C. 25.5,' *CP* 61: 110–11.

Bianco, O. 1967. 'Il personaggio del c. 25 di C.,' *GIF* 20: 39–48.

Verdière, R. 1969. 'La déesse de Tallus,' *Renard* 1: 751–7.
Copley, F.O. 1976. 'C. 25.5,' *Latomus* 35: 416–18.
Papanghelis, T.D. 1980. '*Crux Catulliana* (A Note on 25.5),' *Latomus* 39: 409–11.
Granarolo, J. 1981. 'Encore à propos de la *crux* C. xxv.5: essai de solution,' *Latomus* 40: 571–9.

26

Structure: 4 + 1.

The interpretation of the poem's meaning depends on whether in line 1 we read *vestra* with *O* or *nostra* with *GR*; nowadays the reading *vestra* is generally accepted. Recent editors (F., Q.) tend to dismiss the poem as no more than an excuse for a pun on the two meanings of *oppositus* ('exposed' and 'mortgaged'). It would, however, be well to bear in mind that other poems on Furius, as well as those on Aurelius, harp on the accusation of poverty (cf. poems 21, 23, 24), while not only is the disparaging diminutive *villula* used here, but the amount of the mortgage is almost ridiculously small – which gives a pungent note of sarcasm to the final exclamation. In poem 23, where the point is made that because of Furius' extreme parsimony his needs are few, and therefore he does not need the sizeable loan (between six-and-a-half and seven times the amount of the mortgage!) for which he has asked C., the characterization of Furius as a beggarly pauper is dominant; and this is repeated in poem 24. If *vestra* is a true plural, it may well refer to the starveling trio mentioned in 23.5–6. On the assumption that Furius is to be identified with M. Furius Bibaculus (see however Rudd, referred to at 11.1 n.), this poem might be taken as C.'s indignant reply to certain suggestions in Bibaculus, frs. 1 and 2 M, where the poverty and financially embarrassed condition of Valerius Cato's villa at Tusculum are depicted; *vestra* would then receive heavy emphasis.

1 *vestra*: see App. Crit. *Vestra* is pointed, if this is C.'s answer (see above) to Furius' ungenerous attacks on Valerius Cato, on the grounds of the latter's poverty: '*your* villa, Furius, . . .' There may also (or alternatively) be a link with poem 23; see intr. n.

1–3 The winds (i) cover all the principal points of the compass, and (ii) are arranged more or less in increasing order of length as to their names, with the effect of a blustering crescendo, preceding the anticlimax in line 4.

2 *opposita*: for the pun, see intr. For the meaning 'exposed' cf. Plin. *NH* 17.262 *radices hiberno frigori opponunt*; for 'mortgaged' cf. Ter. *Phorm.* 661, Plaut. *Curc.* 356. *m*'s reading, *favoni*, may be either a correction (cf. 31.5) or merely a slip; G^2 ignores it.

3 *Apheliotes* (a Greek name for the Latin *subsolanus*) was a prosaic navigator's term; used only here in poetry (elsewhere *Eurus*, which is Homer's name for it). Cicero, parodying these 'learned' names used by the *novi poetae*, as well as their frequent indulgence in spondaic hexameter endings, writes the line *flavit ab Epiro lenissimus Onchesmites* (*Ad Att.* 7.2.1).

4 The amount is small: only 15,200 sesterces. Does this imply that the property itself is contemptible, and that in l. 5 Furius is depicted as making a great fuss about very little? (See intr. n.) To speak of such a place as a 'villa' at all was perhaps thought of as ludicrous; Cicero, in an epigram quoted by Quintilian (8.6.73), says *'fundum' Vetto vocat, quem possit mittere funda, / ni tamen exciderit qua cava funda patet.*

5 *pestilentem*, 'unhealthy' (of winds), as in Hor. *Od.* 3.23.5 *pestilentem ... Africum.*

E. Linkomies, 'C. c. 26,' *Arctos* 2 (1931): 71–2.

27

Structure: (2 + 2) + 3.
*R*²'s title *Ad pincernam suum* ('To his butler') sufficiently indicates the poem's milieu and purport. 'The same again, and go easy with the water' – in other words, *amariores* = *meraciores* (N. Rudd, 'The Style and the Man,' *Phoenix* 18 [1964]: 223). In my opinion, a true judgment, so far as it goes, in contrast to Wiseman's (1969: 7–8) view that this is a programmatic poem and that its real subject is poetry; see the Introduction, pp. 8–9. Nevertheless, it is not the whole story. Consider the poem's impact on its first hearers: its novelty and charm; the echoes of Hellenistic epigram; the abrupt and arresting *inger* (F. says 'we have no clue to its associations,' but surely the contexts where the verb is used suggest careless liberality: Plaut. *Pseud.* 157 *tu qui urnam habes aquam ingere, face plenum ahenum sit coquo*); the juxtaposition *vetuli puer*, which of course involves surprise since the affectionate diminutive *vetuli* and the word *minister* alike suggest that an old *man*'s name will end the line; the parodied *lex Postumia(e)* (see l. 3 n.), with another element of surprise; a further surprise in the feminine termination of *magistra (bibendi)*; the kind of repetition (*traductio*) we have in *ebriosa ... ebriosior* (a favourite device of C.'s; cf. 9.10–11, 22.14, 23.18, 39.16, 99.2 and 14; see Riese on 22.14); the bold metonymy in *calices amariores*, and another in *acino*; the 'sound-effects,' as of splashing (*inger: mi*) and hiccuping (*ebriosa: acino: ebriosiores*); the conceit *Falerni minister*; the surprise at the end of l. 5 when we find it is *lymphae* that C. intends to banish; the doubly learned Alexandrianism of *Thyonianus*; metrical effects

such as rhyme (on *i* and *ae* in ll. 1–3) and assonance (ll. 2, 4); and finally the staccato force of the attack on water, with the thin disparaging sounds in *hic ... migrate*. All these touches combine to make of this a witty and in its way unique little poem.

1 After *vetuli* ('good old ...') the reader might be supposed ready, on first acquaintance with the poem, to expect a noun indicating a *person* to follow at once, in view of *minister* (see intr. n.). *Falerni* must surely be to some extent a surprise, even though the adj. *vetulus* is later (in Mart. and Macrob., see Kr. and F.) attached to this wine. Notice the careful juxtaposition of the words *vetuli* and *puer*.

2 *inger* = *ingere* ('popular syncope,' Kr.); the apocope of final *s* is appropriate to compounds of *gero*, a verb which is treated as a close relative of *fero* (e.g., compound adjectives ending either in *-ger* or in *-fer*); and cf. *fer, adfer*, etc. But it is also possible that the abrupt sound of *inger*, followed as it is by the monosyllable *mi*, suggests hasty, 'splashy,' pouring. E. indicated that *ingerere*, of a liquid, means 'ladling out in quantity.'

amariores: in Roman usage, *fortis* and *amarus* are the adjectives regularly used in describing the perceived strength of wine. Both of these words are repeatedly associated with two conditions: the age of the wine, and of course the relative absence of water. Palladius 11.14.11 speaks of wine turning with age from *molle* to *forte*. In Macrobius 7.12.17 the question is raised why a drink (*potio*) taken on an empty stomach seems stronger (*gustatu fortiore sentitur*; and this in turn is exactly equated with *meracior videtur*). When Prudentius pleads for a frugal diet (*Cath.* 3.176), the meaning of *haustus amarus* is quite clearly strong wine, not wine with a particular flavour. For the link between age and *amaritudo*, we may cite Pliny, *NH* 23.40 *fumi amaritudine vetustatem vini indui*, and shortly afterwards *in amaritudinem vinum coit*. There are, it is true, instances where *amarus* has the additional implication of a certain 'bite' or 'tang' – but a pleasant one. We have to ponder the remark of Seneca, *in vino nimis vetere ipsa nos amaritudo delectat*, which Wiseman 1969: 8 dismisses perhaps a little too cavalierly ('Seneca was maintaining a paradox, that unpleasant things can be enjoyable'). In the context (*Ep.* 63.4–7, part of a letter of consolation), Seneca is saying that nobody willingly recurs to what will *really* hurt him to think of – but, while the mention of those we have lost brings with it a certain pang (*morsus*), this itself *habet suam voluptatem*. Seneca immediately quotes Attalus, who used to say *sic amicorum defunctorum memoria iucunda est quomodo poma quaedam sunt suaviter aspera* (i.e., their very tartness is a pleasant thing), *quomodo in vino ...* (see above). The memory of the dead (Attalus went on to say) *non sine acerbitate quadam iuvat*; and so, too, things (fruit and wine) *habentia austeritatis aliquid* (we shall meet this word again presently) please the taste. The passage in Seneca discusses only bereavement, using physical taste as an illustration; it does not seem to me to invoke any proposition about 'unpleasant' things in general.

Pliny, *NH* 15.106, lists thirteen different kinds of wine, among which he places *amarus* next to *austerus*, but clearly distinguishes both from *acer* (Greek δριμύς). Celsus, 2.24.3, appears to make a similar distinction when he suggests that a wine may be *austerum* 'even if it is also' *asperum*. In Galen 11.484ff.,εὐγενῆ ('noble': older and, as we say, stronger) ὀνομάζω τὸν αὐστηρόν, the adjective is contrasted with ἄτονος, ὑδατώδης, ἔκλυτος. The Latin equivalent of ἀστηρός is sometimes *austerus*, sometimes *severus*; Horace uses *severus* of Falernian itself at *Od.* 1.27.9, while in *Sat.* 2.4.24 he calls it *fortis*. (A medical writer links *fortis* with *austerus* in describing the wild plum.) Two pages are devoted to Falernian in A. Tchernia's authoritative *Le vin de l'Italie romaine* (Rome, 1986: 342–3). Here we are informed that there were three types of Falernian: *austerum, dulce, tenue*. The *austerum* itself, however, seemed *dulce* (γλυκύς) when it was contrasted with certain other wines, but (like all types of Falernian, in some degree at least) it was marked by its alcoholic content and lasting powers, qualities to which Galen (11.604) gives the term οἰνώδης. By contrast, a wine that matures quickly and lacks 'body' is called λιπαρώτερος (Galen, *ap.* Athen. 1.26d–f). At all events, Falernian was not *acer*; commenting on Juvenal 13.215–16 *ruga / cogitur in frontem velut acri ducta Falerno*, R.G.M. Nisbet (*MD* 26 [1991]: 78) emends with good reason (and independently, using a quite different line of proof) to *Falisco*.

To return to our poem: lines 5–7 expand on the notion of lack of water, that is, of strength, without introducing any language that could be construed as introducing the notion of 'bitter' in a positively unpleasant sense. Yet, granted that the poem may be credited with unity of theme, this omission would surely be unlikely if the concept of bitterness, with harsh implications, were really intended to be dominant. The opening of our poem suggests Diphilus 58 K εὐζωρότερον ὢ παῖ δός. E.'s excellent note on line 2 should be consulted; he rightly states that 'the common and most accepted view' in antiquity equated ζωρότερον with ἄκρατον and that *amariores* should be taken as virtually equivalent to *meraciores*.

Finally, a mere illustration (which of course lacks any kind of status as a proof). In at least two mutually related Indo-European languages the quality of 'strength' in wine, or tea, is expressed by words, the general sense of which in other contexts would be rendered in English by 'bitter' or 'sharp.' Persian (Farsi) uses *talkh* (or *tond*); Urdu uses *tez*; and there is no other way of saying it. We have seen that, in Latin, *amarus* can refer to strength, and thus be taken as the equivalent of *fortis*; at least in the languages just mentioned, its function (more precisely, the function of its equivalent expression) is wholly to replace *fortis* in the kind of context we are discussing.

3 *Postumiae*: the name is frequently met with in Rome. Guesses can be made concerning her identity. Kr.: 'One Postumia, whose reputation was not unblemished, was the wife of Ser. Sulpicius Rufus, consul in 51.' (Cicero, *Ad Fam.* 4.2.1, at any rate seems to speak of her as a respected *matrona*). Why did C. choose her as the 'mistress of the feast'? Of course, she may have been present at some actual drinking party; but it is just possible that the reader's expectant ear is here treated to another surprise (see line 1 n.): there was a *lex Postumia* – of Numa's time – on the use of certain kinds of wine and the pouring of libations (Plin. *NH* 14.88, quoted only by E.); is the name of P. herself substituted for the concluding part of an anticipated reference to the *lex Postumia*?

4 *ebrioso* (*-se A*) has the advantage of closeness to the transmitted text (the corruption to *ebriosae* being easily explicable as resulting from the proximity of *Postumiae ... magistrae*), and of presenting a more probable epithet ('the berry that goes with, or produces a tendency to, drunkenness'). Because of the following considerations, however, I now believe that A. Statius' *ebriosa acino* is most likely to be right. The manuscript evidence is: (a) in all manuscripts of C., *ebriose* (= *ae*) *acino*; (b) in Aulus Gellius – again, all manuscripts – *ebriose ac in* (with one slight exception: *Parisinus lat. 5763* reads *me* for *in*); but Gellius adds a comment, to the effect that C. *ebriosam dixit*, i.e., 'he wrote <some case – not necessarily the accusative, which will not suit here – of> *ebriosa*.' This seems to mean that C., unusually, gave the feminine gender to *acinus* (= *acinum*, neuter, 'berry'; a substitute for 'grape'). It looks therefore as if the text of Gellius, already corrupt, should be emended to correspond with his comment, and should accordingly read *ebriosa*. We can explain the *-e* (= *ae*) termination in the manuscripts both of C. and of Gellius by the presence of the word *magistrae* immediately preceding: *ebrios(a)e* was assimilated to this, since the following word (*acino*) did not appear to agree with it on account of C.'s irregular feminine gender.

But we have to account for the rest of Gellius' comment, bearing in mind what the manuscripts give. Here I follow L., who observed: 'Gellius starts his discussion with a reference to V. *Geo.* 2.224–5, where, he says, Virgil originally wrote *vicina Vesevo / Nola iugo*, but after quarrelling with the inhabitants of Nola substituted *ora* for *Nola*. Gellius says that from the point of view of sound this was a change for the better, for the hiatus between the two *o*'s is pleasing to the ear (*canoro simul atque iucundo hiatu tractim sonat*). He goes on to quote two passages of Homer which show similar hiatus. The shorter of these (*Od.* 11.596) reads λᾶαν ἄνω ὤθεσκε ποτὶ λόφον; the other (*Il.* 22.151–2) exhibits three instances (ει–ει, η–η, η–η). In each case it is an open hiatus between two identical long vowels. Gellius then proceeds . . . to quote the first four lines of this poem (poem 27) and comment on them. The main point of the comment is contained in the first sentence, and is to the effect that out of liking for the famous Homeric hiatus, C. used in the feminine a noun which was normally neuter. The second sentence shows that the text of C. in this line was already in dispute, by referring to other readings which Gellius dismisses as corrupt. If we look a little more closely at the first sentence, we see that Gellius says nothing about C. changing the form of the noun. Indeed, he might be held to imply that only the adj. was given a feminine inflection, since otherwise he might be expected to give both adjective and noun in their changed forms before the word *dixit*. So it is a reasonable inference from the comment, that what Gellius regarded as the true reading in C. was *ebriosa acino*; and *acino* is the form quite distinctly given in the manuscripts of Catullus.'

Haupt, bearing in mind the remark about 'Homeric hiatus' (whereas -*sa acino* is in fact elided), wished to change the text of Gellius to read (everywhere) *ebria acina* – as being what Gellius wrote, not what C. had written – and the *OCT* editor of Gellius accepts this as the correct version of what Gellius wrote. Haupt's idea was that Gellius knew three versions in the manuscript tradition of C.: *ebria acina* (with 'Homeric hiatus'), *ebriosa acina*, *ebrioso acino*; and that Gellius accepted the worst tradition, represented by *ebria acina*, and rejected the other two as corrupt. Some editors have taken *ebria acina* into their texts of C.; Mynors cites it in his apparatus criticus as being Haupt's emendation of C., whereas Haupt in fact thought *ebriosa acina* to be what C. wrote, and simply 'invented' *ebria acina* as a corrupt reading on which he supposed Gellius' comment to have been based.

Notice that Gellius adds a significant remark on the second of the corrupt readings (as he considers them to be): *nam id quoque temere scriptum invenitur* (treating it as a copyist's blunder). What we find at that point in the manuscripts of Gellius is just such a blunder: the unmetrical *ebriosos*, which Haupt emends to the metrical *ebrioso*! The '-*so* agnoscit Gellius' of Mynors' apparatus is, then, misleading. To quote again from L.: 'The use Mynors has made of Haupt is (a) to ascribe to him a reading which he invented only to reject it, <and> (b) to claim the authority of Gellius for another reading which Haupt invented only to reject it; and he has rejected what Haupt, following Parthenius and others, believed to be the original reading.'

As for the last sentence in Gellius' comment, it appears that he dismissed both *ebrios* (found in some corrupt manuscripts; see the last eight words, *in libros scilicet de corruptis exemplaribus factos inciderunt*) and *ebriosos* (see above) as erroneous readings still in circulation in *some* manuscripts.

We have still, however, not explained Gellius' remark about 'hiatus.' Notice that what he says is this: C., being fond of the *suavitas* of Homeric hiatus, used

the feminine termination *propter insequentis 'a' litterae concentum*. This is
not to say that C. *used* hiatus here. We know that what was special about the
Homeric hiatus was that it brought identical vowels together (see above, on
Virgil), and this was the *concentus* that pleased C. Such *concentus* occurs with
elision as well as with hiatus. The reading *ebriosa acino* in C. will give this
effect. (Gellius, then, says that C. used a feminine ending in the adjective to
duplicate the sound of the opening vowel in the following noun.) If there were
no possible feminine *acinus*, as a substitute for *acinum* (cf. *ulmus*, etc.), then
Gellius' comment would have little or no point.

5 See App. Crit.: at Plaut. *Mil.* 974 the Mss have the same (easy) scribal error as *V*
 has here (*quod iubet* for *quo lubet*). For *abire quo lubet* cf. Mart. 11.16.1–2.

7 *hic*: does this mean 'here' (= *apud nos*, B.) or 'this man'? If the latter, does it
 refer to *Thyonianus*-Bacchus, or (Bolton 1967) to C. himself, meaning '*I* am a
 strict devotee of Bacchus' (where the *-ianus* implies a kind of clientship)? If it is
 an adverb (which is how I should prefer to take it) the contrast with *quo lubet*
 ... *migrate* is clear.

 Thyonianus: since Bacchus' mother (or nurse) was Thyone (= Semele), he could
 be called *Thyonius* (or *Thyoneus*, Hor. *Od.* 1.17.23), but hardly *Thyonianus*.
 Editors say this stands for wine; but since in Latin *vinum* is neuter, we hear
 of *Opimiamum*, *Falernianum*, not *-us*. The usual explanation is that it is here
 made by C. to agree with οἶνος (masc.) in Greek, but as a species of 'Grecism'
 this seems unexampled; V. *Geo.* 2.98 *Tmolius assurgit quibus et rex ipse
 Phanaeus* (quoted by F.) is not a true parallel, since the masculine word *rex*
 dominates the sentence (and its adjectives), and *assurgit* (linked with *rex*) implies
 personification. Probably C. expanded the adj. whimsically (partly for metrical
 reasons); but see the preceding note.

Bolton, J.D.P. 1967. 'Merus Thyonianus,' *CR* 17: 12.
Putnam, M.C.J. 1969. 'On C. 27,' *Latomus* 28: 850–7.
Cairns, F. 1975. 'C. 27,' *Mn* 28: 24–9.
Woytek, E. 1975. 'Nochmals merus Thyonianus (C. 27, 7),' *WS* 9: 75–7.

28

Structure: 5 + 5 + 5.
To Veranius and Fabullus, on the trials of service abroad on a governor's
staff (cf. poems 9, 12, 13, and – especially for Veranius and Fabullus in
relation to Piso – 47).
It is a natural inference from this poem that C.'s own service (to which
he clearly alludes here) under Memmius in Bithynia (57–6 BC) coincided,
or rather overlapped, with Veranius' and Fabullus' service under Piso;

overlapped, because clearly C. was in Rome when they returned (see poems 9 and 12). Perhaps they had been abroad for two years without a break, whereas C. had served for only one (with some additional allowance of time for the sightseeing to which poem 46 looks forward). We must ask *where* they had served. The only internal clue towards identifying the province lies in the words *frigora et famem*, which show that it was not located on the Mediterranean sea-coast. Although there were many Pisos in this period, the choice of L. Calpurnius Piso Caesoninus (Julius Caesar's father-in-law) is plausible (despite Kr.) because of the combination of his name with a reference to Memmius. In 58 BC, the consuls were Gabinius and Piso Caesoninus (F., intr. n. to poem 47), while the *praetor urbanus* was Memmius, later a candidate for the consulship of 54 but condemned for *ambitus* (see F. on 10.13 for a full account). That Memmius, as propraetor, governed Bithynia is a fairly safe inference from lines 7–9; it is not officially recorded what province, if any, he governed as propraetor, but it is reasonable to suppose that a *praetor urbanus* with an ambition to become consul would take up a governorship after his term of office expired (in Memmius' case, 57 BC). As for Piso, he governed Macedonia for two years in 57–5; for l. 5 *frigora et famem*, cf. Cicero, *In Pis.* 40 *ferro, fame, frigore, pestilentia*. Piso's long-term appointment may explain why Veranius and Fabullus returned to Rome after C. See however poem 47, intr. n.

1 *comites* = the members (individually) of P.'s staff (cf. 46.9); *cohors* = the staff itself (as a body); both are quasi-technical terms. Notice how, in ll. 1–2, C. builds up a poetic tricolon increasing in density of meaning as well as in length, from the simple 'companions of P.' by way of 'staff with empty pockets' (lit. 'unladen') to '<and> nothing you couldn't easily manage about *those* little valises!'
 inanis: C. has in mind, as the poem shows, two meanings: *OLD* 5 (of persons), 'carrying no load' (see l. 2), and *OLD* 6, 'poor, penniless.' Cf. e.g., 22.11 n. for another word with double significance in C.

2 *aptis sarcinulis*, 'suitably equipped with *light* baggage-rolls'; *expeditis*, 'in *light* marching order.'

4 *quid rerum geritis*: a colloquial greeting; frequent in Comedy (see the Plautine refs. in F.) and in late authors (Apuleius, Arnobius).
 The *satis* in *satisne* should not be translated 'enough'; the phrase is colloquial: 'did you really put up with . . . ?' Cf. Plaut. *Most.* 76 *satin* (= *satisne*) *abiit neque quod dixi flocci existumat?*
 c(um) isto: the elision is unusual because (i) it is of a monosyllable, other than -*que* (see however Kr. on the 'proclitic nature' of *cum*); (ii) it comes so late in the line; (iii) it is not an elision of a short open vowel.

5 *vappa* is literally wine that has 'gone flat' and lost its taste; hence, a worthless fellow (Hor. *S.* 1.1.104).

-*que et*: cf. 44.15.

6 *patet*, 'is entered.' Cf. Cicero, *Pro Q. Roscio* 5 *non habere se hoc nomen in codice accepti et expensi* ('balance-sheet') *relatum confitetur, sed in adversariis* ('day-book') *patere contendit.*

lucelli: E. points out that Cicero, *In Verr.* 2.3.72 and 106, uses this word of the profits made by the praetor's staff in Sicily.

7 *expensum* = *datum* (line 8). The two instances of a *datum* which (paradoxically) can be seen as *lucellum* – C.'s, and that of his friends – are strictly parallel; *vobis* should be understood in l. 6, to balance *mihi*. As Q. says, the 'profit' for both parties lay in learning what governors are like. Hence the sarcastic advice *pete nobiles amicos!* (line 13).

7–8 *meum ... praetorem* = Memmius (in Bithynia), line 9.

9–10 For the language used, cf. 10.12, where Memmius is described as *irrumator* (*praetor*); not to be taken literally, of course (for this kind of Catullan exaggeration, see intr. n. to poem 40).

10 *trabe*: *trabs*, here = *penis*, has a wide figurative application: cf. 4.3 n.

Clearly there are here two stages of 'correction' by R^2, the first (*trabe*) being picked up by *m*, the second (*trahe*) by m^2. Nothing could better serve to illustrate my contention that we have to identify, by means of m/m^2, two separate R^2 recensions.

lentus, 'unconcernedly' (E.), 'indifferently.'

11 As McKie (206) rightly points out, *X* read *parum al. pari*, whereas *A* had *pari* (with *O*); *X*'s error is due to the proximity of *quantum*. Notice that *X* seems to be the first to acquire the habit of expressing self-correction (often, as here, correction of a casual slip) in the guise of a variant; at a later stage, *m* is especially prone to this.

12 *verpa* = *mentula*; cf. 47.4, where Piso is described as *verpus* (adj.; see n. there) *Priapus.*

History: possibly *urpa A* (and certainly *O*); *verba al. verpa l. urpa X* (R^2m^2), where the first variant is straightforward self-correction by *X*. If this is so, *X* for once offers a double 'variant,' the second variant alone being derived from *A*.

13 For the sarcasm, cf. 73.1–2 (*desine ...*) and passages beginning with *i nunc* in Horace and other poets (see Wickham on Hor. *Ep.* 1.6.17).

14 *at vobis*: for this formula of transition (which often dismisses with a curse, as it were) see 36.18 n.

Notice that, although R^2mG^2 opt for the correction *vobis*, m^2 and G^2 both preserve *nobis*, as a variant, out of sheer loyalty to the exemplar in either case.

15 *opprobria*, 'disgraces' in a concrete sense (so 77.5–6 *venenum* ... *pestis*); meaning praetors who mistreated their subordinates, and in particular both Piso and Memmius.

Romuli Remique, standing for 'the Romans' in general: cf. 29.5 and 9, 34.22–4, 49.1, 58.5.

Syme, R. 1956. 'Piso and Veranius in C.,' *Classica et Mediaevalia* 17: 129–34.

Hiltbrunner, O. 1942. 'Zur Terminologie des römischen Rechnungswesens,' *Hermes* 77: 379–81.

Badian, E. 1985. 'Nobiles amici: Art and Literature in an Aristocratic Society,' *CP* 80: 341–7.

Shackleton Bailey, D.R. 1986. '*Nobiles* and *Novi* Reconsidered,' *AJP* 107: 255–60.

Maselli, G. 1990. 'Livelli espressivi e secante economica nel c. 28 di C.,' *Aufidus* 11–12: 7–23.

29

Structure: 10 + 10 + (2 + 2). See however P. Young Forsyth 1969, who would make two poems of it. This division was first advocated by Sabellicus in his *Ex Catullo*, printed in 1417; see Gaisser 1993: 51 and Appendix 4.

Date: probably late in the year 53; notice that Badian's 1977 emendation to line 20 absolves us from regarding the poem as contemporary with, or antecedent to, Caesar's British expeditions. The subject is the ill-gotten wealth of Mamurra (cf. poem 114); but Caesar, and by implication Pompey (l. 24), are also targets of its invective. The last line became proverbial: see *Catalepton* 6.6.

Q. has voiced the opinion, in his notes on poem 57, that it, not poem 29, is the poem to which Caesar took exception on the grounds that it inflicted *perpetua stigmata* on him (Suet. *Iul.* 73). Q. believes that 'Suetonius implies an appreciable interval between attack and reconciliation'; this I do not altogether follow, unless *perpetua*, 'lasting,' is taken to refer to the past, instead of the probable future (cf. poem 40 *longa poena*, poem 78$^\mathrm{b}$ *fama ... anus*). Since poem 29 is datable to 53 at the very earliest (see Rambaud 1980, quoted above on page 3), we should clearly find a contradiction if we assumed, as Q. and most editors do, that Catullus died in 54 BC; but see the Introduction for compelling arguments showing that the actual date of his death was not earlier than the end of the year 53 BC. In addition, the choice of the iambic metre (in which C. tends to couch his more serious attacks) over the lighter hendecasyllable (see intr. n. to poems 36, 37) points again to poem 29 as enshrining a weightier insult to Caesar than poem 57.

Metre: Pure iambic trimeter (cf. poem 4). To the regularity of the iambics there is (if we discount the proper name *Mamurra*) only one exception – which textual critics have not succeeded in remedying – in the first foot of line 20, where see n.

1 Catullus here characteristically uses two almost synonymous expressions, of which the second is stronger than the first.
quis potest pati? cf. 42.5 *si pati potestis*. For the sentiment cf. Theogn. 58 τίς κεν ταῦτ᾽ ἀνέχοιτ᾽ ἐσορῶν;

2 *impudicus*: roughly equivalent to *cinaedus* or *pathicus*; probably intended as a mere term of abuse. Caesar was a notorious womanizer, but that did not constitute *impudicitia*, which implied homosexuality. Suetonius does indeed (*Iul.* 49) quote from Calvus, Cicero, and Bibulus scurrilous allusions to his alleged relations with Nicomedes, king of Bithynia, but that was a long time ago (80 BC). When these epithets are repeated in l. 10, this time applied directly to Caesar, F. claims in his note that *vorax* does not fit Caesar because he was moderate in eating and drinking. This is indeed reported of him – Suet., *Iul.* 53, says that even his enemies admitted he was *vini parcissimus*, and adds that he was not 'fussy' about his food. But it may have been only for reasons of health that he was abstemious; Cicero (*Ad Att.* 13.52.1) implies that he was ready enough to let himself go when circumstances were favourable. Yet *vorax* need not refer to gluttony (cf. 57.8 *vorax adulter*). It may be meant, in a general sense, of one whose greed extends to everything in sight; cf. Cicero, *Phil.* 2.67 *quae Charybdis tam vorax?* As for *aleo* (a vulgar form, like *ganeo* etc.) = *aleator*, Caesar was a political gambler who spent one fortune to gain another. But the epithets need not be pressed; F.'s quotations (l. 10 n.) show that they were almost automatically bracketed together and used at random for abusive purposes.

3 *Mamurram*: the first vowel is long by nature. See n. on metre, above. B. thinks C. used the licence of abbreviating the first syllable; either this, or the alternative of breaking the succession of pure iambics, would be easier in the case of a proper name.
Comata: a 'half-official' (Kr.) name for Transalpine Gaul (contrast *togata* for the cisalpine province). In Cicero, *Phil.* 8.27, Antony is made to use both *comata* and *togata*; Cicero himself, and Caesar, do not use either.

4 *cū te* (Mss) is palaeographically close to *ante*, the emendation of Statius. Pliny (cited in the *testimonia*) says of Mamurra: '[quem] Catullus dixit habere quidquid habuisset Comata Gallia,' where *habuisset* seems to recall *habebat* in tense, as B. observes. That *uncta* occurs as an adjective in l. 22 is an argument against, rather than for, the acceptance of *uncti* here.
For the lengthened final vowel in *ultima*, cf. 4.9 and 18.

5 *cinaede Romule*: the (degenerate; cf. 58.5) Roman who is, of course, here Caesar (F.) or Pompey (Q.): 'how *can* you put up with it and call yourself a Roman?'

6 *superbus et superfluens*: 'overbearing and over-flush' (F.), 'proud and prodigal' (Q.).

7 *perambulabit*, 'will take a stroll round.' F. points to echoes in Hor. *Epod.* 4.5, 17.41, and (*cubilia*) 5.69.

8 *col. aut Ad.*: the white dove is favoured by Aphrodite (Alexis, fr. 214 K λευκὸς Ἀφροδίτης εἰμὶ περιστερός). So is Adonis, of course. For the older form *Adoneus*, cf. Plaut. *Men.* 144.

11 *eo nomine*: metaphor from bookkeeping (unnoticed by F.): 'on this account'; again l. 23.

13 *diffututa* (cf. 6.13, 37.5, 41.1, making four different compounds in all) here suggests dissipation of energy, leading to exhaustion. Because he had coined the phrase *diffututa mentula* in this lampoon, which soon became famous (observe the number of *testimonia* in the App. Crit.), and applied it to Mamurra, C. took to using *Mentula* thereafter, with a capital M, as a sobriquet for him (see the Index). *Vester* is normally plural in reference, and though there are places in C. where it is hard not to take it as = *tuus* (55.22 and 68.151, for example), it should probably be taken here as making Pompey share the blame for Mamurra; cf. 21 *fovetis*.

15 *quid est alid* ('Surely this is . . . ?'): Colloquial idiom; cf. Cicero, *Phil.* 1.22 *quid est aliud hortari adulescentes ut turbulenti . . . velint esse?* and (more fully) *Verr.* 2.3.71 *quid est aliud capere pecunias, si hoc non est?*
alid: cf. 66.28 *alis*. Use of these forms, in literature at any rate, seems limited to the generation of Lucr., C., and Sallust.

F. translates *sinistra* by 'perverse'; but in view of the question asked in the next line, 'misplaced' would be better.

16 *expatravit*: a very strong word (possibly invented for the purpose of this passage by C.; not attested elsewhere). The translation 'finished off' (F.) is weak; Q.'s 'ploughed through' is better, giving a hint of the erotic undertones of *patrare* (first noticed by Scaliger; Doering equated *expatrare* with *effutuere*). Cf. Suet. *Iul.* 51 *aurum in Gallia effutuisti*. Notice again how C. follows up one expression with another of similar meaning but stronger: 'Hasn't he run through enough already? – hasn't he gormandized enough?'

17 *lancinata*, 'made mincemeat of'; it was probably by squandering his inheritance that he earned the nickname 'the bankrupt of Formiae' (41.4).

18–19 References to M.'s service with Pompey, and with Caesar in Spain in 61 BC.

20 See App. Crit. The line cannot be made into a pure iambic without drastic emendation, such as Owen's, since Latin has no short monosyllables that could be restored in place of the Ms reading *hunc*.

timetur: with dative of that for whom, or which, one fears (cf. Hor. *Od.* 3.27.7–8 *ego cui timebo / providus auspex*). As Badian 1977 points out, it is not the Gaulish or British (enemy) territory for which (out of sympathy) fears are entertained: 'Lines 11–14 show that the British campaign is well and truly over.' Because of Mamurra's way of running through fortunes 'as fast as he makes them' – the second and third fortune consisting of, respectively, Pontic and Spanish *booty* – fears are being entertained for the safety of his latest fortune, consisting in the booty from Gaul and Britain (*Gallicae <praedae> ... et Britannicae*).

21 In my opinion F. (followed by Q.) is right in taking *malum* as an expletive (in this sense, it is frequent in Comedy). 'This bad man' is too feeble an addition to the sense to be plausible as a phrase in C.'s *nugae*.

23 We have to ask how the reading *opulentissime* came into being. It may perhaps be conjectured that an unfamiliar word, *potissim(e)i*, gave rise to a supralinear gloss in favour of the familiar *potentissimi*, in this fashion: *potissimi* (where of course *ul.*, as often, = *vel*, and the gloss amounts to: 'possibly to be taken as *potentissimi*'). For another, quite independent, attempt (by Gordon Williams) to solve a textual problem in C. by suggesting the possibility of a supralinear gloss, see 55.9 n. Note however my reservations expressed there, which apply to the present passage as well. For a further suggestion, this time by B., see 116.7 n. (on *acta / amicta*).

24 *socer generque*: In 59 BC Caesar caused his daughter Julia, who was already engaged, to break off her engagement and marry Pompey. Hence *socer generque* became a set phrase, in verse at least (V. *Aen.* 6.830–31; Luc. 1.289–90, 4.802, 10.417; Mart. 9.70.3).

perdidistis omnia: referring to the breakdown of the republican political system under the recently renewed first triumvirate. The elections of praetors and other magistrates for 55 BC had been so badly impeded by intrigue and faction that they were not held until the year had begun, and then the election of Vatinius and the exclusion of Cato engendered a public scandal; see poem 52, and F.'s notes there (though F. does not see clearly enough that this short political lampoon must be a comment on the election results of January 55 BC). F. suggests that *perdere omnia* had become 'a phrase [cliché] of the opposition,' and that C. echoes it here; see his second n. on this line for quotations showing that the expression had been used in political contexts, by Cicero at least, long before poem 29 was written.

Young [Forsyth], P.R. 1969. 'C. 29,' *CJ* 64: 327–8.
Scott, W.C. 1971. 'Catullus and Caesar (c. 29),' *CP* 66 17–25.
Minyard, J.-D. 1971. 'Critical Notes on C. 29,' *CP* 66: 174–81.
Cameron, A. 1976. 'C. 29,' *Hermes* 104: 155–63.

Badian, E. 1977. 'Mamurra's Fourth Fortune,' *CP* 72: 320–2.

Deroux, C. 1977. 'Un nouveau personnage catullien,' *RBPh* 55: 56–78.

Allen, A. 1983. 'Mamurra's Next Gorge,' *CP* 78: 231–2.

– 1984. 'C.'s Little White Dove [29.8],' *Maia* 36: 243–5.

McCulloch, H.Y. 1984. 'Mamurra, Caesar and Pompey: A Textual Note on C. 29.23–24,' *CW* 78: 110- 11.

Quinn, K. 1985. 'Pompey, Caesar and C. 29,' *AFLNice* 50: 261–8. [Date 55–4 BC.]

30

Structure: balanced (6 + 6) – if the text is sound; see n. on lines 3–4.
A bitter reproach to a friend for deserting the poet in time of trouble. Notice the intensity of the reproach, punctuated as it is by repeated vocatives *in parenthesi* (ll. 2, 3, and 7, after the initial accumulation in l. 1). For equal warmth of emotion in a similar context, cf. Ov. *Tr.* 1.8.11ff. Kr. notes that evidently C. still wishes to regard Alfenus as a friend (which may explain the intensity, as well as the almost wheedling tone of lines 1 and 2); it is not an outburst of dismissive hatred against someone whom C. now regards as an enemy. Kr. also observes that 'the metre forces C. to walk on stilts and strike an academic note which does not suit intimate reproaches.'
Metre: Greater Asclepiad. 'Horace uses this metre in three odes: 1.11, 1.18, and 4.10 – all expository or paraenetic, rather than lyrical or imaginative' (Q.).

1 *Alfenus*: probably Alfenus Varus ('Varus' appears at 10.1 and 22.1); an Alfenus was *consul suffectus* in 39 BC, and so (assuming he did not delay too long beyond the statutory age in attaining the office) he could well have been a close age-fellow of C.'s. This Alfenus, who achieved fame as a jurisconsult, came from Cremona in Cisalpine Gaul – not far from Verona, which is another reason for intimate friendship (now, apparently, betrayed) with Catullus.

   The dative after *false* is unusual: until Sen. *Med.* 654 there is no other instance.

   unanimis, 'loving' as at 9.4, 66.80 (of *one* person; not 'harmonious,' referring to the emotions or opinions of two or more, as we might expect).

   sodalibus: 'generalized' plural (singular in reference).

2 *dulcis amiculi* sounds like a quotation of something Alfenus had said or written. With *dulcis* in this context, cf. 45.11.

   iam: 'is it come to this, that . . . ?' (F.).

3–4 Some editors have supposed a lacuna between these two lines; *nec* without a preceding negative has caused surprise. (Kr.: '*nec* is not exactly equivalent to "not": perhaps *nec tamen* would have been more precise.') Fr. suggests

that *nec*, as a mere negation (= *ne* or *non*), is archaic and belongs to religious
formulae (e.g., at V. *Ecl.* 9.6 *quod nec vertat bene*); see F. for passages where
it is linked to divine disapproval. Regarded in this light, it may be allowed to
stand.

caelicolis, 'heaven-dwellers,' a solemn word for the gods; Kr. suggests that it
was probably coined by Ennius to translate οὐρανίωνες. 'Not pleasing to' is from
Homer (*Od.* 14.83 οὐ μὲν σχέτλια ἔργα θεοὶ μάκαρες φιλέουσιν).

5 *quae*: not referring to l. 4 merely (if it were so, *quod*, which is more normal
when only *one* fact is stated, would be called for). Does *negligis* refer to *facta
impia*? Fr. quotes some similarly elliptical expressions (among which he includes
64.148 *metuere* – but the text there is better served by Czwalina's emendation
meminere: see App. Crit.). He thought of it, therefore, as meaning 'you ignore
the consequences of disloyalty,' and well refers to V. *Aen.* 7.307 *scelus ...
merentem* for a parallel expression. Tr. 'you care nothing for <the consequences
of> your disloyal actions.'

6 See App. Crit. (E. read *dice*, in order to come palaeographically closer to *V*'s
dico; but C. does not use *dice*. In one passage, at 36.16, he uses *face*; but the
language there, part of an address to a god, is studiously hieratic; there are no
such overtones here.)

7 *animam tradere*, 'to commit my life and soul (to you)'; Kr.'s 'mich dir
anzuvertrauen' is hardly strong enough. A friendship that can be called *amores*
(in the next line) does not blench at the mention of 'the soul'; cf. Hor. *Od.* 1.3.8
animae dimidium meae, and for *tradere* cf. *dare* as used at Plaut. *Asin.* 141
amans ego animum meum isti dedi.

9 For *idem* introducing a contrast in behaviour see 25.4 n.

Clearly *X* had *inde al. idem*, the variant being taken from the reading in the
text of *A* while *inde* perhaps resulted from a mere slip; see 28.11 n.

Another instance of *retrahere* is given by F. (Hor. *Ep.* 1.18.58 *ne te retrahas
et ... absis*). The same idea can be found in Cicero, *In Pis.* 70 *revocare se non
poterat, familiaritate implicatus.*

9–10 A *topos*, or literary commonplace; for its history see F.'s n. Usually, of
course, the winds carry off prayers, promises, or declarations: 'strictly speaking,
the wind can carry only *words* away (not *facta*)' remarks Kr.; but he concedes
that the phrase *dicta et facta* is 'an established combination.' Cf., for the τόπος,
64.59, 142; 65.17.

10 *irrita*: also at 64.59.

12 *postmodo* often has an implication of menace (B., Kr.); cf. Hor. *Od.* 1.28.30–1
nocitura postmodo ... fraudem.

Fedeli, P. 1970. 'Il carme 30 di C.,' *Ronconi*: 97–113.
Thom, S. 1993. 'Crime and Punishment in Catullus 30,' *Akroterion* 38: 51–60.

31

Structure: 6 + 5 + 3.

To a villa on Lake Garda: on returning home, after a year in Bithynia. The date is 56 BC. Sirmio appears to have been the summer retreat of C.'s family (see Wiseman 1987); when he implicitly refers to himself as its *erus* (l. 12) he must be using the word somewhat loosely, since in the year 56 his father was still alive (poem 29, which must antedate the reconciliation in his father's house mentioned by Suetonius, *Iul.* 73, is datable to 55 or slightly later by the reference to Britain). This poem offers no evidence in support of the idea that C. made the voyage home from Bithynia in a yacht which he hauled up the Mincio into L. Garda (see the commentary on poem 4).

Notice how, in lines 1–3, C. gradually builds up his claim on behalf of Sirmio: this 'widening of the horizon,' bit by bit, is characteristic of his descriptive method. The language is closely linked to that of poem 46 (written in anticipation of C.'s homeward journey): *linquantur Phrygii ... campi* (46.4) is echoed in *Bithynos liquisse campos*; *mens ... avet vagari* (46.7) in *mens onus reponit* (note the strict rhythmical correspondence here); and we may find a counterpoise to *pedes vigescunt* (46.8) in *acquiescimus lecto.*

The metrical difference between the two poems tells, in its own fashion, much the same tale as the last of these three echoes, inasmuch as the jaunty, lively hendecasyllables of the anticipatory spring poem are replaced by the weary 'limping iambics' that record the journey's end of the tired traveller.

1 *paene insularum*: practically a single word. (Livy uses *paene insula* several times, e.g., 25.11.1, 31. 40.1, 32.31.26; cf. Caes. *BC* 3.40.2). Similarly *paene* is often linked to *puer*, in the sense of 'adolescent' (Cicero, *Ad Brut.* 1.18.3, Ov. *Ex Ponto* 4.3.12, 4.12.20), and occasionally to other nouns (Caes. *BG* 6.36.2 *paene obsessionem*; note F.'s tr.).

2 *ocelle*: whereas at 50.19 this is applied to Calvus as a term of personal affection, here the meaning is extended to general praise of scenery (as in Cicero, *Ad Att.* 16.6.2 *ocellos Italiae, villulas meas*, and *ND* 3.91 *oculos orae maritimae*, of Corinth and Carthage). In this sense the expression occurs in Greek also (Pind. *Ol.* 2.10, Eur. *Phoen.* 802).
  liquentibus, 'clear'; cf. 64.2 *liquidas (Neptuni undas).*
  stagnis, 'pools,' hence 'lakes.'

3 *vasto*: see 64.156 n., and F.'s note here ('conveys the sense of emptiness or desolation').
  uterque: i.e., of salt or fresh water; for the latter, cf. Ov. *M.* 1.276 *convocat hic* (= Neptune) *amnes, qui postquam tecta tyranni / intravere sui, ...* It is

not necessarily implied that there were two separate deities called N.; we are concentrating here on the thing (water in general) for which the god stood, and of that there are two sorts. The distinction between god and thing is not always clear-cut: cf. 3.1 n., and also Hor. *Od.* 3.25.1–2 *Quo me, Bacche, rapis tui / plenum?* Cf. Lucr. 2.472 *Neptuni corpus acerbum* = *salt* water.

4 *inviso*, 'set eyes upon.' Cf., for this meaning, 64.233. Usually = 'pay a visit to,' as at 64.384, 66.20. Cf. 10.2 *visum.*

5 Here, and at 26.2, we should perhaps credit *m* with a (metrical) correction rather than blame him for a slip. *Thyniam*: the accepted name of the province to which C. was posted was Bithynia. By his time the words *Thyni* and *Thynia* were obsolescent, though (as F. notes) *Th.* was 'a metrically convenient alternative': see 25.7 and Hor. *Od.* 3.7.3. In Hdt.'s day the distinction was still clear: 1.28 Θρήικες οἱ Θυνοί τε καὶ Βιθυνοί (though Stein regarded this passage as part of a later interpolation). See Kr. for the boundary between Thunoi in the west and Bithunoi in the east, defined by the rivers Rebas and Psilion.

5–6 *mi ipse credens ... liquisse*: as object before *liquisse*, we must supply the accusative *me*, from the dative *mi* (= *mihi*). Cf. Plaut. *Rud.* 245–6 *vix mihi / credo ego hoc, te tenere;* Prop. 1.1.23–4 *ego crediderim vobis et sidera et amnis / posse Cytaeines ducere carminibus.*

Bithynos liquisse campos: cf. 46.4 *linquantur Phrygii ... campi* (surely an echo; see n. there). Kr. observes that *campos* is surprising in relation to a territory 'largely consisting of mountains'; but *campi* at 46.4 is immediately followed by a reference to the *ager uber* surrounding Nicaea, where C. probably stayed (this city rivalled Nicomedia for primacy), an *ager* described by Strabo (12.4.7, quoted by Kr. on 46.5) as πεδίον μέγα. Kr. himself (46.5 n.) equates πεδίον with *campi.*

8 *mens onus reponit*: cf. 46.7 *mens ... avet vagari*; another echo? (See intr. n.).

8–9 *peregrino labore*: the expression, signifying the hardships of foreign travel, is poetically compressed.

9 *larem*, 'home'; but also, as Kr.'s quotation from Cato, *Agr.* 2.1, reminds us, the god himself, since to greet the *lar* was the very first thing one did on returning to one's *villa*, no matter what the claims of urgent duty, or (as here) one's own state of fatigue, might be. Notice that the final words in ll. 8 and 9 (*peregrino, larem ad nostrum*) are both rhythmically equivalent and in pointed contrast; cf. 58.2 and 3 (*unam ... omnes*).

11 *quod unum est*, 'which of itself alone is <enough to compensate> for ...' Cf. also Cicero, *Ad Att.* 2.5.1 (quoted above, 9.1–2 n.). The second of F.'s two translations ('here is the one thing that is ...') is perhaps not intended to mislead; but mislead it certainly does.

12 *venusta*, 'for Catullus, the adjective of Venus' (F.; see his n. on 3.2). Usually he applies it to persons; here, by a poetic transfer, to a place.

al. bero neither makes sense nor is metrical; therefore it is not a correction by
R^2, but is taken from another Ms (*X*). In such cases, R^2's reading is first picked
up by m^2, not *m*; that is, the variant emerges from a second recension by R^2,
when he more closely ponders *X*.

12–13 See App. Crit. We must accept *gaudente*, otherwise it will be necessary to
take *ero gaude* as meaning (if *ero* is dative) 'rejoice for your master's sake.' This
idiom might perhaps work with a pronoun such as *mihi* (cf. Greek χαῖρέ μοι),
but with a noun it does not appear to be Latin. If *ero* is ablative, and taken with
the reading *gaudete*, neither the ablative at 95.10 nor that at 96.6 is strictly
parallel to the sense required here, since each of these furnishes a positive reason
(Antimachus' tumid writing; your love) for the *gaudium*.

13 The insertion of *o*, accepted by (e.g.) Mynors, is unnecessary and undesirable;
que and *quoque* are confused elsewhere. Kr., who reads *gaudete*, interprets
vosque as = *vos quoque*; but see F. on 102.3, where he favours Vossius' *me
aeque.*

lucidae: *V* almost certainly read *lidie*. Most editors render this as *Lydiae*, and
explain that the lake was in territory traditionally supposed to have been partly
settled by Etruscans, who are (by a further learned allusion) called 'Lydian'
because this people was believed to be Eastern in origin. Since this adjective is
inappropriately applied to the waves, not to the lake, the same editors have to
call this a hypallage (still another touch of learning). But all this is a little too
complicated for the otherwise direct style of the poem; the tortured archaeology
here implied is as implausible as it is pointless in the context. Moreover, if C.
is glad to turn his back on the East and is now rejoicing in his Italian abode, the
'Lydian' touch seems a little out of key. Two things – besides palaeographical
considerations – seem to me to argue for the emendation *lucidae*, which I have
adopted: (i) the soft, repetitive *sounds* in the whole phrase *lucidae lacus undae* –
alternation of the vowels *u* and *ae*, and of the consonants *c* and *d* - – suggest the
lapping of small waves (the alternative *limpidae* falls far short in this respect);
and (ii) the picture is appropriate to the waves, rather than to the water (which
may be, and indeed is, limpid; but it is the wavelets on the rocky shore approaches
that are *lucidae*, 'sparkling with light,' as every visitor to Sirmio can confirm).
Cf. 69.4 for the sound. The reference by some editors to 4.24 is irrelevant,
especially for those who refuse to believe in the probability of a Lake Garda
setting of poem 4; see my commentary on that poem, esp. n. on *limpidae* (l. 24).

14 *est domi*, 'you have in store'; F. has a good note on this idiom.

Delatte, L. 1935. 'Uterque Neptunus (C. XXXI, 3),' *AC* 4: 45–7.
Baker, R.J. 1970. 'C. and Friend in *Carm.* XXXI,' *Mn* 23: 33–41.
McCaughey, J. 1970. 'The Mind Lays by its Trouble. C. 31,' *Arion* 9: 362–5.
Witke, C. 1972. 'Verbal Art in C. 31,' *AJP* 93: 239–51.

Moore-Blunt, J. 1974. 'C. XXXI and Ancient Generic Composition,' *Eranos* 72: 106–18.

Cairns, F. 1974. 'Venusta Sirmio: C. 31,' *Quality and Pleasure in Latin Poetry*, ed. Tony Woodman and David West. Cambridge: 1–17.

Baker, R.J. 1983. 'C. and Sirmio,' *Mn* 36; 316–23.

Vessey, D.W.T.C. 1985. 'Some Thoughts Inspired by Bergk's Emendation *gaudente* in C. 31.13,' *BICS* 32: 101–8.

Cilliers, L. 1987. 'C. 31, 'n Interpretasie (nog eens),' *Akroterion* 32: 75–83.

Wiseman, T.P. 1987. 'The Masters of Sirmio,' *Roman studies in Literature and History*. Liverpool: 313–23, 349–60.

– 1993. 'Sirmio, Sir Ronald and the Gens Valeria,' *CJ* 88: 223–9.

32

Structure: 3 + 5 + 3.

A note to a *meretrix*, requesting an assignation.

C. has chosen to give, on this seemingly unpromising theme, a masterly display of virtuosity in the writing of mellifluous hendecasyllabic verses. Particularly effective is the variety he achieves in distributing words within the line so as to exploit to the full the metre's flexibility. Of the eleven final words in the line, two are of five syllables, three are of four syllables, four are trisyllables, and two are disyllables, with corresponding adjustments in the rest of the line. Notice also the variety among the *breaks* in the lines: seven of them have the usual caesura (line 2, for example), whereas four lines have a diaeresis one syllable earlier. Here, as in many other short compositions, it is possible to verify L.'s opinion that the smoothness of C.'s versification is in inverse proportion to the intensity, the depth, of his emotion. When he feels anything very deeply, he is apt in one way or another to rupture the seams of his poetic medium. In verse of this sort, however, where he is obviously not professing a commitment to anything more than the enjoyment of the passing moment, his technique is exemplary.

1 *amabo* (+ imperative), 'I'll be obliged to you,' 'please' (Plaut., *Men.* 678, *Truc.* 128); obsolete from Cicero onwards.

See App. Crit. Certain forms of the letter *m* (ꝳ) and certain forms of *ch* (cꝳ) or *th* (tꝳ) are palaeographically not dissimilar. The gap in *O* may represent something that the scribe found hard to interpret: perhaps *ipsimilᶦa A*, *ipsi thilá X*, the superscript *i* being interpreted by *G* as a correction of the letter *a* to *i*? Notice how *m²*, reviewing *R*, suddenly realizes that *m* had overlooked *R²*'s variant, and now puts it in as a correction – but does so carelessly, turning *R²*'s *ipsicilla* into *ipsichila*.

ipsimilla. Since in the next line *deliciae* and *lepores* (parallel expressions) are without any suggestion of a proper name, I have dropped the capital *I*, considering the onus of proof to lie with those who would see a name here. Compare Petronius' use of *ipsima*, *ipsimus* at 69.3 and 75.11 (the masc. *ipsimus* occurs in a non-sexual sense at 63.3 and 76.1). *dulcis* here adds a further specification, supported by the two amplifying common nouns *deliciae* and *lepores*.

2 *deliciae*: cf. 6.1.

lepores: cf. 10.1 *amores* (Plaut. *Cas.* 235 *respice, o mi lepos*).

3 *iube* + simple subjunctive is colloquial (e.g., Plaut. *Pers.* 605).

meridiatum: cf. 61.111 *medio die / gaudeat* (of a bridegroom); Ov. *Am.* 1.5, *passim*.

4 See App. Crit. As Kr. points out, the syntax is against *adiubeto*, since *iubere ne* is uncommon; his second objection, however, assumes that *adiubeto* is deemed to govern l. 6, as well as l. 5, which of course is absurd. There is really no need to emend *adiuvato*; Q. translates 'it will be helpful, too, if you will kindly attend to the following.' Cf. Cicero, *Ad Fam.* 5.2.9 *ut ita fieret, pro mea parte adiuvi*.

5 *liminis tabellam*: 'leaf' (of the outer door, for which *limen* does duty).

The R^2 correction is such as must have been obvious to a highly intelligent reader, particularly one of Coluccio's stamp, and need not imply that R^2 took it from X.

6 Probably A and X read *lubeat*. The spelling *lub-* is usual in *OGR* (cf. 17.17, 24.9, 38.7, 61.41, 61. 126, 61.204), but not universal (cf. 2.6, 62.36, 76.14). R^2's correction is natural and easy; notice R^2's other errors in the next line (self-corrected in the first instance, corrected by R^2 in the second), where see n.

7 Of *domi maneas*, for the unmetrical *domi meas*, McKie asks whether Coluccio would have made this change, unless it was prompted by reference to X. The answer, I think, where Coluccio is concerned, is certainly 'yes,' on grounds of common sense, of metre, and of Coluccio's demonstrated grasp of both. Hence we are not surprised to find the R^2 correction in *m*.

8 *novem*: a conventional exaggeration; Kr. quotes Ov. *Am.* 3.7.23 and Philodemus, *AP* 11.30.

fututiones: see 7.1 n. The noun occurs only here (apart from a borrowing by Martial, 1.106.6).

9 *si quid ages*, 'if there's anything doing' (Q.). The future tense, implied in the translation, is of course explicit in C.'s Latin. For the idiom <age> *si quid agis* cf. Plaut. *Epid.* 196, *Stich.* 717.

10 *satur supinus*: C. is apt to use asyndeton of adjectives or adverbs; cf. 1.1, 36.10. See further 46.11 n.

Sabbadini, R. 1912. 'Ipsicilla and Ipsitilla,' *Glotta* 3; 50–1.

Gratwick, A. 1967. 'Ipsithilla: A Vulgar Name, C. XXXII, 1,' *Glotta* 44: 174–6.

Morgan, M. Gwyn. 1974. 'Ipsithilla or Ipsicilla? C., c. 32 Again,' *Glotta* 52: 233–6.

Skinner, M.B. 1980. 'Pertundo tunicamque palliumque,' *CW* 73: 306–7.

Fink, R.O. 1983. 'C., *Carmen* 32,' *CW* 76: 292–4.

Heath, J.R. 1986. 'The Supine Hero in C. 32,' *CJ* 82: 28–36.

Wiseman, T.P. 1987. 'C.'s *belle de jour*,' *Filologia e forme letterarie: studi offerti a F. Della Corte* 2: 375–6. Urbino.

Gratwick, A.S. 1991. 'C. XXXII,' *CQ* 41: 547–51.

33

Structure: unitary. Notice the prosaic articulation of the argument, by means of parenthetical *nam* (after the opening address), followed by *cur* and *quandoquidem*.

C.'s charges against Vibennius (unknown) and his son are the small coin of public pasquil-verse, and are not intended to be taken literally. For clothes-stealing, or its variant, napkin-stealing, see poems 12 and 25; for the accusation against the son, that of being a *cinaedus*, about one in three of C.'s lampoons (as Kr. says) offers some sort of parallel.

1 Q. refers to E.'s informative note on the frequency of thefts from public baths in the Greek and Roman world (the *Digest*, 47.17, has an entire chapter *de furibus balneariis*). Cf. Plaut. *Rud.* 382–4 *qui it lavatum in balineas, quom ibi sedulo sua vestimenta servat, tamen surripiuntur*; Petron. 30.8 has an incident of the same kind.

2 Vibennius is otherwise unknown.

2–3 The comparatives suggest that whereas father and son alike are tainted with both vices, one vice prevails in the father, the other in the son (Kr.).

3 *dextra*: cf. 12.1 n.

4 The word *vorax* is disguised by the spelling (*voratiore*) found in our Mss; it may be that *X*, puzzled by *voratiore* and not at once identifying it as the ablative form of the comparative, added his weak 'variant' (really an attempted correction), which was picked up by $R^2(m^2)$.

5 <in> *exilium*: *in* must be supplied from *in* before *oras*; cf. 4.19 n.
  malas in oras: a variation on the colloquial formula *abi in malam rem* (e.g., Plaut. *Capt.* 877; *Most.* 850 *abin hinc in malam crucem?*).

7 *populo*, 'the public'; cf. 15.6 (= *vulgi*, 40.5), 67.12 and 39, Hor. *Ep.* 1.15.14, Petron. 17.8.

8 *fili*: as Kr. points out, the change from the third-person reference to *patris* in l. 6, to the vocative here, is metrically necessary because the word *potest* would be hard to introduce.

asse: cf. 5.3.

venditare: see also 106.2 (*se vendere*).

Bajoni, M.G. 1993. 'Alcune note a C. 33,' *Euphrosyne* 21: 177–8.

34

Structure: six 4-line stanzas. See Q. for a more detailed structural analysis. A hymn to Diana, represented by the poet as being sung by a choir of boys and girls. Unlike Horace's *Carmen Saeculare*, for example, where there is external evidence (an inscription, naming the poet) that the work was officially commissioned and sung on a public occasion, we have here no such evidence; nor is there any hint, in C.'s text at any rate, that it was designed for a particular festival or was ever publicly recited, though there is nothing in the poem's construction or contents to render this impossible, or even a priori unlikely. It may however have been a purely literary composition, like (as most, though not all, scholars believe) Hor. *Od.* 1.21, a similar hymn addressed to Diana and Apollo. L. devoted part of a lecture to defending and explaining his view that this hymn was written for public performance, though he did not speculate concerning the actual occasion. That view may be summarized as follows:

There is no evidence that in the late Republican period any singing of hymns at public festivals formed part of Roman religion, or was consistent with what we know of its practices; the two instances recorded in Livy (27.37.7, 31.12.9), which Drachmann (1887) dismissed as quite exceptional measures taken in what were believed to be national emergencies, date from 207 and 200 BC, and nothing of the sort is recorded thenceforth until the time of Horace. But Livy himself is for us the only likely source of information about such details – and he stops at 167 BC; if, as is possible, the practice of such hymn-singing resumed and became regular in the meantime, we could not have heard of it in the absence of Livy's text. (Moreover, as Fr. points out, free lyrical compositions in the Greek style are hardly likely to have been heard at Roman religious festivals in that period.) And if there was no tradition of choral hymns to gods, what made C. think of writing one? If it was merely to show that he could imitate the Greeks, why did he not (for example) do something like Anacreon's hymn to Artemis (written in the poet's person, like most of C.'s work)? But C.'s hymn refers specifically to the choir singing it, and to Rome at the end; *could* it be a valid 'literary exercise,' if no such hymns were ever regularly sung in Rome? If there *was* a tradition of choral hymns, why should not this be regarded as a genuine contribution to it? Finally, hymn-singing seems such an improbable diversion from C.'s usual literary preoccupations that it is hard to imagine him writing for this purpose unless he was commissioned to do so.

Wiseman 1985: 99 speculates that Catullus, visiting Delos, might have been asked 'to provide a hymn for the festival of Apollo's sister, with appropriate allusion to the present preoccupation of the Romans in business there.'

Metre: four-line stanzas consisting of three glyconics and a pherecratean (see poem 61, where the stanzas, of five lines each, contain *four* glyconics and a pherecratean). (The only other *original* poem composed in stanzas, in all of C.'s 'polymetrics' [poems 1–60], is poem 11, which is in Sapphics; poem 51, of course, is a translation of a poem by, and in the metre of, Sappho herself, and the metre of poem 11 may well be selected in order deliberately to echo that of poem 51.) The glyconic metre, used in Latin by Ticida (fr. 1 M) and Calvus (fr. 4 M), and found in just one fragment of Varro (*Men.* 437 Büch.), is not employed in Hellenistic poetry; here C. may well have gone directly to Sappho or Anacreon (see Drachmann 1887: 8–10).

There is little in our poem to show that certain stanzas were meant to be sung by girls or boys only. St. 4 certainly does seem more suitable to girls, st. 5 to boys; and if they are read aloud, the sounds (especially the long soprano *i*'s in *Lucina, dicta*) tend to confirm this; but we cannot extend this division to sts. 2 and 3, the second of which is merely a subordinate clause. If C. planned to divide the choir in this way – i.e., by 'gender' – for only two stanzas out of six, he was innovative in doing so.

1 *Dianae ... Dianam* (l. 3). The anaphora is hymnic: Kr. cites Soph. *Ant.* 781–2 Ἔρως ἀνίκατε μάχαν, / Ἔρως ὃς ἐν κτήνεσι πίπτεις, and compares the way in which Philod. *AP* 10.21 is dominated by the repeated Κύπρι.
   in fide: we are her clients (she protects us). Cicero, *Rosc. Am.* 93 *in fide et clientela*, *Planc.* 97 *in fide mea*. Similarly the poet is in the *clientela* of his Muse (1.9 *patrona virgo*; see n. there).

5–6 The reason why *maximi* precedes *magni* is not wholly metrical. We have to consider the hierarchy of gods: it is perilous to praise a subordinate deity without allowing due precedence to the supreme god (Iuppiter), to whom Diana is related as daughter to father. This is why (as B. points out) the normal rhetorical progression by way of climax from the positive *magnus* to the superlative *maximus* is here reversed. This is the first occurrence of the name *Latonia* = Diana (cf. V. *Aen.* 9.405; the form was useful in dactylic metres).
   progenies, a word of epic solemnity, suitable to a hymn.

8 *deposivit* (lit. 'put down') = *deposuit* = *peperit*; the form of the perfect is archaic, and this is appropriate where the setting is that of a hymn. As F. remarks, the

verb *depono* is elsewhere used of giving birth only in the fabulist Phaedrus: 1.18.5 of human birth, 1.19.4 of a litter of puppies. In English, ewes are said to 'drop' their lambs in normal birth, but to 'slip' them if they are born prematurely and suddenly.

olivam: see F.'s note on the Delian tree (an olive in one version of the myth; in another, a palm, if not a laurel). At Ov. *M.* 13.635 the legendary trees, shown to Aeneas, are an olive and a palm; the visitor at Pliny *NH* 16.240 is shown a palm. See also B. and E.

9–10 *montium silvarumque*: cf. Hor. *Od.* 3.22.1 *montium custos nemorumque virgo*, *Carm. Saec.* 1 *silvarum potens*, V. *Aen.* 9.557 *nemorum cultrix*. (Kr. cites Greek parallels.)

11 *saltus*: the belt of open scrub forest above the cultivable level, in the hilly terrain of Italy, was called *saltus* and associated with hunting (*venatio*); cf. Ov. *Ep.* 5.17 *saltus venatibus aptos*. Diana is seen, in this stanza, as the patron goddess of hunters.

saltuum is a correction by R^2, on metrical grounds as well as those of sense.

12 *sonantum* = *sonantium*. The form in *-tum*, being metrically useful, often appears in poetry.

13, 15, 17 *tu* (anaphora): another hymnic feature. (The '*Du-Stil*'; E. Norden, *Agnostos Theos* [Leipzig, 1913], 150 ff).

13 In Italy, Juno (not Diana), with the added name *Lucina*, had charge of human birth; cf. the cry which in Roman Comedy announces a birth 'off-stage': *Iuno Lucina, fer opem*. When the Romans took over the Greek deities and merged them with their own, it was by virtue of this function that Iuno Lucina was identified with Artemis-Diana.

15 Diana (*Trivia*, goddess of the crossroads, lit. the meeting-point of *three* ways) is here associated – as Hecate, i.e., in her 'underworld' guise – with magic.

Notice that R^2 twice seeks to correct by: (i) joining the words (followed by *m*), and subsequently (ii) trying to offer, as a fresh reading, *noto*, without junction (followed by m^2).

15–16 The emphasis is on *lumine*, not on *notho*: 'you are given the name *Luna* because of the light (*lumen*), which is <not your own but> reflected (*notho*).' The words *es dicta* do not amount to a perfect tense; the tense is thought of as essentially present.

17ff. Diana as maker of the lunar divisions of the calendar, regarded as a blessing to farmers. (In one Orphic hymn, Artemis is hailed as χρόνου μῆτερ.)

21 On the double correction implied in the R^2 variant, see the App. Crit. (*OGR* have *que-*; *O* alone has *placet*). It appears that R^2's reading at first seemed to Coluccio to furnish a satisfactory meaning, but that later he reconsidered the matter, perhaps on the basis of a variant such as *al. placet* in *X* (derived from *X*'s inspection of *A*).

21–2 Notice the importance accorded in Roman religion to finding the correct cult
title under which to address the god or goddess: cf. Hor. *S.* 2.6.20 *Matutine
pater, seu 'Iane' libentius audis* (other examples in F.).

22 *sancta* is adj., not participial, since for a *wish* we require present, not perfect,
tense; and there seems to be no parallel for the use of *sancta* as a participle. See
n. on line 16 *dicta*. The adj. *sancti* is used of the gods at 64.268, to distinguish
them still further from the human guests.

23 Merula's suggestion, *Ancique*, still deserves consideration. Diana was, however,
so ancient a member of the company of Roman deities that – apart from
the tradition of all the Mss – *antique* might perhaps be said gracefully to
acknowledge this fact. Also, *antique* would correspond, as F. (following Kr.) says,
to 'the common εἴ ποτε formula of a prayer' (Sappho fr. 1.5 L-P, *Il.* 5.116–17,
Soph. *OT* 164–6).

Zicàri, M. 1970. '*Nothus* in Lucr. V. 575 e in C. 34.15,' *Ronconi*: 525–9.
Németh, R. 1976. 'Der Diana-Hymnus (c. 34) von C. Analyse und Schlussfolgerun-
    gen,' *ACD* 12: 37–45.
Wiseman, T.P. 1985. *Catullus and His World. A Reappraisal.* Cambridge: 96–9.
Scivoletto, N. 1988. 'L' inno a Diana di C.,' *Filologia e forme letterarie: studi offerti
    a F. Della Corte* 2: 357–74. Urbino.

35

Structure: 6 + 6 + 6.
To Caecilius of Novum Comum: come to Verona to receive a friend's
observations on your poem.
'The preoccupation of the poem in general with the writing of poetry
suggests that the *cogitationes* are indeed something of a literary nature'
(L.); see n. on l. 5. B. pointed out that *incohatam* in l. 13, repeated in l. 18,
has a rather emphatic air, suggesting the implication that the poem was by
no means perfect, and thereby hinting that Caecilius ought to welcome the
criticisms which C. was in a position to pass on to him. This still seems the
most reasonable view to take of the poem's purport.

1 *tenero*, implying love poetry; almost certainly in the 'neoteric' fashion, since he
    is a close friend, *sodalis*, like Cinna (10.29). Cf. Ov. *AA* 2.273 (*teneri versus*),
    Mart. 7.14.3 and also possibly 12.44.5, where the C^ reading is *tenero* ...
    Catulle; Lindsay adopts *lepido*.

2 *Caecilio*: otherwise unknown, but possibly an ancestor or relation of the Younger
    Pliny, who bore the name Caecilius and hailed from Novum Comum (3–4).
    papyre: this is the first instance in Roman poetry of the request to a poetical

epistle to 'take' a message, which later became conventional (e.g., Hor. *Ep.* 1.8.1); notice also 36.2 (to the *carta*) *votum solvite*. Cf. V. *Ecl.* 6.12 *sibi quae Vari praescripsit pagina nomen*, for a similar personification of the writing material.

See App. Crit. The agreement of Benzo of Alessandria with *O* is striking. The emendation *cecilio* may accordingly have originated with *X*, though I am more inclined to think that it was entered as a variant in *A* (and ignored by *O*), because such a correction could easily have been suggested by the last line of the poem, even though all the Mss read *caecilia* there. Since *caecilia* would not strike the eye until *occilio* had already been written in line 2, correction by means of a marginal or superscript addition seems possible. *V* had no title here (McKie; see his table on p. 95a) to suggest the correction.

3–4 *Novum Comum* (mod. Como) became a municipality under this name in 59 BC, which helps to date the poem.
Larium: i.e., of Lake Como (*Lago di Como*), the *lacus Larius*.

4 The reading *menia* is attested not only by Benzo but also by Petrarch. (See the Introduction, pp. 27–8, on Petrarch's relation to the tradition of C.). As an emendation by R^2, it is easy, on grounds of sense and metre alike, and possibly independent; $m(^1)$ follows R^2's original correction, as usual. Two further emendations by R^2, both of them sound, will be found in lines 10 and 12.
The reference to Petrarch in the *testimonia* is mentioned by Billanovich 1988: 57. See also Ullman 1955: 195.

5 *cogitationes*, 'thoughts' or 'observations,' often of a critical sort; in this sense, extremely common in Cicero, who uses it about 111 times. Cf. *TD* 1.3.6 *mandare litteris cogitationes*.

6 *amici sui meique*, 'a friend of both of us,' who has either come to stay with C. or, more probably (since the *cogitationes* are already in existence, or so it would seem from C.'s use of *accipiat*), written in a letter to C. giving an opinion on Caecilius' poem. It is not wholly beyond the bounds of possibility that this friend should be Cicero; apart from his interest in new works of poetry, and the generous encouragement he gave to poets (Pliny, *Ep.* 3.15.1 *M. Tullium mira benignitate poetarum ingenia fovisse*; cf. also Cicero's judgment at *Q. Fr.* 2.9.3 on some passages of Lucretius, apparently sent to him for an opinion by his brother Quintus), see the n. on l. 5 above.

7 *si sapiet*, 'if he's wise,' or 'he will show good sense (by coming).' Colloquial; cf. Plaut. *Bacch.* 1001–2, *Rud.* 1391; Ter. *Ad.* 565. It may be inferred from this phrase that C. is 'putting pressure' on Caecilius.
viam vorabit is an unparalleled expression, but it is easily understood ('devour the miles,' or by a different metaphor 'burn up the road'); Cicero, *Ad Att.* 4.11.2, has *litteras vorare*.

9–10 *manus collo iniciens*: of course, as a sign of affection; there need not
be any suggestion of the legal expression *manus iniectio*, used of making
a claim to ownership or possession of something. Cf. 9.8 (n. on *applicans
collum*).

10 *roget morari*: the construction after *rogo* (infin., not *ut* + subjunctive) is
irregular. Occasionally we find *passive* infinitives after verbs of asking, advising,
and so forth. In the active, with verbs other than *rogo*: Cicero, *Sest.* 7 <*res
publica me*> *haec minora relinquere hortatur*; V. *Aen.* 10.439 *soror alma monet
succedere Lauso / Turnum*.

12 *deperit*, colloq., 'is hopelessly in love with' (+acc.) Cf. 100.2. Frequent in
Comedy: e.g., Plaut. *Amph.* 517, *Cist.* 131, Ter. *Heaut.* 525. Also, in a similar
sense, *perire* (45.5).
   impotente, see 4.18 n. See App. Crit. Notice that the quotation in Charisius, *GLK*
1: 134 is prompted by the use by C. here of the unusual abl. form *impotente*
instead of *impotenti*; *V.'s impotentem* is almost certainly wrong (the *-em*
readings in *V* are influenced by *illum*). The early correction by *R*² addresses
itself only to *amorem*, not to *impotentem*.

13 For *quo tempore ... ex eo*, instead of *ex eo tempore ... quo*, cf. 64.73 n.
(V. *Aen.* 2.163, 169, has *ex quo ... ex illo*.)
   legit: the subject of the verb is probably the girl, who was the subject of *deperit*
in the preceding line; also, *misellae* in l. 14 would naturally refer to the subject
of the *quo tempore* clause.

14 *Dindymi domina*: these were probably the opening words of Caecilius' poem
on the *Magna Mater* (l. 18); cf. Martial's reference (11.6.16) to a collection of
C.'s poems entitled *Passer*, and similar references to the work of Lucretius as
Aeneadum genetrix and to the *Aeneid* as *Arma virumque (cano)*.

15 *edunt medullam*: cf. 66.23 *exedit cura medullas*; also (for *medullae*) 45.16, 64.93,
100.7. At 91.6, *me ... edebat amor*.

16 *Sapphica ... musa* (abl.) = Sappho herself, as a poet. (See Ov. *AA* 3.329–30 and
Ex Ponto 4.16.29, quoted in F.'s note; cf. also 68.7 *veterum scriptorum Musae =
veteres scriptores*.)

17 *doctior*: *doctus* implies literary taste and skill, rather than 'learning.' The
effusively exaggerated language of the compliment in 16–17 is characteristic
of C. It is doubtless, of course, aimed at Caecilius, not at the girl, whose emotions,
and even existence, may conceivably be quite imaginary.

Pascal, C. 1921. 'Il carme XXXV di C.,' *Athenaeum* 9: 213–18.
Copley, F.O. 1953. 'C. 35,' *AJP* 74: 149–60.
Fisher, J.M. 1971. 'C. 35,' *CP* 66: 1–5.
Onetti, S., and Maurach, G. 1974. 'C. 35,' *Gymnasium* 81: 481–5.

Akbar Khan, H. 1974. 'C. 35 and the Things Poetry Can Do to You,' *Hermes* 102: 475–90.

Heine, R. 1975. 'Zu Cat. 35,' *Catull, Wege d. Forschung* 308: 62–84.

Buchheit, V. 1976. 'Dichtertum und Lebensform in C. cc. 35/36,' *Lebendige Romania* (Festschrift für H.W. Klein). Göppingen: 46–64.

Basto, J. 1982. 'Caecilius, Attis and C. 35,' *LCM* 7: 30–4.

Fredricksmeyer, E.A. 1985. 'C. to Caecilius on Good Poetry,' *AJP* 106: 213–21.

36

Structure: 2 + 8 + 7 + 3 (l. 1 = l. 20).
The first two and the last three lines are closely linked; between them lies (i) an explanation of lines 1–2, and (ii) the mock-prayer to Venus.

The implications of the first and last line have not always been understood. Surely 'logorrhoea' is what C. has in mind, rather than habits of hygiene which the Romans never knew. For 'logorrhoea' as a characteristic of Volusius, cf. poem 95, where he and Hortensius are joined together as a pair of verbose and mediocre poets in contrast to the succinct and painstaking Cinna.

Here we have the union of Love and Wit at its most complete; it is scarcely possible to answer the question 'is this piece a lampoon (on Volusius) or a lyric?' But the problem of what exactly C. means by *truces iambi* (l. 5) needs some discussion. Many commentators believe it to be possible that C. uses *iambi* here loosely for abusive verses in general, including those in hendecasyllables. It will however be found, I think, that C. never alludes to any single iambic poem under the name of hendecasyllable, or vice versa: 'hendecasyllabos' (12.10) is itself in a poem properly so described, and so also at 42.1; also, more importantly perhaps, when Roman critics refer to 'Catullus in hendecasyllabis,' etc., they mean precisely what they say: Sen. *Contr.* 7.4.7 on 53.5; Atilius Fortunatianus p. 298 on 1.2; Charisius p. 97 on 42.5. Similarly, Verrius Flaccus (*ap. Fest.* 273 L) by 'Catullus in galliambis' refers to 63.68; also Caesius Bassus *de metris* p. 262.19 (frag. 16, Baehrens[1]) speaks of C. 'in anacreonteo ... ades o Cybelle' (63.91). As for the iambic: 54[b].1 *irascere iterum meis iambis*, while the threat is voiced in another metre, obviously *refers to* poem 29, which is in pure iambics – and the repetition of *imperator unice* 29.11 as *unice imperator* at 54.2 clinches the matter (cf. Suet. *Iul.* 73). So also (if it is authentic and not a mistake of Porphyrion on Hor. *Od.* 1.16.22) Fragment 3 *at non effugies meos iambos*. Finally, 40.2 may, and probably does, refer to verses, now lost, ending with *Rauide* (for the syncopation in the hendecasyllabic version, see F. *ad loc.*); it is more likely than otherwise that C. gave the name its normal metrical value at its first appearance in his poetry. Thus nothing whatever makes us suppose, or even suggests, that for C. 'iambi' and 'hendecasyllabi' were interchangeable or overlapping terms. If this is so, we must ask which actual verses (assuming that they are extant) C. may have had in mind here. If these were iambic (in which term of course one must include choliambic) in metre, and objectionable to Lesbia, they must consist either of poem 8 or of poem 37. Now, 8 is either a desperate interior monologue similar in tone to poem 76, or else 'ironic' and designed to elicit Lesbia's sympathy by a kind of play-acting, as some critics have supposed (see intr. n.). In neither case is the epithet *trux* a natural one, considering the wording of the poem. But it is entirely applicable to the very next poem, poem 37; for there Lesbia is depicted, or imagined, in a guise and in a context to which she was bound to take exception. If this is the reference, then 36 and 37 are intended by C. as a pair – and placed together, it may be, rather impishly, if 36 professes to placate Lesbia's feelings. Consider also the parody of an invitation to Venus which occupies lines 12ff.: a stately beginning, with the mention of Idalium and so forth; but by a sudden anticlimax the end descends into mere squalor with 'Dyrrachium the *taberna* of the Adriatic,' which, in the context, is not far from speaking of it as a bawdy-house for sailors. Riese comments: 'Die Bewohner waren *voluptarii* und die *meretrices* zahlreich und "nusquam blandiores" (Plaut. *Men.* 261); deshalb ist Tempelkultur der Venus, obgleich nicht bekannt, doch wahrscheinlich.' It seems, rather, as though C. follows his exquisite list of temples with a deliberate plunge into a kind of bathos, where the connection with 'Venus' is little more than punning; and thus prepares the way for the following poem (poem 37) on the *salax taberna*.

1 It has been conjectured that the name Volusius conceals that of the historian Tanusius Geminus; but this is probably wrong (see F.'s n.). Nowhere is it suggested that Tanusius wrote anything in verse.
cacata carta: does this mean 'verbal diarrhoea' (Fr.) or actual defilement of the papyrus with excreta? The first interpretation, though not impossible, involves a rather violent substitution of *carta* for the words written on it, since Volusius' physical organism can hardly be thought of as producing the papyrus as well as the poem. In the second interpretation *caco* = *concaco*, as at *Apoc.* 4.3, where the late emperor Claudius is depicted as exclaiming *vae me, puto, concacavi me*, and the writer adds: *certe omnia concacavit* (notice the switch to metaphor in the comment). See intr. n., where the former interpretation is preferred (allowing for some poetic laxity in expression).

2 *solvite* (a commercial term), 'discharge.' Cf. 35.1–2 n. for the instrument of an action regarded as the agent.
puella = Lesbia (cf. poems 2, 3, 8, 11, 13, 37).

3 *sanctae*: the adjective is poetical (cf. πότνια in Greek).

5 *vibrare*, perhaps tr. 'brandish.' Often used of a lightning-flash, as at V. *Aen.*
8.524; intrans. at Cicero, *Orator* 234 *non tam vibrarent fulmina illa.*
iambos: these must surely, in the context, be verses personally offensive to
Lesbia (= *mea puella*); and the natural application is to poem 37 immediately
following (and perhaps less directly to the end of poem 8, a poem echoed at
37.12). At all events, poem 29 can be ruled out as too remote from Lesbia for the
purposes of this poem. See intr. n.

6 *electissima* (*pessimi poetae*), i.e., 'the very worst.' The superlative *electissima*
'parodies the common formula of a genuine vow' (F., quoting Eur. *IT* 21
κάλλιστον).

7 *tardipedi deo* = *Vulcano* (i.e., into the fire); there is probably no need to see a
reference to the 'dragging' (choliambic) foot of, e.g., poem 37 (cf. l. 5 *iambos*),
though of course it is tempting to do so (hardly however 'in allusion to the
halting rhythm of *Volusius*' verse,' as E. would have it). The main point of
the phrase lies in parody of the lofty style appropriate to a vow to the gods;
this begins at l. 3 and continues both here and later in the poem, especially in
lines 11–16.
daturam: *se* is understood. This ellipse is often linked to *promises*; cf. for
example Ter. *Andr.* 401 *pollicitus sum suscepturum*. Other references in F.:
Plaut. *Pseud.* 565; Cicero, *Rosc. Am.* 59, *De fin.* 5.31 (with Madvig's n.); V. *Aen.*
2.432, 4.383.

8 *infelicibus*. Festus, *s.v. infelix: felices arbores Cato dixit quae fructum ferunt,
infelices quae non ferunt.* In Virgil the olive is called *felix*, the oleaster *infelix*
(*Geo.* 2.314). Note F.'s passage from Cicero (*Rab. Perd.* 13) for the association
of *arbor infelix* with capital punishment of criminals; cf. Cicero, *Pro Milone* 33
infelicissimis lignis sem(i)ustulatum.

10 The emphasis is on *iocose lepide*: 'and she saw this vow she made to the gods as
a nice touch of wit.'

11ff. A parody (see 7 n.) of the traditional poetic invocation to a god; including
a 'catalogue' of complimentary references, here in the form of a list of places
hallowed by the divine presence (34.13–16 contain another kind of catalogue,
listing the different names and functions of the god, preceded by repeated *tu* as
the references to places here are preceded by repeated *quae*).

12 *Idalium*, with Amathus and Golgi in l. 14; all three were celebrated shrines of
Aphrodite (Venus) in Cyprus.
Urios: the location, and a fortiori the association with Venus, of this place is not
established; but the most likely site is in the vicinity of *Mons Garganus* (Monte
Gargano) between Ancona and the Apulian coast. As for the adjective *apertos*,
this seems to me to suggest simply an open roadstead, in the nautical sense, in
contrast to a safe, well-sheltered harbour. (F.'s explanation, 'exposed terrain,' is

surely misleading.) Pomponius Mela (2.4.66) mentions a *sinus* ('gulf' or here more exactly 'bight') *Urias*, which he says is *extra Sipontum et flumen Aufidum* – where *extra* should probably be taken as indicating the north side of Monte Gargano, south of which lie Sipontum and the river; and he says the bight was *asper accessu* (we think of a similar place in Virgil: *sinus et statio male fida carinis, Aen.* 2.23). At the same spot, Strabo, whose description fits that which I have just quoted, has (at 6.3.9) a certain πολισμάτιον Οὔρειον, though Ptolemy, who at 31.17 mentions both the bight and the city, refers to the latter as Ὕριον. If these sources suggest *Urium* as the name in Latin, why does C. use the form *Urii?* It may be that the two forms coexisted; Pomponius Mela (as Fr. pointed out) himself uses *Thurium* as the name of the place usually known as Thurii.

m's omission of *ad* is careless, but R^2's correcting variant (from Virgil? See p. 42.) is followed by m^1. There is a characteristic restoration of *ad* by m^2, simply in order to preserve by the side of a correction the original *R* reading; we find many instances of this doglike devotion on m^2's part.

13 *Ancona:* Greek accusative, from nom. *Ancon* (Latin form, *Ancona*). If the above explanation of *Urios* is correct (see 12 n.), there may be a particular reason (of contrast) why C. mentions Ancona (which has a good, well-sheltered natural harbour, a very scarce thing on the Adriatic coast of Italy) immediately after the adjective *apertos* (which gains added point).
Cnidum: in Caria; one of its temples was renowned for a statue of the goddess by Praxiteles.

14 *Golgos:* the cult of Aphrodite, established at Golgi in Cyprus, was later transferred to Paphos (also in Cyprus, but surely not the same place as Golgi, *pace* Baehrens; the latter is still *von umstrittener Lage,* as Kr. remarked, but seems to have been close to Amathus).
On the emendation and its history, see 64.96 n.

15 *Dyrrachium:* on the eastern side of the Adriatic, opposite to Brundisium.
tabernam, 'entrepôt, trading city,' as well as 'inn' or 'tavern.' See 37.1 n.
F. drily remarks that '<its> cult of Venus, which is mentioned only here, is not surprising in a large seaport.'
Hadria: a (poetically) 'convenient alternative' (F.) to *mare Hadriaticum.* There was a town called Hadria (or Adria) near the mouth of the Po; it gave its (Greek) name to the sea. Clearly this line contains a humorous anticlimax and surprise, after the last few lines with their parody of the solemn formulae of address to a god. But notice also 37.1 and 10; it is conceivable that C. somewhat impishly drags in the word *taberna* here, if poem 37 = *truces iambi,* as suggested above (see n. on l. 5).

16 The technical terms of commerce ('received and duly credited') blend well with the mention, in the previous line, of a busy commercial city.

17 *illepidum, invenustum:* cf. 10.4.

18 *at vos interea*: formula of transition; cf. 14.21 n. for the adversative (rather than temporal) sense of *interea*. For the transitional *at*, cf. 27.5 (*at vos*); 3.13 and 28.14 (*at vobis*); 8.14 and 19 (*at tu*).

It is hard to explain R^2's *al. venire* (followed by m^2). At all events, G^2 failed to take it from m^2, either because he regarded it as unsatisfactory or because this is one of the very rare instances where the m^2 reading appears to have been unknown to G^2, and may just possibly have been entered after G^2 corrected G on m/m^2.

19 *ruris et inficetiarum*: cf. 22.14.

20 For 'cyclic' repetition of the first line at the end of the poem, cf. poems 16, 52, 57.

Comfort, H. 1929. 'An Interpretation of C. XXXVI,' *CP* 24: 176–82.
Lackenbacher, H. 1935. 'Das 36. Gedicht des C.,' *WS* 53: 156–9.
Buchheit, V. 1959. 'C.s Dichterkritik in c. 36,' *Hermes* 87: 309–27.
Clarke, G.W. 1968. 'The Burning of Books and C. 36,' *Latomus* 27: 575–80.
Ross, D.O. 1973. 'Uriosque apertos, A Catullan Gloss,' *Mn* 26: 60–2.
Østerud, S. 1978. 'Sacrifice and Bookburning in C.'s Poem 36,' *Hermes* 106: 138–55.
Morgan, M. Gwyn. 1980. 'C. and the Annales Volusi,' *QUCC* 4: 59–67.
Townend, G.B. 1980. 'A Further Point in C.'s Attack on Volusius,' *G&R* 27: 134–6.

37

Structure: (5 + 5) + 6 + 4.
For the relationship of this poem to poem 36, see the intr. n. there. The connection of the two poems is suggested also by F. (though he does not print poem 37) and by Q. This poem is further linked, by its four concluding lines, to poem 39 (see nn. there, including the intr. n.). Q. believes poem 39 to be the earlier of the two; see however my n. on 39.1.

1 *taberna*: for *tabernae* as haunts of prostitution (and in this way associated with 'Venus,' 36.15), see Prop. 4.8, and also the *Copa* (*Appendix Vergiliana*), where there is a triad of tutelary deities appropriate to *tabernae*: Ceres, Venus, and Bromius (= Bacchus).
contubernales, a word originally derived from *taberna* = (military) tent, and hence literally 'tent companions,' but now in a general sense either 'fellow-soldiers' or (hence) 'drinking companions.' C. of course plays on the word's etymology; so too does Caelius Rufus in a speech quoted by Quintilian 4.2.123–4 (at a military crisis, C. Antonius is found drunk in his headquarters tent; around him are some young women – *praeclarae contubernales*, as Caelius says).

2 *p. fratres* = <the Palatine temple of> Castor and Pollux, who are usually depicted as wearing prominent caps, *pillei*.

4 *quidquid est*: for the idiom, cf. 31.14 (compare also *quantum est* + genitive, 3.2 and 9.10).

5 *confutuere*, like *constuprare*, *concacare* (see the passage in *Apoc.* cited at 36.1 n., esp. the phrase *omnia concacavit*), *conscribere* (and the *conscribillent* of 25.11), contains the notion of doing something on a large scale, 'in a big way,' 'wholesale.'

   hircos: it has been suggested, without any real evidence, that *caper* = an 'entire' he-goat, *hircus* a 'neutered' goat; but Plaut. *Merc.* 272 (*ego illunc hircum castrari volo*) disproves this notion, since it is hardly possible to take *hircum* proleptically, as meaning 'into a neutered state.' Where *hircus* is employed as a word of abuse, it implies an offensive armpit smell (69.6 *caper* = 71.1 *hircus*), with the corollary that women avoid its possessors. In other words, each of the *contubernales* owns a harem, excluding as undesirable all the other males of the herd.

6 *an* = 'or perhaps,' of 'deliberate vagueness' (L., who compared Cicero, *Ad Fam.* 7.9.3 *Cn. Octavius est an Cn. Cornelius quidam*, *De fin.* 2.104 *Simonides an quis alius*).

   sedetis: cf. 8 *sessores*, 14 *consedit*; C. (in this poem) harps on the word *sedere*, which here means 'hang about,' 'lounge about,' with sexual indulgence in view. Cf. Donatus on Ter. *Adelphoe* 672: *sedere proprium verbum ignaviae et cessationis*.

9 *atqui putate*: 'why, you'd *better* suppose so' (ref. to 7 *non putatis?*).

   G²'s abolition of the gap in the word *atqui* betokens, not any capacity or tendency to emend, but merely loyalty to *m* (see App. Crit. and cf. also l. 17). On the other hand, he has sense enough to decline to follow *m*'s absurd blunder (*amabiliter*) in l. 12 (and at 8.5, where *m* commits the same error).

10 *sopionibus*: Kr. cites *CIL* IV 1700 (a *graffito*) *diced vobis Sineros et sopio <est?>* with the following addition in another hand: *ut merdas edatis qui scripseras sopionis*. In Sacerdos *GLK* 6.461 this rare word is interpreted as = *penis*; at Petron. 22.1, where the Ms reading is *sopitionibus pinxit*, K. Müller prefers to read *sopionibus*, citing this passage of C.

   scribam = *conscribam*; cf. l. 5 n.

11 See App. Crit. For the dative *mi* = *mea* or *meus*, cf. 21.11 n.

12 Repeats 8.5, with the slight change from *nobis* to *tantum*.

13 *pro qua* must mean 'defending whom' (from the assaults or insults of others), not 'pursuing whom' (as a lover).

14 *consedit*: the verb *considere* means to settle down, or establish oneself somewhere. In Virgil's *Eclogues* it is used three times of shepherds (3.55, 5.3,

7.1); in military language it means 'to occupy a position.' Here C. uses it quasi-technically to denote or suggest installing oneself, or 'setting up shop,' as a prostitute – a rhetorical exaggeration as blatant as that by which in poem 58 he depicts Lesbia as indulging in promiscuous sexual activity *in quadriviis et angiportis.*

15–16 A second (and lower) category of lovers is added, as C. adds fuel to the fire of his indignation.

et quidem, 'and what is more ...' Cf. Cicero, *Phil.* 2.43 *duo milia iugerum ... adsignasti et quidem immunia.*

16 *semitarii* (from *semita,* 'lane,' 'alley'; cf. 58.4; see n. on l. 14). Observe the acuteness with which Coluccio Salutati (*R²*) substituted this word, which is otherwise unknown (but obviously correct here) for *R's semithani.*

17 *unus,* 'just any' (cf. 22.10 n. L. wished to add to this Cicero, *Ad Att.* 9.10.2 *Pompeium tamquam unus manipularis secutus,* and *De or.* 1.132 *non mihi modo, qui sicut unus paterfamilias his de rebus* [i.e., *de elocutione*] *loquor, sed etiam ipsi illi Roscio;* both citations are relevant, but I do not agree with L. that the sense in the *present* passage is merely 'one of them,' as it probably is in Cicero, *Pro Milone* 65 *uno de illis*). Note that *une* should not be taken closely with *tu praeter omnes,* since it lies on the other side of the natural break in the rhythm of the line.

18 The rabbit appears on some coins from Spain. The adjective *cuniculosae* (perhaps based on the lore brought out of Spain by Veranius; see 9.6–8) is not merely picturesque; it joins *capillatis* to suggest softness, both by sense and by sound (cf. especially poem 25).

fili, when it is added to the name of a country, is contemptuous (cf. also *terrae filius*).

19 *opaca,* 'bushy' (lit. 'shady').

bonum (cf. l. 14 *boni beatique*), 'a person of rank.'

facit, 'sets a value upon <him as>,' 'makes him out to be,' or 'gives him the label of' (*bonus*). This is a common meaning of *facere;* cf. (e.g.) 10.17.

20 The implications of this line are made clear in 39.17ff.

Hibera ... urina: notice the poetical condensation, or compression, of meaning in the adjective *Hibera,* which really stands for *sicut apud Hiberos mos est.* Is this again derived from Veranius' report on his travels in Spain (see n. on l. 18)? But there exist independent testimonies to the same effect (poem 39 nn.).

Herescu, N. 1960. 'Autour de la Salax Taberna (C., 37),' *Hommages à L. Herrmann.* Brussels: 431–5.

Alfonsi, L. 1978. 'Varia – II,' *GIF* 30: 294–7.

Booth, A.D. 1985. 'Une de capillatis ... Egnati,' *EMC/CV* 29: 111–20.

38

Structure: 3 + 3 + 2.

A complaint (cf. poems 30 and 60) to a close friend (*amores*, l. 6 n.) of neglect in time of mental or, less probably, physical distress. To C. himself a similar request for consolation and support is made by Manlius and answered in 68.1–40.

Q. Cornificius had a career in public life: we hear of him as quaestor in 48 BC, which means that he could be virtually a contemporary of C., possibly a shade older (rather than younger, as F. suggests). He outlived C.; in the end, as proconsul, he died in battle, abandoned by his soldiers, whom he described contemptuously as 'hares in helmets.' He had literary interests, and himself composed poetry: Ovid, *Tr.* 2.435–6, includes him in a list of Latin poets, where he stands among the neoterics (authors of light and amorous poetry); see S.G. Owen's excellent notes on the passage. See E. Courtney *FLP* frs. 1–3 and intr. n., p. 225. On the question whether or not the language used in the poem is or is not particularly associated with illness, three expressions should be examined: *male est* (with dat.); *laboriosus*; and *allocutio*. (i) On *male est*, F. gives several quotations; but he does not notice that the girl who says *excrucior: male mihist* at Plaut. *Cist.* 59 is not ill but in love, nor does he quote Cicero, *Verr.* 2.4.95 *numquam tam male est Siculis quin aliquid facete et commode dicant*, on which see n. on l. 1; (ii) on *laboriosus*, see l. 2 n.; (iii) *allocutio* generally refers to comforting words and naturally applies to a number of situations of which illness is one, bereavement another. At Hor. *Epod.* 13.18 *deformis aegrimoniae dulcibus alloquiis*, the choice of the word *aegrimoniae* makes this look like comforting the sick. But presently we realize that the comforts prescribed are wine and song; and so it becomes evident that here, as elsewhere, the vocabulary of illness has been transferred to a case of low spirits.

1 *male est*: a very general expression, not at all limited to physical or mental illness; cf. Plaut. *Cist.* 59, of a person in love (not ill, as F. seems to suggest); and also Cicero, *Verr.* 2.4.95 *numquam tam male est Siculis* ('they are never in such a bad way') *quin aliquid facete et commode dicant*.

1ᵃ In *R*, there are two stages of emendation by *R*²: (i) repair (*ale* to *male*), (ii) expunction of the entire line.

2 The introduction of *est* after *male* is an original discovery by *R*² (followed by *m*, as is usual in instances of this kind). The correction is incomplete, which is perhaps why *G*² does not follow it. See W.G. Hale, *CR* 3 (1903): 246.

It now seems to me that the line is better without the addition of *est* after *et*, even though Kr. describes the hiatus after *hercule* as 'scarcely tolerable.' To introduce *est* gives a false stress, of an awkward sort; as for the hiatus, this kind of hiatus is quite possible in C., especially after an expletive (see 3.16 n.).

laboriose: *laborare* is certainly used of suffering (as F. says, quoting Cicero, *Ad Fam.* 7.26.1 and 9.23 – similarly *laboriosus*, of sickness: Cicero, *Phil.* 11.8), but also of love: cf. Hor. *Od.* 1.17.19, Prop. 1.6.23

3 *et*, 'and indeed' (Kr.); see on 17.15.

4 For parenthetical *quod minimum est* (here = 'the least you can do'), cf. Suet. *Tib.* 50 *ut relegatae, quod minimum est, offici aut humanitatis aliquid impertiret.*

5 *allocutione*: comforting words, as here, or actions, or even (as at Hor. *Epod.* 13.18) *things*: i.e., practical consolations (*vino cantuque*). Literally, of course, it means 'speaking to, addressing.'

6 *sic meos amores* is clearly elliptical. The difficulty about the tr. supported by Kr. and others ('love' rather than 'beloved person') is that the *plural* of *amor* never seems to bear this meaning elsewhere. If *amores* is personal and concrete, it must mean (as F. points out) 'to think that my beloved Cornificius <should behave so!>' At all events, since ll. 4–5 clearly have to do with Cornificius' neglect of C. himself, it would involve an impossible change of direction to see in *amores* a reference to the very different accusation of rivalling C. in Lesbia's affections.

7 Not *paulum-quid ... allocutionis*, as subject of *iubet* – an idea conceived by Lachmann and apparently accepted by F. in the latter part of his n. – but rather *paulum quid-lubet* (or *quidlubet*) *allocutionis*. The phrase *paulum quid* (allegedly equivalent to *paulum nescioquid*, or to *paulum quidlubet* itself) seems to have no parallels at all. For the ellipse of the verb ('Give me ...'), cf., perhaps, 55.10 (where see n.).

8 Cornificius was in all likelihood a fellow-poet of C., and as such will certainly have admired the 'Cean dirges' (Hor. *Od.* 2.1.38) of Simonides of Ceos. F. cites Quintilian's judgment (10.1.64) *praecipua eius in commovenda miseratione virtus*, as well as Dion. Hal. *De imit.* 2.2.26 on his 'simple pathos.'

Impellizzeri, S. 1937. 'A C. 38, 7–8,' *RIGI* 21: 168.
Copley, F.O. 1956. 'C., c. 38,' *TAPA* 87: 125–9.
Baker, S. 1960. 'C. 38,' *CP* 55: 37–8.
Rawson, E. 1978. 'The Identity Problems of Q. Cornificius,' *CQ* 28: 188–201.

39

Structure: 8 + 8 + 5 (second and third sections introduced by *quare* and *nunc* respectively).

For Egnatius, see the last four lines of poem 37, where he is singled out, among Lesbia's lovers, for the curious habit (attributed to Spaniards) of cleaning his teeth with urine – a practice which is here elaborated on, as explaining the foolish grin which he displays on all occasions (including the most unsuitable) in order to display the whiteness of his teeth. Possibly C.'s Egnatius could be one who, according to Plutarch (*Crass.* 27), escaped from the massacre at Carrhae. Appian (*BC* 4.21) has two Egnatii, father and son, who were put to death in the proscription of 43 BC. It is quite likely that the son was identical with the survivor of Carrhae, and it may be that the father was the Egnatius who, as a junior senator, had served on the jury at the trial of Oppianicus (Cicero, *Clu.* 135). Macrobius, *S.* 6.5.2, mentions – and quotes – an Egnatius who wrote a poem *De rerum natura*. Since he is named in company with Lucretius and Cornificius (see poem 38, intr. n.), he may well have been roughly contemporary with C. The Egnatius mentioned here should probably be identified with this philosopher-poet, in part because of his long hair and beard (on which see 37.17–19), since these attributes were at this period peculiar to philosophers (Hor. *S.* 2.3.35 *sapientem pascere barbam*). There is no reason why, after being in his early youth a philosopher and a poet, he should not have fought at Carrhae a little later. The 'Spanishness' that C. attributes to him should not be taken too seriously. Although it is possible that a man of genuinely Spanish extraction might have found his way into Roman society, particularly in the capacity of a poet (Balbus, the associate of Caesar and Pompey, came from Gades), nevertheless C.'s gibe may merely mean that Egnatius' family had, for example, business interests in Spain. See also Wiseman 1987: 140.

1 It is impossible to say with certainty that poem 37 was composed before this lampoon; but one way to account for the making of poem 39 is to suppose that C. was called upon by his literary friends to explain the last four lines of poem 37, where Egnatius is introduced as a 'Spaniard' (the name is in fact Italian: originally Samnite, then – after the Social War – Roman). See intr. n.
candidos: cf. Cicero, *TD* 5.46 *haec, quae sunt minima, tamen bona dicantur necesse est: candiduli dentes, venusti oculi.*

2 *usque quaque*, 'all over the place.'
 X must have had something like $^{(al.)}_{seu}$ *sei*. Probably *A* (= *O*) simply had *sei*, and *seu* was *X*'s mistake at first, corrected by himself. Notice, once more, how *X* may represent a correction as a variant; see Intr., p. 28.
 For *rei subsellium* cf. Caelius ap. Cicero, *Ad Fam.* 8.8.1 *subsellia rei.* To work on the emotions of the court, even to the shedding of tears, especially in a peroration, was thought to be particularly effective in speeches for the defence.

4 It may be that *X*, who had some critical power, instinctively wrote *pii*, following metre and sense – then glanced back at *A* and saw that in fact the reading of *A*

was *impii* (= *O*). *R*², faced with an obvious lacuna in *R*, probably here at least consulted *X* and found *pii* there. See above, p. 39, on this passage.

6 *quidquid est*, 'whatever *is happening*,' 'whatever the <present> circumstances are.' Contrast Plaut. *Mil.* 311, where the tense of the verb is future: *quidquid est, mussitabo*, 'whatever may happen, I'll hold my tongue.' Not equivalent to *quidquid id est* ('be that as it may').

7 *morbum*, 'weakness.' F. credibly suggests that this is a distortion of the phrase (often in Plautus) *hunc habet morem* ('that's just his way'); *Capt.* 232, *Curc.* 377, *Men.* 338, 573.

8 C.'s condemnation is, as usual, visited more sharply upon lapses from good taste than upon unethical conduct, in spite of the genuine pathos underlying lines 4–5. See F.'s long n. here on the meaning of *urbanum*.

9 *monendum est te mihi*: this impersonal use of the gerund (governing a direct object, here *te*) is, though rare in all periods, not uncommon in Lucr., who uses it nine times.

    Mähly's order *est <te>* is better; it is characteristic of C. to place two pronouns together (cf. 10.1 *Varus me meus*; also Cicero, *In Cat.* 1.25 *ad hanc te amentiam natura peperit*).

10 *urbanus*: not as it is used in l. 8 (where it is an adjective denoting a *quality*; see n.), but in the simple and literal sense, 'a man of Rome.'

11 See App. Crit.: *parcus* would be out of place among the otherwise 'physical' epithets of ll. 11–12. Further, in terms of rhetoric we need a climax (l. 12 being the third *colon* in a triad), not a contrast such as would be implied between *parcus* and *obesus*.

    The variant *al. etruscus* in *R*² (copied by *m*²) must be taken to derive from *X*. It also agrees with the text of Petrarch (see App. Crit.). Now, Petrarch's citations of C. invariably adhere to the tradition represented by *X*, not to the readings of *O*. (For three proofs of this see the Introduction, p. 27: 35.4, 39.16, 65.5.) When I wrote *CE* I entertained the possibility that Petrarch did not own (as Ullman believed) but consulted *X*. More recently it has seemed to me possible that Petrarch might have been responsible for some readings in the margins of *A*, or his copy of *A*. These marginal readings could have been handed down to *X*. Now that Dr McKie has expertly separated the various strands, both original and inherited, that will have made up the fabric of *X*, it is greatly to be hoped that he or another will examine, with an open mind, the possible contribution of Petrarch to *X* (or *A*) in the light of Petrarch's known ways of dealing with other manuscripts of classical authors. For, so far as we yet know, there were few indeed among Humanists of that generation who even in small matters brought to their texts the incisive correcting spirit of which many traces are to be seen in our reconstructed *X*. (That Petrarch did not actually own *X* may now be taken as established by McKie himself; see p. 186 of his dissertation.)

12 *m* originally read *lamuinus*; the virgula on the letter *i*, in its present position, is certainly original. Subsequently, either *m* or *m*² corrected to *lamivinus* by putting a caret mark below and also an *i* above, with a fresh virgula.

14 *puriter* = *pure*, i.e., with clean water; Fest. 293 L *pure lautum*] *aqua pura lavatum*.

lavit, 3rd conj. form for *lavat*. Why does C. prefer it here? It seems to me to be chiefly a matter of sound: the combination of vowels and consonants in *puriter lavit dentes* helps, if read aloud, to suggest the operation of teeth-cleaning better than if *lavat* were substituted. Other eds. either find that the words *puriter lavit* have 'an old-fashioned ring' (Q.), or speculate that they contain 'an echo of a religious formula' (F.).

m follows *R* into error, but sees at once that *R*² has already inserted a correction, and follows it (*m*¹).

16 Geremia (Hieremias) reads *risu* against *O*'s aberrant *risti*, which must surely be an error of *O* himself rather than something that *O* found in *A*. Contrast Benzo at 35.2 (q.v.), exhibiting a reading most probably inherited by *O*. McKie (1977: 93) opines, with high probability, that both Geremia and Benzo used *V*; see Intr., p. 25.

inepto ... ineptior: a typically Catullan repetition; cf. 22.14, 23.18, 27.4, 99.2 and 14, etc. For the sentiment cf. Menand. *monost.* 144 Jaekel (= 88 M) on γέλως ἄκαιρος, and cf. 165 Jaekel (= 108 M). Cf. also Quint. 6.1.38 on those who *intempestive renident* in court.

19 *russam*, colloq. *defricare*: the same verb (usual, no doubt, in describing the cleaning of teeth) is used at 37.20. It is much easier to suppose that the substitution for it of *pumicare* by Apuleius was due to faulty memory than that *defricare* might have lingered in a copyist's mind from 37.20 and consequently caused the true reading, *pumicare* on this interpretation, to drop out of the tradition. (Among other things, the latter view, put forward by L., begs the question of prior composition; cf. l. 1 n.)

For the custom itself, E. quotes Diodorus Siculus 5.33.5 and Strabo 3.4.16.

20 *vester*: here simply = *tuus*, with no plural implication, despite F. (who has a long n.); cf. *te* in the next line. See A.E. Housman, '*Vester = tuus*,' *CQ* 5 (1909): 244–8, an article based on this passage and on 99.1–6.

Small, J.P. 1982. 'Verism and the Vernacular: Late Roman Republican Portraiture and C.,' *PP* 202: 47–71.

Brugnoni, G. 1991. 'C. 39.11,' *RCCM* 33: 81–3. [Throws doubt on the reading *pinguis*.]

40

Structure: balanced (4 + 4).

An attack on Ravidus (unknown) for seeking to rival C. in the eyes of his beloved (*meos amores*). Most of the lampoon is given up to the threat of what C. will do to Ravidus; the reason for it is withheld until the penultimate line. Ravidus is told that he has exposed himself to being pilloried, or worse, at C.'s hands. Despite F., there is surely a clear echo of the famous epigram by Archilochus on Lycambes (fr. 88 Diehl = 172 West: 'Who has driven you out of your wits? You will be a laughing-stock to the whole populace'). The light-hearted, teasing note (of lines 5–6, for example) would be surprising if the beloved were Lesbia; but there are indications that it is, in fact, Juventius. Although the word *amores* in a 'concrete' sense, referring to a person, can be used of a *scortum* (see poem 6 and poem 10, *tui/sui amores*), and also of Acme in poem 45, and even of Thetis in relation to Jupiter (64.27), nevertheless the formulation *mei amores* is elsewhere in C. applied *only* to Juventius – twice at least, in poems 15 and 21, apart from the present passage; excluding, it must be said, the doubtfully 'personal' use of *mei amores* in poem 38. So far as we can be sure, *mei amores* is never applied to Lesbia; and the evidence, so far, points to Juventius. If so, we have already found a strong link between poems 40 and 15. But between these two poems there are in fact other links; for example, only in them does C. use the word *vecors*; only in them, the expression *mala mens*; and (though this is less significant) in both of them the person addressed is characterized as *miser* or *misellus*. And besides these verbal similarities there are others of a non-verbal kind: poem 15, like poem 40, is in hendecasyllables, is addressed to a named person, and ends with a threat of punishment in the event of sexual misbehaviour with the poet's beloved. All three of these also appear in poem 21, which we have already mentioned as a Juventius-poem containing the phrase *mei amores*. From all these similarities it is reasonable to conclude that poem 40 should be numbered among the group of poems concerned with Juventius.

If this is so, it will be worth while to consider whether in *longa poena* (l. 8) C. is not covertly alluding to the physical aspect of the sort of penalty, for proposing to interfere with Juventius, that he makes explicit in the *percurrent mugiles* of 15.19. (A similarly violent punishment is threatened at the end of poem 21, which, as we said, is on the same theme.) Of course, *longa* may imply no more than *omnia saecula* and *fama anus* in 78[b].3–4; but the latter poem is about a *pura puella*, not about Juventius, and the peculiar idiom, characteristic (it would appear) of the Juventius group of poems, is not in point there. It must also be admitted that C. is above all a literary man, and his revenge will *in fact* be a literary one in all of these instances; but the *figures* of *irrumatio*, *pedicatio*, *mugiles*, and so forth, whether C. affects to be the doer or (as at 28.9–10) the victim, are so frequent in his light verse that the presence of double entendre may well be suspected. Otherwise, why the rather tame adjective *longa*, rather than *saeva*, or *digna* (for example)? Archilochus, it may be noted, says emphatically πολὺς ἀστοῖσι φαίνεαι γέλως. But on one level – the power of verse to immortalize for good or ill – the simpler meaning of *longa* is there to be read, and no accretion of ambiguity should be allowed to obscure it.

1 In *m* the rubricator has taken a carelessly written small *q* for an *e*, and has accordingly inserted a large *E*, within which however the small *q* is still visible. Hence the nonsensical *Eue*.

   mala mens = derangement, sickness of mind. Cf. 15.14. For its opposite, *bona mens* (= sanity), F. quotes Sen. *De benef.* 2.14.3, Ov. *F.* 4.366.

   Raude: V has *ravide*. The alternative to reducing this to two syllables by 'syncopation' (cf. Plaut. *Bacch.* 276 *avidi-audi*) is to suppose hypermetric elision of the final *e*, but this never occurs in hendecasyllables.

3 *non bene*: not properly invoked, i.e., under a wrong formula (cf. 34.21–2). Kr. quotes Plin. *NH* 28.11 (in a prayer) *ne quod verborum praetereatur aut praeposterum dicatur* for the conceit 'What god put this idea into your head?' cf. *Il.* 17.469–70; Archilochus (fr. 45 D = 210 West) adds the refinement 'what god, *angry with you*, ...? (τίς ἄρα δαίμων καὶ τεοῦ χωλούμενος;).

   quis deus, not *qui deus*, is normal: see F.'s n. on 61.46. (F. points out that on the other hand Latin always says *scire qui sit*: cf. 17.22.)

   With *advocatus*, *m* appears to stumble into the truth; see l. 1 for his haste and carelessness; also l. 8, where *m* at first writes *poemea*, later expunging the second *e*.

4 *vecordem*: cf. 15.14.

5 *ut* is elliptical: 'are you doing this in order to ...?'

   in ora: in such expressions as this the plural is always used with verbs of motion, the singular with verbs of being, or 'static' verbs, which would require the ablative (*in ore*) instead of the accusative, as here.

6 *quid vis?*, 'what is your object?' (cf. Hor. *S.* 2.6.29 *quid tibi vis?*).

   qualubet, 'somehow or other' (cf. 76.14); here rather more strongly, 'by any means whatsoever,' 'at all costs.'

   notus: cf. Cicero, *Cael.* 31 *cum Clodia, muliere non solum nobili sed etiam nota.*

7 *amores*, in the personal and 'concrete' sense of a beloved person; probably Juventius (see intr. n.).

8 *longa ... poena*: see intr. n.

The correction from the unmetrical *poema* to *poena* is easy, and we are not forced by m^1's variant *al. pena* to suppose that R^2 in his first recension drew *p(o)ena* from X; cf. 42.3, where m^1 has *al. iocum*.

Hendrickson, G.L. 1925. 'Archilochus and C.,' *CP* 20: 155–7.
Németh, B. 1974. 'Zur Analyse von C., c. 40,' *WZRostock* 23: 237–43.

41 and 43

Two squibs, ostensibly directed against Ameana (?), a woman of easy morals and the mistress of Mamurra (*decoctor Formianus*, 41.4 n. and 43.5). It is not easy to assign a date to them. What is certain is that C. has heard gossip in the *provincia* to the effect that A. is as pretty as his Lesbia (43.6–7). This makes it very unlikely that the province in question is Gallia Narbonensis, as E. supposed; it must surely be the cisalpine *provincia*, and the most probable occasion, some visit to that province by Mamurra in Caesar's train while Caesar was wintering there during the years of his Gallic campaigns. The place could be Verona, possibly at the time when Caesar forgave C. for the slur in poem 29 (see nn. there) and resumed his ties of hospitality with C.'s father (Suet. *Iul.* 73). But if so, these two poems must have been composed appreciably after poem 29 itself, which, as we saw, cannot be earlier than the latter part of 55 BC. It should be noted that poem 11, another poem referring – like poem 29 – to Britain, contains C.'s bitter farewell to Lesbia; yet in poem 43 C. is still unwilling to hear unfavourable comparisons of her looks with those of another woman, and she is still *Lesbia nostra*; the fact that the same phrase is used in the sadly dismissive poem 58, in order to recall times and feelings now past, hardly endorses K.'s view (43.7 n.) that here too C. speaks of her with melancholy remembrance, and still less his alternative explanation, that C. has 'patched up' his relationship with her. If she is still in his good graces, a slightly earlier date may then have to be sought. The fact that M. is scoffed at as a *decoctor* does not necessarily reflect the same situation as that in 114.5–6, the context of which (his rich estate at Firmum) is absent here. In the end it is not clear whether the primary target is A. herself, or M., or (by indirection) Caesar.

41

Structure: balanced (4 + 4).

1 See App. Crit. The problem of the name is virtually insoluble, but from 43.6 we can be sure that the girl lived in Gallia Cisalpina. See intr. n.

2 *tota*, 'all of . . .' i.e., 'no less than . . .'

4 is repeated at 43.5. Horace refers to Formiae as *urbs Mamurrarum* (*S.* 1.5.37); cf. Pliny, *NH* 36.48 *Mamurram, Formiis natum, equitem Romanum, praefectum fabrum C. Caesaris in Gallia.*

decoquere (colloquial) = go bankrupt; not quite the same as *conturbare* (5.11 *conturbabimus*), which 'is a technical term for fraudulent bankruptcy with concealment of assets' (F., note *ad loc.*).

5–7 The procedure for dealing with *furiosi* (insane persons) is not relevant to the state of a woman, who would always be under some kind of *tutela*; this is made clear in F.'s note, which is largely directed against the mistaken view held by Kr. and earlier editors. F. is right to add that, even if the point of the passage is not a technical one in the legal sphere, any person who has suddenly become insane needs the care of his or her relatives.

8 *aes imaginosum*, '(polished) bronze, full of images,' i.e., her mirror. (A brilliant emendation; *V* has *et* for *aes.*) P. Beroaldus (*Annotationes Centum*, 1488: c 3) read *solet haec imaginosum*, but perceived *imaginosum* to be a 'novum quidem, sed elegans' way of referring to a *speculum*. See Gaisser 1993: 325 n. 111.

Silvered mirrors were first invented by Pasiteles in the time of Pompey the Great (i.e., approximately in C.'s own generation) according to Pliny, *NH* 33.9.130 (quoted by B.): *(specula) optima apud maiores (nostros) erant Brundisina, stagno et aere mixtis. praelata sunt argentea: primus fecit Pasiteles Magni Pompei aetate.* Cf. also Seneca *NQ* 1.17. 'Bronze is the mirror of the form, wine of the mind' (Aesch. frag. 384, quoted by E.). Q. observes the ascent from a coarse lampoon to 'something near to poetry' in this final phrase. He also well suggests (n. on l. 8) that 'the circumlocution "image-filled bronze" is probably intended as an improvement on Callimachus' description of a mirror as "translucent bronze" (*Hymn* 5.21 διαυγέα χαλκόν).'

Deroux, C. 1969. 'C. et Ameana,' *Latomus* 28: 1060–4.
Forsyth, P.Y. 1977. 'The Ameana Cycle of C.,' *CW* 70: 445–50.
Skinner, M.B. 1978–9. 'Ameana, puella defututa,' *CJ* 74: 110–14.
Bishop, J.D. 1979. 'C. 41,' *SLLRH* 1. Brussels: 217–28.
McDermott, W.C. 1984. 'C., Clodia and Ameana,' *Maia* 36: 3–11.

<h1 style="text-align:center">42</h1>

Structure: balanced (6 + 6) + (8 + 4).

The poem is neatly versified (see intr. n. to poem 32). Notice particularly the use made of word repetition.

H. Usener ('Italische Volksjustiz,' *RhM* 56 [1901]: 1–28) was the first to describe poem 42 as a *flagitatio*, in the technical sense. The chosen target

– thief, perhaps, or debtor – was harassed by the shouting and abuse of an importunate mob. See Fraenkel 1961.

1 *hendecasyllabi* (cf. 12.10) were on the whole selected for light-hearted abuse; for more serious attacks, C. is apt to name *iambi*. See the intr. n. to poem 36.

2 A typically Catullan exercise in emphasis and cumulative exaggeration: notice (i) *quot* followed by *quotquot*, (ii) *omnes* at both beginning and end of the line, (iii) correspondence between the word and the metrical foot, for heavy emphasis (cf. 2.9).

3 *iocum*, used of a person = 'laughing-stock,' as in Petronius 57.4, or (more appropriately here) 'object of contempt,' especially a woman's contempt, as in Propertius 2.24.16.

5 *pugillaria* (the usual form is *pugillares*) = *codicilli*, l. 11 = *tabellae*, 50.2; so called because they could be held in the hand. Ephemeral jottings of any kind, and notes requiring a quick reply, were consigned to these tablets; for a full description, see F.'s long n.

6 For the idiom in *si pati potestis*, F. compares *si dis placet* ('indignant') and 56.6 *si placet Dionae*. For a similarly compressed expression cf. 29.5 and 9 *haec videbis et feres?*
   flagitatio (see intr. n.) was a noisy business (Plaut. *Pseud.* 556 *clamore magno et multo*).

7 *R²'s illa* may be original; but it may just as easily be regarded as the result of an erasure of the virgula in *X*, which was ignored by *GR* under the influence of *quam* (the very fact which presumably caused the error in the first place).

8 *turpe*: neut. as adv., a borrowing from Greek idiom; cf. 51.5, 61.7.
   incedere: gait was regarded as a clue to character: cf. Cicero, *Cael.* 49 *incessu*; contrast *CIL* I² 1211 *incessu commodo*; Ov. *AA* 3.299 *est et in incessu pars non contempta decoris*; Sen. *Ep.* 52.12 *impudicum incessus ostendit*, 66.5 *modestus incessus et compositus*.
   mimice: like an actress (*mima*) in vulgar farces (*mimi*).
   moleste, 'tiresomely, disagreeably' (cf. Quint. 11.3.183 *pronuntiatio molesta*).

11 *putida*, 'disgusting' (the original meaning, 'stinking,' having been by this time lost sight of in such applications as this; cf. *Catalepton* 12.1 *superbe Noctuine, putidum caput*).

12 The omitted line is supplied by *R²* – probably (as with 61.142–6 and 64.353–6) after consulting *X*, but in this case just possibly after reflection on l. 20.

13 *lutum, lupanar*: cf. (as a term of personal abuse) Apul. *Apol.* 74 *lustrum, lupanar*; for *lutum* in this sense, cf. Plaut. *Pers.* 406–8 *oh, lutum lenonium, / commixtum caeno sterculinum publicum, / inpure, inhoneste, iniure, inlex, labes popli*, and (less picturesquely) Cicero *In Pis.* 62 *o tenebrae, o lutum, o sordes*.

14 *si potest quid esse* (*perditius*): for *si quid est* with the comparative, cf. 13.10,
   23.13, 82.2; *V's potes* is understandable, but wrong.
15 *tamen*, 'after all.' *hoc* = what you have tried so far.
16 *potest* <*fieri*>: cf. 72.7 for this ellipse.
17 *ferreo* = *duro* ('brazen' is the usual English equivalent). Notice the growling
   effect of the *r*'s in 16–17 (F.); cf. Lucr. 5.1064–5.
18 *si potestis* really = 'to see if'; i.e., indicative loosely used for subjunctive.
24 *pudica et proba* (ironical): cf. Hor. *Epod.* 17.40.

Perrotta, G. 1931. 'Il carme 42 di C.,' *A&R* 12: 45–58.
Fraenkel, E. 1961. 'Two Poems of C.,' *JRS* 51: 46–53 [Poems 42, 8.]
Augello, G. 1991. 'C. e il folklore. La flagitatio nel c. 42,' *Studi di filologia classica in
   onore di C. Monaco*. Palermo: 723–35.

43

Structure: (with the punctuation in the text) 4 + 4, with repetition of the
fourth line of poem 41 as the fifth line here.
The main *rhetorical* point of the poem is the extended *litotes* in lines 2–4.
On the interpretation in general see the intr. n. to poem 41.

1 *puella*: cf. 41.1.
   naso: cf. 41.3. A long nose was thought of as especially ugly in girls: Hor.
   S. 1.2.93 (*nasuta*).
2–3 *bello pede … nigris ocellis … longis digitis*: for these marks of beauty,
   which the *puella* is said to lack, F. compares Ov. *Am.* 3.3.7 *pes erat exiguus*
   [contrast Hor. *S.* 1.2.93 *pede longo*], Prop. 2.2.5 *longaeque manus*, 2.12.23 *caput
   et digitos et lumina nigra puellae*; add to these Ov. *AA* 1.622 *et teretes digitos
   exiguumque pedem*. Cf. also Hor. *Od.* 1.32.11 and *AP* 37 on *nigri oculi* (in men,
   not women).
4 B. rightly points out that *elegans* is not appropriate to the description of a strictly
   physical defect, and assigns it to her manner of speaking.
5 See 41.4 n.
6 *provincia* = Gallia Cisalpina (in contrast to Rome; the girl, unlike Lesbia, was
   beautiful only by 'provincial' standards – if at all).
   narrat, 'tells the tale' (cf. Hor. *S.* 2.7.5), or simply 'says' (Ter. *Heaut.* 520 '*nil'
   narras?*).
7 *nostra* does not *necessarily* imply that C. was still on good terms with Lesbia,
   though he probably was (see intr. n. to poems 41 and 43, and cf. 58.1).
8 *saeclum*: 'generation,' rather than 'world' (F., who however has a good n. on the
   connotations of the word).

Here *m* is again careless: for *et* he reads *atque*. He corrects himself at once, but annuls his self-correction; this hasty erasure is properly ignored by G^2.

P. Murgatroyd, 'A Note on the Structure and Punctuation of C. 43,' *EMC/CV* 29 (1985): 121–3.

44

Structure: 9 + 8 + 4.

An address to his country-house in the hill country northeast of Rome. C. has been invited to dinner by Sestius (to be identified with Cicero's friend and associate P. Sestius: see F.). He realizes that if he accepts he will be expected to have read – and be willing to praise – his host's latest speech; but, having read it in anticipation of the invitation, he finds that it offends him from a literary point of view. A severe cold comes to the rescue, and enables C. to make his excuses.

A pleasant, straightforward *pièce d'occasion*; but the pun on *frigus*, meaning either 'cold' or 'preciosity of style,' for which, according to F., the poem is 'merely a vehicle,' is not quite everything it possesses in the way of a point. Besides the indications that C. is parodying legal language (no doubt because of Sestius' reputation in the Forum), and also to some extent the archaic formulas of invocations to the gods (since he adopts the form of an address to the abode of his *lares*, so to put it), the reference to a vegetable diet in l. 15 hints obliquely at the connection of Antius (l. 11), the subject of Sestius' eloquence, with a recent attempt to revive the sumptuary legislation, directed against electoral corruption; such laws traditionally (i) aspired to restrict the number of guests a candidate for office (*petitor*: see l. 11) might entertain at the same dinner, and (ii) prescribed that the dishes served at such political entertainments must consist largely of vegetables. Syme 1963 identifies Antius with the author of a *lex sumptuaria* of this kind; see the bibliography below, both for this and for the parodies of legal and sacral language, mentioned above. See also line 10 n.

1 *fundus*: see 6–7 n.

seu Sabine seu Tiburs: cf. Suet. *vita Horati* p. 47 R., quoted by F.: *in secessu ruris sui Sabini aut Tiburtini*; Horace's villa, like C.'s, was not strictly in fashionable Tibur but rather just outside it, in the unpretentious Sabine farming country on the side away from Rome. If you wanted to stretch a point – and flatter the owner – you could call it 'Tiburtine' (Suetonius' *aut*, like C.'s *seu*, implies 'if you prefer to think of it in that way').

4 *pignore*, 'wager,' or 'stake.' Cf. Phaedr. 4.21.5 *a me* (sc. not by Aesop) *contendet fictum quovis pignore.*

5 For *sed* resuming the thread after a parenthesis, cf. 65.15 *sed tamen.*

6–7 *villa*: the habitable buildings of a country estate; *fundus* meant the whole property, including the land.

6 For *esse libenter* (or *iucunde*) = to be glad to be in a place (colloq.), cf. Cicero, *Ad Att.* (five passages quoted by F.), also *Pro Rege Deiot.* 19.

7 See App. Crit.; for *expuli* cf. Hor. *Ep.* 2.2.137 (quoted by F.) *expulit elleboro morbum bilemque.*

9 Hyperbaton is not unusual in C.; cf. 66.18. See 1.9 n. for other references.

10–11 On Sestius and Antius, see intr. n.

10 *dum* (as in l. 9) still chiefly designates time, but has an undertone of causality (later, it became fully causal in meaning). See esp. Cicero, *Ad Fam.* 7.26.2 *dum volunt isti lauti terra nata* (= vegetables) *in honorem adducere, fungos helvellos herbas ita condiunt*, etc. (a passage which comes very close to one part of the poem's underlying content: see intr. n.).

11 See the Introduction, pp. 34–5, for a discussion of R^2's true emendation *orationem* and false emendation (to agree with the supposed *minantium*) *petitorum.*

12 Cf. Hor. *S.* 1.7.1 *Rupili pus atque venenum.* C.'s target, however, is the literary quality of Sestius' speech, rather than its fierceness, as the addition of *pestilentiae* shows; cf. 14.19 *omnia venena*, of bad books.

14 *usque dum*: cf. 61.154.

15 *recuravi* possibly colloq. (Kr.).

    See App. Crit.: the reading *ocimo* (the name of a herb, basil) is an ingenious Humanistic conjecture. It deserves serious consideration, the combination of abstract and concrete being a little uneasy here; even though Celsus, whom F. quotes, recommends *quiescere* on the first day of a cold and *urtica* for coughing, he does not do so in a single breath, or even in the same chapter.

17 The reader naturally and easily links *ulta* with the fem. in *villa*, though strictly speaking the *fundus* (masc.) is still being addressed. But in fact *sinum* in l. 4 is probably thought of by C. as referring to the *villa.*

19 *recepso*: an archaic form (see F.'s n. on the history of the future tense ending in *-so*). Only here in the sense 'take up (i.e., in my hand) again'; otherwise *recipio* in all its forms = 'take back (something I gave away, or else lost).'

20 R^2's attempted correction to *sertio* is ignored by G^2, no doubt as not being an improvement; contrast 45.10.

21 *tunc ... cum*: the *tunc* is emphatic: tr. 'only when.'

    On *tunc* against *tum* in our tradition McKie (281–2) has some interesting remarks. As he says, *tunc* may in any case be preferred here because of its greater emphasis – but also, I think, to avoid the pointless iteration of the *-um* sound (cf. *malum librum*). Cf. 1.2 n., referring to Fr.'s suggestion that C. may have decided to use the unfamiliar feminine form *arida* in order to avoid the repetition *do–do* in *arido modo*.

Karsten, H.T. 1891. 'De Catulli Carmine XLIIII,' *Mn* 19: 222–8.

Haarhoff, T.J. 1934. 'On C. XLIV, 21,' *CP* 29: 255–6.

Murley, C. 1938. 'Was C. Present at Sestius' Dinner?,' *CP* 33: 206–8.

Ronconi, A. 1940. 'Attegiamenti e formi della parodia catulliana,' *A&R* 8: 141–58 = *Studi catulliani* (1953): 193–212, esp. 202–3.

Syme, R. 1963. 'Ten Tribunes,' *JRS* 53: 59.

Jones, C.P. 1968. 'Parody in C. 44,' *Hermes* 92: 379–83.

de Angeli, E.S. 1969. 'A Literary Chill: C. 44,' *CW* 62: 354–6.

Håkanson, L. 1982. 'Miscellanea critica (2),' *Phoenix* 36: 237–42.

Clausen, W. 1988. 'Catulliana,' *BICS* Suppl. 51, *Vir Bonus Discendi Peritus* [Festschrift for Otto Skutsch]. London: 14–15. [Lines 1–7.]

George, D.B. 1991. 'C. 44: The Vulnerability of Wanting to Be Included,' *AJP* 112: 247–50.

45

Structure: 9 + 9 + 8. The last section may be divided as follows:
  19–20 Both Acme and Septimius: good *auspicia*.
  21–22 Septimius (sums up 1–7).
  23–24 Acme (sums up 10–16).
  25–26 Both: good *auspicia*.
The first and second sections are closed by a two-line refrain.

A dialogue of mutual devotion between two lovers. The male–female contrast is brought out on two levels: his rather bombastic asseverations are set against her simple statement that hers is the greater love, and the soprano *i*'s and other vowel sounds, and the liquid *l*'s, of 10–16, make it clear (to the reader aloud) that this is indeed a woman's voice. The name Acme is found on inscriptions, as that of a freedwoman. The Roman name of Septimius suggests that perhaps we have here to do with one of C.'s friends. This small idyll is (as the above brief analysis may suggest) one of the most formally shaped of all C.'s shorter poems. Possibly, as L. suggested, it is modelled on some Alexandrian vignette which is unknown to us. The mise en scène and treatment suggest a wall painting, such as those that have survived (from a later period) at Pompeii and Herculaneum. If, as seems not impossible, C. had such a wall painting in mind when he composed the poem, it would presumably show a couch or settee, a pair of human figures, and Cupids on either side to fill out the picture. The date of composition can be confidently established: line 22 can only have been written in 55 BC, when Britain and Syria were on everyone's lips in Rome, and Britain was thought of as a sort of Eldorado. F.'s commentary on this poem is perceptive, and well worth consulting.

In the absence of punctuation, it is probably safest to take *s. ut ant d.* as a deliberately reversible word group, in which *ut ante* can be read either with what precedes or with what follows. The point of the repetition is that the love between Acme and Septimius goes on endlessly, without any change.

3 *perdite (amare)* colloq.; cf. 104.3, Ter. *Heaut.* 97.

 porro, of the 'indefinite' future; 'on and on' is F.'s translation.

5 *quantum . . .* , elliptical: 'as much as <he loves> who can most ardently love.'

 pote = *potest*. F. has a note on the history of this word.

6–7 Cf. Semonides, fr. 12 D (= 14 West), οὐκ ἄν τις οὕτω δασκίοις ἐν οὔρεσιν / ἀνὴρ λέοντ᾽ ἔδεισεν οὐδὲ πάρδαλιν / μοῦνος στενυγρῇ συμπεσὼν ἐν ἀτραπῷ.

6 *-que*: English prefers 'or' in this and similar phrases. Once again F. gives a full account.

 tosta: cf. V. *Geo.* 4.425 *rapidus torrens sitientes Sirius Indos*, Tib. 2.3.55 *comites fusci, quos India torret.*

7 Kr.[5] refers to an article by F. Wilhelm, *RhM* 57 (1902): p. 606 there discusses the motif in love poetry of an encounter with a savage beast. Cf. Hor. *Od.* 3.27.51–2 *utinam inter errem / nuda leones.*

 caesius = γλαυκός, the greenish colour of a cat's eyes. Apart from this passage, it is only used of humans; Q. (following E.) suggests that C. alludes to *Il.* 20.172, where the lion, attacking a hunter, γλαυκιόων ἰθὺς φέρεται.

8 Gratwick's suggested emendation, which deserves consideration, is defended at length in *CP* 87 (1992): 234–40.

9 *sternuit*: a sneeze was an omen for Greeks also; *Od.* 17.541, Theocr. 7.96. In Latin, Prop. 2.3.24 (reflecting C. here) *argutum sternuit omen amor.*

 approbationem: accus. of internal object (as *omen* in Prop., see above).

10 For *at* as directing the reader's eye to another (part of the) scene, cf. 64.251 *at parte ex alia . . .*

 R[2]'s attempted correction (*ad hanc me*) this time appears to *G*[2] somewhat more plausible than that in 44.20, and is therefore accepted. *G*[2] however ignores the correction in l. 13 below, where *R*[2]'s attempt at restoration, copied by *m*[2], may well be derived from X.

12 To F.'s references for the meaning of *purpureus*, add Irwin 1974, Index s.v. πορφύρεος.

13 *mea vita*: cf. 109.1, and also Cicero, *Ad Fam.* 14.2.3 and 4.1 (to Terentia).

13–16 The words *maior acriorque* in l. 15 should be taken to mean '. . . than yours, Septimius.' From Kr.'s way of expressing himself ('so wahr . . . , so wahr . . .') it might be supposed that he believes l. 14 to carry the main point, seen as a proposal to continue in the service of the *dominus* (= *Amor*; cf. *domina*, of Cybele, 63.13 and 91). But this is not so. Acme simply and beautifully answers Septimius' extravagant utterances (3–7) by the plain statement that *her* love is the greater, and that the measure of this is her desire (l. 14) that the pair should continue indefinitely (*usque*; cf. 109.2, also 3.10 and *serviat usque* at 61.151, 154) in Love's service. (Fr.'s view, that *serviamus* is plural-for-singular and *domino* = Septimius, cannot be right, both because Acme's declaration then becomes tautologous and because *huic* would be an unnatural addition.)

16 *ignis ... medullis*: cf. 35.15, 64.93, 66.23; V. *Aen.* 4.66 *est mollis flamma medullas*.

20 For the asyndeton cf. Tac. *A.* 6.35 *ut ... pulsu armorum pellerent pellerentur*.

22 *Syrias Britanniasque*, generalizing plurals, 'places like Syria or Britain' (see above, 6 n., for *-que* = 'or'), 'any Syria or Britain' (see intr. n. for the probable date of the poem). Syria was a famously rich province (Cicero, *De domo* 23).

23 For *in* = 'in relation to,' of a love attachment, see 64.98 *in flavo hospite suspirantem*, and cf. 61.97–8.

24 *facit*, 'judges, esteems <to be>,' as often in C. Not 'takes his pleasure' as F. translates it.

26 *auspicatior*: the comparative reappears in Plin. *NH* 13.118 *auspicatior ... arbor quae vocatur euonymos*. (The superlative is found in Quint. 10.1.85 *auspicatissimum exordium*, Tac. *G.* 11.2 *auspicatissimum initium*; cf. also Plin. *Ep.* 10.17a.2.)

Pease, A.S. 1911. 'The Omen of Sneezing,' *CP* 6: 429–43, esp. 431–2.

Birt, T. 1919. 'Zum Acme-Gedicht C.s,' *BPhW* 39: 572–6.

Edwards, J.B. 1928. 'The Irony of C. 45,' *TAPA* 59: xxiii–xxiv.

Stearns, J.B. 1929. 'On the Ambiguity of C. XLV. 8–19 (= 17–18),' *CP* 24: 48–59.

Oldfather, W.A. 1936. 'The Sneeze and Breathing of Love,' *Classical Studies Presented to E. Capps* (Princeton): 268–81.

Comfort, H. 1938. 'Analysis of Technique in C. LXV (Septimius and Acme),' *TAPA* 69: xxxiii.

Baker, S. 1958. 'The Irony of C.'s Septimius and Acme,' *CP* 53: 110–12.

Ross, D.O. 1965. 'Style and Content in C. 45,' *CP* 60: 256–9.

Akbar Khan, H. 1968. 'C. 45: What Sort of Irony?,' *Latomus* 27: 3–12.

Dietz, H. 1969. 'Zu C.s Gedicht von Acme und Septimius,' *SOsl* 44: 42–7.

Singleton, D. 1971. 'Form and Irony in C. 45,' *G&R* 18: 181–7.

Tränkle, H. 1972. 'C.s Septimius- und Acme-Gedicht (c. 45),' *Kraus*: 425–36.

Auverlot, D. 1985. 'La réprésentation de la passion dans le c. 45 de C,' *IL* 37: 124–8.

Williams, M.F. 1988. 'Amor's Head-Cold (*frigus* in C. 45),' *CJ* 83: 128–32.

Frueh, E. 1990. 'Sinistra ut ante dextra: Reading C. 45,' *CW* 84: 15–21.

Gagliardi, D. 1990. 'Un sogno ad occhi aperti (struttura e significato del c. 45 di C.),' *CCC* 11: 65–73.

Gratwick, A.S. 1992. 'Those Sneezes: C. 45.8–9, 17–18,' *CP* 87: 234–40. [Read *hoc ut dixit, ut ante Amor, sinistra, / dextra* . . .]

Kitzinger, R. 1992. 'Reading C. 45,' *CJ* 87: 209–12

46

Structure: 3 + 3 + 2 + 3.

A welcome to spring and anticipation of the joys of returning home from Bithynia (date: 56 BC).

C. is at his most exuberant: notice the excited self-address, the ringing sound of the repeated initial *iam*, and the emotional leave-taking in lines 9–11.

For the echoes of this poem's language in poem 31, which marks the poet's homecoming at the end of the journey contemplated here, see the notes on that poem.

Observe the enfolding of themes:

1–3 External (description of the arrival of spring);

4–6 Internal (Catullus and his plans);

7–8 Internal (Catullus and his feelings);

9–11 External (turning to his companions and *their* plans).

1 *egelidos*, literally 'with the chill removed' (Cels. 4.5.4, 18.3 *aqua egelida*). Poets use it for 'mild' (Ov. *Am.* 2.11.10 *gelidum Borean egelidumque Notum*); the opposite meaning, 'excessively cold,' is found at V. *Aen.* 8.610, Manil. 5.131. *tepores*: Kr. points out that this plural occurs also at Lucr. 2.517. For the warm and genial westerly breeze of spring (it began to blow, in most places, as early as Feb. 8–9, according to ancient calendars), cf. 64.282 *aura . . . tepidi facunda Favoni* (= *Zephyri*).

5 *Nicaeae ager*: see n. on 31.5–6. The *campi* of l. 4 are no doubt the 'inland plain' (F. on l. 5) surrounding Nicaea (Strabo's πεδίον μέγα, 12.4.7). Strabo adds that because of the heat (*aestuosae* l. 5) it was not an entirely healthy region in the summer season. C. will have left in the late spring (l. 2).

6 *claras*: most editors interpret this as 'famous.' L. was inclined to translate 'bright,' thinking of the maritime Greek cities with their dazzling marble buildings set off against the blue of the sea. But (e.g.) Horace seems to apply the word *clarus* to the *whole* island of Rhodes (*Od.* 1.7.1); and in C. it seems to be to some extent contrasted (otherwise the change of scene loses its effect) with Nicaea, though that too must have been a city of brilliant *appearance*, reflected in the water of Lake Ascanius; what it lacked, in C.'s day at least,

was a measure of fame (renown) comparable with that of Smyrna, say, or Ephesus.

volemus, simply 'hasten' (whether by land or sea is not implied).

7 *mens*: cf. 31.8 n.

praetrepidans, both intensive and temporal: 'violently fluttering in anticipation.'

vagari, 'be on the move.' Cf. 64.225 *vago malo*, 271 *vagi Solis*.

9 *comites* here = the members of the *cohors* (see 10.10); sometimes they were known semi-officially as the governor's *comites* (cf. 28.1 *Pisonis comites, cohors inanis*). Later, the title became fully official; hence, ultimately, *comte*, 'count.'

10 *longe*, with *profectos*: 'who have journeyed far from home.' As F. shows, *proficisci* 'does not refer exclusively to the start of a journey.'

11 It is possible that C. wrote *diversae variae*; several times he employs two adjectives, or two adverbs, in asyndeton: 1.1 *lepidum novum*; 32.10 *satur supinus*; 36.10 *iocose lepide*; 65.21 *miserae oblitae*, and perhaps (but see n.) 71.4 *mirifice apte*. But do *diversae* and *variae* say the same thing, to an extent that the examples just given do not? For an effective defence of *varie* and a further argument against *variae*, see Cairns 1991.

Elder, J.P. 1951. 'Notes on some Conscious and Subconscious Elements in C.'s Poetry,' *HSCP* 60: 103–4. [Brief analysis of the poem.]

Simpson, C.J., and Simpson, B.G. 1989. 'C. 46,' *Latomus* 48: 75–85.

Cairns, F. 1991. 'C. 46.9–11 and Ancient Etymologies,' *RFIC* 119: 442–5.

Schievenin, R. 1995. 'Il carme 46 di C.,' *Aufidus* 25: 19–30.

47

Structure: 2 + 2 + 3 (articulated by the repetition of *vos*).

On Veranius and Fabullus, see poems 9, 12, and (especially in their relation to Piso) 28. Syme (cited in the bibliography to poem 28) establishes a date for their tour of duty under Piso in Spain. Piso himself has usually been identified with L. Calpurnius Piso Caesoninus, the father of Caesar's wife Calpurnia (though Wiseman 1987: 347 n. 21 dismisses this identification for lack of evidence; see poem 28, intr. n.). If so, his connection with Caesar would in itself not have endeared him to C. For Porcius and 'Socration,' see nn. on l. 1. The picture presented in l. 7 is of course exaggerated (see n. there). For *verpus ... Priapus*, see again poem 28, where C. purports to describe the way in which his own praetor, Memmius, treated him: of course none of the expressions so picturesquely employed amounts to more than the rhetoric of abuse which C. and Calvus, among others of the same 'neoteric' circle, delighted in applying to members of the governing class whom they disliked.

1 The identifications are quite uncertain. 'Socration' may well have been a Greek
in fact; Piso (l. 2) liked having Greeks about him (Cicero, *In Pisonem* 22 and 67).
For the possibility (suggested by Fr.) that C. uses *Socration* as a pseudonym for
the philosopher Philodemus, see F.'s n.
sinistrae <manus>: *dextra manus* = 'right hand' in our (metaphorical) sense,
but C. substitutes *sinistra*, 'thieving hand,' as in 12.1. The word *duae* is not
merely a 'colloquial addition, contributing nothing to the sense,' as Kr. opines,
but serves to add an element of ridicule to the abuse.

2 *Pisonis*: cf. poem 28 on his relations with Veranius and Fabullus, and see the
intr. n.
scabies famesque: in his poems of invective (poem 21, for example) against
Furius and Aurelius, C. uses the contemptuous notion 'starveling' as a part
of his rhetorical armament; here, even if the 'point is just that Porcius and
Socration are not starving, or likely to starve' (F.), it is still available for the
purposes of *diffamatio*. There is therefore no need to follow F. in translating
('most naturally') 'itching greed whose object is the *mundus*.' Whether in C.'s
time *mundus* (the noun) could mean *human* world, as opposed to universe (or
cosmos), in the limited sense in which Lucr. uses it, is discussed at length by F.;
he views with some favour Bücheler's emendation *mundae* (adj. = 'tidy').

4 *verpus* = ψωλός (an Aristophanic word: 'with the prepuce drawn back,' L. and
S.; figuratively signifying 'lustful'). Cf. 28.12 *verpa*; the two poems are linked
by language as well as by subject (cf. 15.14–19 and poem 40; see notes on the
latter).

5 Notice the asyndeton, which, as F. remarks, corresponds to μὲν ... δέ in Greek,
and would be replaced by a subordinate clause (e.g., 'whereas ...') in English.

6 *de die*, as F. says (see his n.), 'implies taking time off the normal [working] day';
his translation is 'in the day-time.'

7 *quaerunt in trivio*: typical Catullan exaggeration; cf. poem 58 (esp. l. 4).
vocationes, 'invitations.' Cf. 44.21 *vocat*, 'invites.'

Giardina, G.C. 1984–5. 'Note a C. [c. 47],' *MCr* 19–20: 193–7.
Dettmer, H. 1985. 'A Note on C. 47,' *CW* 78: 577–9.

48

Structure: (2 + 1) + (1+ 2). Notice the chiastic arrangement of positive and
negative conditional clauses, especially in lines 1–2 and 5–6.
To Juventius: 300,000 kisses. The huge number itself indicates C.'s penchant
for extravagance in language. As I remarked in discussing poem 16, it is the
present poem – not poem 5 or 7 – that is the source of the references there to
versiculi molliculi on the subject of 'many thousands' of kisses (see 16.4 n).

Other poems besides poem 16, notably the (nearby) 15 and 21, and possibly also poem 81 (where see nn.), connect Aurelius at least to C.'s interest in Juventius. (Poem 16 is clearly C.'s reply to a lampoon, or more probably a pair of lampoons, from Furius and Aurelius, which had already been circulated, at least among mutual friends, so that C. feels he must answer them publicly. In spite of the disparaging language C. habitually uses about F. and A., it is clear from poem 11 that they do not regard themselves as his enemies – they say that they will go to the ends of the earth with him – while he for his part is willing to entrust to them, as he professes, albeit somewhat contemptuously, his final message of renunciation, to be delivered to Lesbia.)

1 *mellitos*, colloquial; a favourite word of C.'s; cf. (e.g.) 99.1 (of Juventius) and 3.6 (of Lesbia's pet bird).
 oculos: see 9.9 n.
2 In the elaborately indirect *si quis* ..., C. surely means 'if you yourself should ...' Kr.'s alternative explanation – that C. is hinting that his relationship with Juventius was 'not unhindered' – is too literal, and extends this very slight poem's field of reference too far, to be credible.
3 *milia*, sc. *basiorum*. Notice what Q. calls 'the obsessive repetition' *usque basiare ... usque basiem.*
4 The reading *nec numquam* in *V* cannot be supported, as Q. maintains, by *V*'s *nec ... nullo* at 76.3; see n. there.
5 *aridis*: Kr., rightly dismissing the emendation *Africis*, proposed by Markland (*Ep. Crit.* [1723] 157; see B.), cites Aug. *CD* 4.8 *seges ab initiis herbidis usque ad aridas* (= 'fully ripe') *aristas*; V. *Aen.* 7.720 *densae ... aristae*; and Ov. *M.* 2.213 *seges arida.* (The thickness of the crop is obviously more 'eye-catching' when it is in the ear than when it is still in the blade; so the adj. has point.)
7 *osculationis*: cf. 7.1 *basiationes*, and see n. there.

49

Structure: unitary (a single sentence).
A note to Cicero, professing gratitude. There is no external evidence, either for the occasion of the poem, or for the personal relations between Cicero and Catullus. Much debate has focused on the question whether C.'s gratitude is sincerely meant or 'ironical,' as well as on the other question whether the gift or favour for which Cicero is thanked was literary or forensic. My own view, expressed in an article published some years ago (see Bibliography), can be very briefly summarized as follows. The most important thing in the poem is the insistence (by repetition, at the end of the line) on *poeta*,

together with the answering stress on *patronus* (in the most prominent and emphatic position in the whole poem). We may conjecture that Cicero, who liked at various stages of his life to dabble in poetic composition, has sent C. one of his efforts in this sphere; that he was inordinately vain about them, we know. In reply, C. expresses his thanks, but does not commit himself to the proposition that Cicero is an excellent, or even a good, *poet*; with mock modesty, C. seems to say: I myself am the worst of all poets, yet still a *poet*; while you, Cicero, are indubitably supreme – but as a *patronus*, not (it is implied) a poet. C. is flattered at receiving the literary gift, yet he cannot praise it; in his deft acknowledgment there is a touch of irony (between the lines), yet the poem is not as a whole ironical. Notice that the opening and closing words (*disertissime, patronus*) have a very slight aura of faint praise for the most eminent barrister in the Rome of his day; for the quality of being *disertus*, and the role, successfully exercised, of a *patronus*, are things we might take for granted rather than special badges of distinction, at least in one of Cicero's standing.

On the title, especially in relation to Petrarch's letter to Cola di Rienzo (cited in the *testimonia*), see McKie: 63–4. Petrarch's title for the poem is *Ad ipsum Tullium*, where *V* had (unambiguously, despite Mynors' doubt) *Ad Romulum*.

1 *disertissime*: not quite the same as *eloquentissime*; see 53.5 n.
   Romuli nepotum: this phrase, together with the form of personal address in the next line (*Marce Tulli*), gives the opening a solemn and ceremonious tone hardly in keeping with the modestly expressed note of thanks which is all that the rest of the poem professes to be. See intr. n.

2–3 *quot ... annis*: for this past-present-future formulation, cf. 21.2 and 24.2; in both of these passages it is introduced in a jesting fashion (*scherzhaft*), as Kr. points out; from which it seems likely that here too the tone attending its introduction should be taken as light rather than ponderous.

7 See App. Crit. *omniums* (*R*, self-corrected to *omnium*) may be due, as F. suggests, to false addition of a superscript *s* intended to correct *patronum*; *patronus* (*O*) is certainly right because of the parallel phrase *pessimus omnium poeta* in l. 6.

Harnecker, O. 1882. 'Cicero und Catullus,' *Philologus* 41: 465–81.

Jacoby, K. 1885. 'Zu C.,' *Philologus* 44: 178–82.

Damsté, P.H. 1902. 'Ad Catulli Carmen XXXXVIIII,' *Mn* 30: 394–6.

Schmidt, B. 1914. 'Die Lebenszeit C.s und die Herausgabe seiner Gedichte,' *RhM* 69: 273.

Jurenka, H. 1916. 'Zur Erklärung des Katull,' *WS* 38: 177–80.

Funaioli, G. 1921. 'Il carme 49 di C.,' *RIGI* 5: 147–56 = *Studi di lettera antica* vol. 2 part 1. Bologna (1947): 17–23.

Schmidt, M. 1930. 'Die Komposition von Vergils Georgica' = *Studien zur Geschichte und Kultur des Altertums* 16 (2/3): 186–7.

Melichar, J. 1933. 'Zu Katull 49,' *MVPW* 10: 127–31.

Allen, W. 1936. 'C. LXIX and Sallust's *Bellum Catilinae*,' *CJ* 32: 298.

Salanitro, N. 1938. 'Il carme XLIX di C.,' *Miscellanea di studi latini*. Naples: 77–88.

Romano, D. 1954. 'Il significato del c. 49 di C.,' *Aevum* 28: 222–9.

Wormell, D.E.W. 1963. 'C. 49,' *Phoenix* 17: 59–60.

Ferguson, J. 1966. 'C. and Cicero,' *Latomus* 25: 871–2.

Thomson, D.F.S. 1967. 'C. and Cicero: Poetry and the Criticism of Poetry,' *CW* 60: 225–30.

Gugel, H. 1967. 'Cicero und Catull,' *Latomus* 26: 686–8.

Gagliardi, D. 1967. 'Sul carme 49 di C.,' *P&I* 9: 227–32.

Dinoi, A. 1968. 'Il carme 49 del Liber Catullianus,' *Vichiana* 5: 5–20.

Westendorp Boerma, R.E.H. 1969. 'Once More C. 49 and Cicero,' *GIF* 21: 133–6.

Buchheit, V. 1970. See bibliography to poem 44.

Laughton, E. 1970. 'Disertissime Romuli nepotum,' *CP* 65: 1–7.

Monbrun, M. 1972. 'Encore sur Cicéron et C. Raisons et date d'une rupture,' *Pallas* 19: 29–39.

Basson, W.P. 1980. 'The Riddle of C. 49: Some Notes on Its Interpretation,' *AClass* 23: 45–52.

McDermott, W.C. 1980. 'Cicero and Catullus,' *WS* 14: 75–82.

Deroux, C. 1985a. 'Le plus mauvais de tous les poètes et le meilleur de tous les avocats,' *Hommages à H. Bardon*. Brussels: 124–38.

Deroux, C. 1985b. 'C. et Cicéron, ou les raisons d' un silence,' *LEC* 53: 221–45.

Setaioli, A. 1986. 'Il carme di C. a Cicerone: una messa a punto,' *Studi in onore di A. Barigazzi*. 2: 211–17. Rome.

Tatum, W.J. 1988. 'C.'s Criticism of Cicero in Poem 49,' *TAPA* 118: 179–84.

50

Structure: 6 + 7 + (4 + 4).

To Calvus, a fellow-poet and intimate friend; a glimpse of the *novi poetae* at play (and incidentally engaged in literary creation).

One of the poem's merits consists in exhibiting to us the total emotional commitment that C. brought to his friendships, no less than to his loves and hatreds. It may well be supposed to date from an early stage in C.'s acquaintance with Calvus; the latter, who is still addressed a little formally as *Licini* (despite the term of endearment, *ocelle*, near the end), and is called *iucunde*, becomes *meus Calvus* at 53.3, and *iucundissime* at 14.2. The two poets had, perhaps for the first time, enjoyed a day of leisure together; and C.'s almost juvenile delight in his friend's companionship as they exchanged verses over the wine had so carried him away that out of sheer over-stimulation he was unable to sleep all night. The details of the scene are not of much importance; but *illinc abii* (l. 7) shows that the meeting was not at C.'s house, while the fact that Calvus had to use C.'s *tabellae* (l. 2) suggests that it was not at Calvus' house either. Obviously they met (at a tavern, perhaps?) during the day and parted before the hour of the *cena*, since C. says (l. 9) he lost his appetite for the meal; to speak of their spending the *evening* together, as F. does, is to ignore not only *nec ... cibus iuvaret* but also *otiosi* in the first line: everyone was *otiosus* in the evening, at least in fashionable Roman society, and *otiosi* must therefore (as L. observed) imply that they were enjoying leisure while others worked. For the same reason, a point is made of *otiosum* at 10.2; here, Varus observed C. to be idle in the Forum, where everybody would be expected normally to have some kind of business to transact. Remarkably similar details occur in Cicero, *Ad Att.* 9.10. 1 *cum me aegritudo non solum somno privaret, verum ne vigilare quidem sine summo dolore pateretur, tecum ut quasi loquerer, in quo uno me acquiesco, hoc nescio quid scribere ... institui.*

1 *Licini* = C. Licinius *Calvus*. See intr. n.

2 *lusimus*, 'wrote (trivial or amatory) verses'; cf. (besides V. *Ecl.* 6.1, *Geo.* 4.565, and Plin. *Ep.* 7.9.9, quoted by F.) V. *Ecl.* 1.10 and Hor. *Od.* 1.32.2. For the meaning of *lusi* at 68.17, which some editors identify with that of *lusimus* here, see the n. on that passage.

   tabellis = 42.5 *pugillaria*, 42.11 *codicilli*: small hinged tablets, waxed on one side (and folded together with the waxed surfaces, protected by a raised edge, turned inwards). They were used for short notes or first drafts that could easily be erased with a *stilus*.

3 *convenerat*, 'we had <made> an agreement'; for this meaning, and for the construction with acc. + inf., cf. V. *Aen.* 12.184 *convenit Evandri victos discedere ad urbem.*

   delicatos: for the erotic meaning 'wanton, skittish,' see 17.15 n.

5 *illoc* is an extremely rare form; but it makes a good balance for *hoc*, both in sound and in sense.

   per iocum atque vinum: cf. 12.2 *in ioco atque vino.*

6 *reddens mutua*, 'paying each other out,' or 'each giving as good as he got.'

7 *atque*, 'and so' (continuing the story, as at 64.84).

7–8 *lepore ... facetiisque*; cf. 12.8–9.

9 *miserum*, implying a degree of affection tantamount to love (hence the use of an adjective appropriate to lovesickness); cf. also *incensus* ('set ablaze'), *furore, dolorem*.

11 *indomitus furore* = *indomito* ('uncontrollable') *furore*. (There are so many words in this line ending in *-o* that C. is forced to use this transferred epithet to be grammatically clear; yet B. thinks that C. must have written *-o* and that *V*'s *-us* is a copyist's error.)

13 See 9.6–9 (n.) and 31.8–9 for *hysteron proteron* in C. Fr. adduces 67.44, as alluding to *talking* before *listening*. Cf. V. *Aen.* 4.33 *nec dulcis natos Veneris nec praemia noris* (where, as here, it could be argued that – as B. remarks, p. 255 n. – the more important point is given first).

al. *essem* (R^2m^2) should be attributed to the margins of *X*, who derived it from *A*'s text (cf. *O*); notice R^2's care to identify it as a variant. The confusion is between $\overline{oem}$ and $\overline{eem}$: cf. 63.90, where *GR* are right with *omne* and *O* is wrong with (again) *esse*.

14–15 *postquam* + impf. (after a certain state of things had come into being, as opposed to an action or event at a certain point in time): to F.'s parallels add Sall. *Cat.* 6.3 *postquam res eorum prospera videbatur*.

16 *iucunde*: cf. 14.2 *iucundissime Calve*, and 9.9 n.

18 *audax*, 'over-confident <of my affection>.'
cave, with iambic shortening, as at 10.27 *mane*. Omission of *ne* is colloquial.

19 *despuas*, 'despise,' hence here 'reject'; used in this sense by Plaut. *Asin.* 39 *opsecro hercle ut quae locutu's despuas*.

20 R^2's *ne messis* (copied by *m*) probably represents an independent attempt to make at least a genuine word out of *R*'s nonsensical *mestis*; its agreement with the *O* reading is probably fortuitous.

21 *ve<he>mens* = δεινή, βαρεῖα. Cf. Antim. ap. Strabo 13.1.13 ἔστι δέ τις Νέμεσις μεγάλη θεός (perhaps, as F. suggests, C.'s source here).
caveto: formal imperative, producing a mock-solemn effect which, together with the use of very short sentences, lightens the tone in the ending and so deprives the threat of its harshness.

Pucci, P. 1961. 'Il carme 50 di C.,' *Maia* 13: 249–56.

Scott, W.C. 1969. 'C. and Calvus (Cat. 50),' *CP* 64: 169–73.

Segal, C. 1970. 'Catullan *otiosi* – The Lover and the Poet,' *G&R* 17: 25–31.

Buchheit, V. 1976. 'C. c. 50 als Programm und Bekenntnis,' *RhM* 119: 162–80.

W. Kissel, 1980. 'Mein Freund, ich liebe dich (C. c. 50),' *WJA* 6b: 45–59.

Landolfi, L. 1986. 'I *lusus simposiali* di C. e Calvo,' *QUCC* 53: 77–89.

Burgess, D.L. 1986. 'C. c. 50: The Exchange of Poetry,' *AJP* 107: 576–86.

Williams, M.F. 1988. 'C. 50 and the Language of Friendship,' *Latomus* 47: 69–73.

Evenepoel, W. 1988. 'Humor in de klassike latijnse lyriek (C. 50),' *Kleio* 17: 66–84.

51

Structure: three four-line stanzas, together with a fourth stanza (or else a fragment, metrically similar to the first three, which has become attached to them at some stage in the transmission of C.'s poems).
On seeing Lesbia in the company of a man.

Clearly an adaptation (not, strictly speaking, a translation; see the detailed notes below) of Sappho, fr. 31 Lobel-Page. Conceivably C., on seeing Lesbia with her husband (perhaps at his first meeting with her), fell in love with her on the spot; the encounter in these circumstances, however it happened, seems to have reminded him of the poem by Sappho, which he translated and sent to her as a gift, adapting it during the process of translation in such a way as to suit his needs. (For example, the word *misero*, which corresponds to nothing in Sappho's Greek, appears to have been introduced by C. in order to change the poem's direction by introducing the masculine gender.) The name 'Lesbia' would, then, be added not only as a disguise for the *amour*, but also in order to remind the reader of the poem by Sappho of Lesbos.

The mood of self-reproach which permeates the fourth stanza is an unlikely (to say the least) addition to any poem of courtship. Some scholars (e.g., Fr.) have maintained that it was added by C. when he rewrote the poem (if he did) towards the end of his life, after his final renunciation of Lesbia (cf. poem 11, in the same metre), in a spirit of self-disgust. Others would exclude it from the poem. No certainty has yet been attained: see the bibliography for a variety of conflicting views and arguments.

1 *mi*: see App. Crit. (*V*'s unmetrical reading, *michi*, is the result of the common substitution of a familiar for an unfamiliar form of a word.)
   par deo: not, as Kr. takes it, 'godlike in strength' (so as to bear your proximity without, for example, swooning), but 'godlike in happiness' (cf. l. 5, where *misero* = 'lovesick' of a frustrated infatuation).

2 Nothing in Sappho's poem corresponds to this line; but C. likes to 'cap' a statement by going further in the same direction (see, in a very different genre, the intr. n. to poem 40, referring to 15.19).

   In *si fas est* I do not find a 'characteristically Roman conventional formula of caution' (F.) or 'the cautionary formula which such near-blasphemy requires,' as L. put it, but a frequently used poetic way of saying 'if it is possible' (cf. the use of *nefas* in Hor. *Od.* 1.24.20 *quidquid corrigere est nefas*). See P. Cipriano, *Fas e Nefas* (Rome, 1978), where three passages are quoted (Cicero, *De domo* 113 *negabis fas esse duos consules in hac civitate inimicos rei p.*; Prop. 1.12.19–20; and Cicero, *Ad Fam.* 5.12.8 *neque enim fas esse arbitror quicquam me rogantem abs te non impetrare*) in which it is out of the question to take *fas* in any sense other than 'possible,' and three more (Naevius *ap.* Gell. 1.24.2; Ov. *F.* 3.313ff.; and *M.* 9.385–6) where the impossibility clearly originates in the nature of the universe. See also C.A. Peeters, *Fas en Nefas* (Utrecht, 1945; with English summary), 131–5, on *fas* = 'possible' and *nefas* = 'impossible.'

3 *adversus*, partic. used as prep. before *te* (Sappho's ἐνάντιός τοι). A heavy break in the sense before the final syllable would spoil the line.

   identidem has in terms of meaning no equivalent in Sappho, who instead has πλάσιον ('close by'). F's remark, '*identidem* generalizes what is a particular situation in Sappho's poem,' is somewhat misleading in relation to the statement as a whole, since Sappho's ὄττις is potentially much more generalized than C.'s *ille* (which surely must, in this context at least, be particular). C. regards, or at any rate professes to regard, the man who sits beside Lesbia as *habitually* doing so – as being, in effect, her *vir*.

5 *misero*: C. replaces καὶ γελαίσας ἰμέροεν, 'with your lovely laughter,' by *dulce ridentem*, which is shorter; and the connective καί, which was required because of the preceding ἆδυ φωνείσας ὑπακούει, 'listens to your sweet utterance,' is omitted by C., who (moreover) condenses the last three words into *et audit*. All this makes room for the addition of *misero*. Notice the masculine gender of this word, which of course gives a completely new aspect to the poem (considered as a translation).

   quod: R²'s correction (given as a variant: Intr., p. 42). -ꝗ(-*que*) is often confused in Mss with abbreviated *quod*. Cf. e.g., 63.10.

6 *eripit sensus*: cf. V. *Aen.* 2.736 *eripuit mentem*. L. regarded C.'s *eripit sensus mihi* as 'stronger than Sappho's delicate feminine phrase' (καρδίαν ἐν στήθεσιν ἐπτόαισεν); but it should be observed that at 66.25 *sensibus ereptis* is applied to a young bride, and so it probably is not here particularly related to the gender of *misero*, though it is not certain that L. meant to imply this.

   simul = *simul ac*; cf. e.g., 22.15, 64.31, 99.7.

7 *Lesbia* (pseudonym): C. apparently seeks to convey to the reader (i) that he is translating Sappho, the poet of Lesbos, and (ii) that he now bestows on his own beloved the name 'Lesbia.'

   est super = *superest*; for the inversion, cf. V. *Aen.* 2.567 *super unus eram*.

8 See App. Crit. Our present text of Sappho fr. 31 *LP* contains the result of researches into Aeolic dialect which have replaced the infinitive φώναισ· for the φώνας of the [Longinus] text in which the poem was preserved. If the corruption from infinitive to genitive had occurred by the time of C., Ritter's *vocis in ore* would seem to be supported as the most likely supplement for the missing line. In 1922, when he wrote the preface to the first (1923) edition of his commentary, Kr. pronounced that *vocis in ore* was 'a fairly safe restoration.' In his n., he quotes Theocr. 2.108 (of Simaitha, when she first encounters Delphis) οὐδέ

τι φωνῆσαι δυνάμαν. It is simpler, and more sonorous, than Parthenius' *quod loquar amens*, or any alternative restoration that has hitherto been suggested. Nevertheless it is still possible that some scholar may suggest a new supplement, with an infinitive in C. corresponding to φώναισ· (assuming this to have been the current reading in his day).

10 The first appearance of the reading *flamma* might be attributable to *Laur.* 33.13, or else to *Sen.*, if it could be proved that either Ms is in fact earlier than Paris 7989; see nn. in the Table of Mss, items 22, 78, and 95.

11 *gemina*: abl. with *nocte*; transferred epithet. For other examples of enallage, cf. 6.10–11 *quassa lecti argutatio*, 7.5 *Iovis aestuosi*, 64.50 *priscis hominum figuris*, 340 *vago certamine cursus*, 359 *caesis corporum acervis*. (In all of these instances, however, a true participle or adjective is involved, not merely a numeral.) An emendation deserving some consideration is Schrader's *aures geminae, teguntur* (with change in punctuation), though it must be allowed that if it were to be adopted, *geminae* would be no more than a weak metrical filler, adding nothing to the sense. (See now Vine 1992: n. 23, who prefers *gemina* for the same reason.) F.'s note, which begins by condemning *gemina nocte* as 'a piece of <Hellenistic> sophistication which seems suspiciously out of place,' somewhat inconsistently ends by conceding the possibility that C. 'has allowed a reminiscence of an Alexandrian conceit to intrude on Sappho.'

12 The fourth stanza of Sappho's poem is not translated (or at least only partially used) by C. Why not? There are in fact good reasons that might have prompted him to stop translating (fairly loosely, in ll. 1–7; rather closely, in ll. 9–12), as follows: (i) Sappho's fourth stanza has three feminine inflexions in its four short lines (including ἔμ᾽ αὔτᾳ in l. 16, recovered from a papyrus and first published in 1965; see Campbell 1982: 80 and 198); (ii) at least one of the symptoms described in it – χλωροτέρα δὲ ποίας ἔμμι – is, or at least might be considered, unlikely to be used of a male; (iii) by l. 12 the poem, whether of Sappho or of Catullus, has reached a point at which it can stop without appearing to be incomplete. Vine 1992 suggests that C.'s third stanza 'compresses' Sappho's third stanza together with some things taken from her fourth stanza.

13–16 See intr. n.

13 *tibi molestum est*, 'is giving you trouble.' The phrase is often used of medical conditions (Cicero, *Ad Fam.* 7.26.1, Hor. *Ep.* 1.1.108); where the afflictions of love are concerned, a closer parallel is to be found in Cicero, *Cael.* 44 *amores et deliciae ... quae firmiore animo praeditis diutius molestae non solent esse.* Editors quote Ov. *Rem.* 139 *otia si tollas, periere Cupidinis arcus.*

14 *exultas nimiumque gestis*: there are two passages in Cicero where these two verbs are linked together (*TD* 4.13, 5.16). Both of these passages, as the editors say, are physical in reference, having to do with uncontrolled restlessness and wanton desires; B. quotes the following definition, from Donatus' commentary

on Ter. *Eun.* 555: *'gestire' est motu corporis monstrare, quid sentias; constat autem a pecudibus ad homines esse translatum.*

15 *reges ... et ... urbes*: Q. and Lattimore 1944 refer to Theogn. 1103–4, F. to E. Fraenkel on 'Hellenistic moralizing about the effects of *otium* on the life of a community' (*Horace*, pp. 212–13).

Goldbacher, A. 1907. 'Das 51. Gedicht des C.,' *WS* 29: 110–15.

Amundsen, L. 1933. 'Catulliana I. Zur Sappho-Übersetzung C.s,' *SOsl* 12: 70–4.

Ferrari, W. 1938. 'Il carme 51 di C.,' *ASNP* 7: 59–72.

Tietze, F. 1939. 'C.s 51. Gedicht,' *RhM* 88: 346–67.

Lattimore, R. 1944. 'Sappho 2 and C. 51,' *CP* 39: 184–7.

Mariotti, S. 1947. 'Nota a C. c. LI,' *Paideia* 6: 303. [But see A. Riese's 1884 edition *ad loc.*]

Borszák, I. 1956. 'Otium Catullianum,' *AAntHung* 4: 211–19.

Kroymann, J. 1956. 'Zu C. c. 51,' *Festschrift für F. Sommer*. Berlin: 20–1.

Katičić, R. 1958. 'Die letzte Strophe in C.s Carm. 51,' *ZAnt* 8: 27–32.

Kidd, D.A. 1963. 'The Unity of C. 51,' *AUMLA* 20: 298–308.

Pavese, C. 1963. 'Due noterelle greco-latine. I,' *SIFC* 35: 117–18. [Lines 11–12; cf. Schol. Aesch. *Sept.* 782, p. 61 D.]

Alfonsi, L. 1965. 'Nota catulliana,' *Latomus* 24: 409–10.

Fredricksmeyer, E.A. 1965. 'On the Unity of C. 51,' *TAPA* 96: 153–63.

Akbar Khan, H. 1966. 'Color Romanus in C. 51,' *Latomus* 25: 448–60.

Woodman, A.J. 1966. 'Some Implications of *otium* in C. 51.13–16,' *Latomus* 25: 217–26.

Elder, J.P. 1966. 'The "Figure of Grammar" in C. 51,' *The Classical Tradition: Literary and Historical Studies in Honor of H. Caplan*. Ithaca, NY: 202–9.

Wille, G. 1967. 'Die innere Einheit von C.s c. 51,' *APhA* 2: 83–4.

Jensen, R.C. 1967. 'Otium, Catulle, tibi molestum est,' *CJ* 62: 363–5.

Lejnieks, V. 1968. '*Otium Catullianum* Reconsidered,' *CJ* 63: 262–4.

Frank, R.I. 1968. 'C. 51: *Otium* versus *Virtus*,' *TAPA* 99: 233–9.

Levin, D.N. 1969. 'Propertius, C., and Three Kinds of Ambiguous Expression,' *TAPA* 100: 221–35.

Deroux, C. 1971. 'Pour un commentaire de l'Ode à Lesbie,' *LM* 7 (31–2): 1–8.

Copley, F.O. 1974. 'The Structure of C. c. 51 and the Problem of the *otium*-strophe,' *GB* 2: 33–6.

Kinsey, T.E. 1974. 'C. 51,' *Latomus* 33: 372–8.

Wilkinson, L.P. 1974. 'Ancient and Modern: C. 51 Again,' *G&R* 21: 82–5.

Colaclides, P. 1978. 'Note sur la strophe finale du c. 51 de C.,' *Philologus* 122: 327–8. [Cf. Soph. *Ant.* 295–9, 672–5.]

Shipton, K.M.W. 1980. 'C. 51: Just Another Love Poem?,' *LCM* 5: 73–6.

Lund, A.A. 1981. 'Zum Verstandnis des Sappho-Gedichtes (C. 51),' *Maia* 33: 147–9.

Baker, R.J. 1981. 'Propertius' Monobiblos and C. 51,' *RhM* 124: 312–24.

Fredricksmeyer, E.A. 1983a. 'C. 51 and 68.51–6: An Observation,' *CP* 78: 42–5.

– 1983b. 'The Beginning and End of C.'s Longus Amor,' *SOsl* 58: 63–88. [Especially poems 51, 11.]

Itzkowitz, J.B. 1983. 'On the Last Stanza of C. 51,' *Latomus* 42: 129–34.

Knox, P.E. 1984. 'Sappho, fr. 31 L-P and C. 51. A Suggestion,' *QUCC* 17: 97–102.

Lefèvre, E. 1988a. 'Otium und τολμᾶν: C.s Sappho-Gedicht c. 51,' *RhM* 131: 324–37.

– 1988b. 'Paulus Melissus' Parodien von Sappho 31 LP und C. 51. Beobachtungen eines altphilologisches Lesers,' *Litterae medii aevi. Festschrift für J. Autenrieth*. Sigmaringen: 329–37.

Edwards, M.J. 1989. 'Greek into Latin: A Note on C. and Sappho,' *Latomus* 48: 590–600.

Segal, C. 1989. '*Otium* and *Eros*; C., Sappho, and Eur. *Hippolytus*,' *Latomus* 48: 817–22.

Marinone, N. 1991. 'L'acufene di Saffo e di C.,' *Studi di filologia classica in onore di C. Monaco*. Palermo: 115–19.

Vine, B. 1992. 'On the Missing Fourth Stanza of C. 51.' *HSCP* 94: 251–8.

Miller, P.A. 1993. 'Sappho 31 and C. 51: The Dialogism of Lyric,' *Arethusa* 21: 183–99.

52

Structure: cyclic, with enclosing repetition of a complete line.
On the corrupt state of politics at Rome.

In 55 BC, the probable date of the poem, the magistrates came into office immediately on their election, since political obstruction had prevented elections being held in 56 *for* 55. As L. noted, the natural time to protest about the sort of riff-raff who are obtaining office is when they have just been elected. In a normal year, someone who had just been elected as aedile would not yet be sitting in a curule chair, but in 55 he would. Notice also that the person referred to as Nonius must be occupying a curule chair for the first time. In the next line, Vatinius 'swears falsely' by his consulship (so he is not yet consul – which in any case did not come about until 47 BC – and is saying 'as surely as I *expect* to be consul,' most naturally when he is praetor already; as he was in 54 BC; he may have been on the list of future consuls, facetiously referred to by Cicero, *Ad Att.* 4.8a.2). One candidate for identification as 'Nonius' is Nonius Sufenas; but as he was tribune in 56, he could not have held any office in the following year, 55. Another is Nonius Asprenas, who could indeed have been aedile (or praetor) in 55; he was of proconsular status, probably *legatus pro consule*, under Caesar in 46, which is the first year in which we hear anything definite about him, as Łinderski 1971 remarks.

Metre: Iambic (not pure iambic, as found in poem 4 and, with an exception, in poem 29).

1, 4 *emori*, 'die outright.' The expression is typically extravagant; it need not imply that C. was fatally ill when he wrote it. Cicero, *Ad Fam.* 14.4.1 *te cupio videre et in tuo complexu emori*, addressed to his wife Terentia, is certainly gloomy in tone, but does not carry the implication that the writer is on the point of dying; nor does *emori cupio* at Ter. *Heaut.* 971 imply this of the speaker, Clitipho (cf. *Phorm.* 956 *emori hercle satius est*). It follows that no inference can safely be drawn for the date of C.'s death from an attempt – even a successful attempt – to fix the year to which this poem refers. (See the following n. on Nonius.)

2 *Nonius*: on his identification, as well as the date of the poem, see intr. n. See also the n. on 29.24.

struma: Boethius (see App. Crit.) says that there was a certain Nonius 'whom Catullus calls a *struma*.' Since there is no reason for supposing Boethius to be in error, the clear implication is that *struma* is here a common, not a proper, noun; there is no such person as Nonius Struma.

3 *peierat*, 'swears falsely.' The text of *V* gives *perierat*, pluperfect indicative from *pereo*, because of the scribe's unfamiliarity with the less common word, at least in its classical form of the Republican period; *peierare* came to be ousted by *periurare*, which was also the medieval form (hence the remark in *OLD*: 'N.B. The MS. evidence for these forms is often unreliable'). Notice also that *V*'s error in reading *novius* in l. 2 is corrected by Pliny and others who quote the line: see the Testimonia and the App. Crit.

Taylor, L.R. 1964. 'Magistrates of 55 BC in Cicero's *Pro Plancio* and C. 52,' *Athenaeum* 42: 12–28.

Łinderski, J. 1971. 'Three Trials in 54 BC – Sufenas, Cato, Procilius – and Cicero, *Ad Atticum* 4.15.4,' *Studi in onore di E. Volterra* 2. Milan: 281–302.

Barrett, A.A. 1972. 'C. 52 and the Consulship of Vatinius,' *TAPA* 103: 23–38.

Cornacchia, G. 1973. 'Considerazioni formali sul carme 52 di C.,' *BStudLat* 3: 89–91.

Granarolo, J. 1976. 'C. LII. Simple fronde ou pessimisme sans merci?' *Mélanges offerts à J. Heurgon.* Paris: 333–9.

Traina, A. 1985. 'Strutture catulliane: il c. 52,' *AFLNice* 50: 269–72.

Maisonobe, J.F. 1985. 'A propos de C. LII,' *AFLNice* 50: 273–82.

<h1 style="text-align:center">53</h1>

Structure: unitary.

A glimpse of Calvus in the courts. Date: probably, though by no means certainly, 58 BC, when Calvus was twenty-three or twenty-four years old.

(Tacitus, *Dial.* 34.7, implies that Calvus was not much, if at all, older than twenty-two). F. has a long historical introduction where, of the three prosecutions of Vatinius, he rejects that of 56 BC and leaves the question open as between 58 and 54. See Gruen 1966, who in a long article identifies the trial with that of 54 BC, mentioned by Cicero, *Ad Q. F.* 2.15.3.

1 *nescio quem*, 'someone or other.'
   corona, 'the circle' (of spectators, surrounding the open colonnades of a basilica where a trial was being held).
2 *mirifice*, 'wonderfully *well*'; note that the second adverb is always implied – but *merely* implied, never expressed – in this locution, which is a great favourite with Cicero. Cf. 84.3 (where again, as usual, it means 'wonderfully well'); see however 71.4 n. for an apparent exception.
   Vatiniana (*crimina*, l. 3) = the charges *against* Vatinius. The date of this prosecution is most likely to have been 58 (rather than 56 or 54) BC; see intr. n.
3 *G²* characteristically preserves, as a 'variant,' *m*'s careless error (*carmina* for *crimina*).
   explica<vi>sset, 'had laid out' (lit. 'unrolled').
4 *manusque tollens*, as a sign of astonishment; cf. Cicero, *Ad Fam.* 7.5.2 *sustulimus manus*.
   The *R²* reading (*inanius*) surely came from *X*; cf. *G*'s *inanus*).
5 *di magni*: cf. 14.12.
   salaputium: clearly a vulgar word, though otherwise unknown; perhaps wholly or partially obscene in content (connected probably, if so, with *salax* in a sexual sense, and just possibly with *praeputium*; the connection, suggested by Kr. and some other editors, with *putus* = 'boy,' on the grounds of Calvus' diminutive stature – *parvulus statura*, Sen. *Contr.* 7.4.7 – seems less likely, because of the quantity of the first syllable, though the context does seem to suggest – see the n. on *disertum* below – that an allusion to Calvus' smallness, or insignificant appearance, is contained in the word).
   disertum: editors have failed to observe that this adj. bears the full force of a predicate: supply *est*, and translate, not 'an eloquent little runt!' but (much more trenchantly, with an effect of climax and surprise) 'the little runt can <actually> make a speech!' Notice that *disertus* means 'articulate' rather than – in the full sense – 'eloquent.'

MacKay, L.A. 1933. 'C. 53.5 "di magni, salapantium disertum,"' *CR* 47: 220.
Comfort, H. 1935. 'The Date of C. 53,' *CP* 30: 764–76.
Bickel, E. 1953. 'Salaputium: Mentula Salax,' *RhM* 96: 94–5.
Gruen, E.S. 1966. 'Cicero and Licinius Calvus,' *HSCP* 71: 215–33. [55 BC.]
Knobloch, J. 1969. 'C. 53.5 and Cicero,' *RhM* 112: 23–9.

54

Structure: unitary (54^b should be regarded as a separate poem, or fragment). On some unsavoury followers of Pompey and Caesar (cf. poem 29, where both are attacked).

Some name must appear in the role of the person addressed; it would be strange to leave that person anonymous while naming his associates. The word *rustice* appears in *V*'s text; there is no reason why the required name should not be found in it (see l. 2 n. and App. Crit.).

1 *Otho*: unknown, like Libo (l. 3; but see n. there for a conjecture) and Sufficius. Possibly to be identified with L. Roscius Otho; see Neudling 1955: 135–6.
caput: Q. follows Lenchantin's edition in suggesting that perhaps *caput* (by itself) = *caput mentulae*. This transferred meaning seems however to receive no convincing support. *Priap.* 83, line 5 of which Lench. cites, links *caput* to *penis* throughout, but does not equate them, and the interpretations of Calvus' epigrams which Q. adduces are implausible. It is possible that Otho is indirectly represented as a *fellator*, which in Ps.-Cicero, *Invect. in Sall.* 18, seems to be the meaning of *c(h)ilo* (= one *cui frons est eminentior, ac dextra sinistraque veluti recisa videtur*).
oppido, 'exceedingly'; Quintilian, 8.3.25, says that this word had recently become obsolete. The dependence of G^2 on *m* is well illustrated by his election of *m*'s deviant spelling (*opido*) in this line.
2 See App. Crit., where I propose *at mi* for *V*'s *et eri*. At 67.6, B. in his commentary (p. 484) suggests *facta era rite* for *V*'s *facta marite* ('ER pro M repositis').
Rustice: coins attest to the existence of the name Rusticus in the Republican period (e.g., the moneyer M. Aufidius Rusticus = *RE* Aufidius 35), though it occurs much more commonly in the Empire. (See Crawford 1974: 262.) A. Guarinus, whose text reads *at en rustice*, notes: 'Vide, inquit, o rustice, quo modo libo iste immundus . . . ,' which may or may not imply that he took *Rustice* as a proper name, as Puccius apparently did. The annotation by Puccius (see App. Crit.) may go back to Pontanus; see J.L. Butrica, *Res publica Litterarum* 3 (1980): 5–9. Some Mss of ca. 1460, e.g., *Vic.* (= No. 122) and *Harl.* 2574 (= No. 49), had already offered *et en*.
3 *Libonis*: possibly the Pompeian, L. Scribonius Libo (consul, 34 BC); see Neudling 1955: 102–3.
4 *si non omnia*: i.e., 'I think you and your friend Sufficius should at least take exception to the squalid habits of Libo, as well as noticing Otho's tiny head <as you already do>.' Observe that whereas *est* (l. 1) records a fact – apparently recognized by both C. and Rusticus, and perhaps already mentioned by the latter – *vellem* expresses a wish for something else to be taken into account; hence

the emphatic position of *at* (l. 2), separated from the rest of the clause by the parenthetical *mi Rustice*.

5 *recocto*, probably 'rejuvenated' in a general sense (Petron. fr. 21 *anus recocta vino*), rather than alluding in a literary way to the story of Medea and Aeson (Ov. *M.* 7.159–93).

Mazzoni, G. 1938. 'At non effugies meos iambos (C. LIV),' *A&R* 6: 207–13.

Neudling, C.L. 1955. *A Prosopography to Catullus* (Iowa Studies XII). Oxford.

Deroux, C. 1969. 'C. 54.2,' *Latomus* 28: 645–8.

Crawford, M.H. 1974. *Roman Republican Coinage* (Cambridge): Index, s.v. M. Aufidius Rusticus.

Tandoi, V. 1976. 'L'arguzia del carme 54 di C.,' *SIFC* 48: 5–28.

Forsyth, P.Y. 1987. 'C. 54: A Note,' *CW* 80: 421–3.

54$^{\rm b}$

Structure: unitary distich.

On Caesar (cf. poem 29, and note the repetition of *imperator unice* from that poem). The date, therefore, is after 55 BC, the year to which – or shortly after which – poem 9 can be confidently dated. C. will not give up attacking Caesar, despite the latter's protests. Cf., perhaps, poem 93, especially the phrase *velle placere*.

1 *iterum*: after poem 29, since the words *imperator unice* (line 2 here: *unice imperator*) are borrowed from that poem (line 11). Note that poem 29 is in *iambi*; see next n.

iambis: for the threat of *iambi*, cf. (e.g.) 40.2. See also 36.5.

2 *inmerentibus*, 'innocent' (Q.).

unice imperator = Caesar; see line 1 n.

55

Structure: possibly 5 + 5 + (2 + 2) + 5 + 3; but the poem appears to be unfinished.

This and its companion piece (poem 58$^{\rm b}$) have much in common. Both are on the same theme (the search for Camerius); both show the same metrical peculiarity; both (but especially poem 58$^{\rm b}$) have the look of unfinished work; and at least up to the end of the nineteenth century editors tended to unite them, generally by inserting 58$^{\rm b}$ somewhere near the middle of 55, either before or after l. 13 (see F. on the history of these transpositions). But even if C. in principle himself arranged the collection as we have it (see the

Introduction), the last nine or so poems of this, the 'neoteric' or 'polymetric' part of the book, beginning with poem 54, look (more than anything else in the rest of the opus, except possibly poem 116, where see nn.) like gleanings from his notebook which an editor has posthumously inserted (and here it is particularly interesting that in the British Library Ms *Harl.* 2525 of Terence, fol. 11ʳ, 52.1 is quoted as being *prope finem primi operis*; see Intr., p. 7); and our two poems in particular could well be taken to represent 'work in progress,' respectively a draft for a poem about the elusive Camerius (which was intended to be longer than the length of the surviving fragments) and – poem 58ᵇ – part of an alternative draft, in a still more inchoate state. The date is 55 BC or later; see line 6 n. On the identity of Camerius (a friend of Catullus, probably from Cisalpine Gaul, and a Roman citizen) see Wiseman 1976.

Metre: an apparently experimental mixture of regular hendecasyllable with (in the majority of lines) a kind of decasyllable line achieved by resolution of the second and third syllables of the second foot into a single long syllable.

1 *si non molestum est*, 'if it isn't any trouble'; a polite phrase (Plaut. *Rud.* 120, Ter. *Ad.* 806, Cicero *Ad Fam.* 5.12.10, *Phil.* 2.41), used here with a tinge of irony.

2 *tenebrae* = 'lurking-place.' The word contains a hint of disreputable behaviour (so also *OLD* s.v., 1 b); e.g., Cicero, *Sest.* 20 *ex diuturnis tenebris lustrorum ac stuprorum.* Palladius' substitution of *latebrae* is unnecessary.

3 See App. Crit. *Campo ... minore*: the location of this *Campus minor*, apparently the same as *Campus Martialis*, is uncertain; see B. and F., and esp. Wiseman 1980: 183–6, who finally endorses a site near the Porta Caelimontana, on the Mons Caelius. The objections of Richardson 1980 are adequately met by Wiseman.

4 *R²*'s correction (given as a variant) is pretty certainly original (note the agreement of *OGR*); *m* at first missed the correction, probably through haste, but almost immediately noticed it and corrected it himself (*m¹*). Corruption of *in* to *id* was easy because *idcirco* is a familiar and common word.
Circo = the Circus Maximus, near the Forum. See Wiseman 1980.
libellis: no wholly convincing explanation has been given, either of what this means, or why C. should expect to find Camerius there. The best is still Scaliger's: 'bookshops,' defended by Wiseman. See F.'s n. Non. Marc. 134 alleges that *ligellum* = *tuguriolum*, citing Plaut. *Aul.* 301, where however the proper reading is *tigillo*; Guarinus refers to both Plautus and Nonius in support of his (more likely, his father's) emendation. But 'huts,' presumably as the squalid abodes of vice, could only with difficulty be interposed among the public places mentioned in lines 3–6.

te in omnibus: the *e* is short; such shortening of 'unaccented long syllables in hiatus' (F.; see his n.) belongs to colloquial speech (*sermo cotidianus*).

5 The temple C. has in mind is obviously the Capitoline temple of Jupiter. *sacrato*: simply = *sacro*, 'consecrated to.'

6 *Magni ambulatione* = *portico Pompei*. This *porticus* was dedicated in 55 BC, which of course gives a *terminus post quem* for the composition of the poem. F. (quoting Ov. *AA* 1.67, 3.387, and Prop. 4.8.75) notes its popularity as a place for 'girl-hunting.' Wiseman 1980 adds Prop. 2.32 and three passages in Martial.

7 *femella*: this form is otherwise unknown, but it is almost certainly colloquial; there is, however, an entry in Isidore's *Origines* (ca. AD 600) under *femellarius*, in the sense of 'womanizer.' Words that 'went underground' for several centuries in this manner usually belonged exclusively (and originally) to the colloquial idiom, which preserved them.

8 *vultu sereno*, of the *femellae*: they 'looked blank' when confronted with C.'s questions. (*vultus* = 'expression,' as seen by others; not 'regard' or 'look' or 'gaze,' which anyway would give poorer sense here.)

9 See App. Crit. On *en* in second place, see Skutsch 1969: 43 n. 10.

The suggestion by Gordon Williams *ap. F.* (that *iratus* was what C. wrote, and a scribe added *vel -te* above the line) has some merit, but (i) there are only very tenuous grounds for supposing supralinear glosses to have crept into the text of C., (ii) a reasonable motive for changing *iratus* to *irate* seems hard to discern. *usque*: 'I kept on calling to them, demanding an answer.' Foster 1971, reading *ipse*, would tr. 'alone,' i.e., 'without my friends' help.' But *usque* gives easier sense; and the line is surely corrupt enough to justify the substitution.

10 *Camerium*: the verb ('give me ...') is in ellipse, which is a further colloquial touch. The *e* in the name is short by nature (58^b.7), but could be lengthened 'by position' if the following *i* were to be treated as consonantal; the word *principium* is so treated by Horace, *Od.* 3.6.6.

In lines 9–10, Goold suggests 'aufertis ... puellae?' This makes good sense, but the corruption into *avelte* is hard to explain.

11 *nudum reducta pectus*, in spite of F.'s strictures on its possible meanings, should be admissible – in poetry – in the sense of *cum reducta veste pectus nudavisset*.

It is difficult to decide between the supplements that have been offered. Riese's is not palaeographically inferior, since *cl* and *d* are often confused, and the *c* may well be explained as the beginning of an unfinished *d*. The same kind of merit attaches to Fr.'s *nudum reclude pectus*.

12 *em* or *en*? See App. Crit. *em* (short *e*) is possible, and a hiatus after it is normal (Lindsay, *Early Latin Verse*, 243, quoted by F.). However, F. also rightly points out that in this poem (and, it could be added, in its metrical fellow, 58^b), the first foot, apart from the proper name in l. 10, is regularly spondaic, which tends to establish *en*.

13 *Herculei*, gen.; the *-is* form was also current (Cicero, *De fin.* 2.118: see Varr. *LL* 8.26 [on the two forms] *cum utrumque sit in consuetudine*). For the proverb itself, cf. Plaut. *Pers.* 2, Cicero *Acad.* 2.108.

14 *tantone* ... I now read this as a statement, not a question (see F.'s n. on *tanto ... negas* as an 'inverted consecutive,' and cf. 22.11 and 17.). For *in*, cf. Lucr. 3.295: <the lion> *effervescit in ira*.

15 *ubi sis futurus*, 'where I can find you.'

16 See App. Crit. It is understandable that m^2 should correct *crude* in *m*; what is remarkable is that in going over *R* he should carefully preserve the original error (*crude*) and enter it as a variant in the parent Ms. See McKie: 128, 203–4.
   luci, originally written *lucei*, is almost certainly right: (i), as often happens, the unfamiliar *-ei* is changed to *-et*; (ii) the noun *luci* provides a contrast to *tenebrae* in l. 2.

17 *lacteolae*: possibly colloquial (elsewhere only in late authors).

18 *si tenes* (continuous present tense), 'if you *go on* holding ...'

19 *fructus amoris*: cf. Prop. 3.20.30 *fructu semper amoris egens*.

20 There were two opposed views about this: C. of course urges the one that suits his purpose. Cf. (e.g.) Plato, *Symp.* 182d λέγεται κάλλιον τὸ φανερῶς ἐρᾶν τοῦ λάθρᾳ, but also Prop. 2.25.29–30 *quamvis te diligat illa, in tacito cohibe gaudia clausa sinu*.

21 *palatum*, here of speech, not taste: Hor. *S.* 2.3.274, Ov. *Am.* 2.6.47.

22 See App. Crit. *V* has *vestri sis*, which of course is nonsense. To emend the former word, and so read *nostri sis*, yields F.'s translation, 'so long as you are not detaching yourself from my love'; but surely at the end of this particular poem *particeps esse amoris* must mean 'share the secret of (someone's) love'; and in this poem, too, the whole argument is about Camerius' concealment of *his* love. There is no hint, so far, that C. is anxious to blurt out an affair of his own. It would be entirely possible for Camerius simply to produce the girl – and thereby to reveal his secret – without having to say a word (which is what seems to have troubled F.). R^2's attempted correction *nostri* obviously depends on acceptance of *sis*; see p. 42.

Barwick, K. 1928. 'Zu C. c. 55 und 58ª,' *Hermes* 63: 66–80.

Foster, J. 1971. 'C. 55. 9–12,' *CQ* 21: 86–7.

Peachy, F. 1972. 'C. 55,' *Phoenix* 26: 258–67.

Camps, W.A. 1973. 'Critical and Exegetical Notes,' *AJP* 94: 131–2. [Lines 6–10.]

Slater, W.J. 1974. 'Pueri, turba minuta,' *BICS* 21: 133–40.

Wiseman, T.P. 1976. 'Camerius,' *BICS* 23: 15–17. [Criticism of Slater.]

Rawson, E. 1978. 'The Identity Problems of Q. Cornificius,' *CQ* 28: 188–201, esp. 190 n. 16. [Criticism of Slater.]

Richardson, L., Jr. 1980. 'Two Topographical Notes,' *AJP* 101: 53–6. [*campo minore*.]

Wiseman, T.P. 1980. 'Looking for Camerius: The Topography of C. LV,' *PBSR* 48: 6–16. [= *Roman Studies* (1987): 176–86.]

Wiseman, T.P. 1981. 'Camerius Again,' *LCM* 6:155. [Further criticism of Slater.]

56

Structure: 4 + 3.

Whether the incident which C. professes to record really happened or is fictitious, the way in which he presents it is perhaps modelled, as Kr. suggests, 'on epigrams such as those that have for their pattern Strato, *AP* 12.222.' But (to translate Kr. further) 'C. gives a wholly personal character to the conventional motif: *inter alia*, he involves his friend Cato, and in doing so is at least not reluctant to play on the jingle *Cato–Catullum*.'

Who, in fact, is Cato? M. Porcius Cato (of Utica) seems an unlikely recipient of this particular communication, even though (according to Plutarch, *Cato Minor* 7) he composed *iambi* and thus might have been considered by C. as a practitioner of one of his own kinds of poetry and hence as at least a potential friend (to say with Fr. that he 'was probably associated with C.'s circle' may be going too far). Another possibility is Valerius Cato, a fellow-poet of C.'s and a member of the 'neoteric' movement.

1 For the colloquial *o rem*, cf. Cicero, *Ad Att.* 6.4.1 *o rem totam odiosam!* The slightly diversified repetition of this line at l. 4 is characteristic of C.; cf. 8.3 and 8 (also 8.5 and 37.12). Cf. Archilochus 168 W 2–3 χρῆμά τοι γελοῖον ἐρέω κτλ.

2 *tuo* of course refers to *auribus* as well as to *cachinno*; cf. 68.1, where *acerbo* must refer both to *casu* and to the preceding *fortuna*.

3 *ride*: intransitive; not, of course, taking *Catullum* for object.
   quidquid amas: a more pointed form of the regularly used idiom *si me amas*, 'pray have the goodness to.' Kr. quotes Gell. 12.1.23 *quidquid ita educati liberi amare patrem atque matrem videntur*, 'whatever *apparent* filial affection there is in children so raised' (i.e., by a wet-nurse).
   Cato: the vocative is inserted in a tightly bound phrase; cf. 87.2.

4 For this colloquial use of *nimis* = 'very,' cf. 43.4.

5 *deprendi*, 'caught in the act' (cf. 62.35 *comprendis*).
   Take *pupulum puellae* together: 'my girl's little boy-servant.' To take *puellae* as dative is, as Kr. remarks, equally hard in grammar and in sense.
   Calphurnius printed *pupullum* in the dedication to his 1481 edition, but the correction was carelessly left out by the printer. See Gaisser 1993: 37, 295.

6 *trusantem* = *masturbantem*. For *trudere* in a similar sense, cf. Mart. 11.46.3.
   The existence of the verb *trusare* is implied by the expression *mola trusatilis*;

there is no need to change *V*'s reading (see App. Crit.) to *crisantem*, which in any event is used only of women.

si placet Dionae (where *si* is, as Kr. claims, roughly equivalent to *sic*): 'so help me Venus' might be the nearest colloquial equivalent in English. Strictly speaking, Dione is Venus' mother, not Venus herself; for the indirect allusion to a person by the mother's name, cf. 27.7 n. (*Thyonianus*). Notice also V. *Ecl.* 9.47, where Caesar is referred to by the adjective *Dionaeus*, as son (descendant) of Venus.

7 Although *V*'s reading is *pro telo*, we must take *protelo* (abl. of *protelum*) adverbially, 'in tandem,' 'in quick succession' (where something follows behind something else, in single file as it were, and swiftly). See Lucr. 2.531 and 4.190, with Bailey's notes. B. paraphrases it here as *uno tenore*.

rigida (= *mentula*; cf. the use of the participle *tenta*, without a noun, in much the same sense at 80.6); cf. Mart. 9.47.6 *in molli rigidam clune libenter habes*; Petron. 134.11 *nisi illud tam rigidum reddidero quam cornu*; *Priap.* 45.1 *rigidus deus* = Priapus.

cecidi = *pedicavi*. The verb *caedere* may perhaps have been chosen, as Kr. suggests, because it has overtones of punishment: *loris caedere* is the regular Latin expression for 'to flog.' The same ambiguity appears in *Priap.* 26.9–10, where the god Priapus says *solebam / fures caedere quamlibet valentes*. For *caedere* in a sexual sense, see *OLD* s.v. *caedo*, 2.

Housman, A.E. 1931. 'Praefanda,' *Hermes* 66: 402. [Lines 5–7.]

Buchheit, V. 1961. 'C. an Cato von Utica,' *Hermes* 89: 345–56.

Scott, W.C. 1969. 'C. and Cato,' *CP* 64: 24–9.

Tanner, R.G. 1972. 'C. LVI,' *Hermes* 100: 506–8.

Fehling, D. 1974. 'Gegen die neueste Aüsserung zu C. 56,' *Hermes* 102: 376. [Criticism of Tanner.]

Rockwell, K. 1975. 'O rem ridiculam!,' *CP* 70: 214.

Shackleton Bailey, D.R. 1976. 'O rem ridiculam!,' *CP* 71: 348.

Verdière, R. 1985. 'L' étrange aventure du 'Pupulus',' *RPh* 59: 189–93.

Decreus, F. 1986. 'La notion de valeur esthétique. Application au poème 56 de C.,' *Philosophica* (Univ. of Ghent) 38: 77–105.

57

Structure: 5 + 5. For the 'cyclic' effect obtained by repeating the first line at the end of the poem, cf. poems 16, 36, 52.

This lampoon, directed against Caesar and Mamurra, perfectly illustrates the needlessness, and indeed the impossibility, of supposing that sexual slanders (which were the current coin of political and public invective in that period) are meant as anything more than an elaborate form of abuse.

(Even the verses chanted by Caesar's own soldiers at his triumphs spoke in similar terms, with Nicomedes, king of Bithynia, in the place of C.'s Mamurra.) If one wished to reproach someone for immoral behaviour, one would of course take care not to seem implausible by accusing him simultaneously of passive homosexuality and the seduction of other men's wives – both of which were standard topics of triumph verses. If, however, the real object was to express dislike of, or opposition to, a person in the public eye, Roman custom dictated that all kinds of bizarre charges might be added to the burden of the indictment. Because of the rhetorical convention involved here, and because really serious accusations against Caesar, related to Mamurra and his activities under Caesar's command in Gaul – accusations of substance, which have nothing to do with the rhetorical tradition – are made in poem 29, I am inclined to disagree with Q. and to suggest that poem 29 is more likely than poem 57 to have been the composition that first offended Caesar (see nn. to that poem).

Alexander Pope must surely have had these lines in mind when he wrote (in *A Further Account of the Condition of Edmund Curll*): 'At the Bedstead and Bolster, a Musick-House in Moorfields, / Two translators in a bed together.'

1 *pulcre convenit* + dat., 'they get on splendidly <together>.' The *mG*² reading *pulchre* arises simply from a preference in the matter of spelling; cf. 61.191, where *OGR* spell *pulcre* but *m* changes to *pulchre*.

2 *-que* is postponed, and really belongs to *Mamurrae*; to say with E. (approved by Q.) that from its position between the names it 'distributes the vice equally to both' is grammatically dubious, to say no more. For *pathicus* and *cinaedus* together, as words of abuse, cf. 16.2; B. correctly points out that *pathicus* is somewhat wider in scope of meaning, but for practical purposes here the two are synonymous. The gossip that became attached to the name of Caesar, in which he figures as *cinaedus*, is (as Q. reminds us) retailed by Suetonius (*Iul.* 49).

3 The *macula Formiana* was probably financial (41.4 *decoctoris Formiani*). Caesar too had debts that exposed him to prosecution (Suet. *Iul.* 18). But there may be an underlying association of debt with luxury, and hence with vicious self-indulgence; cf. 29.2 (note *aleo*), 6–7.
   utrisque, plural (as in l. 6), instead of singular (as elsewhere in C.) of two people: Plaut. *Amph.* 223 *utrique imperatores*; Caelius in Cicero *Ad Fam.* 8.11.1 *utrisque consulibus* (so Livy 27.22.2). See *OLD* s.v., 3 b.

6 *morbosi*: it seems to me wrong to take this with *gemelli* (= *testiculi*), punctuating without a comma after *pariter*. The whole squib represents Mamurra and Caesar as an egregious *pair*, as like as peas; and we ought to see in lines 6–7 a series of increasing *cola* within the exposition of this theme.

7 Observe the superiority of *O*'s reading here. The word *lecticulus* is attested by Celsus 2.12.2 in a medical context; note *morbosi* in the preceding line. The 'cosy' effect (L.) of its juxtaposition with the other diminutive in *-ulus* (*erudituli*) is of course deliberate. For the literary ('grammatical') interests of the pair, notice (i) Caesar's *De analogia*, (ii) poem 105 on Mamurra.

Suet. *Aug.* 78 refers to *lecticula lucubratoria*; cf. also Plin. *Ep.* 5.5.5 for a similar use of *lectulus*.

8 For the extended sense of *vorax*, cf. 29.2 n.

adulter: Suet. *Iul.* 50–2 (containing inter alia the scurrilous verses to this effect sung at Caesar's triumph). On Mamurra, see 29.6–8.

9 See App. Crit. (It may be right to omit *et*; possibly, as B. suggests, *sociei* became *societ* and was later expanded by doubling of the *i*.) Tr. 'rivals who <nevertheless> also <have the benefit of each other's> share in.'

Birt, T. 1896. 'C. und Petron,' *RhM* 51: 468–70.
Scott, E.A. 1976. 'Gemelli (C., c. 57.6),' *RhM* 119: 349–51.
Lebek, W.D. 1982. '*Gemini* und *gemelli*: Anthologia Latina² (Riese) 457.8 und C. 57.6,' *RhM* 125: 176–80.

58

Structure: unitary (single sentence).
A communication to the Caelius of Verona mentioned in poem 100: C. has heard that Lesbia, whom he once loved with all his heart, is living an abandoned life with her lovers in Rome.

Like poem 11, this renunciatory poem is addressed not to Lesbia herself, but to someone else. It is nevertheless the saddest and the bitterest in tone of all the Lesbia poems; notice the heartbroken repetition *Lesbia illa, illa Lesbia*. C.'s disillusionment is complete. The repetition of the name, together with the reference to himself in the third person (cf. poem 8 for the pathos involved in this), and the declaration of his own devotion, are all associated with the past (perfect) tense in *amavit*; but with *nunc ... glubit* (the poem's only other verb) we turn to the harsh present, and the poem ends, as poem 11 also does, with a sudden shower of cold realism in the shape of ugly words. The phrase *Remi nepotes* clearly implies that Lesbia is in Rome; it also suggests that neither C. nor Caelius is there, certainly not Caelius. Of course, *glubit* (and the surrounding language) should by no means be taken literally; 'Lesbia' (whoever she was) was no prostitute (cf. 37.14 and see n. there.) It is a typical piece of Catullan passionate exaggeration.

1 *nostra* = *mea*; cf. 43.7. Here again *m* seems to have blundered into the right reading.

2 *unam*: compared by F. (on 10.17) to *unus* with superlative or comparative. What we should think of, also, is 31.11 *quod unum est pro* . . .; Lesbia outweighed (in herself alone) all others in the eyes of C.

3 *plus quam se atque suos*: besides Cicero, *TD* 3.72 (quoted by Kr. and F.), cf. *Brut.* 295 *hunc quem tu plus quam te amas*.

4 *quadriviis*: Prop. 4.7.19 *saepe Venus trivio commissa est*.

angiportis, 'alleys, lanes' (between two houses). *m* heedlessly misses R^2's correction, and reads *agi-* with *R*.

   m alters *R*'s unmetrical reading to *-viis* (a typical example of his independence in correction).

5 *glubit*, 'peels' (of *verpi*, etc.; *sens. obsc.*)

magnamini Remi nepotes, 'the (degenerate) descendants of great-souled Remus.' The mock-epic language enhances the brutality of the picture. For *Remi nepotes* (= present-day Romans) there are parallels: see 28.15, 29.5 and 9, 34.22, 49.1. Clearly C. is at Verona when he hears the news of Lesbia's goings-on *in Rome* (the last line is designed to make this point); Caelius, a Veronese friend (see 100.1–2), is with C. at Verona, in all probability. The date is likely to be close to, or somewhat later than, that of poems 41 and 43 (see the intr. n. to both poems).

   GR offer some evidence of an abortive attempt at correction on the part of *X*. We can plausibly reconstruct the archetypal (*A*) reading as follows: *magna*amiremi/ni** (*O* supposed that this meant that the *ni* should be added at the end, and so did *X*, who however tried to make a word out of *amiremini*.)

   The reading *magnanimos Remi* makes (it seems) its earliest appearance in *Ven. Marc.* 12.28 (No. 116), a Ms apparently of the 1460s. Jocelyn 1979: 87 attributes it to *Vat. Lat.* 1608, which is firmly dated as late as 1479.

Pearse, P.J. 1910. 'Miscellanea: C. 58.1,' *PCPS* 85: 6–7. [Punctuate: Caeli Lesbia, nostra Lesbia illa.]

Lenz, F.W. 1963. 'Catulliana,' *RCCM* 5: 62–7.

Bodoh, J.J. 1976. 'C. 58,' *AC* 45: 627–9.

Penella, R.J. 1976. 'A Note on (de)glubere,' *Hermes* 104: 118–20.

Arkins, B. 1977. 'C. 58.5,' *LCM* 2: 237–8.

– 1979. '*Glubit* in C. 58.5,' *LCM* 4: 85–6.

Jocelyn, H.D. 1979. 'C. 58 and Ausonius Ep. 71,' *LCM* 4: 87–91.

Skutsch, O. 1980. 'C. 58.4–5,' *LCM* 5: 21.

Randall, J.G. 1980. 'Glubit in C. 58; Retractio,' *LCM* 5: 21–2.

Sobrino, E.O. 1984. 'Catulo, c. LVIII,' *EClas* 26: 189–91.

58^{b}

Structure: impossible to say, as the poem gives a strong impression of being an unfinished draft; see on poem 55.

Theme: the search for Camerius. There is no logical syntax to be found by any rearrangement of the lines; F.'s long intr. n. states, and grapples with, the many difficulties.

Metre: experimental; see the metrical note on poem 55 for a brief discussion.

1 *fingar*, 'if I were to be moulded into the shape of,' rather than 'if I should think of myself as,' the mechanical giant Talos. Talos, an invention of Hephaestus, patrolled Crete as an automatic watchman and defender, in the service of Minos.

2, 3 See App. Crit. Muretus' transposition of these two lines does not help much in producing a logical syntax which really cannot be established by any rearrangement of the poem (see F.'s long intr. n.). Part of the trouble is that neither Ladas (the Spartan runner who died at the moment of victory in the Olympic games, Paus. 3.21.1) nor Perseus – both of them fleet of foot – has much to do with Talos. It might be better if *fingar* and *ferar* came in successive lines and *ego* were allowed to dominate the lines ending in *Perseus* and *bigae*, the latter being taken as nominative plural, its normal form (genitive singular would be irregular; there is an example in Varro, *Men.* 93 Büch, of *quadriga* as a singular, but probably not in the genitive case; see however Prop. 2.34.39, admittedly a corrupt line, and 3.9.17 *est quibus Eleae concurrit palma quadrigae*).

4 *Rhesi niveae* ...: cf. *Il.* 10.437 λευκότεροι χιόνος, θείειν δ᾽ ανέμοισιν ὅμοιοι.

5 *plumipedas*: the word is otherwise unknown. Perseus, in his search for the Gorgons, was helped by the gift of a pair of sandals from the Nymphs.

6 B. (followed by Cazzaniga) punctuates with a colon at the end of l. 6 and a comma at the end of l. 7, so that *quos ... dicares* more clearly = *quos si dicares* (though I think other punctuations too may have this interpretation in view: both Kr. and F., who do not adopt it, quote Cicero, *De off.* 3.75 *dares hanc vim M. Crasso, ... in foro, mihi crede, saltaret*); notice that thus we avoid the grammatical difficulty of pres. imperative *require* followed by the historic tense in *dicares*.

7 *Pace* F., the story of Aeolus, who tied the winds in a bag (Homer, *Od.* 10.17ff.), is surely in point here; *dicares* = 'made <them> over to' (exactly as Aeolus did to Odysseus); whereas the reading *iunctos* (which is – apart from *G*^{2} – a Humanistic conjecture, not in the text of *V*; see App. Crit.) would have to do, not with putting winds in a bag, but with harnessing horses or other animals. Notice that *vīctos*, as written (carelessly) in *m*, could easily be read as *iūctos*; hence *G*^{2}'s error, which in this case at least is certainly not due to conjecture.

8–10 *defessus … quaeritando*: cf. Plaut. *Amph.* 1014 *sum defessus quaeritando,*
   Epid. 197 *per omnem urbem sum defessus quaerere, Merc.* 805 *defessus sum*
   urbem totam pervenarier.
8 *medullis*: cf. Plaut. *Stich.* 340 *at ego perii, quoi medullam [medullas A] lassitudo*
   perbibit.
9 *peresus* (and notice *medullis*, l. 8): cf. 66.23 *exedit cura medullas.*

Comfort, H. 1935. 'Parody in C. LVIIIa,' *AJP* 56: 45–59.
Benediktson, D.T. 1986. 'C. 58[b] Defended,' *Mn.* 39: 305–12.

59

Structure: unitary (single sentence).
A defamatory pasquil: not a fragment, like (apparently) several of the poems
in its immediate vicinity, but a studied construction, the first line based
on a *graffito*, such as those found on the walls of houses in Pompeii; of
these, Q. quotes three (*CIL* IV 2421, 1427, 2402; Fr. gives the text of the
second and third): *Rufa ita vale quare bene felas; Salvia felat Antiocu luscu;*
Ionas cum Fileto hic fellat. On this opening, as Q. puts it, 'is built an
elaborately phrased sentence, in which Rufa's reputation is torn to shreds
with a detachment that renders the lurid imagery all the more telling.' No
identification is possible for those, like ourselves, who do not know the local
circumstances; but for those who did, the woman who is the target is very
carefully singled out by name, husband's name, place of origin, and name
of paramour. For a lengthier and more elaborate squib of the same kind, cf.
poem 67.
   Since the woman is described as coming from Bononia, the events of the
poem must be supposed to take place elsewhere; possibly in Verona (cf. again
poem 67).

1 *Ruf<ul?>um*: the name is not certain. For another pair of names that jingle, as
   this does with *Rufa*, cf. 56.3. Since the entire composition has to do with the
   woman's behaviour, not the man's, it is quite likely that his name has been
   invented to fit hers (if indeed it is a name; the word *rufulus* designated a kind of
   military tribune, and in C.'s time Bononia was an advanced military base). By
   naming her husband, and calling her *Bononiensis*, C. appears to wish to identify
   the woman. Several editors cite *CIL* IV 2421, on 'Rufa' (text in intr. n.; B. would
   read *quam bene* for *quare bene*).
   See App. Crit. The evidence of *O* points to *X* as the source of *R*[2]'s variant *al.*
   fellat.

2 Characteristically, C. extends his *diffamatio* by adding something else to Rufa's discredit: she is a *bustirapa* (Plaut. *Pseud.* 361), though there is no suggestion that she is additionally a *moecha* by trade, as Q. suggests (which would remove the intended horror of *uxor Meneni*); *tunderetur* (l. 5) = *vapularet*, 'she was being hammered,' without any implication of sexual relations.
sepulcretis occurs only here.

4 Cf. Ter. *Eun.* 491 *e flamma petere te cibum posse arbitror*, Tib. 1.5.53–4 *ipsa fame stimulante furens herbasque* [*escasque* Muretus] *sepulcris / quaerat et a saevis ossa relicta lupis.*

5 *semiraso ustore*: the *ustor*, described as *sordidus* by Lucan, 8.738, was the slave of the *libitinarius*. The fact that he is *semirasus* suggests that he is in fact a *fugitive* slave (Apul. *Met.* 9.12): half the runaway's head was shorn, as a means of recognition.

60

Structure: unitary (single-sentence address).
A single-sentence outburst of indignation at the unkind dismissal, by a friend, of C.'s appeal for sympathy and perhaps for help in an extremity of despair. It is not (explicitly, at any rate) connected, as poem 38 seems to be, with illness of mind or body; rather, the situation appears to be like that which we have encountered in poem 30. The name of the person addressed is not stated; but it is fairly clear that she, or he, is addressed in terms traditionally appropriate to an object of love rather than of mere friendship. As Weinreich 1959 points out, even though part of the topos goes back to *Iliad* 16.33–5 (Patroclus to Achilles: 'child of sea and rocks, not of Peleus and Thetis') – cf. V. *Aen.* 4.365–7 – much is due to Euripides, *Medea* 1342–3 (cf. 1358–9 and also *Bacchae* 988–90); the topos is usually applied to love relations. Notice also that C. here uses the choliambic metre, which as a rule he reserves for serious attacks (apart from poem 31, where the 'limping iambic' is chosen for special reasons); it is unlikely, therefore, that the lines are no more than an 'exercise' in a literary genre. Weinreich's belief that Lesbia is the addressee is supported by Lieberg 1966. The material appears to be used again at 64.154–7 (see line 1 n.).

1 For a (possible) reworking of the same notion in a different context by C., cf. 64.154–6. F. illustrates the history of the concept from Homer (*Il.* 16.33–5), Virgil (*Aen.* 4.366), and Ovid (*M.* 8.120–1). Cf. also Eur. *Med.* 1342–3.
Libystinis: see App. Crit., and notice *m*'s independence in the matter of spelling. Cf. V. *Aen.* 5.37 and 8.368 *Libystidis ursae* for another form of the adjective.

Libyssae occurs at 7.3. For the form *Libystinus* cf. Macrob. 1.17.24 (the only other instance in Latin).

2 *Scylla*: the picture given of her is Hellenistic (as in Lucr. 5.892, V. *Ecl.* 6.75, *Aen.* 3.426–8), not the Homeric one of *Od.* 12.85.

4 *novissimo*: this meaning of *novissimus* (= *extremus*) is rare (except in Tacitus: to F.'s three citations or references, namely *A.* 6.50, 12.33, 15.44, add the closing words of *Agric.* 45 *novissima in luce desideravere aliquid oculi tui*). Among poets, Statius has (in the same sense) *novissima verba* at *A.* 1.381. Cf. the use of *novissime* (adv.) at Catullus 4.24.

5 *contemptam haberes*, 'treat with contempt'; B. and Kr. compare Plaut. *Cas.* 189 *vir me habet pessumis despicatam modis*. Cf. Plaut. *Bacch.* 572, Ter. *Eun.* 384. As E. puts it, 'the combined verb and participle are not simply = the verb alone, they give the idea of permanence or settled determination.'

 We may plausibly reconstruct *A*'s reading as follows: *contĕtam* (perhaps hard to read; notice how G at first hesitates, and even O has second thoughts).

Weinreich, O. 1959. 'C. c. 60,' *Hermes* 87: 75–90.
Lieberg, G. 1966. 'C. 60 und Ps. Theokrit 23,' *Hermes* 94: 115–19.

61

Structure: (45 + 30) + 45 + (30 + 30) + 115 (including gaps in text) as follows:

Lines	Number of lines		
1–45	45	Invocation to Hymen	
46–75	30	Praise of Hymen	Hymn (formal in style)
76–113	45	Praise of the bride (reassuring her)	
114–43	30	} *Deductio* {	*Fescennina iocatio*; to the bridegroom
144–73	30		Address to the bride (encouraging her)
174–end	115	*Epithalamium* (properly so called)	

Place of the action: In 1–113: at the bride's former home. A chorus of girls (companions of the bride), assembled there, is called upon by the poet, acting as *choragus* or choirmaster (cf. Aristophanes, *Ran.* 372ff.), to invoke Hymen as the god of marriage (36–45).

 In 114–73: during the progress of the torchlight procession escorting the bride from her old home to the new (*deductio*). At l. 149, she comes within sight of the bridegroom's house; at l. 173, she arrives there. The Fescennine verses are deemed to be spoken by or on behalf of a male chorus (friends of the bridegroom).

In 174–228: at the bride's new home. The chorus of boys and youths, which has accompanied her, is still present; but the poet (who has acted as master of ceremonies throughout) may now, perhaps, speak with his own voice, rather than as *choragus* – notice the first person singular in l. 209 – as he gives the final blessing on the wedded pair, in the shape of a wish for children.

For a thoroughgoing analysis of the poem, and an especially penetrating account of its use of different kinds of language in its functionally differing component parts, see Fedeli 1972.

In artistry the sixty-first poem is one of the most successful, while in atmosphere it is surely one of the happiest, of C.'s compositions. It was written to celebrate the marriage of a pair whom C. evidently knew: one Manlius Torquatus (see ll. 16, 209, 215), who is most likely to have been L. Manlius Torquatus, praetor 49 BC (see F.) and who may or may not be the same as the Manlius of 68ᵃ (= 68.1–40), and his bride, whose name is given in the Mss as Iunia (l. 16) Aurunculeia (l. 82). (Since each of her names, as given, represents the *nomen* of a *gens*, there is a great deal to be said for Syme's suggestion of *Vibia*, as a known *praenomen*: cf. *ILS* 7819 [Praeneste], for example.) The affectionate, not to say tender, way in which C. – or his poetic persona – addresses and seeks to reassure the bride (who like many Roman brides was clearly very young) suggests that she may have been at least distantly related to him; the bridegroom, on the other hand, is mentioned much more briefly and more distantly. Such a *praenomen* as Vibia would strongly suggest central Italian origins; if C. belonged (as has been suggested) to a branch of the Valerii who came north to Verona from that region in the disturbances after the Social Wars, a family connection (perhaps two generations removed) is not unthinkable.

That the poem was designed for recitation or 'performance' – by a pair of choirs – at the actual wedding ceremony, is in the highest degree unlikely, for several reasons. (i) Philodemus, *De Musica* (ed. Kemke) 68.37–40, writing about 50 BC, says of his time νῦν δὲ δή σχεδόν καὶ παντάπασι καταλελυμένου τῶν ἐπιθαλαμίων – i.e., the singing of epithalamia (at weddings) had died out, or virtually so. (ii) As Fedeli remarks towards the end of his monograph (p. 128), little or no regard is paid in poem 61 to the conventions of the ceremony; most of the significant ritual acts of a Roman wedding are totally ignored. (iii) The poem is not fully dramatized; it is in parts, and to a considerable extent, a descriptive monologue.

Professor T.P. Wiseman (1985: 199) nevertheless appears to suggest that poem 61 was indeed 'an actual choral ode to be sung simultaneously with, and as a part of, the ceremonies it describes,' which seems to encounter all three of the objections I have just raised. Moreover, an ode should maintain a public, rather than drop intermittently into a private and colloquial, level of *language*; nor should it have, as a separate and distinguishable element, a hymn to Hymen. In two publications, both cited by Wiseman 1985: n. 71, Professor F. Cairns suggests – though to all appearance merely en passant – that poem 61 is to be classed as a choric ode, 'though without necessarily implying anything about performance in real life,' as W. puts it; but (as Fedeli has shown in great detail) the originality of Catullus is such that, for all his awareness of literary tradition, it is hard indeed to squeeze him within the template of generic composition.

In the time of Catullus the lustre of Sappho's name attached to an entire book of epithalamia, composed for real persons. When the form was revived in the Hellenistic age, we *know* that this was done as a literary exercise because (as F. has pointed out in his introduction to this poem) the only surviving example, Theocritus XVIII, celebrates the marriage not of flesh-and-blood mortals but of characters in myth. In C.'s generation we know of glyconic epithalamia by Ticidas and by Calvus (a single short fragment remains from each of these). Calvus, like C. in poem 62, at least experimented also with hymeneal 'songs' in hexameters. Here too the revival of the form was surely a matter of artistic interest, rather than of social utility. When Ovid later said (*Ex Ponto* 1.2.131–2) to his friend Fabius Maximus

> ille ego, qui duxi vestros Hymenaeon ad ignes,
> et cecini fausto carmina digna toro,

he is still sufficiently under the spell of tradition to say *cecini*; but of course the epithalamium in question was never meant to be sung (and it would not in any case have been sung by an individual).

Metre: A stanza, not of three glyconics plus one pherecratean, as in poem 34, but of four glyconics plus one pherecratean (cf. Anacreon, frs. 1 and 2 D). Synaphea is observed – i.e., within the stanza the lines are regarded as merging into each other without a break so that *syllaba anceps* is not permitted at the end of the line (except at the end of the stanza). Corinna (*Suppl. lyr.* 2 D) similarly maintains synaphea, though in her stanza the glyconic has a different form. The Mss show one exception to this (line 185 *est tibi*); modern editors transpose (to *tibi est*), as it is thought unlikely that C. would in this one place have broken a rule elsewhere so strictly observed, and it was just as easy and natural to write *tibi est*. There may be one instance of a short syllable ending a glyconic, if the Ms reading is correct, at line 215 *omnibus*; but this is not really surprising, since lengthening of short syllables ending in a single consonant occurs in Latin poetry even within lines. For *-us* lengthened before a vowel cf. 64.334, where the transposition *tales umquam*, printed in the first edition of my text, spoils the balance of this line and the next; in Virgil, cf. *Geo.* 2.5 *gravidus autumno*, 4.453 *non te nullius exercent*, *Aen.* 4.64 *pectoribus inhians*. Elision between lines is allowed. In the refrain, the second *io* could be either one syllable without elision, or two syllables with elision; but since it must be a monosyllable at the beginning of the line, clearly it should be read as a monosyllable each time it occurs. In general, *io* can in Latin be treated either as a disyllable (with vocalic *i*) or as a monosyllable (with consonantal *i*); for a similar flexibility cf. V. *Aen.* 1.288 *Iulius a magno dimissum nomen Iulo*. *Io* is a disyllable in Ov. *M.* 5.625 *et bis 'io Arethusa, io Arethusa' vocavit*; but it is a monosyllable in Mart. 11.2.5 *clamant ecce mei 'io Saturnalia' versus*. Note that in the Ovidian passage there is hiatus before disyllabic *io*; this would not be allowed before monosyllabic *io*, where the *i* is consonantal. Likewise, a short syllable ending with a consonant is lengthened before monosyllabic *io*.

(NOTE: In the detailed nn. on this poem, Fe. = Fedeli 1972.)

1 Notice the hiatus, which frequently occurs after an exclamation, and particularly after the exclamation *o*.

   C. is the first Roman poet to use displaced (postponed) *o* (Fe. 24).

2 The god of marriage (Hymen) is described as the offspring (*genus*, a solemn word) of Urania. See Estevez 1977/78, who points out that if the name of a Muse must stand between *cultor* and *genus*, three Muses are available, each of whom is attested in antiquity as Hymen's mother: Terpsichore, Calliope, Urania. But the first two names will not produce the trochaic opening which, in glyconics, C. overwhelmingly prefers. More important is this: *Aphrodite Urania* stands for pure, or wedded, love (note the frequency of *bonus* etc. in this poem; cf. 180 n.); this, and the association of the 'iunctura' *Aphrodite Urania*, might themselves suffice to cause C. to select this particular Muse (for Muse she is, as the mention of Helicon shows) in preference to others. Callim. fr. 2a.42ff. gives Urania.

3 After mentioning the god's abode and parentage, C. adds a *qui*-clause; this 'relative-style' is closely linked with the technique of the 'cletic' hymn (Fe. 23).

5 Fe. and others would read *Hymen o*, since the collocation *o Hymen* seems not to occur in Greek; cf. also poem 62. (Clearly ll. 4–5 were wrongly divided, *hymen* at the end of 4 being transferred to the opening of 5.) In that case, *Hy̆men* in 4 will be followed by *Hȳmen* in 5 (cf. again poem 62). But, as F. points out, C. prefers a trochaic opening (above, n. 2, and F. 238).

8 Scholars are divided on the question whether the comma should follow *cape* (B., Kr., Fe.) or *laetus* (Fr., Mynors). Fr. quotes *cape laetus* from Hor. *Od.* 3.8.27 and *cape tura libens* from [Tibullus] 3.11 = 4.5.9, also *accipe laetus* from Statius

S. 3.4.7 (and a similar expression is found at V. *Aen.* 6.377, *cape dicta memor*). Cf. esp. 64.393 *acciperent laeti divum*. On the other side, Kr. and Fe. rely on Plato, *Legg.* 4.712b ἵλεως εὐμενής θ᾽ ὑμῖν ἔλθοι and *h. Orph.* 6.10 βαῖνε γεγηθώς, passages that Fe. regards as decisive. Fr. quotes several instances of *huc huc*, claiming that when this phrase occurs it is always at the beginning of a clause, as at 64.195 (though even he explains *laetus* as 'also to be taken ἀπὸ κοινοῦ' with *huc huc*). The punctuation adopted in the text appears to be supported by the otherwise usual division of the line, in this poem, after the third or fifth syllable, as Kr. points out.

9 *niveus*: a new word, much used by C. (Fe. 27 n. 1).

10 *luteum*, 'red'; cf. 188 n.

11 *excitus*: Kr. equates this with ἀνακληθείς, 'summoned,' probably rightly despite the objection by Fe. (27 and n. 2), who follows *TLL* ('laetus, bono et erecto animo').

13 *R²*'s correction is independent (followed by *m*), and essentially metrical.

14 The wedding god himself is called upon to dance; usually, this action is assigned to choirs of young people.

15 The purely Roman ritual that caused Parthenius to conjecture *spineam* is described by F. But the symbolism of pine torches at a wedding is familiar in poetry and art; and indeed 'torches' may stand for the wedding itself (64.25 and 302).

16 *namque* = γάρ (the *reason* for invoking the god is an essential part of the hymn; Kr. compares Ar. *Ran.* 876–83).
Iunia: the objection to *V*'s reading is that the bride will be given two gentile names, which is unparalleled. See the intr. n. on Syme's suggestion (*Vibia*).
Manlio must be right. See the Ms readings at line 215, and the mention of Torquatus 209; this family did not use the name *Mallius* (cf. Cicero and Livy for the spelling).

17 *colens*, of a god's abode: cf. 1–2, recalled here (still in prayer style). *colere* is not exactly = *custodire, servare*, as Fe. (following *TLL*) asserts.

18–19 *Phrygium ... iudicem*, Paris. 'Phrygian' = Trojan, cf. 63.2 n., 64.344 n., and Callim. *H.* 5.18. For this 'Alexandrian' style of learned allusion, cf. 2 *Uraniae genus*.

19–20 *bona ... alite*. Although the terms *auspex* and *auspicium* were still employed in connection with love and marriage (45.19 and 26), the taking of auspices, in the literal sense (i.e., from the flight of birds) was by C.'s time obsolete so far as weddings were concerned: see Cicero, *De div.* 1.28 (quoted by eds. and Fe.). For metaphorical *alite* = *auspicio*, cf. Hor. *Epod.* 10.1 *mala soluta navis exit alite* and the passages quoted here by F.

21 *floridis*, a 'poetic' word (Fe. 33).
velut: cf. l. 102 and 64.105 n.
enitens, in a literal sense (of flowers etc.) is rare (see Fe. 33).

22 The myrtle had both a connection with Venus and a special relation to the
Judgment of Paris (Fe. 32).
Asia: not the Roman province of Asia (Ă-), but the coastal region of Lydia,
around the mouth of the Cayster and the city of Ephesus (not 'the Maeander,' as
F. has it). Kr. translates 'Orient,' rejecting the Cayster allusion; but see Fe. 33–4.

23 *Hamadryades*: properly tree nymphs, but here = nymphs in general.

25 Metrically unique (spondee for dactyl in the second foot); but *roscido ... umore*
seems a natural 'iunctura' (cf. Pliny *NH* 9.38); a similar metrical substitution
occurs in poems 55 and 58 $^{\rm b}$; and *nutriuntur honore* (Mähly; rejected by Fe.
30 n. 2) would give feeble sense, even though the deponent form (cf. V. *Geo.*
2.425, where Mynors reads *nutritor*) is attested as correct by Priscian. See F. for
a metrical parallel from Seneca, and for Wilamowitz' explanation (namely that
apparent, though not real, parallels are to be found in such Greek glyconic lines
as Anacreon, fr. 11 D σύρίγγων κοϊλώτερα).

26 *age* is (like ἄγε in Greek) common in requests.
aditum ferens: prayer-style; cf. 43; also 63.47 and 79 *reditum ferre*.

27 *perge* + infin. simply implies the notion of haste (examples in Kr.); F.'s 'set about
leaving' is hardly right. At V. *Geo.* 1.16, a god is similarly called down from his
dwelling-place.
linquo (for *relinquo*) is archaic (Fe.).

27–30 *Thespiae ... frigerans ... Aonios*: these three words seem to have been
invented by C. (Fe. 38). They refer, of course, to Mount Helicon and its
surroundings (for the location of *frigerans Aganippe*, see Paus. 9.29.5).

31 *ac* is identified by Ross 1969: 28–9 as 'a connective of archaic formality.'

31–3 With this punctuation, *novi coniugis* is an objective genitive, related to
cupidam, which agrees with *dominam*. I see nothing against this. Kr., following
M. Bonnet, has no comma at the end of 32, and would make *cupidam* (*mentem*)
predicative, in close association with *amore revinciens*; i.e., the bridegroom's
mens passes from 'desire' to 'love' under the impulse of Hymen. But if this is so it
is hard to see how *revinciens* is connected to *voca*. B., again, wished to read *cupidi
novam* (with a comma after *novam*), leaving *mentem* unmodified; *coniugis
cupidi* was to be a possessive genitive, depending on *novam domum*; but the
order would then become unnatural, with no gain in meaning. Kr., punctuating
as B. did, suggested taking *coniugis novi* ἀπὸ κοινοῦ with *domum* and *cupidam*,
which is forced and improbable. F. seems to misinterpret Wilamowitz, as quoted
by Fr. (in his *Nachträge*).

32 On the meaning of *cupidus* see Biondi 1979 (with Granarolo's review).

34 *huc et huc* = *huc illuc*; cf. Hor. *Epod.* 4.9.

36 *vosque* = *vos quoque*; cf. possibly 102.3 *meque* (*V*; but see text and n.), and
perhaps (if Bergk's *gaudente* is rejected) 31.13.
simul, 'in unison with me.'

38 *in modum* appears to mean, not 'in time' (= *in numerum*), but 'in tune' (see examples in Fr., and cf. F.).

41 *ut*: notice that *quo* need not always be used in clauses of purpose involving a comparative.

42 *citarier*: there are five instances in poem 61 of the archaic infinitive in *-er*; elsewhere in C. this occurs only at 68.141 (but see App. Crit. and n. there). The verb *cito* belongs to the vocabulary of prayers, as do *munus* (in this sense) and *bonus*, used of gods (Fe.).

44 *bonae Veneris*: cf. line 195, and see Alfonsi 1967.

45 *coniugator*: a hapax eiremenon, apparently invented by C. (though Calvus, fr. 6 M, has *cara iugavit corpora conubiis*; and cf. *coniugare* at Cicero, *De off.* 1.58).

46 *quis deus* is regular and normal, whereas *qui deus* is unattested in poetry and very rare in prose (Fe. 43 n. 1).

46–7 The Mss have *amatis/est*, which is of course unmetrical. The most widely accepted emendation is Bergk's *est ama/tis* (though the only other division of a word between two lines can be justified as a very special case – the need to include the bride's own name at some point in a poem on her wedding; cf. 82 n.). Those who accept it (including Fr., Kr., Mynors – but F., who prints Mynors' text, has serious doubts about it and urges a solution on the lines of Haupt's *anxiis est* – and also Fe.) cite, as a parallel, 45.20 *amant amantur*, which will not serve (see B. and F. for cogent objections). Bergk (*Philologus* 16 [1860]: 619) and Fe. (44) refuse to accept *anxietas* as appropriate to the lover who has a prospect of happiness, though Fe. admits that there are passages where the epithet *anxius* is used of persons in love (e.g., Cicero, *TD* 4.70, *Ad Att.* 2.24.1); but Fe. claims that such passages refer to fears that the love will be short or the lover unfaithful, and that such feelings are not in point here. Yet the next two stanzas seem to refer to various specific forms of anxiety experienced even towards the time of the wedding (see 51 n.); and not much is to be gained by pointing out that *anxius* is not exactly synonymous with *timens* (54). When Fr. asserts 'Hier ist … von glücklicher Liebe die Rede,' he is probably thinking of 45.20, to which he at once refers, rather than ll. 46–7, which (with *est petendus*) seem to cover the entire course of love; see also his own citations, especially those from Ovid. On the whole it seems right to adopt Haupt's emendation, or something of the sort. The reading *amatis* at the end of 46 can be explained as prompted by *amantibus* at the end of 47.

51 *tremulus*: surely not 'of the shakiness of age' (F.; cf. 'der greise Vater,' Kr.), either here or in 68.142, which F. quotes in support. In the latter passage it clearly means 'anxious' (Munro 1905: 193), and is appropriated to the natural tendency of a parent to worry about the young (indicated by *suis* in the present passage). Here, too, it must mean 'anxious'; see the foregoing n. Cf. 64.242 and

379 for the adj. *anxius*, similarly applied; Prop. 2.22.42 *geminos anxia mater alit*. A Roman father would often be under forty years old at the time of a daughter's wedding, since girls married very young; that he should be *tremulus* because of age could hardly be a sufficiently typical circumstance to serve in a poem such as this. If 'anxious' is the proper translation, then *suis* can be taken ἀπὸ κοινοῦ with *tremulus* and *invocat*.

    m's careless error *remus* is characteristically preserved, as a variant, by G^2.

53 *zonam solvere* (cf. 2ᵇ.3) = ζώνην λύειν (*Odyssey* 11.245; see 2ᵇ.3 n.), which however is said to the *bridegroom*; but cf. Eur. *Alc.* 177–8 (with κορεύματα), *AP* 7.324 ζώναν λυσαμένα of the bride who allows the bridegroom to untie it. C.'s sources are, as Fe. remarks, literary, not antiquarian. *soluunt sinus* implies shaking out the folds of the garment when the confining ζώνη is loosened.

54 *timens*: Fr. supports the Ms reading by several quotations; notice especially Hor. *Ep.* 1.16.65 *qui cupiet metuet quoque* (cf. also Kr.).

54–5 The unfamiliar, because archaic, spelling *novos* (in the nominative) produced *V*'s *maritos*. Cf. 53.3, where *Calvos* has similarly produced *meos*.

56–8 Much the same sentiment appears in 62.21–4; though the expression there is stronger, voiced as it is by a choir of girls with a point to make in the singing contest in which the are opposed to the youths. There is no necessary allusion here to the tradition of 'capture' associated with a Roman wedding.

56 *manus*: editors (and Fe. 48) have seen in this word a reference to the legal expression *conventio in manum*, denoting a bride's transfer from the tutelage of her father to that of her husband; but the husband's legal assumption of (singular) *manus* was, as F. notes, 'obsolescent or obsolete' in C.'s time; the poetic value of such a notion is hardly evident; and, what is more important, the plural (*manus*) here suggests otherwise.

61 *nil potest sine te*: hymn-style (see refs. in Kr.).
    m's *nil* is metrically sound. Why, then, does m^2 feel obliged to add – and invent – *al. nihil*? Simply, it seems, to make the point that *if R*'s *nichil* were a valid reading, then it ought to be spelled *nihil*.

61–75 The last three stanzas of the invocation to Hymen are well annotated by E. (summarized by F. as follows: 'the blessings of marriage in the relation of man to woman, in the family, and in society.'). Notice especially Cicero, *De off.* 1.54, quoted by E. as a parallel.

64 *volente*, used in the 'sacral' sense, of divine approval.

65 *m*'s error (-*per*-) agrees with *O* by mere accident.

66 *quit* (R^2m^2) = *O*; it was probably in the margins of *X*. (Unrevised *CE* has '*corr. R*,' wrongly.)

67 *dare*, properly said of the mother (e.g., at V. *Aen.* 1.274, quoted by F.).

68 *nitier*: for the idea, cf. Eur. *IT* 57; also Cicero, *Cael.* 79 *unico filio nititur*, Sen. *Contr.* 2.1.7.

72 *queat* should not be replaced by an indicative; the imagined country which 'had no marriage rites' (71) is purely hypothetical, and such a country can hardly be the subject of a categorical statement in this context.

praesides: only freeborn citizens could serve in the legions; but the distinction made here is not that between legitimate and illegitimate children, since presumably, in a country where marriage (and hence the concept of legitimacy) was unknown, the disqualification of the illegitimate would not apply. Rather, what C. appears to say is that but for the institution of marriage, with its several advantages, many people would not have children at all (L.).

76 Fe. (56, and 117 n. 2) would take *ianuae* as vocative plural, 'admitting Callimachean influence and comparing *h. [2] Apoll.*, line 7,' and also because 224 (below) answers to 76 (presumably, therefore, because of the plural *ostia* in 224).

77 Since in 94–5 the words *faces quatiunt comas* again occur, with *viden* (or *vide ut*) clearly addressed to the bride (92 *nova nupta*), it is likely that here too *viden ut* is addressed to her. If so, it could scarcely follow immediately upon *adest* in the third person. Those who retain *adest* must take *viden ut* as a 'stereotyped formula' (F. on 62.8), similar in form but addressed to *several* persons, which seems less satisfactory. Notice that the doors have just been opened – this is a new section of the poem – and the bride is about to appear for the first time; *ades* need not be a command, but at most a request, repeated in successive stanzas (in the form *prodeas n.n.*) until she appears. Notice also that *viden ut* is followed by the indicative, being 'quasi-poetical' (F.); the phrase is colloquial (as the 'iambic shortening' of the second syllable demonstrates), and Virgil seems to follow C. in using it in this way.

78 *comas*: an ancient metaphor, applied to comets, flames, etc.

78–9 Apparently the last two lines of one stanza have been lost, together with the first two of the next. They probably alluded to, or described, a struggle in the bride's heart between maidenly bashfulness (*pudor* 79) and desire. She is clearly the subject of *audiens* 80, and equally clearly inclines more towards bashfulness.

79 *tardet = tardescit* (cf. 4.26, where *senet = senescit*); not necessarily subjunctive, as Kr. holds.

80 *audiens*, 'obeying'; cf. V. *Geo.* 1.514 *neque audit currus habenas.*

82 *Au-*: it is permissible to divide between two lines a *name* that cannot otherwise be fitted into glyconics; cf. 46–7 n.

84 *femina*, 'woman,' significantly; the word denotes married as well as unmarried (64.143, Fr.). Its use may serve to reassure the bride, whose girlish diffidence forms the context of the passage.

85–6 There is no reason to see (with B., E., Fe., and others) a specific reference to the morning after the wedding. More prosaically expressed, what is said is: 'no fairer woman has ever lived.' Mention of dawn (*venientem* = *surgentem*) adds a touch of hopefulness. Cf. V. *Aen.* 7.218.

86 *viderit*, past tense: 'never in history' (including myth, no doubt). Usually it is the Sun, or Dawn, that 'sees'; cf. Eur. *Hec.* 635, Callim. *H.* 3.249 (Kr.).

88 *divitis*: *Iliad* 11.68 ἀνδρὸς μάκαρος κατ' ἄρουραν.

89 *stare*, 'stand up straight' (B.).
flos hyacinthinus, for *hyacinthus*, has (according to Ronconi, quoted by Fe.) an 'intonazione culta.' The comparison is a traditional topos; see L. Alfonsi, 'Sul nuovo Anacreonte' (P. Oxy. 22.2321), *Aegyptus* 35 (1955): 201–5.

92–3 *si videtur*, a polite (though colloquial) idiom; cf. *sodes*, etc.
audias n. v., 'hear our request' (prayer formula).

94 See the App. Crit. Those (B., for example) who believe that the reading *vide ut* conveys more urgency than *viden* may compare 62.12 *aspicite ut*. On C.'s use of *viden (ut)* see G. Pascucci, *SIFC* 29 (1957): 174–96. The unmetrical reading *viden ut* is probably an unconscious echo of line 77.

   R^2 makes an easy and obvious correction (apart from metre) of *R*'s *viden et*; R^2's *viden ut* (= *G*) is independent of *O*'s *videri ut*, and probably independent of any marginal correction in *X*, since satisfactory support from *O* is not forthcoming.

97 *non* governs the whole stanza: 'it is not true that ...,' i.e., 'you need not fear lest ...' *tuus* is also important; see the tr. below. The order produces a studied distribution of emphasis. There is also a hidden compliment to the bride: 'because of your beauty and attractiveness, it will certainly not be *your* husband ...' This point is underlined at the close of the stanza: observe what is said in 100–1, and notice the echo of *tuus* in *tuis*.
in + abl. is stronger than simple ablative: 'in the person of ...'

98 *deditus*: cf. Lucr. 3.647.

102 *lenta*, 'pliant.' It was, of course, the vine that was 'sown beside' the tree, rather than vice versa; but the ambiguity may not be merely poetical. Cf. Cato *Agr.* 32.2 *vites ... adserantur*, Varro *RR* 1.16.6 *vitis adsita* (glossed *iuxta satus*, B.). Perhaps tr. 'growing beside.' As Fe. (64) remarks, C. here takes a traditional Greek motif and uses Roman images to express it.
   For *vult* in *O*, see line 21.

107 Cf. Ticidas, fr. 1 M.
   There is another lacuna here, probably of three lines only, and it is hopeless to try to fill it (for attempts to do so, see Fe. 67 n. 3).

108 *candido* either (of the bed) = *eburneo*, or quite possibly of a human being: cf. 9–10 *niveo pede*; also 64.162–3, and 68.70–1.

109 *quae* = *qualia*.

110–12 *quae ... gaudeat*, purposive: 'for him to enjoy.'
vaga, 'as the night passes.'

114–48 The bride emerges from the house she is leaving; the *pueri* raise their torches to accompany and guide her in procession (*deductio*) to the house of the bridegroom. As they move, they utter the *fescennina iocatio*, traditional banter addressed directly or (as here, in part) indirectly to the newly married couple, and ritually seen as a device for warding off the evil eye (*fascinum*). Notice that the poet calls on *pueri* only; not the *virgines* (37), for whom this rough banter was considered unseemly. Cf. Varro *Men.* 10 *pueri obscenis verbis novae nuptulae aures returant.*

117–18 The words *io H.H. io, io H.H.* will serve as a refrain at the end of each stanza from 136 to 183. *io* is probably a monosyllable at both places in the refrain; theoretically it might at the second occurrence be treated as disyllabic, with elision; but uniformity has a prior claim. In Ov. *M.* 5.625 (quoted in the intr. n.), the anguished effect of the repetition demands such uniformity, though the former *io* could in theory be regarded as monosyllabic. Cf. Mart. 11.2.5 for *io* as a monosyllable.

    See App. Crit., and observe that *GR* (and from line 175 onwards, *O* also) add a superfluous *io* to the second line of this refrain each time it occurs, thus rendering it unmetrical, while *O* omits the line itself at 138, 143, 148, 153, 158, 163 (at 138, *GR* also omit the line; at 148, *G* omits it). These additions and omissions indicate, of course, that the metre was simply not grasped.

120 *R²*'s attempted correction (unexceptionable on purely palaeographic grounds, but of course inferior in sense to *iocatio*) is original. For other corrections by *R²*, see lines 121 and 139.

121 On the scattering of *nuces* at weddings, see Serv. *ad Ecl.* 8.30 (*sparge, marite, nuces*): Servius has a variety of explanations (fertility ritual included), showing that the Romans themselves had inherited no clear account of it.
linquere nuces (cf. Schol. Pers. 1.10) is a figurative expression for putting childhood behind one; cf. 125–6 *satis diu lusisti nucibus.*

122 *audiens*: several nineteenth-century scholars repudiated this reading because 'hearing' a mere report is not in question; the *concubinus* knew of the wedding in advance, and is now attending it. So Fe. (79) defends the interpretation *audiens = intellegens* here, citing *TLL.* Nevertheless, *audiens* in the literal sense may be right; the *concubinus* is among the listeners to a lengthy *fescennina iocatio* – poetically shortened by C. – which made much of the transference of the bridegroom's affections from the *concubinus* himself to the bride. The genitive *domini* has also been questioned, on the grounds that it is the emotions of the *concubinus* that have been 'betrayed,' and that therefore we should read *domino* (dative of agent); see Fr.'s n. Cf. however [Ov.] *Ep. Sapph.* (= *Ep.* 15) 155 *Sappho desertos cantat amores*, where *desertus* = 'given up.'

123, 125, 128, 130, 133 *concubinus*: the word is repeated in derision, since he has ceased to be this.

127 The form of the ancient cry, uttered at weddings, was *Talasio*: Livy (1.9)
implies that this was a dative, and so much is also to be inferred from Plut.
Rom. 15.2 τὸν Ταλάσιον ἐπᾴδουσι; Martial however seems to regard *Talasio* as
a nominative form (see *OLD* s.v. *Talasio*). Clearly C. treats it as dative, with
servire. Does *lubet* 126 refer to the bridegroom's wish for himself or for the
concubinus (= *lubet domino te servire Talasio*)? The former interpretation
(with *domino* understood) may seem to strain the Latin; but it is hard to see
in what sense the *concubinus* might be said *servire Talasio*, and hard also to
supply with confidence a dative for *lubet*. Schrader (*Emend.*, 10) suggested
iubet, taking *Talasio* (nominative) as its subject; but *iubet* would then lack an
object, and *servire* a subject, so not much would be gained. Perhaps, reading
lubet, translate: 'Our (general) desire (at this moment, *iam*) is to serve Talasius
[= Hymenaeus, see Plut. *l.c.*]'; that is, 'What we are about now is the joyful
celebration of a real wedding' (and your child's-play, ll. 125–6, is superseded).

129 *vilicae*, the wives of the bailiffs (supervisors) of slave-operated farms, were
proverbially 'dragons,' of whom the young slaves might well be terrified – with
the exception of the master's *concubinus*, in whose eyes they might be said
sordere (= 'be despised,' cf. V. *Ecl.* 2.44 *sordent tibi munera nostra*).

131–2 In Martial 11.78.4 (quoted by F.) the bride herself is satirically depicted
as snipping off the long effeminate locks of her husband's favourite slaves:
tondebit pueros iam nova nupta tuos. Some editors (e.g., Fr.) take *tondet os* as
implying shaving; but Martial at least cannot mean this.

134 *diceris*: present (*-ĕris*) or future (*-ēris*)? Surely present: the jesting (*iocatio*)
at the bridegroom's expense is something for (and of) the wedding day only;
it would be contrary to the spirit of the occasion – in bad taste, indeed – to
prophesy at his marriage that, once married, he will be said to prefer male
slaves to his new bride. Translate: 'They are saying you find it hard to refrain;
but (from now on) refrain you must!'
    male = *aegre*; cf. V. *Geo.* 1.360 *male temperat unda carinis* (B.).

134–6 *te ... abstinere*: cf. esp. Plaut. *Curc.* 37 *dum ted abstineas nupta, vidua,
virgine, iuventute et pueris liberis, ama quidlubet*.

139 The emendation to *soli*, commonly attributed (as by Fe., p. 80 n. 2) to A.
Statius, already appears (more than a century earlier) in *Cod. Par. Lat. 8233*
(No. 83 in the Table of Manuscripts). The required meaning (*solus = caelebs*) is
not elsewhere attested, and *sola* yields perfectly good sense: 'Yes, we are aware
that you have experienced only those <sexual indulgences> that to bachelors
are permitted by custom, <such as your relationship with the *concubinus*>,
(and that you have not sought to taste the forbidden fruit of other kinds of
liaison – [see 134–6 n.]); but (140–1) to a married man even such *permitted*
pleasures (*ista eadem*) are forbidden.' On the plural *licent* see F.

144 R^2's 'late' correction *tuus* is not picked up by m^2 and is therefore missing from G^2. Because the lines (142–6) were in the margin of *R*, and in a second hand (R^2) at that, it seems as though m^2 did not treat them as part of the text, and thus ignored *corrections* by R^2 contained in them (even though *m* had not of course overlooked R^2's basic text of the lines).

144–6 Leaving the *fescennina iocatio*, and turning to the bride (in preparation for the new scene that opens with 149), the poet-as-choirmaster adopts a different tone: delicacy replaces ribald banter; yet a humorous note, or undertone, remains. Cf. Williams 1958: 22. The advice to the bride to be *morigera*, normally delivered by the *pronuba*, is here transferred to the poet and subjoined to the *fescennina iocatio* (Fe. 87).

145 *cave ne*: S.G. Owen, on the basis of 50.19, proposed *deneges*; it may be that (as L. suggested) he saw *cave*, without *ne*, as a poetic use of colloquial idiom. (Owen's text of Catullus, with a few notes, was published in a limited edition [London, 1893], and hardly merits inclusion in the Introduction or in the Bibliography; it is mentioned only here and at 29.20.)

146 *ni*: archaic form of *ne* (final). See F., who finds in its use here a 'desire to avoid having two *ne-* clauses depending on the same verb,' whereas Fe. (87) regards the deliberate archaism as marking a change of style (hence tone) from the familiar language of the *fescennina iocatio* to the fresh address to the bride.

　R^2, followed by *m*, makes an unnecessary correction here through failure to understand that *ni = ne*.

149–63 The procession arrives at the bridegroom's house; 149 *en tibi* is 'deictic.'

149–51 Fe. (90) points to the use of elevated style here, as contrasted with the return to a familiar style in 154–61.

149 *en* ('deictic'), for *em*, was coming into use in C.'s time; see B., who compares 55.12 (cf. my n. there). Cicero would have said *ecce tibi*.
　ut potens, 'how rich' (*potens = opulentus*); B. compares Cicero, *Cael.* 62 *mulier potens*; cf. also Hor. *Od.* 1.35.23 *potentis domos*.

151 *serviat*, 'be at your service': cf. Ov. *Ep.* 4.164 *serviat Hippolyto regia tota meo* (Fr.).

153–4 Notice that here, for once, the refrain is placed parenthetically within a sentence-clause.

155 *tempus* (rare in the singular, in this sense) for *caput*.
　On *m*'s intermittent attachment to the diphthong *ae* (he reads *aetas* here), see de la Mare and Thomson 1973: 189–90. At 53.4 and 64.50, for example, *m* changes *R*'s *hec* to *haec* (cf. 76.15 and 16), and similarly *que* to *quae* at 61.151, 68.91, 69.5.

156 *annuit*: indicative, because it is a *general* statement about old age. The frequent nodding of the head, which (as F. says) looks like a continuous 'Yes,' is

poetically equated with loss of authority and consequent readiness to give in to everyone. Cf. Ov. *Ep.* 19.45–6 (quoted by F.) *adnuit illa fere non nostra quod oscula curet, sed movet obrepens somnus anile caput.*

159 For the custom of carrying a bride over the threshold of her new home (to avoid the bad omen of a stumble there), see E.'s notes. (It may well be that there is no reference here to carrying her, and that she is merely urged not to stumble.)
transfer has two objects (*limen*, after *trans*; *pedes*, after *fer*).

161 *forem* = the doorway as a whole, including lintel (hence *subi*) and threshold (hence *rasilem*). L. suggested that *rasilem* might be an adjectival 'transference' of the general notion of smoothness, alluding to the Roman custom of greasing the doorposts; but I find this notion over-subtle, and it is neither necessary nor desirable to strain for archaeological comprehensiveness in this poem (see intr. n.). Professor Christopher Brown first drew my attention to K. Latte's article in *Glotta* 32 (1953): 35–6, which suggests that C.'s phrase owes something to Sappho, fr. 117A (Voigt) = Hesychius Ξ 85, ξοάνων προθύρων· ἐξεσμένων, quoted by Vossius with reference to Hesychius. See now Campbell 1982: 140 and 141 n.

164–6 There are two principal interpretations: (i) the husband has dined (with guests) in the *atrium* of his house and is still at table (*accubans*) when the bride arrives (E. and Riese); the chief prop of this theory is the argument that in C.'s time *accubo* could only mean 'recline at table'; (ii) the husband is caught sight of inside the house, whether or not he has participated in the *deductio* until its arrival there; if not, he may have left the procession and gone ahead (Fr. supposes him to have entered the house while his bride paused to anoint the doorposts, a traditional rite for which no place is otherwise given); he is now seated, alone, on a *torus* (165) of some kind, to await the bride's arrival. Against the linguistic argument in (i), Fe. (93 n. 1) quotes *TLL*. Fe. also points out that even if there could have been a *cena nuptialis* in the bridegroom's house, by Roman custom the bride was present throughout (92 n. 2; to Fe.'s references add Plaut. *Curc.* 728 and Cicero, *Ad Q.F.* 2.3.7, both quoted by E.). As for the question whether the bridegroom is supposed to have taken part in the procession, the fact that he is addressed by the *pueri*, at l. 135 for instance, does not necessarily imply his presence. The *torus* is certainly not the marriage bed (which is in an inner room; see 176–85), nor is it just any couch; Pasquali (see F., and esp. Fe. 93 nn. 5 and 6, and 94) supposed, probably rightly, that it is the *lectus genialis*, archaically and poetically seen as the object within the *atrium* that best symbolizes both the dignity of the bridegroom's house and his eager reception of his bride.

166 *immineat* = *inhiet*. F. quotes Ov. *M.* 1.146 and *Culex* 90; add Livy 30.28 *in propinquam <spem> imminebant animis*, and ἔγκειμαι as used in Theocr. 3.33

(the latter quoted by Fr.). The word implies both a physical and an emotional 'inclination.'

170–1 Cf. 35.15, 45.15–16, 100.7; also (probably of jealousy) 77.3.

170 See App. Crit. *uritur*, of *flamma*, would be most unusual; as Kr. remarks, one would expect – the other way round – *pectus uritur flamma*. Hence I have adopted Goold's suggestion, *urit in*.

171 *penite* (V), as an adverb, would be unique. It may be supposed to have arisen, or been coined (perhaps by C.), from *penitus*, which appears as an adjective in Plautus (see F.), but is normally indeclinable and is used, in the form just given, as an adverb. O. Skutsch (see App. Crit.) proposed to read *perit en*, which is decidedly tempting. Fe., however (91–2), accepts *penite* against Skutsch, seeing an artistic purpose in the accumulation of exaggerated expressions of passion, applied to the husband, which further serve to emphasize the bride's bashfulness and reserve.

175 The use of the singular *praetextate* (though by custom two *praetextati* accompanied the bride, while one bore the torch) has been explained as an adaptation of the Roman ritual to the Greek, which allowed for only one παράνυμφος. It is arguable that in ll. 174–6 this youth is seen by C. as accompanying the bride to the very door of the *thalamus*, whereas by the Roman custom the responsibilities of the *praetextati* ceased at the door of the house. On these points see Fe. 97. But the latter conclusion is not strictly necessary (the procession may have halted at the outer door, 161–76); and it should at least be borne in mind that *only* the singular of the word *praetextatus* will fit the glyconic line (Fr. understates this by saying 'leichter'), while in poetic address a singular may perfectly well deputize for a plural.

It is tempting, but unnecessary, to suppose that R^2 – here followed by m – drew his correction from X; it is well within Coluccio's own capacity, as a glance at his many original emendations will show.

176 X's false reading *adeant* may well be due to a notion, carelessly entertained, that *viri* is plural and therefore the verb should agree with it.

179 For the missing syllable (metrically indispensable), B. suggested *o*, which might appear to be more easily lost (as at 114; cf. 1.9) than *vos*; but (as Fr. said, admitting this), the repeated *io*'s, immediately preceding and presently to follow, make *o* unlikely.

180 *cognitae*, i.e., sexually known (*cognoscere* = γιγνώσκειν) (cf. *Gen.* 24.16: 'And the damsel was ... a virgin, neither had any man known her'). The adverb *bene* is added 'to show' (as L. put it) 'that a word of doubtful respectability' (Ov. *Ep.* 6.133 *turpiter illa virum cognovit adultera virgo*) 'is being used in a good sense'; *bene = honeste*, cf. Ov. *Ep.* 13.117 *lecto mecum bene iunctus in uno.*' Cf. 197 *bonum ... amorem.*

185 β (*Cod. Paris. 7989* = Table of Mss, No. 78, dated 1423), which was written by a scholar for his own use, corrected *R*'s *est tibi* (the only example in poem 61 of hiatus between lines); β², about a century later, clearly wanted to revert to the *textus receptus*. Bentley should not be credited with the correction.

187 On *vult*, see ll. 21 and 102. *R*² (*m*) makes a miscorrection; *G*² is doubtful, and, though he accepts it, he repeats *G*'s *vult* as a variant reading.

188 *luteum* here = 'red' (cf. 10). Fr. points out that the poppy was a symbol of fertility, quoting Ov. *M.* 11.605 and *F.* 4.151.

189–98 A larger transposition: this time of stanzas, not merely of words.

189–90 *ita ... caelites*: cf. 66.18 *ita me divi ... iuerint*, and also 97.1; a colloquial phrase (Kr. compares Cicero, *Ad Att.* 1.16.1).

195 *bona Venus* (cf. line 44; also lines 61–2): see Alfonsi 1967, who gives a convincing account of the overtones, both social and religious, of the phrase in question.

197 A plausible miscorrection by *R*²(*m*) is adopted by *G*².

199–201 For the figures of sand and stars as representing finite but uncountable numbers, cf. 7.3; C. is the earliest Latin author to use the sand in this way, but Plautus has the figure of the stars (Fe. 108). Greek philosophy made use of the figure to represent finite, but uncountable, numbers; see Cicero, *Acad.* 2.110.

201 *subducat* must, despite E.'s opinion and F.'s uncertainty on the question, be jussive, not potential subjunctive; otherwise the verb of the relative clause (*qui ... vult ...*) would have to be in the subjunctive as well.

203 *ludi*, 'lovemaking'; cf. 68.17 n.

204 Notice how the opening repeats the close of the preceding line; cf. 92.

205 *date*: cf. 67 n.

207 *nomen = genus; nomen* also does duty as the subject of *ingenerari* (E.). The point of *indidem* ('from the same stock') is that C. hopes that such an old, and distinguished, family may not have to resort to the too-common Roman expedient of adoption.

210 *R*² corrects, on first principles I think; the change from *et* to *e* is easy and obvious.

213 ς *michi ante* Mss (not far from the correct reading, though this was never divined before Scaliger). Scan *sēmĭhiāntĕ* (- ˘ - ˘).

215 See 16 n. on the reading *Manlio* (*maulio* O), here and elsewhere.

215–16 Two words give rise to difficulty: (i) *insciens* (*V*), which scarcely appears to make sense; (ii) *omnibus*, which breaks the synapheia prevailing in the sequence of glyconic lines, since it (uniquely, for poem 61) ends the line with a doubtful quantity. (i) was early dealt with (ς*η*) by substituting *insciis*; Lachmann suggested the archaic spelling *inscieis* as the source of the corruption to *insciens*. (ii) is usually set right by transposition (see App. Crit.); Fe. (111 n. 2) accepts the simple exchange of *insciis* and *omnibus*. I have however decided to print *obviis*. It can be defended in terms of palaeography, since at 64.109 *O* has *obvia*, while *GR* have *omnia*. Moreover, *omnibus* may seem exaggerated; the son will be recognized by *some* people who have not met him before, namely those who know his father; but surely not by *all* strangers. Cf. however – in a similar context – Ov. *Tr.* 4.5.32 *quilibet*.

On the whole question, Fr. has some useful remarks on pp. 263 and 278–9. See also F.

217 *V*'s *-am* is due to assimilation to *pudicitiam. suae*, as a correction, is better than *suo*, which has already appeared, in the same stanza, at 214.

219–23 'The point of this stanza seems to be that as the previous stanza has expressed the hope that the son of this pair will resemble his father, it is the bride's turn to have something said about her; so the slightly forced analogy of Telemachus and Penelope is brought in to express the hope that he will derive good moral qualities from his mother' (L.). Cf *Odyssey* 1.215ff.; '*bona* = human (mother), *optima* = divine (hero-mother),' B. For the poetic fame of *Penelopea fides* see Ov. *Tr.* 5.14.35–6.

223 *Penelopaeo*: on the spelling, in Greek and in Latin, see A.E. Housman, *J. Phil.* 53 (1914): 54ff. (esp. 73).

224 *claudite*: cf. *pandite* 76. The 'circle' is completed here; and this repetition of the idea helps to prove that C. himself considered lines 1–75, addressed to Hymen, as a thing apart from the principal narrative action of the poem.

virgines: notice that C. does not give any function at this point either to the Greek or to the Roman *pronuba*. But who are the *virgines*? It may be significant that in 76 the door is *ianua*, clearly a house-door; here the appropriate door is that of the *thalamus*. (Believing it to be the *Haustur*, Fr. identifies the *virgines* as domestic slaves, who must close it from within). Fe. (118–19, q.v.), pointing out that an epithalamium was by literary tradition assigned to a choir of maidens, identifies the *virgines* here with those of l. 37. But the antiquarian question is, once again, of little significance, although it might be thought that the poem's action is rounded off more neatly if there is only one such choir.

225 *at* often 'preludes a change of addressee' (B.).

*R*²'s correction is not original, or he would almost certainly have written *boni*. *O*'s *bonlei* must surely have appeared as a reading in *X* also; *R*², by half-correcting (with the sense of *boni* in view, yet preserving the *-ei* ending of the Ms tradition), shows his uncertainty. See also p. 39.

226 *bene vivite* = *felices, concordes vivite* (a traditional formula of general goodwill, on taking leave of the couple; cf. the Greek wish for ὁμόνοια). C. is not 'moralizing,' as ll. 227–8 (cf. next note) clearly show; see Fe. (119).

227 *munere*, 'function' in a sexual sense. Cf. Claudian, *Epithal. Pallad. et Celerinae* (*carmina minora* 25) 130, who makes Venus say – at the end of an epithalamium – *vivite concordes et nostrum discite munus*.

Wheeler, A.L. 1930. 'Tradition in the Epithalamium,' *AJP* 51 (1930): 205–23.

– 1934. *Catullus and the Traditions of Ancient Poetry* (Berkeley, 1934; repr. 1964): 183–213.

Pighi, G.B. 1948/49. 'La struttura del carme LXI di C.,' *Humanitas* 2: 41–53.

Williams, G. 1958. 'Some Aspects of Roman Marriage Ceremonies and Ideals,' *JRS* 48: 16–29.

Alfonsi, L. 1967. 'Nota catulliana,' *Aevum* 41: 153. [On *bona Venus*, ll. 44, 62, 195.]

Fedeli, P. 1972. *Il carme 61 di C.* Fribourg; reprinted 1981; English translation, *Catullus' Carmen 61*. Amsterdam, 1983.

Grilli, A. 1972. 'Nota a un frammento tragico adespoto [160 N²] e C., carme 61,' *Studi classici in onore di Q. Cataudella* 3. Catania: 95–7.

West, M.L. 1973. *Textual criticism and editorial technique* . Stuttgart: 132–41. [Lines 189–228.]

Pearce, T.E.V. 1974. 'The Role of the Wife as Custos in Ancient Rome,' *Eranos* 72: 16–33, esp. 16–22.

Lieberg, G. 1974. 'Observationes in Catulli carmen sexagesimum primum,' *Latinitas* 22: 216–22.

Estevez, V.A. 1977/78. 'The Choice of Urania in C. 61,' *Maia* 29/30: 103–5.

Mayer, R. 1979. 'On C. 61.116–19,' *PCPS* 25: 69–70. [Lines 109–12: no need to emend *medio*.]

Biondi, G.G. 1979. *Semantica di 'cupidus' (Catull. 61.32).* Bologna. See the next item.

Granarolo, J. 1980. Review of G.G. Biondi, *Semantica di 'cupidus' (Catull. 61.32), REL* 57 (1979, published 1980): 415–21.

Harrison, S.J. 1985. 'C. 61.109–13 (Again),' *PCPS* 31: 11–12.

Greenwood, M.A. 1988. 'More Thoughts on C. 61,' *LCM* 13: 80.

62

Structure: (excluding the one-line refrain): (G = girls; Y = youths). The usually accepted structure is as follows:

```
4   +  4  +  8       5  +  5  +  (?) +  (?) +  9(10?) +  10      8
Y      G     Y       G     Y     G       Y      G          Y     Y(?: see Goud 1995)
  1–10      11–19      20–31        32–8            39–58        59–66
  Introduction        |————————Singing-match————————|          Epilogue
                             (carmen amoebaeum)
```

N.B. Where I have written (?) twice in the first line, Goud 1995 would substitute 6(+?) in each instance; see his article.

Notice that both the introduction and the rest of the poem end with a pointed statement, eight lines long – the first by way of challenge, to open the debate; the second to claim victory and to draw the moral. Both of these are commonly supposed to be uttered by the youths. Goud has a quite different attribution of the epilogue: see his article.

This poem, like poem 61, is concerned with a wedding; or rather with the theme of marriage, since there is nothing to tie it to a particular wedding or even to a definite place. (At the outset, the geography is vaguely Greek.) What it has in common with poem 61 is a delicate approach, here made explicit in the epilogue, to an unmarried girl (perhaps, in this poem, representing – as it were – all unmarried girls) to persuade her to enter into marriage. This explains why the youths dominate the debate, and even the preparation for it in ll. 11–18; unless they are destined to win, the cause of marriage is lost. All this is evident. What is also evident is that the composition is in its essence a singing-match, of the kind developed by Theocritus and found in Virgil's third and seventh Eclogues. With this genre goes a strong interest in near-mathematical symmetry (for which see the diagram above, though in the second of the three strophe-antistrophe episodes of the *carmen amoebaeum* the text is so heavily damaged that we can only guess how many lines should be given to the girls and youths respectively). According to the rules, the utterance of each singer, or choir, should be answered by the respondent(s) in the same number of verses, but with greater force. At the end, the continuation of the victor's song (perhaps with no pause, this time, for the dividing refrain) disturbs the balance of the two sides, yet can be weighed against the opening lines; moreover it has, as we have said, a generalizing function, revealing that which it is the intention of the poet to say by means of the poem as a whole.

On the history of *T* (No. 80 in the Table of Mss), a Carolingian manuscript (*Codex Thuaneus*, an anthology) which from Catullus contains poem 62 only, see the Introduction, pp. 23–4.

1 *Vesper* = Venus, as the 'evening star' (the first celestial body to become visible as the sky darkens); also, but at other times (35 n.), the 'morning star,' Ἑωσφόρος (= *Lucifer*).
   Olympo = *caelo* (not the mountain; cf. *Oetaeos* 7 n.).
2 *tollit*, not of course implying a genuine stellar 'rising.'
4 Notice the lengthening in *dicetur*, before the Greek word *hymenaeus*, and followed by a strong 'caesura' in the fifth foot: cf. 64.20, 66.11; also V. *Aen.* 7.398, 10.720; and similarly before *hyacinthus*, V. *Ecl.* 6.53, *Geo.* 4.137, *Aen.* 11.69 (F. on 64.20).

6 Because of *T*'s garbled *consurgi eretera*, some scholars have wished to transfer the question-mark to the end of the line and read *consurgere* (Mowat; see E.) or *consurgier* (Radke 1972), on the grounds that l. 7 becomes easier to understand if it gives the girls' explanation of the boys' action in rising (l. 6). Against it stands the *V* reading, and also the poet's possible desire to establish antithetical expression in the girls' and boys' 'strophes' at this stage. The case for change is not quite made, since (i) the *V* reading can be taken pretty well in the required sense, and (ii) *contra* more naturally applies to the second group, who *rise to face* those who have already risen.

7 *nimirum*, 'no doubt <because>.'
Oetaeos: it is true that Mount Oeta is in Thessaly, and the very mention of the name sets the imagined scene of the poem in Greece. But we must not suppose, with E., that this shows *Olympo* (l. 1) to refer also to a mountain. In fact, 'Oetean' is as symbolic, or metaphorical, as 'Olympus' (= sky): the region of Trachis, including Oeta, was the birthplace and home of Heosphorus (Ἑωσφόρος), or *Lucifer* (see l. 1 n.), whose son Ceyx was king of that realm (Ov. *M.* 11.268ff.). Cf. V. *Ecl.* 8.29 (and Servius ad loc.) for a typical example of reference to Oeta in connection with *Lucifer* or *Vesper*; for further examples see F. For the corruption of *ignes* to *imbres/imber*, or *vice versa*, see Tib. 1.1.48 (where the generally accepted *imbre* is independently attested only in the *Florilegium Gallicum*); cf. F. Della Corte, *GIF* 20 (1967): 105–9 (supporting *imbre*, with refs.) and A. Chetry, *GIF* 14 (1961): 349–54 (supporting *igne*). See also Rosemary Burton, *Classical Poets in the Florilegium Gallicum* (Frankfurt, 1983): 18, who gives further references. Corruption of *imber* to *ignis* appears at Lucr. 1.784, 785, Germ. *Arat.* fr. 3.63, and Valerius Flaccus 5.415. At Lucr. 1.744, *imbrem* has been suggested for *ignem OQ*. Fr. has a long note on the phenomenon. See the Introduction, p. 23, for the importance of this reading in *dating* the common source of *T* and *V*.
ignis is used of a star's light at Hor. *Od.* 3.29.18 (Kr.).

8 *sic certest*, colloquial: 'Yes, that's it'; cf. 80.7. (*R*² attempts an original correction and is very nearly successful.)
viden ut is also colloquial (cf. 61.77 n.), and also formulary: notice its application to a number of people.

9 *vincere*: Kidd 1974: 32 defends *visere*, which he translates 'to look at a sight worth seeing'; but see F. on this tr. Moreover, the youths are not going to sing *of Hesperus*, as F. suggests (nor is there any proof that the girls believe it, wrongly), but of something intangible, namely attitudes to marriage. It is important that the whole of lines 1–18 should be seen to establish the context of a singing-match; *visere* would detract from this. I cannot agree with Kidd's objection to *vincere*, that it '<makes> the line anticipate the contest-theme, which is properly introduced in the next stanza and does not belong here,' or

with his claim that 'the emendation has in fact foisted on C. a rather inept line.' In any case, following its regular meaning, *par est* = rather 'it is likely <that they will win>' than 'it is worthwhile <to look at>.' In other words, the leader of the girls is warning them that they face a determined opponent who, as things stand, looks like winning.

11 As at 68.39 (where see n.), the *non* applies to the whole clause: 'it is not true that ...'

aequales (*-is*, the accusative form in *TV*, is surely due to *nobis*, or else arises from false agreement with *palma*), 'age-fellows' (Greek ἥλικες), often used (in poetry) by young people in referring to one another; cf. Pacuv. 113–14R² *hymenaeum fremunt aequales*.

parata est, 'lies in store' or 'is ready-made' (see F.).

12 Notice the simple haplography by which, in *V*, *-tata* becomes *-ta* (hence the corruption).

12–14 The girls' expression (*adspicite* ...) is one of intense concentration on a well-rehearsed (*meditata*) song.

14 The genuineness of the line is attested by *T*: see App. Crit. The indicative *laborant* should be left; it is unusual in this kind of relative clause, but cf. Plaut. *Trin.* 905 *novistin hominem? – Ridicule rogitas, quicum una cibum capere soleo* (Fr.). For parallel passages, otherwise with the subjunctive, see Kr. and Fr. Cf. also F. on 64.157, where again the indicative is used.

15 *nos*, adversative: 'while we, for our part, ...'

alio ... *alio*. Editors disagree as to whether this means 'we think of one thing while we listen to another,' or 'our minds are distracted (i.e., not, like the girls', concentrated), and so are our ears' (with *alio* repeated for emphasis); I prefer the latter (perhaps they have been thinking of the banquet, as Kr. suggests) – it is hard to see the exact force of *divisimus aures* on the former interpretation. For *mentem/animum dividere*, cf. V. *Aen.* 4.285.

17 *nunc* and *saltem* should be taken together.

convertite (*T*), 'bring to bear,' is much the better reading; it is doubtful whether *committite* could really mean 'concentrate.'

22 *retinentem*, 'clinging to' <the embrace of her mother>.

24 The Augustan poets also use this comparison (perhaps following C.?); examples in F.

27 *desponsa* ... *conubia* refers to the ceremony known as *sponsalia*; the *sponsio* was a kind of contract ('giving away,' before the wedding day) between the bride's father and her *fiancé*. It may be that *viri* and *parentes* are 'generalizing' plurals (F.), only one *vir* and one *parens* being involved; less likely is the explanation that *viri* means the fathers of both, and *parentes* the mothers of both (Schulze, Fr.). See Serv. Sulpic. on *sponsalia, ap.* Gell. 4.4, for the basis of the former view.

28 Take *quae* (repeated) with *conubia*. E. supposes that *ante* implies that the bride's father made his commitment first, the bridegroom later; but of course *ante* belongs to both parts of the clause; cf. ll. 15, 42 (and 44, 53, 55), 58.

 The verb *pepigere* is repeated; notice the change of form (cf. V. *Ecl.* 10.13–15, quoted by F.). For the meaning of *pepigere*, cf. Val. Fl. 8.154 *nil tecum pepigere parentes*.

29 *iunxere*, as at 78.3 *iungit amores*; F. quotes Cicero, *De or.* 1.37 *conubia coniunxisse*.

32 The following passage, of five lines or slightly more, was omitted, no doubt because the writer's eye leapt from one line beginning *Hesperus* ... to another. It probably contained a claim by the girls that the evening star of the wedding night should be considered as a thief, robbing maidens of their virginity. See Kidd 1974: 30, who finds a source for the youths' reply in Bion. fr. 8.6–7 οὐκ ἐπὶ φωρὰν ἔρχομαι, οὐδ᾽ ἵνα νυκτὸς ὁδοιπορέοντος ἐνοχλέω. On *custodia* = φυλακή (the abstract word), see Wistrand 1961.

32b Clearly, one line – just possibly more – has been lost at the beginning of the youths' reply. A balance of six lines against six would meet every requirement. As Goud 1995 suggests, probably the similes in lines 39–58 were intended as climactic, and therefore constituted the longest sections of the singing-match.

33 *tuo adventu* is contrasted with *nocte* (= the dead of night, as opposed to the evening and early morning).

34 *idem* seems to endorse the false notion (conventional in poetry) that Venus could be the evening star of one day and the morning star of the next.

35 The reading *eosdem* (see App. Crit.) must be very old, since *T* has *eospem*. A case can be made for it, on the grounds that *mutato nomine* is enfeebled if the actual name follows, and that the name *Eous* is not positively required. On the whole, however, the emendation may be allowed to stand. See Cataudella 1970/2 for a possible Callimachean model (perhaps taken from the *Hecale*) for this line. *comprendis*: there is no reference to 'furtive' *amours* here.

37 *R*²'s *quid tum*, though presented as a variant, is a correction (there is, of course, no link with *T*'s differently spelt *quittum*. *m*² carelessly copies it as *quid tñ* (*tamen*), so that *G*² – who already sees *tamen* in *G* – can do no more than borrow *m*²'s *quid* to replace *G*'s *quod*.

39ff. For the image of the flower in the enclosed garden, cf. Sappho fr. 105(c) L-P οἶαν τὰν ὑάκινθον κτλ. (possibly from an epithalamium), and with this also cf. the end of poem 11. Lines 39–47 have been compared with Soph. *Tr.* 144–9 by Alfonsi 1970, and by Akbar Khan 1971, who also points to Eur. *Hipp.* 73–81.

40 *ignotus*: see Akbar Khan 1971.

 convolsus (*T*): cf. 64.40 *convellit*. *R*²'s *contusus* is a heroic, but unsuccessful, attempt at original correction.

41b Spengel's suggested lacuna of one line is well defended by Goud 1995.

42 *optavere*: 'gnomic' aorist in Greek, here for the first time adapted to the Latin perfect (Kr.). The line is clearly imitated by Ovid, *M*. 3.353–5.

45 *dum ... dum*, 'while ..., so long ...' (explained by Quintilian, 9.3.16; notice that Quint., quoting from memory, has *innupta* instead of *intacta* – just as he gives V. *Ecl*. 1.2 as *agrestem tenui* instead of *silvestrem tenui*). Cf. the Greek ἕως ... τέως (Callim. *H*. 4.39 τόφρα μὲν ... τόφρα δὲ), and (in Latin) V. *Ecl*. 8.41 *ut vidi, ut perii* (from Theocr. 2.82 ὡς ἴδον, ὡς ἐμάνην). See F.'s long n.
castum florem, a condensed expression for *florem castitatis* (Kr.); cf. 68.14 *dona beata* (see n.).

See App. Crit.: R^2 makes an attempt at correction that plainly suggests itself; it is no more likely to depend on X than the same reading in O and G is likely to depend on T.

49 *vidua*, of the vine (not 'married' to a supporting tree): cf. *marita*, of a house-door, 67.6 n.; Hor. *Od*. 2.15.4 *platanus caelebs*, and cf. 4.5.30 *vitem viduas ducit ad arbores*. Training vines on trees planted in rows for the purpose was not unknown in Greece, but much more common in Italy (Cato *Agr*. 32.2 *arbores facito ut bene maritae sint*), and certainly not known in Sappho's Lesbos.

51 *T*'s reading (*perflectens*) is preferred by Della Corte 1976, who claims that *deflectens* describes the wrong method of propagation.

53 As Kr. points out, the poet's desire for symmetry (here, correspondence to l. 42) has affected the thought, making it a little strained and artificial. B. deplores *iuvenci*, and would read *coloni*; but cf. V. *Geo*. 2.354–7, where the soil of the vineyard must be kept clear of weeds by surface harrowing between the rows – as is done, with the aid of mules, in tobacco-growing areas of South Carolina.

R^2 originates a correction which happens to agree with O but is metrically called for in any case.

54 *si forte*, 'when once ...,' or 'it has only to be united ... and ...'
maritā is to be preferred to *marită*; (i) the rhythm is stronger, (ii) C. avoids short *a* at the end of a line. It might be argued that if *marito* = 'as a husband,' we then have the required emphasis on the husband – and 'any husband,' even a vegetable husband-figure, needs a masculine termination. However, Courtney 1985 makes a strong case for reading *maritā*.

56 Goud 1995: n. 9 demonstrates that Weber was right to read *innupta* here.

58 The true comparative force lies in *minus invisa* (the father has a daughter off his hands); it is – claims Kr. – transferred to *magis cara* (not really a comparative, but a parallel phrase, is sought – the poem is full of these). The bride, in fact, simply by becoming *cara* to her husband, becomes less *invisa* to her parent. But the previous line shows some emphasis on *par* and *maturo*; the girl has made a good marriage (*par*), at the *right* time, and so is both relieving her parents *more* than if it were otherwise and also *more* likely to make a happy marriage than if she chose the wrong person or left it too late. If, therefore, we ask 'dearer than

what?' the answer is 'dearer than she would have been without *par conubium maturo tempore.*' On the metrical peculiarity of the line (pyrrhic word after trithemimeral caesura, in a hexameter beginning with a trochaic word), see Kr.

G^2, who misses the R^2 correction, is already hurrying; see below, 64.319 n.

59 It is tempting to read *At* for *Et*, because of *T*'s *tua* (suggesting the archetypal reading *ETTV*). See, however, Fraenkel 1955, who points to the formula καὶ σύ.

Goud 1995 argues, on the ground of symmetry with lines 11–19, that an additional line (58c) has been lost in addition to the refrain. This prompts him to call for the retention of *nec*, as well as *V*'s *tua*, in line 59, assuming a prior prohibition in the lost line.

60 *pugnare*: sc. *cum eo* (or *ei*, with poetic dative as in 64).

For *ne* + imperative (archaic), cf. 61.193, 67.18.

61 *ipse* is added by R^2 (followed by m^2) from *X*; *G* does not omit the word, so no action is called for on the part of G^2.

63 The reading *patris est* is suggested by the reading in *T*, and avoids the difficult quantity in *patri*.

See the Introduction, p. 24; *X* ventures an emendation of the unmetrical reading in *A* (which is reproduced in *O*), adding a word to make the line metrical, the result being *data pars data* – a good example of early critical tinkering with the text, applied to *X*.

64 *duobus* of course refers to her parents; but 'to fight against two' is a proverb (πρὸς δύο μάχεσθαι): Plato *Phaedo* 89c, *Legg.* 11.919b.

65 *iura*, figurative (in the case of the mother).

Knapp, C. 1896. 'A Discussion of C. 62.39–58,' *CR* 10: 365–8. [Lines 39–58.]

Perelli, L. 1950. 'Il Carme 62 di C. e Saffo,' *RFIC* 28: 289–312.

D'Errico, A. 1955. 'L'epitalamio nella letteratura latina, dal fescennino nuziale al c. 62 di C.,' *AFLN* 5: 73–93.

Fraenkel, E. 1955. 'Vesper adest,' *JRS* 45: 1–8.

Merkelbach, R. 1956. 'Boukoliastae (Der Wettgesang der Hirten),' *RhM* 99: 124–7.

Wistrand, E. 1961. 'De Catulli carmine 62 v. 33 sqq. interpretandis,' *Eranos* 59: 49–53.

Davison, J.A. 1968. 'A Marriage Song of Sappho's (S 104 and 105)' [and poem 62], *From Archilochus to Pindar*. New York: 242–6.

Alfonsi, L. 1970. 'Nota Catulliana,' *StudClas* 12: 139–40. [Poem 62 and Soph. *Trach.* 144–9.]

Akbar Khan, H. 1971. 'Observations on Two Poems of C.' [62, 51], *RhM* 114: 159–78.

Cataudella, Q. 1970/2. 'Callim. fr. 291 Pf.,' *MCr* 5/7: 155–63. [Line 35.]

Radke, A.E. 1972. 'Zu C. c. 62, 6–7,' *Hermes* 100: 117–20.

Kidd, D.A. 1974. 'Hesperus and C. LXII,' *Latomus* 33: 22–33.

Della Corte, F. 1976. 'Catullo, la vite e l'olmo,' *Maia* 28: 75–81.

Stigers, E.S. 1977. 'Retreat from the Male: C. 62 and Sappho's Erotic Flowers,' *Ramus* 6: 83–102.

Nethercut, W.R. 1979. 'The Art of C. 62,' *SLLRH* 1. Brussels: 229–38.

Commager, S. 1983. 'The Structure of C. 62,' *Eranos* 81: 21–33.

Courtney, E. 1985. 'Three Poems of C.: (1). Poem 62 and Its Greek Background,' *BICS* 32: 85–8.

Pennisi, G. 1992. 'C. Valerii Catulli, Epithalamium carmen LXII,' *Studi latini e italiani* 6: 45–52.

Goud, T. 1995. 'Who Speaks the Final Lines? C. 62: Structure and Ritual,' *Phoenix* 49: 23–32.

63

Structure:

(11	+	15	+	12)	+	(11	+	24	+	17)	+	3
narr.		orat.		narr.		narr.		orat.		11 narr. enclosing 6 orat: 4 + 6 + 7		prayer

The above diagram shows how I interpret the movement of the poem. For other analyses see Q. (who offers alternatives), Guillemin 1949 ('a tragedy in three acts'), Schäfer 1966, Oksala 1969 ('two acts'), and Courtney 1985. It seems to me that Guillemin has correctly pointed out the importance of the break at line 38: with her, I would separate Day 1, which ends there, from Day 2 (in my view = *all* that follows, to l. 90) in terms of the action. (I cannot follow Courtney in regarding ll. 27–49 as a single continuous narrative.) On the above analysis, there are two movements and a coda; each movement encloses a speech between two narratives, with the following difference: in the second movement, the third section (ll. 74–90) does indeed contain eleven lines of narrative, to balance ll. 39–49, but splits those 11 lines to insert between them a brief speech by Cybele. (That is, the tripartite and symmetrical structure of *each* movement is reproduced in miniature in the third section of the *second* movement. The effect of this, as it seems to me, is to accelerate the poem's tempo towards the end – a not undesirable development in a poem that ends with *incitatos* and *rapidos*.)

   The themes may perhaps be described as follows:

Day 1: Access of religious frenzy, resulting in enslavement to the goddess by self-mutilation;

Day 2: Remorse, and desire to flee (with a backward glance at lost happiness) followed by re-enslavement.

In the coda (ll. 91–3) the poet, acting as a sort of tragic *choragus*, reflects upon the events just described, and repudiates the *furor* that prompted Attis to act as he did. Notice how the word *furor* itself takes up the explanatory phrase *stimulatus ... furenti rabie* in l. 4. As critics have in various ways pointed out, the whole poem is linked together by repetitions of this kind.

The Phrygian legend of the Great Mother, with or without the inclusion of her love for the shepherd Attis and its consequences, made from its very introduction an enormous impression on both the Greek and the Roman public. In the case of Rome, we can date its arrival quite precisely, from a moment in 204 BC, during the course of the war against Carthage, when in response to a demand by the Sibyl a meteoric stone purporting to embody the presence of the goddess was brought by ship to the mouth of the Tiber and afterwards solemnly installed, with appropriate ceremonies, in a Roman temple; the festival of the *Megalensia*, held in April, dates from this time. The whole story is given, in an entertaining form, by Ovid (*F.* 4.179–372). Every Roman of C.'s generation must have been familiar with the annual processions of eunuch priests, accompanied by music played to strange percussive rhythms, in honour of Cybele. Lucretius (2.594–628) both describes these graphically and interprets them as an allegory of nature and the works of man; Varro gave an account of them, using appropriate metre (see below) in his satire *Eumenides*, on the madness of fools (fragments 131 and 132 Bücheler, also Astbury 1985). That this form of worship, which continued for ages, was always regarded as highly exotic and never quite naturalized, is shown by the fact that the hymns to the deity were always in Greek (Serv. *ad Geo.* 2.394). Strange and barbarous, too, were the emasculated priests; no citizen could be a member of the college, or take an active part in the rites (D.H. *Ant.* 2.19.4–5).

Who was the Great Mother, and who was Attis? In the persons of both of them, as we should expect from a legend so important and so widespread, there was a good deal of syncretism. Cybele (the name, like that of Agdistis which she also bore, is derived from a place) was early identified with Rhea, as mother of gods; it is perhaps for this reason that her lover Attis sometimes appears as Zeus. The emperor Julian, who in his oration devoted to her (*Or.* 5, *de Syria Dea*) offers an intellectualized, neoplatonic interpretation of the myth, confers on Attis a role similar to that of Helios. Other identifications include that of Cybele as Demeter; her lament for the dead Attis and also – in some versions – his resurrection suggest Persephone, not to mention Adonis (an anthropological 'classic,' J.G. Frazer's *Adonis, Attis and Osiris*, is included in his *Golden Bough*). In the earlier part of the twentieth century, research suggested that all of these were originally vegetation deities having to do with crops and seasons. Sometimes Attis appears to be another name for Dionysus-Sabazios. As becomes clear from the long passage in Diodorus Siculus (3.58–9), of which E. in his introductory note gives a slightly abbreviated text, the traditional story of Cybele has a strongly musicological aspect. With or without the help of Marsyas, she invented an Eastern style of music and dance, together with its appropriate instruments: tambourines, cymbals, and a kind of flute. For many generations, in the minds of Romans orgiastic music (as they thought of it), as well as unrestrained bodily gestures and comportment, were associated with the service of the cult. Even in the Neronian period, the name of Attis conjured up both metrical and moral licence (Pers. 1.93 and 105); and the compositions by the emperor himself, named in the epitome of Dio Cassius (61.20.2), consist of a 'Bacchae' and an 'Attis.' Slightly later, Martial (2.86.4–5) affects to despise the metre of Attis-poems as *mollis debilitate galliambon*.

In literary history the crop of dithyrambic verse attesting the cult is meagre (E. offers a few fleeting references). What interests us most is that in the high Ptolemaic period of Alexandrian poetry, when Philetas' pupil Hermesianax recorded the tale of Attis and the Great Mother, he used not the galliambic metre but elegiac couplets (Powell 8 = Paus. 7.17.9; there is no valid reason why this should have formed part of the *Leontion*). Wilamowitz did indeed suggest (*Hermes* 14 [1879]: 194–9, and *Hellenistische Dichtung* 2 [Berlin 1924]: 291–5) that the text of Hephaestion (second century AD), *Enchiridion* 12.3, taken with the sixth-century commentary attributed to Georgius Choeroboscus, shows that this composition derives directly from a species of galliambic hymn, addressed to Cybele and 'anaclastic' in its rhythms, that had considerable popularity in the Alexandrian period; in other words, that it closely imitates a model. But the integrity of Hephaestion's text itself has been effectively impugned, and Wilamowitz' contention can no longer be taken as established; see below, on 'Metre.' If Caecilius' work on the same theme, which forms the subject of poem 35, began (as seems not unlikely) *Dindymi domina*, obviously that, too, was in a metre other than galliambics.

As nearly all editors point out, whereas Ovid's Attis is still *Phryx puer*, as he is in the Attis myth in general, C.'s is very much a Greek; see lines 63–7. In this, he is unique; he has neither predecessors nor followers, as far as we can tell. Why, then, did C. give the name of Attis to a Greek who crossed the sea to serve a goddess whose votaries ritually made themselves eunuchs? For it was never claimed that the Attis of the myth was other than Oriental. In the language of the cult, however, as it was taken over by the Romans from its centre, Pessinus in Phrygia, the name 'Attis' was certainly one of two given to the chief priests, under the influence of the legend in its prevailing form; the other was 'Battacos.' Polybius (22.20), supplying this information as far as Pessinus itself was concerned, adds that the delegates whom those two high-priests sent out to represent them were known as Γάλλοι (Gallus, the name of a river in Phrygia, to drink the water of which caused madness – see Ov. *F.* 4.364 – is also the name of a second youth who bears a part sometimes in the legend of Attis). Consequently, in Rome the eunuch priests of Cybele were called Galli (sometimes in the feminine; cf. line 12, where *Gallae* = Γαλλαί) and the name 'Attis' was easily transferred to the leader, or local high-priest, of any troop of them. The inscription (*ILS* 4161) of a certain C. Camerius Crescens describes him as *Attis populi Romani*. Since the hero of our poem is exactly the leader of just such a troop of (prospective) Galli, the name of Attis is quite naturally assigned to him.

There are differing versions of the Attis-Cybele story in Diodorus Siculus and in Ovid (see the references above). In both, Attis appears as Cybele's youthful lover. In Ovid he is led to vow eternal constancy to her – a vow which he presently broke with a nymph, who was duly slain by Cybele; after which he castrated himself out of remorse. In Diodorus, on the other hand, there is no castration; Attis was killed by Cybele's father when it became evident that she was with child by him; and this drove her insane. In this condition she wandered over the mountains, wildly lamenting Attis. The setting in the wilderness finds an echo in C.'s poem. Commentators, however, do not always point out clearly that two geographical areas are involved: the original 'Phrygia,' in the Troad, with Mount Ida as its feature (hence the description of the Trojans as 'Phrygians,' with the consequent claim of the Romans, as sons of Aeneas, that they should have the *Idaea mater* among their gods: Ovid *F.* 4.272); and on the other hand the later, historical Phrygia, containing Mount Dindymon or Dindyma, where Pessinus lay. In the poem, although the action takes place in the former area, some of the names derive from the other.

On the degree and kind of originality C. brought to the writing of poem 63, Courtney 1985 is highly suggestive (see the end of his article for remarks on the metre). Of course, the worship of Cybele was by C.'s time a recognized theme for poetry (Lucretius' fine lines have already been mentioned). But whereas the typical Alexandrian poem on Cybele-worship would probably have been full of the details of the cult, with allusions to the underlying myths, C.'s poem (whether or not there is a model behind it) goes a step further, in a direction taken by much of his poetry: it is clearly in essence a tragedy, as Guillemin 1949 (see above) and others have described it, involving the principal character in a deed of blind fanatical devotion, and his subsequent repentance. The emotions arising from this situation are minutely analysed – this, indeed, is Alexandrian – but with a degree of personal passion added by the poet himself. For this tragedy the religion of

Cybele serves as hardly more than a suitable pretext and framework; and it is perhaps significant that the only touch of myth in the whole poem, and a merely passing one at that, is the reference to Pasithea in line 43. As Fr. observes, if C. had a model he has far surpassed it; Fr. goes on to cite, as an example of the superiority of Roman poets to their models, Virgil, who in *Geo.* 1.351–463 patterned his poem on Aratus (*Phaenomena*); similarly, he adds, the *Attis* 'ist mir stets als der stärkste Beweis für das Genie des C. erscheinen.'

Metre: Galliambic. In Greek, no doubt some models existed for a hymn or other poem to Cybele in ionic metre, which was so closely and particularly associated with Cybele-worship that it was called 'galliambic' or μητρῳακός. A pair of lines in this metre is quoted by Hephaestion (12.3), in a metrical treatise of the second century AD, and a scholium on his work tells us that 'Callimachus also used it,' which implies that the two Greek galliambic lines Hephaestion has just quoted (reproduced below) are not in fact by Callimachus (not merely that 'there is no proof that the lines … are by Callimachus,' as F. says, ibid., n. 1).

Hephaestion (see above) definitely states that the basis is Ionic; and this basis will be assumed in what follows. The question has, however, been debated since antiquity. As Mulroy 1976: 69–70 remarks, in the first century AD Caesius Bassus (*GLK* 6.261) entertains the possibility of analysing it as essentially a pair of iambic lines each beginning with an anapaest (and the second, of course, catalectic). Some modern editors, Q. for example, also follow this analysis.

The ionic foot is the equivalent of three long syllables, either the first or the last syllable being resolved into two short syllables. The alternatives are:

    ⌣ ⌣ - - (Ionic a minore)

    - - ⌣ ⌣ (Ionic a maiore).

The galliambic began as an ionic tetrameter catalectic, since the two lines referred to above, which Hephaestion quotes, are quite straightforward ionics, using both major and minor:

Γαλλαὶ μητρὸς ὀρείης φιλόθυρσοι δρομάδες
αἷς ἔντεα παταγεῖται καὶ χάλκεα κρόταλα.

Note that the first foot of the first line has the three long syllables without any resolution. In the second half of line 2 the use of an ionic a maiore followed by an ionic a minore catalectic produces the run of short syllables which most obviously characterizes the handling of the metre in Catullus. But – some time before C. employed it – it had developed another characteristic feature. By a process known as *anaclasis*, the last syllable of one foot and the first of the next were interchanged. Thus, the characteristic form of the first half of the line became, instead of ⏑ ⏑ – – | ⏑ ⏑ – –,

⏑ ⏑ – ⏑ | – ⏑ – –.

The first, or at least the earliest surviving, explanation of the term *anaclasis* is to be found in Marius Victorinus (*GLK* 6.93, quoted in Mulroy 1976: 63), writing in the fourth century. But it is clear from Hephaestion's text (12.1 and 14.7, if we avoid the now suspect text of 12.3: see Mulroy, art. cit.) that he was familiar with anaclastic ionics a minore, which he describes as a 'mixed' (ἐπίμικτον) kind; only, at 12.3 he is simply trying to establish that galliambics are in fact ionics a minore, and to make this clear he cites two lines of the 'pure' as opposed to the 'mixed' variety.

Having accepted this, we may now look at *anaclasis* itself. Observe that it means, in effect, shortening the first foot by the equivalent of one short syllable, and compensating for this by adding an equivalent amount to the second foot. In the second half of the line, the process was repeated, so that the third foot was again ⏑ ⏑ – ⏑. This left the catalectic foot with – ⏑ ⏓; but the standard form of the line *resolved the long syllable* into two short syllables, giving the run of four short syllables and a *syllaba anceps* (– ⏑ – ⏑ | ⏑ ⏑ ⏑ ⏓) which appears in the second of Hephaestion's two specimen lines, quoted above, and which – as we have already noted – is strongly characteristic of the metre as used by C.

The standard form of C.'s galliambics, then, is the form we can observe in the first line of the poem:

sŭpĕr āltă | vēctŭs Āttīs | cĕlĕrī ră | tĕ mărĭă;

and (with our text) 66 of the 93 lines are of exactly this pattern. Notice that there is a firm diaeresis at the end of the second foot (only in line 37 is there even so much as an elision there), and there is no *syllaba anceps* at this point; that is, the last syllable must be definitely long, either by nature or by position. At the end of the line, on the other hand, we can have either long or short; and these final longs or shorts are, in fact, fairly evenly distributed throughout the poem. (The business of making – so to put it – two lines into one, as the fixed diaeresis shows, reminds us of the priapean metre as it is used in poem 17.)

So far we have discussed the standard form of the line, which (as remarked above) accounts for 66, or 65, of the 93 lines in the poem. (To the *OCT*-based list given by Ross 1969: n. 15, we should add lines 54 and 61.) The remaining 27, or 28, lines, which are not of the standard pattern, contain a total of 36 or 37 variations, four lines (76, 77, 86, 91) having two variations each and two lines (22, 73) having three each. All these variations, except one (see below), consist of simple substitutions of two shorts for one long, or vice versa. Taken in the order in which they occur in the line, they may be grouped as follows:

(a) one long syllable replacing two short syllables at the beginning of the first foot: eleven instances (lines 5, 15, 17, 22, 26, 40, 67, 73, 77, 82, 86);

(b) long syllable of the first foot resolved into two short syllables, making five consecutive short syllables: three or four instances (lines 23, 48, 70, and 63 if *mulier* is read);

(c) the first long syllable of the second foot resolved into two short syllables: eleven instances (lines 4, 22, 27, 30, 31, 63, 69, 76, 77, 78, 91);

(d) long syllable replacing two short syllables at the beginning of the third foot (the first foot of the second half): six instances (lines 18, 22, 34, 73, 83, 86);

(e) a long syllable instead of two short syllables at the beginning of the last foot, making the second half of the line identical with the first, except for lacking a syllable at the end: five instances (lines 14, 35, 73, 76, 91).

Finally, the exceptional variation noticed above: in line 91 the first foot of the second half of the line has its long syllable resolved in the same way as happened in the first half in variation (b). This, however, is combined with variation (e); consequently, we are not embarrassed by an intolerable sequence of *seven* short syllables. All that happens is that the 'balance' of the second half of the line is reversed, with the five short syllables coming first.

If we were to accept *V*'s *omnia* at line 54, there would be an additional variation, taking the form of rejecting the use of *anaclasis* and reverting to the original ionic a minore basis. To put it another way, the short syllable at the end of the first foot and the long syllable at the beginning of the second foot are interchanged. This occurs in line 54 if we follow the Ms reading *omnia*; but see my text, which reads *operta*, so that the line is of the standard form. Why the first half of line 54 will not do in this non-anaclastic form is made clear in Courtney 1985. In any case, *omnia* makes 'next to no sense' (Skutsch 1976).

It must not be thought that C. adopted these variations only as a means of avoiding technical difficulties when he could not convey what he wanted to say in lines of the standard form. They often alter the tone of the poem very effectively, the most notable instance being in l. 73, the last line of A.'s speech, in which he sadly sums up his remorse at his act of self-mutilation. Here, variations (a), (d), and (e) are combined; the result is a line that conforms rather to an iambic than to an ionic pattern (iambic dimeter catalectic + iambic dimeter dicatalectic).

1–11 On these lines, regarded from a literary point of view as the prologue to an 'Alexandrian' poem, see Fedeli 1979.

1–5 Notice the rapidity with which C. reaches the situation on which he wishes to focus our attention. We are not told initially who Attis was, or why he crossed the sea. His journey from Greece (as it turns out) towards the sacred groves of the goddess takes three lines; the religious frenzy and the act of self-castration are disposed of in two more. For the rest of the poem, the subject will be the emotional turmoil and inward conflict arising from lines 4 and 5. The companions of Attis – not until l. 11 do we understand that he was not alone – are a shadowy chorus, introduced only to hear his thoughts; narrative and monologue alike are his alone.

2 *Phrygium* vaguely, of the Troad; see the intr. n. Mount Ida lay at not too great a distance to the east of this, the original 'Phrygia,' and was covered with forests; cf. *nemus* here with 52 *Idae ... nemora*. As F. remarks, 'the Trojans are *Phryges* in Virgil (*Aen.* 2.191, 9.599) and Ida is *Phrygia* (*Geo.* 4.41)'; but Ennius before him had *Bruges* (= *Phryges*) of the Trojans. Cf. also 61.18–19 n.

4 *ibi*, probably temporal: 'thereupon, then'; cf. ll. 42 and 48.
animis (pl.): B. and Fr. wish to read *animi*; but it is hard to see why the *s* should have been added, unless to make *amni* (see App. Crit.) agree with *vagus*; cf. 61.217 *-am suam* (*V*). E. and F. quote V. *Aen.* 8.228 *furens animis*; but F. too is inclined to read *animi*, as a 'limiting genitive,' of which he quotes examples, each with an adjective (e.g., *ferox animi*). E. suggests that the plural may be intended to suggest a divided state of mind, both here and in the *Aeneid*.

5 *ili*, genitive from a missing nominative form *ilium* (the plural, *ilia*, denoting much the same as the vague English 'loins,' is well attested). On the strength of Servius, *ad Ecl.* 7.26 and *Aen.* 7.499, Lachmann, followed by E., supposed the nom. sing. to be *ile*, and hence read *acuto ... pondere silicis*; but 'sharp weight' is strange, and might seem irrelevant to the observation). Translate as if *pondera* = *testiculos* (see Fr. for examples), with *acuto silice* (*silices*, *V*) as abl. of instrument. Cf. Ov. *Fasti* 4.241 (of Attis) *onus inguinis aufert*. On the problem of the text, Bianco 1970 is worth consulting, though I do not agree with his solution. It is possible that the archaic form *ilei* (Bergk's conjecture) may at one time have stood in the text; this might, through unfamiliarity, have been copied as *ilet*, ultimately with the result we observe in *V*'s reading. (The addition *-as* may come from an initial error for *ac*, which the scribe forgot to expunge.)

7 The corruption of *maculās* (= *-ans*) to *maculas* must have occurred at a period when the letter *n* was represented by a virgula. It has nothing to do with pronunciation, as E. supposes.

9 To read *tuum, Cybebe* (instead of *tubam Cibelles* or *Cybebes*) secures a better balance (with repetition) between the two halves of the line, and also avoids the

change in mid-line from third to first person. The second syllable in the form *Cybebe* is long (Serv. *ad Aen.* 10.220). It is curious that C. uses two different forms of the name in this poem (cf. 12 *Cybĕlĕs*), but understandable in view of the extreme difficulty involved in writing Latin galliambics: see n. on metre (above). On the text, see Scott 1973 for an interesting suggestion.

initia: cf. Prop. 3.3.28 (*tympana ... , orgia Musarum*); other references in F. Perhaps 'the instruments of your mystic rites' (*initia = mysteria*).

Notice again *m*'s interest in spelling (*tymp-*, *cyb-*); cf. ll. 35, 68, 84, 91.

12ff. (etc.) On Attis' monologues, see Fedeli 1978.

12–20 The companions of Attis, who like him have undergone ritual emasculation (17), are urged to follow him into the mountains where Cybele has her dwelling.

12 *O* reads *Cibelle(s)* with two *l*'s at 68 and 76 (where it is unmetrical), as well as at 12, 20, 35, 84, and 91, where it is metrical. Such (erroneous) doubling of intervocalic consonants is characteristic of *O* (e.g., 101.10 *ave atque valle*); it does not show either that *O*'s exemplar is metrically superior or that the scribe of *O* knew, or cared, whether his text was metrically correct.

13 *m*, reading *dindimenee*, is careless, and *G*² follows him into error. Contrast l. 15, where the false correction *excute* by *R*²(*m*) leads to a metrical fault; here *G*² does not follow.

Dindymenae (of Cybele): cf. 35.14 n.

14 *celeri* is a superfluous addition in *V*. Lachmann supposed that *celer* was the missing word in 74 and that it somehow strayed, fetching up here – though he does not explain how. F.'s suggestion is much better: that it is 'perhaps a misplaced marginal correction of the unmetrical *celere* in l. 1.'

See the App. Crit. Politianus earlier deleted *celeri* in the margin of *1472*; see Gaisser 1993: 405.

15 *sectam ... (ex)secutae*, tautological 'internal' accusative. (*R*²'s mistaken attempt to 'emend' *execute* to *excute* fails to recognize that in Latin texts the *s* is often dropped after *x*; e.g., *expectare = exspectare*.)

16 *truculenta pelagi*: the idiom (n. pl. + gen. sing.) is extremely common in Lucr. (e.g., 1.86 *prima virorum*, 5.35 *pelagique severa*; other references in F.), but unparalleled in C. himself, though not therefore to be rejected; the change to *pelago* is unwarranted.

17 How unfamiliar the word *evirastis* was can be deduced from the fact that only *G* preserves it; *OR* (independently, perhaps) change it to *evitastis*.

18 'Make glad the heart of the mistress-goddess with your frantic dervish-dances.' (Take *erae* with *animum*.) *R*² corrects boldly.

19 Here *G*² reads *cedat*, as in *Rm*, but adds *al. cedit* above. That is, he doubts whether the text he sees in *m* is right; cf. 61.187 n.

21 *cymbalum*: archaic genitive plural; cf. *Hiberum* 9.6 n.

22 Cf. Stat. *Th.* 6.120–1 *signum luctus cornu grave mugit adunco / tibia.*

23 *Maenades*: the language of one 'orgiastic' cult is often transferred to another. E. gives a quotation from the *Etymologicum Magnum* which shows the term Γαλλαί (*Gallae*) being applied to the worshippers of Bacchus; this of course reverses the substitution of *Maenades* for *Gallae* in our passage. Strabo (10.3.18) quotes Aesch. *Edoni*, fr. 56 N, as showing the identity of the cult of Cybele with that of Dionysus.

27–49 For a good analysis of these lines see Fedeli 1977.

28 *m* reads *th asus*; *m*² reads *th asiis*. The gaps in place of a third letter in each instance represent the scribe's doubt – which he hoped to resolve later – whether the word should be spelt *thy-* or *thi-*. The *-iis* termination is derived by *R*² (followed by *m*²) from *X*; it is metrically wrong as well as meaningless, and it is therefore most unlikely to have been an original correction.

31–3 On the heifer simile, see Glenn 1973.

31 *animam agens*: here to be taken literally, 'panting, breathing with difficulty.' Because so often this is a terminal symptom, the phrase comes to mean 'breathing one's last,' and in most of its occurrences it bears this connotation; see examples in F.

32 Because of its implication of *human* companionship, *comitatus* (or *-ta*) is usually linked with a person, not a thing, in the ablative (F. gives two exceptions to this). But notice E.'s sound observation that in Lygdamus (= [Tib.] 3) 2.13 *matris comitata dolore = comitata matre dolente*; on this analogy it could be argued that here *comitata tympano* simply = *comitata Gallis tympana gerentibus*. Fr. points out that *comitata tympano*, in relation to *dux*, reminds us clearly of 15 *duce me mihi comites*.

34 *rapidae*: cf. 93 *rapidos*.

35 The cretic rhythm of *lassulae*, combined with the *languor* (cf. line 37) of the (unexpected) diminutive, gives an effect of weariness (see B.).

36 *sine Cerere*: they are so tired that they cannot trouble to make a meal (Kr.).

37 'Drowsy sleep covers their eyes *with* wavering weariness'; not abl. abs. (To express their inability to keep their eyes open, C. repeats the notion of drowsiness, in different phrases.) On the elision at the natural diaeresis in the line, between *languore* and *oculos*, see Knobles 1971; it 'turns the line into a blur,' thereby expressing exhaustion.

38 *V*'s reading is *mollis rabidus*: either *mollis* must be changed to *molli*, or *rabidus* to *rabidi*. Clearly the antithesis implicit in the chiastic juxtaposition of ... *molli* / *rabidus* ... works better, and is more in the manner of C. in this poem, than the complicated expression *mollis rabidi furor animi* – especially since the division is pointed by the position of the caesura.

39–43 Five lines are devoted to describing the rise of the Sun and consequent awakening of Attis. The description is highly 'Alexandrian'; possibly it may follow some Callimachean precedent, though evidence for this is lacking. What cannot be denied, in any case, is the contribution made by these lines to the poem's *atmosphere*; this is true especially of line 43, where see the n.

39 *oris aurei*: possessive genitive, with *oculis*, not 'genitive of description,' as F. would have it. L. argued to the contrary as follows: (i) a 'descriptive' genitive usually (though not always) depends on nouns that are themselves descriptive, denoting a species (e.g., *homo*) rather than an individual (*Caesar, Sol*); (ii) there is a *general* distinction of meaning between genitive and ablative, corresponding to the basic usages appropriate to these two cases: the gen. tending rather towards 'consisting *of*,' the abl. towards 'accompanied *by*.' Thus it is more usual to find a genitive applied to description related to the *whole* of the subject (e.g., *vir optimi ingeni*), while if only a part, especially an external aspect, of the subject is in question, the abl. is more commonly used (e.g., the familiar *senex promissa barba*, where the gen. would be surprising). In the light of all this, *oris aurei Sol* (which is a proper name, like *Somnus*, as ll. 39–43 show) would not do. (Sol's *os aureum* is not *all* of him, but only a part.)

40 *lustravit*, taken with *oculis*, = 'surveyed' (not 'illumined,' as E. takes it, comparing Lucr. 5.575 and 693; but in both of these passages the all-important abl. of instrument is *lumine*). A close parallel is furnished by Ap. Rhod. 1.519–20:

> ... ὅτ' αἰγλήεσσα φαεινοῖς ὄμμασιν Ἠώς
> Πηλίου αἰπεινὰς ἴδεν ἄκριας.

album: as L. noted, the morning twilight, in the Mediterranean, fills the sky with a milk-white glow for about half an hour before the sun rises; i.e., the sun rises to meet a *white* sky.

43 Pasithea (one of the Graces), wife of Somnus (Hypnos): *Iliad* 14.267–76 (see F.). She is an obscure figure in mythology; C. is again being 'Alexandrian,' both in the learned reference and in his manner of extending the simile in a way that, while it is 'digressive,' adds to the artistic exquisiteness of the simile itself. (It increases the effect of the personification of *Sol*.)

45 See App. Crit. Although *ipsa* appears in A. Guarinus' text, Gaisser 1993: 95 and esp. n. 106 has now shown that this must be a misprint, as his comment is based exclusively on *ipse*. The correction to *ipsa* can be found in a seventeenth-century Ms in Florence (Table of Mss, No. 32).

46 *quis* = *testibus*; for the polite euphemism, cf. *pondera* 5 n. (Kr. quotes Ov. *Fasti* 4.240 *ah, pereant partes, quae nocuere mihi.*)

47 *rusum*: slightly colloquial, for *rursum*. The form is used by Lucr., but was much less familiar to scribes than *rursum*; hence the corruption. Cf. Cic. *Ad Fam.* 8.8.3 *postulante rusus Appio* (where M reads *postulanter usus*).

48 *maria vasta*: taken together, the words are descriptive of the 'sundering' sea, dividing the youth from his homeland. The same underlying notion is to be found in poem 64 (where see Thomson 1961) and poem 101.

49 *R²*'s variant (*al. miseriter*) was not picked up by *m*, but only by *m²*. (Cf., e.g., 64.28 *al. neutūne R² bis.*) As for *maiestates* (*R²m²*), it must ultimately be due to something in *A*; it makes no sense, but cf. *magestates* in *O*. *G²* does not follow; he is already missing much through haste (cf. 64.319 n.).

50 *mei*, gen. sing. of *ego*; C. could of course have used *mea*, with lengthening of short final *a* before *cr-*, but the genitive is to be preferred (F.) because it gives more emphasis to the verbal force of *creatrix* (stronger than in the other noun, *genetrix*, which is conventionally 'poetical' for *mater*).

m's carelessness (he wrote *genitris* at first) is self-corrected; in its corrected form, *m*'s reading is adopted by *G²*, as usual; but *G²* then sees that *G* itself embodies the improvement, with better spelling.

51 On *erifuga*, see Fasce 1979.

52 *O*'s retention of *tetuli* here, against *X*'s erroneous *retuli* (standing for *rettuli*, of course), helps to establish Calphurnius' emendation *tetulit* at line 47.

54 *furibunda*: probably to be taken as feminine singular, referring to Attis; there will be no contradiction with the masculine form of *miser* 51, which of course refers to Attis *before* emasculation. Accordingly, *miser* cannot show that *furibunda* is neuter plural ('the furious lairs of wild beasts,' an unlikely phrase in C., though perhaps less so in a poet of the Silver Age). There also arises the question whether *omnia* can be right, involving as it does a unique reversion to the ionic a minore rhythm (see the intr. n. on metre); if it is not, and if an adjective must be substituted for it, then that adj. must qualify *latibula*, and it would be awkward (to say the least) to burden the same noun with a second adjective. All these considerations seem to me to point to feminine singular *furibunda*.

55 *reor* (indicative): cf. 1.1 n.; also V. *Aen.* 4.534 *en quid ago?* Here, it may be argued that the meaning of the verb helps the reader to tolerate the indicative: 'what do I think?' is virtually equivalent to 'what am I to believe?'

56 *sibi* is not a 'stopgap,' as F. says, but an example of a tendency shown by C. to use the dative of the personal pronoun in place of the possessive (and as an equivalent to it): e.g., 37.11 *puella nam mi*, 21.11 *mi puer*; also line 6 of this poem (*sibi*), 39.18–19 *sibi ... dentem*, and 10.23 *in collo sibi*. Certainly the dative here has no function *except* as a virtual equivalent to the possessive.

58 *remota*: to be taken not with *nemora* (Kr.) but with *ego* (F.).

60 The word spelled *gyminasiis* in this line (cf. also Varr. *RR* 1.55.4) seems to recur in its shortened form at 64. If the text is correct, this may be a combination of metrical pressure (see 9 n.) and the search for variety. *m* (who at first wrote *ginnasiis*) corrects his own text independently (*gimnasiis*, *m¹*), and is virtually followed by *G²*, who has *gymnasiis*.

62 The second *quod* is, of course, a postponed relative.
obierim, 'passed into <on my way>.'

63 The line begins with the present and goes back by stages to A.'s childhood. The verb *fui* can be taken as meaning 'I have been <all those things, including what I am now>,' though F. considers (as Wilamowitz did; see E.'s n.) that we should read (with *V*) *ego mulier* and interpret thus: 'I, who am <now> a woman, have been ...' But the expression is surely strained; it is better to emend, in the interests of consistency in Attis' list.
adulescens = ἔφηβος.

64 *fui ... eram*: editors have been suspicious of the disagreement in tense (B. suggested *mei* for *fui*); but cf. V. *Aen.* 12.147 *qua visa est fortuna pati Parcaeque sinebant*. Notice also that *fui* belongs in part to the previous line, where it had a purely perfect sense.

65 The plurals, of course, do not refer to number but merely show, by an idiom, that these events occurred repeatedly at a single spot. Fr. cites for comparison Ov. *M.* 6.373–4 *saepe in gelidos resilire lacus* (several leaps into *one* lake only!).

67 *ubi*, 'whenever,' with the subjunctive in a 'frequentative' temporal construction, is rare. Cf. 84.1 *si quando ... vellet*, with F.'s n. there. In the present passage, however, F.'s citation from Hor. *Od.* 3.6.41 is not a good parallel, since there the syntax is complicated by subordination of the clause to the infin. *portare*, and this in its turn is governed by *docta*.

68 *deum*, poetic (or 'generalizing') plural for singular: cf. 10.10 *praetoribus*. Cf. Fr. for several Greek and Latin parallels, including four from Euripides.

70 *viridis* does not contradict 'snow-clad'; as C. visualized the shrine, it was on a well-forested mountain mass, close to the snow-line. Using the adjective as he does, he may possibly have remembered Callimachus, *H.* 3.41.

71 *columinibus*, 'peaks,' an alternative spelling for *culminibus* (cf. 60 *gyminasiis/gymnasiis*).

73 Notice the *rallentando* (with pathetic effect) imposed by the slow, heavy rhythm; C. uses the greatest possible number of long syllables permitted to him by the normally light and rapid galliambics.
iam iam(que) merely = 'now' (with emphasis). F. well notes: 'The implication, often conveyed by *iam iam* ..., of an action so imminent that it seems to have happened already ... is not present here.'

74 *hinc*, 'from him'; cf. perhaps 68.10 *hinc*, 'from me,' in a letter, and 116.6 *hinc*, 'from me,' in what purports at least to be a letter. See Fr.; he cites Ov. *F.* 4.230, where *hinc* = *ab ea*, as well as passages from Livy (1.58.8) and Tacitus (*A.* 11.10). He also points out that the exchange of *huic* and *hinc*, though frequently occurring in the text of other authors, is not elsewhere found in that of C.

75 *geminas ... aures*: F. claims that the adj. lacks 'any special force'; but his quotations seem to show that this kind of expression is quite often used to

emphasize a powerful impact made on the senses. (Cf. 51.11–12 *gemina teguntur lumina nocte*.)

deorum, a 'generalizing' plural; see above, l. 68 n.

77 The choice of *saevum* is a matter of taste; but when you have embarked on a phrase like *pecoris hostis* it is perhaps better to stay in the realm of poetic periphrasis than to come down in mid-phrase to questions of port and starboard, or nearside and offside. For *saevus* as a conventional epithet applied to lions, see Lucr. 3.306.

See App. Crit. The exact date of the sixteenth-century (post-Aldine) manuscript in Florence, known as *Laur. Ashb. 973* (No. 25 in the Table), is uncertain; but marginal notes, by the first scribe, are dated after 1548 by a quotation on fol. 47ʳ from the *Annotationes* of F. Robortellus (Gaisser 1992: 260).

81 The natural history of lions that lash themselves into a fury with their tails had a long life; see especially F.'s quotation from Pliny (*NH* 8.49).

82 In his n. on 36.16 (but not here), F. suggests restoring *face* in our present passage; it seems to me unnecessary to do this.

84 *religat*, 'unties.'

85 See F. on 81, quoting Pliny's account of *incitamenta* in lions.

Take *rapidum … animo* together: cf. Cicero, *Ad Q. F.* 1.1.38 *animo incitari*, of anger.

m's *adortalis* could be due to careless copying of *R*; but the later reading in *R*², reproduced in *m*², probably depends on a variant or correction in *X*.

86 The rhythm of the line is, here too, modified in order to obtain a special effect; compare line 73.

87 *umida* and *albicantis* refer to the foam-spattered appearance of the sand at the edge of the water where sea meets shore.

88 *marmora pelagi*: cf. 16 n. for the idiom (n. pl. + gen. sing.).

88, 89 Lachmann's attempt to substitute the feminine forms (see App. Crit.) for those in *V* should be rejected. Cybele sees Attis as rebelling against her *imperia* by his complaints, and she regards him, *qua* rebel, as a man, using the masculine at lines 78 and 80. A man, of sorts, he still is at the moment of pursuit and before he is overtaken (lines 88–9); but when the punishment has taken effect, his feminine condition recurs, presumably for good (line 90).

90 *O*, in all probability, misread *A*'s o̅e̅ as e̅e̅; cf. 50.13 n.

91 The punctuation adopted in the *OCT* seems to spoil the rhythm, and even the meaning, of the line, which should contain a balanced series of ritual invocations. Cf. Prop. 3.17.35 *dea magna Cybebe*.

m's careless reading *dindimenei* is, as usual, followed by *G*²; subsequently, *m*² looks at *R* afresh and sees the superiority of *R*'s reading, but (instead of altering the text) reintroduces that reading *as a variant* on the earlier mistake.

92–3 Notice how this poem, like poem 64, ends with a 'moralizing epilogue.' The concluding prayer is an instance of Alexandrian technique (see F.'s n., which quotes two examples, taken from the hymns of Callimachus). The deep passion of C.'s utterance however adds a personal note to his use of the conventional device.

92 *era* = πότνια. Cf. Callim. *H.* 3.136.

93 *rapidos* seems better than *rabidos* because it is closer in meaning to *incitatos*, and such antithetical but tautologous repetitions are characteristic of the style of this poem (Fr.).

Weinreich, O. 1936. 'C.s Attisgedicht,' *Mélanges Cumont*. Brussels: 463–500.

Elder, J.P. 1940. 'The Art of C.'s *Attis*,' *TAPA* 71: xxxiii–xxxiv.

– 1947. 'C.'s *Attis*,' *AJP* 68: 394–403.

Guillemin, A.M. 1949. 'Le poème 63 de C.,' *REL* 27: 149–57.

Oksala, T. 1962. 'C.s Attis-Ballade: über dem Stil der Dichtung und ihr Verhältnis zur Persönlichkeit des Dichters,' *Arctos* 3: 199–213.

Schäfer, E. 1966. *Das Verhältnis vom Erlebnis und Kunstgestalt bei C.* Wiesbaden: 95–107.

Sandy, G.N. 1968. 'The Imagery of C. 63,' *TAPA* 99: 389–99.

Oksala, P. 1969. 'Das Geschlecht des Attis bei C.,' *Arctos* 6: 91–6.

Ross, R.C. 1969. 'C. 63 and the Galliambic Meter,' *CJ* 64: 145–52.

Bianco, O. 1970. 'Sul testo del v. 5 del c. 63 di C.,' *Ronconi*: 35–9.

Sandy, G.N. 1971. 'C. 63 and the Theme of Marriage,' *AJP* 92: 185–95.

Knobles, C. 1971. 'A Significant Elision (Cat. 63.37),' *CP* 66: 35–6.

Glenn, J. 1973. 'The Yoke of Attis,' *CP* 68: 59–61.

Scott, R.D. 1973. 'C. 63.9,' *CP* 68: 214–15.

Rubino, C.A. 1974. 'Myth and Mediation in the Attis Poem of C.,' *Ramus* 3: 152–75.

Skutsch, O. 1976. 'Notes on C.: (3) Anaclasis in Galliambics,' *BICS* 23: 20–1. [See Courtney 1985.]

Mulroy, D. 1976. 'Hephaestion and C. 63,' *Phoenix* 30: 61–72. [Important: see intr. n. above.]

Fedeli, P. 1977. 'Dal furor divino al rimpianto del passato. Tecnica e stile di C. 63.27–49,' *GIF* 29: 40–9.

– 1978. 'Struttura e stile dei monologhi di Attis nel carme 63 di C.,' *RFIC* 106: 39–52.

– 1979. 'Il prologo dell' *Attis* di C.,' *Traglia* 1: 149–60.

Fasce, S. 1979. 'Attis erifuga,' *Maia* 31: 25–7.

Salanitro, N. 1979. 'Lingua e stile nella poesia menippea,' *Traglia* 1: 351–73, esp. 369–73.

Traill, D.A. 1981. 'C. 63: Rings around the Sun,' *CP* 76: 211–14.

Shipton, K.M.W. (Kirsty). 1984. 'Attis and Sleep: C. 63.39–43,' *LCM* 9: 38–41.

Courtney, E. 1985. 'Three Poems of Catullus: (2) How C. Came to Write the Attis,' *BICS* 32: 88–91.

Shipton, K.M.W. 1986. 'The *iuvenca* Image in C. 63,' *CQ* 36: 268–70.

– 1987. 'The 'Attis' of C.,' *CQ* 37: 444–9.

Martina, M. 1987. 'Odisseo, Attis e l' amore. Nota a C. 63, 48,' *Aufidus* 3: 15–19.

Näsström, B.-M. 1989. *The Abhorrence of Love. Studies in Rituals and Mystic Aspects in C.'s Poem of Attis*. Stockholm.

Kirby, J.T. 1989. 'The Galliambics of C. 63,' *SyllClass* 1: 63–74.

Granarolo, J. 1991. 'C., Poésies, LXIII 12–34,' *Vita Lat.* 121: 18–26.

Libri, A. 1992. 'Catullus 63.54,' *Studi latini e italiani* 6: 53–8.

Skinner, M.B. 1993. 'Ego Mulier: The Construction of Male Sexuality in C.,' *Helios* 20: 107–30.

64

For centuries, poem 64 has occasionally been referred to as 'The Epithalamium of Peleus and Thetis'; but this title or subtitle is inaccurate, since an epithalamium is (literally) a marriage *song*, whereas this is a narrative poem – with descriptive passages — *about* a marriage. Admittedly, it contains a kind of epithalamium in the 'Song of the Fates,' lines 323–81 – R^2 inserts the title *Epythalamum thetidis et pelei* before line 323 – but we are not therefore entitled to designate the entire poem an epithalamium. As a whole, however, it purports to be an elaborate account of a mythical marriage between a hero and a goddess, a marriage to which there are many allusions in ancient poets. It is by far the longest of C.'s extant works and perhaps – in its final form — one of the latest in date: (i) it seems to contain, almost though not quite entirely within its 'Ariadne episode' (see below) echoes of Lucretius, who died – leaving his work unfinished – about 54 BC; (ii) its structure (see below) is clearly a developed version of that of poem 68[b]; (iii) its artistic technique on the whole seems mature; (iv) lines 154–7 look like a reworking of a theme abruptly stated in poem 60, one of a group of obscure poems or fragments appended, it seems, to the first *libellus* (see Intr., p. 8). It recounts the 'heroic' myth, familiar in literature and art, of the first encounter and wedding of the mortal Peleus, an Argonaut, with the sea-nymph Thetis. Their union was celebrated above all as a meeting of the human and the divine; and this aspect is emphasized, not only by careful descriptions of the two kinds of wedding guests, mortal and immortal (and the fact that the gods attended Peleus' wedding was from Homer onwards his unique distinction among men), but also by two meditative passages near the poem's opening (22–30) and at its close (384–408), both of which suggest or record the contrast between the blessed age of the Heroes, when the gods visited assemblies of mortals, and the degenerate present, when they no longer do so. Within this narrative are contained two long episodes, each of which again is carefully placed between pairs of two-line transitional passages leading into the episode (50–1, 303–4) and subsequently out of it again (265–6, 382–3). The former episode, represented as a description (*ecphrasis*) of the coverlet of the marriage bed, and containing the story of Ariadne, is particularly long; indeed, its length (213 lines at least) amounts to more than half of the poem. In its turn it is cut up into several scenes, including that of Theseus' departure from Athens for Crete and his subsequent return after abandoning Ariadne (207–50), and the description of the arrival of Bacchus and his followers in pursuit of Ariadne after her desertion (251–64), this being implicitly (see Townend 1983) another marriage of human and divine persons. Besides descriptive passages and internal 'flashbacks' in the narration, the episode also contains long speeches: not only Ariadne's extended lament on her desertion, but also a twenty-three-line speech by Aegeus, father of Theseus, to his departing son. In the second episode, the structure is simpler: the Song of the Fates, sung at the wedding, is merely extended into the future with a prophecy of the birth of Achilles from this union, and the celebration of the fame that awaits him as a warrior.

Structure: As will now be clear, what we have in this poem is a more complicated version of the concentric-ring or 'Chinese box' structure, first met with in poem 68[b]. The chief difference is that, whereas in poem 68[b] there was a single *omphalos* or centre-piece, around which the 'rings' were more or less symmetrically arranged, this poem should really be explained in terms of two *omphaloi*, namely the Lament of Ariadne and the Song of the Fates. See my 1961 article (cited in the bibliography) for details, and for a comparative diagram of the two poems. For poem 64 itself, there are helpful diagrams at Traina 1972: 149 and Traill 1981: 233. On the poem's structure and also C.'s use of verbal 'signals' to mark off the sections of the poem as its movement advances, see most recently the incidental remarks relating to poem 64 in Courtney 1985: 92–4.

Scholars in general attribute the poem to a genre they have agreed to call 'epyllion,' or small-scale epic, a term possessing – in the sense in which they use it – 'no ancient authority,' as F. says, and 'first used by Haupt, in a lecture on this poem, in 1855' (p. 272, n. 1; for a fuller history and bibliography see Most 1981: 111 n. 2). There is no doubt, however, that the thing exists, both in Hellenistic and in Latin literature, and that it is distinguished from other genres by certain characteristics belonging to its way of telling a story, as well as (to some extent) in the stories – or parts of them – it chooses to tell. If we seek to describe it, we at once encounter the difficulty that C.'s poem is the only survivor of a group of such epyllia known to have been written by the neoteric poets in Rome, others being the *Io* of Calvus, the *Zmyrna* of Cinna (see on poem 95), the *Glaucus* of Cornificius, and possibly one by Valerius Cato. Even in Greek, very few poems identifiable as epyllia survive: two by Theocritus (13, 24), another (25, 'Heracles the Lion-slayer') under the name of Theocritus, and one by Moschus (2). The question is how far C. made innovations in the genre, how far he followed its laws or the practice of an individual model (or models). Certainly no other extant epyllion shows the enormously long 'insert narrative,' outweighing the rest of the poem, which we find in poem 64. Other unusual features in C.'s treatment will be mentioned below.

Before we go further it will be useful to mention certain peculiarities of the epyllion in general which distinguish it from the traditional, or Homeric, narrative poem. The most arresting of these is the reduction of important constituent events in the story to the barest mention in passing, or to mere allusion, or even total suppression, in favour of picturesque description, emotion and psychological interpretation (especially when there is a possibility of innovation, such as giving a 'new twist' to the motives attributed to a character in a story; for an example of this, see the n. on 2^b.1). Romantic settings, and the replacement of personal names by allusive phrases, are frequent. Often an obscure version of a myth or fable is preferred to the familiar one. Sometimes – more of this later – there is a story within a story, and it may be hard to see how the two are connected. All of this applies to poem 64.

Why did C. elect to write an epyllion? Speculation begins at this point, since (as already remarked) we are unable to compare his effort in this genre directly with those of Calvus or Cinna or any other contemporary poet. Most scholars hold either that he had to show his skill in a now fashionable kind of composition, simply in order to justify his position in the neoteric movement (and consequently we ought to view the resulting poem as mere 'art for art's sake'); or else that for some reason he wished to set off the tale of a happy marriage (though in certain particulars he was as far as we know the first to represent the union of Peleus and Thetis in this way) against the tormented affair of Theseus and Ariadne, resolved as it was by the final intervention of Bacchus; or, thirdly, that he wished to represent the Heroic age, seen in the light of a familiar myth, as really un-heroic and already corrupt, so that even the ostensible praise of that age in the introductory part of the poem and in the 'moralizing epilogue' becomes ironic. This third view now has a numerous following (Kinsey 1965, Curran 1969, Bramble 1970, and others; see however Dee 1982 for an effective counter-argument); but traces of irony, which ought surely to be discernible elsewhere in the poet's works, are extremely hard to demonstrate securely, so that it must be approached with some degree of reserve. If we cannot quite accept it, then on first principles we have still to face certain novelties in C.'s narrative. Apart from the *felicitas* of the marriage, and the fact that Thetis is not unwilling to wed Peleus (contrast *Il.* 18.434 πολλὰ μάλ' οὐκ ἐθέλουσα), and the removal of the scene of the wedding from Mount Pelion to the palace at Pharsalus – which in itself has been taken to indicate a major source in Hellenistic court poetry, perhaps describing a Ptolemaic nuptial feast – C. makes free with his myths in many other particulars. For example, Apollo and Artemis absent themselves from the wedding (see 301–2 n.), while Chiron brings unusual gifts to it; the *Parcae*, not the Muses, sing the *epithalamium* with its prophecy of Achilles; Bacchus (called by his cult title, Iacchus) does not come upon, and suddenly fall in love with, the sleeping Ariadne, but brings his noisy rout all ready to capture her; the punitive tribute of youths and maidens sent from Athens is apparently increased (l. 78; cf. Plut. *Thes.* 15); all the inhabitants of Delphi come out to meet Bacchus (l. 392); Nemesis is a war-goddess alongside Ares and Athena (ll. 394–5); and Minos, the proverbially just ruler, is paradoxically *iniustus* (l. 75). Finally, Zeus is said to have yielded Thetis to Peleus as a bride (27), and when Prometheus (at first sight surprisingly, for a minor god) attends the wedding (294–7), we hear nothing of the act that justifies his inclusion, namely the warning he promulgated to the effect that the son of Thetis would be greater than his father, which effectively ruled out Zeus, unless *sollerti corde* (l. 294) hints at this.

Besides this preference for the unusual over the usual version, poem 64 is strongly characterized by the taste for allusiveness already mentioned as a trait of Hellenistic composition. For example, the goddess Athena is indirectly referred to, as *incola Itoni* (228), and Artemis as *unigena cultrix montibus Idri* (300). Here *unigena* = γνωτός, reminding us of the same equation at 66.53, where γνωτός is the original adj. in Callimachus, corresponding to C.'s *unigena*. (Similarly, at 66.44, *progenies Thyiae* = ἀμνάμων Θείης in the restored papyrus text of Callimachus, though whether it indicates the sun or a wind is uncertain; see n. there). Other allusive phrases (they are too numerous to list) include the following: *Rhamnusia* = Nemesis 395 (Callimachus, *H.* 3 [*Dian.*] 232 Ἑλένῃ Ῥαμνουσίδι is of course not quite parallel, since Helen is in fact named); *Amphitrite* = sea 11, *Minois* = Ariadne 60, 247; *Gortynia* = Cretan 75 (unless this is intended as a learned or antiquarian substitution for *Cnosia*); *Cecropia* = Athens 79, 83; *quae regis Golgos etc.* = Aphrodite 96; *germanus* = the Minotaur 150; *Gnosia Cecropiae* 172; *perfidus nauta* = Theseus 174; *Erectheus portus* = Piraeus 211; *tereti aere* = with cymbals 263; *Haemonides* = Thessalian maidens 287;

lenta soror Phaethontis = poplar 291; *pater divum* = Zeus 298; *Opis natus* = Zeus 324; *Pelopis tertius heres* = Agamemnon 346; *urbis Dardaniae vincla* = the walls of Troy 367; *Thyiades* = Bacchants 391.

There is, however, an instance of allusiveness on a larger scale, to which Forehand 1974 and, more systematically, Townend 1983 have drawn attention. This involves on the poet's part 'the assumption that the story is already familiar to the reader and that it is therefore unnecessary to relate it in full' (Townend 1983: 25). Townend proceeds to point out that such a reader was intended 'to fill in the story of how Ariadne became the bride of Bacchus and was installed on Olympus, with her garland set up as a constellation in the sky.' He describes the fact that nothing is said about this further development as 'a major aposiopesis,' and suggests that we may be prompted to look for a similar aposiopesis – in his words, an 'unstated climax' – in the 'outer story' of Peleus and Thetis. This he finds in its abrupt cutting-off before the anciently attested *finale* of the wedding celebration, when Eris (who had not been invited) 'crashes' the feast and provokes the contest among the goddesses which will result in the Judgment of Paris and ultimately in the Trojan War; this story, first recorded at the beginning of the *Cypria* in the Trojan Cycle of post-Homeric epic poems, was, we must suppose, familiar to the circle of educated Roman readers for whom C. wrote.

Modern editors like to proclaim the demise of the theory, voiced by Riese in 1884, that poem 64 is a translation of a poem by Callimachus; and several echoes of rival poets at lines 30, 102, 139, and 160ff. (see nn.) prove at least that it is not entirely this. Even the later theory advanced by Wilamowitz (*Hellenistische Dichtung.* 2 [Berlin, 1924]: 298), that C. composed poem 64 and other long poems independently but under strong influence from various Alexandrians, has lately been doubted ('generally discredited,' Q. in relation to poem 63; see however Courtney 1985 on poems 62 and 63). Yet quite apart from the homage to Callimachus involved in C.'s translation of the *Coma Berenices* (poem 66), we have found reason to consider the possibility that poem 4 may follow closely a Callimachean *Phaselus Berenices*. We now have to reckon with the argument set out by Thomas 1983 that the major impulse that moved C. to compose a particular kind of epyllion may still be traced to Callimachus, and specifically to his *Victoria Berenices* (a companion piece to the *Coma*), which in 1977 emerged in fragmentary shape from a Lille papyrus. Putting together V. *Geo.* 3.1–48, Prop. 3.1, Stat. *S.* 3.1, and poem 64 itself, Thomas concludes that the *Victoria Berenices* embodied an experiment in 'ecphrastic epyllion' of just the sort we have sketched (*ecphrasis* denoting the literary description, at some length, of an object, such as the shield of Achilles in *Il.* 18.478–617). Poem 64 is noteworthy, even among 'ecphrastic' poems, not only because the 'episode,' in Callimachus as in C., seems to dominate the poem both in length and in interest, but also in that the characters depicted on the coverlet – a work of art – are not merely *shown*, but come to life, act, and move as though they were involved in a normal poetic narrative and not a merely 'static' description. This, too, is part of the experiment; pointing this out, Thomas reminds us that Callimachus (*Aet.* inc. lib. fr. 114) represents a statue of Apollo 'which conducts a conversation with the poet.' He also strives (not without success, in my opinion) to show that Virgil and later poets revert to a more restrained kind of ecphrasis, whereas the experimental vein of Callimachus was absorbed, in its original uncompromising essence, by Catullus alone, on whom the mantle and manner of Callimachus descended.

To sum up. Although both the original motivation and the developed orientation of this poem are at present still debatable, for reasons already given, nevertheless C.'s allusive method, which both on a larger and on a smaller scale is thoroughly Hellenistic, together with the way in which he directs his *ecphrasis* towards narrative rather than mere description, seem to reintroduce into the debate the possibility, even the probability, that he received his initial impulse from an ecphrastic epyllion by Callimachus, later than the *Hecale* (see T.B.L. Webster, *Hellenistic Poetry and Art* [London, 1964]: 309); the *Victoria Berenices* (now extant in part) has been suggested by Thomas as providing this impulse. From a purely literary aspect, then, poem 64 represents the emulation by a Roman poet of the learned elegance and allusive technique of the Alexandrian *Kleinepos*. It remains to ask, as many critics continue to ask, whether we are to find in it a statement of that poet's personal values. In a long and late work, it might even be thought surprising if no indication of those values were to be discovered. Here too there is room for debate. But if we do not limit ourselves to the 'moralizing' finale of the poem (383–408), and compare the expressions given emphatic utterance in poem 64 as a whole with those similarly treated in the more intimate among the short poems, we may be driven to some conclusions. Both in the story of the wedding and in that of Ariadne, C. seems to lay stress on the notion lying behind the word *fides* (and, as at 335 and 373, on its cognate *foedus*), and to associate this idea with the beneficent presence of the gods, who are seen as its guarantors. It is to the *caelestum fides* that Ariadne appeals when she is wronged by a mortal, Theseus (191); and he, the guilty party, is emphatically *perfidus* (133, 174; notice the word *fidelis*, negated in 144, and also *periuria* at 135 and 148, *fallax* in 151). At the wedding-feast, the Song of the Fates is, in line 322, heavily stated to be beyond accusations of *perfidia* as it celebrates the *concordia* of the happy pair – here again, a condition guaranteed by the divinity present both in the union itself, and in those who utter the prophecy. As a corollary, the poet at once makes the point that when mortals forsook *pietas* and banished Justice (Themis) by their actions, they lost the goodwill of heaven, so that the gods no longer came openly among them. In this sense, poem 64 has many clear links with the language used in the shorter poems; consider poem 76, for example, on *pietas* and *sancta fides*, or poem 30 on the opposite notions. One is tempted, accordingly, to agree with those who have designated poem 64 as one of the 'poems of *fides*' (see, e.g., Traina 1972: 152–6). Further, C.'s careful assertion that the homes of the heroes were *castae* (a word here linked with *pietas*, as *vitam puriter egi* is in poem 76) is a statement which should be carefully pondered by those critics who believe that C.'s principal intention in the poem is to denigrate the Heroic Age and its values – particularly in view of line 23b, if that line is correctly restored. Here, too, C. should probably receive the benefit of any doubt as to whether or not he has imposed on his inherited material, however various that may be, his own unifying force.

Metre: Dactylic hexameters, with some admixture of 'spondaic hexameters' (ending in a double spondee). As F. (3 n., following Kr.) observes, poem 64 contains thirty σπονδειάζοντες (only four fewer than in the whole of Virgil); but – as he does not notice, or at least does not mention – twenty of these spondaic endings occur in the first 120 lines. In the next 130 lines, there are none. They begin again in the description of Bacchus and his followers, and in lines 251–301 there are nine. In the last 106 lines of the poem there is only one σπονδειάζων, at 358. The reason for this uneven distribution becomes fairly obvious after a glance at the divisions into which the poem falls. It is in passages of description that the poet feels the need for technical flourishes such as this. In emotional (that is, rhetorical) writing, such as the lament of Ariadne or the speech of Aegeus, they would be out of place. Something should also be added concerning the source from which C. derived this metrical device. Spondaic endings, in Latin verse, might be due either to imitation of Ennius (as sometimes in the *Aeneid*) or to Hellenistic fashion. Since Ennius' time, Roman poetry had been learning to do without them; but the neoteric movement had brought them back into favour as an imitation of the verse rhythms of the Hellenistic poets, and it is this influence which caused C. to adopt them, and not that of Ennius, to whom indeed he seems to acknowledge by imitation no more than the smallest debt. C.'s versification in the greater part of poem 64, and especially in its two speeches, is remarkably smooth and flowing, differing from Virgil's later development of the hexameter mainly in two respects: the prevalence of end-stopped lines, making for a somewhat monotonous sequence on which Virgil's metrical periods were certainly an improvement, and the frequency of diaeresis after the fourth foot, which Virgil used more sparingly (more often when the phrasing closely linked this foot with what followed; thus Virgil might have written line 124, where *ardenti* is closely followed by its noun, more readily than a line like 131; cf. however *Geo.* 1.323 and other passages). See F.'s n. on line 5 for the way in which C. too often burdens his lines, and makes them prosaic, by the excessive use of participles (thirty-two instances of this in lines 1–131, a passage of narrative), whereas Virgil 'prefers paratactic structure with finite verbs.'

1–5 The proper names create an atmosphere of romance (Geymonat 1982), while *quondam* (cf. *olim* 77) underlines the remoteness of the myth. See l. 2 n. on *dicuntur*.

Notice how C. rushes *in medias res* at the very beginning; B. rightly identified this as an 'Alexandrian' trait. Cf. the opening of poem 63 for a similar impression of rapidity; see nn. there.

1 *quondam* (see n. above) is strongly emphasized by the double caesura, preceding and following it (see Traina 1972, who points to its 'nostalgic resonance' and its implied or – as at 139, 143 – explicit contrast with *nunc*).

prognatae, an archaic word (*Scipionum elogia*, CIL I² 7 line 2 *Gnaivod patre prognatus*), but fairly freely used by poets (e.g., Hor. *S.* 1.6.78, 2.1.26) and prose writers in formal phraseology, as when Caelius in Cicero *Ad Fam.* 8.15.2 refers (facetiously) to Julius Caesar as *Venere prognatus*. The language of poem 64 is, however, far from being generally archaic; it is on occasion prosaic or colloquial or both, but archaisms are introduced deliberately when epic or religious solemnity is sought.

pinus, like *nasse* (for *navigavisse*, cf. 66.46), of course seeks to suggest the novelty of seafaring by the want of proper words for ships and sailing; cf. *decurrere* 6, *volitantem ... currum* 9.

2 *dicuntur*, like *fertur* 19, and *perhibent* or *ferunt* in 76, 124, 212, and also poem 2ᵇ and 68.109 *ferunt* (cf. *Il.* 2.783 φασί), expresses (as Kr. remarks) C.'s dependence on tradition, though (as F. adds) 'the tradition he follows may be an unusual one.' Similarly Callimachus says (*H.* 5.56) μῦθος δ' οὐκ ἐμός, ἀλλ' ἑτέρων.

3 *Phasis*, the river, stands for the realm of Aeetes in Colchis.

The *R²* emendation, for such it is (despite *al.*), suggests prompting by the reading now found in *O*; *X*'s version with -*sc*- is a less likely source. Two other factors bearing on this successful remedy are Coluccio Salutati's interest in metrical matters and his learned acquaintance with the geography of Greek myths.

Aeetaeos: poem 64 contains thirty 'spondaic' hexameters (ending - - | - -), a remarkable proportion; Virgil has only thirty-four in all. Twenty of these are in ll. 1–120, none at all in ll. 121–50. In the description of Bacchus and his rout they reappear: ll. 251–302 have nine, but after that – in 106 lines – there is only one, a proper name at 358. In using them, C. intends (as a glance at these passages will show) to achieve an effect which he considers appropriate to description, rather than to the more rapid and uniform pace of narrative. Often a spondaic line makes a closing cadence to a kind of 'paragraph' within the poem; the word *fines* occurs here, not accidentally.

4 Both ideas and expression are resolutely epic.

Argivae: a covert reference to the ship Argo, the name of which was derived by Ennius and others from the city of Argos; whereas Apollonius Rhodius, for example, derived it from Argus, the name of the builder. (C. seems to insist on the notion that Athena, who sometimes appears in the legend as an adviser to Argus, built the ship with her own hands: cf. 9–11.) A third derivation, from a word meaning 'swift,' may have been preferred by C., who repeatedly uses adjectives such as *cita* 6, *volitantem* 9, *celeri* 53; see Thomas 1979, who however may go too far in identifying as C.'s major poetic purpose the 'correction' of his predecessors in matters such as etymology. (Thomas' argument had already been advanced in 1972 by Traina, who suggested that C. here contradicts Ennius and answers his etymology with one based on νῆα θοήν, and further refutes the derivation from the builder's name by attributing the building of the Argo to Athena alone.)

lecti iuvenes ... robora pubis: cf. V. *Aen.* 8.518.

5 *avertere*, 'win away,' of cattle-reaving and other forms of heroic robbery.

6 The rhythm is striking: a molossus (- - -) followed by dactyls for speed.

vada salsa: cf. V. *Aen.* 5.158. C. is the first to use the poetic word *vada* for 'sea'.

decurrere: Virgil has *currere* (transitive) of the sea at *Aen.* 3.191, but also *decurrere* (intransitive) at *Aen.* 5.212.

See App. Crit. *m*'s reading, *decurre*, is characteristically careless.

7 *verrentes*: the easy metaphor of 'sweeping' (cf. Eng. 'sweeps' for large oars) goes back to Ennius, *Ann.* 384 V^2 = 377 Skutsch. Cf. V. *Aen.* 3.208, 6.320.

palmis, 'oars,' another metaphor; cf. 4.4 *palmulis*.

8 *diva*: Athena 'Polias' (or πολιοῦχος), the *keeper* of the Acropolis; as goddess of handicrafts (weaving, shipbuilding, etc.), she participated in the building of the Argo: see 4 n.

retinens, 'occupying (κατέχουσα),' cf. Lucr. 4.412–13 *terrarum milia multa quae variae retinent gentes*.

9 *ipsa*: Ap. Rhod. 1.111 αὐτὴ γὰρ καὶ νῆα θοὴν κάμε.

10 *carinae*: not 'keel' but (curved) hull. The ribs and keel were of hardwood, to which the strakes (of softwood, usually pine) were bent and attached. The same technique was naturally employed to make the Trojan horse (V. *Aen.* 2.16, 112).

11 *proram* is added in the margin of *O*; but the text gives *post eam*, written with a compendium which might fairly easily be confused with that standing for

prae. (At 153 and 194, *O* gives *post-* instead of *prae-*; at 145 it may be inferred that the common source of *OGR* did so.) Both L. Schwabe, in his Berlin edition (1886) and R.J. Tarrant (*Texts and Transmission*, ed. L.D. Reynolds [Oxford, 1983]: 45 n. 17) suggest that here *O* confused the compendium for *post* with that (found in *G* and in *R*) for the *pri-* in *primam*; 'quo facto' (as Schwabe remarks) 'ex *post mam* scriba interpolavit *post eam*, denique sensu loci seductus idem addidit in marg. illud *proram*, quasi id reponendum esset.' The page of *O* is reproduced in Merrill's edition (1893), p. ix. Close examination of *O* shows that *O*¹ has here deleted the oblique cross-stroke of *e* (in order, presumably, to convey the appearance of an original *proram* in the text). Notice that he has also practically deleted the virgula over final *e* in *Amphitritē* at the end of the line, trying to make sense of his *proram*; in other words he realized that if you have *proram* as object to *imbuit* you cannot keep *A(m)phitritem*, and accordingly changed the name to the nominative case. Mynors (followed by Zicàri 1978: 33) is clearly wrong in reporting *O*'s only reading as *proram* (the top two lines on the page, reproduced in Merrill's facsimile, give ample evidence of *O*'s manner of writing *ea* and *ra*). It should be added that nothing, here or elsewhere, obliges us to believe in a 'second hand' in *O* (Professor A.C. de la Mare has kindly confirmed this for me); *O*¹ must bear the responsibility for all the alterations and the (few) marginal variants.

In confirmation of *prima* (against *proram*), Zicàri 1978: 139 cites Prop. 3.15.5–6 *illa rudes animos per noctis conscia primas / imbuit* ...

Amphitrite, a nymph, the wife of Poseidon/Neptune, stands here for the surface of the ocean, just as 'Neptune' is the sea itself in l. 2 (cf. 31.3 n.). For the Greek accusative in *-n*, cf. 74.4 n. and 102.4.

12 *proscidit*, not merely 'ploughed' but 'ploughed [virgin soil] for the first time'; so the concept of novelty (1–5 n.) is maintained.

13 *remigio*: to be taken concretely, '<a set of> oars,' rather than abstractly, 'the act of rowing.'
incanuit is preferable to *incanduit*: the oar-beaten waves 'became white' rather than 'became shining.'

14 *feri*: cf. 63.40 *mare ferum*. With this reading, defended by Puelma 1977 and O'Connell 1977, *vultus* is nominative in apposition to *Nereides*, as A. Guarinus noted. The nymphs reflect in their faces the wildness of the waves around them – a stronger image than we can find in *freti* ... *gurgite*. Emendation to *freti* would really require *emergere* to be transitive, a doubtful usage (*pace* Fr., F. and *TLL*). *OLD* brackets 'tr.'; in all the passages cited, the text is challenged (at Manil. 1.116 Bentley conjectured *evincere*, which Goold appears to adopt when he translates 'surmount,' though he prints *emergere*). At *Dirae* 57 *emersere* may be intr.; see Richmond 1962: 44, who cites Vahlen's strong rebuttal of Haupt's argument for transitive *emersere* in C. For the principle underlying the

balanced apposition (in asyndeton) of *feri vultus, aequoreae Nereides*, cf., for example, 14.14–15, or the adverbs placed 'in tandem' at 36.10 and perhaps 71.4 (where see n.).

15 *monstrum*, with of course no implication of size; merely 'a strange phenomenon.' *admirantes*, of surprise, not of love (V. *Aen.* 8.91–2 *mirantur et undae, miratur nemus insuetum*, linked with *monstrum*; Cicero, *ND* 2.89, summarizing Accius: *admirans et perterritus* – of the Argo). The breathless amazement of the nymphs is suggested by the spondaic ending (B.). See Thomas 1982: 159 and 161.

16–18 A. Balland (*Mélanges J. Heurgon* 1 [1976]: 1–11) has an interesting comparison of these lines with an inscription from Algeria ending *optavi nudas videre Nymphas, vidi* (see n. 25 for a long discussion of the text of line 16).

16 A omitted *haud*; O went further, and omitted *atque* as well. A's reading may have been *atque illa*. To change *atque* to *ante* ('never before,' Fr.) is unnecessary: novelty is implied.

   On Sabellicus' suggestion *haudque alia* (published in 1497, but apparently datable a few years before Av.) see Gaisser 1993: 49.

18 *nutrices* in the sense of *papillae* is unique in Latin, but must be accepted. Hesychius indicates a similar use of τίτθη in Greek, but literary instances are wanting.

19–21 Repetition of *tum* suddenly introduces into the description a note of emotion; cf. 46.1–2, 7–8 (*iam*).

   The version of the story given by C. is unusual; hence no doubt his insistence that he relies on tradition; see above, line 2 n. In *Il.* 18.433–4, Thetis says of herself καὶ ἔτλην ἀνέρος εὐνὴν πολλὰ μάλ᾽ οὐκ ἐθέλουσα, and this was the agreed version in the older sources. In Ovid, *M.* 11.221–65, Peleus has to conduct a difficult courtship under several metamorphoses before Thetis finally gives up. Other differences (chiefly chronological, having to do with the voyage of the Argo) are listed in F.'s n.

20 *tum*: a good example of *m* stumbling into the truth. Later he notices his 'mistake' and returns to *R*'s erroneous reading.

   It may be claimed that only Peleus apparently falls in love at first sight, whereas Thetis merely consents; but there is no doubt that C. regards their love as mutual (cf. 334–6). In the present passage, C.'s encomium on their wedded happiness is generalized into the praise of an *age* of happiness. Some recent writers have suggested that C. deliberately 'undercuts' the picture he presents of Thetis' marriage as a happy one; but why then should he so firmly defy tradition by making it happy in the first place? At all events the notion of 'love at first sight' is found only in C.'s version of this story.

21 Most editors suppose that *pater* = Jupiter, who relinquished the hand of Thetis, but Mayer 1980 has made a good case for taking *pater* as referring to Nereus. If he is right – and I think he is – it may be added that there will be an

implied contrast with the elopement of Ariadne in 52ff., especially 180–1, and particularly if (as is by no means certain) *parentis* 159 = Minos (see n.).

22 Coluccio's metrical interests are the source of an R^2 correction which – exceptionally – is not picked up by G^2 from *m*.

23 *deum genus*: cf. Ap. Rhod. 3.402 θεῶν γένος.

    See App. Crit. Here we have, in *matre*, another attempted R^2 emendation (unsuccessful this time) in the guise of a variant reading.

23[b] Peerlkamp's supplement to the broken line, recovered from the Veronese scholia, establishes in the text a triple *salvete*, together with repeated *vos*; in these respects, it may be held to be supported by *Ciris* 195–8, where we find threefold *gaudete* combined with repeated *vos*. Fr., who admits the imitation in the *Ciris*, nevertheless asserts (p. 329) that a third *salvete* is very unlikely because each of the appositions (*deum genus, bona matrum progenies*) has already received a *salvete*. Cf. further the triple χαῖρε in Callimachus, *Hymn [1] to Zeus* 90–3 (where note the context), and also cf. Ap. Rhod. 4.1381ff., 1773ff.

24 C.'s promise to address the heroes 'often' is hardly fulfilled, except by the brief mention in lines 384–6, which open the *envoi*, or moralizing epilogue, to poem 64. It appears to be a traditional compliment, not to be taken literally; cf. the concluding line of *h. Hom.* 2, 3, 4, 6, 19, 28, 30 αὐτὰρ ἐγὼ καὶ σεῖο καὶ ἄλλης μνήσομ' ἀοιδῆς, and a variant in 25, 27, 29, 33; also Theocr. 17.135 χαῖρε ἄναξ Πτολεμαῖε, σέθεν δ' ἐγὼ ἴσα καὶ ἄλλων μνάσομαι ἡμιθέων. If so, non-fulfilment of the promise is scarcely evidence of late date in C.'s life – or works – for this poem.

25 *eximie*: here taken with *aucte*, of Peleus; cf. *decus eximium* 323, where see n.; observe that *columen* 26 is answered by *tutamen* (similarly formed) at 324.

For *taedae* = *nuptiae* (a poetic, and metrically convenient, metaphor which C. is the first to use) cf. l. 302 and also (in the singular) 66.79.

aucte, 'endowed, blest'; cf. 66.11, where the reading *auctus* receives support from the present passage. Cf. Callim. *H.* 3.34 ἀέξειν.

X's *thetis* must be a slip, not a correction; observe how the line ends, and note also that, in the text as transmitted, only three lines have intervened since the triple repetition of Thetis' name at 19–21. The emendation *taedis*, against the vulgate *thetis*, is claimed for B. Guarinus by his son.

26–30 A concentration of legendary (hence 'romantic') names closes the Address to the Heroes that forms the first section of the poem; for the same phenomenon at the opening of the Address, see 1–5 n.

26–7 *ipse, ipse*: the use of epanalepsis (frequent in poem 64, see F.) here expresses either delight or (possibly) wondering disbelief, of a sort that is close to delight.

28 *te-ne*: -*ne* suggests (like *ipse* in l. 27) incredulity: 'did she actually ...?' Cf. *Ciris* 313–14 for this kind of question.

Nereine: C. uses a Greek form (Νηρίνη); elsewhere in Latin it is always *Nerine*.

The variant *al. neptine* is not much more illuminating than *nectine* (in the text); yet it was faithfully copied by m^1, and hence it passed to G^2. When R^2 came to look at the passage again, he added — in a different ink, and in a slightly altered style of writing – a second variant, *al. neutūne*, which was again picked up – by m^2, but not this time by G^2 – and which amounts to little more than an admission of R^2's inability to penetrate the corruption of the text. This is a clear example of the sort of instance where the obvious palaeographical difference between m^1 and m^2 can help us to distinguish chronological strata (not necessarily separated by many years) in the R^2 contributions to R.

29–30 Notice that the grandparents give their consent (cf. 21 n.).

30 *Oceanus*: According to E. it was Riese who first suggested that this line is imitated from Euphorion fr. 122 Powell ὠκεανός, τῷ πᾶσα περίρρυτος ἐνδέδεται χθών. See Powell 1925: 51 on the attribution.

mari (here in a non-emphatic position, and used of the waters of Ocean) is an everyday, rather prosaic word for 'sea,' which C. generally avoids in poem 64 despite the large part played in the poem by the thing itself, for which 'epic' language is generally employed. Cf. however lines 155, 269, and *marinas* 16.

31 *optatus* is a word appropriated by C. almost invariably to themes of marriage; so its connotations in 22 above may perhaps include some trace of this colouring. *finito = definito*, 'appointed.' Livy has the idiom *diem finire* (35.7.3, 39.17.2, 45.12.7).

luces, 'days'; both Kr. and F. take this as poetic plural ('a metrical expedient,' F.), actually signifying 'day,' but B. (who with *O* reads *optato finitae*) does not. In this particular, he seems to me right. The wedding *celebrations* must have lasted for several days (cf. Stat. *Theb.* 2.307 *bisseni dies*), and where in ll. 16, 325, and 376 the word *lux* (sing.) = 'day,' it is twice applied to events other than the wedding and once to a specific performance during the actual wedding ceremony.

32 *tota*, to be taken poetically, not literally (as by editors who would eliminate the conjecture *Haemonisin* 287 because this line seems to show that every soul in Thessaly attended the wedding): for a similar exaggeration cf. Prop. 2.6.2 *Graecia tota*.

35 *Cieros* is surely right; we need a place (a city of Thessaly itself, like those that are mentioned in 35–6) from which the crowds stream (on foot), and to which they return on foot (*ad se ... pede discedebant* 277). The island of Scyros, however closely associated with Peleus and his family, hardly qualifies for festive depopulation in the aftermath of the Argo's maiden voyage. For a defence of *Scyros* see Giangrande 1976: 111–12.

m, who is interested in spelling and often prefers *y* to *i* (cf. 61.18), cannot here decide whether to write *syros* or *siros*, and at first, therefore, leaves the space for the second letter vacant; but presently he makes up his mind and writes *sy-*.

Pthiotica: cf. 211 *Erectheum* for the spelling; the first of the two aspirates in Greek was replaced by a simple (*tenuis*) letter.

Tempe: on C.'s geographical displacement of the Vale of Tempe (which is in the extreme north of Thessaly, whereas Phthiotis is in the extreme south) see F., who finds a precedent for the error in Callim. *H.* 4.112 Πηνειὲ Φθιῶτα. The two important towns mentioned in l. 36 lay in the central plain of Thessaly, Crannon to the northwest and the more distant Larissa to the north of Pharsalus.

37 *Pharsalum*: after l. 36, and (as E. was the first to point out) the lack of a preposition and the use of *coire*, we need the name of a town here; so Pontanus' emendation is virtually unassailable, despite Fr.'s long and eloquent note setting forth all possible arguments for retaining the Ms reading.

38–42 For the random description of rural activities suspended during a festival cf. Tib. 2.1.5–8, but, as F. says, C. exaggerates the interruption, at least in ll. 38 (*mollescunt*) and 42.

39 *humilis*: not a conventional epithet, but designating, apparently, a particular kind of viticulture. On the operations described here see Cressey 1977.

40 The four spondees suggest hard work (Kr., who cites Norden on V. *Aen.* 1.420).

41 *frondatorum*: usually = 'tree-pruners' in general. In the present instance, however, perhaps 'vinedressers'; cf. Servius on *Ecl.* 1.56 *frondator* (Kr.). Alternatively, olives may be thought of (Fr.); they were regularly pruned, and as a major crop would balance the vine in C.'s picture.

umbram, here singular; more usually plural, as at V. *Geo.* 1.156–7 *ruris opaci falce premes umbras.*

42 Cf. l. 7 for this kind of line (two adjectives, two nouns, and a verb) as marking a pause at the end of a 'paragraph.'

43 *ipse* as often, = 'the master,' 'the owner.' Virtually a noun at 3.7 *suam ipsam*, 'its mistress,' and at 114.6, where *ipse* ('the owner') is balanced against *saltus* ('the estate').

quacumque is not quite 'simple relative' as Fr. would have it; tr. 'wherever.' *recessit*, i.e., 'there is a perspective of.' Kr., who cites V. *Aen.* 2.299–300, remarks that the palace forms a separate quarter of the city, like those of Alexander's successors. Perhaps the picture owes something to Callimachean influence?

45 *mensae*: probably dative, to balance *soliis*.

46 *gaudet* (lit. 'rejoices'): cf. 31.12 (and also 64.284 *domus risit*); Lucr. 3.894 (*domus*) *laeta.*

gaza, 'treasure,' an exotic (Persian) word (first used in Latin by C. and by Lucr. 2.37); here linked with *regali*, which also has exotic overtones. Cf. V. *Aen.* 1.637–8 *domus interior regali splendida luxu / instruitur*, and in general compare with Catullus the whole passage 637–42, especially the mention of *fortia facta patrum* as an element in the decoration (below, line 51, *heroum virtutes*).

47 *pulvinar*, '[ritual] couch'; the word belongs to the high epic vocabulary and is
used for a religious object; but its adjective, *geniale*, brings the concept at once
to (Roman) earth, since the *lectus genialis* was in the *atrium* of the reader's own
house: *mediis* (48) reinforces this reference (the custom was purely Roman).
Because of Thetis' divine nature (*divae*), her *lectus genialis* can be poetically
described as a *pulvinar*.

48 *Indo dente*: cf. l. 45 *candet ebur soliis* amd 61.108 *candido pede lecti* for ivory
inlay as a decoration of articles of furniture.
politum, 'adorned' (Lucr. 5.1451 *daedala signa polire*); Varro *RR* 3.2.9 speaks of
a *villa ... polita opere tectorio eleganter.*
conchyli: the murex, identified with the 'purple' made from it. Similarly, *fucus*
is primarily a potent red vegetable dye, but because of its wide employment
comes to stand for any dye at all. (For details see F.)

49 Red-white contrasts are especially popular with Roman poets (e.g., Hor.
S. 2.6.102–3); cf. also the strong contrast between dark and bright, above
(ll. 41–4), and the choice of the word *variata* in l. 50 to mean 'elaborately
decorated' (this last preserves or parallels a Greek expression; cf. the description
of the furnishings at the wedding of Ptolemy Philadelphus in Athen. 5.179b,
especially the mention of περιστρώματα ποικίλα).

50 *haec* is *m*'s reading (*hec V*). *m*'s interest in spelling (cf. l. 35 n.) often leads
him to substitute diphthongs for the medieval contractions: see de la Mare and
Thomson 1973: 189–90. G^2 here follows *m*, as usual.
priscis, 'ancient' (hypallage: *priscis h. v. f. = priscorum h. v. f.*; cf. 359, and 51.11).
Notice the emphasis placed on remoteness.

51 *virtutes*, not 'qualities' but 'heroic deeds.' Cf. 68.90, and also *Aen.* 1.565–6. See
also above, n. on l. 46. Editors have noticed the absence of the *virtutes* from the
description of the 'coverlet'; they are mentioned in the explanatory *narrative* of
105–11, but do not seem to be represented on the 'coverlet' itself.

52–267 C. seems to describe by stages a visual scene: Ariadne in a central position;
Theseus, embarked, vanishing over the horizon (perhaps to the left); Dionysus
arriving *parte ex alia* (251) with his followers.

52 *namque* introduces a new tale or scene: cf. 212, and *nam*, e.g., at 76 and 105.
fluentisono, a word otherwise unknown; editors compare *clarisonus* 125, 320,
and *raucisonus* 263. According to *Od.* 11.325, Ariadne met Theseus Δίῃ ἐν
ἀμφιρύτῃ (cf. Callim. fr. 601 Pf. ἐν Δίῃ, τὸ γὰρ ἔσκε παλαίτερον οὔνομα Νάξῳ);
but *fluentisonus* can hardly be intended by C. as a direct translation of ἀμφίρυτος
(E.) or even πολύφλοισβος (perhaps after Ennius; Kr.'s suggestion).
Diae: was this the modern Dhia, a few (five and a half) miles off Herakleion (and
thus near Knossos), or Naxos? From our sources it is clear that two divergent
accounts of the desertion of Ariadne by Theseus have been fused together,
most likely because of the dissemination of the Naxian legend describing

the encounter of Dionysus and the sleeping Ariadne. Dhia, which is barren, rock-bound, and precipitous especially on its northern side, lies on a direct course from Crete to the Piraeus, whereas Naxos does not. Yet C. seems to think of Naxos; it may be that his choice is determined solely by the literary tradition, but in fact Naxos possesses gently sloping beaches (*arena* 57) to which Ariadne might run down from the hilltop, whereas the northern coast of Dhia does not. Moreover, because of its vastly greater distance from Crete itself, Naxos is more easily reconciled with 178–9. (On the topography of both places, see *Admiralty Mediterranean Pilot* vol. 4, 7th ed., 1941, pp. 44, 146.) Alexandrian scholarship defends the Naxian claim by asserting that Naxos was earlier known as 'Dia' (Callim., quoted above), while a scholiast on *Od.* 11.321 makes the contrary assertion that Dia was once known as 'Naxos.' Neither statement seems to rest on more than a desire to resolve the conflict in the myth.

53 *celeri* is surely not simply a conventional epithet, like Homer's θοαί of ships (even when they are beached, as Fr. remarks), but expresses Ariadne's feelings: 'How quickly he leaves me!' Notice the atmosphere of swift motion created at the poem's opening, and see Thomas 1982.
classe: in a work of art, we may guess, only one ship would be shown (see Fr.'s long n.). In poetry *classis* may be used of a single vessel. Despite Kr. and F., *puppes* (l. 172) may well be poetic plural.

54 The line begins with an adj. and ends with its noun. This happens 27 times in poem 64, and also occurs in the *Ciris* and the *Culex*; elsewhere, it is less common (G. May, *De stilo epylliorum Romanorum* [Kiel, 1910]: 2–7; statistics, p. 5).
gerens in the sense of 'bearing, carrying' is archaic.
furor in the sense of erotic passion is used by C. at 50.11 and 68.129; in this poem the pl. at 94 refers to *homines* in the plural; only here is the plural used of one person.

56 *utpote* (cf. 67.43) is prosaic; see B. Axelson, *Unpoetische Wörter* [Lund, 1945], for this and similar elements in the vocabulary of poem 64.
As McKie has suggested, *A* probably gave, for *quae*, an ambiguous *que*: when this follows a word, *O* (and here *G* also) presents it as if it were a conjunction (ꞯ). On *tunc* (*O*) and *tum*, see 10.3 n.

57 *sola*, 'deserted' (ἔρημος, Callim *H.* 4.243); below, lines 154, 184.

58 The rhythm of this line, avoided by all later poets (but see 68.157), seems appropriate to a description of rowers tugging at their oars.
immemor: Ariadne regards Theseus as culpable because of his 'forgetfulness' (for *immemor* in this sense, cf. 30.1) towards her; but the further act of 'forgetfulness' that led to his father's death (207ff.), and thus recoiled on him in punishment for the first lapse, was visited upon him by the gods in response to Ariadne's curse. Thus, even though at this stage he became a puppet of heaven, he is still thought of as guilty from Ariadne's point of view (which for C. is

central). Editors have created unnecessary difficulties here in terms of an issue between determinism and moral responsibility, with varying corollaries about C.'s attitude to the gods and to heroic values. On *immemor, memor*, as keywords in poetry of this kind, see Jackson 1913: 50.

59. Cf. Theocr. 29.35 αἰ δὲ ταῦτα φέρην ἀνέμοισιν ἐπιτρέπηις, Nonn. 47.271 συνθεσίας δ' ἀνέμοισιν ἐπέτρεπεν. Similarly 30.10, 70.4.

60 *alga* ('seaweed') for beach. Emendation to *acta* ('cliff'), as proposed by B., is unnecessary; see 52 n. Of course Ariadne's awakening, and her running to the beach, could not both be shown on the *vestis*, unless this contained several panels showing the same figures in different situations – a proposition for which there is insufficient other evidence (see however 63 n.), and which it is hard to accept because C. not only (i) recurs to the same scene after digressing, but also (ii) in handling his material sometimes appears to adopt the method of narrative, and not of description at all: for a stylistic aspect of this distinction, see l. 3 n.
Minois (Greek form), 'daughter of Minos' – Ap. Rhod. 3.998. Coluccio's knowledge of mythical names (see l. 3 n.) prompted his emendation.
ocellis: diminutives are frequent in the tale of Ariadne, where they are not merely metrically useful but as a rule pathetic in effect.

61 C. likens the figure of Ariadne, as depicted on the *vestis*, to that of a Bacchant *carved in stone*: this in itself suggests that at this point he conceives himself to be *describing* something fully visualized. Perhaps we may be tempted even to concede B.'s claim that he has, or may have, a particular statue in mind.
prospicit in epanalepsis, for pathetic effect: cf. 26–7 n. (anaphora), and also 63–5 *non*.

62 Abbreviated forms of *et* and *con* (= *cum*) are closely similar; the mistake occurred in *A* and is clearly visible in *O*'s reading. *R*² corrects (*suo Marte*).
curae = πάθη (Kr. cites Plaut. *Epid.* 135 and *Pseud.* 21).
fluctuat: for the metaphor, cf. 65.4; for a related simile, see 68.3. V. *Aen.* 8.19 *magno curarum fluctuat aestu* is surely borrowed from C.; see also Lucr. 6.33–4 *et genus humanum frustra plerumque probavit / volvere curarum tristes in pectore fluctus.*

63ff. I.e., emotion removes concern for personal appearance.

63 *flavo*: in Greek legend, blond hair is characteristic of heroes and heroines.
mitra can mean either a snood to bind the hair, or else a cap (see Fr.) worn by girls at night, by older women in the daytime also (Eur. *Hec.* 923–4); thus the hour of waking is at once suggested for this scene, though it is not made explicit until 122. See Tatham 1990, who says: 'In Greek literature, a "mitra" is any piece of cloth worn by women in various ways to tie up their hair,' and points out that for the Romans it remained a Greek word for a Greek article of dress. Tatham further suggests that it had a Bacchic association which 'is to be actualised at the end of the story.' Partly because Ariadne loses her clothing in

63–7 but is still clothed in 129, Fr. (pp. 341–2) thought 58–70 a later addition. Or does the discrepancy rather point to different scenes on the *vestis*? See l. 60 n.

64–5 *velatum pectus, papillas*: internal accusatives. See F.'s excellent note on the poetic usage underlying these lines.

65 *lactentis*, literally 'full of milk' (whereas *lactantis* = 'giving milk, suckling'): here, however, a conventional epithet, merely indicating external shape. W.S. Watt, *LCM* 9 (1984): 131, translates 'milk-white' here and at Petronius 86.5 (he suggests reading *lactens pectore* at Mart. 12.38.4, comparing 14.149.2 *niveo pectore*).

66 The dactylic opening suggests rapidity; followed by the 'lapping sound' (B.) of the spondaic ending, with several *l*'s.

    Perhaps *delapso e* stood in *A*, as McKie suggests; but it is possible that *A* had *delapsẽ* (the o being a mistaken correction, influenced by *corpore*); hence the *OGR* readings.

67 *ipsius*, 'their owner' (cf. 43 n.).

68 *neque tum*, deliberate anaphora (Kr.), imitated at *Ciris* 116.

69 *vicem* (= *sortem*), 'their lot,' 'what happened to them.'

69–70 Rhetorical second-person address, for 'liveliness' (Kr.). Cf. 253 and 299; 4.13, 68.105. The address to the heroes at 22–4 is not in the same category, *pace* Kr.; but he is right in saying that the personal address lends 'a warmer tone' to the story. Later poets inherit this Hellenistic device; F. cites E. Norden, *Aeneid VI*, 122 and 126.

    Notice the repetition of the idea in *pectore – animo – mente* (and the triple *toto / tota*, for additional emphasis). Alliteration 'binds the phrase together' (B.).

71 This kind of pitying exclamation (cf. 94) is common in Hellenistic poetry, and is often associated with situations in which the gods of fate, Tyche for example or (as here) Aphrodite, interfere in human affairs (Kr.).

72 *Erycina*, originally the cult title of a goddess (= the Phoenician Astarte) of Eryx in Sicily; later she was adopted at Rome (with a temple of her own) and of course identified with Venus. To name her by this exotic cult title is in the Hellenistic mode; cf. *incola Itoni* 228 n.
serens: editors compare Soph. *Ajax* 1005 ὅσας μοι κατασπείρας φθίνεις.
curas, here of love, as at 2.10, 66.23, 68.18 and 51.

73 The text is problematical (see n. above, and also 81 n.). It should be noted that Theseus is credited with physical strength; cf. Plutarch, *Thes.* 3, 6, 12, which relate how he had to prove his sonship by lifting the sword of his father Aegeus from its hiding-place under a heavy rock. The adjective *ferox* generally implies not 'ferocity' but youthful strength, energy, and high spirits; observe the emphasis on *ferox* 247 and also *fervida virtus* 218 in contrast to Aegeus' age and infirmity. For these reasons, and because *ex* does not appear in the Mss (and the syntax of *illa t., ferox quo ex t.* is awkward),

some consideration should perhaps be given to such a reading as *ferox qua* (sc. *tempestate*) *corpore* (cf. *corpus* 81); *co-* and *te-* are palaeographically close. (In the text, however, I have preferred Fröhlich's *qua robore*.) See V. *Aen.* 5.318, and Fr. on 66.31–2. Kr. has another argument against *ex*: 'it is a question of the *moment when* Venus sows her cares in the heart.' For *qua tempestate*, cf. 66.11.

74 *curvum litus* occurs in Accius (fr. 569 R².).

As editors point out, the name *Piraeus* is anachronistic; but its three bays must have been used from early times, and C. would have been hard pressed to describe them by any other name that his readers could recognize.

75 *iniusti*, from an Athenian point of view; Plut. *Thes.* 16. The Athenians, knowing the reputation for justice which Minos enjoyed, left it to him to assess the appropriate penalty to be exacted for the death at Athens of his son Androgeon (Apollodorus 3.15.8). His decision – the human tribute of youths and maidens – abolished that reputation in the eyes of the city on which it was imposed (Plut. *Thes.* 15–16).

Gortynia, merely 'Cretan' (cf. V. *Aen.* 11.773, *Ciris* 114, Stat. *Theb.* 4.530, Claudian *VI cos. Hon.* 634 *semiviri Gortynia tecta iuvenci*).

See App. Crit. It is not altogether easy to decide between *templa* and *tecta* (? > *tepta* > *tēpta*). Both words are used of royal palaces. For *tecta* see lines 37, 246, 276, and Claudian (above, with *Gortynia*); V. *Aen.* 7.668 *sic regia tecta subibat*. For *templa* editors cite Enn. *Androm.* 92 V² *o Priami domus, saeptum altisono cardine templum*. F. defends *templa* on the grounds of the generalized use of the word by Lucretius to mean regions or abodes, and of a similarly generalized application in Plautus (*Mil.* 413), and I believe he is right.

76–9 The tribute (75 n.) was to be paid either annually (V. *Aen.* 6.21) or every nine years (Plut. *Thes.* 15.1). To end it was, of course, the purpose of Theseus' voyage. On the whole *solitum* tends to suggest 'annually.'

76 *peste*: Plut. *Thes.* 15.1 (νόσος ἐνέσκηψε), Diodorus Siculus 4.61.1.

77 Androgeon, the son of Minos, was killed while visiting Attica; Minos accused the Athenians of his murder, invested the city, and imposed the human tribute in the story. See V. *Aen.* 6.20–2 *pendere poenas Cecropidae iussi (miserum!) septena quotannis corpora natorum*.

The adjective instead of gen., for metrical convenience (cf. 368; also 44.10, 53.2, 68.74, and V. *Aen.* 2.193 *Pelopea ad moenia*), is in a form unattested in extant Greek, which knows only the form Ἀνδρογέως. Prop. (2.1.62) has the accusative *Androgeona*. Kr. however suggests that the longer form used here by C. may exactly reproduce the opening of some Greek line.

78 *electos*, a conventional epithet (cf. *lecti* 4), in no way indicating selection by lot. *decus* implies beauty.

78–80 The three consecutive spondaic line-endings are unique in Roman poetry;
cf. in Greek Theocritus 13.42–4; also cf. Aratus 419–21, 953–5. Other references
(Callim., Ap. Rhod., Euphorion) are given by Kr. and F.

79 *Cecropiam*: 'city of Cecrops,' the mythical early ruler of Athens. It was Theseus
himself who later, as king, introduced the name *Athenae*. Hellenistic poets
revived the archaic adjective-name (used three times in poem 64), both for
its metrical convenience and as an antiquarian flourish. Cf. Callim. *H.* 4.315,
Ap. Rhod. 1.95.
daps: in epic style, for a *religious* meal (cf. *pulvinar* 47 n.). Diodorus Siculus
(4.61.3) has βορά.

80 *angusta*: another piece of Hellenistic-type learning, probably introduced in order
to show that the poet (C. or a predecessor) is aware how much smaller the city's
compass was before Theseus' 'synoecism' of Attica, and consequently how much
heavier – in proportion to its population – the tribute would have seemed.

81 *ipse* = *ultro* (B.) – referring to the variant story in Apollod. *Epit.* 1.7 (Kr.):
'Theseus, some say, a *voluntary* sacrifice …' Cf. Plut. *Thes.* 17 (quoted below,
83 n.), Hyg. *Fab.* 41.
corpus, see 73 n. (E. notes the emphasis on Theseus' physical beauty).

82 *optavit*, here = 'chose, elected.'
quam = *quam ut* (parallels in E.).

83 *proicere*, 'cast away' (Plut. *Thes.* 17.2 ἐπέδωκεν ἑαυτόν).
funera nec f., 'living corpses,' in imitation of Greek paradoxical expressions with
a-privative attached to the second word (χάρις ἄχαρις, τάφος ἄταφος); cf. V. *Aen.*
9.490–1, Lucr. 5.326, and also Lucr. 5.993 *vivo … busto*.
Cecropiae (gen.) *funere* Ov. *Ep.* 10.99–10. Cf. M. 8.231 *pater infelix nec iam
pater*.

84–5 Notice the 'musical' quality of these lines, with *l* and *n* alternating to suggest
a smooth voyage (84.8 n.). Multiple assonance and alliteration culminate in the
harsh *s*'s and *r*'s of distaste; see poem 84 (passim, with notes).

85 *magnanimum* is usually taken as = μεγάθυμον, in a pejorative sense, equivalent
to *superbum* – again from the Athenian point of view; cf. 75 n. But Cressey
1981, supported in this instance (though opposed overall) by Matthews 1981,
argues cogently that here (and in Ennius) *magnanimus* simply = ὀλοόφρων.
At 58.5 and 66.26, *magnanimus* has either a simply good sense, or an ironic
sense by which a good primary meaning is presupposed. For a contrary view, see
Giangrande 1984, who calls *m.* = ὀλοόφρων 'a nonexistent meaning,' and would
take *m.* as simply indicating 'the hero,' referring to Minos' military past.

86ff. Love at first sight – as is usual in ancient poetry; Ap. Rhod. 3.275ff. seem to be
recalled by C., even though Apollonius' lines have to do with Medea, not with
Ariadne.

86 *lumine*, 'eye(s)'; cf. *lumina* 92 and 233.

87 'Generic motif' (Kr.), because Pasiphae is in herself 'not the most charming of
   mothers' (Fr.).

89 *quales = tales quales.*
   Eurotae (*europe*, Mss): the emendation is almost certain, but the literary
   ancestry – if any – of this allusion is unknown. For a different 'specification' of
   myrtus cf. 61.22 (*Asia*).
   progignunt, 'engender.' B., who suggested *praecingunt*, thinking perhaps
   of 67.33, where he reads *praecurrit* (*percurrit* Mss; see n.), himself prints
   progignunt (in text and commentary). Conversely, F. prints *praecingunt* but in
   his note prefers *progignunt*, comparing line 1 *prognatae.*
   myrtus (not *-tos*) of the whole shrub, not merely the flower. In Laconia there
   were myrtles sacred to Aphrodite (Paus. 3.22.12).

90 *colores* = flowers of every hue (*distinctos*, an adjective usually applied rather
   to the earth as being 'picked out' by flowers, as at Ov. M. 5.266 *innumeris
   distinctas floribus herbas*; cf. *Culex* 70–1 *tellus ... vere notat dulci distincta
   coloribus arva*).

91 *declinavit*: spondees for reluctance (to tear the eyes away); cf. 76.15
   pervincendum.
   Editors cite the passage where Medea's love rekindles on Jason's appearance
   (Ov. M. 7.86–8 *spectat et in vultu veluti tum denique viso lumina fixa tenet ...
   nec se declinat ab illo*).

92 For alliteration on *c*, cf. 117.
   For love as a fire, cf. Callim. *Ep.* 43.5 ὤπτηται μέγα δή τι, Ap. Rhod. 3.287
   φλογὶ εἴκελον.

93 Take *funditus* with the preceding clause. (Editors cite *atque* as 'postponed';
   wrongly, I think.)

94 Apostrophe to Eros; *heu* should be taken with the whole clause. Cf. Ap. Rhod.
   4.445–9 σχέτλι' Ἔρως, μέγα πῆμα, μέγα στύγος ἀνθρώποισιν, ἐκ σέθεν οὐλόμεναί
   τ' ἔριδες στοναχαί τε γόοι τε.
   immiti corde, 'cruelly'; not 'in the heart,' as E. takes it.

95 *sancte puer*: cf. *sancta Venus* 36.3, 68.5. In such addresses *sancte/a* is, as Kr.
   remarks, a literary rather than a cult title, corresponding to δῖε or μάκαρ.

96 *quaeque etc.* = Venus (Aphrodite). (Theocritus 15.100, cf. – for the indirect
   allusion – 16.83; Ap. Rhod. 1.411; see above, 36.12 n.)
   Golgos: cf. 36.14. On the three claimants to the paternity of this emendation (Av.,
   Polit., and H. Barbarus) see Grant 1992: 267–9 and n. 37. See also Ribuoli 1981.
   Idalium: cf. 36.12 and 61.17.
   For the 'relative style' in prayers, see E. Norden *Agnostos Theos* (Leipzig,
   1913): 168.

97–8 *incensam* (with *mente*) ... *iactastis fluctibus*: ancient poets are relatively
   unabashed by such mixed metaphors as this; *incensam* has wholly shed its literal
   meaning.

98 *in*, 'over,' 'on account of.' Numerous parallels are given by F.

  flavo, cf. 63 n.

  hospite, 'stranger' (cf. 81.4) rather than 'guest.'

  suspirantem: the spondees suggest sighing (Fr.); also the repeated *s*, surely.

99 As Kr. well remarks, 'Even the slaying of the Minotaur is introduced not as narrative but from the angle of the psychological effect on Ariadne.'

  timores: probably a poetic plural (cf. Lucr. 2.45, 5.46), rather than the kind of plural that designates repeated instances. To seek to determine whether Ariadne's fears are 'apprehensive' or 'erotic' (Fr.) seems academic.

100 See App. Crit. It may be better to read *quam tum*, especially in view of C.'s penchant for *tum* in this poem. Fr. finds in *quanto* a 'powerful climax'; but that reading would find more plausible support in the desire to keep *V*'s text wherever it yields tolerable sense.

  fulgore (auri): cf. 81.4. Several editors point out that Mediterranean complexions have a yellowish tinge when they 'pale.'

101 *contra* = *in*; cf. V. *Aen.* 5.124, 370.

102 Probably imitated from Ap. Rhod. 4.205 ἠὲ κατηφείην ἢ καὶ μέγα κῦδος ἀρέσθαι; cf. 3.428–9 τῶ καὶ ἐγὼ τὸν ἄεθλον ὑπερφίαλόν περ' ἐόντα τλήσομαι, εἰ καί μοι θανέειν μόρος.

  appeteret, 'deliberately seek' (anything, including death). Cicero, *In Milonem* 81 *praemia laudis ... petenda*; Sen. *Ep.* 24.23 *appetere mortem*. The alternative reading, *oppeteret*, is often applied to *mors* – so much so that *mortem oppetere* is in some degree a set phrase for 'to die' – but could not be transferred, as here, to such an object as *praemia*.

  laudis, either 'of glorious action' or 'consisting in praise.'

103 It is best to take *frustra* (adv.) as an addition to the notion contained in the adjective *ingrata*, and as coming under the general force of *non*. For the less likely punctuation and meaning (, *tamen frustra*,), cf. 68.118 *tamen indomitam*.

104 *tacito*, variously interpreted as 'silent (sc. in order to escape her parents' notice)' or 'hushed in adoration (of the beloved)'; the latter seems more probable. Cf. perhaps Pind. *P.* 9.98 (172) ἄφωνοι.

  succepit is said, on insufficient grounds, to be 'prosaic' (so B.); but see the poetic parallels quoted by Fr.

105–11 An elaborately 'Homeric' simile, for which F. cites Greek models (Homer, Ap. Rhod.). The geographical exactitude is a Hellenistic touch.

  brachia, 'branches' (the metaphorical content is extinguished, as when we speak of the limbs of a tree).

  Tauro: a great mountain range on the northern boundary of Cilicia. Its forests are still dense, with a heavy growth of conifers at the higher altitudes.

106 *conigeram* (= *coniferam*, V. *Aen.* 3.680); a word unknown elsewhere.

  sudanti cortice (= 'resinous,' but expressed more picturesquely) is of course little more than a decorative addition.

107 *contorquens*, 'wrenching round,' hence 'plucking out'; V. *Geo.* 1.481 (*silvas*).
robur, 'trunk'; V. *Aen.* 4.441.

108 *eruit*; followed by a highly effective pause.
radicitus: cf. πρυμνόθεν, Ap. Rhod. 4.1686.

109 *quaeviscumque* Ellis: not in his *editio maior*, but first in *Philologus* 49 (1890): 270. Fr. cites Lucr. 3.388 *cuiusviscumque animantis* and Mart. 14.2.1 *quoviscumque loco potes hunc finire libellum* in support. It has at any rate the advantage of sound over the tripping rhythm of Fink's 1963 suggestion (mentioned by Q.) *lateque cacumen it obvia frangens*.

110 For *saevum* ('the fierce creature') as a noun, cf. 63.85 *ferus*.

111 This may echo the Greek line (from Callimachus?) quoted by Cicero, *Ad Att.* 8.5.1 (πολλὰ μάτην κεράεσσιν ἐς ἠέρα θυμήναντα). For the shape of the line, cf. above 42 n. (but observe that here the formula is varied inasmuch as the adverb *nequiquam* replaces one of the usual two adjectives).

112 The 'labyrinth' is, of course, now commonly identified with the many-roomed palace at Knossos.

115 Notice the distinctive rhythm of this line: it has no masculine (full) caesura, a distinction carefully imitated by Virgil, *Aen.* 5.591; when, however, Virgil came to imitate it a second time (*Aen.* 6.27 *hic labor ille domus et inextricabilis error*) he smoothed away, as he sometimes does, the metrical irregularity in his chosen model.

116 *primo carmine*: of course not poem 64 as a whole but the 'episode' of Ariadne.
The self-interruption is in the manner of Hellenistic narrative poetry (E.; Kr. and F. compare Ap. Rhod. 1.648 ἀλλὰ τί μύθους Αἰθαλίδεω χρειώ με διηνεκέως ἀγορεύειν;).

117 *ut*, 'how' (ὡς). The order of the words *linquens genitoris filia vultum* (*vultus* = *conspectus*, as B. says) suggests an affectionate relationship; the point is made more explicitly in the second clause (*c. complexum*), and the third clause is still more emphatic, in obedience to the 'law of increasing *cola*.' Against *all* these (variously stated) decrees of family emotion, Ariadne sets in the balance her single, overmastering love for Theseus (120). For the rhetorical juxtaposition cf. 78.6 *patruus patrui*; Kr. and F. cite Cicero, *Deiot.* 2 *qui nepos avum in capitis discrimen adduxerit*.

118 *consanguineae* = Phaedra (who later married Theseus). A famous painting at Delphi showed her together with Ariadne (Paus. 10.29.3). 'Why does C. not suggest the other sisters?' asks Kr. But C. is not really thinking of Ariadne's actual family situation (if he were, the affectionate reference to the Minotaur as 'brother' would surely strike any reader as odd), but of an idealized set of relationships — granted of course that the 'loss' of her 'brother' is recognized in l. 150; it has even been suggested that C. has Medea, rather than Ariadne, in mind at this point in the story.

119 *in*: see 98 n., and cf. Prop. 1.13.7 *perditus in quadam*.

deperdita: 35.12, 100.2 n.

laetabatur seems right, both palaeographically and rhetorically; see the n. on 117 for the gradual climax in expressions of affection (*vultum – complexum – deperdita laetabatur*). To introduce lamentations here would sound a false and discordant note. Moreover, *lamentata est* is, as Fr. observes, 'palaeographically impossible.' He adds – and it is a caution which would-be emendators ought to heed: 'Die Verschreibungen und Fehler in den Handschriften des C. bilden ein Art System ...' The reading *lamentata est* has been revived by Clausen 1977. Varro Atacinus, fr. 7 M, *curis experdita lamentatur*, might seem to suggest the reading *lamentata est* (or *lamentatur*) here; but grief is not the theme of ll. 117–20 (see above).

120 *praeoptarit*: three syllables, as in Plaut. *Trin.* 648 and Ter. *Hec.* 532 (a synizesis later avoided, Kr.).

121 *ut vecta* was in *A*; *O*'s omission of *ut* was a mistake. This seems more probable than metrical or other emendation by *X*.

122 *venerit* is a sound supplement: Fr. gives a useful list of passages to illustrate his contention that *vectus* often precedes *venio*. S. Bailey 1994: 16 rejects *venerit* for Laetus' *placido* on statistical grounds, to me unconvincing. If one wanted an adjective I would suggest *lasso*, to describe Thetis' surely troubled sleep (cf. 63.35–7)

devinctam: cf. Lucr. 4.453–4 *suavi devinxit membra sopore somnus*, 1027 *somno devincti*.

McKie: 263 gives *deiuncta O*, incorrectly I think.

lumina, internal accusative (see F.'s n. on lines 64–5).

123 Notice the repetition of *immemor* from 58.

coniunx, 'betrothed' (often used of love relations, like γάμος: examples in Kr.); or else ironically for 'husband' (cf. 182 *coniugis ... fido ... amore*).

m makes a slip (*in nemori*), corrected by *m²*; but *G²* still reproduces *m*'s error as if it were a legitimate variant – a good example of his excess of loyalty to *m*. Yet it is due precisely to this loyalty that the correct reading enters *G* at line 126, for example. See line 130 for an example of *G²*'s occasional — limited – exercise of critical judgment.

124 *m*'s fit of carelessness continues; he writes *prohibent*. Again *m²* corrects.

furentem: see 54 n.

125 *clarisonas*, used again at 320 of the voice of the *Parcae*. Like a number of other unusual words in poem 64, this is paralleled in Cicero, *Aratea* 526 (280), quoted by E.

e pectore Mss: supported by Lucr., who does not use *ex p*. (Fr.).

125–6 Notice the change from perfect to present infinitive, which seems purely metrical.

126 The rhythm of the line suggests effort (cf. 40 n.).

127 *vastos*, 'desolate' as well as 'huge'; cf. 156.
protenderet: cf. Cicero, *Acad.* 2.80 *intendi acies longius non potest*; Nonius reads at Lucr. 1.66 *oculos tendere*. *G²* does not follow *m* (who follows *R* in reading *protenderet*); either he did not see the abbreviation, or he regarded the prefixes as equivalent.

128 *salis*, 'sea' (a kind of metonymy, helped by the addition of *tremuli*).

129 On the fact that Ariadne is here clothed despite 63–7, see n. on 63. The grammatical 'numbers' are reversed: the chiton is the *tegmen* (sing.) *surarum* (pl.) (Kr.). According to B., Ruhnken was the first to cite Ap. Rhod. 3.873–4 ἂν δὲ χιτῶνας λεπταλέους λευκῆς ἐπιγουνίδος ἄχρις ἄειρον.

130 *hoc* was in *A*, *hec* apparently in *X* (possibly as a superscript variant, *hŏc*).
extremis, 'dying' (B. quotes Prop. 3.7.55 *extremis dedit haec mandata querellis*) rather than 'zuletzt brach sie in Klagen aus' (Kr.'s alternative explanation).

131 C., unlike Virgil (except for good reason at *Aen.* 4.328), does not exclude diminutives from his epic style of writing.
Frigidulos heightens the pathetic effect sought by C. as a poet in the Hellenistic tradition.
udo ore: abl. of 'attendant circumstances' (F., who translates 'with tear-stained face').

132 *sicine*: see 77.3 and F.'s n. there; also cf. Plaut. *Rud.* 251, Prop. 3.6.9. B. points out how rare it is, at least after the Comic poets, in this sense ('Really … ?').
R², correcting *V's avertam*, adds the original reading *below* (feeling his correction to be somewhat bold); this *m* picks up, but *m²* reproduces *R²'s avertam* as a variant, and *G²* (who, though overawed by *m*, is not stupid) apparently sees the correction as inevitably right.

132–4 The shrillness of Ariadne's indignant outburst is reflected in the repeated *i*-sounds. For this device, cf. Ov. *AA* 1.536–8 *perfidus ille abiit; quid mihi fiet? ait; / quid mihi fiet? ait; sonuarunt cymbala toto / litore et adtonita cymbala pulsa manu* and (for a similar contrast in the vowels) Ov. *F.* 4.242, describing Attis' emasculation, which seems to take place in mid-line: *nullaque sunt subito signa relicta viri*. Cf. also 45.13–14 (n.).

132–201 As editors point out, there are three parts to Ariadne's 'lament': (i) 132–63, reproaches to Theseus; (ii) 164–87, depiction of her abandoned and hopeless state; (iii) 188–191, prologue to prayer, followed by (192ff.) a prayer for divine vengeance.

The opening part of Ariadne's speech recalls Medea (cf. 118 n.). Schmidt 1967: 491 n. 6 points out that the 'motif of humble service' (by Ariadne to Theseus) reappears in Nonnus, but with a difference: whereas C. ends his pursuit of this theme with the spreading of Theseus' bed, N. ends it only with the singing of the actual wedding song for a new bride. It may be suggested that C. is psychologically more convincing here, but S. does not draw this conclusion: he infers that C. is abbreviating a traditional account (which N. preserves in full) in order to end this part of the 'coverlet story' with *a* coverlet, observing the colour equation (*purpurea* 163 = *roseo* 49).

133 *ī* (for *in*) was simply omitted by *O* (after *-i* of *liquisti*). It seems hardly necessary to raise and dismiss (as McKie: 254 does) the possibility that *A* might have caused the omission and *X* restored the word.

135 *X* had *ah* (misread by *R*, who writes *ab*). *m* is careless in writing *ad*; *m²*, even while correcting, fails to pick up *R²*'s *ah*, or at least writes it as *ab*; *G²* sees that *ah* (*G*) is right, and so does not follow *m²*.

   devota, in a pejorative sense, 'under sentence of cursing' (E.) to the *di inferi*; cf. Hor. *Epod*. 16.9 *impia perdemus devoti sanguinis aetas*.

136 *R²* invented his correction.

   flectere: cf. Ov. *M*. 9.608–9 *duram flectere mentem*.

137 *fuit clementia praesto*: cf. Cicero, *Phil*. 13.13 *intellegitis animum ei praesto fuisse*.

138 *mitescere* results from a failed attempt at correction, by *X*, of *A*'s *mirescere*, which made no sense but is nevertheless preserved by *O*, whose garbled text often, though by no means always, points the way to the truth when both *O* and *X* are faulty.

139 *non haec = non talia*; cf. V. *Aen*. 11.152 *non haec ... dederas promissa parenti*. With the wording cf. Ap. Rhod. 4.357–9 τῶν δ' οὔτι μετατρέπῃ, ὅσσ' ἀγόρευες χρειοῖ ἐνισχόμενος; ποῦ τοι Διὸς Ἱκεσίοιο ὅρκια, ποῦ δὲ μελιχραὶ ὑποσχεσίαι βεβάασιν; and esp. Nonn. 47.368–9 οὐ τάδε μοι κατέλεξεν ἐμὸν μίτον εἰσέτι πάλλων, οὐ τάδε μοι κατέλεξε παρ' ἡμετέρῳ λαβυρίνθῳ, indicating a common Hellenistic source for the passage (Kr.).

   See App. Crit. for a notable example of a metrical stopgap, now found in *G* and *R*. *nobis* must be either an accidental substitution by *X*, not noticed as erroneous by him because metrically satisfactory (McKie: 269), or else a relatively weak attempt to fill a gap in the line, where *O* has *blanda*. Therefore, Prof. Courtney suggests that *X* took his *A*-readings from a copy of *A* – (x?) in my Stemma – rather than directly from *A* as *O* did. It is possible that (x?) inadvertently dropped the word *blanda* because of the preceding letters *ondā*, as Richmond seems to have suggested; I have failed to trace his note.

139–40 *blanda ... voce*: cf. Ennius, *Ann*. 50 *V²* [= 49 Skutsch], *blanda voce vocabam* (see *O*'s text).

140 *V*'s *misere*, if adverbial, is rejected by common sense; if it represents *miserae*, there is no convincing parallel for *iubeo* + dative (B., F.). It was probably assimilated to *mihi* (F.).

141 This line, with its feminine caesura in the third foot, could easily be read as the two concluding lines of a stanza such as we find in the wedding poem, poem 61, thus:

> sed conubia laeta, sed
>> optatos hymenaeos.

Virgil, imitating it (*Aen.* 4.316) – with slight changes, as usual – recognizes its distinctive rhythm. Notice the ('very rare,' B.) secondary caesura in the fifth foot; another example of this, likewise justified by a Greek word following, is at V. *Geo.* 1.437 *Inoo Melicertae.*

conubia: cf. 158. I doubt if the 'poetic' plural here is prompted, as Kr. (followed by F.) suggests, by Greek γάμοι, λέκτρα. Metrical convenience seems more likely.

142 Cf. V. *Aen.* 9.312–13 *aurae / omnia discerpunt et nubibus irrita donant,* where *irrita* has the same 'proleptic' sense as here; in prose, B. compares Livy 28.29.4 *auferat omna irrita oblivio.* For the language cf. Prop. 1.8.12 *neve inimica meas elevet aura preces.*

143 *nunc iam*: Guar.'s emendation (for *V*'s *iam tum*) is rendered certain by *nunc quoque* in Ov. *F.* 3.475 (quoting C.'s line): *nunc quoque 'nulla viro' clamabo 'femina credat.'*

viri, 'any [particular] male.'

145 *quis* ('for *quibus,*' as Coluccio Salutati remarks: see App. Crit.): construction according to the sense (notice the sing. *viro*). With *quis animus = quorum animus* cf. 193–4 *quibus frons,* 307 *his corpus.*

  *R*²'s *pro quibus* is an original grammatical note (not in *G*; hardly *X* or *A* – there is no trace of it in *O* even though in the same line *O* has a gloss on his own *apisci*). It is carefully reproduced by *m*², and from *m*² by *G*².

postgestit: *GR* (and perhaps *O*, but see below). For confusion of the compendia for *prae* and *post*, see line 11 n. The correction cannot be due to *X* (see McKie: 256); it appears to be original to *R*² (followed by *m*, not merely *m*²). McKie wrongly reports, in the table on p. 109 of his dissertation, that *R* reads *pregestit* and *m* reads *pregesti*; there is a very small *t* above the *i*, added perhaps by *m*¹. Therefore this line should not figure in his list (p. 112) of *m*'s errors that eluded detection when checked on *R*.

  Hieremias, unlike *X*, has the correct prefix; his text is usually close to that of *O* (his *aspici* is close to *O*¹ and remote from *GR*); did *O* intend to write *prae*- here? Cf. 194, where *O* has p̄portat (properly = *postportat*).

apisci = adipisci (archaic; twice in Lucr. Cf. 150 n. on *crevi*).

145–6 As Achilles Statius (Estaço) observed in 1566, Aristotle (*Rhet.* 2.21) says that 'generalized [universal] statements, where there is in fact no universal truth involved, are appropriate above all to abusive speech (σχετλιασμὸς καὶ δείνωσις)' [καθόλου δὲ μὴ ὄντος, καθόλου εἰπεῖν μάλιστα ἁρμόττει ἐν σχ. καὶ δ.]. B. quotes Terence (*Andr.* 459–60, *Hec.* 58–9) to illustrate this.

148 *metuere,* the *V* reading, is probably influenced by *metuunt* 146; *meminere* is less strained.

149 *certe*: cf. V. *Aen.* 1.234 ('introducing a reminder which justifies a grievance,' F. on 30.7).

turbo (in a metaphorical sense): cf. Ov. *M.* 7.614 *miserarum turbine rerum*, *Am.* 3.15.6 *militiae turbine factus eques*. B. and Fr. add examples from other poets down to Apuleius.

lecti is O's own error; see l. 121 n.

150 *germanum*: Ariadne exaggerates; strictly speaking, the Minotaur was her half-brother.

crevi, archaic. Such archaisms in C. at least are often prescribed by metrical necessity, especially those consisting in substitution of simple for compound verbs. Cf., e.g., lines 145 *apisci*, 227 *dicet*; also 37.10 *scribam*, 66.4 *cedant*.

150–1 Notice the change of construction in *potius amittere ... quam ut d<e>essem*.

152–3 Imitated from *Iliad* 1.4–5 αὐτοὺς δὲ ἑλώρια τεῦχε κύνεσσιν οἰωνοῖσί τε πᾶσι. See Zetzel 1978, who argues that C. read δαῖτα, with Zenodotus, at line 5 (instead of πᾶσι); and that he substituted *praeda* for (say) *cena* on the strength of Aristarchus' objection to δαῖτα, namely that elsewhere in Homer the word is used only of the food of human beings, not that of animals.

153 See nn. on ll. 11 and 145. *V* may have bequeathed to *A* some such reading as *p̃da* (where an accidental gap before the letter *d* may have prompted *A* to suppose *prae* to represent a whole word, not a mere prefix, and so tempted him to emend by means of a superscript *e*); or else *p̃da* results from emendation (with superscript *d*) by *X* of *p̃ea* in *A* (and in *V*).

154–6 Cf. poem 60 for this 'topos,' and cf. Eur. *Med.* 1342–3.

155 Cf. *Il.* 16.34–5 γλαυκὴ δὲ σε τίκτε θάλασσα πέτραι τ' ἠλίβατοι, ὅτι τοι νόος ἐστὶν ἀπηνής.

156 *vasta*, here 'dreadful.' See F.'s n. on this, and cf. Lucr. 1.722 *vasta Charybdis*. V. *Aen*, 7.302–03 imitates C. closely: *quid Syrtes aut Scylla mihi, quid vasta Charybdis / profuit?* See also Lygdamus [= Tib. 3] 4.85–91.

m reads *sylla*. His preference for spelling with *y* is ignored by *G²*.

On *-que* and *-quae*, see 56 n. As McKie: 279 points out, it seems that *X* inserts the punctuation found here in *GR*, which makes it more likely that he made the further change of *-que* to *-quae*.

157 *dulci* may be a conventional epithet (as perhaps at 215 if the text is sound) rather than an allusion to the hopes outlined at 141; cf. however 120 *Thesei dulcem ... amorem*, a passage which, it may be, C. recalls here.

158–63 Editors quote Nonnus 47.390–5, a passage so strikingly similar to this that it argues (see on 139 above) a common source. Extant sources of influence include *Il.* 3.409–11, Eur. fr. 132 N².

159 *parentis*: Aegeus or Minos? Editors disagree. It is true that Aegeus is later represented by C. – to the reader – as no harsh parent. But is Ariadne supposed to understand this? She is searching (excitedly) for reasons to account for the

actions of Theseus, and in her anger finds one that is discreditable to him: he has abandoned her because he was the kind of man to fear parental disapproval. (Her own relations with her father are treated as affectionate *for the purposes of this speech*.) In such a light as this, the unqualified *parentis* may more naturally be taken to mean 'your father.' As for Minos, even supposing his hostility, he has evidently not foreseen the elopement, or he could surely have prevented it.

A third suggestion has been revived by Professor Gaisser; it may be summarized thus. The *parens* is not Aegeus (since no such 'advice to marry' is recorded of him); also, C. would not have called him *priscus* since he was still alive. [See however *OLD* s.v. *priscus* 3 (b).] Rather, the *parens* is Cecrops, who first instituted marriage in Athens. (This however rests on the authority of Trogus, and seems remote from the passion of Ariadne, though in other respects it deserves consideration.) L. Richardson 1963 suggests Pittheus. Cressey 1979 backs Minos.

The identification of *parens* with Cecrops is first found in Sabellicus, *Ex Catullo*; see Gaisser 1993: 408.

160 *vestras*, 'of you and your family.' (This again seems to point to Aegeus as having some interest in the matter.) It may possibly be = *tuas*, as Kr. takes it, referring to his n. on 68.151, which cites 39.20 and other passages. See F. on 39.20 for a lengthy discussion, in which he generally dismisses for C. the equation *vester* = *tuus*; I find it hard to accept his view, at least in relation to 39.20 and 99.6.

161 *iucundo*, a word nearly always associated by C. with love or close friendship: cf. 284 *iucundo . . . odore*, at the scene of the wedding.

162 The liquid sounds support the pictured action. Cf. *Od.* 19.387–8; also Pacuv. fr. 244–6 R², which well illustrates the meaning of *permulsi* (. . . *ut pulverem manibus isdem quibus Ulixi saepe permulsi abluam lassitudinemque minuam manuum mollitudine*).

vestigia in the concrete sense is not uncommon; see *OLD* 3. The adj. *candida* is of course proleptic; notice *pulverem* in the passage quoted.

163 *vestis*, of any fabric: cf. 234 (of a sail).

On the conclusion of this line, as dividing the lament of Ariadne into two 'disparate' sections, see Schmidt 1967.

164 Observe that *sed quid ego* is repeated from 116.

Both *sed* and *auris* are original corrections by *R²*; in the second instance *V*'s error is due, no doubt, to the spelling *aureis*, which B. would restore.

165 *extenuata* (*X*) is a failed attempt at correction, *X* being unfamiliar with the rare (and poetical) verb *exsternare*; cf. 138 n.

auctae, 'endowed with' (cf. 323 *decus . . . virtutibus augens*, where see n.; also 25 *taedis felicibus aucte*, 66.11 *novo auctus hymenaeo*, and Cicero,

Ad Att. 1.2.1 *filiolo me auctum scito*). Lucr. ends a line with *sensibus auctas* (3.630).

166 *missas*, 'uttered.' Kr. cites Lucr. 3.931 *si vocem rerum natura repente / mittat;* he also points out that Lucr. ends a line with *reddere voces* (4.577). There are especially close verbal links between Lucr. and C.'s 'Ariadne episode' (see also the foregoing n.).

167 I.e., Theseus is now almost half-way to Athens.

168 *vacua ... in alga*, a poetically compressed phrase, in which *alga* = 'beach' (cf. 60).

170 *etiam* goes with *invidet-aures* (taken together as one verb), not of course with *nostris ... questibus.*

171 'Would that ... not': the familiar opening of the *Medea* (Euripides, Ennius).

See App. Crit.: notice Petrarch's agreement with Macrobius here against the surviving Mss of C.

172 Here *O* agrees with Macrobius (see previous note); but this time the agreement lies only in a doubled consonant (habitual in *O*).

Gnosia = Cretan (cf. *Gortynia* 75), as commonly in poetry, e.g., Virgil. Clearly, the conjunction of the two adjectives is contrived in order to enhance the atmosphere of myth.

174 *religasset*: 'tied up,' the usual meaning of *religo*, is appropriate to *O*'s reading *in Creta* (see App. Crit.). 'Untied,' i.e., 'cast off,' would suit *in Cretam.* Only at 63.84, however, is the latter meaning attested (see however *OLD* 5, which adds 'apparently'); and even there E. rejects it and B. has doubts. See below.

Gratwick 1979 would read *intortum*, which is ingenious, but (i) Ariadne need have no general objection to such an action by Theseus, except in Crete, (ii) *O* offers *in Creta*, (iii) to qualify a rope as 'twisted' seems here a dull and pointless addition; contrast 235, where a nautical operation is prescribed in detail.

Probably *O* dropped the virgula, present in *A*, as he does below in lines 190, 237, and 291, and also at 34.21, 46.4, 58^b.7, 63.42, 65.14, 67.10, 68.41, and 86.1; the opposite happens at 36.14, 63.55, 64.231 (where *O* is right), 67.45, 68.31, and 98.4. That the virgula was added in *X* here (McKie: 282), by assimilation to *funem*, seems much less likely (see below). On the rival merits of *Creta* and *Cretam*, scholars are still divided. The expression *religare in Cretam*, meaning (as we should put it) 'weigh [anchor] for Crete,' is, however, doubtful Latin. McKie (loc. cit.) suggests that an adjective, balancing *funem*, is required in place of *in Cretam*; but to say 'would that the sailor had never tied up his ship' is surely insufficient, even in the context of the preceding lines; what must be said is '... never tied up *here.*'

175 *O* often takes ħ (*hic*) to be ħ (*hec*): cf. line 269 (*hec O, hic V*) and also 44.13, where *O* takes ħ as *hoc.* Generally, in the case of *hoc* the downward stroke, or

dot, touches the shoulder of the curve (ħ), whereas with *hec* it comes short of it and turns in towards the vertical stroke.

176 *m*'s initial carelessness (in writing *requirisset*) is later corrected by means of a small superscript *s* (m^2), which G^2 apparently did not notice.

hospes, again 'stranger' (cf. 98 n.; V. *Aen.* 4.10 *nostris successit sedibus hospes*), but in this particular context perhaps also 'guest.'

177 *quo me referam ... at ...*: cf. Cicero, *De or.* 3.214 (text in B.): a familiar sequence in rhetoric. In poetry, cf. esp. Eur. *Med.* 502–5 νῦν ποῖ τράπωμαι κτλ. Ovid (*M.* 8.113–18) expands the same self-debate: *nam quo deserta revertar, etc.*

Idaeos: of Mount Ida, which dominates western Crete. Its remoteness across the ocean, expressed in three ways in 178–79, suggests that C. thinks of Ariadne's desertion by Theseus as occurring in Naxos (52 n.). The case against the reading *Idomeneosne* (or *-usne*) rests (apart from the grammatical form, on which see F.) not so much on the anachronism (Idomeneus belonged to the next generation) as on the fact that in mythology Idomeneus 'never appears as the proper representative of Crete' (Kr.). R^2's wrong guess at correction of *idoneos* is adopted, as usual, by m^2G^2 in the form of a variant.

179 Here, as at 174 and presently at 183, *O* is a far better witness than *X*.

180 *quem ve* (R^2's original correction) is missed by *m*, inserted by m^2; and absent again in G^2, G^1 having already made an alteration in the *G* reading.

180–1 At this point, Ariadne feels unable to turn to her father for help because of her elopement with Theseus who killed her half-brother; however, as already suggested (118 n.; see also 117 n.), in this highly rhetorical speech of Ariadne's C. may really have in mind an idealized family situation, perhaps not without some influence from the *Medea* of Euripides (476ff.); as Kr. suggests, this literary reminiscence would serve to justify the notion that paternal help might have been forthcoming.

182 Editors find it odd that Ariadne should even propose to herself the possibility of finding consolation in the faithful love of a *coniunx* when the matter concerning which she is to be consoled is the very faithlessness of that same *coniunx*. But this argument is slightly pedantic. Ariadne's words here suggest lines 117–20, in which family affection (later recalled in 180–1) is set in the balance against her overpowering love for Theseus who is presently (123) to be described as her *coniunx* just after he is shown to have deserted her. In other words, *coniunx* in both passages has ironical overtones, and C. is quite aware of the paradox.

incurvans, 'bending,' a sign of urgent haste (*lentos* is graphic, possibly proleptic; at all events not merely conventional). For this notion, cf. Ap. Rhod. 2.591–2 ἐπεγνάμπτοντο δὲ κῶπαι ἠύτε καμπύλα τόξα, V. *Aen.* 3.384 *lentandus remus in unda,* Ciris 461 *flectitur ... remus.*

184 Palmer's clever emendation may prompt the suggestion that the history of these words ran as follows: nullo loco colitur (*locus* inserted in a misguided attempt to supply a noun; the order is at all events disturbed) > nullo loco ̣colitur ̣(the wrong *co* being expunged first, and the corrector forgetting to erase his dots afterwards) > nullo litus.

sola here of course = 'deserted' (*OLD* 3). To the idea of loneliness and desertion all four lines, 184–7, are devoted: Nature herself indicts Theseus.

185 *m* follows *R* into an error (*pater*) that R^2 had failed to reflect upon, with results too absurd even for G^2.

186 *nulla spes*: an example of 'lengthening by position.' Notice the pause after a monosyllable at the end of the fourth foot; the effect is abrupt, suggesting shock.

186–7 The triple repetition of *omnia* is solemn and arresting.

letum (in epic style) = *mors*. With the line ending cf. V. *Aen.* 1.91 *intentant omnia mortem.*

190 *multam*: this word, originally meaning a fine, was extended – by the poets, apparently – to signify punishment of any kind.

194 *exspirantis* (accus.) *iras* = snakes, the outward embodiment of inward wrath.

praeportans: the verb occurs twice in Cicero, *Aratea*, in a literal sense (209 and 430 Traglia), and once in Lucr. (2.621 *telaque praeportant violenti signa furoris*, where the last two words are close in meaning to C.'s *pectoris iras*).

For *O*'s reading see the notes on lines 11, 145, 153.

195 *huc huc*: cf. 61.8–9, in an invocation.

R^2's correction of *R* is metrical in character.

196 '*vae! misera* ist sehr matt gegenüber den kommenden *inops, ardens, amenti caeca furore.* Viel energischer und somit passender wäre das *vae miserae!* der Itali' (Fr.). E. reads *miserae*; see his reasons. See also Thomson 1970.

197 Notice the asyndeton (characteristic of C.).

198 *quae quoniam*: a relative pronoun + *quoniam* frequently occurs in Lucr., usually though not always at the opening of a line (1.21, 607, 626, 893; 2.95, 478, 512, 522, 748, 808; 3.538, 794; 4.63, 1092; 5.138, 150). Cf. also Lucr. 3.57 *nam verae voces tum demum pectore ab imo.* See above, 166 n.

200 *quali* ... *tali*, echoed in 247–8 (*qualem* ... *talem*), after fulfilment of the curse.

201 *funestet* = 'pollute with death.'

202–48 Theseus returns home; his forgetfulness (see 58) causes the death of his father Aegeus, and so Ariadne's curse (200–1) is accomplished. This episode within the episode of Ariadne is yet a semi-independent narrative, containing as it does the long speech by Aegeus (215–37).

203 *factis*, poetic plural (for a single deed; cf. perhaps 51 *virtutes*, of the slaying of the Minotaur).

204 *annuit*: the 'nod' of Zeus, implying both assent and power, is Homeric
(*Il.* 1.528–30 νεῦσε Κρονίων … μέγαν δ᾽ ἐλέλιξεν Ὄλυμπον). Notice the
etymological word-play in *annuit-numine*. Cf. V. *Aen.* 9.106 *annuit et totum
nutu tremefecit Olympum*. Although *numen* means a (physical) 'nod' in two
passages of Lucr. (2.632, 4.179), the adj. *invicto* (conventional, of Iuppiter:
Hor. *Od.* 3.27.73, Ov. *F.* 6.650) shows that the meaning here is partly
'transferred' (B.).

205 *motu*: answering to *nutus*, the abstract noun implicitly contained in *annuit* 204.
In support of Heyse's *quo motu* see Stat. *Theb.* 7.3 (of Iuppiter) *concussitque
caput, motu quo celsa laborant*. Cf. also Ov. *M.* 8.780.
horrida, often used by C. of the sea: cf. 4.8, and 64.270 *horrificans*; Lucr. 3.835
horrida contremuere. Fr. takes it as *epitheton ornans*, probably rightly (against
F., who compares Hor. *Od.* 3.24.40 and translates it by 'ruffled'); Fr. points
out that *micantia* 206 must be *epitheton ornans*, since 'the stars do not shine
by day.'
    McKie: 254 wrongly reports *O* as reading *Quo tunc*; *quomodo* is merely
abbreviated.

206 *concussit*, 'caused to shiver.'
mundus, 'the firmament,' as in Lucretius and in earlier Latin writers generally.
(Lucr. 5.514, 1204–5, also links it to the words *micant sidera, micantes stellae*.)

207 *caeca*, (i) 'dark, impenetrable,' (ii) 'blinding.'

208 *consitus*, of any growth that impedes access or vision. Metaphorically, at Plaut.
Men. 756 *consitus sum senectute*.

209 *quae mandata*: cf. 232, 239 *haec mandata*; 239 virtually repeats the whole of
this line ('eine Erinnerung an die Wiederholungstechnik der alten epos,' Kr.).

210 *maesto*, 'grieving'; the *dulcia signa* would have removed Aegeus' otherwise
settled grief.
sustollens, not merely 'raising' but 'hauling up' in a nautical sense (cf. the
passages in Lucr. quoted by E.). *R²* corrects, *suo Marte*, on metrical and
linguistic grounds.

211 *Erectheum … portum*: a Hellenistic 'learned' periphrasis, even if 'Piraeum'
would be anachronistic; see 74 n.

212 *classi*, for *classe*: cf. 66.46. See 64.53 n. for content.
divae, Athena.

213 *R²* corrects, from his knowledge of myth (l. 3 n.), followed by *m* (who is not in
turn followed by *G²*, to whom the form *egeus* may have made no sense).

215 It is hard to decide between *longa* (*V*) and *longe*. See however 217 n. For Fr.,
not only are 'life' and 'long life' the same thing in the mouth of the aged A.,
but men as they age cling more and more to the ideal of longevity (he quotes
τὸ ζῆν γὰρ οὐδεὶς ὡς ὁ γηράσκων ἐρᾷ). This may well be psychologically closer
to the truth than Housman's

Life, to be sure, is nothing much to lose;
   But young men think it is, and we were young. (*More Poems* xxxvi)
The story of Theseus' upbringing, at a distance from Aegeus, who first set eyes upon him in his extreme old age, was familiar; cf. Plut. *Thes.* 12.

   In support of *longe iucundior*, cf. 68.159 *longe ... carior*, in a passage (159–60) where the sentiment is similar.

217 There is some merit in Avantius' *extremae*; but, besides the unanimous testimony of *OGR*, the fact that line 216 (and, if we should read *longa*, line 215 also) follows the pattern (in which an adjective after the penthemimeral caesura fits a noun at the end of the line) that would then be repeated, tends to tell against it.

218 For *fervida virtus*, implying youth and strength, and the 'play' on *fervida-ferox*, see 73 n.

219 *cui* R²*m*= *O*, but may well be original since it is a fairly obvious correction of R²'s *quem*.
languida, i.e., weakened by age; cf. 188 *languescent lumina*.

220 Prop. 2.15.23 has *oculos satiemus*. Cf. *Od.* 11.452–3 υἷος ἐνιπλησθῆναι ... ὀφθαλμοῖσιν.

221 McKie: 252 argues for error by *O*, not preservation of *A*'s reading (see 149 *lecti*), on the grounds that the evidence related to *laetor* (etc.) points to consistency of spelling in *A*.

224 Cf. V. *Aen.* 12.611 *canitiem immundo perfusam pulvere turpans*, clearly imitated, with V.'s characteristic variations, from C.
infuso: again an obvious correction, made by R² and followed by *m*.
foedans: cf. *Il.* 18.23–4 κόνιν ... χεύατο κὰκ κεφαλῆς χαρίεν δ' ᾔσχυνε πρόσωπον.

225 *vago*, 'moving,' often of *regular* motions (as in *vagus Sol*); hence, to tr. 'wandering' can often mislead. See 271 n.
lintea, poetically used of a sail (4.5, and 243 below) or any other cloth (12.3, 64.163 n.).

225–37 The sponge-fishers of Kalymnos told Freya Stark that when they left harbour in the spring their wives accompanied them to the quay; and when every man had sailed, the women exchanged their usual white kerchiefs for black ones, to wear until their husbands returned. See *The Lycian Shore* (London, 1956): 38.

226 *incendia mentis*: the same phrase occurs at Val. Flacc. 7.243. For *incendium* = (mental) turmoil, cf. Plaut. *Merc.* 590. With V. *Aen.* 9.500 *incendentem luctus* (of the mother of the dead Euryalus) cf. *Od.* 20.353 οἰμωγὴ δὲ δέδηε.

227 *carbasus*: yet another indirect way of saying 'sail.' (See also 234 *vestem*.)
   R²'s attempted correction *obscura* is followed by *m*. Renaissance humanists sometimes wrote Latin verses on the assumption that the *i* in *dicare* was, or

could be, long; e.g., George Buchanan, in his Horatian ode *Calendae Maiae* (*Miscellaneorum liber*, 11, line 3); is Coluccio also under this impression? (*Obscura* must be intended by him as an additional epithet qualifying *ferrugine*.)

On *ferrugine*, indicating (almost always) a hue that was *vicinus purpurae subnigrae* (Servius *ad Aen.* 9.582), see F.'s long n. Add (for the sake of the distinction it appears to make) *SHA* [Julius Capitolinus] *Vita Maximini iunioris* 30.3 *lorica ... non ut solet ferrugine sed tota purpureo colore infecta*.

228 *incola Itoni* = Athena, who had a cult in Thessaly (Phthiotis: Paus. 1.13.2), with a derivative cult in Boeotia (Paus. 9.34.1); the cult title would be recognized in Athens.

m's spelling (*ithomi*) agrees with *O*'s, but its cause lies in carelessness, not imitation.

The reading *itoni* is attested in Hermolaus Barbarus' *Castigationes Plinianae* (1492), *ad N.H.* 4.27. See Grant 1992: 269–70.

229 *has* is not quite impossible if we punctuate with a comma after *genus*; but it is less satisfactory in terms of sound (*s*'s), and the movement of the line is unduly arrested.

sedes ... Erecthei, cf. 211. *Il.* 2.547–8 δῆμον Ἐρεχθῆος μεγαλήτορος, ὅν ποτ' Ἀθήνη θρέψε Διὸς θυγάτηρ.

230 *tauri*, a word chosen in ironic reminiscence of 150 and 181. To Ariadne, the Minotaur is a 'brother'; to Aegeus, he is merely a 'bull.'

231 *facito ut*, 'see to it that you ...' Kr. and F. cite Cicero, *Flacc.* 57, V. *Aen.* 12.438.

memori: again ironic (230 n.), since the adjective *immemor* applied to Theseus has been established in the reader's mind already (123, 135).

See 174 n. on omission of the virgula – here, in *tū* – by *GR*.

232 *R²*'s correction is easy and obvious. *m*'s careless error *obliferet* is preserved (together with its *m²* correction) by *G²*.

235 *intorti*, 'twisted,' i.e., plaited in manufacture; of ropes or cables. Cf. V. *Aen.* 4.575 (*tortos*) and Ov. *M.* 3.679 *intortos funes*.

sustollant: cf. 210 (n.), a line of which we are meant to be reminded, just as *invisent* 233 reminds us of *visere* 211. *A*, and probably *X* as well, had *sustolant*; *G*'s *subs-* is surely a mistake. *R²* corrects to *sustollant*, followed as usual by *m*.

236 Editors debate the nature of the concept denoted by *gaudia*. Fr. takes it as concrete (meaning 'you'), comparing 2.5 *desiderio* (where however see n. for other interpretations); E. (followed by B.) claims it as abstract, 'the joy of which the white sail is the sign.' It is surely not too much to assert that both aspects of meaning are present in the noun, *gaudia*, however purely 'concrete' the verb *agnoscam* may be.

237 *aetas*, 'day' (cf. Stat. *Th.* 3.562 *crastina aetas*).

We can here say with confidence that both *A* and *X* read *sistent* (*sistēt*, *A* at least). Notice the independent corrections by *G*¹ and *R*¹ of their own texts. On *O*'s omission of the virgula found in *A*, see 174 n.

As F. notes, the expression *reducem sistere* 'belongs to formal religious language'; see his three examples (two from prose, one from the *Aeneid*). Cf. also *CLE* 19.8 *tu me meos reducem sistito* (Kr.) and Livy 29.27.3 (B.).

239 *R*²'s correction is an acute one for his period.

239–40 The point of the simile is hardly the rapidity with which clouds are blown away from a peak, so much as the completeness with which they are blown away. Kr.'s objection to it assumes the former interpretation.

240 *nivei* = *nivalis, nivosi*: unusual, but not unparalleled, though elsewhere in C. it always means 'snow-white.'

241 *ut*, 'while.'
For *prospectum peto* cf. V. *Aen.* 1.181. Pac. *trag.* 96 and Acc. *trag.* 407 R² have *prospectum aucupo*.
arce: C., by choosing this word (unqualified), surely adopts the version of the legend in which the scene is set on the south side of the Acropolis (Paus. 1.22.5, cf. D.S. 4.61.7), not at Cape Sounion (Sunium) as in Stat. *Theb.* 12.624–6.

242 Instead of correcting the careless error (*etiam* for *in*) in *m*, *m*² puts in the true reading – from *R* – as a variant.

243 *inflati*: there is no need to emend this to *infecti*; the reader is well aware that the dark sail was still hoisted.

245 *G*¹'s correction is not considered adequate by *G*², who insists on *m*'s spelling (*imm*-).
fato: *O*'s mistake is similar to that at 221 (insertion of *c*; see n. there). Since *fato* and *facto* differ little in their effective meaning in this context, *X* had little reason to wish to emend, as McKie: 264 points out, comparing l. 326.
Cf. Ov. *M.* 13.260 *fatisque immitibus*.

246 *domus ... tecta*: cf. 276 *vestibuli ... tecta* (where the reading *vestibuli*, which has been questioned, receives some support from the present passage). Take *funesta* [= *funestata*; cf. 201 *funestet*] ...*paterna morte* together; the house of mourning is polluted (cf. Cicero, *De legg.* 2.55 *quae finis funestae familiae, quod genus sacrificii Lari vervecibus fiat*; with *Lari* compare the reading *penates* at 404 below, where there is a similar notion of pollution – see the n. on *scelerare* there).

247 Apropos of Ariadne, *luctus* refers not to grief at her own ill-treatment but to the bereavement she has suffered in the death of the Minotaur; *luctus* is correctly defined as 'dolor externus' (*tristitia de amissione carorum*, Aug. *de serm. dom.* 1.2.5; *TLL* 7.2.1737ff.). The point implied here is that the Minotaur was as close to her in affection as Aegeus was to Theseus; see again 150, 181.
Minoidi: the short final *i* is exceptional; there is another example at 66.70, and

a very few in Statius (*A.* 1.285 *Palladi, Th.* 3.521 *Iasoni, S.* 4.2.28 *Doridi*). On Greek forms in general, see F.'s n. on line 3.

248 *immemori*: cf. 231 n. The word serves forcefully to link the story of Ariadne, and of her curse, with that of Aegeus (in which the curse was fulfilled), since grammatically it can be taken both with *obtulerat* and with *recepit*.

249 *prospectans*: cf. 241 *prospectum*. R^2's correction (*aspectans*) is essentially metrical, depending on the (false) reading *tamen*; some doubt about it is implied by his subsequent addition of *al.*; *m* accepts the *corrections*, but m^2 shares the doubt and therefore inserts *al. pro*.

Observe how here, at the end of the story of Ariadne and Theseus, both *prospectans* and *cedentem* are deliberately recalled from its beginning (52–3).

250 *curas* = 'love' (cf. V. *Aen.* 4.1), not 'fear of death, etc.' (as B. takes it).

251–64 After Theseus departs, 'Iacchus' (= Bacchus, the god Dionysus) comes, with his followers, in search of Ariadne.

251 *parte ex alia*: the other side, that is, of the scene depicted on the *vestis*.

252 'Nysa-born': the adjective may well have been coined by C.; it is otherwise unknown. Sileni were elderly followers of Bacchus/Dionysus; Muretus (followed by B.) quotes Diod. 3.72.1: '... the aristocrats of Nysa, who are called Silenoi. For Silenos was (he says) the first king to rule in Nysa.' Diodorus puts Nysa in 'Arabia' (3.66.3), whereas *plerique Indiae ascribunt*, according to Pliny (*NH* 6.79); but earlier (*Iliad* 6.133) it is situated in Thrace. As E. notes, 'Apollonius [Rhodius] 4.431 speaks of Dionysus as the prince of Nysa when he woos Ariadne in Dia, a passage which may have been in C.'s memory.'

253 R^2, with *te*, corrects (*suo Marte*), followed by *m*.

254 For O. Skutsch's emendation see *Philologus* 106 (1962): 281–2. An argument which can be added to his defence, but which he does not use, is that *V*'s *qui* represents an original *quoi* = *cui* (see my n. on 1.1). In further support of *cui* ... *furebant*, cf. Claudian, *De IV. cos. Hon.* 605 <*Bacchi*>, *cui furerent*.

255 *euhoe*, an interjection, attached to the construction only loosely and parenthetically, but thought of, perhaps, as a kind of object to the participles in the line. Cf. V. *Aen.* 7.389 *euhoe Bacche fremens*.

256 The thyrsus was wound about with ivy or vine-leaves; its point (*cuspis*) was hidden in these and in a large pine-cone.

257 The Thy[i]ades, or Maenads (women of Delphi: see 390–1) were believed to indulge in such violent acts as these under the influence of the Bacchic frenzy: Eur. *Bacch.* 739 (σπαραγμός).

259 *obscura* = *occultata*, i.e., treated as a participle, 'hidden in.' The other interpretation regards *obscura* as anticipating the meaning of 260, less probably; B. sits on the fence, with a preference for the second.
cavis, a word used of any *enclosing* box, river bed (95.5), or other bounded space.

celebrabant, not 'celebrated' (as Fr.), but 'thronged about' (in procession).

orgia, sacred objects (a cult word); in Sen. *Herc. Oet.* 594–5 they are concealed in *cistae* (another religious term, in this sensè). The word is also used, more commonly, in the extended sense of 'rites' in mystery religions and in the cult of Dionysus.

260 *audire*, 'hear of.'

profani, the uninitiated (Hor. *Od.* 3.1.1 *profanum vulgus*) = οἱ ἀβάκχευτοι, βέβηλοι, ἀτέλεστοι. Cf. Ov. *AA* 2.601 *quis Cereris ritus ausit vulgare profanis?* (and see the dialogue between Pentheus and Dionysus in Eur. *Bacch.* 471–4).

261–4 Notice the onomatopoeia in these lines; cf. in this respect the similar description in Lucr. 2.618-20.

261 *proceris ... palmis*, 'with hands held high'; E. mysteriously finds 'tapering fingers' implied here.

Here, and in the next fifteen lines or so, *m* is remarkably careless; at 264 he omits *tibia*.

262 *tereti ... aere* = cymbals (rounded in shape).

Possibly *tinnitus A, tinǹitus X*? (hence R^2m^2). McKie: 271 speaks of 'dittography' in *X*.

For *tinnitus ciere* cf. V. *Geo.* 4.64 *tinnitusque cie*.

263 *bombus* is a deep vibratory hum, such as certain low-pitched wind instruments (the old-fashioned *tromba marina*, for example) produce. For the word, cf. Lucr. 4.546, the corrupt text of which also contains the words *raucum, barbara*, and (dubiously) *cita*.

264 *barbara* here = Phrygian. Cf. 63.22 *tibicen ... Phryx*.

Notice how the shrill *i*-sounds in the middle of the line represent the *timbre* of the instrument (Kr.); see above, 132–4 n.

265–6 sum up the 'coverlet story,' 267–8 announce the transition to the second stage of the wedding feast, attended by the gods of varying degree.

267–8 *spectando ... expleta est*: for the idiom cf. 219–20. It has an 'epic' resonance; cf. *Od.* 4.47 αὐτὰρ ἐπεὶ τάρπησαν ὁρώμενοι ὀφθαλμοῖσιν.

268 Seeking, as he often does, to reform *R*'s spelling, *m* proceeds to alter the R/R^2 reading from *cepit* to *coepit*. See 344 n.

Here *decedere* is not merely 'depart' but (deferentially) 'yield place to' or 'make room for.'

269 *hic*, 'at this point.' For *O*'s mistake cf. 175 n.

269–77 Notice the subtle rhythmical effect, in this descriptive passage, of the pauses (*rallentandi*) brought about by spondaic line endings (269, 274, 277) or line openings (269, 272, 274, 277). For 269–70, cf. *Iliad* 4.422ff. and 7.63; but, as E. points out, it is not merely imitation or translation on C.'s part. Fr. suggests that C. here conflates two images, one from *Iliad* 4.422ff. and one from Aesch. *Agam.* 1180ff., but with the difference that whereas Homer and Aeschylus mention growing waves C. merely says that the waves succeed one another more and more rapidly.

270 *O* alters his first (faulty) reading, but not to the reading of *X*. McKie: 264 is right in suggesting that *O*'s exemplar read *proclivis*; he further suggests that *proclivas* was *X*'s emendation.

horrificans: cf. θρίξ, of a breeze ruffling the sea (*Il.* 7.63).

271 *limina Solis*: similarly V. *Aen.* 6.255; cf. *Od.* 24.12 Ἠελίοιο πύλαι. On the adj. *vagi* ('onward-moving,' cf. 277 *vago pede*), F.'s n. should help to counter the frequent mistranslation of *vagus* as 'wandering.' Kr.'s tr., 'rasch,' is hardly less misleading.

272 McKie: 258 cites *O*'s reading as *elementi*, which I do not see.

273 *leviter*: cf. 84.8 n. (where a contrast is implied with the sibilant storms of the Ionian sea; see my intr. n. to that poem).

275 *purpurea*: cf. Cicero, *Acad.* 2.105 *mare ... quod purpureum videtur*. On the meaning of *purpureus*, see Edgeworth 1979, and also F. on 45.12. Further, cf. Irwin 1974: 18 (on πορφύρεος as indicating 'sheen' or 'iridescence'). It should be noted that in *SHA* (Julius Capitolinus, *Vita Maximini iunioris* 30.3) *purpureus color* is contrasted with *ferrugo* (see above, 227 n.).

procul should probably be taken with the sentence as a whole (E.) rather than limited to *nantes* in its reference, as Kr. would have it.

For the sense of *a*, cf. 66.63 *uvidulam a fluctu*; F. quotes Cicero, *Acad.* 2.105 *a sole collucet*, of the sea (see his n.).

276 *tibi* (*m*, for *V*'s *tamen*) is simply another example of *m*'s carelessness, 'corrected' by m^2 to *R*'s unmetrical *tamen*, but inserted by the hand of m^2 as a variant – really a correction – between the lines of *R* itself, no doubt because it fits metrically; G^2 also adopts it.

vestibuli ... regia tecta: if the reading is correct, an instance of hypallage; cf. 246 *funesta domus ... tecta*. The reading *vestibuli* was, however, doubted by Munro, *JPh* 11 (1882): 124. (As he remarks, Schrader had proposed *vestibulo* or *vestibulis*.) He hesitantly suggests *sic tum, vestis ubi, linquentes*, citing V. *Aen.* 7.764 *pinguis ubi ... ara Dianae*.

278 By *Peli* (*Pelei* in the Mss) the genitive form of the name of Mount Pelion of course is meant; but the scribe of the archetype probably thought of the word, in the context of this poem, as the genitive of the name Peleus which occurs elsewhere in poem 64 (we find *Pelei* at 382). There is no need to have recourse to the archaic form of the genitive (in which *Pelei* = *Peli*).

279 Chiron was a local Thessalian god (of Pelion, where he dwelt in a cave); Peleus is sometimes represented as his grandson or (more often) protégé (Kr.). Especially, he helped Peleus to win the hand of Thetis; hence he came to the wedding (as Prometheus did, 294, for a similar reason). As his wedding gift, he is usually said to have brought a spear of ash (*Iliad* 16.143; other refs. in Kr.),

but different gifts are indicated here on the pattern of Eur. *IA* 1058ff.: that they
are flowers is 'a characteristically Alexandrian touch' (F.), and Kr. suggests
that C. intends by them to heighten the atmosphere of a courtly Hellenistic
marriage feast. On this point, cf. Reitzenstein 1900: 87 (on line 293).

280 *ora*, 'region, district,' rather than 'sea-coast,' even though the mountain ranges
are in fact quite close to the sea.

282 *aura ... tepidi ... Favoni*: cf. 46.1–3 (Favonius = Zephyrus). Cf. Lucr. 1.11
genitabilis aura Favoni; Callim. *H.* 2.81–2 ἄνθεα ... τόσσα περ Ὧραι ποικίλ᾽
ἀγινεῦσι Ζεφύρου πνείοντος ἐέρσην.

With *parit*, *m* stumbles into the true reading; later, m^2 (characteristically)
returns to *R*'s *perit*. G^2, however, preserves *m*'s unintended correction. For the
occasional confusion by scribes between *facundus* and *fecundus*, see the Ms
readings of Hor. *Ep.* 1.5.19.

Ellis, in his *Oxford Classical Text* (1904), supporting *parit* against Housman's
aperit, cites Ov. *AA* 3.185–6 *quot nova terra parit flores, cum vere tepenti /
vitis agit gemmas*.

283 *R*'s *curulis* (*corulis OG*) is accepted by *m* (hence by G^2), *faute de mieux*; but
when R^2 (later) has a good emendation of his own to produce – disguised as a
variant, it should be observed – m^2 adopts it. It is hard to believe that if *corollis*
had already been visible in *R* on *m*'s first reading, *m* would not have seized
upon it. Because of this and similar instances, I find it impossible to relinquish
altogether my thesis of two R^2 recensions, distinguishable by means of $m(^1)$
and m^2.

284 *risit*: cf. 31.14; *h. Hom.* 2 (Demeter) 13–14 κηώδει δ᾽ ὀδμῇ πᾶς οὐρανὸς εὐρὺς
ὕπερθεν γαῖά τε πᾶσ᾽ ἐγέλασσε κτλ.

285 <*a*>*l. os*: a (late) correction by R^2, picked up by m^2.

285–6 The anaphora of *Tempe* is linked with the enlarged description appended as
if by an afterthought in 286 (where notice the 'hanging' effect of the spondaic
close).

286 Does R^2's correction derive from *X*? Probably not, because of the change in
spelling and word division taken together with the fact that *m* (not m^2) adopts
it.

287 *V*'s reading plainly conceals *some* Greek dative plural, and *Haemonisin* on the
whole best fits sense, rhythm, and the appropriate sequence of vowel sounds.
We need a dactylic opening, to suggest the *choreae*, and most of the names of
nymphs suggested by editors are palaeographically remote from *minosim* of
the Mss.

claris recommends itself by alliteration. The *choreae* had elements of song as
well as dance; Fr. quotes a gloss: *chorea: graece saltatio cum cantilena classium
concinentium*. Cf. Tib. 1.3.59 *choreae cantusque vigent*, Dracont. 6.32 *cantare
choreas*.

288 *vacuus* = 'empty-handed,' as in Juv. 10.22 *cantabit vacuus coram latrone viator*. E. compares κενέος (*Il.* 2.298, *Od.* 15.214) and κενός (Soph. *OC* 359).
ille: E. translates 'in his turn, as *his* gift' (in contrast to the flowers brought by Chiron). More subtly, F. identifies here a 'pictorial' use of *ille* ('there he was, with trees in his hands').
tulit = *attulit*. See 150 n. on C.'s use of simple, in place of compound, verbs.
radicitus, 'roots and all'; this extension of meaning would surely not seem objectionable in a poet, though Nisbet 1978: 111 (following L. Herrmann) wishes to substitute *radicibus*.

289 *laurus*, characteristic of the Vale of Tempe.

290–1 The poplar alone (unless with V. *Ecl.* 6.62–3 we are to take the *Phaethontiades* as having been metamorphosed into alder-trees; Fr., in fact, thinks C. has them also in mind) receives an elaborate periphrasis. Otherwise, only the *laurus* are allowed more than a single adjective. Notice how variety is achieved in the descriptions of the five trees, so that the effect of a catalogue is avoided.

292 Note *circum* (all the walls were covered); not = 'round about' on the *outside*, which would deprive line 293 of sense.
contexta: *m* misses *R²*'s correction.

294 *sollerti*, 'inventive'; used here as a purely conventional epithet of Prometheus (cf. Hes. *Op.* 48 and *Th.* 546 ἀγκυλομήτης), since it is not relevant to the present context. Prometheus, like Chiron, had earned his invitation, by promoting the idea of the marriage: after being released from his bonds, he warned Zeus what the consequences of marrying Thetis would be, inasmuch as the son of Thetis was fated to be greater than his father; whereupon Zeus ceased to be a suitor and Peleus took his place (Aesch. *PV* 768).

295 Traces (*vestigia*) – not to be confused, as by some editors, with the *tokens* of his punishment that Zeus made him wear (Prob. on V. *Ecl.* 6.42, quoted by Kr.).

297 For the effect of the spondaic line ending cf. 286.
persoluit, 'paid in full'; cf. Aesch. *PV* 112 τοιῶνδε ποινὰς ἀμπλακημάτων τίνω.
praeruptis: cf. Aesch. *PV* 4 πρὸς πέτραις ὑψηλοκρήμνοις.

298 The final -*que* is elided into the next line. Up to and including C., this is very unusual; Virgil however adopts it, and in him it is frequent. Heinze (on Hor. S. 1.4.96) traced it to Callim. *Ep.* 41.1 Pf., where a line ends οὐκ οἶδ' (Kr.).
   With *divum, m* once more stumbles into the truth; *m²*, consulting *R*, relapses into *divi*. In reading *gratisque, m* is again careless (but is followed by *G²*, as usual).

299 *caelo*, ablative of separation, taken with *advenit* (B. punctuates *advenit, caelo* and would translate 'in heaven,' taking *caelo* with *relinquens*; but then *advenit* becomes jejune, and the pause after it stronger than the meaning justifies).

300 *unigena*, 'sister' (ὁμομήτρος),' not 'only child' (μονογένης), since her brother is mentioned with her. As F. points out, *unigena* at 66.53 translates Callimachus' γνωτός.

cultricem montibus: for the construction, cf. *incola littoribus* 66.58, and also perhaps 64.184 *colitur nullo tecto*. If the reading *Idri* is right (which is at least doubtful), the phrase *c. m. Idri* must refer to the Hecate cult in Asia Minor.

301–2 At *Il*. 24.62–3, Hera says the great gods (= *divi*) all came to this wedding, including Phoebus Apollo himself: πάντες δ' ἀντιάασθε, θεοί, γάμου· ἐν δὲ σὺ τοῖσι δαίνυ' ἔχων φόρμιγγα. Why then in C.'s poem are Apollo and his sister absent? Several answers have been given, as follows: (i) because, as the reader knows, Achilles, the future offspring of the marriage, was to be slain in due course by Apollo; (ii) because Apollo and Artemis/Hecate – but why these two alone? – saw the union of Thetis with a mortal as a *mésalliance* (301); (iii) because the wedding of Peleus, which in some accounts was associated with storm and darkness, must be regarded as a ceremony held by torchlight in murky gloom, devoid of *sun* and *moon* (this, it might be added, would give point to the figure *taedas* in 302). Plainly (ii) must be taken very seriously because of the *nam*-clause in 301–2, which also seems to militate against (i) because of its greater emphasis on *Peleus* as unworthy; but (iii) deserves more attention than modern editors have given it – it was Marcilius who first advanced it – and might be combined with (ii) and possibly regarded as an attempt by C. to reconcile his sources by offering a mythical explanation for the tale of a storm-darkened wedding. For a discussion of the problem see Knopp 1976: 211.

302 Here *m*'s careless version (*tethidis*) is not followed by *G²*, in contrast to 298 (*gratis*) and 307 (*hic*). The correspondence in the spelling of *O* and *m* is accidental; *thedas* is due to the proximity of *Thetidis*.

303–4 The transition to the Song of the Parcae.

303 *flexerunt artus*: an extremely dignified equivalent for 'sat.' Cf. κῶλα κάμπειν, γόνυ κάμπειν, in Greek tragedy: Aesch. *PV* 396 (γόνυ), Soph. *OC* 19 (κῶλα). Lambinus, on Hor. *Od*. 1.27.8 *cubito remanete presso*, quotes C.'s line, and also Serv. on *Aen*. 7.176, for the perception that gods and heroes sat at table, instead of reclining as Greeks and Romans did in historical times.

304 *constructae*: unusual prefix, for metrical reasons; see parallels in Fr. B. would read *sunt exstructae*, arbitrarily, while Kr., recognizing that *con-* is strictly appropriate to *dapes in mensa* whereas Latin says *exstruere mensam dapibus*, compares *oppidum moenibus circumdare* with *moenia oppido circumdare*.

305 *cum interea* is often purely adversative (95.3); editors claim that here it is 'simply temporal' (F.), but it seems to me *slightly* adversative: 'whereas apart, yonder, the aged Parcae <did not sit down to dine but> ...'

307–19 This lengthy description of the Parcae is indulged in for its own sake (the love of minute detail is of course Hellenistic) and as a conscious digression, though it enhances the atmosphere of the wedding scene. To invest mythical and divine figures with the outward frailties of everyday mortals, and to show them in common tasks on a domestic scale, is very much in the vein of such Alexandrian writers as Callimachus. It is not easy to recover the peculiar piquancy it possessed for the ancient mind.

308 C. furnishes the white robes of the Parcae (for which see Plato *Rep.* 617c, a passage first cited by A. Statius) with a 'purple' border, for the sake of the red-white contrast, dear to Roman poets in particular, which he develops in the juxtaposition *roseae niveo* (309). For a defence of *V*'s order *roseo niveae* see P. Flobert, *REL* 54 (1976): 142–51.

310 Properly, *carpere* is applied to (e.g.) *pensa* (V. *Geo.* 1.390) or *vellera* (*Geo.* 4.335; cf. below, 319); here, however, as editors remark, the concrete verb is extended in application to the abstract *laborem*.

311 *R*²'s correction is metrical in intent.
amictum, 'covered,' i.e., metaphorically 'clothed' (as, at 63.70, places are 'clothed' with snow).

312 *supinis*, 'upturned' (in 313 the thumb turns *down*ward).
fusum, 'the spindle,' which is kept turning evenly on its axis by its *turbo*, or 'whorl,' a kind of heavy disc encircling the spindle and acting as a flywheel to steady it.

315 *atque ita*, 'and then' (καὶ οὕτως). B., who finds it hard to explain *ita* when something *new* is involved, would read *ibi*, comparing 66.33; but cf. the passages adduced by F. on l. 84. The teeth pluck surplus wool from the thread, with the result vividly shown in 316–17.
dens: for the abrupt (stressed) monosyllabic word at the end of the line, with its effect of suddenness, cf. 68.19 n.

316 *morsa*, as a noun, is unique; cf. *tenta* 80.6, perhaps *condita* 66.74; *mansa* in Cicero, *De or.* 2.162.

318 *candentis*: picturesque, not symbolic.

319 *vellera*: the word is used here of raw wool waiting to be spun. The minor correction of spelling by *R*² (*m*) is not followed in *G*², who perhaps is already hurrying; a few pages later he virtually stops adding corrections (see 66.67 n.).
virgati: only here in its literal sense ('made of willow-twigs'); elsewhere, by transference, always with the meaning 'striped' (E., F.).
X's *custodiebant* is a wrong (and metrically inferior) 'correction' (to the regular form of the verb) of *A*'s *custodibant*, preserved by *O*.
calathisci (Greek diminutive), an uncommon word in Latin, at least in its diminutive form (B. cites Petron. 41.6 as the only other instance, whereas *calathus* occurs in several instances).

320 *haec*, a feminine form, regular in Comedy but otherwise rare; for instances, other than those in Cicero and Virgil questioned by F., see Fr. Cf. Puelma 1977: 172–4.

321 *divino*, here in the fairly common sense (*OLD* 6) of 'prophetic.' Cf. V. *Aen.*
3.373 *canit divino ex ore sacerdos.*

323–81 The Song of the Fates, with the Hellenistic device of a refrain, occurring
after passages of three to five lines (cf. Theocr. 1, V. *Ecl.* 8). The song is
Hellenistic also in devoting more lines to its central section in praise of Achilles,
the future son of the union, than to the marriage itself, with which it begins and
ends. For this 'enfolding' technique as a characteristic of poem 64, see the intr. n.

323 *decus*: editors are divided over the meaning. Is it 'beauty,' 'personal distinction,'
or 'ancestral glory'? Much depends on what sense we feel we must give to
augens: F. renders it by 'enhancing,' and claims that *decus* means 'either the
inherited distinction of Peleus' race … or perhaps his own physical beauty,'
but in the second case it is a little difficult to come to terms with the notion
of 'enhancing.' (Kr. suggests 'enhances *the impression of* his beauty'; can this
really be extracted from the Latin?) B. says simply 'beauty,' quoting such
passages as V. *Aen.* 4.150 and Stat. *A.* 1.290. Unless we translate *augere* as
'complement' (165 n.), it seems better to take *decus* as 'inherited distinction,'
bearing in mind Nepos, *Timoth.* 1.1 *a patre acceptam gloriam multis auxit
virtutibus.*

324 Cleared up by Housman 1915; but notice the first step taken by the Humanists,
who replaced *tutum* with *tu tamen* (see App. Crit.), or with *columen.* (At line
26, Peleus is referred to as *columen Thessaliae.*) Emathia was a district of
Macedonia near Pella, but the name was freely used by poets (it was easy to
scan in hexameters, Kr.) for Thessaly also; e.g., Lucan 1.1, V. *Geo.* 1.492. See
OLD s.v., 1a, 1b.

    Housman 1915 was the first to point to *Il.* 24.61 Πηλέϊ, ὃς περὶ κῆρι φίλος
γένετ' ἀθανάτοισι.

Opis natus = Iuppiter (Plaut. *Mil.* 1082 *Iuppiter ex Ope natust*).

325 The rhythm is Lucretian, not Virgilian (spondee corresponding to fourth foot).

327 The words of this refrain are recalled by Virgil, *Ecl.* 4.46. For the refrain in
general, see 323–81 n.

subtegmina, a term from weaving; here used of (merely) spun yarn only 'by
anticipation' (F.).

quae fata sequuntur: cf. Theocr. 24.70 ὅ τι μοῖρα κατὰ κλωστῆρος ἐπείγει.

328 *iam*, 'at last' (Fr.), not 'straightway' (as E.); cf. 61.127, 176, 184, (195); also
62.3, 18.

maritis here = 'bridegrooms.'

329 The word *coniunx* is used in this part of the poem without any of the overtones
it had acquired in the story of Ariadne (182 n.).

330 *flexanimo* (a word used twice by Pacuvius, once in passive and once, as here, in
active sense), 'that sways your heart' (cf. θελξίφρων). Cf. V. *Geo.* 4.516 *nulla
Venus,non ulli animum flexere hymenaei.*

331 It is characteristic of C.'s 'Hellenistic' style that even so stately a prophecy as this can accommodate the rare diminutive *languidulos*, with its erotic significance (cf. A. Riese, *Anth. Lat.* 33.2).

    so(m)nos: either *V* or *A* has apparently omitted a virgula, as *O* does from time to time (see 174 n.).

332 For this type of line structure, and its function in closing a 'paragraph,' see 42 n.

334–6 C. habitually combines the concepts *amor, foedus*: see for example 87.3–4. Notice also the equation here between *amor* and *concordia*, and cf. 66.87–8, and line 336 n. The emphasis in 334–6 on the *concordia* prevailing in this marriage runs counter to the older tradition that Thetis left Peleus shortly after Achilles was born (cf. Ap. Rhod. 4.875–9). On C.'s motivation in stressing the unbroken concord between Peleus and Thetis see esp. Reitzenstein 1900: 90; he points out that if Thetis is to have a formal (even courtly) wedding, then mention of ὁμόνοια becomes part of the ritual. See also l. 279 n.

334 Notice the lengthening of *-us in arsi* (if *V* is right); cf. 62.4, 64.20, 66.11, though admittedly all of these precede forms of the Greek word *Hymenaeus*. See however the parallels in Fr., p. 263 (Hor. *Od.* 3.24.5, 4.7.20, *Ep.* 1.6.40; Ov. *AA* 1.389; Prop. 2.8.8, 2.24.4; V. *Geo.* 2.5, 4.453; *Aen.* 4.64, etc. As he says, there is a kind of anaphora between *tales contexit (amores)* and *tali coniunxit (amantes)*; cf. 143–4 *nulla viro ... nulla viri*. The transposition *tales umquam* is now, however, generally accepted.

336 F. has a useful note on the synizesis in *Peleo*.

    qualis concordia (substituted for *quale foedus*): cf. 96.2–3 *dolore ... desiderio*.

338 *expers terroris* = ἄφοβος, ἄτρεστος (but the Greek sobriquets are post-Homeric; cf. θυμολέων, *Iliad* 7.228) (Kr.).

339 Cf. *Iliad* 13.289, where it is said of Meriones:

    οὐκ ἂν ἐν αὐχεν' ὄπισθε πέσοι βέλος οὐδ' ἐνὶ νώτῳ

    ἀλλά κεν ἢ στέρνων ἢ νηδύος ἀντιάσειε

    πρόσσω ἱεμένοιο κτλ.

    m has *ut* in place of *haud*: an example of initial carelessness on the part of *m*, duly corrected (from *R*) by *m*².

340–1 For the proverb, cf. Plaut. *Poen.* 530 (Kr.). In Homer, Achilles is πόδας ὠκύς.

    flammea (metaphorically, of speed): cf. *ignea*, e.g., V. *Aen.* 11.718 *pernicibus ignea plantis*.

341 *G*² does not follow *m/m*² (ρvertis, ρvertit), either because he sees no reason here to reproduce *m*'s careless error and *m*²'s subsequent half-correction or simply (perhaps more probably) because he was beginning to correct more hurriedly (319 n.).

343 For this account of the Trojan War in a few words, cf. *Culex* 304–6.

344 *Phrygii Teucro*: mythological romance continues, in the substitution here of old epic names for 'Trojan.' Cf. V. *Aen.* 2.325–6 (*... Dardaniae. fuimus*

Troes, fuit Ilium et ingens gloria Teucrorum), for similar variation in names (πολυωνυμία).

Notice *m*'s insistence on spelling (*phrygii*); cf. 61.18 and elsewhere. The variant *al. teuen* ($R^2m^2 = O$) is assigned to X by McKie: 272, probably rightly, though it hardly improves the *tenen* of X's text; but if McKie is right, it is clear that X inserts it out of pious duty to A rather than from any conviction of its emendatory merit. So attested, this tendency of X should be borne in mind. McKie: 265 attributes O's divergent *manebunt* to error, believing that the line as a whole is too meaningless to make X-emendation probable. Accepting his conclusions, we may suppose this succession: teucro manabunt sanguine teuen *A*; teucto [error] manebunt [error] s. teuen *O*; teucro manabunt s. tenen (al. teuen) *X*; teuero [error] manabunt s. tenen *G*; teucro manabunt s. tenen *R*; *m* (*primo*) as R (or else *m* saw R^2's variant – see below – and ignored it; but this, though it does not occur in a passage where *m* is careless, is not in character); al. teuen *add.* R^2 (from X); m^2 follows R^2; G^2 follows m^2.

345 *longinquo = longo* (of time), not 'far-off.' Cf. Enn. *Ann.* 413 V^2 (= 406 Skutsch) *longinqua aetas*. Caesar (*BG* 5.29.7) speaks of *longinqua obsidio*.

346 *periuri*: P. bribed Myrtilus, the charioteer of Oenomaus, with the offer of half his kingdom as reward for an act of sabotage which should enable P. to win a race and thereby his intended bride, Hippodamia. This done, P. defaulted on his promise by putting M. to death and so incurring the curse on 'Pelops' line' (Hyginus, *Fab.* 84). E. provides a handful of references to the myth.

tertius heres, Agamemnon. There were two versions of the family tree. The shorter of these, Pelops–Atreus–Agamemnon, is found generally in Homer and in the tragedians. But in order to justify the expression *tertius heres* we must understand C. to be conforming to the alternative version, by which either Thyestes (as in *Il.* 2.105–8, most likely his ultimate source here) or Pleisthenes (as in Hesiod, fr. 194 Merkelbach-West^3, Stesichorus fr. 15 D = 219 [42] Page *PMG*) is inserted between Atreus and Agamemnon. The learned periphrasis (see intr. n. for other examples of this in poem 64) is of course Hellenistic in character; but by adopting it the poet also doubtless wishes us to realize that he has in fact followed the less familiar version of the legend (to do so being itself an Alexandrian habit).

348–60 It should be remembered that Achilles says of himself (*Iliad* 18.122–4) καὶ τινα Τρωιάδων καὶ Δαρδανίδων βαθυκόλπων ... ἁδινὸν στοναχῆσαι ἐφείην (imitated here). Perhaps the nearest approach in English literature to the sentiments at least outwardly expressed here is to be found in Thomas Love Peacock's *The War Song of Dinas Vawr* (q.v., passim):

... spilt blood enough to swim in;
We orphaned many children,
And widowed many women.

348 *clara facta* are virtually a synonym for *egregiae virtutes*; cf. 51 n., and line 323.

350 *incultum ... solvent*: *solvere crinem* not = tearing the hair out (see Ov. M. 11.682, where *solvere* is contrasted with *scindere*), but allowing it to be unkempt and unbound. Cf. V. *Aen.* 11.35 *maestum Iliades crinem de more solutae*.
crinem: both *O* and *X* are wrong here: *O* blunders, inverting *n* and *m*; *X* emends to *crines* in order to fit the supposed meaning of *civium*, which (we may add) has itself been 'emended' by *X* from *in civum A* (= *O¹*).

351 *putria*, 'frail' (i.e., disintegrating with age): see *OLD* 1, and cf. Hor. *Epod.* 8.7 *mammae putres*, a phrase that surely supports the emendation.
variabunt, 'will bruise' (mark with bruises); cf. Plaut. *Poen.* 26 *ne et hic varientur virgis et loris domi*. For beating the breast as a sign of grief, cf. *Il.* 18.30–1 χερσὶ δὲ πᾶσαι στήθεα πεπλήγοντο.

353–5 A 'Homeric' simile; cf. *Il.* 11.67–71 οἱ δ᾽, ὥς τ᾽ ἀμητῆρες ἐναντίοι ἀλλήλοισιν ὄγμον ἐλαύνωσιν ἀνδρὸς μάκαρος κατ᾽ ἄρουραν πυρῶν ἢ κριθέων ... ὡς Τρῶες καὶ Ἀχαιοὶ ἐπ᾽ ἀλλήλοισι θορόντες δῄουν.

353 *praecerpens*, 'mowing down before him' (as he walks forward swinging his scythe).
messor (*O*) gives the more specific sense; *cultor* (*GR* = *X*) may result from accidental substitution by *X* of a word of similar meaning. *X* is habitually more inclined than *O* to replace a word by another word, presumably through negligence (McKie: 273). Notice also that *messor* is supported, as Kr. remarks, by the Homeric ἀμητῆρες (see the foregoing n.).

354 *flaventia*, 'in a ripe, yellow state' (livelier than the corresponding adjective *flava*; the same kind of difference exists as between *candens* and *candidus*). The phrase *sole sub ardenti* also helps to make the picture more concrete and arresting (Kr., F.). Compare with it the effect which C. obtained by adding the adj. *aridis* to *aristis* at 48.5, where see the n.

355 *Troiugena*: like *Graiugena*, an ornamental Grecism from a form ending in -γενής.

357 *testis erit*: for the concept of the scene of action 'testifying to' the warrior's prowess cf. Hor. *Od.* 4.4.37–38 *quid debeas, o Roma, Neronibus / testis Metaurum flumen*. Further examples in F.; but read Prop. 3.7.21 for 4.7.21.
unda Scamandri: shortening of the final vowel in *unda* is borrowed (as Kr. suggests) from *Iliad* 20.74 ἄνδρες δὲ Σκάμανδρον); cf. Prop. 3.1.27, if G. Wolff's restoration *cum prole Scamandro* is right.

359 A traditional notion (*Iliad* 21.15–21 and 218–20). Kr. asks why C. chooses to celebrate the *virtutes* of Achilles by singling out this berserk massacre (and by the death of Polyxena, 362) rather than by (e.g.) the slaying of Hector, as we might expect. No wholly convincing answer has yet been given; see the bibliography for attempts to do so.

360 Cf. Lucr. 3.643 *permixta caede calentis* (also 5.1313); no doubt borrowed from
Ennius by both Lucr. and C.

    m's *flumine* is due simply to error; *m*² adds the reading of *G* (*lumina*) as
well as that of *R* (*flumina*), both as variants, and is (as usual) followed by *G*²,
even in error; but *G*² does not add *vel flumina*, as *m*² does, perhaps through
haste (see 319 n.). Where does *m*² obtain the *G* reading? There is little if any
other evidence that *m* saw *X*. It would not be uncharacteristic if *m*² intended to
write only *al. flumina* but, when he saw that he had carelessly written *lumina*,
simply added *vel flumina* to correct himself (judging that there was hardly
room for the addition of the letter *f*).

362 *morti* = *mortuo*; i.e., to Achilles after his death. *m. quoque* = *etiam mortuo*.

363 *teres*, of a rounded 'barrow' or tumulus. Cf. *Od.* 24.80–2, of the joint burial place
of Achilles and Patroclus, with that of Antilochus nearby: ἀμφ᾽ αὐτοῖσι δ᾽ ἔπειτα
μέγαν καὶ ἀμύμονα τύμβος χεύαμεν κτλ. (and Strabo 13.1.32 Ἀχιλλέως καὶ ἱερόν
ἐστι καὶ μνῆμα πρὸς τῷ Σιγείῳ, Πατρόκλου δὲ καὶ Ἀντιλόχου μνήματα).

364 *perculsae* (*V*) is more appropriate for a beheaded victim (cf. 370); *percussae*
would fit the other account (Eur. *Hec.* 567), in which Polyxena is *stabbed* to
death, but *perculsae* (of a heavy blow: 'pole-axed,' for example) would not.

366–7 *copiam ... solvere* (instead of *solvendi*): for this construction cf. V. *Aen.*
9.484 (B.).

367 *urbis Dardaniae ... solvere vincla*: cf. *Il.* 16.100 and *Od.* 16.388 (Τροίης
κρήδεμνα λύειν).

    Neptunia vincla = the walls built by Poseidon, who says in Eur. *Tro.* 4–7 ἀμφὶ
τήνδε Τρωικὴν χθόνα Φοῖβός τε κἀγὼ λαΐνους πύργους πέριξ ὀρθοῖσιν ἔθεμεν
κανόσι. Cf. also *Il.* 7.452–3 and 21.446–7.

368 *Polyxenia*: for the old idiom by which adjectives replace the genitive of
personal names, cf. 77 *Androgeoneae*; also 14.3 *Vatiniano* (and 53.2 *Vatiniana*),
44.10 *Sestianus*, 61.223 *Penelopaeo*, 66.8 *Bereniceo*, 66.60 *Ariadnaeis*, 68.74
Protesilaeam. Notice that *quae* in l. 369 clearly relates to the implied *Polyxenae*.

369 *victima*, usually of *animal* victims (and therefore deliberately chosen here, for
horrific and pathetic effect). So also in Eur. *Hec.* Polyxena compares herself to a
(sacrificial) calf (*Hec.* 206, cf. 526), as E. notes.

370 *summisso poplite* (where *poples* = 'knees'): cf. Lucr. 1.92 *terram genibus
summissa petebat*, but also 4.952–3 *poplitesque cubanti / saepe tamen
summittuntur virisque resolvunt*. Eur. *Hec.* 561 has καθεῖσα πρὸς γαῖαν γόνυ.

372 The conclusion of the Song *appears* unconscious of the cruelty of at least some
aspects of the scenes that have been described. Whether this is irony on C.'s
part, or merely subscription by him to what he sees as an epic convention, has
been much debated in recent years; see the introductory note.

    amores iungere is a set phrase (78.3, Tib. 1.1.69).

373 *coniunx, felici foedere*: see n. on 329. (For the play on *coniunx* and *coniungere*,
cf. 329, 331.) B., followed by Kr., believes that in *felici* the 'original' meaning

('fruitful' or 'fertile') comes through, presumably because the occasion is a wedding; this may well be doubted.

374 *iamdudum*, 'now at last' (cf. *iam* 328 n.), taken with *dedatur*, rather than with *cupido*; in the latter case its meaning would be 'now for a long time.'

376–7 At this point C. sees his poem as an 'Epithalamium' (its traditional title in the intermediate heading found in the Mss), at least to the extent of introducing an element of 'fescennine' erotic jesting; cf. 61.119ff. The young bride's childhood nurse, who is a party to all her secrets, applies on the morning after the wedding a popular test of consummation: the thread that would measure her neck yesterday is today too short to do so.

   esterno (O) seems likely to have been the *reading* of A, and *ext-* (X) a correction, of the wrong sort, offered by X himself.

379–80 The other side: if the test just mentioned shows that the marriage is still unconsummated, the bride's mother fears that there has been a quarrel and may be a breach (*discordis puellae secubitu*), and so loses hope of grandchildren. (B. perversely sees the prospect of a divorce *due* to sterility.)

379 *anxia*: cf. the nn. on 61.46 *anxiis*, 51 *tremulus*.

380 *secubitu*: cf. 61.101 *secubare*.
   mittet = desistet (Fr.).

382 *praefantes*, 'uttering'; with an overtone of prophecy perhaps, though this is not (as might be expected) its primary meaning. *Praefari* is a 'sakrales Wort' (Fr.), indicating either (i) to dictate or rehearse a religious formula to another person (as in Livy 5.41.3, 39.15.1), or (ii) to pronounce the prescribed opening words that are to be followed either by further religious formulae or by a ritual act (in this instance the marriage ceremony; see B.). Cf. Livy 45.5.4.
   Pelei: C. elsewhere uses the Latin dative in *-eo* (cf. 336 n.), but seems here to adopt the Greek form (see Fr.'s n.). To take *Pelei* as genitive in *felicia P. carmina* is less attractive. B., who considers the use by C. of two different Greek forms impossible, would emend to *Peleo*.

383 *divino*, 'foretelling,' cf. 321 n.

384–408 The 'moralizing epilogue,' as editors and critics often describe it, which recalls the praise of the heroic age at the outset of the poem (1–30) and contrasts it with the present.

384 *praesentes*, in the religious sense (as used of a god 'occupying' a shrine, etc., with full *numen*). See Puelma 1977.
   castas: notice the stress on this word and also on *pietate* 386, considered in the light of 397–406, q.v. Notice esp. Germanicus, *Arat.* 107–10, quoted by E.: *mediis te* [= Justice] *laeta ferebas / sublimis populis, nec dedignata subire / tecta hominum et puros sine crimine, diva, penates / iura dabas.*

385 *mortale = mortalium* (transferred epithet).
   coetu, a word repeated at 407. Cf. 66.37 for dative in *-u*.

386 *caelicolae*: cf. 30.4 n.

387 *fulgente*: a conventional epithet, general in meaning and without particular
implications for the decoration of the temple at Olympia.
revisens (*V*): the idiom *revisere in* is doubtful; hence B. proposed *residens*. See
however Puelma 1977: 175–80.

388–9 E. cites Callim. *H.* 2.77–9 ἐν δὲ πόληϊ θῆκε τελεσφορίην ἐπετήσιον, ᾗ ἐνὶ
πολλοὶ ὑστάτιον πίπτουσιν ἐπ' ἰσχίον, ὦ ἄνα, ταῦροι.

389 The traditional 'hecatomb.' Cf. Ov. *Tr.* 2.75 *fuso taurorum sanguine centum*,
and the refs. in Owen's n. ad loc.
   See App. Crit. The reading *procurrere currus* (cf. V. *Geo.* 3.18) has been
defended, e.g., by Cressey 1980a. But *terra* makes it unlikely. Cf. Ov. *M.* 2.347,
5.122 (*procumbere* with *terrae* or *terra*), V. *Aen.* 5.481 *procumbit humi bos*.
Terra would be a 'meaningless addition' (E.) if we read *procurrere currus*.

390 *vagus*, perhaps 'on his progresses,' bearing in mind Eur. fr. 752 N² Διόνυσος ὃς
θύρσοισι καὶ νεβρῶν δοραῖς καθαπτὸς ἐν πεύκασι Παρνασὸν κάτα πηδᾷ χορεύων
παρθένοις σὺν Δέλφισιν. On the pediment of Apollo's temple at Delphi reliefs
of Apollo himself (with the Muses) were balanced by others showing Bacchus
(together with the Thyiades); cf. Lucan 5.73 *mons Phoebo Bromioque sacer* (B.).

391 The *Thyiades* were the celebrants of Dionysus; they accompanied him in his
'rout' (*thiasus*). B. gives numerous *testimonia*.
evantis egit: cf. Prop. 2.3.18 *egit ut euhantis dux Ariadna choros*.

392 *Delphi* here = the inhabitants.

393 *acciperent ... divum*: cf. 373 *accipiat ... divam*: a phrase of religious
(including marriage) ritual; and the same may to some extent be said of *laeti*
in such contexts: cf. 61.8 (in an invocation to the god Hymen), where see n. on
the punctuation.
lacti (*V*) must be wrong: it does not agree with the idea underlying *fumantibus*,
and would hardly enhance the reverent tone of the passage; Cressey 1980b
supports *lacti*, but the argument for it is exceedingly slender without evidence
for milk offerings at Delphi itself, apart from the points already made.
   G² made two changes: first he altered *c* (from *m²*'s *al. lacti*) to *e*; then he
expunged *a*, thus returning to *m*'s *leti*.

394 *Mavors*: the archaic form of the name, used in a solemn epic context. 'Epic'
stylistic value is also claimed for the defining phrase *belli certamen*: editors
cite Lucr. 1.475, 5.1296, and V. *Aen.* 10.146. But it should be noted that this
phrase appears in a letter from Plancus to Cicero, *Ad Fam.* 10.18.2, while Cicero
himself has *proelii certamen* at *Rep.* 2.13.

395 *Tritonis era* (τριτογένεια, *Iliad* 4.515) = Athena: τριτώ in Aeolic dialect = 'head'
(of Zeus, from which Athena was born) (B.). Later a place name was sought;
rapidi suggests a river, and the names of rivers occur among the candidates
(Hdt. 4.178, Paus. 9.33.7, etc.; see E.). A lake is much less likely, esp. with

rapidi: Lake Triton, in Libya, which has been suggested, was *torpens palus* (Lucan 9.347).

Rhamnusia: B.'s emendation *Amarunsia* (Artemis: from Amarynthus in Euboeia) takes account of the fact that the alternative reading *Rhamnusia* (66.71, 68.77) is a cult title of Nemesis, invariably a goddess of justice, never of war (her shrine at Rhamnus in Attica lay alongside that of Themis); and also of the consideration that if the name of Rhamnusia-Nemesis were to be mentioned here it must mean what it means in the other two passages which I have just quoted (so that Wilamowitz' attempt to suggest that Artemis too was at some times, and for some authors, known as Rhamnusia becomes irrelevant). See however Skinner 1984, who has adequately dealt with B.'s arguments. Notice also that while Hesiod (see next n.) refers to Nemesis, C. (397 n.) alludes to Themis.

397–406 Cf. Hes. *Op.* 182–201, a similar picture of 'contemporary' degeneracy, with particular emphasis, as here, on injustice and on violations of family ties.

397 *scelus*, like *scelerare* (404 n.), implies moral pollution.

iustitium ... fugarunt: a reference to Themis, the last of the gods to flee from Earth and from the presence of human beings. Cf. Aratus 133 δὴ τότε μισήσασα Δίκη δείνων γένος ἀνδρῶν ἔπταθ' ὑπουρανίη.

398 In a manner which is characteristic of C., *cupida* concisely introduces a further statement, of a causal sort, by way of a simple adjective, or participle; cf. 65.21 *miserae oblitae*.

399–401 Notice the insistent effect of three self-contained lines, making statements of the same kind, and each beginning *with the principal verb*. To this add the verbal repetitions (*natus, frater*) noted by F. See also 403 (end of my n.).

399 Cf. Lucr. 3.72 *crudeles gaudent in tristi funere fratris*. V. *Geo.* 2.510 (*gaudent perfusi sanguine fratrum*) combines Lucretian language with C.'s *fraterno sanguine*. Cf. above, 181 *respersum ... fraterna caede*; C.'s reminiscence of that line is deliberate, whatever we make of Ariadne's attitude to the Minotaur.

401 *funera*: poetic plural; cf. *sepulcra* 368.

nati, not *gnati*, for metrical reasons, though elsewhere in the poem C. prefers the archaic form.

402 V's reading, *innuptae ... novercae*, would be paradoxical, since the girl would become *noverca* only after her marriage. If we take *noverca* in a proleptic sense, we attribute to C. a phrase which, with its rather strained 'poetic' condensation of ideas, might be credible in terms of the sophisticated rhetoric of the Silver Age – of Statius, for example – but is far from the generally straightforward idiom of C. The double restoration, involving *nuptae* and *novellae*, uses language and forms familiar to us from C. himself: apart from his love of the diminutive in such contexts, *nova nupta* ('bride') appears several times in poem 61, and at 66.15, and surely says what C. is on all counts most

likely to have said at this place. Cf. also 67.23–8, and perhaps 17.14 *cui cum sit viridissimo nupta flore puella.* For a counter-argument see Puelma 1977: 181–90; also Giangrande 1975: 109–11.

It may be possible to defend the reading of the Mss (*novercae*) as follows: a father desires his son's death, because he himself wishes to be free to marry a girl of about his son's age or even younger; but as things are she will not accept the father's proposal, because so long as the son remained alive she would, embarrassingly, be his stepmother. But (as already noted) this pregnant 'future' meaning burdens the word *novercae* (translated 'who would then become a stepmother') far too much for C.'s relatively direct manner; and in general the notion is too complicated.

403 *ignaro* ... This, of course, cannot be meant to recall Oedipus and Jocasta. Much of the debate about C.'s meaning hinges on the question whether he had in mind a contemporary Roman situation or a story from Greek mythology. For lines 401–2, editors quote Sall. *Cat.* 15 (a father disposes of his son in order to clear the way for his own marriage), sometimes comparing also Cicero, *Cluent.* 27; for 403–4, on the other hand, mythical parallels (though never exact) are easier to find. There are the stories of Hippolytus and of Phoenix, which have at least something in common with this passage; there is a story, closer to it, in Ov. *M.* 7.386, concerning an obscure Menephron who *cum matre concubiturus erat* (though here the son is not *ignarus*). The story of Myrrha's incestuous love for her father is also told by Ovid (*M.* 10.298–502); more to the point perhaps, it had earlier been told at great length by C.'s contemporary and friend Cinna in his *Zmyrna* (cf. poem 95). Apart from such indirect literary incitements as this, it seems doubtful whether any concretely visualized situation, whether mythical or historical, was in C.'s mind. Most probably ll. 403–4 are simply an imaginatively expanded chronicle, or list, of further offences against the family. Observe the special indignation implied by C.'s epanalepsis (*impia ... impia*) as he recounts the culminating atrocity just before the summing-up in line 405.

404 *penates*, an early emendation, is (despite Kr.) probably right: the *di parentes* embody the spirits of departed ancestors, not the active principle of home (*parentes* may have been accidentally copied from 400). For the 'polluted house' motif, cf. 246–7 (Aegeus' death makes the *domus funesta*): the final paragraph resumes several key words and ideas from the rest of the poem, and there may well be deliberate recall here. N.B. also 67.23–4 *conscelerasse domum* (cf. *scelerare* in this passage), where the context should be observed. V. *Aen.* 3.42 has the same verb: *parce pias scelerare manus.*

For the most forceful statement of the argument in favour of *parentes*, see Kr.

405 *fanda nefanda*, an established asyndeton, at least in terms of its idea; asyndeta
by contraries are very common. Cf. V. *Geo.* 1.505 *fas versum atque nefas.*
omnia ... permixta: *omnia miscere* is another established phrase: cf. *perdidistis
omnia* 29.24.
furore: the concluding lines of poem 63, which 'moralize' as do those of
poem 64, include the wish: *procul a mea tuus sit furor omnis, era, domo.*

406 *iustificam*: a unique form, 'epic' in sound and shape. As Kr. suggests, such
(pseudo-archaic) compound verbs tend to be invented by poets for metrical
convenience: e.g., *regificus* (Enn. *scen.* 96 V²), *largificus* (Lucr. 2.627); Ovid has
several ending in *-ficus.*
avertere recalls the same verb, used in a different sense, at the very beginning
(l. 5).

407-8 On the part of the gods, notice the difference between seeing (*visere*, 'set
eyes on,' also 'pay a visit to') and being seen. Here, as elsewhere in the poem,
C. appears to share with Lucretius a few ideas, as well as several expressions
(though the latter may, as often as not, go back to a common source in Ennius).
The notion of 'touching' denoted by *contingi* may just possibly (see Fr.'s n.,
though I think he exaggerates) have some reference to the Epicurean doctrine
that the gods cannot impinge on human life because their substance is remote
from ours, both in place and in its degree of subtlety and freedom from the
constraints imposed by intermixture with the grosser particles of matter, and
therefore changes in our body's texture (and its destiny) cannot be caused by
them. (See Lucr. 5.146–55.) But while such ideas may well have formed part of
the contemporary climate of thought, they do not constitute the *point* of C.'s
conclusion. For further discussion see the intr. n. to the poem.

Note on the bibliography to poem 64: The enormous amount of scholarly literature
that has gathered around poem 64 would seem to justify a slightly different kind
of bibliography. Where items that I have included contain general comments on
the poem, so far as these can be separated from discussions of particular lines or
passages, and where those comments seemed to me unusually important, I have
briefly summarized them in square brackets preceded by an asterisk (*[. . .]).

Reitzenstein, R. 1900. 'Die Hochzeit des Peleus und der Thetis,' *Hermes* 335:
73–105. *[The wedding scene is strongly influenced by Alexandrian court poetry;
hence the transference of the locale to Pharsalus.]
Pascal, C. 1904. 'Il carme LXIV di C.,' *SIFC* 12: 219–27. *[Why do Apollo and
Artemis absent themselves from the wedding? Because C. has in mind a torchlight
procession (*taedae*). (Neither this, nor the related explanation that it was
inappropriate for sun and moon to desert their stations, fully accounts for lines
301–2).]

Jackson, C.N. 1913. 'The Latin Epyllion,' *HSCP* 24: 37–50.

Housman, A.E. 1915. 'C. LXIV. 324,' *CQ* 9: 229–30.

Ramain, G. 1922. 'Sur la significance et la composition du poème 64 de C.,' *RPh* 46: 135–53. *[C., uniquely, wishes to show that the love between Peleus and Thetis was a source of mutual happiness, blessed by the gods, symbolizing legitimate marriage; contrast the story of Ariadne (condemned by C.), where all is wild and disordered. What C. does in poem 64 is to attempt to transfer to poetry the principles of *visual art*.]

Morpurgo, A. 1927. 'Il c. 64 di C.,' *RFIC* 5: 331–43. *[The story of Ariadne, centrally placed in the poem, is treated as a distant, fabulous view; cf. Pompeian wall-painting.]

Perrotta, G. 1931. 'Il c. 64 di C. e i suoi pretesi originali ellenistici,' *Athenaeum* 9: 177–222 = *Scritti minori* (1972): 63–147.

Latte, K. 1935. 'Der Thrax des Euphorion,' *Philologus* 90: 129–55, esp. 151–5.

Murley, C. 1937. 'The Structure and Proportion of C. 64,' *TAPA* 68: 305–17. *[C.'s habit of abrupt transition is taken from *pictorial* technique (cf. Ramain 1922 and Morpurgo 1927). Ariadne's tale fills out, rather than interrupts, the main story <of Peleus and Thetis>.]

Hutton, J. 1942. 'C. and Ovid,' *CW* 36: 243–5. *[Good remarks on Ariadne's lament; cf. Ov. *Ep.* 10.]

Waltz, R. 1945. 'Caractère, sens et composition du poème 64 de C.,' *REL* 23: 92–109. *[The reason for the poem's complicated structure, if not due to Hellenistic models, lies in C.'s taste for the kind of myth that allows him to display both vivid colours and psychological analysis.]

Cova, P.V. 1949. 'La composizione del c. 64 di C.,' *Convivium* 5: 209–23.

Klingner, F. 1956a. *Römische Geisteswelt*[3]. Munich: 210–20.

– 1956b. *Catulls Peleus-Epos* = *Sb. Bay. Ak. Wiss.* 6. *['Lyricized epic.' The Ariadne-Dionysus story is 'only a doublet' of that of Peleus and Thetis (but cf. Floratos 1957).]

Boucher, J.-P. 1956. 'À propos du Carmen 64 de C.,' *REL* 34: 190–202. *[The object of the poem lies in the expression of C.'s sensibility in all directions. (Sometimes C.'s pictures run away with him.) There is no 'key,' no dominant idea, or moral antithesis; it is 'only a story.']

Floratos, C. 1957. *Über das 64. Gedicht C.s.* Athens. *[The absence of Apollo and Artemis: the 'contradiction' of a blessing on the wedding from a god who is to slay the son of the marriage would have been avoided if C. had made Apollo attend but not utter the prophecy; but the strongly entrenched tradition of Apollo as the actual prophet forbade this solution.]

Beyers, E.E. 1960. 'The Refrain in the Song of the Fates in C. c. 64 (v. 323–381),' *AClass* 3: 86–9. *[C.'s purpose is to condemn Achilles. Artistic qualities in the Song; function of the refrain.]

Putnam, M.C.J. 1961. 'The Art of C. 64,' *HSCP* 65: 165–205. *['Nothing less than the complete scope of the poet's imagination' (cf. Boucher 1956). 'The love-elegy was not yet available as a vehicle for C.'s personal statement … He was not ready to interpret the present by myth as Propertius does … The only way … was through the long epic tale.']

Thomson, D.F.S. 1961. 'Aspects of Unity in C. 64,' *CJ* 57: 49–57.

Richmond, J.A. 1962. *The* Halieutica *ascribed to Ovid*. London.

Fink, R.O. 1963. 'C. LXIV, 109.' *AJP* 84: 72–4. [Read *lateque cacumen it obvia frangens*.]

Richardson, L. 1963. 'A Note on C. LXIV, 159,' *AJP* 84: 74–5.

Vrugt-Lenz, J. ter. 1963. 'Die singenden Parzen des C.,' *Mnemosyne* 16:262–6. *[C.'s innovation in the song was to substitute for the Greek *motif* of a marriage song, sung by the *Moirai*, a *carmen* of the *Parcae*, certainly likewise sung at a wedding but containing a soothsaying on the Roman pattern.]

Kinsey, T.E. 1965. 'Irony and Structure in C. 64,' *Latomus* 24: 911–31. *[C. is 'ironic' at the expense of heroic legend.]

Webster, T.B.L. 1966. 'The Myth of Ariadne from Homer to C.,' *G&R* 13: 22–31.

Schmidt, E.A. 1967. 'Ariadne bei C. und Ovid,' *Gymnasium* 74: 489–501.

Curran, L.C. 1969. 'C. and the Heroic Age,' *YCS* 21: 169–92. *[C. wishes to show the darker side of the heroic age.]

Bramble, J.C. 1970. 'Structure and Ambiguity in C. LXIV,' *PCPS* 16: 22–41. *[The unity of poem 64, which as a whole undercuts the initial atmosphere of heroism.]

Santo, L. 1970. '*Unigenam … prolem* (Marullo, *Hymni naturales* I. 1, v. 50),' *QIFL* 1: 61–101.

Thomson, D.F.S. 1970. 'C. 64, 196,' *RhM* 113: 89–91.

Vessey, D.W.T.C. 1970. 'Thoughts on the Epyllion,' *CJ* 65: 338–43.

Traina, A. 1972. 'Allusività catulliana (due note al c. 64),' *Studi classici in onore di Q. Cataudella* 3. Catania: 99–114, reprinted in *Poeti latini (e neolatini)*. Bologna (1975): 131–58.

Daniels, M.L. 1972. 'The Song of the Fates in C. 64: Epithalamium or Dirge?,' *CJ* 68: 97–101.

Giangrande, G. 1972. 'Das Epyllion C.s im Lichte der hellenistichen Epik,' *AC* 41: 123–47.

Granarolo, J. 1972. 'Liens entre le baroque décoratif et la poésie à la fin de la République romaine,' *Euphrosyne* 5: 429–35.

Harmon, D.P. 1973. 'Nostalgia for the Age of Heroes in C. 64,' *Latomus* 32: 311–31.

Forehand, W.E. 1974. 'Catullan Pessimism in Poem 64,' *CB* 50: 88–91. *[The absence of Apollo and Artemis/Diana is a first hint of discord: we think of Discord's golden apple (she was not invited); the eventual result is the Trojan War, grimly prophesied here.]

Giangrande, G. 1975. 'The Stepmother-Motif in C.,' *Eranos* 73: 109–11.

– 1976. 'Catullus 64.35,' *LCM* 1: 111–12.

Forsyth, P.Y. 1976. 'C.: The Mythic Persona,' *Latomus* 35: 555–66, esp. 558ff.

Knopp, S.E. 1976. 'C. 64 and the Conflict between *amores* and *virtutes*,' *CP* 71: 207–13.

Clausen, W. 1977. 'Ariadne's Leave-Taking: C. 64.116–20,' *ICS* 2: 219–23.

Cressey, J. 1977. 'Ploughing for Grapes: C. 64.38–42,' *LCM* 2: 153–4.

Konstan, D. 1977. *Catullus' Indictment of Rome: The Meaning of C. 64*. Amsterdam.

Martin, P. 1977. 'Encore et toujours le Carmen LXIV de C.,' *IL* 29: 93–101.

O'Connell, M. 1977. 'Pictorialism and Meaning in C. 64,' *Latomus* 36: 746–56.

Puelma, M. 1977. 'Sprachliche Beobachtungen zu C.s Peleus-Epos,' *MH* 34: 156–90.

Wiseman, T.P. 1977. 'C.'s Iacchus and Ariadne,' *LCM* 2: 177–80.

Zetzel, J.E.G. 1978. 'A Homeric Reminiscence in C., ' *AJP* 99: 332–3.

Cressey, J. 1979. 'Find the Knave: Catullus 64.159,' *LCM* 4: 137–8.

Thomas, R.F. 1979. 'On a Homeric Reference in C.,' *AJP* 100: 475–6.

Fourcade, J. 1979. 'Dolor Catullianus (II),' *Pallas* 26: 77–102.

Gratwick, A.S. 1979. 'Quam lepide lexeis compostae: C. 64.174,' *CQ* 29: 112–16.

Edgeworth, R.J. 1979. 'Does "purpureus" Mean "bright"?,' *Glotta* 57: 281–91.

Cressey, J. 1980a. 'The Text of C. 64.389,' *QUCC* 4: 69–71.

– 1980b. 'Two Textual Notes: C. 64.393 and Thucydides 4.48.3,' *LCM* 5: 69–70.

Forsyth, P.Y. 1980. 'C. 64: Dionysus Reconsidered,' *SLLRH* 2. Brussels: 98–105.

Mayer, R. 1980. 'On C. 64.21,' *PACA* 15: 16–19.

Duban, J.M. 1980. 'Verbal Links and Imagistic Undercurrents in C. 64,' *Latomus* 39: 777–802.

Glenn, J. 1980–1. 'Ariadne's Daydream (C. 64.158–63),' *CJ* 76: 110–16.

Cressey, J. 1981. 'C. and Minos (64.85),' *LCM* 6: 19–21.

Matthews, V.J. 1981. 'C. 64.85,' *LCM* 6: 283–4 [an answer to Cressey].

Kubiak, D.P. 1981. 'C. 64.1–2,' *AJP* 102: 41–2.

Dee, J.H. 1981. 'Iliad 1.4f. and C. 64.152f.: Further Considerations,' *TAPA* 111: 39–42. *[C. was 'primarily interested in the literary and emotional effectiveness of each part of his poem'.]

Most, G.W. 1981. 'On the Arrangement of C.'s Carmina Maiora,' *Philologus* 125: 109–25.

Traill, D.A. 1981. 'Ring-Composition in C. 64,' *CJ* 76: 232–41. *[Structure: see Table 1, p. 233.]

Thomas, R.F. 1982. 'C. and the Polemics of Poetic Reference,' *AJP* 103: 144–64. *[Conflation of literary allusions, as a technique of 'multiple reference.']

Dee, J.H. 1982. 'C. 64 and the Heroic Age: A Reply,' *ICS* 7: 98–109. *[Contrary to an 'emerging consensus,' C. does not imply disapproval of the 'brutal deeds' of the Heroic Age, and there is no 'consistent and serious morality' in the poet's approach to his subject-matter.]

Geymonat, M. 1982. 'Onomastica decorativa nel carme LXIV di C.,' *MD* 7: 173–5.

Granarolo, J. 1982. *Catulle, ce vivant*. Paris (esp. 161–5).

Townend, G.B. 1983. 'The Unstated Climax of C. 64,' *G&R* 30: 21–30. *[p. 23: 'There is enough similarity of structure in the two poems (poems 68 and 64) to make it inconceivable that C. did not intend the reader to make his own inference about the bearing of his two stories <in poem 64> upon one another. In many respects the elegy 68 is a more helpful guide to the interpretation of 64 than any of the extant epyllia, among which that of C. stands out as unique in complexity and … subtlety.' Is the Peleus-Thetis story the main theme, or only a 'frame to the more interesting story of Ariadne'? Contradictions in the wedding story are shown by Bramble 1970 …' There can be no doubt that C. has undercut his ostensible purpose at every point'. C.'s allusive technique relies on the reader's previous knowledge of the story: 'every reader is aware that, as the Fates sing their prophecy, the scene is being set for the irruption of Eris, leading inexorably to the Judgment of Paris, the Rape of Helen, and the Trojan War … The story goes back at least as far as the *Cypria*, including … the Apple of Discord. Eris <in the traditional story> makes her appearance precisely at the point where C. breaks off his account to moralize.' Thus there is an 'unstated climax' in poem 64. (See also Forehand 1974.)]

Thomas, R.F. 1983. 'Callimachus, the *Victoria Berenices*, and Roman poetry,' *CQ* 33: 92–113, esp. 112–13. *[The coverlet story is unique as an *ecphrasis*, inasmuch as the 'figures involved … come to life and speak, acting … like characters in a narrative poem.' Callimachus is a likely source for this 'experiment' in 'ecphrastic epyllion.']

Weber, C. 1983. 'Two Chronological Contradictions in C. 64,' *TAPA* 113: 263–71.

Skinner, M.B. 1984. 'Rhamnusia Virgo,' *Classical Antiquity* 3: 134–41. *[There is a discordant note in the Song; it is intended to shock: 'The ostensible nostalgia for a happier age is qualified by the grim ironies of the concluding mythic scene.' The reader was expected to know the plot of the *Cypria*, especially the account of Peleus' wedding (cf. Townend 1883).]

Hubbard, T.K. 1984. 'The Unwed Stepmother: C. 64.400–2,' *CP* 79: 137–9.

Giangrande, G. 1984. 'A Non-Existent Problem in C.,' *MPhL* 6: 45 [line 85].

Cairns, F. 1984. 'The Nereids of C. 64.12–23b,' *GB* 11: 95–101.

Watson, P.A. 1984. 'The Case of the Murderous Father: C. 64.401–2,' *LCM* 9: 114–16.

Courtney, E. 1985. 'Three Poems of C. (3),' *BICS* 32: 92–100, esp. 92–4.

Arkins, B. 1985. 'C. 64.287,' *Latomus* 44: 879–80.

Tartaglini, C. 1986. 'Arianna e Andromaca (da Hom. *Il.* 22.460–72 a Cat. 64.61–7),' *A&R* 31: 152–7.

Deroux, C. 1986a. 'Mythe et vécu dans l'épyllion des Noces de Thétis et de Pelée,' *Hommages à Jozef Veremans*, ed. F. Decreux and C. Deroux. Brussels: 65–85.

– 1986b. 'Some Remarks on the Handling of Ekphrasis in C. 64,' *SLLRH* 4. Brussels: 247–58.

Tränkle, H. 1986. 'Die Stellung der Aegeusgeschichte in C.s 64. Gedicht,' *Kontinuität und Wandel* [in honour of F. Munari]: 6–14.

Forsyth, P.Y. 1987. 'C. 64.400–2: Transposition or Emendation?,' *EMC/CV* 31: 329–32. *[Adversely criticizes Hubbard 1984.]

Boës, J. 1988. 'Le mythe d'Achille vu par C.,' *REL* 64: 104–15.

Clausen, W. 1988. 'Catulliana,' *BICS* suppl. 51, *Vir Bonus Discendi Peritus* [Festschrift for Otto Skutsch]. London: 15–17.

Blusch, J. 1989. 'Vielfalt und Einheit. Bemerkungen zur Komposition von C. c. 64,' *A.A.* 35: 116–30.

Fusaro, M. 1989. 'Lessemi e modelli compositivi nel C. 64 di C.,' *Atti Acc. Pelorit.* 65: 211–18.

Allen, A. 1989. 'C. LXIV. 287–8,' *Mn.* 42: 94–5.

Dyer, R.R. 1989. 'C. 64.401–2,' *Latomus* 48 (1989): 877–8.

O'Hara, J.J. 1990. 'Vergil's *Acidalia mater* and Venus Erycina in C. and Ovid,' *HSCP* 93: 335–42. [line 72].

Courtney, E. 1990. 'Moral Judgments in C. 64,' *GB* 17: 113–22.

Tatham, G. 1990. 'Ariadne's Mitra: A Note on C. 64.61–4,' *CQ* 40: 560–1.

Lesueur, R. 1990. 'Catulle: étude littéraire du poème LXIV,' *Vita Lat.* 120: 13–20.

Romano, D. 1990. 'C. a Nasso. Un' ipotesi sulla genesi dell' episodio di Arianna nel c. 64,' *Pan* (St. Ist. Filol. Lat.) 10: 5–12.

Hunter, R. 1991. 'Breast Is Best: C. 64.18,' *CQ* 41: 254–5.

Granarolo, J. 1991. 'C. et l'âge d'or,' *Studi di filologia classica in onore di C. Monaco.* Palermo: 687–92.

Traill, D.A. 1992. 'The Text of C. 64.24,' *CP* 87: 326–8. [Read *vos ego saepe memor.*]

Grant, J.N. 1992. 'Pietro Bembo as a Textual Critic of Classical Latin Poetry: "Variae Lectiones" and the Text of the "Culex,"' *IMU* 35: 253–303, esp. 268–71.

Laird, A. 1993. 'Sounding Out Ecphrasis: Art and Text in C. 64,' *JRS* 83: 18–30.

Kragerrud, E. 1993. 'The Spinning Parcae: On C. 64.312,' *SOsl* 68: 32–7.

Rees, R. 1994. 'Common Sense in Catullus 64,' *AJP* 115: 75.

Shackleton Bailey, D.R. 1994. *Homoeoteleuton in Latin Dactylic Verse.* Leipzig.

65

Structure: 4 + (10) + 4 + 6 (unitary, single-sentence; because of the long parenthesis on the death of C.'s brother, the main clause does not begin until line 15).

A kind of dedication, in the form of a letter, written to Hortensius Hortalus, accompanying a translation from Callimachus (poem 66) which had evidently been requested (65.17 *tua dicta*). Influenced, it may be, by the translation just completed, this poem too is written in a somewhat 'Alexandrian' manner; notice especially the typically Hellenistic simile at the end. Its structure is (considering its modest length) remarkably intricate, encapsulating a second theme within the first; we find this kind of structure, more elaborately developed and on a much larger scale, in poems 64 and 68. The poet begins by saying that he has been kept from literary creation by a lasting sorrow over the recent (line 5, *nuper*) death of his brother. Next, he gives utterance to his grief in a direct address to the brother he has lost. After ten lines (probably no more) of emotional outburst, occasioned by this thought, he returns to his primary theme by saying that he has managed to complete, and is sending to Hortalus, a translation which will show that the latter's request has not been forgotten; and the notion of 'forgetting' prompts him to add the delicately worked simile with which the poem closes. Clearly the composition has what Eduard Fraenkel called 'double orientation,' consisting as it does of an *epicedion*, addressed to one person, within a dedication to another. For this reason, and also because of the literary decoration with which it is here associated, the lament for the brother (despite the depth of feeling it conveys) makes less of an impact than the starker language of poem 101.

The address to the lost brother is so similar to that in poem 68[a], written apparently in Verona (68.27), that it is not unlikely that this poem (with poem 66) was also composed in Verona before C. went to Bithynia; a pair of early poems, then. On the identification of (Hortensius) Hortalus, see the intr. n. to poem 95.

1 *etsi me* ... 15 *sed tamen*: cf. *Ciris* 1 *etsi me* ... 9 *non tamen*. S. Mariotti (*Humanitas [Coimbra]* 3 [1950–1]: 371–3) contends that this is deliberate repetition.

See App. Crit. For the reading *defectum* cf. Ov. M. 9.154 *vires defecto reddat amori*, Val. Flacc. 7.116 *solo maeret defecta cubili*, as well as German. *Aratea* 65 *defecta labore*, and Lucilius 639 M *doloribus confectum corpus*. The R^2 variant can scarcely have been original: it offers no metrical or other advantage that might have appealed to Coluccio. Either A or X had something like *de͏fectum* (*con*); if so, then *con-* should perhaps be regarded as a suggested emendation. Against *defectum*, Kr. urges that it is used more of physical than mental affliction (contrast Cicero's *dolore conficior*, quoted by F.); less plausibly, E. suggests that the *other* sense of *defectum*, 'abandoned (by),' makes the word 'an awkward one and less likely therefore to be used <here>.'

2 *doctae virgines*, the Muses; *doctae*, 'proficient' as artists, not 'learned'; the word is transferred (B.) from poets to their patrons, the Muses.

3 *fetus*, 'offspring,' but used of any product. (Associated with *virgines*, the word
has of course practically ceased to be recognizable as a metaphor.)

4 *mens animi*, 'the thought of the mind,' is almost an Epicurean technical term
(see n. on 64.408); Lucretius uses it four times. The *animus* is, as to its matter, a
concentration (in the human breast) of soul atoms, individually identical with
those of the *anima* or life substance, which are more widely dispersed over
the body; *animus* is distinguished from mere *anima* by a capacity for thought,
emotion, etc., while *mens* appears to be thought of as *animus* in its functioning
aspect.

5 Parthenius' insertion of *in* deserves serious consideration. If *Lethaeo gurgite*
is instrumental ablative, *mei* is awkwardly separated from *fratris* by a noun
phrase depending on *manans* and *alluit* (on which it depends) in the next line;
in gurgite would of course merely say *where* the action occurs. The final *i* in
Lethaei (Mss) may also reflect *ī = in*.

On Petrarch's adherence here and elsewhere to the *X* version of the text
against that of *O*, see the Introduction, p. 27.

6 *pedem*, 'poetic' singular; in 64.104, *labello* is no more metrically obligatory than
pedem here, but C. elects it; cf. 61.9–10, 68.70.

7 On the Trojan shore, the 'Rhoetean' grave was that of Ajax, the 'Sigean' that of
Achilles (cf. 64.363). At V. *Aen.* 6.505, a cenotaph is set up for Deiphobus at
Rhoeteum; the ritual there (triple *conclamatio*, cf. *ter voce vocavi*) is the same as
that of poem 101 (*frater … frater … frater*), where see nn.

R^2's emendation is original. It is picked up by m^2, not by m; this to me implies
that it belongs to the later stratum of R^2 corrections; nor is this surprising, for
the obvious source of its invention lies in the references to Troy in 68.88–9,
where the Mss invariably testify to *Troia*, and where the context is again related
to the death of C.'s brother. Note again *m*'s preference for spelling with the
letter *y* (*Troya*). In *m*'s *retheo* the coincidence with *O* is fortuitous, and probably
due to simple carelessness; m^2 returns to the reading of *R*.

9 The Humanistic supplement *alloquar, audiero numquam … loquentem* appears
in some fifteenth-century Mss (the earliest of which, ca. 1430, is item 58 in
the Table: see Zicàri 1978: 85 n. 14), though the line is missing in *OGR*. Some
editors have accepted it as genuine, filling the gap with *tua* (or *te*) *facta* (or
fata, or *verba*); *facta* might be suggested by 9.7. The repetition *alloquar …
loquentem* is however clumsy. At the same time, to suggest, as Fr. does, that
the variation of tense in *alloquar, audiero* is beyond the capacity of Humanists,
is to underestimate them. On the supplement see E., *Commentary*[2]: 354–5
(Excursus). For the marginal variant *verba*, replacing *fata* in the supplement,
see Zicàri 1978: 84–5 (= 1958: 83). On the attribution of the supplement to
Tommaso Seneca see Mynors x–xi (footnotes).

10 *vita … amabilior*: cf. 64.215, 68.106.

12 *maesta tua ... morte*, taken together (*maesta* participially, 'saddened';
   B. compares 64.379), though F. takes *t.m.* with *canam*, as 'ablative of external
   cause.' The process of corruption from *morte canam* to *morte tegam* (*V*) would
   imply that at some stage *canam* was shortened to *cam*, and *mortetecam* became
   -tegam. For interchange of *c* and *g*, cf. Clausen 1976: 42 on poem 1, referring
   to 36.14: 'GOLGOS was corrupted to COLCOS in late antiquity'; thus E.'s
   argument against *canam*, that *c* and *g* are not confused in the tradition of
   Catullus, appears to be invalid. Because of the proximity of *morte*, it would
   hardly be possible to accept *tegam* and take it as referring to the coming simile
   of the nightingale, which sings in the shade (*Odyssey* 19.520).

14 The myth has two forms. In Homer (*Od.* 19.518–23), Aëdon, daughter of
   Pandareos (king of Crete) married Zethus, who jointly ruled Thebes with
   his brother Amphion; having no children, and being therefore jealous of
   Amphion's wife Niobe, she attempted to kill Niobe's eldest son, but by mistake
   murdered her own son *Itylus* instead. In the later version, Philomela, daughter
   of Pandion (king of Athens) had a sister Procne, who married Tereus; Tereus
   later committed rape upon Philomela, and the sisters combined to kill *Itys*, son
   of Procne and Tereus, and to serve him as a meal to his father. Then before
   Tereus could take revenge, occurred the metamorphosis into birds: Procne to
   a swallow, Philomela to a nightingale, Tereus to a hoopoe. C. uses the later
   legend, but the earlier form of the name (Itylus); the word *Daulias*, connected
   with Tereus (king of Daulis in Phocis), points to the later myth. In fact, as E.
   points out, the name of Daulis is derived from δαυλός (a dialect word for δασύς,
   'thick,' of foliage), and so can be naturally connected with the nightingale, which
   sings from deep leafy cover.

   *R*²'s correction is very close to the truth; but *m*'s carelessness in transcribing
   causes him to retain the reading of *R* (*Baiula*), whereas *al. Baulias* (*m*²) is
   perhaps the result of an attempt to copy *R*²'s *al. Dauilas* (*R*'s capital *D*'s and *B*'s
   are very similar in outline). Notice *Baiulas* (*G*², from *m*); *G*² is uncertain about
   this word, and adds to it what he takes to be *m*'s original reading.

16 *carmina*, 'verses' (not implying *several* poems). At Prop. 4.7.83, *carmina* refers
   to a two-line inscription in elegiacs; in the words spoken by Cydippe at Ov. *Ep.*
   20.235, the phrase *mea carmina* denotes a single versified epistle.
   Battiadae = Callimachus (a name he gave himself both as a patronymic and also
   because Battus was the hero-founder of his city, Cyrene).

   *R*²'s attempted correction is not followed by *m*, who in this part of the book is
   often careless in omission; *m* fails to notice the very small *b* (see App. Crit.).

17 *nequiquam*: not implying that the winds betrayed their trust, but as a
   (characteristically Catullan) parallel expression to *credita ventis*, 'in vain,
   entrusted to the winds.' Cf. 64.164, where also *nequiquam* is virtually
   superfluous; similarly, perhaps, *irrita* 64.59. Cf. also 30.9–10.

19–24 The concluding simile (based on the notion of 'forgetting'; see intr. n.) gives
   Hellenistic grace and charm to an otherwise slightly awkward letter of excuse.
20–1 *O* has a fit of carelessness, but corrects himself (twice).
21 *miserae + oblitae*: cf. perhaps 64.57 *desertam in sola miseram se cernat harena*.
23 *atque*, 'and suddenly –' (cf. V. *Ecl.* 7.7).
   decursu, spondaic, 'a sudden check' (E.), throwing the quick movement of the
   preceding dactyls into relief, as the apple comes to rest.

Kaiser, L.M. 1950. 'Waves and Color in C. 65,' *CB* 27: 2.
Van Sickle, J.B. 1968. 'About Form and Feeling in C. 65,' *TAPA* 99: 487–508.
Offermann, H. 1975. 'Der Flussvergleich bei C., c. 68, 57ff.,' *Philologus* 119: 67–9.
   [*Anhang:* on 65.1–18.]
Horn, H.-J. 1978. 'El carmen 65 de C.,' *Helmantica* 29: 377–82.
Tromaras, L.M. 1981. 'C. 65.6–12,' *Hellenica* 33: 169–74. [With summary in
   French.]
Block, E. 1984. 'Carmen 65 and the Arrangement of C.'s Poetry,' *Ramus* 13: 48–59.
Lausen, S. 1989. 'The Apple of C. 65: A Love Pledge of Callimachus,' *C&M* 40:
   161–9.
Hunter, R. 1993. 'Callimachean Echoes in C. 65,' *ZPE* 96: 179–82.

66

Structure: 14 + 24 + 40 + (10) + 6.
For an analysis of the structure see Kidd 1970: 45. Kidd's analysis is recalled
and summarized in Courtney 1985: 92–3.

This poem is a translation from Callimachus (cf. poem 116 for a reference
to others); from its position, we may say that it is almost certainly the
work which poem 65 was designed to accompany. The fact that it is a
translation implies, inter alia, that it is of only very limited value for the
criticism of Catullus as a poet; even the language (together with the poem's
structure and rhythms: see F. for examples) is often carefully adapted to
that of Callimachus. Until not so many decades ago, only a few short scraps
of the Greek original survived; but groups of complete lines, about 30 in
all, were published from papyrus discoveries, first by G. Vitelli (in 1929)
and subsequently (with substantial additions) by E. Lobel (in 1952). The
result of these discoveries was to show that the translation was as close
as could possibly be expected from a poet of strong original genius (see
Herescu 1957). Whether Catullus added lines 79–88 out of whole cloth is
debated; see Nicastri 1969/70 for a penetrating discussion which exposes
weaknesses in Pfeiffer's account. It is obvious that any work on this topic
dating from before 1929 can be ignored.

Why did Catullus choose to translate this particular poem? The key may lie in lines 21–22 ('et tu non orbum luxti deserta cubile / sed *fratris cari flebile discidium*'). It has long seemed to me that these two lines, which may or may not have had their equivalents in Callimachus' poem (but it is more likely than not that they had), could be applied to C.'s great sorrows at the time of poem 65 (ll. 5–8) and of poem 68ᵃ, if that is contemporary (as seems probable; see above). Kidd 1970: 40–2 has independently come to the conclusion that these two losses – separation from Lesbia and (especially) the brother's death – may constitute the relevance for C. of Callimachus' poem. In this connection it should be observed that at 65.12 Catullus says, addressing his brother, 'semper maesta tua carmina morte canam.' In the poem that immediately follows this declaration, lines 21–2 alone seem to fulfil it, albeit indirectly.

Of the Callimachean original, F. (intr. n. to poem 66) well remarks: 'The piece is gallant court-poetry, characteristically Alexandrian in its parade of allusion, drawn from astronomy, history, and mythology, in its compressed and selective handling of incident, in its playful and arch sentimentality, and in its interest in the psychology of love.' It could perhaps be added that whereas in the first three of these four characteristics of the genre Callimachus shows more elaboration, more artifice, than Catullus, in the last of them, namely psychology, Catullus seems far to surpass Callimachus in terms of vividness and force (see Luppino 1958); not surprisingly, since for him (as in poem 63, for example; see the introductory note to that poem) psychology often occupies the very centre of the stage, relegating myth, as such, to the wings.

Historical note (see the genealogical stemma in F., intr. n., p. 329): Ptolemy I (a Macedonian; one of the leading *Diadochoi*) took the title of king of Egypt in 305 BC, and reigned until his death in 283. He and his third wife Berenice (also Macedonian born) were deified as θεοὶ σωτῆρες; hence the name *Soter*, by which the first Ptolemy is generally known. His successor, Ptolemy II, was married twice, each time to a person named Arsinoe; of these the second was the stepmother of the first. Arsinoe I was a daughter of Lysimachus, king of Macedon, by his first wife; Arsinoe II, Ptolemy's sister, initially went to Macedon as the second wife of Lysimachus; but after his death in 281 she returned to Egypt. Having become the most influential person in the land, she fabricated an accusation against the reigning queen, Arsinoe I, and so brought about the latter's disgrace and exile. Next, she took advantage of the Egyptian tradition of the marriage and joint rule of brothers and sisters to persuade Ptolemy to make her his queen. By this time she was at least forty years old, and there were no children of the marriage. She took the name of Arsinoe Philadelphus; the joint rulers were deified as θεοὶ φιλάδελφοι, whence this Ptolemy came to be known as *Philadelphus*. Arsinoe II was further deified under the name of Aphrodite Zephyritis (lines 54–8, where see nn.).

Ptolemy III, later known as Euergetes, was a son of Ptolemy Philadelphus by Arsinoe I, but was adopted by Arsinoe II, and so always referred to himself as a 'son' of the θεοὶ φιλάδελφοι. In 247 his father adopted him as joint ruler, and his reign was calculated from that date, not from his father's death in 245. He had a sister named Berenice ('Berenice C' in Fordyce), who in 251 was married to Antiochus II, king of Syria. The 'Berenice' of our poem, however, is another person; to place her we must turn for a moment from Egypt to Cyrene, where Ptolemy I had installed as governor a certain Magas, son of his queen Berenice by her former husband and hence half-brother to Ptolemy II. Magas, however, made Cyrene practically independent of Egypt; his rule there, first as a satrap of Egypt and later as king, lasted from 308 to 258. In his old age he had a daughter named Berenice (Berenice II, or 'B' in Fordyce); he betrothed her to the son of Ptolemy II, as a natural and easy way of reuniting Cyrene with Egypt after his death. But his plans for this marriage were frustrated by his widow Apama, a Seleucid princess, who sought a husband for her daughter not in Egypt but in Macedon (hoping no doubt for a son-in-law who would after all keep Cyrene independent). The prince who turned up was known as Demetrius 'the Fair' (ὁ καλός). Apama herself succumbed to his charms and, having duly married him to her daughter (who was still very young), she took him as a lover. Berenice then reacted with unexpected firmness: she broke in on her husband and her mother and had Demetrius killed on the spot (the *bonum facinus* of line 27). This was regarded as a heroic exploit on the part of a girl defending her outraged virtue, and it opened the way for her marriage with Ptolemy (III), which took place shortly after he was given the title of king. Ptolemy and Berenice were half-cousins: they had one grandmother in common, Berenice I ('A' in Fordyce), who was the mother of Magas by one husband (a Macedonian named Philip) and of Ptolemy by another. Since they had a blood relationship, and since the former king and queen had been brother and sister, it was easy to call them also 'brother and sister,' and the Canopic decree in fact calls Berenice the ἀδελφή of Ptolemy. Hence the word *fratris* (line 22); it can of course mean 'cousin', but in view of these facts it may just as well be translated 'brother.' Hyginus confuses the two Berenices: see 45–64 n.

The marriage of Ptolemy III's true sister Berenice ('Berenice C' in Fordyce) to Antiochus of Syria (see above) had been made possible by the exile of Antiochus' first wife Laodice, who was given in consolation a part of Asia

Minor to rule over, in partnership with her two sons. But when Antiochus died in 246 she was not satisfied with this. In order to establish the succession of her own eldest son, she sent agents to Antioch with orders to murder Berenice and her infant son. The murder of a daughter and a grandson of Ptolemy II was regarded in Egypt as an act of intolerable provocation. Leaving his bride, the newly wedded Ptolemy at once set out on a punitive expedition to Syria. The young bride, Berenice II, dedicated – so ran the legend – a lock or tress of her hair in the temple of Aphrodite Zephyritis (= Arsinoe II: see above), so making a vow to ensure her husband's safe return. Presently, however, it was reported that the lock of hair had disappeared from the temple; whereupon the court astronomer Conon promptly and tactfully discovered it in the sky, and gave the name Βερενίκης Πλόκαμος to a group of seven stars, located between Leo and Boötes. And Callimachus, as court poet, sanctified the discovery with a poem, the *Coma Berenices*. (A statement in the *Suda* that the reign of Ptolemy III dated from 271 for a time caused scholarship to attempt to date the setting of the *Coma* too early; but papyri have established the fact that a joint reign began in 266 and ended in 258. Since there was a gap of eleven years after this before Ptolemy III was associated with his father as joint ruler, it is clear that the first joint ruler was not this Ptolemy but an elder brother who died in youth.) *

1 The first line of Callimachus' poem (Fr. 110.1 Pf. Πάντα τὸν ἐν γραμμαῖσιν ἰδὼν ὅρον ᾗ τε φέρονται) is not complete in sense (it is quite likely that the first word in the second line was ἀστέρες), and it is more complicated than the first line in the version by Catullus. The general meaning is that Conon had plotted the movements of all the celestial bodies on a series of star charts. Barrett 1982 defines γραμμαῖσι as 'lines used in diagrammatic representations of the constellations, in which stars of major magnitude are joined by straight lines,' citing the scholium on Aratus 190; he therefore seeks to defend the Ms reading *despexit*, in the sense 'looked down at' (on the charts, instead of looking up at the sky); but it is hard to believe that C.'s readers would easily take the point.

2 *obitus*, 'setting,' is first found as a term of astronomy in Cicero's *Aratea*, which C. knew and used (see n. on 64.125). Notice the corruption to *abitus* (a more familiar word) and then to *habitus*.

3 Conon had a special interest in eclipses (Sen. *Nat.* 7.3.3).

* This historical note began as an abridged and to some extent updated version of a much longer note put together by L., originally on the basis of data given in E. Beavan's *History of Egypt under the Ptolemaic Dynasty*. For a fuller account see Marinone 1984: 13–27.

4 *cedant*, 'move on' (through fixed phases). In the context of line 63, *cedentem* translates ἀνίοντα (see n.). On these technical terms, see Traglia 1955 and Marinone 1980.

5 None of the three variant readings attested by R^2 makes sense; none, therefore, is the result of attempted emendation.
Latmia: the cave where the moon (*Trivia* = Diana) visited her lover Endymion was on Mount Latmus (in Caria).
relegans, 'banishing' (F.). The myth explains the moon's occultations.
R^2's variant is interesting. The reading of Ms *A*, perhaps *sublam^{n}ia*, has been corrected by *X*, who adds a superscript *i*, thus: *sublam^{l}^{n}ia* (perhaps trying at the same time to erase the *n*, but not completely succeeding; hence *GR sublimia* and also the variant in R^2). See also p. 40

6 *gyro* = 'orbit.' Notice *guioclero* (*V*); *guio* = *guro* (*gyro*), while *clero* is surely not, as Fröhlich suggested, a corruption of *circo* (a gloss on *gyro*), but more simply (E.) a duplication of *devo-* in *devocet* (*cl* and *d* are endlessly confused).
aerio (Mss): the spelling should be kept. Aristotle (see Kr.) locates in the orbit of the moon the boundary between ἀήρ and αἰθήρ; thus *aetherio* would be no more appropriate.

7–10 The scholium on Aratus which gives us Callimachus' text is quoted in a distorted version by older editors (E., Fr., Kr.), who wrongly supposed therefore that it was made up of parts of three lines. C.'s translation is in fact quite close, though longer than the Greek. It is just possible that Vossius' <in>, brought in to account for the *n* in *V*'s *numine*, is unnecessary: cf. 59 *in numine V*. If so, *fulgentem clare* will be heralded by *lumine* two lines before (but the syntax becomes more congested). B.'s *in limine* is recommended by F. (who however turns down *limine* at l. 59, because the Greek there seems to read φάεσιν, 'lights').

9 See App. Crit. Haupt's *cunctis* is defended by Courtney 1985: 92, on the strength of verbal echoes, within a balanced structure, of lines 9–10 in 33–4, taking account of Callimachus' πᾶσιν ἔθηκε θεοῖς See however Marinone 1984: 118. (He regards Haupt's emendation as a *soluzione semplicistica*.) Lee, in his edition, accepts and prints *cunctis*.

9–10 *multis ... dearum ... pollicita est* translates πᾶσιν ἔθηκε θεοῖς. This Greek phrase cannot imply a 'pantheon' (Kr.), since there is no trace of a pantheon at Alexandria before 205 BC (Pfeiffer). C. uses the feminine; from 54–8 it is clear that the deified Arsinoe, known as Aphrodite Zephyritis, was a likely target of the lock's homage, though C. does not limit the dedication to her alone.

11 *novo auctus hymenaeo*: use of a Greek word permits the Latin poet to exercise Greek metrical freedom (lengthening, or strong caesura, in the fifth foot, as well as hiatus) in its vicinity: cf. V. *Ecl.* 6.53, *Geo.* 4.137, *Aen.* 11.69; see 62.4 n. Hiatus in the fifth foot is also allowed before a Greek word, e.g., at V. *Geo.* 1.2.81, *Aen.* 3.74.

12 *iverat*: the first vowel in *ierat* would be short, even if Mss of Terence (and Plautus, *Amph.* 401) give *īerat* and so on.
   Assyrios, vaguely, for *Syrios* (cf. F. on 68.144); see the Historical Note. Kr. points to a similar example of geographical vagueness at 64.324 (*Emathia* = Thessaly, instead of Macedonia).

13 *rixa*: cf. Prop. 2.15.4. The phrase *n. rixa* probably translates ἐννυχία ἀεθλοσύνη in Callimachus (echoed in *AP* 5.293.18, Agath.; see Marinone 1984: 127).

15 The substitution of *anne* for *atque* (*V*) is called for by the sense. Of the two parts of a single question, linked by *V*'s *atque*, one would require an affirmative, the other – the second – a negative answer. But with *anne* the question becomes an alternative: do brides dislike the idea of marriage (*Venus*), or are the tears they shed (dismaying their parents, l. 16) only feigned, not real? For they do shed them (cf. 61.80–2), and in fact they *are* feigned (l. 18).

17 *thalami*: if the reading *parentum* is kept, as it should be, *thalami* will refer to the bride's parental home: cf. 61.76–106, which contain the notion of 'reluctant' weeping (see previous n.) and are certainly supposed to be uttered at the house the bride is leaving. Nisbet 1978: 105 claims that 'after *novis nuptis* the *thalamus* can refer only to marriage' (meaning, presumably, the bride's new home); but cf. once more 61.76–106, with its refrain *prodeas, nova nupta*.

18 The hyperbaton in this line is an extreme instance of a poetic mannerism both Greek and Latin; see F.'s long note. Other examples of hyperbaton in C. include 44.9, 57.8, 64.101; see also 1.9 n.
   iuerint (= *iuverint*): as with *ierint* (= *iverint*), when the intervocalic *u/v* is omitted the preceding vowel (in this case, *u*) is shortened by the influence of the vowel that now immediately follows; cf. Prop. 2.23.22 (Fr. gives several well-attested instances of this form, taken from Cicero's letters).

19–20 'I came to understand this fact (that brides' tears are feigned, l. 18, and Venus not disliked by them, l. 15) through the deep distress that Berenice showed when her new husband went off to war.'

21 *fratris*: see Historical Note. Cf. (Fr.) Cicero, *Phil.* 2.99 *uxori et sorori tuae*, of Antony's wife, who was also his cousin; and Ov. *Ep.* 8.27–8:

   quid quod avus nobis idem Pelopeius Atreus,
   et si non esses vir mihi, frater eras.

   But F. may well be right in suggesting that 'the reference is to the formal honorific style which described the Egyptian king's consort as his sister.'
   Note *R*²'s attempted correction, disguised as a variant.

23 See App. Crit. B.'s *ut*, which he defends on the rather pedantic grounds that the anguish was not felt *only* at the moment of departure, is adopted by Kr. because, as he puts it, 'die Erinnerung an den schweren Abschied ist so lebendig, daß nur Ausrufe den Eindruck wiedergeben können.' *V*'s *cum* need not be disturbed; it goes well with the preceding lines.

24 The phrase *toto pectore* must surely be taken with the words *tibi … sollicitae*, which enclose it. F., believing that it might just as easily be taken with *mens excidit*, cites 68.25 (but notice *de* there). Translate 'to you in your all-pervading anxiety.'

    The R^2m^2 variant (= *O*) may point to an emendatory suggestion in *X*. McKie: 281 n. implies or states (i) that *A*, like *O*, wrote *tunc*; (ii) that *X* first wrote *nunc*, in error, but added a correcting variant, *al. tunc*, which has made its way into R^2. Cf. 44.21 (*tunc R, nunc G*, corr. G^1; therefore *tunc A*); here McKie gives a different account, apparently involving *tum*, which I find some difficulty in accepting.

25 <*te*> is the only possible supplement; it has in its favour (i) palaeography ('double haplography'), (ii) the need of an object for *cognoram*, (iii) the frequently occurring sequence *at certe* (10.14, 65.11).

26 Here *magnanimam* plainly translates μεγάθυμον, as Pfeiffer suggests; cf. n. on 64.85. It is possible that in this line the intended reference is not to the *bonum facinus* but to an earlier episode (Hyg. *Astr.* 2.24), when as a young girl she turned the battle for her father; thus (*pace* F.) *two* instances of her courage are given. See Marinone 1984: 144–5 and 23 n. 29.

28 See App. Crit. Pietro da Noceto (b. 1469) preceded Robortellus as a teacher of Greek and Latin at Lucca (Marinone 1984: 147).

    alis (archaic) = *alius*; cf. 29.15 *alid* (and Lucretius similarly, in a number of passages). Translate 'which no one else, *even* one stronger than you were then, would dare to do'; this appears to support 26 *a parva virgine magnanimam*, but see 26 n. Emendation to *fortius* is unnecessary, and would flatten the expression. For this kind of idiom see Fr. on 4.18 *impotentia* (= 'wild at *other* times').

29 That is, you were brave enough to perform the *bonum facinus* (27), but broke down and wept when your husband went to fight.

30 For Avantius' suggestion, *tersti*, which has a good deal of merit, cf. perhaps 99.8 *abstersti*.

31 *quis deus*: the regular form (cf. 61.46 n.). Translate 'What god <was> so potent as to change you <in this way>?' The use by C. of the *quis-tantus* idiom, the validity of which F. supports here by examples taken from the *Aeneid*, is not brought out by his translation 'who was the great god who changed you?'

    Cf. Prop. 1.12.9–10, where La Penna 1955 sees the influence of the Callimachean couplet underlying C. here.

33 *cunctis divis*: see lines 9–10 n.

34 *Iliad* 23.146–7 seem to show that the bull's sacrifice was part of what was vowed, rather than an accompaniment of the vow itself.

35 R^2's correction is fairly obvious; m^1 picks it up. *redd-* is due to carelessness; the coincidence with *O* is, once more, accidental.

    For the idiom *reditum ferre* cf. 63.47, 63, 79; for the form *tetuli* cf. also 63.52.

36 *Asiam*: probably in a wide sense, including not merely Asia Minor but Syria.
(Since the word *Asia* does not occur in the works or fragments of Callimachus,
we clearly cannot know what he meant by it.) The inscription (*OGIS* 54), referred
to by F. and quoted by E., mentions 'Asia,' and also Cilicia and Pamphylia; the
eastern victories of Ptolemy's campaign were historically the most significant,
though of course he did not literally 'add them to the boundaries of Egypt' itself
(l. 36). Notice the tense of *addiderat*, suggesting rapid and final conquest.

37 *m*'s preferred spelling (diphthongs *cae-*, *coe-*) is twice imitated by G^2.

38 *novo munere* = 'new function' (i.e., as a constellation); the *pristina vota* had to
do with the Lock's dedication in a temple, not with its catasterism, which came
later.

39 Cf. the famous adaptation in V. *Aen.* 6.460 *invitus, regina, tuo de litore cessi.*
The repetition of *invita* stresses the pain (and cruelty) of separation, which
dominates the *emotional* content of C.'s poem, especially in the following
section. See the intr. n., referring to l. 22, and observe there the strong word
discidium; cf. also 51–2.

40 The Greek is close: σήν τε κάρην ὤμοσα σόν τε βίον. Cf. V. *Aen.* 4.492–3 *testor
... te ... tuumque ... caput.*

41 *quod* refers to *caput*. Read the words in the order *quod si quis inaniter adiurarit,
digna ferat* ('let him reap a just reward').

43 The story of the canal dug by Xerxes is cited as an outstanding demonstration
of the power of iron tools, but the rhetoric with which C. presents it is highly
exaggerated: *maximum in oris* is not true, even if (i) *progenies Thiae* means
the north wind (cf. next n.), and (ii) *oris* refers only to the northern districts
of Greece; see F. on 45–6 (and to his n. on 43 add V. *Aen.* 7.563–4 *locus
multis memoratus in oris*). Again, *eversus* (of Mount Athos itself) is a great
overstatement (repeated as admittedly hyperbolic by Ovid, *M.* 11.554–5).
Cf. V. *Aen.* 1.43 *disiecitque rates evertitque aequora ventis* (of winds furrowing
the sea), Val. Flacc. 7.75 *everso campo* (of ploughing). The canal merely cut
through the narrow isthmus joining the peninsula of Athos to the mainland. In
a court poem, of course, gross exaggeration is allowed in the – direct or indirect
– service of compliment.

44 The papyrus is interpreted by Pfeiffer as reading ἀμνά]μω[ν Θείης ἀργὸς
ὑ]περφέ[ρ]ετ[αι, where clearly ὑπερφέρεται = C.'s *supervehitur*. Bentley, who
followed Vossius in reading *Thiae*, took this name to indicate the Sun (whose
mother was Θεία, according to Hesiod and Pindar). Cf. V. *Aen.* 7.217–18 *quae
maxima quondam extremo veniens Sol aspiciebat Olympo*, where *quae maxima*
may suggest a reminiscence of C.; if this is so, Virgil interpreted C. as Vossius
was later to do. Pfeiffer, however, doubted that the Sun could be represented
as 'carried over' a mountain north of Greece and far from Egypt. He pointed
to the gloss Θείας ἀμνάμων (= 'grandson' or 'descendant') in the *Suda*, quoted

from Callimachus, *Hecale*, with reference to the north wind (Boreas); Boreas was the son of Aurora and the grandson of Thia and Hyperion. Accordingly, he reconstructed the line as it is given above. For *clarus*, '<sky->clearing,' as epithet of Boreas, cf. V. *Geo.* 1.460 *claro ... Aquilone* (cf. *Iliad* 19.358 αἰθρηγενέος Βορέαο). For identification of a person by metronymic, cf. 64.324 *Opis nato*, where Latin *Ops* = Greek *Rhea*. Against Pfeiffer's interpretation stand (i) V. *Aen.* 7.217 (quoted above as appearing to support Vossius and Bentley), (ii) the rather difficult notion of a wind 'carried over' a mountain; see however lines 53–4, which refer to a wind (Zephyrus) as a 'winged horse.'

45–64 The Greek runs:

Βουπόρος (= ὁ ὀβελίσκος, schol. *P. Oxy* 2258) Ἀρσινόης μητρὸς σέο, καὶ διὰ μέ[σσου

Μηδείων ὀλοαὶ νῆες ἔβησαν Ἄθω.

Callimachus here extravagantly calls Mount Athos 'Arsinoe's obelisk' or 'spit' (βουπόρος) – cf. 'Cleopatra's needle' in London – possibly with reference to Arsinoe's Macedonian connections; C., however, omits this fantasy. Kidd 1970: 42, after Lenchantin, prefers to ignore the scholiast and to emend βουπόρος to βούπορος, translating 'great passage' ('Bosporus'). On μητρὸς σέο, it may be added that the scholiast remarks: '"mother" is said κατὰ τιμήν, since she was the daughter of Apama and Magas,' correctly, which dismisses – and perhaps explains? – Hyginus' error (*Astr.* 2.24) about her parentage. See G.L. Huxley, *JHS* 100 (1980): 189–90 on βουπόρος.

45 *peperere* is both poetically and palaeographically the best of the emendations hitherto proposed for *V's propere*.

R²'s *al. cumque* (= O) is essentially a metrical 'variant' (really a correction); it is not adopted by G², who is already in haste (see 64.319 n.) and will presently (67 n.) cease to add variants and corrections, except for a very few isolated instances. It is not necessary to suppose that X introduced for the first time the reading *al. cumque*, though McKie: 204–6 believes that he did. Cf. p. 40.

48 Politianus, who proposed *Chalybum*, spelt it thus (with his own hand) in the margin of Bibl.Corsin. Inc. 50. F. 37. His later adoption of the Greek spelling (*Misc.* 1.68; cf. A. Guarinus, fol. 87ʳ, and see Zicàri 1978: 37 n. 14) may have been due to a desire to avoid hiatus; but cf. the nn. on 67.44 and 99.8. (All the Mss here offer readings that end in -*um*). For hiatus after *m*, and also elision, at the diaeresis of the pentameter, cf. 67.44, and possibly 97.2; and see M. Zicàri, *Phoenix* 18 (1964): 193–205 (= *Scritti*, 1978: 203–19). It may be that C. would in any case have avoided using a wholly Greek proper-name form, ending in -*on*, almost immediately after the intensely Roman *Iuppiter*. Initially I proposed to read *Chalybum* in the present edition; but in the end I have with much hesitation decided on *Chalybon*, on purely subjective grounds of euphony. Zicàri (art. cit., 1964, n. 19) points to 'the crudity of the morphological Grecism, extremely rare

outside of book-titles, and in C.'s own period supported only by Varro, *Men.*
101 Büch.: *Arcadon.'*

To the reading in R (*celitum*), R^2 made two corrections: (i) *celorum* (cf. *O*'s
celerum), (ii) *celtum*, which is an attempted correction, essentially metrical in
nature, based on *celitum = caelitum*. The most likely reading in X seems to be
celitum, s. s. al. celerum (did X, or A, emend to *celitum* for the meaning's sake?);
R^2 will thus have noticed *celerum* in X but changed it to *celorum* (= *caelorum*)
for the sake of metre, adding the further correction *celtum* (at a relatively late
stage, if we may judge from the sequence R^2m^2).

50 The emendation *stringere* is supported by -s at the end of *ferris* in V.

51 *abiunctae*, 'cut off' (genitive sing., agreeing with the genitive concealed in *mea*;
this is proved by the Greek, which has ν]εότμητόν με). Cf. line 22 *fratris ...
discidium*, and see 39 n.

52–3 The reference is to Zephyr, half-brother of Memnon as a son of Aurora; the
Greek has Μέμνονος Αἰθίοπος ... θῆλυς ἀήτης.

53 Bentley's suggestion *nictantibus* ('flashing' or 'winking') has been revived by
Martyn 1974; he considers that it translates κυκλώσας in Callimachus, *Aetia*
fr. 110.51–3. Bentley's parallels, which he quotes, are Lucr. 6.836 *nictare
insistereque alis* (*nixari* Lachmann, rightly) and V. *Aen.* 4.252 *nitens ...
alis*. B. notes: '*pennis nutantibus sive trepidantibus*: Apul. *Met.* 6.15 *libratis
pinnarum nutantium motibus*, Cicero *Arat.* 88 *tremebundis pinnis*, Ovid M.
1.506 *penna trepidante.'* Palaeographically, the change is not particularly likely;
more important, the word in fact means 'winking' and does not seem fully
transferable to the supposed meaning; further, the verb *nitens* quoted by Martyn
from *Aen.* 4.252 (see above) is surely less than relevant, an objection that applies
also to *nixari* in Lucr. 6.836 as emended by Lachmann.

54 *arsinoes*: the R^2 variant (= O) may well have originated in X.
Locridos: Bentley's conjecture is supported by P. *Oxy.* 2258 (see F.; also notice
that the schol. in the papyrus seems to contain the word Λοκρίς). But the other
papyrus, *PSI* 1092, reads Λοκρικός, and when it was published in 1929 Statius'
Locricos was for a time preferred; Kr.'s ed.² reveals hurried substitution of -*cos*
in the plates. V's *elocridicos* seems to show traces of an alternative reading,
though its explanation remains obscure; but in any case it ends in -*os*, which
must be taken to support *Locridos*, since C. would surely have written *Locricus*,
not -*cos*, in the nominative case. See the arguments for Λοκρικός in Callimachus
given by Hansen and Tortzen 1973: 46. On Zephyr as Λοκρός (Eustathius, p.
223 Müller), and the explanation thereby furnished for the phrase 'Arsinoe the
Locrian' (because of her temple at Zephyrium), see Forsyth 1972. Marinone 1989
argues strongly against Bentley's reading.
ales: V has *alis*, which might seem to support Statius' emendation *alisequus*
(on the model of *pedisequus*); this was defended by Housman 1929 before the
papyrus unmistakably revealed the word ἵππο[ς]. Thus Zephyrus, a wind, is

certainly Arsinoe's 'winged horse'; and Zephyrus flies in the service of Aphrodite Zephyritis. S. West, *CQ* 35 (1985): 63 n. 13 would restore ἱππότ', 'rider.'

55 *m*'s *is quia* is careless and unmetrical; it is corrected by *m*², yet *G*² feels obliged to restore *m*'s mistaken original reading as a variant – unreflectively because in haste? Cf. 64.319 n.

56 *advolat* (*GR* = *X*) is clearly a mistake derived from *X*'s other mistake *advolat* (for *avolat*) just above; *O* has the right reading in line 55, and also in 56 (where *X* added a variant). *X* must surely have thereafter introduced *collocat*, as a variant, from *A*, to mend the metre; he could hardly have guessed *independently* at the very word which we find in *O* (McKie: 205 and 207).

58 Since in the Greek (. . . Κανωπίτου ναιέτις α[ἰγιαλοῦ) the first word is missing, the unmetrical *gracia/gratia* has been variously emended. B., followed by F., insists on *Graiia* (= *Graia*); but in this form it would surely have to be scanned *Graīiă*, which again does not fit. The Greek cannot be filled out by Γραῖα (Vitelli 1929) or Φθία (Pfeiffer 1932), because the final *a* in adjectives of this kind is long. Consequently, Pfeiffer afterwards (in his edition of Callimachus) suggested that ἧκε (see 57 n.) may have stood there (and not in 57). In any case the juxtaposition of *Graia* ('Greek' from the Egyptian point of view; in fact, Arsinoe was Macedonian) with *Canopeis* gives an attractive antithesis; *grata*, in comparison, seems flat, as even its defenders (e.g., Mariotti 1972: 59) admit. *Canopeis* is the true Latin form; *Canopitis*, as neuter abl. plural, would point to a non-existent nominative, and offers little if any palaeographical advantage (though Mariotti defends it). C. had no need to adhere letter by letter to the Greek form of a name: cf. 44 *Thiae* = Θείας, and perhaps also 48 n. (on *Chalybum*). The sequence may be this: *canopeis*[?] *V*; erroneously *canopicis* (*c* for *e*) *A*; hence *canopicis GR*(*X*), *conopicis* (another mistake) *O*. The regular Latin form (which appears in my text) is, as already stated, *Canopeis*; and it is not far from the presumed *V* reading.

59 This line, in *V*, is quite corrupt. Any restoration should seek to preserve *vario*, which both yields good sense and is to some extent called for, as an adjective, to balance *lumine*. The argument for Fr.'s *hic liquidi* was well explained by G.P. Goold, *Phoenix* 12 (1958): 93–116 (in a review of Mynors' *OCT*); its weakness (which is also that of Lafaye's *hic dii*, deriving *ven ibi* from a gloss *vel divi*) is that the line seems overburdened with its two adjectives. The reading *lumine* derives support from the Greek, restored as φάεσ]ιν ἐν πολέεσσιν. F.'s translation 'shifting lights,' for *vario lumine*, seems unhappy.

60 Ariadne's garland = the Corona Borealis; *corona* goes with *ex A. t.* On the legend, see Ovid, *Fasti* 3.459ff., M. 8.178.

61 Clearly, the true reading (*nos*) was in *X*, and probably in *A*. *O*, who is erratic throughout this passage (see l. 58), is to be discounted as a witness to the archetype here.

62 C.'s conceit is his own elaboration (cf. Callim.'s simple Βερενίκειος καλὸς ἐγὼ
πλόκαμος), and – as Marinone 1984: 218 remarks – it lingers over the parallel
with Ariadne.

63 *uvidulam* is preferable to *umidulam*, as meaning 'drenched' (with 'pathetic'
diminutive) by sea-spray; *umid-* is merely 'slightly damp'; and the Greek has
ὕδασι] λουόμενον. Stars were pictured as rising from, and setting in, the ocean:
cf. B. on 67–8. Pfeiffer, defending ὕδασι against δακρύσι, for which, as he says,
there is not enough room in the papyrus, quotes Nonnus (of a star's rising):
ὕδασι λουόμενος. Cf. perhaps Matthew Arnold, *Sohrab and Rustum*, sub fin.:
'[waters] ... from whose floor the new-bathed stars / Emerge ...' The *Coma* is
imagined as first rising from Ocean to its destined place in the sky. For *cedere*
= 'rise towards a height,' cf. Cicero, *Arat.* 475, where the Greek text of Aratus
(694) has ἀνελίσσεται, and see Traglia 1955: 436.

 R^2's *virid-* is an instance of a fairly common phenomenon, namely an
unsuccessful attempt on his part (followed as usual by *m*, and hence by G^2) to
correct a nonsensical word in *R*.

 uvidulam should surely be credited to B. Guarinus, whose son (in 1521) reads
-*um* in the text but annotates thus: *uvidulam] sic legendum, non uvidulum,
pater existimat, cum ubique de caesarie non de crine loquatur.*

65 For the postponed *namque* see 23.7 n.

66 Callisto, daughter of Lycaon, was a huntress and a follower of Artemis. She had
an amorous entanglement with Zeus, in punishment for which Hera changed
her into a bear, with the not entirely fortuitous result that she was shot – and
killed – by the goddess. Zeus, however, metamorphosed her into the celestial
'Great Bear' (Ov. *M.* 2.409ff., *Fasti* 2.155ff.; Apollod. 3.8.2). (L.)
iuxta (*V*) is unlikely to have been altered in quantity to *iuxtă* by C.; but if we
accept the correction *iuncta* we must also accept *Callisto* as dative (= Καλλίστῳ),
and not only are there no parallels to this form but Serv. *ad Aen.* 7.324 says
of *Allecto* that 'we use only three cases in this declension, namely genitive
Allectus, nominative and accusative *Allecto*.' It is true, on the other hand, that
the 'rule' just quoted is twice broken by Hyginus (*Fab.* 14 and 224: genitives
in -*o*), and Fr. quotes dative *Erato* from *CIL* IX 747; this type of Greek name
seems to have 'embarrassed' Roman writers, as Fr. remarks. In laying down this
'rule' about *names*, Servius may have forgotten an isolated instance; this seems
more likely than violation by C. of the regular vowel-quantity in an everyday
preposition.

67 B.'s desire to remove the comma after *occasum* hardly takes proper account
of *Odyssey* 5.272 ὀψὲ δύοντα Βοώτην (cf. Germ. *Arat.* 139 *tardus in occasum
sequitur sua plaustra Bootes*), though he mentions it. The phrase *vix sero* is a
Graecism, μόλις ὀψὲ (B.). Heliacal rising and setting are referred to. Notice how
the rhythm of the first part of l. 68 suggests slowness.

G^2, seeing that m's *boethem* (due to carelessness) is without any meaning, corrects on the basis of G, so that his version (*boothem*) is a compromise between G and m. It is not necessary to suppose that he ever saw R (here or elsewhere).

After this point, G^2 abandons variants, and has very few corrections indeed: only those at 67.46 (and possibly l. 44 also); 68.86; 101.1; and lastly 103.3, which, though given in the form of a correction, essentially reproduces the m^2 variant *al. numi*. McKie's observation (p. 124) that the variants in G^2 'stop after poem 66' is perhaps not sufficiently exact; they had in any case been 'thinning out' before (see l. 45 n.).

69–70 *me nocte* ... As F. explains, she is in the sky, the floor of heaven, by nights, and at dawn returns to 'Ocean.' (Tethys was Ocean's wife.)

70 *Tethyi*: the papyrus has ιτη, possibly preceded by ιη (as suggested by Lobel); hence πολιῇ (-ηι) Τηθύι may have been written by Callimachus in the same relative position in the line as is occupied by C.'s *canae Tethyi*, an exact translation.

71 *pace*, and 74 *quin*, are both corrections (original) by R^2; but *quin* (picked up by m^2, and so probably belonging to the later stratum of R^2's work) is, it could fairly be said, less obvious than *pace*, which is found already in m.
Rhamnusia virgo = Nemesis. Cf. 50.18–21.

72 *non ullo* ... *timore*. The Greek has οὔτ]ις ἐρύξει / βοῦς ἔπος. The last two words, βοῦς ἔπος, given by the scholiast probably from the opening of the pentameter, must have had something to do with the proverb βοῦς ἐπὶ γλώττης, indicating total (prudent) silence, though the point here is that the truth will not be concealed under any threats whatever.

74 See App. Crit. *vere* might perhaps be kept (there are eight instances of this adverb in the text of *V*); but Watt, repeating the arguments of Nisbet 1978: 105, rejects both *vere* and *veri*, though for Nisbet's *imi*, accepted by Goold, he substitutes (in my opinion, rightly) *nostri* (*nr̄i*) as palaeographically preferable. He gives a parallel for the corruption, and justifies *nostri* = *mei* by other instances from Catullus himself.

75 Marinone 1984 comments on the pathetic effect of the epanalepsis (with chiasmus) *me afore* ... *afore me*, intensified by *semper*, the effect of which is emphasized by its position at the end of the line.

77 Against the conjecture *Hymenis* see B. Rehm, *RhM* 90 (1941): 346–51.

77–8 'In company with which (i.e., *vertice*, 'her head'), while she was a girl, in time past, I drank many simple [unmixed] oils (*vilia* = λιτά), not [yet] enjoying any unguents [such as are used by married women].' Two alternative punctuations are possible: with, or without, a comma after *fuit*. The Greek, which runs thus

> ... κορυφῆς ...
>
> ἧς ἄπο, παρ[θ]ενίη μὲν ὅτ᾽ ἦν ἔτι, πολλὰ πέπωκα
> λιτά, γυναικείων δ᾽ οὐκ ἀπέλαυσα μύρων

on the whole suggests keeping the comma in C. (notice the rhythmical parallel between the two hexameters in Greek and Latin: $- \smile \smile \mid - \overset{\smile}{\smile} \mid - \overset{\smile}{\smile} \mid - \smile \smile \mid - \smile \smile \mid - \overset{\smile}{\;}$, where παρθενίη … ἔτι and *dum* … *fuit* occupy the same positions in the line). On the same grounds, I now find, Clausen 1970: 87 defends the comma. Unless we accept Morel's *nuptae* for *una* (an unlikely corruption and perhaps, with *unguenta*, an unlikely phrase; but see the elaborate article, Marinone 1982, which ends by recommending it), we must suppose (what comparison with Callimachus suggests) that *unguenta* by itself is meant by C. to indicate perfumed unguents, suited to married women, as opposed to the *vilia* of girlhood (see Callim. *H.* 5.15–16, 25, quoted by F.); the alternative is to suspect, with Pfeiffer, that *omnibus* conceals an adjective expressing the content of γυναικείων and meaning 'suited to the married state.' For a modern argument against the reading *vilia* see Kidd 1970: 44–5; for it, Nicastri 1969/70: 25. The rhythm of the line, imitated from Callimachus (see above), with its heavy pause after *fuit*, may suggest that *expers* should be taken closely with *ego*, rather than with *virgo*. Were it not that Callimachus distinguishes between the λιτά, used when Berenice was a girl, and the 'womanly perfumes' of the pentameter, we should be tempted to translate *omnibus expers unguentis* by 'who *am now* deprived of all unguents [whatsoever],' and if we regard C. as a free translator we may still do so. Much depends on whether the Callimachean μέν … δέ must be taken to have been imitated; I am inclined to think that C. considered it unimportant, and dropped it.

77–83 Berenice was famous for her enthusiastic encouragement (σπουδή is Athenaeus' word) of the manufacture of perfumes in Alexandria; see F. on 77f. This gives additional 'courtly' value to these lines, so far as they existed in Callimachus (on which question, see the next n.).

79–88 The lines are wholly absent from the text of Callimachus as we have it. Either C. used a different text from ours, or he imported ten original lines into what was otherwise at least a fairly close translation. There are two main reasons for supposing Callimachus to have written them: (i) as the rest of the poem is a translation, and its theme is very far removed from C.'s usual topics, it would be puzzling if he were to have originated these ten lines, and only these (for an attempt to deal with this difficulty, see Horváth 1962: 351–6); (ii) the passage seems to continue the 'promotion' of Berenice's perfume industry; cf. ll. 80–3, which urge wives to use libations of ointment on every occasion when they sleep with their husbands (and see the foregoing n.). Nicastri 1969/70, after an exhaustive inquiry (in which *inter alia* he dismisses Pfeiffer's idea that Callimachus published two different versions of his poem), shows the very high probability that the lines were in the Greek text seen by C. and were removed before our papyrus was copied in the sixth to seventh centuries; he tentatively, but not implausibly, suggests that a prudish transcriber objected to l. 81 but found he must remove all ten lines to avoid an obvious break. Putnam 1960, like Horváth (and also L. Ferrero, *Introduzione* 23–4 and n. 30, together with F. Della Corte and others), believes the lines to be a 'moralizing' addition by C. The argument for C.'s originality rests largely on psychological grounds; I found it interesting but unpersuasive. Putnam's great service is to show the increase in the emotional intensity of C.'s language, compared with that of Callimachus.

79 'You, whom marriage has joined' (note the tense): i.e., already-married women, not brides. If the meaning were 'on your wedding night,' as F. suggests, what would be the point of the reference to adulterous wives in 84–6?
   quam (see App. Crit.): a desperate, and unsuccessful, attempt by *R²* (reproduced by *m²*) to remedy *quem*, a word that makes no sense here; writing *quam* as he does, *R²* must be thinking of *post* (*R*'s reading) in l. 80.

80 *non*, for *ne* (cf. Ov. *Ep.* 16.164 *non . . . puta*, *AA.* 3.129, *Ex Ponto* 1.2.106 *non adimat*), is not quite on all fours with *non siris* (*V*'s text) at line 91 below, where see n.; the words *non prius* are closely linked, a fact that provides a further argument in favour of B. Guarinus' emendation.
   unanimis, simply 'loving'; cf. 9.4 n.

82 *onyx* = a jar made of onyx; cf. Prop. 2.13.30, 3.10.22, Hor. *Od.* 4.12.17. For the nature of 'onyx,' see F.; 'yellow' onyx resembled alabaster.

83 See the App. Crit. *R*'s unique reading *qu[a]eritis*, whatever its source, is of the utmost importance for establishing the dependence of nearly all the *deteriores* on *R*, not on *G* which, like *O*, has *colitis* (Introduction, p. 33). Presumably it comes (by a slip) from the following *qu[a]e*, unless *qu[a]e* was accidentally omitted in *X* and then written above *col-*. Since it fails to scan, some late Mss, which derive from *R*, replace it with *petitis* (*quaerere* = *petere*, more or less). Alternatively, the source of the reading in *R* may be as follows: colitisque [?] *V*, colitisꝗ*A*, colitis que *X* (seeking to mend the metrical fault arising from taking *que* as a connective instead of a relative); *X*'s correction was then accepted by *G* but misunderstood by *R*, who – with typical lack of thought and of feeling for metre – supposed that the correction was intended by *X* to prescribe a change of verb; *m* then followed *R*, but preferred his own diphthongal spelling. If this account should be correct, it would seem probable also that *X*'s exemplar wrote the letter *l* in a way that allowed *X* to read it as *r*; if so, that exemplar was not a very old Ms. (See the Introduction, pp. 25–6, for the date of *A*.)

86 *indignis*, the true *correction* (disguised as a variant by *R²*; adopted into the text by *m*) is metrically sound and also adequate in sense. But *R²* later (followed by *m²*) found it necessary to add, as a second variant (ultimately, from *A*), the absurd and unmetrical *indignatis* that we see in *O*. If the genesis of *indignatis* were to reside in an attempt by *X* to cure by a variant the weakness of *indigetis* (the presumably sole reading inherited from *A*, on this theory), we should be hard pressed to explain its presence in *O*; it must in this case be supposed that

A himself added the variant *al. indignatis* (see above, p. 40), and that *X* simply copied both text and variant together, and finally that *GR* took only the reading in the text, neglecting the variant.

87 *magis*, 'rather,' in adversative sense; see 73.4 n.

91 *sanguinis* (*V*) can hardly be right (see however Marinone 1982: 20 n. 76, and 1989: 390); blood-sacrifices are not appropriate to Berenice's lock: *unguen* = *unguentum* (l. 78), but the word is unfamiliar, and its form would suggest *sanguen* to the copyist.

  ne or *non*? B. conjectured that an original reading *ne siris* (*siris* Lachmann) was corrupted to *uestris*, leaving a syllable to be supplied, and that *non* was inserted to fill this up (since *sed* seemed to demand a preceding negative). This is more usual Latin than *non* + subj.: cf. however the instances of the latter quoted by F., and also l. 80, where *non* precedes an imperative (but see n. there). For a sound defence of *ne siris* see Courtney 1982: 49–50.

92 The choice between *affice* and *effice* is linked to the reading and interpretation of lines 93–4.

93 *proximus*: the (very fragmentary) Greek line can be reconstructed as beginning γείτονες ἔστωσαν. Hydrochoos (= Aquarius) and Oarion (= Orion) were the subject, according to the scholiast; they must have occupied part of another, perhaps the following, line. If so, C. has apparently squeezed into his final line what Callimachus took a whole couplet to express; hence, perhaps, C.'s obscurity. It does seem that *largis a. m.* balances *expertem non siris esse*. If with *V* we read *effice*, and also *cur iterent*, in the sense 'keep repeating,' and if, putting a comma at the end of 93, we treat *coma regia fiam* as quoting what the stars say as a result of the *larga munera*, then we achieve good sense (see Kidd 1970 on punctuation and meaning). And (we must further ask) why should Orion be next to Hydrochoos, normally 120 degrees off? Are we to explain this as meaning (i) that the stars will keep saying 'I want to become a royal tress, even if the constellations have to crowd together so that O. is next to H.,' or (ii) that they keep saying 'I want, etc.,' even if this (universal) demand on their part involves congestion among the stars? In either case, 'become a royal tress,' to make sense of the whole, would mean 'become part of the Coma Berenices' – so that it would not (surely) be true to say that O. is close to H., but rather that both of these constellations (together with many others) finally cease to exist in so far as the desire of their stars to desert them for the Coma is fulfilled. This intricate conceit would, one might think, need more than Callimachus' two lines to clarify, and C.'s single line leaves it uncharacteristically obscure. Alternatively, reading *affice*, we may accept Lachmann's palaeographically dubious emendation *corruerint*, with a stop at the end of line 92; the sense could then be paraphrased, 'would that the heavens should fall into confusion, so that O. shone next to H. – gladly should I face this, so long as I might

become *once again* a royal tress' (note that the italicized words are not implied
by *fiam*, as Kidd points out; and this might tempt us to accept Markland's
emendation *iterum* for *utinam*). B., however, has argued against Lachmann's
reading, maintaining that the expression *corruerint* indicates the total collapse
of the stellar universe and is therefore too violent for the context. But it may
be that for C. the operative part of the verb consists of the prefix *con-* (= *cum*);
in a few passages, e.g., Lucr. 6.824 and perhaps Curt. Ruf. 3.3.18, the root
idea of 'rushing [together]' seems to replace the acquired meaning 'collapse';
cf., possibly, *V*'s reading (*corruerit*) at 68.52 (but see n. on the text there).
B. further claims that it would do the Coma no good to have her wish granted –
presumably because she is already a *celestial* 'Coma'; but this is to deny C. the
right to a certain measure of elliptical expression, due to the translator's need to
compress his original here, and perhaps it is also to forget the loyalty shown by
the Coma in ll. 39–40. As it is, the changes in the lines are very abrupt; the effect
is staccato, and the sense hard to follow. In general, what is meant is surely that
the Coma would like to abandon its place in the sky and be once again a tress on
its mistress' head, and cares not a whit if this were to leave a gap in the heavens
and cause major dislocations among the stars – the whole, of course, by way of
extravagant compliment to Berenice. (For the case against *corruerint*, see Kidd
1970: 46; also Gutzwiller 1992.)

Vitelli, G. 1929. 'Frammenti della "Chioma di Berenice" di Callimaco in un papiro
della Società Italiana,' *SIFC* 7: 1–12.

Housman, A.E. 1929. 'C. 66.51–4,' *CR* 43: 168.

Fraenkel, E. 1929. 'Kallimachos und C.,' *Gn.* 5: 265–8.

Prescott, H.W. 1929. 'The New Fragment of Callimachus' Coma Berenices,' *CP* 24
(1929): 290–2.

Pfeiffer, R. 1932. ΒΕΡΕΝΙΚΗΣ ΠΛΟΚΑΜΟΣ,' *Philologus* 87; 179–228, esp.
211–19.

Rehm, B. 1934. 'C. 66 und der neue Kallimachosfund,' *Philologus* 89: 385–6.

Barber, E.A. 1936. 'The Lock of Berenice: Callimachus and C.,' *Greek Poetry and
Life: Essays Presented to Gilbert Murray*. Oxford: 343–63.

Mette, H.J. 1955. 'Zu C. 66,' *Hermes* 83: 500–2.

Traglia, A. 1955. 'Sopra alcune consonanze fra il c. 66 di C. e gli Aratea di Cicerone,'
Studi in onore di Gino Funaioli. Rome: 434–8.

La Penna, A. 1955. 'De Propertio et Callimacho adnotatiuncula, ' *Maia* 7:134. [Line
31.]

Herescu, N.I. 1957. 'C. traducteur du grec et les parfums de Bérénice (C. 66.77–78),'
Eranos 55: 153–70.

Luppino, R.A. 1958. 'Esegesi catulliana e callimachea,' *RFIC* 36: 537–49.

Putnam, M.C.J. 1960. 'C. 66.75–88,' *CP* 55: 223–8.

Axelson, B. 1960. 'Das Haaröl der Berenike bei C. und bei Kallimachos,' *Studi in onore di L. Castiglioni*. Florence: 13–21.

Horváth, I.K. 1962. 'La technique de traduction de C. à la lumière du papyrus de Callimaque retrouvé à Tebtunis,' *AAntHung* 10: 347–56.

Merkelbach, R. 1967. 'Kallimachos, Locke der Berenike 69–76,' *ZPE* 1: 218.

Nicastri, L. 1969/70. 'C. traduttore del *Plokamos*. Il problema dei vv. 79–88,' *AFLN* 12: 5–29.

Kidd, D.A. 1970. 'Some Problems in C. LXVI,' *Antichthon* 4: 38–49.

Forsyth, P.Y. 1972. 'C. 66.54. A Note,' *CJ* 68: 174–5.

Mariotti, S. 1972. 'C. 66.58,' *SCO* 21: 56–9.

Hansen, P., and Tortzen, C.G. 1973. 'Berenikes plokamos – Coma Berenices,' *Museum Tusculanum* 20: 29–54.

Cassio, A.-C. 1973. 'L' incipit della Chioma callimachea in Virgilio,' *RFIC* 101: 329–32.

Martyn, J.R.C. 1974. 'C. 66.53,' *Eranos* 72: 193–5.

Marinone, N. 1980. 'Conone, Callimaco e C. 66.1–6,' *Orpheus* 1: 435–40.

– 1982. 'I profumi di Berenice da Callimaco a C.,' *Prometheus* 8 (2): 1–20.

Barrett, A.A. 1982. 'C. 66.1: *Dispexit* or *Despexit*?,' *RhM* 125: 135–7.

Marinone, N. 1984. *Berenice da Callimaco a C.* (= *Ricerche di storia della lingua latina*, 17). [Pp. 103–285 contain a detailed and valuable commentary on the poem; plates give its text in *O* and *G*.]

Courtney, E. 1985. 'Three Poems of C.: (3.) C. 68 and Its Compositional Scheme,' *BICS* 32: 92.

West, S. 1985. 'Venus Observed? A Note on Callim. fr. 110,' *CQ* 34: 61–6.

Muth, R. and Töchterle, K. 1986. 'Berenike ohne Parfums?,' *Hommages à J. Veremans*. Brussels: 224–7.

Zwierlein, O. 1987. 'Weihe und Entrückung: die Locke der Berenice,' *RhM* 130: 274–90.

Marinone, N. 1988. 'C. 66.57–62,' *Filologia e forme letterarie: studi offerti a F. Della Corte* 2: 349–58. [At line 59 read *sidere uti (ubi* Vossius*) vario*.] Urbino.

– 1989. 'Richard Bentley e la *Chioma di Berenice*, ovvero la fortuna degli emendamenti,' *Mnemosynum. Studi in onore di A. Ghiselli*. Bologna: 383–91. [Important for text and apparatus. Editors have in general overestimated the value of Bentley's suggestions.]

Bajoni, M.G. 1990. 'Ales equos: C. 66.54 e Callimaco 110 Pf., 52–54,' *Aevum antiquum* 3: 163–7.

Edwards, M.J. 1991. 'Invitus, Regina,' *AC* 60: 260–5.

Helmes, L. 1992. 'Myrrh and Unguents in the *Coma Berenices*,' *CP* 87: 47–50.

Gutzwiller, K. 1992. 'Callimachus' *Lock of Berenice*: Fantasy, Romance and Propaganda,' *AJP* 113: 359–85. [An important article, which *inter alia* defends *V*'s reading in line 93.]

Hollis, A.S. 1992. 'The Nuptial Rite in C. 66 and Callimachus' Poetry for Berenice,' *ZPE* 91: 21–8.

Kershaw, A. 1993. 'A! at C. 66.85,' *Papers of the Leeds International Latin Seminar* 7:27–9.

Griffith, R.D. 1995. 'C.'s *Coma Berenices* and Aeneas' Farewell to Dido,' *TAPA* 125: 47–59.

67

Structure: *8 + 6 + (2 + 1 + 1) + (10 + 2 + 18)*.
(Notice the generally increasing length of the Door's utterance – *italicized* above – under the interlocutor's encouragement.)
A dramatic duologue (Q.'s description) between an interlocutor (the poet?) and a house door, recounting a piece of local gossip, of a scandalous sort, concerning a woman whose identity and history would be known to the inhabitants of Verona and Brixia – and perhaps other towns in the surrounding territory – in C.'s generation, but hardly to those of Rome at that time, and certainly to nobody since. The name of the person alluded to in the last four lines (by hints that would sufficiently identify him to other citizens of Verona) has been carefully disguised; a lawsuit has already been involved, and it is quite on the cards that another may threaten.
Even without 'the labors of generations of scholars' (Badian 1980: 81), it is not particularly hard to reconstruct from purely internal evidence the bare outlines of the story, so far as they are relevant to an understanding of the poem. The door is that of a house in Verona (l. 34). It now belongs to Caecilius (l. 9), whose name is mentioned by C. merely for the purpose of identification, though there is also an implication of respect and friendship on the Door's part, and of friendship on the poet's part, in l. 9. (There is no reason at all why the Caecilius of this poem should not be identified with C.'s fellow-poet Caecilius, who in poem 35 is called, or perhaps recalled, to Verona by C. from the embrace of his lady love at Novum Comum; see Hallett 1980, n. 3.) Caecilius acquired the house (whether by purchase or inheritance does not matter) from the son of Balbus (l. 3; the name of the son, whether or not it was also Balbus, is again irrelevant). Old Balbus was well served by the Door, as the traditional guardian of female purity (ll. 1–4). But there were ugly rumours after Balbus died and his son brought to the house a bride from the not-far-distant town of Brixia: 'they say she came here a virgin; but really she had a former husband [in Brixia] who was impotent, and in fact it was her father-in-law who deflowered her, whether through an incestuous passion for the young bride or because the older man was called in to perform the sexual act of which the husband was

incapable by nature.' Besides this (the Door adds) she had other lovers at Brixia ('How do I know this, you may ask, when I am fixed in this doorway and can't go out to hear the talk of the forum? Because I heard the woman gossiping with her maids when she thought I couldn't overhear'). Names of the Brixian lovers emerged during this whispering; and the woman also mentioned another man, whose name the Door will not give explicitly, 'ne tollat ... supercilia' (l. 46), and who presumably lives in Verona and is the particular cause of the Door's feeling that she herself, as a servant who must keep *fides* to Balbus as her late employer, is blamed by all and sundry (ll. 10–14) for admitting the son's wife's adulterers and thus bringing shame on the house.

Doors involved in dialogue are not unknown in Latin literature; another example is Propertius, 1.16. The chief attraction of this poem lies in the skill with which C., treating the Door 'as if it were a living being' (Lenchantin, intr. n.), endows it with all the characteristics of a female servant who, bursting with gossip but determined (at first) to be both loyal and discreet, has a stream of secrets gradually extracted from her by persistent questioning. The structure (see above) reflects the accelerating tempo of her willingness to communicate what she can barely restrain; the thematic development of the poem lies in her change of attitude, and it holds the reader's attention because of the suspense produced by this, together with the humorous detachment by means of which the interlocutor gains his perhaps not altogether laudable ends.

1 The mood of teasing irony in which the interlocutor addresses the Door is established at once; *iucunda* (stressed by repetition with the parallel nouns *viro* and *parenti*, emphasized by the caesura) is used in a general, conventional sense, not as especially applicable to the *vir* of the poem or to any particular *parens*. The adjective *iucundus* is employed by Catullus, normally of human beings, in contexts suggesting a relationship of warm friendship or affection (cf. the n. on 9.9); its repeated use in this line indicates at the outset of the poem that the Door is to be regarded as a 'human' character, an idea developed throughout (see intr. n.). Here it is *iucunda* to husband and father as safeguarding the chastity of females.

2 Greetings and compliments continue, still in general terms (Kr.).
   auctet (= *augeat*) is an archaic form suitable to the language of benedictions; for the archaic verb, and for the phrase *bona ope*, cf. 34.23–4 *bona sospites ope*.
   ope: the pentameter ends in a short open syllable; later poets avoid this.

3 Notice that the first appearance of the word *ianua* in the poem is deferred to this line, which of course generates suspense – and indeed surprise, since the reader will naturally assume that a person, rather than a (personified) thing, is to be

addressed. Cf. the effect of *Falerni* at the end of the first line of poem 27, and see n. there.

benigne, 'generously' (contrast *maligne* in l. 5).

Balbo: for this name and others, see intr. n.

4 *olim*, 'formerly,' need not suggest a distant past (a connotation it acquired only in the 'Silver Age'). *olim cum* is virtually equivalent to 'at that time when,' of a moment *other than the present*. Cf. Plaut. *Mil.* 1–2 *curate ut splendor meo sit clupeo clarior / quam solis radii esse olim quum sudumst solent.*

ipse senex: it might be better to regard *ipse* ('the master'; cf. 3.6–7 *suam ipsam*) as the noun, *senex* as the adjective here. Cf. 61.179 *senibus viris*, and also 9.4 *anum matrem*, 68.46 *carta anus*. Probably at 2.9 *ipsa* should be taken as = 'your mistress.'

5 *rursus = per contra*, not 'once again'; cf. 22.11.

nato, Fröhlich's emendation (for *voto*), is still energetically disputed. For the spelling *nato* (rather than *gnato*) see Badian 1980: 83 n. 5.

See App. Crit.: notice *O*'s disregard of metre.

6 *porrecto* suggests that the Door 'became married' only a short while after the old man's death.

Badian's ingenious defence of his suggested reading *pacta*, based on his interpretation of the situation described here, may be deemed to have a kind of forerunner in Baehrens' *pacta era rite*. Against this, however, stands *ipse* (line 4), which at this point must surely imply 'alone.'

marita: Kr. compares Livy 27.31.5 *maritas domos*, and points to similar expressions at 68.6 *lecto caelibe* and Ov. *F.* 1.36 *vidua domus*.

7 *agedum* ('come, now!') is colloquial. Cybele uses it (to a lion) at 63.78.

nobis = mihi; cf. line 18 *nos ... nobis*.

8 *veterem* is almost certainly to be taken with *fidem* (notice the metrical division of the line) rather than with *dominum*.

9 The Door's naming of Caecilius, together with the following phrase including *nunc*, suggests that Caecilius, the present owner of the house, is neither the *senex* nor his son (see intr. n.).

ita ... placeam, 'so may I ...,' to emphasize the Door's assertion.

11 *quisquam ... quicquam*: cf. 73.1. This kind of emphasis is slightly archaic and colloquial; similarly *pote* (= *potest*), for which see 17.24 n.

12 No wholly convincing restoration of the line has been offered, but the general sense is clear: 'everyone blames everything on me, the Door' (see lines 13–14). Among more recent attempts at restoration, Lee's suggested version of 11–12,

> ... quicquam
> vere, etsi populi vana loquela facit,

deserves mention; might it be improved by the insertion of *id* after *etsi* or after *populi*?

For *populi* sing. with *qui* pl., cf. Cicero, *Acad.* 2.32.103 *Academia ... a quibus*, and see J.S. Reid *ad loc.* for parallels (the idiom is, as Reid says, 'remarkably frequent' in Livy; and he cites Madvig on *De fin.* 5.16).

R² attempts a correction (not disguised as a variant), but can hardly be said to follow it through. Either *m*, who is careless throughout the poem (cf. ll. 22 *substulit*, 25 *suieque*, 26 *quod meo* for *quod iners*, 42 *cum aliis* for *R's cum conciliis*), garbles *R²*'s 'correction' *isti* by changing it to *istis* (note that *m²* reverts to *isti*), or else *R²* at first allowed *R's* unmetrical *istius* to stand, having nothing better to suggest (and *m* simply misread *istius*) but later *R²* tried to mend the metre with *isti*, and was accurately followed by *m²*. The second explanation seems better, since *m* and *m²* do not very often give differing versions of a single *R²* reading.

16–17 After *non satis est*, we have to understand something like *oportet* before *facere*.

17 *qui* (ablative), 'How?' Cf. Plaut. *Men.* 786 *qui cavere possum?*, *Most.* 641 *qui scire possum?*
laborat, 'tries hard.' *scire laboro* should be taken as either archaic (Lucil. 349–50 M *labora discere*) or colloquial (Hor. *Ep.* 1.3.2 *scire laboro*).

20 *prior*, 'first, formerly' (probably not to be taken with *vir* in the sense 'her former husband,' even though in fact he seems to have been the person in question: see intr. n.). For *prior = prius*, see K.F. Smith's note on Tib. 1.4.32.

21 *sicula = mentula.* For *hasta* in the same sense, cf. *Priap.* 43.1 and 4.
For *beta*, used symbolically for flaccidity or languor, Kr. refers to the emperor Augustus' personal substitution of a verb *betizare* for the commonly used *lachanizare* (Suet. *Aug.* 87.2), and quotes Automedon, *AP* 11.29.3–4, where λάχανον is mentioned similarly.

23 *V's illius* would have to be scanned with the second syllable long, unlike all other genitives in *-ius* in C. (see below). Further, if we take *pater-illius* and *gnati-cubile* together, the expression becomes awkward. B.'s *illusi* ('deceived' or 'tricked') is palaeographically easy to accept. The principal arguments against *illius* are these: (i) C. scans *illĭus* at 3.8, 10.31, 11.22, 61.219, 64.348, 66.85, and 68.44; also *ullĭus* 4.3, *unĭus* 5.3, *totĭus* 17.10; (ii) the burden on *illius*, before a strong pause in the line, does not seem to fit C.'s verse technique. B.'s emendation calls for less displacement than Scaliger's, and the *ille* in the latter seems awkward (we have *illam* in l. 20) and of dubious relevance (the father should be introduced as a fresh *persona* here).

24 For *miseram conscelerasse domum* (implying the pollution of a household by sexual misconduct) cf. 64.404 n. (*divos scelerare penates*).

25 *mens*, 'disposition,' as often (see 65.4 n.).
caeco, of a passion that blinds the judgment. Cf. Hor. *Od.* 1.18.14 *caecus amor sui.*

26 *natus* = *gnatus*; the *n*-form is used here for metrical reasons (64.298 n.).

27 *unde unde*, 'from some source or other,' cf. Hor. *S*. 1.3.88 (but see B.'s objections). The omission of the second *unde* is the simplest way to explain the unmetrical reading in *V*.
  foret virtually = *esset*. Cf. 4.5, 63.46, 66.61, 68.40, 68.116, 99.13.
  nervosius illud: cf. Petron. 129.8 *recipies ... nervos tuos si triduo sine fratre dormieris* (Fr.).

29 *Egregium*: ironical affectation of surprise and admiration; cf. V. *Aen*. 4.93 *egregiam vero laudem et spolia ampla refertis*. Notice the addition in parataxis of *mira pietate* to *egregium*, which is characteristic of C.: cf. 71.4 n.
  narras: colloquial; cf. Ter. *Andr*. 466 *bonum ingenium narras adulescentis*, Cicero *Ad Fam*. 9.16.7 *quem tu mihi ... narras?* Later, as Kr. says, the idiom became obsolete.

30 *minxerit*: again a euphemism. Cf. Hor. *S*. 2.7.51–2 *sollicitum ne / ditior aut formae melioris meiat eodem*.
  gnati ... gremium, properly 'that ... which *belonged* to his son.'

32 *Cycneae*: the restoration of *V*'s *chinea* is probable, though not certain, but during much of Brescia's history this prominent hill (*specula*), the modern *Castello*, has apparently been known as *colle Cigneo*, *Cigno*, or *Cicneo*. The story of Cycnus and Phaethon is certainly domiciled in the Po valley (Ov. *M*. 2.367–80), but appears to have no particular link with Brescia: see Richardson 1967: 430–1, who suggests retaining *Chynea* (*chinea*, Mss), and refers in support of this to a name concealed in the Virgilian *crux* at *Aeneid* 10.186.
  supposita: the *a* is (rather awkwardly) lengthened by position. Cf. 17.24 *pote stolidum*, 63.53 *gelida stabula*, 68.186 *nulla spes*, Tib. 1.5.28 *pro segete spicas*. Petreius' *supposita in specula* probably represents an attempted correction by a local antiquary, as B. suggests for J.C. Zanchi (see No. 113 in the Table of Mss). For *supponere* in this sense, cf. Petron. 116.1 *haud procul suppositum arci sublimi oppidum*, where *impositum* is the Ms reading but *sup-* (Büch.'s conjecture) is – independently, it seems – urged by Fr.; see Fr.'s palaeographical explanation.

33 The debate between the Humanistic emendation *praecurrit* on the one hand, and *V*'s *percurrit* on the other, has a topographical dimension, since the Mella, though close to Brescia, does not flow through the ancient city (see Tozzi 1973). The reading *Mello*, for *Mella*, has probably been assimilated to the gender of *flumine* (Fr., p. 434). Tozzi, reading *percurrit* (*praecurrit* first appears in *Trinc*. and not, as he claims, in *Ald*.¹ and *Ald*.²), concludes that by *Mella* C. meant the Garza (a tributary). He supposes, after Lenchantin, that in antiquity the name Mella was (sometimes) given to both rivers, since they eventually meet in one bed (p. 492). In view of the distance (over a mile) of the Mella proper from the outmost limits of the ancient city, he may well be right, and demonstrably right

if only there were other evidence for the sharing of the name. This solution, in an
earlier version, is one of two commended by Zicàri 1978: 134–36, the other being
the substitution of *praecurrit* for *percurrit*; Zicàri himself, however, offers a
third way out, leaving *percurrit* and changing *quam* to *qua*. See Carratello 1988:
333 n. 65, whose defence of Zicàri's emendation has now persuaded me.
flavus is a conventional epithet of rivers, not to be taken too seriously; cf. V. *Aen.*
9.816 (Kr.).

34 See Giangrande 1970 for his attempt to substitute *matronae* (= the erring
woman, whose lovers are mentioned in the latter part of the poem) for *Veronae*.
In fact, Billanovich 1988: 35–6 shows, from an echo in a much later text, that the
true reading is after all *Veronae*. Though he seems unaware of Giangrande's
article, this does not affect the outcome. Since there are no good grounds for
replacing *meae* with *tuae*, the Door must be supposed, if we accept *V*'s reading of
the line, to be situated in Verona (see the intr. n.). The reading *tuae*, championed
by Scaliger, has however been defended by some modern scholars (Riese, for
example, and also Rambelli 1957: 65–88).

   On what is meant by *mater*, in terms of the personal relations between heroes
or founders, transferred in myth to their cities, see Wiseman 1987: 324–36.

36 *malum … adulterium*: cf. 61.97–8 *mala … adulteria*.

38 For *abesse* with simple ablative of separation, cf. 63.60.

39 *auscultare*, colloquial (Ital. *ascoltare*).

41–2 Overhearing by the house door of a whispered (*furtiva voce*) conversation in
which the woman confesses her sins to her maids (hardly in the entrance hall!)
is, though implausible, a way out of the question asked by C. in 37–40; whereas
the interlocutor can pick up the stories circulating in the streets (3 *dicunt*,
5 *ferunt*, etc.), how can the *door* pick up gossip, fixed to the house as 'she' is?
(C., however, does not brood over the intrinsic probabilities of the situation.)

44 *speraret* (or *speret*) = 'suppose.' The argument for the emendation *speraret* does
not depend solely on the avoidance of hiatus, as Richardson 1967: 431 supposes;
the sequence of the tenses of verbs from 41 *audivi* to 45 *addebat* has some weight
also. On hiatus in C.'s poems written in elegiac couplets, with a defence of the
hiatus that would result in this line from adoption of the reading *speret*, see M.
Zicàri, 'Some Metrical and Prosodical Features of Catullus' Poetry,' *Phoenix* 18
(1964): 193–205.

45–8 This elaborate periphrasis is no doubt intended to identify (for readers already
acquainted with the local scandals) the person whom the Door, like C., is
unwilling to name. For a P. Cornelius Balbus (married to a Caecilia) and a
C. Cornelius *Longus* at Verona in the early imperial period, see Wiseman
1987: 342.

46 Although it is almost invariably R^2m^2(not m)G^2 that yield a reading otherwise
found in *O*, which suggests that in these instances R^2 took the reading from an

alteration found by him in *X*, we need not be troubled by the sequence R^2mG^2 = *O* here; the correction can easily be supposed to have suggested itself, and the agreement with *O* is probably fortuitous.

47–8 The situation appears to be this. The person attacked, being disappointed of a legacy which was contingent upon his having natural heirs, caused his wife to simulate pregnancy, and at the same time secretly adopted a child, which he subsequently gave out to be his own. The deceit was suspected, and a lengthy lawsuit was the result.

Cahen, R. 1902. 'C. LXVII,' *RPh* 26: 164–80.

Kroll, W. 1904. 'C.s 67. Gedicht,' *Philologus* 63: 139–47.

Magnus, H. 1907. 'C. Gedicht 67,' *Philologus* 66: 296–312.

Giri, G. 1909. 'De Catulli carmine LXVII,' *RFIC* 37: 527–47.

Wick, M. 1913. 'Il carme 67 di C.,' *Atti, Reale Acc. di Archeologia* (etc.) *di Napoli* 2: 1–46.

Perrotta, G. 1927. 'Il carme della *Ianua* (C. 67),' *Athenaeum* 5: 160–90.

Copley, F.O. 1949. 'The "Riddle" of C. 67,' *TAPA* 80: 245–53.

Rambelli, G. 1957. 'C., carme 67,' *Studi di filologia classica*. Pavia: 65–88.

Horváth, I.K. 1960. 'Chronologica Catulliana,' *AAntHung* 8: 351–5.

Richardson, L., Jr., 1967. 'C. 67: Interpretation and Form,' *AJP* 88: 423–33.

Giangrande, G. 1970. 'C. 67,' *QUCC* 9: 84–131.

Mazzarino, S. 1970. 'Note di storia giuridica in territorio cenomano e problemi di storia culturale veneta,' *BIDR* 73: 35–57.

Tozzi, P. 1973. 'L' antico corso del fiume Garza e C. LXVII.32–33,' *RIL* 107: 473–98.

Billanovich, G. 1974. 'Terenzio, Ildemaro, Petrarca,' *IMU* 17: 1–60, esp. 47ff.

Hallett, J.P. 1980. '*Ianua iucunda*: The Characterization of the Door in C. 67,' *SLLRH* 2. Brussels: 106–22.

Badian, E. 1980. 'The Case of the Door's Marriage (C. 67.6),' *HSCP* 84: 81–9.

Macleod, C.W. 1981. 'The Artistry of C. 67,' Δεσμὸς κοινωνίας: *Scritti di filologia e filosofia per Gianfranco Bartolini nel secondo anniversario della scomparsa 1979–1981*, ed. G. Fabiano and E. Salvaneschi. Genoa: 71–87.

Ribuoli, R. 1981. 'Sull' attribuzione di una congettura catulliana: "Golgos" 36.14 e 69.46,' *Orpheus* 2: 357–9.

Forsyth, P.Y. 1982. 'A Note on C. 67.12,' *CJ* 77: 253–4.

– 1986. 'C. 67: poeta chiarissimo?,' *Latomus* 45: 374–82.

McGready, F. 1986. 'On C. 67,' *MPhL* 7: 119–21.

Camps, W.A. 1987. 'Notes on C. and Ovid,' *CQ* 37: 519. [Lines 7–14, esp. line 12: read *verum istuc populi fabula iniqua facit*.]

Billanovich, G. 1988. 'Il Catullo della Cattedrale di Verona,' *Scire litteras* = *Bayerische Akad. d. Wiss., Phil. - Hist. Klasse, Abh. N.F. 99*. Munich: 35–57, esp. 35–6.

Carratello, U. 1988. 'Il carme della *ianua*,' *Filologia e forme letterarie. Studi offerti a F. Della Corte* 2.321–38. Urbino.

Murgatroyd, P. 1989. 'Some Neglected Aspects of C. 67,' *Hermes* 117: 471–8.

Forsyth, P.Y. 1989. 'A Note on C. 67.32,' *CW* 83: 30–1.

Kilpatrick, R.S. 1992. 'Two Notes on Roman Elegy: C. 67 and Propertius 1.9,' *The Two Worlds of the Poet. New Perspectives on Vergil*, ed. R.M. Wilhelm and H. Jones. Detroit: 296–302.

68 (a and b)

One poem or two? After a century of heated debate, modern scholarship is predominantly inclined towards separating 'poem 68' into two poems: see for example Wiseman 1974b and Courtney 1985; *contra*, Sarkissian 1983. Fordyce, who succinctly outlines some but not all of the objections to uniting them, wisely observes: 'If they had stood apart in our text, they would have been accepted as referring to two quite different situations and there would have been no temptation to connect them.'

Poem 68[a] is presented as a letter to a friend. Its language and style, accordingly, are correspondingly prosaic and 'everyday'; contrast again 68[b], where they are those of an art poem, in line with Hellenistic canons of taste (elaborate similes, use of myth, the display of geographical and other learning, and so forth). This is one reason for separating the two poems in terms of composition; other, perhaps more cogent, reasons will be given below. Yet because they are adjacent to each other it is tempting to seek for *some* relationship between them. One view of such a relationship was expressed by Vretska 1966: 327–8, following (substantially) Della Corte 1951 and Wohlberg 1955. He maintains that the two poems were deliberately juxtaposed. This juxtaposition, however, may have led to the interpolation of lines 91–100. Catullus (one can imagine, though certainty is impossible), responding to the request for a poem, may first have composed his poem of refusal, based on his situation at the moment. Then, however, he remembered an earlier composition which he happened to have ready to hand (for touching-up?) in a *capsula* (line 36), and added it after inserting the interpolation as a connection of thought. (So 68[b] was sent off as a gift, *faute de mieux*.)

This not altogether implausible account can be reconciled with the way the text is set out here: 68[b] appears with a capital letter at its head (and an implied interval, though in *CE* this was concealed by its beginning at the top of a page); contrast the lack of a capital at line 149, where (as most scholars agree) a new poem does *not* begin. See below on the general question of unity versus division.

For establishing *unity* in composition, it is of no importance that 68ᵃ and 68ᵇ are found together in the Mss, without any break between them, and under a heading ('Ad Mallium') which on the Ms evidence can apply only to ll. 1–40; the same situation applies in other parts of the collection, especially towards the end. Wiseman 1974b: 89 cites poems 101–16, which are run together under a heading, *fletus de morte fratris*, that applies only to the first of them. Some evidence even suggests that the heading goes back no further than *R*², and thus does not possess manuscript authority; and that it was taken from the form of the name as it is first encountered in *R* (see line 11). In poem 61 the bridegroom's name, which is Manlius (l. 215) Torquatus (l. 209), appears in l. 16 as *Mallius*; at line 215 we find the reading *Maulius* in *O* (cf. the variant *al. mauli* in *R*², here at 68.11). (Clearly *Malli*, or *Mali*, could represent *Manli* at 68.11 and 30.) See however McKie, esp. 62, 86, 89.

In 68ᵃ the name in ll. 11 and 30 begins in *V* with a consonant; in l. 11, at least, it must do so because of the open vowel just before it. It is no remedy to drag in the 'Allius' of ll. 41, 50, 66, and 150, by reading *mi Alli* (or *mi, Alli*) at l. 11; the elision of the *i* at this position, in this metre, will simply not do (and certainly not as a result of conjectural emendation); there are only two or three instances of such an elision before a vowel in the very much looser satiric hexameters of Horace and Persius, and none at all in those of more formal poets. In 68ᵇ, on the other hand, the opposite is true; at line 41 the name must begin with a vowel, for two reasons: (i) to make possible the elision of *m(e)*, and (ii) to give *iuverit* an object, which it has to have. Moreover, *V*'s reading *quam fallius* (*QVAMFALLIVS* at some stage of the transmission) must come from *QVAMEALLIVS*. The other names given in 68ᵇ are: 50 *alli* or *ali*; 66 *allius* in *O*, with *vel manllius* in the margin, but *manlius* in *X*, who clearly has here made a critical choice, as he sometimes does, taking *(vel) manlius* from *A*, the common parent of *O* and *X*, where evidently the variant appeared as such; *O* does not invent variants for himself, but simply copies what he sees – or thinks he sees. We must therefore come to terms with the fact that 68ᵃ and 68ᵇ are addressed to different people, and that the faint similarity between their names (one of which began with a consonant, the other with a vowel) is simply accidental.

There are other reasons for separating the poems. They cannot have been addressed (in the first instance) to the same person at the same time, because the circumstances of the people concerned are not the same: in 68ᵃ, lines 1–6, the addressee is living a forlorn bachelor life, whereas in 68ᵇ (l. 155) he receives a message of goodwill in association with his lady love (*tua vita*). Further, the virtual repetition of 68ᵃ lines 20–24 at 68ᵇ lines 92–6 is very much harder to accept in two poems (or parts of a poem) written at the same time and to the same person. It may be added that the verse-technique of

68^a differs from that of 68^b in at least one important respect, namely the frequency of elisions. In 68^b, if I calculate correctly, an average of one elision occurs every 1.6 lines (cf. the elegiac epigrams, poems 69–116, in which the corresponding figure is 1.9); but in 68^b there is only one for every 2.4 lines (2.6, in lines 41–148), or less if we consider lines 89–100 as a later addition (cf. here the long poems 67, 64, 66, which have one elision every 2.5, 3.1, and 3.1 lines respectively). If 68^a and 68^b are parts of a single composition, this difference has to be explained.

(a) Lines 1–40
Structure: 10 + 20 + 10.
A letter to Manlius, containing a negative reply (*recusatio*) to Manlius' request to C. for two kinds of solace, erotic and literary, in a time of personal distress.

A complete and self-sufficient poem, possibly (though by no means certainly) referring to 68^b, but in no way structurally determined by it. See especially Vretska 1966, who (though his analysis is somewhat too schematic) has properly located (pp. 319–20) the pivot on which the poem revolves in the second-person address to the lost brother (ll. 21–4). This will remind us of poem 65 (see intr. n. there); in both instances it gives a certain circularity of structure, or at least an 'enclosing' type of structure, to a short elegiac poem. It does not follow that the relationship, in date of composition, of 68^b to 68^a should be presumed to resemble that of 66 to 65; we have seen that the brother's recent death seems to give a suitable context for both 65 and 66; whereas, as between 68^a and 68^b, the word-for-word repetitions (20, 22–4; 92, 94–6), whatever they may indicate (see below), are hard to reconcile with the notion of virtually simultaneous composition.

1 *quod*, 'as for the fact that ...,' a common formula of epistolary style; cf. 27 *quod scribis*. Kr. compares Cicero, *Ad Att.* 3.7.1 *quod me rogas ... , voluntas tua mihi valde grata est*.
   acerbo must of course be taken to qualify in sense both *fortuna* and *casu*.
2 *conscriptum*, 'bedewed' or 'smudged,' rather than 'penned'; Cf. 25.11 *conscribillent*, 37.10 *scribam*.
   hoc (implying 'which I have in front of me') does as much as anything to prove that lines 1–40 are a genuine letter-in-verse. The loose periodic style (fourteen lines before a major pause) is another epistolary touch.
   epistolium, as a Latin word, occurs only here and twice in Apuleius (*Apol.* 6 and 79). In Greek, however, ἐπιστόλιον is regularly used.

3 For the figure of shipwreck, applied to love, cf. Philodemus *AP* 10.21.6 σέο
πορφυρέῳ κλυζόμενον πελάγει. Other applications of the figure can be found, e.g.,
in Cicero's description of Catiline's followers (*Catil.* 2.24 *illam naufragorum
eiectam ac debilitatam manum*).

4 *mortis limine*: cf. the Lucretian (2.960, 6.1157) *leti limen*; neither expression,
however, need be supposed to refer to the gates of the underworld, as Kr.
suggests.

5 *sancta Venus:* a cult title; cf. 36.3, where F. has a helpful note.

6 *lecto caelibe*: cf. 67.6 (of the *ianua*) *es* ... *facta marita*. It is not necessary to
suppose that Manlius is suffering from bereavement, or a tiff: his trouble is
unrequited love.

7 *veterum*: the implication is that Manlius has asked C. for a *new* poem.

9 *quoniam*, 'inasmuch as.' *m* (reading *quero* for *quoniam*) is singularly careless
here, as he is elsewhere in this passage; cf. ll. 22, 34, 38, 39, 42, 53, 59, 63, 70.
(Readings in *CE*, App. Crit.) Here m^2 corrects by reverting to *R*'s reading, giving
the correction as a variant.
me tibi dicis amicum does not suggest close friendship.

10 Notice the careful disjunction, by means of *et ... et*, between the *munera
Musarum* and the <*munera*> *Veneris*. The two complaints made by Manlius
in 5–8 (he finds it hard to sleep alone, and older books give no solace in his
wakefulness) are taken up in reverse order.

Elision at the diaeresis of the pentameter is not avoided by C. except (under
Greek, especially Callimachean, influence) in poems 65 and 66; Kr. and F. both
point to lines 56, 82, 90 below.
Musarum: for the expression 'gifts of the Muses' Kr. and F. cite Archilochus,
fr. 1 D (= 1 West) Μουσέων ἐρατὸν δῶρον, Theognis 250 ἀγλαὰ Μουσάων
δῶρα, and for 'gifts of Aphrodite' Hesiod *Sc.* 47 τερπόμενος δώροισι πολυχρύσου
'Αφροδίτης, while F. points also to Anacreon, who in fr. 96 D (= 2 West) has
both: Μουσέων τε καὶ ἀγλαὰ δῶρ' 'Αφροδίτης συμμίσγων.
hinc = *a me* ('colloquial,' Kr.); cf. 63.74 n., 116.6 n., and the use of *hunc nostrum*
at 109.2 and perhaps of *istinc* at 76.11.

11 The natural explanation of R^2's *al. mauli* seems to be that it was the variant
reading of *X*, ignored by *GR* because it was unhelpful (not yielding a name), and
that this in turn represents a faulty transcription by *X* of something like *m{a}li*
in *A*.

12 *odisse* = 'have a distaste for'; cf. Prop. 1.1.5 and 3.8.27.

14 *dona beata*, 'gifts to be expected from *one who is* happy' (transferred epithet).

15–26 Bearing in mind the distinction referred to in 10 n., these ten lines seem to
have nothing to do with literature; certainly they need not be taken as referring
to poetry, even to love poetry (see 17, n. on *lusi*).

15 *vestis ... pura* = the *toga virilis*, or youth's badge of maturity, exchanged for
   the *toga praetexta* of childhood. The idea behind 15–18 is expressed also by
   Propertius 3.15.3–4:
>   ut mihi praetexti pudor est ablatus [*Heinsius*; velatus *codd.*] amictus
>   et data libertas noscere amoris iter.

17 *lusi*, 'I played the lover.' (Not 'I composed love poetry'; C. is still talking about
   munera Veneris rather than those of the Muses. See 33 n.).
   est dea nescia nostri: the usual form of the expression implies that the lover 'has
   knowledge of' the god or goddess of love, not the other way about; the *Ciris*
   (242) plainly imitates C.'s unusual way of putting it.

18 'bitter-sweet'; cf. Sappho L.-P. 47 (γλυκύπικρος, of Eros), and Meleager, *AP*
   12.81.2 τοῦ πικροῦ γευσάμενοι μέλιτος.
   The word *curis*, as used to describe a lover's state of mind, may comprehend
   both extremes – of bitterness and sweetness – and it is to make this clear that C.
   amplifies it with *dulcem ... miscet amaritiem*. There is no such tautology as B.
   supposes.

19–21 Notice the repetition of *frater(na)* in three successive lines; cf. 91–3, and also
   poem 101, where *frater* is thrice repeated at four-line intervals and at the same
   place in the line. This is probably intended to suggest the rite of *conclamatio*:
   cf. V. *Aen.* 6.506 *ter voce vocavi*, Ov. *Fasti* 3.563–4 *terque 'vale' dixit, cineres
   ter ad ora relatos / pressit*. See further 101.2 n.

19 *studium*, 'pursuit' (again with no literary overtones, but simply of love or
   flirtation).
   Notice the sense of abruptness given by the monosyllable at the end of the
   line, followed by the heavy pause at the end of the first foot in l. 20.

20–1 *m*'s correcting tendency is well exemplified in these lines.

21–4 The repetitions of *tu* etc. reinforce the effect of those mentioned in 19–21 n.

23 Kr. compares Eur. Alc. 347 σὺ γάρ μου τέρψιν ἐξεῖλες βίου.

25 *interitu*, abl. of cause; cf. line 87 below (*raptu*), and also 14.2 and 65.12.
   tota de mente fugavi, 'completely banished from my mind'; for other examples
   of this Latin poetic idiom see F.

26 *haec studia* = 19 *hoc studium*. As Kr. says, the pl. is used here for the sake of
   concinnitas with *delicias*.

27 Wiseman 1974b: 96–100 has made an eloquent plea for regarding the words
   'Veronae turpe <est>, Catulle [= V], esse' as a direct quotation from Manlius'
   letter to C. This would avoid the difficulty involved in assuming that C. means
   one *esse* to do duty for two (= Veronae esse turpe Catullo esse). On the other
   hand, that C. should introduce a direct question in this way, at least in the
   second person – even if not, as here, using the vocative – would be easier to
   accept if there were at least one really valid parallel instance in the works of a

poet. Of Wiseman's five citations in n. 52 from Cicero's letters, one (*Ad Att.* 12.25.2) is limited to one word, as is 12.34.3; 8.15.2 and 12.1.2 are proverbial and non-personal in expression; and at *Ad Fam.* 5.2.3, which is perhaps the closest, *ita* is inserted to introduce the citation. See also line 28 n. for a further objection to Wiseman's view.

28 *quod* here surely = 'inasmuch as,' not 'the fact that,' following *quod* = 'as for the fact that' in line 27. Wiseman's translation 'As for … the fact that' disguises this. Notice also that *non turpe* in line 30 must directly contradict *turpe* in line 27.

hic would mean 'in Rome' (not Verona), if we were to adopt the view that a direct quotation is involved, and assume (as Q. does) that the quotation continues to line 29. On Wiseman's view (see line 27 n.) it refers to Verona; this, I think, is right. F., who would expect an indirect quotation to follow *quod scribis*, deals fairly with the difficulties inherent in his own assumption but still thinks direct quotation 'unparalleled and improbable.'

quisquis either = *quisque*, 'everyone' (on the analogy of the neuter *quidquid* = *quidque*), or (more probably with such a phrase as *de meliore nota*) we are to understand *est*, as F. suggests. Here he is supported by Wiseman.

de meliore nota, 'out of the top drawer' (the metaphor in Latin has to do with choice wines, as in *nota Falerni*, Hor. *S.* 1.10.24). The same metaphorical use is found in a letter from Curius (Cicero, *Ad Fam.* 7.29.1) and in Petron. 116.5; F. also cites Sen. *De benef.* 3.9.1.

29 If we regard *Veronae … esse* as a quotation (see 27 n.), it may be possible to read *tepefactat* with R^2, rather than *tepefactet* with Bergk; but the choice between emendations is of little moment, and even in that case the subjunctive seems on the whole preferable; the reason is not so much given as a fact, as imputed by C. to the mind of Manlius. R^2's attempted (and almost successful) correction is of course partly, though not wholly, metrical in character.

  For the shortening of the second syllable in *tepe-* see F.'s n. on 64.360 *tepefaciet*. The word *tepefactare* is elsewhere unknown, but F. points to two instances of the analogous *frigefactare* in Plautus (*Poen.* 760, *Rud.* 1326).

30 *non est turpe, magis miserum est*: cf. Cicero, *De Har. Resp.* 49 *miserum magis fuit quam turpe*.

magis, 'but rather'; cf. Lucr. 2.1086 *non … unica, sed numero magis innumerali*, V. *Ecl.* 1.11 *non equidem invideo, miror magis*.

30, 32, 34 Kr. points out that in these pentameters there is punctuation in the second half of the line, contrary to C.'s unvarying practice elsewhere in his longer elegiac poems (and indeed in the epigrams, except at 110.4); he correctly attributes this to the relatively loose style of a versified letter.

31 *ignosces* ('polite' future), 'please forgive.' Hor. *S.* 1.9.72; with *igitur*, at Prop. 1.11.19.

32 *cum nequeo*: temporal (cf. perhaps line 8), but (as Kr. suggests) here close enough to the causal sense to approximate the archaic *cum*-causal.

33 *nam*: elliptical, as F. notes. In this transition we merely imply the second request, and explain why the second request also cannot be met.
scriptorum: probably from *scripta*, not from *scriptores*. Notice that *nam* is used, transitionally, as passing to a new subject: 'now, as for <the other topic> ...' In ll. 15–30, C. has very carefully explained why he cannot accede to Manlius' request for *munera Veneris* (10); now he turns to the request for poetry (*munera Musarum*), and let us remember that it was *new* (original) poetry that M. had in mind (7 n.). Four lines are now devoted to C.'s reason for being unable to do as M. wishes, in this respect also. He has no great *copia scriptorum* with him at Verona. It seems artificial to suppose that C. needs a whole library to cope with a friend's request for lines to take a vexed mind 'out of itself'; after all, the friend presumably knew C. was at Verona, away from Rome and from his books. Nor should we imagine that M. expected C. to sit down there and then and compose a long, learned work for which histories and encyclopaedias were indispensable. The very phrases used in 39–40 (*petenti copia posta est: ultro ego deferrem, copia siqua foret*) seem to suggest furnishing something that is ready to hand. Accordingly, what C. says is most likely this: 'I have only a small *capsa* here, with just a few rolls <of work, *scripta*, brought with me> (for revision?).' Cf. Horace, *S.* 1.4.22–3 (*capsis ... scripta*) and *Ep.* 2.1.268.

34 *hoc*, 'probably ablative' (Kr. and F.).
capsula, diminutive of *capsa*, which = *scrinium* (14.18), 'a cylindrical box in which *volumina* stood on end' (F.).

36 *sequitur*, either 'accompanies me whenever I come here' or else loosely (in 'conversational' epistolary style) for *secuta est*.

37 *quod cum ita sit*: prosaic. Cf. Juvenal 5.59.
mente maligna, 'out of a grudging disposition.' Cf. 10.18 *non mihi tam fuit maligne ...*
id facere, colloquial (cf. 85.1 *id faciam*, and see n.).

39 *non* probably negates the whole clause; C. has to refuse *both* requests. His reasons for doing so are clearly given in two phases, 15–32 and 33–6, where see nn.
copia posta est (= *posita est*), 'has been put at your disposal'; a fresh coinage, on the analogy of *copia facta est*. For the whole expression cf. Seneca, *Ep.* 39.1 *sed utriusque rei copiam faciam* (to which Kenneth Quinn kindly drew my attention).

40 *ultro deferre* ('to volunteer') is a set phrase; cf. Hor. *Ep.* 1.12.22 *si quid petet, ultro defer.*

(b) Lines 41–160

Structure: variously described as 'cyclic,' 'mesodic,' 'omphalos' or 'Chinese box' arrangement of themes (e.g., abcdedcba; see for example the plan set out in Kr.⁵: 219).

The groups of lines are balanced, with mathematical symmetry (or an approach to it) around the central section in lines 87–104:

Lines	87–90	91–100	101–4
Theme	Troy	Brother's death	Troy

For the question whether the apex passage, 91–100, originally formed part of the poem, see above: Copley 1957 and others have pointed out that the reader can pass from 90 to 100 without interruption of the sense. Lines 41–50 are usually regarded as an introduction, containing the name Allius at its beginning and end; lines 149–60 are for the most part similarly seen as a kind of conclusion or *envoi*, again addressed by name to Allius and roughly balancing the introduction in length. For an important discussion of this 'conversational scheme,' together with that of 68ᵃ, see Courtney 1985, who gives parallels.

41 *deae*, the Muses (Il. 2.485 ὑμεῖς γὰρ θεαί ἐστε). The fact that the Muses are formally addressed at this point serves powerfully to show that a separate composition (in some sense at least) begins here, and that it has more of the character of a work of art than lines 1–40; see intr. n.

42 Notice the emphatic, almost excited, repetition of *iuverit*.

   m at first mis-writes *iuverit* as *iuveret*; then *m*² 'corrects' him with *viveret*, apparently without consulting *R*'s already correct reading.

43 To read *nec*, with *V*, would intolerably break up the logical progression from 41 to 45.

   *m*²'s senseless variant (*al. r*, i.e., *aeras*) can only be explained as the result of *R*'s imperfectly drawn *t* (fol. 30ᵛ), which indeed does distinctly resemble an *r*. This tends to show how slavishly *m*² (in contrast to *m*) seeks to recapture all that he sees in *R*.

44 *caeca*, 'blinding' as well as 'dark'; 64.207 n.

45 The opposite of the usual claim of a poet to be the mouthpiece of the Muses (Callim. *H*. 3.186, Theocr. 22.116). B. has seen the point: the theme of this poem is so personal and private to C. that the Muses cannot be expected to know it and to prompt the poet; they have to be told about it first.

46 *anus*, adjective; cf. 9.4 *anumque matrem*, and especially 78ᵇ.4 *fama ... anus*; also 67.4 n., where *ipse senex* = 'the old master.'

47 Both *G* and *R* leave a space, indicating a lacuna of one line; *O* leaves no space. Humanistic supplements began to be added in η-class mss (Zicàri 1958: 83 = 1978: 84).

48 *magis ... atque magis*; but cf. 38.3 and 64.274 *magis magis*.

49 *sublimis*, 'aloft.' The adj. (not particularly appropriate in this context) is conventional; Hes. *Op.* 777 ἀερσιπότητος ἀράχνης. See however the App. Crit. for Nisbet's suggested emendation *subtilis aranea* (which may perhaps receive support from Prop. 3.6.33 *putris et in vacuo texetur aranea lecto*, though he does not cite or mention this passage).

Allusion to a neglected inscription is used, in a somewhat different context, by Propertius (2.6. 35–36; cf. 3.6.33).

Post v. 49 See App. Crit. The earliest of the δ-class Mss, No. 58 in the Table, retains the line.

51 *duplex*, probably in the sense of 'wily.' See Nisbet and Hubbard on Hor. *Od.* 1.6.7, where 'the word is a pejorative translation of Hom. *Od.* 1.1 πολύτροπον.' The strongest Latin parallel is Ov. *Am.* 1.12.27 *vos* (writing tablets) *rebus duplices pro nomine sensi*. There is no reference to the bitter–sweet antinomy of l. 18, which as Kr. remarks is already too distant (considerations of unity apart). *Amathusia*, 'the goddess of Amathus' (36.14 n.) = Aphrodite, or Venus.

52 *V*'s *corruerit* would mean 'has ruined': *corruere* as a transitive verb is very rare; the few transitive instances listed in *OLD* 4 are archaic, though Lucr. has one. If Lachmann's emendation at 66.93 (see n. there) should be right, C. would there use it intransitively; he does not employ it elsewhere. It was however pointed out by W.S. Watt, *LCM* 9: 1984, that C.'s imitator Martial never uses *ruere* transitively but seven times intransitively. But *torruerit* has support from 100.7 *cum vesana meas torreret flamma medullas*, as well as perhaps from the sense of *arderem* in line 53. The repetition of the metaphor hardly seems disastrous; C. is fond of heightening and expanding an image. For *torrere* of mental anguish, cf. Lucr. 3.1019, Hor. *Od.* 3.9.13.

in quo ... genere: 'in what category'; a discreet allusion to the fact (made explicit in 143–6) that C.'s love for 'Lesbia' was adulterous. F.'s 'in what matter' is hardly adequate.

torruerit: cf. 100.7, and note *arderem* in l. 53.

53 *Trinacria rupes*, 'the Sicilian rock': a typically 'Alexandrian' periphrasis for Mount Etna. As a figure for amorous passion it appears also in Hor. *Epod.* 17.30–3, Ov. *Rem.* 491, *Ep. Sapph.* 12.

54 Again, a geographical reference of a somewhat learned kind. The Pass of Thermopylae ('hot gates,' i.e., the pass which had hot springs, Hdt. 7.176 θερμὰ λουτρά) was in Malis, and adjoined Mount Oeta.

55 *neque* postponed, as often in C., e.g., below at line 116.

56 *imbre*, 'shower' (of tears); frequent in Ovid (B., E., F. cite *Tr.* 1.3.18).

57–66 See intr. n. The choice is between regarding 57–62 as referring to what precedes or to what follows; if the latter, then *hic* (63) must be changed to *ac*, which is both unwarranted and palaeographically unconvincing. See the thoughtful article by Offermann 1975; he points out from other passages that it is sometimes C.'s way to move from theme to theme by a sort of association of ideas, which produces a certain artistic tension when set against conscious articulation of the progress of the thought. It seems more poetical to let the image of tears (*tristi imbre*) grow into that of a mountain stream as it enters the plain, than to insist (after F. Skutsch) that the two similes at 119–34 must for the sake of symmetry be balanced by two similes here; and the necessary *ac* at 63 represents a weakening of the forceful effect obtained by *hic*.

If we punctuate as I have done, it can be supposed that C. may have in mind *Il.* 9.14–15 ἵστατο δάκρυ χέων ὥς τε κρήνη μελάνυδρος, ἥ τε κατ᾽ αἰγίλιπος πέτρης δνοφερὸν χέει ὕδωρ.

60 Nisbet's objections to *densi* are worth considering; see *PCPS* 24 (1978): 114 n. 49, and *MD* 26 (1991): 84–5.

61 The reading of *A* may perhaps have been double: possibly *viatorŭm*, *X* taking the *i* to be a correction; *X* is hardly an emendator of sufficient acumen to make this correction for himself. If *O*'s *-rum* is pure error (which might otherwise seem possible), it is hard to account for the adoption of the unhelpful variant *-rum* from *X* by *R*[2].

lasso sudore: 'poetic' transferred epithet.

62 *hiulcat* may be a coinage of C.'s (Venantius Fort. 6.10.6 *per hiulcatos agros*; cf. however V. *Geo.* 2.353 *hiulca ... arva*).

65 Castor and Pollux are the sailor's protecting deities: cf. 4.27, where notice the repetition of *gemelle*, curiously parallel to that of *iam* here.

prece Pollucis implorata = *Polluce precibus implorato* (Kr.). Cf. V. *Aen.* 11.4 *vota deum*.

66 See the Introduction to *CE*, p. 22; as I there suggest, both *allius* and *manl<l>ius* probably go back to the source of *OGR*, i.e. to *A*.

67 *is ... isque ... isque*: A.'s services to C. are now listed in detail. (Repetition of *is* for deliberate emphasis, Kr.)

limite, 'pathway.'

68 *dominam* goes closely with *domum*, as at 61.31. If Fröhlich's conjecture *dominae* is read, Lesbia is then introduced before her 'dramatic epiphany' in line 70 (Kinsey 1967: 43), which spoils the effect.

69 *ad quam*: *ad* = *apud*, or French *chez* (of the *domina*).

communes = *mutuos* (despite the objections of Kinsey 1967); cf. Lucr. 4.1195–6 *communia gaudia*, followed by *mutua gaudia* 1206.

exerceremus: the plural prepares the reader for the scene where Lesbia enters the room, without making any premature statement.

70 *molli ... pede*: cf. Prop. 2.12.24 *ut soleant molliter ire pedes*.
candida, 'dazzling,' 'shining.'

71 *trito*, 'well-worn'; cf. εὔξεστος.

72 *arguta*, 'squeaky,' of any high-pitched sound. For the adjective, and its associations in respect to hearing and other senses, see F. (to his *De oratore* reference, add Aul. Gell. 1.5.2). There is a considerable literature of love poetry celebrating the sound of the beloved's shoe or slipper, and it appears to be of world-wide extension.

73ff. Like Propertius after him (e.g., Prop. 1.3), C. is moved by the vision of his mistress to an extended mythological simile.

74 Protesilaus' marriage to Laodamia lasted one day, after which he went to Troy and – first of the Greeks to leap ashore – perished there. There is no trace in the legend of a neglected sacrifice in connection with Protesilaus' house; Homer (*Iliad* 2.701) merely says that it was half-finished (ἡμιτελής) when he went to war. It has recently been suggested that the *hostia* (76) is Iphigeneia, and that this reference serves only to 'date' the marriage just before the Trojan War: see Thomas 1978. But 77–8 tell against this interpretation, as Van Sickle 1980: 91 points out.

76 *hostia*: see 74 n.
caelestis ... eros = the gods.

77–8 For the interjected personal wish cf. 63.91–3 (and also cf. the poet's greeting to the heroes at 64.22–4).

77 *Rhamnusia virgo* = Nemesis; cf. 66.71 n. (also 50.20). If *A* had *ranusia*, both *O* and *X* will have deviated from it in characteristic ways.

78 For *R*'s *quod*, *m* has *quam*, influenced doubtless by *tam* in 77; *m²* adds *al. quod*, thus once again (cf. 9 n.) showing the correction as a variant.
invitis eris, 'against the will of the gods.' Cf. 76.12 *dis invitis*.

79 *pium cruorem* = the blood shed in sacrifice by *pii mortales* (transferred epithet).

81 *coniugis ... novi*: cf. *nova nupta* 61.91, etc. (also 64.402 n.).
novit is obviously wrong and unmetrical; the *R²* variant appears to be an attempt to gain a more plausible sense, but it is of course still unmetrical.

82 *una atque altera*, here = one, followed by another (as in Cicero, *Cluent.* 38 and 72). Elsewhere sometimes = 'one or two' (refs. in F.).

85 *quod* = *abruptum coniugium*.
non longo tempore abesse, si = 'was not to be long delayed, if ...'
V's *abisse* is perhaps influenced by *isset* 86.

86 *miles*, 'as a soldier.'

87 *raptu*, abl. of cause (cf. above, 25 n.).

89 *Troia ... /Troia*: with the epanalepsis, Kr. and F. compare 64.61–2 *prospicit, eheu, / prospicit*. Cf. 99 below, and see the intr. n. on the Troy passages, as well as line 92 n.

Kr. points out how the spondaic line ending expresses a tragic thought which could have been avoided by inversion of the two words; V. *Aen.* 10.91 begins *Europamque Asiamque.*

90 *acerba*, 'bitter' because unripe, premature.

cinis in transferred sense (feminine, as at 101.4 and in Calvus 15, 16 M and Lucr. 4.926; cf. 101.4 n.).

91 See App. Crit. Heinsius' *quaene etiam* has been successfully overturned by Courtney 1982: 50. Rather than obelize *V's que vetet id*, I have hesitantly come to accept Watt's arguments (see 'Sources') for accepting Marcilius' *quae nunc et.*

92 Cf. 20; notice also that 94 = 22, and compare 95–6 with 23–4.

See App. Crit.: *O* is not the source of the correction in G^1R^2, which is easy and obvious.

93 Cf. Lucr. 3.1033 *lumine adempto animam moribundo corpore fudit,* V. *Aen.* 6.363 *per caeli iucundum lumen at auras.*

97 *nota sepulcra*: cf. the use of *noti* at 79.4.

98 *cognatos = cognatorum* (another 'transferred' epithet); see Prop. (quoted below) and also Stat. *S.* 2.4.22 *cognata funera.*

The dread of being buried in distant foreign soil was grounded in the belief that the welfare of the soul after death depended on the performance of the appropriate cult acts by one's kin; Kr. cites Prop. 3.7.9–10 (*et mater non iusta piae dare debita terrae / nec pote cognatos inter humare rogos*) and Ov. *Tr.* 31–46. See Kr.'s n. on l. 97 for other passages.

compositum, 'laid out (for burial),' or (F.) 'laid to rest' (*OLD* 4 c).

100 *extremo* = at the furthest edge of the world, as in 11.2 *extremos Indos.* Ovid speaks thus of his place of exile (*Tr.* 3.3.13 *lassus in extremis iaceo populisque locisque*).

101 For the resumptive *tum*, taking up the thread of 86–8, and for the suggestion that 89–100 are a later insertion, see the intr. n.

102 *penetralis* (connected with *Penates*, see Cicero *ND* 2.68) *focos*: the central hearths of their houses. Editors from B. onwards cite Cicero, *Har. Resp.* 57 *deorum ... abditos ac penetralis focos* and V. *Aen.* 5.660 *rapiuntque focis penetralibus ignem.*

103–4 Notice the displaced order of words: *libera* ('unchecked') in 103 goes with *otia* in 104.

105 *tum* refers back to 85 and recurs to the story of Laodamia. (See intr. n.)

106 Cf. 64.215 *iucundior ... vita.*

107 *coniugium* (abstract for concrete), 'husband.' Notice that this single word has strayed into the next couplet (a sign of undeveloped elegiac technique).

amoris: take with *aestus* (Fr.) rather than with *barathrum.*

108 *barathrum*: deep drainage holes, leading to underground channels (mod. Greek *katavothra*) are a feature of northwest Arcadia; some of them were

attributed to Heracles. Pheneus was a city to the southwest of Mount Cyllene in Arcadia.

110 *emulsa*, 'drained out.'

111 For the metaphor in *montis ... medullis*, cf. V. *Aen.* 3.575 *viscera montis*.

112 *audit*, 'is said to,' in imitation of the Greek use of ἀκούειν (cf. Hor. *S.* 2.7.101). By analogy with *cluere* (Kr., F.), used here (and here only) with infin. *falsiparens Amphitrioniades*, 'he who was falsely said to be Amphitryon's son' (= Heracles, who was really begotten by Zeus). The compound adjective seems to be derived from Callimachus (ψευδοπάτωρ, *H.* 6.98, but in a different sense). As Kr. and F. point out, the line is wholly Greek in effect.

113 The references to the legends of Heracles continue with the slaying of the Stymphalian birds.
certa = 'flying straight,' 'unerring' (of an arrow at Hor. *Od.* 1.12.23). *Stymphalia monstra*: the crane-like birds of Lake Stymphalus are called *monstra* by C. because they ate men (as B. points out). Since the lake was close to Pheneus (above, 108 n.), C. fancies that the subterranean channels that drained the floods near the town (attributed by legend to Heracles, though not as one of his labours) were constructed by H. at the same time as he happened to be in the area in order to deal with the birds. Only E. notes that a Stymphalian bird appears on denarii of the *gens Valeria*.

114 *eri*: Eurystheus, who enjoined upon Heracles the labours the completion of which conferred immortality on the hero, gave Heracles his orders but was *deterior* all the same, as Heracles himself remarks in *Od.* 11.621 (μάλα γὰρ πολὺ χείρονι φωτὶ δεδμήμην, ὁ δέ μοι χαλεποὺς ἐπετέλλετ' ἀέθλους).

115 *pluribus ut ...*; i.e., the number of the gods who entered heaven was to be increased by one when Heracles achieved deification (and hence, immortality). His second reward, the hand of Hebe, is mentioned in the next line.

115–16 *Od.* 11.602 αὐτὸς δὲ μετ' ἀθανάτοισι θεοῖσι τέρπεται ἐν θαλίης καὶ ἔχει καλλίσφυρον Ἥβην.

117 C. returns again to address Laodamia.
altus amor: cf. Theocr. 3.42 βαθὺν ἔρωτα.

118 *tamen indomitam*, 'even untamed as you were,' a common metaphor for the unwedded maiden (παρθένος ἀδμής, *Odyssey* 6.109). For the idiom, see 64.103 (alternative punctuation). F. here refers to Munro on Lucr. 3.553 and Housman on Lucan 1.333.

119 Cf. V. *Aen.* 4.599 *confectum aetate parentem*. Virgil has many clear echoes of poem 68; cf. 108 with *Aen.* 3.421–2 *imo barathri ter gurgite vastos / sorbet in abruptum fluctus.*
   See App. Crit.: here we have another instance of a variant in *X* (reproduced in *R²m²*, though with substitution, perhaps by *R²*, of *neque* for *nec*) which

covers a mere slip (*causa* for *tam*) made by *X* himself. *X*'s variant gives, as usual, the text of *A*.

119–28 Two figures for the depth of Laodamia's love. They might seem a little superfluous; but, as Kr. points out, they balance, in the poem's structure, the two similes for C.'s own passion in lines 53ff. The first (a grandparent's delight in the late appearance of a grandson to be his direct heir) seems linked to Pindar, *Ol.* 10.86–90 ἀλλ' ὥτε παῖς ἐξ ἀλόχου πατρὶ ποθεινὸς ἵκοντι νεότατος τὸ πάλιν ἤδη, μάλα δέ οἱ θερμαίνει φιλότατι νόον· ἐπεὶ πλοῦτος ὁ λαχὼν ποιμένα ἐπακτὸν ἀλλότριον, θνᾴσκοντι στυγερώτατος and more remotely to *Il.* 9.481–2 Καὶ μ' ἐφίλησ' ὡς εἴ τε πατὴρ ὃν παῖδα φιλήσῃ μοῦνον τηλύγετον πολλοῖσιν ἐπὶ κτεάτεσσι. The second is the familiar image of two doves (see 125–8 n.).

119–24 The expression *carum caput* may have been borrowed from C. by Virgil (*Aen.* 4.354) and Horace (*Od.* 1.24.1–2). For the brief picture of the grandfather's pleasure in the fact that his daughter has at last presented him with an heir to the family fortune (which by the *Lex Voconia* could not be bequeathed to a female if the testator was included in the census, i.e., was financially of some substance), cf. the lines on the bereaved mother at 39.4–5.

122 *testatas*, for *testibus confirmatas*, of a will ('signed and sealed').

123–4 The distant relative is seen as a *captator* (legacy-hunter), a type for which the Roman satirists had a special distaste: for the metaphor in *volturium* cf. Plaut. *Trin.* 101 *sunt alii qui te volturium vocant.*

123 *impia* = contrary to family *pietas*.
derisi, 'made a laughing-stock' (F.), looks forward to the result.

125–8 Another metaphor for the depth of Laodamia's love. Editors compare (from poetry) Prop. 2.15.27–8 *exemplo iunctae tibi sint in amore columbae, / masculus et totum femina coniugium* and (from prose) Pliny, *NH* 10.104 *<columbae> coniugii fidem non violant communemque servant domum.*

126 *compar*, 'mate.'
improbius, 'more shamelessly.'

128 *multivola*, 'promiscuous' (cf. 140 *omnivolus*, of Jupiter).

129 *furores*, 'passion' (plural because several instances have been given). Although *furores* (cf. 64.54 and 94) might be applied to the amorous passion of doves in the second simile, it can hardly suit the grandfather's affection in the first; however, Kr. is probably right in suggesting that it applies loosely to both.

130 *conciliare* (*OLD* 1 b) means 'to bring a woman to a man as a wife (or mistress).'

131 *cui* postponed. As Kr. points out, such displacements occur in colloquial language when more emphatic words or phrases claim priority, and poets use them freely; he cites 51.5, 62.13–14, 64.8, 66 and 216.
aut paulo: the restriction surprises us, but is common in Latin: Cicero, *ND* 2.118 *nihil … aut admodum paululum*; Hor. *Ep.* 1.15.33–4 *nil aut paulum*

abstulerat; F. explains *paulo* (instead of *paulum*) with *concedere digna* by the fact that *c.d.* stands in place of *minor*.

132 *lux mea*, cf. 160. For this intimate expression of affection cf. Cicero, *Ad Fam.* 14.2.2 *mea lux, meum desiderium* (to his wife).

133–4 For the picture, cf. poem 45, with its refrain.

134 *candidus*, of Amor: Prop. 2.3.24 (B.).

For an exhaustive discussion of the phrase *crocina candidus in tunica*, see Mantero 1979.

135 F. has a good n. on the emotional significance of the poet's references to himself in the third person; he cites Propertius (2.8.17) and Ovid (*Tr.* 3.10.1, *Pont.* 1.7.69) as well as C.

136 *verecundae*: 'discreet' (i.e., not shameless). The future tense of *feremus* should be noted; it may be that C. suggests that he will tolerate her *furta* so long as she is discreet, and does not overdo them. Recent attempts to defend Büchner's 1950 reading *verecunde* (adverb) have hardly succeeded; *verecunde ferre* seems an unlikely combination, and the sense suffers. Against *verecunde* see, e.g., Bickel 1950, Holleman 1970, Bauer 1975; for *verecunde*, see Reynen 1974 and Bright 1976.

137 On *stultorum* it may be remarked that in poem 17 and at 83.2 it is the protesting cuckold who is called 'stupid'; B. proposed *tutorum* here, claiming that the *s* may be a duplication of the final letter of *simus*, but the change is hardly justified.

138 *caelicolum*: for the form cf. 64.355 *Troiugenum*. Notice that here, unusually, the sentence begins with the pentameter (Kr.).

138–9 C. here bends the myth to serve his purpose; Juno is not traditionally so tolerant (Fr.).

140 *V's facta* need not be changed: cf. Prop. 1.18.25–6 *omnia consuevi timidus perferre superbae / iussa, neque arguto facta dolore queri*. The Humanist who suggested *furta* may possibly have had in mind Prop. 2.30.28 *dulcia furta Iovis*.

141 *componier*: the archaic passive infinitive elsewhere exists in C. only in poem 61. Perhaps for this reason, and because *componere* is the reading of *V*, the end of this line frequently appears in the late Ms tradition in the form *componere fas est*. But the change from *fas* to *(a)equum* would be hard to explain. Gordon Williams 1968: 712 implicitly denies the presence of a lacuna by printing *nec ... est* as a parenthesis; but the imperative *tolle* (142) does suggest a lacuna.

143 *nec tamen*, 'and in any case ... not.' As Kr. and F. agree, the *nec* here cannot be shown to respond to the *nec* in 141, which 'was perhaps answered by a lost *nec* or *et*' (E.).

144 The perfume is a concrete presentation of the garnishing, for a bride, of her bridegroom's house.

Assyrio = (vaguely) 'Eastern.' Cf. 6.8 *Syrio fragrans olivo*. C. is by no means alone in apparently confusing the two adjectives; Horace has *malobathro Syrio* (*Od.* 2.7.8) and *Assyria nardus* (*Od.* 2.11.16). For a careful account of the history of the words in question see the nn. by Nisbet and Hubbard on these two Horatian passages.

145 See the App. Crit. As suggested there (the suggestion is mine, not Landor's), abbreviations for *mira* and *media* may have been confused. Though the notion behind *mira* may seem 'romantic' to modern eyes, it is quite unlike C. to cut across his meaning by introducing it. A doubtful alternative to *media* (not noticed by editors) might be *pura*, on the basis of V. *Ecl.* 9.44 *pura sub nocte*. *munuscula*: both here and at 64.103 the diminutive virtually stands for *munera*. Metrical convenience, and possibly the liquid sound that C. likes to attach to feminine utterance (cf., e.g., 45.13–16), may have prompted him to use it.

148 The reading *dies* is possible; see however F. For the 'attraction' of the relative, cf. 153 (where *plurima* goes with *munera* 154) and 64.208–9. *candidiore*: cf. 107.6 n.

149 *quod potui*: contrast 32 *nequeo*. The epilogue (149–60) must be attached to the poem in praise of Allius (68^b), not to the letter to Manlius (68^a).

See the App. Crit. *O* is not really at home with his compendia; cf. 64.153. For the palaeographical distinction between the compendia for *h(a)ec* and *hoc*, see 64.175 n.

150 *multis ... officiis*: cf. 42 *quantis ... officiis* (echoed here, along with Allius' name).

151 *vestrum*: 'your family's'. Cf. 64.160, where *vestras* and *potuisti* are juxtaposed. Kr., however, takes it as = *tuum*. *robigine*: cf. 49–50 (only a slight change of metaphor). There is also, in *nomen* and the idea of oblivion, an echo of line 43.

153 Themis, goddess of justice (= Dike, the last of the goddesses to leave the earth); associated with Nemesis (their shrines, at Rhamnus in Attica, lay beside each other and were virtually one). *piis* (treated here as a noun): *pietas* is a human quality especially linked with Themis. Cf. 64.386 *nondum spreta pietate* (and 403–4 *impia ... impia*), 406 *iustificam ... mentem avertere deorum* (i.e., when *pietas* was abandoned by men).

155 *tua vita*: cf. 132, 160, *lux mea*; also 45.13, 109.1.

See App. Crit. (*R*¹ makes an obvious correction, but in so doing he introduces a fresh error, which is in turn corrected by *R*²).

156 *domus ... domina*: cf. 68 *domum ... dominam*. The parallelism implies that *domina* here denotes 'the lady of the house,' not 'my mistress' (= *era*). This would tell against the restoration *in qua nos lusimus*, adopted by Lee and others. *lusimus*: for this meaning of the word, cf. line 17 n.

157–8 The text is corrupt, but it appears that a further person is gratefully recorded as having procured for C. an introduction – perhaps to Lesbia, perhaps to Allius – even before the house was made available for the assignation.

157 This line is described by Mynors as a *locus conclamatus*. In order to keep some kind of sense in the last sentence of such a long poem as this, in *CE* I adopted, very hesitantly, Lipsius' emendation. In support of his reading, *terram dedit auspex*, cf. Varro *LL* 7.6 *templum … dicitur … ab auspiciis in terra … (8) in terris dictum templum locus augurii causa quibusdam conceptis verbis finitus.* For the role of *auspices* in matters of love, cf. 45.19, 26. Perhaps this particular *auspex* is poetically seen as fulfilling the office of an *augur* and delimiting – *augurii causa*, in a manner of speaking – a *templum terrestre* (the house). But I now regard this explanation as too controversial, and have abandoned it.

The spelling of Scaliger's reading is taken from his 1577 edition. Cf. *OLD* s.v. *trado* for the form *transd-*. Lee adopts *te tradidit* as from Scaliger. See further Wiseman 1974a, who would read *vobis me tradidit*, supposing a name (now lost) to end the line.

159 As parallels to the expression *mihi me carior*, F. cites two passages from Ovid (*Tr.* 5.14.2, *Pont.* 2.8.27) and one from Cicero's letters (*Ad Att.* 3.22.3).

Vahlen, J. 1902. 'Über C.s Elegie an M.' Allius,' *SPAW* 44: 1024–43 (= *Ges. Schriften* 2.652–74).

Guglielmino, F. 1915. 'Sulla composizione del carme LXVIII di C.,' *Athenaeum* 3 (1915): 426–44.

Hartman, J.J. 1916. 'De Catulli carmine LXVIII,' *Mn.* 44: 88–99.

Howald, E. 1918. 'Zu C. 68a,' *BPhW* 38: 141–4.

Jus, L. 1927–28. 'De duodeseptuagesimo carmine Catulli I & I,' *Eos* 30 (1927): 77–92 and *Eos* 31 (1928): 63–77.

Prescott, H.W. 1940. 'The Unity of C. 68,' *TAPA* 71: 473–500.

Barwick, K. 1947. 'C.s c. 68 und eine Kompositionsform der römischen Elegie und Epigrammatik,' *WJA* 2: 1–15.

Salvatore, A. 1949. 'L' unità del carme 68 di C.,' *GIF* 2: 36–49.

Büchner, K. 1950. 'C. 68, 136,' *MH* 7: 14–18.

Bickel, E. 1950. 'Era Verecunda: C. 68,136,' *RhM* 93: 384.

Della Corte, F. 1951. *Due studi catulliani*. Genoa. [For poem 68 see pp. 134–42.]

Pepe, L. 1953. 'Il mito di Laodamia nel carme 68 di C.,' *GIF* 6: 107–13.

Salvatore, A. 1955. 'Le poème 68 de C. et le problème de l'élégie latine,' *Phoibos* 6/7 (1951/52 and 1952/53: published 1955): 7–55.

Wohlberg, J. 1955. 'The Structure of the Laodamia Simile in C. 68b,' *CP* 50: 42–6.

Copley, F.O. 1957. 'The Unity of C. 68: A Further View,' *CP* 52: 29–32.

Pennisi, G. 1959. 'Il carme 68 di C.,' *Emerita* 27: 89–109 and 213–28.

Godel, R. 1965. 'C., poème 68,' *MH* 22: 53–65.

Vretska, K. 1966. 'Das Problem der Einheit von C. c. 68,' *WS* 79: 313–30.

Kinsey, T.E. 1967. 'Some Problems in C. 68,' *Latomus* 26: 36–53.

Hering, W. 1970. 'Die Komposition der sog. Allius-Elegie (C. c. 68,41ff.),' *WZRostock* 19: 599–604.

Holleman, A.W.J. 1970. 'Lesbia als Verecunda Era (carm. 68, 136),' *Hermeneus* 41: 192–4.

Wilkinson, L.P. 1970. '*Domina* in C. 68,' *CR* 20: 290.

Hering, W. 1972. 'Beobachtungen zu C. c. 68,41–160,' *ACD* 8: 31–61.

Skinner, M.B. 1972. 'The Unity of C. 68: The Structure of 68a,' *TAPA* 103: 495–512.

Macleod, C.W. 1974. 'A Use of Myth in Ancient Poetry,' *CQ* 24: 82–93, esp. 82–8.

McClure, R. 1974. 'The Structure of C. 68,' *CSCA* 7: 215–29.

Reynen, H. 1974. 'Rara verecundae furta feremus erae,' *MH* 31: 149–54.

Wiseman, T.P. 1974a. 'C. 68.157,' *CR* 24: 6–7.

– 1974b. *Cinna the Poet and other Roman essays.* Leicester: 77–103 (see also 70–6).

Monbrun, M. 1975. 'A propos du poème 68 de C. Quelques considérations sur la métrique et l'ordre des mots,' *Pallas* 22: 23–41.

Baker, R.J. 1975. '*Domina* at C. 68.68: Mistress or Chatelaine?,' *RhM* 118: 124–9.

Bauer, J.B. 1975. 'Erae furta verecundae,' *WS* 9: 78–82.

Offermann, H. 1975. 'Der Flussvergleich bei C., c. 68,57ff.,' *Philologus* 119: 57–69.

Solmsen, F. 1975. 'C.'s Artistry in c. 68: A Pre-Augustan Subjective Love-Elegy,' *Monumentum Chilonense: Studien zur augusteischen Zeit. Kieler Festschrift für E. Burck.* Amsterdam: 260–76.

Bright, D.F. 1976. 'Confectum Carmine Munus: C. 68,' *ICS* 1: 86–112.

Gantar, K. 1976. 'Einige Beobachtungen zu C. c. 68,71–73,' *GB* 5: 117–21.

Levine, P. 1976. 'C. c. 68. A New Perspective,' *CSCA* 9: 61–88.

Phillips, J.E. 1976. 'The Pattern of Images in C. 68.51–62,' *AJP* 77: 340–3.

Shipton, K.M.W. 1978. 'C. 68,' *LCM* 3: 57–64.

Thomas, R.F. 1978. 'An Alternative to Ceremonial Negligence (C. 68.73–8),' *HSCP* 82: 175–8.

Yardley, J.C. 1978. '*Copia scriptorum* in C. 68.33,' *Phoenix* 32: 337–9.

Mantero, T. 1979 '*Crocina candidus in tunica,*' *Traglia* 1. Rome: 161–92. [Line 134.]

Della Corte, F. 1979. 'Arguta solea,' *RFIC* 107: 30–34 (= *Opuscula* 7 [1983]: 57–61). [Line 72.]

Pasoli, E. 1980. 'Appunto sul ruole del c. 68 di C. nell'origine dell'elegia latina,' *Actes du colloque 'L'Élégie romaine: enracinement – thèmes – diffusion,' mars 1979* (= *Bulletin de la Faculté des Lettres de Mulhouse,* fasc. X). Paris: 17–26.

Dee, J.H. 1980. 'C. 68.155–60: An Observation,' *CW* 73: 420. [Discussion of Macleod 1974.]

Williams, G. 1980. *Figures of Thought in Roman Poetry.* New Haven: 55–61. [On C.'s similes.]

Van Sickle, J. 1980. 'C. 68.73–8 in Context (vv. 67–80),' *HSCP* 84: 91–5.

Tuplin, C.J. 1981. 'C. 68,' *CQ* 31: 113–39.

Most, G.W. 1981. 'On the Arrangement of C.'s Carmina Maiora,' *Philologus* 125: 109–25, esp. 116ff.

Bright, D.F. 1982. 'Allius and Allia,' *RhM* 125: 138–40.

Papanghelis, T.D. 1982. 'A Note on C. 68.156–57,' *QUCC* 11: 139–49.

Sarkissian, J. 1983. *Catullus 68: An Interpretation*. Leiden.

Woodman, A.J. 1983. 'A Reading of C. 68A,' *PCPS* 29: 100–6.

Fredricksmeyer, E.A. 1983. 'C. 51 and 68.51–6: An Observation,' *CP* 78: 42–5.

Shipton, K.M.W. 1983. 'A House in the City: C. 68.68,' *Latomus* 42: 869–76.

Brenk, F.E. 1983. 'Lesbia's arguta solea: 68.72 and Greek λιγύς,' *Glotta* 61: 234–6.

Németh, B. 1984. 'Communes exerceremus amores, C. 68.69,' *ACD* 20: 43–7.

Hubbard, T.K. 1984. 'C. 68. The Text as Self-Demystification,' *Arethusa* 17: 29–49.

Cavallini, E. 1984/85. 'C. 68.70ss.,' *MCr* 19/20: 191.

Capponi, F. 1984/85. 'Note filologiche' [68.157], *QCTC* 2–3: 17–34.

Courtney, E. 1985. 'Three Poems of C.: (3). C. 68 and Its Compositional Scheme,' *BICS* 32: 92–100.

Shipton, K.M.W. 1985a. 'C. 68 and the Myth of Agamemnon,' *Latomus* 44: 55–71.

– 1985b. 'A Successful *kômos* in C.,' *Latomus* 44: 503–20.

Schilling, R. 1985. 'La paronomasie domum-dominus dans l'élégie 68 de C.,' *AFLNice* 50: 284–91.

Poliakoff, M. 1985. 'Clumsy and Clever Spiders on Hermann's Bridge (C. 68.49–50; *Culex* 1–3),' *Glotta* 53: 248–50.

Shipton, K.M.W. 1986. 'The *iuvenca* Image in C. 68,' *CQ* 36: 268–70.

Lain, N.F. 1986. 'C. 68.145,' *HSCP* 90: 155–8.

Allen, A. 1986. 'Sacrificial Negligence in C.,' *Latomus* 45: 861–3.

Shipton, K.M.W. 1987. 'No Alternative to Ceremonial Negligence (C. 68.37ff.),' *SO* 62: 51–68.

Forsyth, P.Y. 1987. 'Muneraque et Musarum hinc petis et Veneris: C. 68A.10,' *CW* 80: 177–80.

Brenk, F.G. 1987. 'Arguta solea on the Threshold: The Literary Precedents of C. 68.68–72,' *QUCC* 26: 121–7.

Heath, M. 1988. 'Catullus 68[b],' *LCM* 13: 117–19.

Milanese, G. 1988. 'Non possum reticere (C. 68A. 41),' *Aevum antiquum* 1: 261–4.

Powell, J.G.F. 1990. 'Two Notes on C.,' *CQ* 40: 199–206. [On poem 76 and on 68.27–30.]

Allen, A. 1991. 'Domus data ablataque: C. 68.157,' *QUCC* 37: 101–6.

Edwards, M.J. 1991. 'The Theology of C. 68[b],' *Antike und Abendland* 37: 68–81.

Lefèvre, E. 1991. 'Was hatte C. in der Kapsel ... <68A> ...? Zu Aufbau und Aussage der Allius-Elegie,' *RhM* 134: 311–26.

Simpson, C.J. 1992. 'A Note on C. 68A.34f.,' *LCM* 17: 12.

Arkins, B. 1992. 'Two Notes on C.: I. 68.145 [Read *mira*]; II. Crucial Constants in
C.: Callimachus, the Muses, Friends and Enemies,' *LCM* 17: 15–18.

Feeney, D.C. 1992. 'Shall I Compare Thee ...? C. 68B and the Limits of Analogy,'
Author and Audience in Latin Literature, ed. Tony Woodman and J. Powell.
Cambridge: 33–44.

Fear, T. 1992. 'Veronae Turpe, Catulle, Esse,' *ICS* 17: 245–63.

Kershaw, A. 1993. '*A!* at C. 68.85,' *Papers of the Leeds International Latin seminar*
7.27–9.

Fear, T. 1993. 'Another Note on C. 68a.34f.,' *LCM* 18: 4.

Simpson, C.J. 1994. 'Unnecessary Homosexuality. The Correspondent's Request in
C. 68a,' *Latomus* 53: 564–5.

Clauss, J.J. 1995. 'A Delicate Foot on the Well-Worn Threshold: Paradoxical Imagery
in C. 68[b],' *AJP* 116: 237–55.

69

Structure: 4 + 4 + 2 (statement; explanation; conclusion to be drawn).
The theme is 'personal hygiene'; cf. poems 71, 97. Yet it is delicately
written, using no vulgar terms: a fitting opening poem for a series of some
fifty elegiac epigrams characterized by exquisite artistry, particularly in the
manipulation of sounds, no matter what the subject may happen to be. The
language is very slightly colloquial (*femina, neque mirum*); there is one
hapax eiremenon (*perluciduli*). A 'cyclic' effect is obtained by the use of
repetition (*quare, admirari*) to link the concluding couplet with the opening.
Like many of the epigrams, this repays reading aloud because so much of its
effect depends on sound-arrangement: in the second couplet, for example,
the 'feminine' *i*'s (cf. poem 45 nn.) together with the liquid *l*'s (cf. poem 25)
contrast with the harsh *r*'s in l. 6 and the disapproving *m*'s in l. 7.

On the question who 'Rufus' is, see intr. n. to poem 77. Noonan 1979
ingeniously sees the poem as a kind of allegory, with Bestia as a proper
name; but this view hardly takes adequate account of the prima facie relation
of poem 69 to poem 71 (echoes, both in theme – odour – and in language:
caper = hircus).

3 *non si*, 'not even if' (cf. 48.5 n., 70.2 – where F. has a useful n. – and 88.8).
rarae, 'choice,' 'exquisite' (probably not referring to the fineness of the textile).
labefactes: literally, 'undermine' a building, to impair its stability; hence
'seduce.'

4 *perluciduli*, 'transparent' (*hapax eiremenon*). Notice the melodious repetition of
(chiefly liquid) consonants in the line. (At 31.13, if *lucidae lacus undae* is right,
it deserves the same praise).

6 *valle*, 'hollow.' Cf. Ar. *Eccl.* 12 μηρῶν μυχούς, Auson. Epigr. 87.5 *valle femorum.*
   caper: cf. 71.1 (and 37.5) *hircus*. On the supposed distinction in meaning between
   caper and *hircus*, see n. on 37.5. Cf. Ov. *AA* 3.193 *ne trux caper iret in alas.*

7 *omnes* (sc. *feminae*, or *puellae*).

8 *quicum* as a feminine form (cf. 66.77) is archaic.
   bella puella cubet: also at 78.4.

9 *crudelem ... pestem*: the phrase is used at 64.76 to describe the Minotaur. As
   often happens in C.'s short poems, overstatement (which here begins with *mala
   bestia*) works up to a climax of rhetorical extravagance.

10 *admirari*: the repetition (from line 1) produces a cyclic effect.
   fugiunt: the indicative in indirect question (for *fugiant*) is colloquial; cf. 61.78
   (Kr. gives other references).

Dane, N. 1968. 'Rufus redolens,' *CJ* 64: 130.
Noonan, J.D. 1979. '*Mala bestia* in C. 69.7–8,' *CW* 73: 155–64.
Cairns, F. 1992. 'C. 69.9–10 and Ancient "Etymologies,"' *RFIC* 119: 442–45.

70

Structure: balanced (2 + 2).

As poem 69 is echoed in poem 71, so does poem 70 find thematic and
linguistic echoes in poem 72; because 72.1–2 mention Lesbia, we know
poem 70 also has to do with her. For the mode of expression there are Greek
precedents: Callimachus, *Ep.* 25 Pf. = *AP* 5.6; Meleager, *AP* 5.8 (cf. 5.24 and
12.70); see Laurens 1965. Ultimately the manner is Callimachean, though
the mere repetition of *dicit* should not be given undue weight. Skiadas 1975
draws attention to a contrast: C. is 'involved,' whereas Callimachus is not
(cf. poem 72, which, as F. notes, is 'clearly personal').

   The poem records a period of disillusionment in C.'s affair with Lesbia;
she ranks him still above all possible rivals, or says she does, but he for
his part begins to realize how little such 'oaths' are worth. Here again (see
poem 69) the succession of vowel sounds and consonantal sounds produces
much of the poem's charm: notice the sudden change from (mostly) sweet to
harsh consonants in l. 4. Many of the epigrams contain, or hint at, a proverb
(ll. 3–4 here; cf. poems 93, 94, 100, 113, 115).

1 *nulli* = *nemini*. (Later writers, such as Livy and Tacitus, revert to *nulli*, perhaps
   under the influence of poetry.)
   mulier: a very general term ('woman' or 'wife'), in colloquial use (hence Italian
   moglie); here employed to contrive a repetition within the perfectly general
   statement contained in line 3.

nubere: Editors suggest, on the whole rightly, that *nubere* can be used of a tie other than marriage; but passages like Plaut. *Cist.* 43 (of a *meretrix* who *cottidie viro nubit, nupsitque hodie, nubet mox noctu*), where the meaning is extended *ad hoc*, do not really support this claim (as Kr. points out, in the *Cistellaria* context, just before these words occur, the talk had been of legitimate marriage).

2 *non si*: cf. 69.3 n.

Iuppiter etc.: proverbial; cf. Plaut. *Cas.* 323; also Ov. *M.* 7.801, which may echo C. here. See 72.2.

petat, of a suit: cf. V. *Aen.* 12.42 *conubia nostra petentem*.

4 The proverbs speak of 'writing on water' (εἰς ὕδωρ γράφειν, Soph. fr. 742 N²; cf. Plato, *Phaedr.* 276c), or else of 'letting the wind (or water: *ventus et unda* at both Prop. 2.28.8 and Ov. *Am.* 2.16.45–6) carry one's words away'; but 'writing on the wind' is unparalleled. C. has simply conflated the two expressions (cf. 30.10) in a poetic ellipse.

Laurens, P. 1965. 'À propos d'une image catullienne (c. 70.4),' *Latomus* 24: 545–50.

de Venuto, D. 1966. 'Il carme 70 di C. e *Anth. Pal.* 5.8 di Meleagro,' *RCCM* 8: 215–19.

Skiadas, A.D. 1975. 'Periuria Amantium: Zur Geschichte und Interpretation eines Motivs der augusteischen Liebesdichtung,' *Monumentum Chilonense: Studien zur augusteischen Zeit. Festschrift für E. Burck*. Amsterdam: 400–18, esp. 407–9.

Miller, P.A. 1988. 'C. 70: A Poem and its Hypothesis,' *Helios* 15: 127–32.

71

Structure: 4 + 2 (*nam*).

On 'personal hygiene' (poem 69 n.). It is surprising, in view of C.'s usual practice, to find no name given. (Palladius' *iure bono*, which E. calls 'tame,' is needed to balance *merito*.) Possibly it continues, under *aemulus*, the attack on Rufus of poem 69; if so, is it addressed to C. himself?

1 'If anyone deserves to be physically handicapped in his social life, it's that rival of yours.'

iure bono: a loose poetic equivalent for the prosaic formula *optimo iure*.

sacer, 'accursed' (cf. 14.12).

obstitit, 'has got in the way' (of his success with girls).

On *qui* or *qua* for *cui* see 1.1 n. *R²*'s *al. quo* is an attempted correction, ignored by *m*, who shows signs of haste towards the end of the book (for example, he omits the word *aliquem* at 73.2).

2 *tarda*, in active sense, 'hindering.' Horace borrows the phrase *tarda podagra* (*S.* 1.9.32).

podagra: the second syllable, (unusually) treated as long here, is short in line 6. Here *m* agrees with *O*; but *m*'s correction of *R* is easy and obvious – and independent.

3 *exercet amorem*: not simply = *amore fruitur*, as at 68.69 (which would apply to one's *own* love), but here 'meddles in *your* love.'

vester can mean *tuus*, even in the proximity of *te* or *tuus*; cf. 39.20–1. But C. may, as Kr. suggests, be thinking (together) of the person addressed and his *puella*.

4 *mirifice*, a work much used by Cicero (111 instances are quoted in *TLL*), never seems merely to intensify another adverb, but always to be self-contained in its meaning ('wonderfully *well*,' etc.); the parallel with θαυμασίως ὡς, drawn by Nisbet 1978: 109, does not seem to be supported by usage. For this reason – and because the placing of two adjs. or advs. in tandem is a feature of C.'s style – in *CE* I thought it right to enclose *apte* between commas: 'has acquired both troubles to a remarkable degree – and appropriately, too!' At Lucr. 4.462 *mirande multa* and Quint. 3.5.14 *mirabiliter multa*, the adverb is used to intensify, not a second adverb, but an adjective. The nearest parallel, in a sense, is Gellius 16.6.9 *nimium quantum audacter*, though, besides being late, it has nothing to do with *mirifice*. After much hesitation, and in view of the passages cited from Lucr. and Quint., I have now deleted the commas. See n. on 53.2.

6 *odore*: cf. 69.9 *nasorum ... pestem*.

perit: for this (less than literal) meaning, cf. 14.14.

Castiglioni, L. 1940/1. 'Decisa Forficibus,' *Rendic. Ist. Lomb.* 74: 389–418.
Kaster, R.A. 1977. 'A Note on C., c. 71.4,' *Philologus* 121: 308–31.

72

Structure: balanced (4 + 4); see Davis 1971 (three sets of structural patterns, based on contrasts).

Related to poem 70 (q.v.); but also to poems 75 and 85, in which the thought expressed here, especially in ll. 5–8, is progressively condensed. The great change from poem 70 lies in the use of tenses: poem 70 is entirely in the present (*dicit*), but a main factor in the working of poem 72 is the steady progress in time from past state (*dicebas*) to completed action (*dilexi*; *cognovi*) to present situation (*es*). As Davis points out, there are two further contrasts: Lesbia's feelings (1–2 only) against C.'s; and romantic love (for which C. finds a new kind of expression, l. 6) in opposition to sexual desire. It is of course C.'s discovery of Lesbia's infidelity (only a future possibility in poem 70) that finds expression in *te cognovi*; nevertheless, he still burns with passion. For the device of 'advancing anaphora,' by which *te* steadily advances towards the beginning of the line, producing an effect of excitement and climax, see poem 83 n. Notice how in the last two lines, where there is no further reference to *te* or *me*, the expression becomes general; cf. poem 70 for this (in some other epigrams, e.g., poems 73, 107, 110, 111, the general statement comes first). The opposition between *quondam* ... *nosse* in l. 1 and *nunc* ... *cognovi* in l. 4, with its deliberate repetition of the same, or a cognate, verb in a quite different sense, is sharply pointed.

1 *dicebas*: cf. 70.1 and 3 *dicit*.
   nosse ... *tenere*: both words have generally amorous overtones, but neither refers to a specific sexual act. With *nosse* we should supply *velle* from l. 2.
2 Cf. 64.28 *tenuit*.
   Iovem: cf. 70.2 n.
3 *dilexi*: the choice of a word indicating (as is evident from what follows) a supra-sensual kind of affection is deliberate: see line 4. At 6.5, the word has an earthier connotation, being applied to a *scortum*.
4 *generos*: note the 'extension' of family implied by this.
5 *cognovi*: a true perfect tense, 'I have come to understand you,' almost (in the context) 'I have found you out.' The central importance of the changes of tense in the poem is well brought out by Davis.
6 *vilior* and *levior* have here much the same meaning: Lesbia has lost C.'s respect (Tac. *H.* 4.80 *paulatim levior viliorque haberi*).
7 For the device of a short question suggesting dialogue, see 6.13 n. (also 85.1 *fortasse requiris*, 'perhaps you are asking me').
   qui, instrumental (ablative) – 'how?' – as in phrases like *qui fit, qui possum*.
   potis est = potest <fieri> (cf. 76.24 for *potis est*, 42.16 and 76.16 for *potest*).
   iniuria, 'wrong,' the opposite of *ius*; not 'injury,' which in English tends to suggest physical violence (or, by a metaphor, 'injured' feelings). In C. it begins to have the connotation of unfaithfulness, especially on the part of a mistress, which it retains in the Augustan elegists; F. quotes Prop. 2.24.39, 4.8.27, and Ov. *M.* 9.150.
8 *bene velle* = 'the feelings of ordinary friendship,' according to F., who cites Plaut. *Pseud.* 233 *iam diu ego huic bene et hic mihi volumus et amicitia est antiqua*. Kr., too, interprets *bene velle* as originating in the sphere of friendship; but in addition to the passage already quoted he cites two further Plautine passages, from which Q. properly deduces the meaning 'be fond of': *Truc.* 441 *egone illam ut non amem? egone illi ut non bene velim?*; *Trin.* 437–8 *quid agit filius? / bene volt tibi*.

Harmon, D.P. 1970. 'C. 72.3–4,' *CJ* 65: 321–2.
Davis, J.T. 1971. 'Poetic Counterpoint: C. 72,' *AJP* 92: 196–201.
Kubiak, D.P. 1986. 'Time and Traditional Diction in C. 72,' *SLLRH* 4. Brussels: 259–64.

73

Structure: 4 + 2 (*ut* ...) (a general statement, followed by a particular application).

Ingratitude and hostility on the part of one who had regarded C. as an intimate friend. The person referred to here may well be the Caelius of poem 100; cf. l. 6 *amicum* with 100.6 *unica amicitia*. Rufus of poem 77 is another candidate (not Alfenus of poem 30, despite Kr.; something more than simple neglect is in point here). Of all poems in this category (complaints about breach of friendship), the present one is – as L. remarked – the most emotionally charged. In the last line, the multiple elisions are pathetic; any slight awkwardness is deliberate, as though the poet wished, thereby, to show his distress (reflected also in the repeated *m*-sounds).

For the restoration of the imperfect l. 4, see the n. below. Some editors prefer to read <*prodest*>, *immo* ... But with this text the first, and more emphatic, contrast of *prodest* would be with *taedet*, not, as the editors wish, with *obest*. For the repetition *taedet, taedet*, see l. 4 n.

1 *desine*: notice the use of the imperative to express 'a general rule' (Kr., who compares 28.13 *pete nobiles amicos*, and also the formula *i nunc*).
   quoquam quicquam: repetition for emphasis.
2 *aliquem*, 'somebody or other,' not merely (as Kr.) = *quemquam* ('any single person'): see F. on 76.7, especially his tr. of Cic. *Red. Sen.* 30 *difficile est non aliquem, nefas quemquam praeterire*, 'it is difficult not to leave out someone or other; it is wrong to leave out any single person.'
   pium, 'loyal' in friendship.
3 *omnia sunt ingrata*, 'every kindness one does is wasted.' Kr. well compares Plaut. *Asin.* 136 *ingrata ... omnia intellego quae dedi et quod bene feci*; other references will be found in F., whose alternative explanation (in which *omnia* = 'the world'; cf. 89.3 n.) is perhaps too general for the context.
   fecisse benigne, a more elaborate way of saying *bene fecisse*; cf. 76.1 *benefacta* (Cic. *Ad Fam.* 13.67.1 has *plurimis ... benigne fecisti*).
   Est (*ē*, omitted after the final *e* of *benigne*) must be restored if Avantius' reading is adopted in l. 4; it is needed to balance *sunt*.
4 For the repetition *taedet, taedet* cf. 64.26–7 *ipse, ipse*, and 107.4–5. The enjambement, if we accept *prodest* (or any of the other words supplied at the beginning of the line), is somewhat heavy for C. in epigrams of this length and type, and should be avoided if possible. A scribe who was capable of omitting one word might easily omit another (see l. 3); this is merely an observation, for of course as an argument it has no weight. The opposition *obesse-prodesse* is obviously familiar: see *TLL* 9.2.265.35–72. Here, however, the first – and the

more emphatic – contrast implied in <prodest> would be with *taedet*, rather than with *obest*.

Notice R^2's attempt at metrical correction, an attempt based on the archetypal (A) reading *magisque magis*.

magis = potius ('instead,' 'rather'), as at 68.30. F. cites also V. *Ecl.* 1.11, Prop. 2.3.53, to illustrate the acquisition by *magis* of the 'adversative' sense which (as he rightly says) it bears in later Latin.

5 *gravius = acerbius*: cf. Caes. *B.C.* 1.5.4 *gravissime acerbissimeque (decernitur)*.
urget: cf. Tib. 2.1.79 *quos hic graviter deus urget*.

6 R^2 at first leaves *R*'s *habet* in place, but later – in the margin – offers a metrical correction, which is accepted (as a variant, *because* it is marginal in R^2) by m^2. If *habuit* had been there for *m* to see, it is very unlikely that he would have missed it.

See the ingenious, if not wholly convincing, explanation for the large number of elisions in this line (parody of a metrical fault by the offender, who had written the same line with *te* for C.'s *me*), offered by Postgate 1932.

unum atque unicum: as Kr. says, the fact that Aulus Gellius (18.4.2) and Apuleius (*M.* 4.31) treat this pleonasm as a formula suggests that they regarded it as archaic.

Postgate, P.E. 1932. *PCPS* 151–2: 6.
Oldfather, W.A. 1943. 'The Most Extreme Case of Elision in the Latin Language?,'
   CJ 38 (1943): 478–9.

74

Structure: 4 + 2 (*nam*, postponed).
The first of a cycle of abusive poems on Gellius (poems 80, 88, 89, 90, 91, 116). From poem 116, probably the earliest of them, with its mention of *tela ista* and its reference to the possibility of appeasing Gellius with literary offerings, it seems that G. was himself an epigrammatist, and at least to that extent C.'s literary rival; he was also his rival in the matter of a *magnus amor*, probably Lesbia (see poem 91). Probably he was L. Gellius Publicola, son of the consul of 72 BC, and consul himself in 36 (if so, his uncle may have been the Gellius mentioned adversely by Cicero, *Pro Sestio* 110). For his alleged incest with his stepmother, see Val. Max. 5.9.1. When he was a member of Clodia's circle, in 56 BC, he seems to have been doubly linked with the prosecution of Caelius, as (i) married to the sister of the prosecutor, and (ii) possibly the stepson of Polla, against whom Caelius was charged with fraud (R.G. Austin on *Pro Caelio* 23).
The point of the poem, namely that '*fellatio* precludes conversation' (Gaisser 1993: 72), was first made by Parthenius (line 5 n., *nam qui*

irrumatur et fellat tacere cogitur); cf. Politianus, *Miscellanea* I.83 *coepit irrumare patruum, eoque pacto tacere coegit, quoniam loqui fellator non potest*. Both passages are quoted in Gaisser 1993: 311 n. 21.

1 *R's lelius* appears in *m*. The variant *al. Gellius* was surely taken by R^2 from the margins of *X*. It looks therefore as if *X* had, in his text, the erroneous *lelius* of *GR*. Notice that *O* has *tellius* at 89.1. For the spelling of the name cf. also 80.1, 88.1 and 5, 90.1, and 116.6. It is not, however, likely that *O* has here corrected *Gelius* to *Gellius* on the basis of any or all of these passages; consistency in spelling is not *O's forte*, as will be evident from the App. Crit.
Gellius: see intr. n.
patruum: the Romans thought of the *patruus* as a 'Dutch uncle,' apt on occasion to scold the young; see Cicero, *Cael.* 25 (quoted by Kr.).

2 *delicias*, 'naughtiness' (cf. 50.3 *delicatos*). As Kr. points out, Cicero (*Cael.* 27) calls one section of the speech *against* Caelius 'deliciarum obiurgatio.'

3 *perdepsuit = futuit*; see *depsit* at Cic. *Ad Fam.* 9.22.4 (discussing the use of improper language). Giselinus, in the 1569 Plantin edition, attributes the correction to 'Cauchus et alii.' Scaliger claimed it for himself. See Gaisser 1993: 414–15.

4 Harpocrates (har-pe-chrod) was the god Horus (Hor), son of Isis and Serapis; in works of art he was depicted as an infant, hence with finger in mouth; but this came to be interpreted as a gesture, counselling silence. Cf. 102.4 n. (On the spelling -*en*, see A.E. Housman, 'Greek Nouns in Latin Poetry,' *J.Phil.* 31 (1910): 236–66.)

5 *fecit = effecit* (cf. 98.6).
irrumat: 16.1 n.

6 *nunc* should really be included in the main clause, but the meaning is clear.

Kitchell, K.F. 1986. 'Et patruum reddidit Harpocratem; A Re-interpretation of C., c. 74,' *SLLRH* 4. Brussels: 100–10.

75

Structure: balanced (unitary: *huc ... ut ...*).
See n. on poem 72 for poem 75 as an intermediate stage in compression of thought between poem 72 and poem 85. The tenses (see on poem 72) are now reduced to two: perfect and present. The opposition between *fieri* and *facere*, which forms the principal contrast in poem 85, is already made explicit here, though less concisely and in a more laboured way. Notice, in this poem, the fact that the first halves of ll. 1 and 3 show some measure of rhythmical correspondence, whereas ll. 2 and 4 do not correspond (in

rhythm) at all. This gives a certain variety; the somewhat unusual elision of the *e* in *amare* (at the diaeresis) both helps this variety and adds a touch of pathos.

1 *huc ... deducta ...* (3) *ut*, 'led to the point where ...'

The rhythm of this line, and the character of *mea Lesbia* as a kind of set phrase (5.1; 87.2; cf. *mea puella*), seem to require the punctuation I have given. To isolate *Lesbia* in a parenthesis in the fifth foot seems to me awkward both in sound and in sense.

culpa: To some extent at least, this word is probably intended to bear the developed sense of 'sexual misconduct' (cf. 68.138–39), for which Q. cites V. *Aen.* 4.19 and 172.

2 *officio*, 'devotion' (e.g., to friends; cf. 68.12) – here shown as the result of *pietas* in adhering to the *foedus amicitiae* (109.6 n.).

ipsa suo: C.'s devotion turns out to have been misplaced, hence misguided and self-destructive.

3 *bene velle*: cf. 72.8 n. For the contrast, Kr. quotes Theogn. 1091–4, Lygd. [=Tib]. 3.6.55–6.

4 desiflore *m*. Another example of *m*'s carelessness (71.1 n.); *m*² writes *al. desistere*, thus restoring *R*'s reading, and here (as often) disguising the restoration as a variant.

omnia si facias: that is, if you should prove to be *capable de tout*. Theocr. (23.11) has πάντα ποιεῖν in the same sense; cf. Bion 2.25 and also (as Kr. suggests) πανοῦργος.

76

Structure: either two-part – (8 + 8) + (6 + 4) (see Q.) – or, as I prefer, three-part – e.g., (6 + 3 + 3) + 4 [bridge passage] + (6 + 4), or 8 + 8 + 10, as in Stoessl 1977, who has a useful discussion of the structure.

Despite the apostrophe and appeal to the gods in ll. 17–26, this poem is really a soliloquy, or interior dialogue (of the poet with himself). The moment it depicts is surely earlier than that of poem 11: there, C. faces, with firmness and detachment, the fact that his love for Lesbia is dead, whereas here he is still gripped by a passion he knows to have outlived its time. The emotional crisis is precisely that of poem 8 (q.v.), but (as is usual in the epigrams) the treatment is more reflective, less 'direct' and 'passionate' than in the polymetric poems 1–60; cf. for instance poem 86 with poem 43 for a relatively trivial example of this difference in treatment. Some critics call poem 76 an elegy; but in spite of its comparative length it lacks the wide sweep and (especially) the kind of interior development we associate with

the true love elegy, and I should prefer to describe it as an extended epigram.
Like poems 72, 75, and 85, it is inspired by C.'s conflict of emotions over
Lesbia and the feeling that his love for her has been one-sided (cf. poem 87,
where see n. on the past tenses) – though this latter idea cannot be made
explicit in the brief compass of poem 85. As in poem 8, C. detaches himself –
as a rational being – from his infatuation, but with a struggle. If there is any
going beyond the mood of poem 8, it is that, as F. says, 'here it is not the
happiness that C. remembers . . . he has passed beyond recrimination and is
obsessed by his own undeserved suffering . . . his despair is final, and there
is no thought of reconciliation.' (In the still later stages of the relationship,
as reflected in poems 11 and 58, C. turns – having formally repudiated
Lesbia – to something like pure repulsion and bitterness unmixed with
any nostalgic feeling whatever.) Notice here the stress on *fides* – loyalty, a
personal attachment, whether to a *patronus* on the part of a *cliens*, or to the
gods (cf. 34.1; and the poet is a kind of *cliens*, bound by *fides* as *pius poeta*
to his patroness the Muse: 16.5 n.; a bad poet is *impius*, 14.7), or to a trusted
friend or beloved person. C.'s claim to be *pius*, to observe *fides*, is neither
self-satisfied nor illusory; it is more like a formula of invocation, asserting
the sine qua non of a rational and constant practice of *fides*, without which
one simply could not appeal to the gods to show and to exercise their kind
of *fides* in return. See, for this, Ariadne's words at 64.191, *caelestum fidem
comprecer*; such *fides* is 'the feeling of responsibility the gods have for those
in their care' (Henry 1951: 53).

1 *benefacta*: cf. 73.3 *fecisse benigne* (*benefacta*, in a sense 'active' in meaning =
'benefits conferred,' whereas *beneficia* include – and usually mean – benefits
received; cf. the title of Seneca's treatise *De beneficiis*).

2 *pietas* denotes, as E. rightly says, the performance of human obligations that
have a divine sanction (such as discharging promises or oaths, as well as vows);
F.'s definition, 'conformity to divine will,' is unsatisfactory.

3 *in ullo*: see App. Crit. (For a clear instance of *in* omitted by the copyist, see 87.3,
where the preceding *m* makes the source of the corruption obvious.) *Pace* Quinn,
V's dubious *nec numquam* at 48.4 should not be cited in support of a double
negative here, since, as F. remarks, the two negatives are not separated.

5 Fr.'s *manent tum* – *manentum* is O's reading – has something to commend it (it
is adopted by Lenchantin). In support of Fr., Levens argued that '*tum* answers
to *si*, as often; cf. 15.17, 64.231.' (In both of these passages, however, *tum* is a
connecting particle that points the way to a future or virtual future; I do not find
them relevant here.) L. went on to maintain that with *tum* 'the rhythm is much
more Catullan; he uses elision to charge his lines more heavily <with emotion>.'
This is true, and so common in C. as to need no particular illustration. For elided

tum, cf. 100.6 (with Palmer's reading; see text and App. Crit. there); similarly, *iam* is elided both in this poem at lines 10, 18, 23, and elsewhere (e.g., at 8.9). *parata*, 'won,' or 'earned' (in the past, according to B., who observed that *in longa aetate* should, if it refers to the future, be expressed by *in* + acc.); but C. is surely thinking of a long *future* extent of life. The order of the words in the line suggests taking *in longa aetate* with *manent*.

6 For *O*'s confusion of the compendia for *hec* (ħ) and *hoc* (ħ), cf. 64.175 n. and 68.149 n.; also lines 15 and 16 below.
ingrato: cf. 73.3 for the meaning. At 1.9, however, it means 'ungrateful.'

7 *cuiquam*, 'to any single person,' F. (he aptly quotes Publilius *ap. Sen. Dial.* 9.11.8 *cuivis potest accidere quod cuiquam potest* and Cicero, *Red. Sen.* 30 *difficile est non aliquem, nefas quemquam praeterire*). Sometimes *quisquam* is used after *si* (which occurs in l. 1. here); cf. 96.1, 98.1, 102.1.

9 *quae*: see App. Crit. (If we read *-que*, the transition to the next section of the poem will bisect the couplet 9–10, and the connection itself with the preceding section loses its force.)
perierunt credita: suggesting a bad debt, to be written off as a loss. Cf. Seneca, *De benef.* 1.1.1 *sequitur enim ut male collocata <beneficia> male debeantur, de quibus non redditis sero querimur; ista enim perierunt cum darentur.*

10 There are several instances of hiatus in C., but this apparent example occurs just before the diaeresis of the pentameter. In emending, we should retain *iam amplius* – in that order – since these words 'are regularly placed together, in verse as in prose' (F., who gives examples from Cicero and Virgil). As we have seen, this poem contains several elided monosyllables (above, l. 5 n.).

11 With *animo, offirmas* is intransitive (F. quotes Plaut. *Stich.* 68 and Ter. *Eun.* 217 for instances of this). Notice the rewriting by Ovid (*M.* 9.745), who in three words (*quin animum firmas*) deliberately eliminates two of C.'s elisions. On the prevalence, or at least frequency, of elision in this poem (and a suggested reason for it), cf. the notes on lines 5 and 10 above. Notice also that Ovid goes on to say *teque ipsa recolligis*, which supports E.'s *te ipse* here. F. also quotes Ov. *Tr.* 5.7.65 *meque ipse* (the vulgate reading, i.e., that of the *dett.*; but Merkel and Owen, unnoticed by F., read *sic meque* with the Codex Gothanus) *reduco a contemplatu semoveoque mali.* The emphatic 'both – and' of *teque reduc et* ... *desinis* would be pointless. *istinc* = from that situation of yours' (cf. 116.6 *hinc*).

O's reading is here slightly better than the reading of *X*; probably *A* had *istincteque* and *X* turned *e* into *o* by a slip.

For George Buchanan's emendation see his *De Prosodia* (*Opera Omnia*, 1715, vol. 2, part 5).

12 *dis invitis*: that is, 'when Heaven itself opposes <the love that makes you *miser*>' (cf. Prop. 1.1.7–8 *et mihi iam toto furor hic non desinit anno / cum tamen adversos cogor habere deos*).

13 Kr. quotes Menander fr. 726 (Koch; = fr. 544 Körte) ἔργον ἐστὶ … μακρὰν
συνήθειαν βραχεῖ λῦσαι χρόνῳ. See the references in Posch (on poem 93) 1979:
329 to various studies of this fragment.
longum subito, 'an emphatic collocation' (Q.).

14 *efficias*, 'you must do (this)'; jussive subjunctive, as at 8.1 *desinas*.

15 *pervincendum*: the heavy (spondaic, one-word) ending suggests difficulty. As
Kr. points out, such endings are much more common in the hexameters of
poem 64 (30 in 408 lines) than in C.'s elegiac couplets (12 in 373 ll., of which 8
are in the long poems 66, 68); noting this, F. describes the use of the device in
poem 64 as a 'Hellenistic mannerism.' See his long n. on 64.3.

15, 16 Notice how the closely similar compendia for *hec* and *hoc* (cf. l. 6 n.) have
led our Mss into error (corrected by R^2, *suo Marte*).

16 *m* corrects *R*'s *faties* to *facies*; *facias* (*G* = *X*) is evidently unknown to him.
pote … *non pote*: 'polar expression' (Kr., F.: see the parallels, Plaut. *Trin.* 360
and Sen. *Medea* 567, quoted by F.). For the form *pote* = (*fieri*) *potest*, cf. 1.23
and see 45.5 n.

17 *si* with the indicative = *si quidem* (Greek εἴπερ); used in prayer formulae ('*since*
you …,' stressing the *fact* of the deity's quality or action; not '*if* you …'),
it has almost the same function as *tu* (cf. 34.13–20) or *vos* in the traditional
invocation. (The use of *si* with the indicative in poem 96 similarly appears to
express confidence rather than, as certain critics have suggested, scepticism;
see n. there.) One might tr. 'if, as is the case, …'

17ff. For the appeal to the gods, cf. 109.3ff.

18 R^2's correction *extrema* has been defended (Virgil, in two passages, has *extrema
iam in morte*), but so has *extremam*, on the supposition that C. wishes to avoid
a string of ablatives. Palaeographically, there is little to choose between them.

19 *puriter*: this form of the adverb, instead of *pure*, is archaic, as F. points out here;
see, however, his note on 39.14, where 'solemn' connotations are less obviously
in place. C.'s use of the word here implies that his hands are clean in relation to
Lesbia: the central idea seems to be that of integrity in conduct (to be classified,
no doubt, as a species of *pietas*). Total sexual abstinence outside C.'s affair with
Lesbia is not claimed; what *is* claimed is that while C. was in love with Lesbia he
was wholly faithful to her.

20 *pestis ac pernicies* (a kind of set phrase, e.g., in Cicero – *Rab. Perd.* 2 [quoted
by F.], *In Cat.* 1.33, *De off.* 2.51 – cf., for instance, Lucil. 77 M) = *morbus*,
l. 25. C. can now see what is left of his love as a morbid affliction, needing
a cure.

22 *ex omni pectore*, 'completely from my …' (F.; for parallels, see his n. on 68.25).
R^1's instant self-correction is followed by *m*. There appear to be no instances
where such R^1 corrections are noticed only by m^2.

23–4 For a complete contrast in tone, cf. Ov. *Am.* 3.14.1–2 *non ego ne pecces, cum
sis formosa, recuso, / sed ne sit misero scire necesse mihi.*

23 See App. Crit. (*me ut me* is *V*'s unmetrical reading, so that the two possible restorations *me ut* or *ut me* have equal standing). I now prefer *ut me*, for the reasons that were given by L., as follows: (i) *me*, since it is not emphatic, should not be outside the subordinate clause; (ii) juxtaposition of the words *contra me* would too strongly suggest that *contra* must be taken as a preposition; (iii) palaeographical probability: the copyist, having omitted *ut*, writes it after *me* and then adds another *me*, forgetting to delete the former.

24 *potis*: here neuter. For the history of *potis/pote*, see Kr. on 72.7 and F. on 45.5. The form *potis* was dying out in C.'s time.

25 *ipse*, contrasted with *illa* (1.23); a contrast emphasized by the asyndeton, as Kr. observes.

26 *R²*'s correction *mi* for *mihi* is, of course, metrical in nature. For the confusion of compendia (*hec* and *hoc*) see above, line 6 n.

Pepe, L. 1950. 'Si vitam puriter egi: Sul carme 76 di C.,' *GIF* 3: 300–9.

Henry, R.M. 1950. 'Pietas and Fides in C.,' *Hermathena* 75: 63–8, and 76: 48–57.

Traina, A. 1954. 'C. e gli dei. Il carme 76 nella critica più recente,' *Convivium* n.s. 1 (1954): 358–68.

Oksala, P. 1958. '*Fides* und *pietas* bei C.,' *Arctos* 2: 88–103.

Wille, I. 1964. 'C.s Gedicht 76 als Spiegelbild seines Liebeserlebnisses und seiner Liebesdichtung,' *Das Altertum* 10: 89–95.

Akbar Khan, H. 1968. 'C. 76: The Summing-Up,' *Athenaeum* 46: 54–71.

Moritz, L.A. 1968. 'Difficile est longum subito deponere amorem,' *G&R* 15: 53–8.

Bishop, J.D. 1972. 'C. 76: Elegy or Epigram?,' *CP* 67: 293–4.

Dyson, M. 1973. 'C. 8 and 76,' *CQ* 23: 127–43, esp. 136–43.

Bodoh, J.J. 1974. 'C. 76,' *Emerita* 42: 337–42.

Leeman, A.D., and den Hengst, D. 1976. 'C.'s Carmen 76,' *Lampas* 9: 244–68.

Cassata, L. 1977. 'Le gioie della buona coscienza (C. 76.5–6),' *A&R* 22: 1–14.

Stoessl, F. 1977. *C. Valerius Catullus: Mensch, Leben, Dichtung*. Meisenheim: 204–7.

Pietquin, P. 1986. 'Analyse du poème 76 de C.,' *LEC* 54: 351–66.

Skinner, M.B. 1987. 'Disease Imagery in C. 76.17–26,' *CP* 82: 230–3.

Powell, J.G.F. 1990. 'Two Notes on C.,' *CQ* 40: 199–206, esp. 199–202.

Scivoletto, N. 1991. 'La protasi del c. 76 di C.,' *Studi di filologia classica in onore di C. Monaco*. Palermo: 737–43.

Vine, B. 1993. 'C. 76.21: ut torpor in artus,' *RhM* 136: 292–7.

77

Structure: 4 + 2 (question and answer).

On the theme of false friends, cf. poems 38 and 73. As to the identity of 'Rufus,' see Noonan on poem 69 (with reservations expressed in my n.) and

Arkins 1983. See also Wiseman 1974: 107–8, on the difficulty of choosing among the many men of senatorial rank who bore the name Rufus.

The poem is interesting because of its sound-values (*s-*, *m-*, and especially *o-* in l. 2), and its use of word-repetition, or virtual epanalepsis (*frustra, eripuisti, eheu*); cf. poem 83 n. on 'advancing anaphora,' which produces an effect of increasing agitation and climax.

1 *m*'s reading is correct, though whether for the right reason is hard to say (cf. 76.26 *pro pietate*). In view of *m*'s interest in spelling, however, he should perhaps receive the benefit of the doubt.
frustra ac nequiquam: as Kr. points out, *nequiquam* is the more poetic word of the two. They are not quite synonymous: *frustra* contains the notion of disappointment, whereas *nequiquam* simply denotes 'to no effect.'
credite amice, 'believed to be a friend': the noun is 'attracted' into the case of the participle. *amico* may possibly be the result of *X*'s attempt to 'emend.'

2 *cum*, 'to the accompaniment of ...'; cf. 40.8 *cum longa ... poena*. F. quotes Plaut. *Rud.* 710 (*cum pretio*), *Bacch.* 503 (*cum malo*).
pretio, 'cost'; *malo*, 'damage, hurt.' For *malo*, in contrast to *lucro*, see Plaut. *Men.* 356.

3 *sicine* (cf. a similar reproach at 64.132), 'is this how ...?'
intestina perurens: cf. *subrepsti* – it is clear that the false friend Rufus is seen by C. as undermining his life (5–6 *crudele venenum vitae*) from within. The phrase *intestina perurens* appears to be associated with the notion of jealousy. For *intestina* of 'the inward parts' cf. Plaut. *Pseud.* 343 *sine ornamentis, cum intestinis omnibus*. On the whole phrase, see the discussion in Fedeli's article on poem 30, p. 112.
m, who writes *subrepti*, has almost blundered into the truth; his agreement with *O* is fortuitous. As a sign of *m*'s haste, notice that he was about to write *istina* (and then corrects himself).

4 *ei misero*: cf. 68.92. As F. points out, *miser* is often 'strengthened by an interjection' (64.71 *a misera*; Tib. 1.8.23 *heu misero*. Cf. also 64.196 n. On the text: for the emendation of *si mihi* to *ei mihi*, cf. Lygd. (= [Tib.] 3) 6.33.
omnia nostra bona: almost certainly = <life with> Lesbia (see l. 3 n.); *omnia bona* alludes to her at 68.158.

6 Although the expression *pectus amicitiae* (*V*'s reading here) occurs in Statius (*S.* 4.4.103) and Martial (9.14.2), what is needed here is a continuation of direct invective.
pestis = 'blight, poison'; it is linked with *subrepsti*, as *subrepens* at 76.21 is linked with *pestem* in the preceding line.
amicitiae = the friendship between C. and Rufus (though in line 4 *omnia nostra bona* is at least likely to include C.'s affair with Lesbia; cf. 68.158 *omnia ...*

bona). See n. on *intestina perurens*, line 3. The word will naturally be taken to refer back to *amice* (l. 1); therefore, to take it of C.'s love for Lesbia, characterized as *sancta amicitia* in 109.6, seems less likely (despite Q.).

Arkins, B. 1983. 'Caelius and Rufus in C.,' *Philologus* 127: 306–11.

78

Structure: unitary (three-part, with repetitions). Notice the effect of (i) the substitution of *stultus* for *bellus* in l. 5, (ii) the 'elegant' (Q.) chiasmus in l. 4, (iii) the juxtaposition *patruus patrui* in l. 6.

Gallus, acting as matchmaker in a climate of 'liberated' morals (pointed by the poet's use of fashionable language such as *bellus, lepidus*), demonstrates (l. 6) to his brothers the possibility of adultery between two different generations of a single family, the woman belonging to the older. But he is a fool, since he forgets that he too has a wife and a nephew (and hence may himself qualify for the cuckold's horns, if his teaching is accepted).

Should be separated from poem 78[b] for three reasons: it seems complete in itself; the themes have little, if anything, in common; and poem 78 is in the third, poem 78[b] in the second, person.

'Gallus' has not been securely identified; this name appears in many families in Cisalpine Gaul. B. hesitantly suggested, with reference to Valerius Maximus 5.9.1, that the *filius* of l. 2 might be the Gellius of poem 74.

3 *homo bellus*, κομψός, 'elegant, smart' (often joined, as here, with *lepidus*, cf. Plaut. *Capt.* 956). Cf. 81.2 *bellus homo*; 24.7 *homo bellus* (where Kr. translates 'netter Kerl,' quoting Varr. *Men.* 335 and Cic. *Ad Att.* 1.1.4).
iungit amores, 'makes a match' (the phrase has physical implications: cf. 64.372 *coniungite amores*; Tib. 1.1.69 *dum fata sinunt, iungamus amores*).
5 *videt*, 'is aware' (cf. 36.9).
6 *patruus*: For the Roman view of the *patruus* as an unofficial *censor morum* within the family, see 74.1 and n.

Giangrande, G. 1976. 'C.s Gedicht auf Gallus,' *Eranos* 74: 170–3.
Milanese, G. 1988. 'Su C., carme 78: unità, ideologia, linguaggio,' *Maia* 40: 251–61.

78[b]

Structure: (probably) 4 + 2. The poem is unlikely to be a displaced continuation of any other, such as 77, 80, or 91; more likely, it is a damaged six-line composition (the opening *sed nunc*, 'but, as it is, ...' strongly suggests that it originally began with *si*, followed by a pluperfect or imperfect subjunctive of the 'unreal condition').

The tone differs from that of poem 78 (see n. there); and the tendency to repeat in the pentameter a word or sound of the hexameter, which can be seen in poem 78, is absent here. Notice the sounds: *s*, *p* (the latter in ll. 1–2); they have an almost onomatopoeic effect (hissing and spitting). The vocabulary of l. 2 is almost identical with that of 99.10 (and that of l. 3 with that of 99.3); but of course the occasion is different. The juxtaposition of *purae pura*, and the interwoven arrangement adj.-adj.-noun-noun in 1–2, are rhetorical.

1 Cf. 21.10 *nunc ipsum id doleo, quod* ...

2 *savia* (unusually) = 'lips'; cf. Plaut. *Mil.* 94.
comminxit: cf. 99.10.

3 For the threat of lasting poetic vengeance cf. 12.10–11, 40.6; for the poet's power to confer immortal *praise*, cf. 68.41ff.
verum ... *feres*: cf. 99.3 *verum id non impune tuli*.

4 *qui sis*: cf. Ter. *Eun.* 66 *sentiet qui vir siem*, Ov. *Pont.* 4.3.2.
fama ... *anus*: cf. 68.46 *carta* ... *anus* (in a similar context, as Kr. remarks). The word *anus* is an adjective, as at 9.4 *anumque matrem*: compare the use of *senex* at 67.4, where *ipse senex* should be translated 'the old master,' not 'the old man himself.'

Once again the coincidence between *O* and *m* is fortuitous. With *qui scis*, *m* nearly blunders into the truth; cf. 77.3 n. *R*[2] corrects *R*'s *tanus*; *m* adopts the correction as his text, but insists on preserving *tanus* as a variant, even though it is nonsense.

79

Structure: semi-unitary (balanced) 2 + 2. Notice the effect of the repetition of *pulcer* from l. 1 to l. 3; in each instance, before the strongest pause in the line.

Because of the scandal recorded in Cicero, *Ad Q.F.* 2.3.2 (*versus obscenissimi in Clodium et Clodiam*), this poem makes a strong prima facie case for the identification of C.'s Lesbia with Clodia Metelli, sister of P. Clodius Pulcer. Wiseman 1969 doubts the identification, though he does not altogether dismiss it; Skinner 1982 rejects Wiseman's doubts, which 'rest entirely on a tenuous supposition about the date of composition of the Lesbia-poems.'

1 *quid ni?* (sc. *pulcer sit*): 'a rather colloquial expression on the lines of *quippe, utpote qui*' (Kr.)

2 *te . . . tua*: rhetorical hyperbole. *cum tota gente tua* merely goes one step beyond *te*; cf Ar. *Ran.* 1408. There is no suggestion that Lesbia seriously considered marrying C. but turned him down because he belonged to a family that was socially beneath hers.

3 *vendat*, 'sell as slaves'; another hyperbole (absurd, of course). Cf. Kr.'s citations of Plaut. *Mil.* 23 (*mancupio dabo*) and *Apoc.* 11.3 (*tria verba cito dicat et servum me ducat*).

4 *notorum* (see App. Crit.) = 'acquaintances'; cf. Ter. *Eun.* 238 *noti me atque amici deseruerunt*, Hor. *S.* 1.1.84–5 *te vicini oderunt, noti, pueri atque puellae*.
   tria: standing vaguely for a small number (cf. *Apoc.* 11, quoted at line 3 n.). Acquaintances avoid his kiss of greeting because of his habits, which include some kind of action involving *infamia oris* (see the passages cited by Kr.).
   m's careless error (*reperierit*) is at once self-corrected, it seems.

Skinner, M.B. 1982. 'Pretty Lesbius,' *TAPA* 112: 197–208.
Forsyth, P.Y. 1985. 'Catullus 79,' *Latomus* 44: 377–82.
Tatum, W.J. 1993. 'C. 79: Personal Invective or Political Discourse?,' *Papers of the Leeds International Latin Seminar* 7: 31–45.

80

Structure: balanced (double question and answer) 4 + (2 + 2). As Kr. says, to the question in lines 1–4 is given, first a provisional answer (5–6) and then a final answer.

The language appears artificially exalted and 'poetical,' especially in lines 2, 4, and 6. Curran 1966, who calls this a 'poetic obscene-invective,' compares it with poem 97 (q.v.). A literary convention is burlesqued, or parodied, in the service of a violently abusive attack on Gellius.

1 *quid dicam . . . quare*: cf. Cic. *S. Rosc.* 94 *permulta . . . dici possunt quare intellegatur* (Kr.).
   rosea labella: cf. 63.74 (where the language is generally elevated and 'epic').

2 *hiberna candidiora nive*: cf. Il. 10.437 (λευκότεροι χιόνος) – again 'epic.'

1–2 are rightly described by Q. as marked by 'sham lyricism' (see my nn. on the language) which 'is undercut by the concluding line of the poem.'

3–4 *quiete / e molli*: the stylistic mannerism, with a postponed preposition inserted between noun and adjective (Kr. sees this as a relic of archaic poetic practice), and the end of the line coming between noun and adjective, is very rare in C. For the language (*quiete molli*) cf. 63.38 and 44 (Q.; he describes it as 'high style' here).

longo die, 'when the day is long,' that is, in summer, when Romans took a lengthy siesta, sometimes appropriated to love-making (cf. 61.111); the adj. *longo* is therefore not 'superfluous' or 'idle' (*müssig*), as Kr. claims.

5 *nescioquid certe est*, 'surely there's something up'; cf. V. *Ecl.* 8.106–7 *bonum sit! nescioquid certe est, et Hylax in limine latrat.*

5–6 *an vere ... vir*: 'sham high style' (Q.).

6 *tenta* (sc. *membra*) = *rigida* 56.7 (Kr. compares 64.316 *morsa*, 66.74 *condita*, for this kind of 'Substantivierung').

The reading of *O* was probably that of *A*, misinterpreted at first by *X*, who however corrects himself – or offers another interpretation (he does not feel sure enough about the meaning of *tenta* to substitute it for *tanta*); this alternative is apparently added from *X* by *R*[2] (followed by *m*[2]).

7 *sic certe est*, 'why, of course!' (cf. 62.8); the dawning recognition of a situation.
Victor: otherwise unknown.
clamant (sc. *id factum esse*); of signs, cf. 6.7 *clamat.*

7–8 *rupta ilia*: cf. 11.20 n.
sero = semine.

8 Through carelessness, *m* replaces an *e* with an *a*; neither reading being comprehensible, *m*[2] first gives the *R* reading as a variant on *m*'s mistake, then takes the further step of abolishing its 'variant' status and accepting it into the text.

Curran, L.C. 1966. 'Gellius and the Lover's Pallor: A Note on C. 80,' *Arion* 5: 24–7.

81

Structure: unitary, with two-line exclamatory ending added; hence 4 + 2. For an interpretation of the whole poem, see Zicàri 1955. He points out that for these verses (deploring Juventius' interest in a stranger from a dull and distant town) to have point, Juventius himself must belong to a good Roman family. References in C. to 'provincial' origin are as a rule malicious (though 100.2, in an early poem with a Veronese setting, and 39.13, which is neutral, are exceptions). The phrase *in tanto populo* makes it clear that the poem was written in Rome. It is possible that the *hospes* was either Furius (as A. Couat, *Étude sur Catulle* [Paris, 1874], p. 98, thought) or more probably Aurelius, if the words *inaurata statua* contain a pun. Certainly, *if* C.'s Furius is Furius Bibaculus (see 11.1 n. and 26, intr. n.), who came from Cremona, he is not the *hospes* (from Pisaurum) of this poem. For Furius and Aurelius in relation to Juventius, see poems 15, 16, 21, 23, 24. There is an echo of tragic style in l. 3 (probably parody: see n.); notice the sharp contrast with the colloquial (and immediately preceding) *iste tuus*. Alliteration on *p* and *c* suggests, as usual, disapproval.

1 *popul(o)*: the only instance in C. of the rare elision of the last syllable of an anapaestic word between the fourth and the fifth foot of a line.

2 *bellus homo*: cf. 24.7, and see 78.3 n.
tu: the pronoun is stressed, reproachfully (cf. 3 *iste tuus*, 5 *tibi ... tu*).
inciperes, 'proceed to': Plaut. *Bacch.* 565 *occiperes ... amare*; 68.88 *coeperat ... ciere*. 'Must you go and ... ?'

3 *iste tuus*: cf. 71.3 (at 17.21, which is cited here by Q., I read *merus*).
moribunda sede. i.e., a dead-and-alive spot. For an amusing comment, see Zicàri 1955: 62 n. 23; he himself lived at Pesaro (Pisaurum). The phrase *m. ab sede P.* is surely a parody on the source (Accius?) of *Aen.* 3.687 *augusta ab sede Pelori*.

4 *hospes*: not, as Kr. suggests, because Juventius lived at (or frequented) the friend's house in Rome, but rather in the sense of 'stranger' (*advena*). Notice *in tanto populo*, line 1: 'with all the crowds of people at your command in the City, must you choose an outsider from Pisaurum?'
inaurata p. statua: the comparison seems forced, unless a covert allusion to the name *Aurelius* is intended; see intr. n.

5 *cordi est*: for this colloquial idiom cf. 44.2 and 95.9 (also 64.158, in Ariadne's outburst of emotion addressed to Theseus).

6 On *quod* (*quid*) editors are sharply divided. The case for reading *quid* is made by Kr., who cites Plaut. *Truc.* 425 (*aliquid munusculum*) and *Amph.* 364 (*quid nomen tibi est?*) as examples. F. quotes *Poen.* 829 *quid genus* (cf. Gell. 9.13.4), but maintains that these 'rare examples in early Latin' hardly support *V*'s *quid* here.
facinus facias: again colloquial, of a discreditable action; cf. 110.4 *facis facinus*. Kr. cites Cicero, *De fin.* 2.95 *vide ne facinus facias cum mori suadeas*.

Zicàri, M. 1955. 'Moribunda ab sede Pisauri (Nota a C. 81),' *StOliv* 3: 57–69 (= *Scritti*, 1978: 187–99).
Massimi, A. 1957. 'Nota catulliana,' *GIF* 10: 336–8.

82

Structure: balanced (unitary; note detailed symmetry).
As F. says, this appeal to 'Quintius' (see l. 1 n.) not to steal C.'s love away reads as if Lesbia were meant; but surely more than this can be said. The phrase *carius oculis*, twice used here, reappears as *carior oculis* in poem 104, which also associates it with *mea vita*; and a few short poems later, at 109.1, *mea vita* occurs in the vocative, in a context where it must certainly refer to Lesbia.

It seems as if Quintius has offended C. since poem 100 (in which C. names him in a particularly friendly way) was written. Notice the excited triple repetition of *oculis*.

1 *Quinti*: cf. poem 100; possibly the brother of the Quintia who appears in poem 86 (but see n. there).

  There are 27 examples in C. (15 in elegiacs) of a pyrrhic word following trithemimeral caesura; the rule, from Callimachus onwards, is that such lines must not begin with a trochaic word. To this rule C. adheres strictly. See 64.21 and Kr.'s n. there.

2 *m*'s original error *aud* (corrected by *m²*) fortuitously agrees with O.
  carius … oculis: cf. 3.5 *plus … oculis suis amabat*, 104.2 *carior … oculis*. Note the expansion, in line 2, of an idea expressed in line 1; this is typical of C.'s manner of writing. Cf. for example 22.13 *aut si quid, etc.* Kr. compares Plin. *Ep.* 1.18.4 *nam mihi patria, et si quid carius patria* [*patria om. β*], *fides videbatur*.

3 *eripere*, 'snatch away' (cf. 77.4–5), seems colloquial; *eripere oculos* occurs at Plaut. *Rud.* 759.
  ei, monosyllable; Pl. and Ter. have *ēi, ĕi,* or *ēī*; Lucr. has only *ēī*, and later poets generally avoid the dative (and the genitive; see however poem 84.5) of this pronoun (Ov. *Hal.* 34 has *ēī*).

4 *seu quid*: cf. 13.10 *(seu = vel si)*.

Forsyth, P.Y. 1975. 'C. 82,' *CJ* 70: 33–5.

83

Structure: broken order (conversational).

One of the earliest Lesbia poems; the husband is mentioned only here and at 68.146. The fact that he does not come into the picture after this early stage tends to help the identification of Lesbia with Clodia Metelli, whose husband died suddenly in 59 BC. In the scene depicted in this poem, C. is not present (otherwise there would be no point in either *oblita* or *meminit*). For the point made here, cf. poem 92; and with both together, cf. Prop. 3.8, especially lines 9–10, 19–20, 28.

  The mule is cited, not because it is sterile or because it is proverbial for stupidity or obstinacy – which would have little relevance to this passage – but because of its excessive patience and complaisance; cf. 17.25–6 *supinum animum … ut … mula* (it will bear any burden and accept almost any treatment, lacking the proper pride of the horse, for example), making it a suitable figure for the indifference of the husband (cf. Plaut. *Most.* 778–2, and see Kitchell 1979). With *nihil sentis* (associated with *mule*) cf. the simile at 17.20, of a felled tree: *(velut alnus) tantundem omnia sentiens quam si nulla sit*, and a few lines later (26) *ut … mula*.

  For the juxtaposition *Lesbia mi*, cf. poems 87 and 92.

1 *viro*: see intr. n.

mala dicit = maledicit, 'abuses'; cf. 92.1 *dicit male*. Kr. quotes Ter. *Andr.* 640 *ingeram mala multa* (cf. *plurima* here).

1–3 Note the climax of indignation, expressed not only by the replacement of *viro* by *fatuo* and then of *fatuo* by *mule*, but also by the steady movement of these nouns towards the beginning of the line so as to shorten the interval between them (a device I have called 'advancing anaphora').

3 *mule*: see the foregoing n., from which it *ought* to follow that *mulus* signifies – as apparently it does at Juv. 16.23 *mulino corde Vagelli*, though (as F. notes) not elsewhere in Latin – stupidity or foolishness, rather than stubbornness (poem 17, on one who is *insulsissimus, merus stupor, stolidus*, ends with the word *mula*: the subject of the poem is to shed his *supinus animus* just as a mule sheds its shoe). See however intr. n. Levens defended *mulle* (*V*: see App. Crit.) = 'mullet,' claiming rather implausible support from the *Paroem. Graeci* (Μύλλος πάντ' ἀκούει) and from Hesychius *s.v.* Λύλιος ἢ Μύλλος.

nihil sentis, 'aren't you aware of *anything*?'

nostri of course = *mei*.

4 *sana*, 'heart-whole,' 'fancy-free.' F. quotes Sulpicia ([Tib.] 3.12 = 4.6.17): *uritur* (cf. line 6 here) … *nec, liceat quamvis, sana fuisse velit*. At Lucr. 4.1075, *sani* is contrasted with *miseri* (both in terms of love): *purast sanis magis inde voluptas / quam miseris*.

No doubt the reading in *A* was *sanna*; the erroneous double consonant in *O* might be attributable to *O*'s habit – characteristic of fourteenth-century manuscripts written in northeast Italy – of doubling, if it were not for the mistaken *samia* in *X*. After examining *A*, *X* writes a correcting suggestion.

It may be, however, that the single *n* is the work of *R*², who (as McKie: 286 points out) is a more scholarly corrector than *X*.

gannit, 'grumbles' (lit. 'snarls'); used primarily of animals (esp. dogs), but transferred to human beings (Varro *LL* 7.103, quoting Plautus).

obloquitur, 'reviles' (cf. Plaut. *Curc.* 41), not 'interrupts' (Q.), since both *oblita* and *meminit* rule out the possibility that C. is present in person.

5 *acrior*, 'more to the point' (Merrill); the clause is prosaic in sound (Kr.) and colloquial in its use of *res*.

6 *uritur*: 'burning' is of course one of the most common metaphors for love in C., as in other poets (see the next note).

coquitur: the quotations in Kr. and F. may be taken to support this reading (strange as it may appear when literally translated); its purpose must be to reinforce and amplify the metaphor contained in *uritur*. See however Herescu 1950, who dismisses it as a useless correction. In support of *loquitur* is the contrast with *si … taceret*.

Garrod, H.W. 1919. 'Mule, nihil sentis (C. 83.3),' *CR* 33: 67–8.

Fehrle, E. 1933. 'Zum 83. Gedicht des C., ' *PhWoch* 53: 445.

Herescu, N.I. 1950. 'Les médisances de Lesbie (C. 83.6),' *Latomus* 9: 31–3.

Zarker, J.W. 1969. 'Mule, nihil sentis (C. 83 and 17),' *CJ* 64.4: 172–7.

Rockwell, K.A. 1969. 'C. 83.3: Mule, nihil sentis,' *CJ* 65: 27.

Kitchell, K.F. 1979. 'Mule, nihil sentis? The Origin of the Insult in C. 83,' *Univ. of S. Florida Language Qtly.* 18: 33–4.

84

Structure: balanced (6 + 6).

On Arrius' uncouth way of speaking. Datable, with some confidence, to the end of 55 BC; see n. on l. 7. The matter of proper aspiration was being debated by grammarians in C.'s time, perhaps because the rules, or practices, were changing: Cicero says (*Orat.* 160) that he himself in youth had pronounced without aspiration some words which had since come to be aspirated; cf. Quint. 1.5.20. Nigidius Figulus, who is quoted by Aulus Gellius (13.6.3) as pronouncing that *rusticus fit sermo si aspires perperam*, belongs to C.'s generation – as, more or less, does Julius Caesar, whose treatise *De analogia* contained a chapter on aspiration. One reason for the uprush of *rusticus sermo* in Rome itself may have been the influx of rural 'Italians' into the city after the Social Wars. On this, and on the identification of Arrius himself, F. has a long intr. n. The most likely candidate, on the whole, is still the Q. Arrius of Cicero, *Brut.* 242; both as a 'familiar figure in the courts' (F.) and as Crassus' right-hand man he fits the context of l. 7. If so, Cicero's description (*infimo loco natus ... sine doctrina, sine ingenio*) shows clearly enough the grounds for C.'s dislike of him. In fact it was evidently not in aspiration alone that Arrius offended the ear: the letter *s* plays a part in the poem which has been ignored. That letter causes a great deal of hissing and spluttering, until Arrius departs for Syria: the 'sigmatism' immediately ceases, and line 8 relieves us of it completely; but it comes back in l. 10, and works up to a renewed climax in l. 12. To C., the *s*'s sounded like a gale at sea; for *leviter* (cf. l. 8) of a raging sea diminishing, see Jones 1956. The word *postilla*, and the form *audibant* (which occurs in Lucr. 5 and 6), are somewhat archaic.

From what we have said, it should be clear that the poem works on two levels simultaneously: C.'s attack on Arrius for his *s*'s is merely heard; the other – aimed at his aspiration – is overt.

1 *si quando ... vellet*: a 'frequentative' temporal construction which, 'almost unknown in early Latin, was coming in at this period: it occurs 25 times in Cic.,

14 times in Caesar' (L.). The subjunctive takes the place of the indicative; in this construction *si* is less common than *cum*. Cf. (with *ubi*) 63.67.

commoda, 'advantages,' but also – as a popular euphemism – 'perquisites'; see Vitruvius (in his *Praefatio*, 2); by his time this meaning had become established. Pontanus' spelling (-mm-) appears in Ms No. 113 in the Table.

3, 4, 11 Politianus: for his spelling, and in general his marginalia (dated 1473 in the *subscriptio*) in Bibl. Cors. Inc. 50 F 37, see Gaisser 1993: 71 and 311 n. 14.

3 *mirifice*, 'wonderfully *well*.' Normally (especially in Cicero) this adverb stands by itself, in the sense just given. In *CE* I took it so at 71.4; but see now the n. on that line.

sperabat, 'flattered himself.' F. ('schmeichelte sich,' Kr.).

4 *quantum poterat*, 'as loudly (and emphatically) as he could'; 'for all he was worth.'

insidias: does this refer to 'Parthian shots' (cf. 11.6)? If so, this would connect with l. 7.

5 *liber*: if *V*'s reading is correct, it should be explained as follows. Arrius' uncle (on the maternal side, like all the relations mentioned here; A.'s father, it is implied, had married beneath him) either became free or claimed to be free, and was the first of his line to achieve this status. C.'s statement is then a piece of (characteristically exaggerated) invective, with the aim of broadening the field of disparagement; it need hardly be supposed to reflect the truth. Bell 1915 suggested reading *Liber* (= Bacchus, 'a heavy drinker'), a suggestion also made by Levin 1973 and by Baker and Marshall 1975. But Nisbet's *semper* is very attractive.

7 Crassus departed for Syria just before the end of 55 BC (possibly in winter storms, suggests Kortekaas 1969); thus the mention of Syria here yields a probable date. It is interesting that Cicero finished, and no doubt 'published,' the *De oratore* about November 55; F. quotes *De or.* 3.45 (perhaps parodied by C.; at any rate it is possible that he could have newly read it), where another Crassus in the same family is made to speak of the antique pronunciation used by his mother-in-law Laelia, *ex quo sic locutum esse eius patrem iudico, sic maiores*; these words, with their repeated *sic*, are strikingly similar to ll. 5–6.

hoc: see App. Crit. (*hic* looks like a 'correction' by *X* of *hec* in *V*; cf. 67.37 for another possible 'correction' of exactly the same kind which had a better result).

leniter et leviter: Kr. quotes Gell. 18.9.7 (on a matter of pronunciation) *lenius leviusque*. The two words are (as he remarks) often joined together for the sake of the alliteration.

8 *-iebant* will not scan. The scribe adopted the regular spelling, disregarding metrical considerations; cf. 51.1 *mi(c)hi*, 14.14 *misisti*. Note that in this line the ('stormy' or 'windy') hissing of the *s*'s, which imparts a touch of sigmatism to the rest of the poem (see intr. n.), is temporarily suspended.

9 *postilla* is archaic.

10 *horribilis*, with an implication of rough seas; cf. 4.8 *horridam*, and perhaps 11.11 *horribile aequor* (but the text is doubtful). See intr. n.

Bell, A.J. 1915. 'Note on C., 84,' *CR* 29: 137–9.

Harrison, E. 1915. 'C., LXXXIV,' *CR* 29: 198–9.

Schuster, M. 1917. 'Zur Deutung des Arriusepigramms,' *WS* 39: 76–90.

Jones, D.M. 1956. 'Catulli Nobile Epigramma,' *Proc. Cl. Assoc.* 53: 25–6.

Ramage, E.S. 1959. 'Note on C.'s Arrius,' *CP* 54: 44–5.

Einarson, B. 1966. 'On C. 84,' *CP* 61: 187–8.

Kortekaas, G. 1969. 'Arrius en zijn uitspraak van het latijn,' *Hermeneus* 40: 269–86.

Levin, D.N. 1973. 'Arrius and His Uncle,' *Latomus* 32: 587–94.

Baker, R.J., and Marshall, B.A. 1975. 'The Aspirations of Q. Arrius,' *Historia* 24: 220–31.

– 1977. '*Avunculus liber* (C. 84.5),' *Mn.* 30: 292–3.

– 1978. '*Commoda* and *Insidiae*: C. 84.1–4,' *CP* 73: 49–50.

Vandiver, E. 1990. 'Sound Patterns in C. 84,' *CJ* 84: 337–40.

85

Structure: unitary monodistich (see below).

This poem represents the ultimate stage in a process of condensation of thought and expression, earlier stages in which are represented by poems 72 and 75. Its merits are strength and economy. Images, which are often held to be the lifeblood of poetry, are wholly lacking, except for the long-extinct metaphor in *excrucior*. The 'figure of grammar' is another matter; see Colaclidès 1969. A notable feature is the heavy proportion of verbs: 'quand la tension est extrême, les verbes dominent,' remarks J. Bayet (*Fondation Hardt, Entretiens.* Vol. 2 [Geneva, 1953]: 33). Of the structure it may be said, 'while the form is dual, the idea it expresses is triple' (D. Daiches, *The Study of Literature* [New York, 1948]: 148). In the first place, we have a triad of increasing *cola*, with pauses after *amo* and *requiris*. Again, each line is internally divided by two pauses: in l. 1, the second of these comes after *faciam*; in l. 2, the second comes after *fieri*. This serves to emphasize, as well as to mark, the main contrast on which the poem hinges: not the contrast *odi–amo*, as is commonly supposed, but the much more potent one between the active and passive forms of the verb *facio*; see n. on l. 2. In terms of rhythm, the choriambic phrase *odi et amo* is exactly balanced against the concluding verb *excrucior*; taken together, these two summarize the poem. The prosaic *fortasse*, and the conversational tone of *id faciam* (cf. Hor. *S.* 1.1.64, where *id* in *id facit = miserum esse*), are well suited to the 'dialogue' in very plain terms which occupies the middle ground of the couplet. For a view of the 'interlocutor' (the subject of *requiris*) as being C.'s 'ideal self,' see Bishop 1971. The anticipated question, however, is both a poetical and a rhetorical device, and need not strictly be taken to embody the notion of a dialogue.

1 *quare id faciam = quare oderim et amem* (F.); *id faciam* is colloquial.

    R's self-correction is not clear enough to prevent *m* from following at first (he is already in great haste); but *m* corrects himself no less quickly, seeing the erasure and the superscript letter *o*. This is better than supposing, as McKie: 200 does, that here *m* deliberately follows *R*, erasures and all (a procedure more suited to the character of *m²*).

2 Contrast Ovid's much less powerful *odero, si potero; si non, invitus amabo* (*Am.* 3.11.35; the line is bracketed as spurious by Kenney, following Heinsius).

    fieri is not, as Kr. says, the exact equivalent of *me id facere*; on the contrary, the *passive* nature of the event is strongly stressed by contrast with the active in the question (*faciam*). What we have to supply with *fieri* is not *a me* but *mihi*: 'It's *happening to* me (and I can't help it).'

    excrucior: cf. 76.10, 99.12, and 66.76 *discrucior*.

Colaclidès, P. 1969. 'Grammaire et Poésie: C. 85,' *EMC/CV* 13: 65–8.

Bishop, J.D. 1971. 'C. 85. Structure, Hellenistic Parallels, and the Topos,' *Latomus* 30: 633–42.

Triantaphyllopoulos, J. 1979. 'C. 85,' *RhM* 112: 98.

Colaclidès, P. 1981. 'Odi et Amo – Une Lecture Linguistique de c. LXXXV de Catulle,' *Contemporary Literary Hermeneutics and Interpretation of Classical Texts* (ed. S. Kresic). Ottawa: 227–33.

Verdière, R. 1985. "Odi et amo. Étude diachronique et psychique d'une antithèse,' *Hommages à H. Bardon*. Brussels: 360–72.

Decreus, F. 1986. 'Le poème 85 de C. et les épigrammes 28, 35 et 19 (Pf.) de Callimaque,' *Hommages à Jozef Veremans*. Brussels: 48–56.

Hommel, H. 1986. 'Topos und Originalität in C.s Zweizeiler (c. 85),' *Studien zur Altengeschichte* .... Siegfried Lauffer ... I–III. Rome: 421–36.

Ferguson, J. 1987. 'C. 85,' *LCM* 19: 138.

Arkins, B. 1987. 'A New Translation of C. 85,' *LCM* 12: 118.

Nussbaum, G. 1987. 'Odi et Amo – Again (C. 85),' *LCM* 12: 148.

Arkins, B., and Egan, D. 1988. 'Another Translation of C. 85,' *LCM* 13: 61–2.

Greenwood, M.A. 1988. 'More Thoughts on C. 85,' *LCM* 13: 80.

86

Structure: 4 + 2 (with repetition).

Lesbia's beauty surpasses mere good looks, however perfect; for she is – over and above good looks – charming in every possible way. Comparison with poem 43 shows on a small scale the difference in treatment between the 'polymetric' poems and the epigrams (cf. poem 76 n.); and the tone is certainly more reflective here. The charm of these few lines is attributable largely to their rhythmical variety, especially as between the central couplet and the other two. Notice the major and minor pauses, and the numbers of syllables in the words at the ends of pentameters.

This is the only mention of a 'Quintia' in C. On her identity, see l. 1 n.

1 It may be that Q. is the sister of Quintius in poem 82 (who has been identified with Quintius of Verona, mentioned in poem 100), but the name is not at all uncommon, and it is easier to suppose that Lesbia is here compared with another well-known 'society' woman in Rome. (Of course Quintius and Quintia *might* have moved to Rome from Verona after poem 100 was written). Kr. suggests that Quintia need not have come to Rome, since 'C.'s Veronese friends who lived in Rome (cf. 82) could make this comparison (for themselves)'; but this interpretation seems too restrictive. The identification is not of any great importance.

multis, 'in the eyes of ...'

1–2 *candida, longa, recta*: for these traits cf. Hor. *S.* 1.2.123–4.

2 *recta*, 'upright' (cf. 10.20 *rectos*); of a 'good carriage.'

sic, 'if it is put like that, in just those terms' (F. illustrates at length, chiefly from Cicero, this 'pleonastic' use of *sic* or *ita*).

singula, 'severally.'

3 *illud formosa*, that expression 'beautiful.'

formosa: nominative (outside the construction): cf. Prop. 1.18.31 *resonent mihi Cynthia silvae*, Ov. *M.* 15.96 *aetas cui fecimus aurea nomen*. More frequently, a quoted word is inflected as part of the grammatical structure of the sentence. On the meaning of *formosa*, F. (p. 378) has a long and useful note.

4 *sal*, 'piquancy': of sexual attractiveness (as at Lucr. 4.1162), rather than (verbal) 'wit' as at 13.5 and 16.7. The adj. *salsus*, in the same sense, is sometimes paired with *venustus*; Cicero, *ND* 1.79 (on the beauty of the actor Roscius): *hoc ipsum* (a squint) *salsum et venustum <Catulo> videbatur*.

5–6 *cum ... tum*, 'not only ... but also'; prosaic, as Kr. remarks.

6 *surripuit veneres*: cf. Nonnus, *Dionysiaca* 16.44–5 παρθενικὴ γὰρ κάλλος ὅλον σύλησεν Ὀλύμπιον.

veneres (pl.): cf. Plaut. *Stich.* 278 *amoenitates omnium venerum et venustatum*.

(The principal argument against writing *veneres* with a small *v* lies in the possibility that C. may partly have had in mind Callim. fr. 200a Pf. τὰς Ἀφροδίτας ὑπερφέρει πάσας; but *surripuit* embodies a different concept.)

87

Structure: balanced (2 + 2), with repetition.
Complete in itself, and not to be attached (as Scaliger suggested) to poem 75. One part of what is said in poems 72 and 75, which found no room for inclusion in the brief utterance of poem 85, is the subject of this poem: the one-sidedness of C.'s past love for Lesbia (note the emphasis on the perfect tense: *amata es; fuit; reperta est*). In the change of person, associated with repetition, F. sees 'emotion struggling with the restrictions of form.' For the stress C. lays on his own *fides*, see poem 76 n. The sting of this epigram lies, of course, in *ex parte mea*.

2 *vere* goes with *dicere*. In the light of *tantum ... quantum* it cannot be right to punctuate, as Kr. does, at the end of line 1.
 es: see App. Crit. (*V*'s *mea est* is perhaps influenced by line 4). Change of 'person addressed' would drive a wedge between the two couplets; F.'s defence of *est*, based on the order of the words in l. 2, is hardly strong enough to answer this objection.
3 *in* is omitted due to preceding *m* (76.3 n.)
 tanto V, under the influence of the neuter *foedere*.
 fides, foedere: cf. 76.3 n.
4 On the harsh diaeresis following *ex* (which separates noun from preposition) see 76.18 n. (also 111.2).

Heuze. P. 1987. 'À propos du c. 87 de C.,' *CEA* 20: 53–61.

88–91

A quartet of epigrams against Gellius (on whom see intr. n. to poem 74) accusing him of incest with his (step)mother and sister (*germana*, 91.5).

88

Structure: balanced (question and answer) 4 + 4. The poem is 'punctuated,' so to speak, by the repetition of *Gelli* at the same place in each quatrain.
 For the parody of mythological language (see l. 6 n.) immediately after the pointedly prosaic *ecquid*, cf. 81.3 n.; there is bathos at the end as well.

For the spondaic first halves of pentameters cf. poem 69 (last line) and 89.4 and 6; in all these places the heavy effect sounds censorious.

1 As Kr. points out, if Gellius = L. Gellius Publicola (poem 74 n.), then *mater* = 'stepmother.'

2 For this meaning of *prurit*, cf. Plaut. *Stich.* 756 *numquam ... vinces quin ego ibidem pruriam.*
abiectis: cf. 66.81 *nudantes reiecta veste papillas.*
pervigilat = παννυχίζει. Kr. quotes Plaut. *Curc.* 181 *Venerin pervigilare te vovisti?* (though there is, as he notes, no connotation of a 'religious' vigil here; cf. also 68.8).

3 Cf. 74.3–4 *patrui perdepsuit ipsam uxorem.*

4 *ecquid = num* (colloquial; cf. 10.8 *ecquonam ... aere*); Plaut. *Asin.* 900 *ecquid matrem amas?*
suscipiat: the full expression was *scelus in se suscipere* (Cicero, *Phil.* 11.9).
m restored *tantum*, not altogether out of fidelity to *R* (McKie: 200), but because he misunderstood the intention of *R*'s correction (thinking that *R* desired to change the *a*, not the *t*) and for that reason failed to see that it was an improvement.

5 For the emphasis that always attaches to *o* with voc., Kr. cites 24.1, 28.9, 33.1. *Tethys*, linked with her husband Oceanus at *Il.* 14.201; cf. 64.29–30, 66.68 and 70. By a similar metonymy, at 64.11 *Amphitrite* = sea. Tethys is *ultima* as dwelling with Oceanus at the farthest boundary of earth; cf. 29.4 *ultima Britannia* (and also perhaps 11.11–12, though the text is disputed).
Notice *m*'s independence in correction (see n. 4 above).

6 *genitor nympharum*: cf. *Il.* 21.196–7 (Oceanus as father of πάντες ποταμοὶ καὶ πᾶσα θάλασσα καὶ πᾶσαι κρῆναι καὶ φρείατα μακρά – i.e., of all waters).
The word *genitor* belongs to the elevated language of epic (see intr. n.).
nec ... abluit: for the notion, see especially – apart from *Macbeth* – Kr.'s quotation from Sen. *H.F.* 1326.

7 *nihil quicquam*, colloquial; cf. Plaut. *Bacch.* 1036.
ultra: cf. Cic. *Verr.* 2.5.119 *estne aliquid ultra, quo crudelitas progredi possit?*

8 *non si*: introducing an ἀδύνατον (cf. 48.5).
voret: cf. 80.6 for this sense (implying *fellatio*).

89

Structure: 4 + 2.
On Gellius' *latera effututa* (6.13), once again in a context of incest. Cf. poem 80. The repetition of *tam* (five times in the first three lines) produces an effect of crowding and excitement.

1 *quid ni (sit tenuis?)*: 'why, of course he is!' For the opening, cf. 79.1 n. But (as Kr. remarks) here the relative clause is not independent: it is a preliminary clause leading to *quare ... macer* (line 4); the *cui* is taken up by *is*.
bona, 'obliging,' in a sexual sense; cf. line 3 *bonus*, 'complaisant' (of a husband); and 110.1 *bonae ... amicae* (cf. Tib. 2.4.45 *bona quae nec avara fuit*).

2 *vivat*: with personal qualities (here *valens*, 'sexually active,' for which cf. 61.227) *vivere* acts as an 'intensified' *esse* of the copula; cf. also 8.10, 10.33.

3 *omnia plena*, '(for him) the world is full of ...'; possibly a parody of Thales (D-K 11 A 22) πάντα θεῶν πλήρη ('the world is full of gods'). But *cognatis*, in the next line, is an addition by way of surprise, typical of C.'s manner: 'not only girls, but girls of his own family.' Strictly speaking the uncle's wife is *adfinis* to Gellius, not *cognata*; but the stepmother (see 88.1 n.) and sister are *cognatae*, and so all three can (as a group) be loosely referred to in this way.

4 *R²*'s correction shows concern for metre as well as for sense.

5 *ut*, 'even though.'
attingat, 'lay hands on' (in a sexual sense); cf. 67.20 *non illam vir ... attigerat*.
tangere = *attingere*. For another example of a simple verb repeating – more or less – the meaning of a preceding compound verb, cf. 10.15 and 20, where *comparasti* reappears in *parare*.
quod fas tangere non est: this would cover, as Kr. says – quoting Gaius, *Inst.* 1.59 – both *incestum* with the stepmother and sister, and also *adulterium* with the uncle's wife.

6 *quantumvis quare ... invenies*, 'you will find entirely sufficient grounds ...' Cf. 80.1 *quid dicam quare*.

90

Structure: 2 + 4 (*nam*) – unusual.
This epigram is ostensibly concerned, like those on either side of it, with Gellius' incestuous sexual relationships. If so, it 'peters out' feebly (which is not the way of C.'s epigrams) on a small detail of the fire-worshipping cult, and the last line adds nothing to the meaning and could well be dispensed with. But it is possible that it has (at another level) a secondary theme, which is also the theme of poem 116, namely Gellius as an ineffective *poet*. The word *carmine* (l. 5) may mean either a sacral formula or a poem. If the words *omentum pingue* can also be taken ambiguously, either as 'fatty entrails' in the literal sense, or as 'thick, stupid trash' in the Callimachean sense of παχὺ γράμμα (*pingue* being the precise Latin equivalent of παχύ), then Gellius' poems might well become an acceptable offering upon the altar fires in the same way as those of Volusius in poem 36; cf. 36.16 *acceptum* with l. 5 here (*accepto*). If C. has in mind here Callimachus,

Aetia 1.23–4 ἀοιδέ, τὸ μὲν θύος ὅττι πάχιστον θρέψαι, τὴν Μοῦσαν δ᾽ ὠγαθὲ λεπταλέην, a literary interpretation of this passage seems all the more likely. By his incestuous birth, Gellius' son will be qualified to become a *magus* and so to find favour in the eyes of the gods by making burnt offerings of his father's *pingue carmen*. And why *omentum*? The answer is doubtful, but in Suetonius, *De viris illustribus*, fr. 104 Reifferscheid, a certain kind of *omentum* is included in a short list of writing materials that were, says Suetonius, formerly used, the other materials included in the list being *carta* and *membranae* (both mentioned by C., whom Suet. duly names); next, the mallow-leaf which C.'s friend and fellow-poet Cinna tells us *he* used for poems (Suet. quotes Cinna's lines to this effect immediately afterwards); and finally the palm-tree leaves on which the Sibylline books were written (unless it was linen) – and that is all. If the other materials in Suet.'s list were used in the time of Cinna and Catullus, it may be supposed that *omentum* also was used then, for the same purpose.

As for *liquefaciens*: on this interpretation the implication must surely be that Gellius' παχὺ γράμμα can only become *liquidum carmen* in the dissolving fires of the altar. (Cf. Clausen's interpretation of 95.5–7 – *GBRS* 5 [1964]: 190 – in which Volusius' turbid, as well as turgid, verse is likened to the muddy waters of the River Po, while by contrast the poetry of Cinna has a clarity that resembles the waves of the Satrachus.) If so, the epigram contains more than one ambiguity; and it ends on a rousing double entendre which, perhaps unexpectedly, is in no way sexual but is wholly literary in its nature.

1 *magus*: for testimonies to the belief that the *magi* were in fact born from such unions, see Kr.'s notes to this poem.
   matris: cf. 88.1 n.
   nefando: cf. 89.5 *fas ... non est*.
2 *aruspicium*: attributed to the Chaldaeans rather than to the *magi* (Kr.)
4 *relligio*: this spelling, familiar from Lucretius, is by Kr. compared with the 'epic' lengthening of the first syllable of words that begin with three short syllables; possibly, he adds, there is some influence from forms beginning in *re-*, such as *rettuli, reddo*. It is of course metrically convenient, especially in dactylic verse such as the Lucretian hexameter.
5 *gratus*: V's *gnatus* is not impossible, but *gnato* in line 3, referring to another person, makes it awkward and open to suspicion.
   accepto, 'acceptable'; often linked with the adjective *gratus*, especially in religious contexts; cf. 96.1 *gratum acceptumve sepulcris*.
   carmine: for the *magi* as ἐπαοιδοί see Kr.'s n.

6 *omentum*: the caul, or fat, surrounding the entrails of an animal. See Kr. for
some details of the cult. The sacred fire was of course the central object of
Zoroastrian worship as practised by the *magi*.
liquēfaciens: for the long second syllable cf. 64.360 *tepēfaciet*.

Németh, B. 1979. 'Zur Interpretation von C.s 90. Gedicht,' *ACD* 15: 43–50.

91

Structure: (6 + 2) + 2. For useful remarks on the language, see Fedeli 1970:
112–13 on poem 30.
Of the abusive Gellius epigrams of this group (i.e., omitting poem 116),
poem 91 is the least coarse in its language, as well as the longest. It connects
Gellius with one for whom C. cherished a *magnus amor* (l. 6; see also
l. 2) which was consuming him; it is difficult not to identify this person
with Lesbia. Perhaps for this reason, it alone, among the Gellius poems, is
written in an 'elevated' style, besides being distinctly purer in tone than its
neighbours. Gellius had at one time been a friend to C.; see line 7 of this
poem, where *multo usu* may suggest a shared interest in poetry, and also
116.2–3, where C. still hopes to win back his friendship by means of gifts (or
translations?) of the poems of Callimachus; but since then he has become a
rival in love.

Skilful use of the vowel *o*, of elisions, and of repetitions, makes the second
line brooding and sorrowful when it is read aloud.

1–2 The surprising statement is made at the poem's beginning, not at its end: after
studiously abusing Gellius, C. now declares that he believes he can depend on
G. not to betray him, at least in the matter of his love. And why? Then comes
the bitter explanation: C.'s beloved is *not* related to G., who is (perversely)
attracted only to women who are his own blood relations, and to no others
(lines 5–6).

2 There are three awkward elisions here. These elisions coincide, as often, with
indications of tension and unhappiness within C. Notice that they are all on the
letter *o*.
misero: cf. 99.15 (of C.'s love) *misero ... amore*; also 76.12 (of C. himself).
Similarly 45.21 *misellus*, of one in love.
nostro = meo. It does not disagree with the singular *cognossem*: cf., e.g., 68.149
tibi, 151 *vestrum*, 83.1 *mi*, 3 *nostri*.
perdito, in a strong sense, 'fatal' (as we speak of a 'fatal infatuation'). At 104.3
perdite amarem is a little weaker, merely 'love you to distraction' (colloquial
exaggeration).

3 *bene*: take with *cognossem*.
constantem, 'consistent,' 'dependable.'

4 *probro*, 'scandalous conduct'; cf. 61.99 *probra turpia persequens*.

5 *neque quod* = *quod nec*; the order of the words is inverted for metrical reasons. There are similar slight inversions at 63.62 and 64.68; Kr. cites Tib. 1.2.77.

6 *edebat*: cf. 77.3 *intestina perurens*, 35.15 *ignes ... edunt medullam*, etc. In the short epigrams, though hardly ever in the long elegiac poems, C. occasionally ends the first half of the pentameter with a monosyllable, somewhat awkwardly (72.2, 76.8, 83.6, 87.2, 107.2, 109.2).

7–9 These lines should be read with care. As Kr. notes, Gellius is represented as having turned out to be so evil and faithless that *precisely* a long acquaintance (*multus usus*) is for him all the greater reason to betray a friend. Previously, C. had been unable to think that this was possible. The language, as Kr. observes, is prosaic throughout.

10 *culpa*, 'guilty action'; *scelus*, 'crime' (cf. 88.7).

<h1 style="text-align:center">92</h1>

Structure: balanced (2 + 2).
Closely linked to poem 83, but showing (as L. pointed out) a further stage in the development of the relationship (notice the words *semper, umquam, assidue* as signs of this). Characterized by repetition-with-variation (*Lesbia mi, Lesbia me; dispeream nisi amat, dispeream nisi amo*).

1 *dicit male*: cf. 83.1 n. The dative *mi* = 'against me' (cf. 2 *de me*), not 'to me.' C. is probably not present; see 83.4 n.

2 *dispeream nisi*: a kind of colloquial oath (for the form, cf. *moriar si*).
nis(i) amat: in general, elisions in the last two feet are avoided (see Kr. on 66.25).

3 *quo signo? quia* ... 'how do I know this? Because ...' This kind of *short* question, immediately answered, belongs to *colloquial* rhetoric. For *signa* = manifestations of love, cf. Prop. 3.8.9, Ov. *Am.* 2.1.8.
sunt totidem mea, 'I have exactly the same set of symptoms' (cf. Dunbabin 1917).

3–4 *deprecor illam assidue*, 'I am for ever running her down.' Aulus Gellius, 7.16.2–5, glosses *deprecor* in this passage of C. by *detestor, exsecror, depello, abominor*. Gellius' whole chapter is of great interest as 'the earliest example we have of Catullan exegesis' (Gaisser 1993: 13). Although this meaning for *deprecor* is unusual, notice Cicero, *In Cat.* 1.27 *ut ... patriae querimoniam detester ac deprecer*, which (as Kr. suggests) is not too far off.

4 *R*²'s 'variant' *al. amat* (taken up by *m*²) must depend on *X* (but *G* ignores it). It cannot, in all probability, come from Aulus Gellius, otherwise *R*² would have

added lines 2 and 3, which Gellius (like *O*) preserves. See the discussion in the Introduction, p. 43.

Dunbabin, R.L. 1917. 'Notes on Latin Poets: C. 92.3,' *CQ* 11: 136.

93

Structure: unitary monodistich. See Campanile 1975 for a useful analysis. To Julius Caesar: 'I have no desire to please you, or even to know the very first thing about you.' Not, surely, a mere expression of indifference; the pointed language suggests that C.'s epigram is a reply to some communication from Caesar (perhaps a polite request to C. to desist from attacking a friend of his father). What was the ground of C.'s offence? Possibly poem 29 (see the echo of *imperator unice* in 54[b]); or 57; or even poems 41 and 43, as lampoons directed against Mamurra, though this seems less likely; not, at any rate, the 'Mentula' poems, which arise out of poem 29 apparently because C. could no longer afford to assail Mamurra under his real name (which, if we could assume it to be probable, would again point to poem 29 as the source of the trouble and the cause of Caesar's complaint).

The language is studiously offhand; see notes on l. 1. Of the proverbial expression in l. 2 it may be remarked that C. is much more apt to introduce proverbs into his epigrams than into either the 'polymetrics' or the long poems: see also poems 70, 94, 102, 105, with only one example (at 22.21) in the rest of the collection. (At 94.2 and 98.2 and 100.3, C. announces a proverb as such; see also 94.1–2 n. on the use of *vere* and *certe*.)

It may (or may not) be sheer accident that, among several quotations of C. in Quintilian, the two which are 'unattributed' (Wiseman 1985: 260), this one (at 11.1.38) and that at 9.4.141 (quoting 29.1), both refer to attacks on Caesar (here significantly described as *insania*; see 11.1.38, where also the phrase *aliquis poetarum* suggests a rather contrived forgetfulness as to the offending poet's identity).

1 *nil nimium studeo*, 'I'm none too anxious' (colloquial in language and tone). Cf. 43.4 *nimis*. Originally, *nimium* meant the same as *valde* (Kr., F.). This is a survival of that meaning.

velle placere, perhaps 'try to please'; *velle* is not, as Kr. would have it, wholly pleonastic; see the examples in F.

(Notice how the word *Caesar* is dropped into the most *un*emphatic position in the line.)

2 *scire*, etc.: this can be paraphrased 'know the first thing about you.' A proverb: see intr. n. Cicero, *Phil.* 2.41 *albus aterne fuerit ignoras*; cf. Apul. *Apol.* 16. The

origin of the phrase can just possibly be seen in Phaedr. 3.15.10, where it is a lamb that asks concerning its mother: *unde illa scivit, niger an albus nascerer?* *ater*, 'swarthy' (in complexion); cf. 39.12 *Lanuvinus ater*. There is of course no equation *albus* = 'good' and *ater* = 'bad'; see Campanile 1975: 38. Posch 1979: 322–6 gives a thoroughgoing account of the meaning of the phrase ('indifference' in general, the terms *albus* and *ater* being external, rather than moral, in reference). Ingemann 1981–2 challenges this view, claiming that a moral application would be more interesting; such application he finds in the Greek terms λευκός = homosexual, μέλας = manly (Ar. *Thesm.* 30–5 and 191). But he seems to miss, or ignore, the fact that C. is saying, above all, 'I don't greatly *care* to know ...'

See App. Crit. According to Avantius, Parthenius (in his lectures on Quintilian) was first to suggest *sis ater an albus*. For this and other claims (including that of Beroaldus, *Annotationes centum*, 1488) to have found or invented the correction, see Gaisser 1993: 103 and n. 135.

Campanile, E. 1975. 'Una struttura indoeuropea a Roma,' *SSL* 15: 36–44, esp. 36–9.
Posch, S. 1979. 'Albus an ater homo. Zu C. c. 93,' *Serta Philologica Aenipontana* 3. Innsbruck: 319–36.
Ingemann, V. 1981–2. 'Albus an ater – a double entendre in C. 93?,' *Classica et Mediaevalia* 33: 145-50.

94

Structure: unitary monodistich.
'Mentula' here and at 105, 114.1, and 115.1, can hardly be anyone but Mamurra, in view of 29.3 and 13. For the rather contrived pun on the name (see n. on l. 2) cf. 115.1 and 8. Notice in l. 1 the alliteration on *m* (a sound often used by C. to convey disapproval).

1 As variations on the punctuation adopted here (see the next n.), it is possible (a) to place a full stop at the end of the line (as Mynors does), so that *Certe* answers the question *moechatur?*; or (b) to take *moechatur* as a statement (Kr.); or else (c) to punctuate as follows: '*Mentula moechatur.*' *moechatur mentula certe.* (Schuster, Eisenhut). Against (a), the strong punctuation before a final spondee makes it decidedly preferable to continue the sense of *certe* into the next line; cf. 98.3, 100.3. See Norden on V. *Aen.* 6.389. Kr. may be right in suggesting that a stop after *certe* would weaken the effect of the chiasmus in the line.
1–2 *certe hoc est quod dicunt*, 'this undoubtedly is an example of the proverb ...' Cf. Ter. *Heaut.* 520 *quod dici solet*. In the passage 100.3–4 (*hoc est, quod dicitur, illud fraternum vere dulce sodalicium*), notice the use of *vere* to point

the proverb, as *certe* is used here; this is why – with *V* – I read *vere*, not *vero*, at 115.8 (where *mentula magna minax* appears to be a parody of a well-known Ennian tag, *machina magna minax*); see n. there.

2 *ipsa olera olla legit*: the proverb is otherwise unknown, but there is in it a verbal jingle which relates somehow to Varr. *LL* 5.108 *ab olla olera dicta*. Here the point is that 'Mentula' (which C. pretends to be a real name, instead of a nickname apparently invented by himself) cannot help behaving as a *mentula* would.

95

Structure: (4 + 4) + 2. The case for detaching lines 9–10 (= 95^b) as do many editors, including Q. (but not F., though he prints the text of Mynors, who does so), still finds its most persuasive exponent in Leo (1903). The desire to segregate the two lines is associated with the mention of Antimachus (Hor. *AP* 146), a Greek poet who was the type of long-windedness (see F.); editors feel that if he enters poem 95 in company with Volusius, C. will seem to admit that Volusius too was a popular poet. If 9–10 are detached, the name of some Greek poet (set against that of Antimachus) can be inserted to fill the gap in the text. There is, however, no other instance of C. writing a purely literary epigram about the poets of the past, such as lines 9–10 (= '95^b') would then become. Leo tried *Catonis*, in order to obtain a personal reference; but if the contrast is between a Roman poet and a Greek, why should not the Roman poet selected for the purpose be Cinna, and the couplet remain attached to the poem as we find it? If we take l. 9 as referring to Cinna, either *sodalis* or *poetae* will do as a supplement: cf. 10.29–30 *meus sodalis Cinna*, and 35.1 *poetae tenero, meo sodali*. The objection to linking Antimachus with Volusius largely disappears if we recognize that *two* contemporary poets, Hortensius and Volusius, have been mentioned adversely. Both alike were long-winded; so in the last line, instead of bringing in either of them by name, C. mentions a third poet, the classic example of long-windedness: Antimachus. Since A. did in fact enjoy considerable popular esteem, C. makes the point that if the public likes his kind of verbose poetry it is welcome to it, but he (as a Callimachean) prefers something shorter. Even if we infer that C. implicitly admits that Volusius enjoyed some popularity, this is not really inconsistent with ll. 7–8, since C. is then claiming that these fluent, voluminous works may be more acceptable to the public, because more easily intelligible, than a poem like the *Zmyrna*, but that they will prove to be ephemeral. See n. on l. 9.

The 'Hortensius' of this poem must either be the same person as 'Hortalus' of poem 65, or belong to the same family, since these two names invariably

go together. Was he however (as is usually believed) quite certainly to be identified with the famous orator, Q. Hortensius Hortalus, who was eight years older than Cicero and a whole generation older than C.? Although Kr. ('kaum zu zweifeln'), F. ('must be'), and Q. ('Doubtless') all think so, the evidence for the identification, set out as follows, is by no means compelling.
(i) Plutarch, *Luc.* 1.5, recalls that Hortensius wrote ποίημα καὶ λόγον – no doubt the poem was a narrative – on the Marsian wars (90–85 BC); but this appears to have been in his youth, before C. was born. (He drew lots with young Lucullus whether these should be in Latin or Greek.)
(ii) Pliny, *Ep.* 5.3.5, lists some well-reputed public figures, who composed erotic or salacious verses; and since the name of Hortensius is included in this list together with that of Cicero, it is clear that the orator is meant.
(iii) Ovid, *Tr.* 2.441–2, giving a list of poets, says: *nec minus Hortensi, nec sunt minus improba Servi carmina.* (See S.G. Owen ad loc.) Servius is also included in Pliny's list, (ii) above. Hortensius' poems are by Aulus Gellius (19.9.7) grouped with those of Laevius, Cinna, and Memmius, and are there described as *invenusta.*

Erotic verse – (ii) and (iii) above – is seldom written in a bulky format; and there seems to be a contrast in l. 3 between neoteric concision and the diffuseness of Volusius' Ennian-type *Annals*, with Hortensius in the latter camp. There is also some suggestion that 'Hortensius' had little better to do than turn out vast quantities of verse. That the successful and famous orator commanded so much leisure seems a priori unlikely. He had, however, a son, who is known to us only from references to his profligate character in Cicero's letters; this son would have been of C.'s generation. The family was wealthy, and so literary pastimes were well within the son's reach. Alternatively, it is not impossible that the references in Ovid and Gellius – (iii) above – are to the son, not the father, and that *he* was the 'neoteric' literary friend to whom C. wrote poem 65 and sent poem 66, but that the father, in his declining years, being less active in the courts and in politics, reverted to his youthful weakness for writing (and publishing) Ennian epic. [The arguments in this note apply of course to the defence of *V*'s reading. But I would now accept *Hatriensis*; inter alia, *Paduam* gives it 'local' support.]

1 It is a measure of *O*'s weak grasp of Latin that the scribe can write *mensem* although *nonam* has the feminine inflection. Further, *hiemem* in line 2 makes it certain that *messem* is right.

2 *edita <est>* is the principal verb (with *denique* as adverb, implying eager anticipation); subordinate clauses are *post … quam coepta est* and *cum interea … F.*, who apparently cannot accept the 'omission,' regards *mittetur* (line 5) as the main verb, following Kr.; but the stylistic awkwardness of adding one

more *est* at the end of the line is obvious, and the poet's concern to avoid such awkwardness would surely justify the omission.

3 It is likely that in the omitted line 4 a genitive followed *milia*; and a noun, in agreement with *uno*, must be understood. Fröhlich's conjectural supplement *versiculorum anno quolibet ediderit* is at least as plausible as any other.

interea has here the adversative sense ('H., for his part . . .'), not the temporal sense 'in the meantime.'

5 See App. Crit. (*V.*'s unmetrical reading was almost certainly influenced by *Zmyrnam cana* in line 6.)

cavas: the adj. is used of a river running between the walls of a gorge it has cut (and in general of a channel or hollow, or that which it encloses). Cf. V. *Geo.* 1.326 *cava flumina crescunt*, of rivers rising to overflow the beds that normally contain them.

Satrachi: this river in Cyprus was the very home of the legend of Zmyrna. Clausen 1964: 189 has made the point that the S. was a clear, fast-flowing river, *Padua* the opposite – slow and muddy – and that this contrast illustrates a difference of styles between Callimachus and his opponents, of whom (perhaps) Antimachus may be taken as a representative. He quotes the lines put into Apollo's mouth by Callimachus (*Hymn* 2.108–12).

> Ἀσσυρίου ποταμοῖο μέγας ῥόος, ἀλλὰ τὰ πολλὰ
>
> λύματα γῆς καὶ πολλὸν ἐφ᾽ ὕδατι συρφετὸν ἕλκει.
>
> Δηοῖ δ᾽ οὐκ ἀπὸ παντὸς ὕδωρ φορέουσι μέλισσαι
>
> ἀλλ᾽ ἥτις καθαρή τε καὶ ἀχράαντος ἀνέρπει
>
> πίδακος ἐξ ἱερῆς ὀλίγη λιβὰς ἄκρον ἄωτον.

6 *cana . . . saecula*: cf. 78^b.4 *fama . . . anus* (see n.). Tr. 'the generations <as they grow old and white-haired> will long continue to . . .' More commonly it is the literary work itself that is said to become old: Cicero, *De legg.* 1.1, tells us that Scaevola said of Cicero's poem on Marius *canescet saeclis innumerabilibus*. Catullus has simply altered the image. For the prediction, in general terms, cf. Cinna fr. 14 M (on Valerius Cato): *saecula permaneat nostri Dictynna Catonis*.

7 *ipsam* = 'no further afield than'; implying perhaps either that V. was a native of those parts (near the mouth of the Po) or (less probably) that his *Annals* took account only, or chiefly, of events in that area.

8 *laxas . . . tunicas*: see my article (1964); papyrus sheets were not used to wrap fish in antiquity (at any period); and moreover C. clearly has cookery in mind. The adj. *laxas* simply implies that an abundance of sheets was available for this purpose.

9 Some Mss from the third quarter of the fifteenth century, for example No. 38 in the Table, read *sunt* (no doubt the result of a conscious decision to emend): it is adopted by Lee. E. correctly attributes the reading *sunt* to one Ms (No. 38) and incorrectly to another (No. 45).

sodalis and *Catonis* seem to be the two leading survivors, in the general view of editors, among the many supplements that have been proposed. If *sodalis* is accepted and taken to refer to Cinna (see 10.29–30, and cf. 35.1–2 where C. speaks of another fellow-poet, Caecilius, as *meus sodalis*), then obviously 95 and '95[b]' (lines 9–10) must be read as a single poem. See the quotation from Cinna, referring to Cato himself, quoted above in n. 6, where the language is so similar to that of 95.1 (*mei = nostri*) and 6 (*saecula pervoluent*) that the fusing of all ten lines of 95 into a single poem appears inescapable. Leo 1903 however points to the wide appeal predicated of the *Zmyrna* in 95, contrasted with the restricted appeal for which the fellow-poet is consoled in '95[b],' as an argument for the division of the poem and for the supplement *Catonis*. As the text will show, I now read lines 1–10 as a single poem. I am also inclined on the whole to accept B. Guarinus' long-neglected supplement *poetae*, taking C. to refer to Cinna. Taken with *mei*, this expression would imply both 'the poet we have been speaking of' in lines 1–8 (a value that has generally been attributed to *V*'s reading *meus* at 17.21) and also 'my fellow-poet and friend.' It may further be suggested that in such a purely literary context as this the social overtones of the word *sodalis*, appropriate enough in poem 10 (where the embarrassed poet has to create the impression that Cinna's slaves are 'as good as' his own), are somewhat less relevant.

10 *Antimachus:* his long-windedness was proverbial (see Schol. on Hor. *AP* 136). But, apart from Plato's resolute championship, A. was generally popular (hence *populus gaudeat*), and his reputation as an epic poet stood next to that of Homer (Quint. 10.1.53). There is no contradiction between short-term popularity and permanent acceptance – by 'learned' critics, at least – as a literary giant: cf. Callim.'s remark σικχαίνω πάντα τὰ δημόσια (*Epigr.* 28.4) and his expressed desire to follow untrodden paths (fr. 29). (Prop. 3.3.24 *turba maxima* suggests the Callimachean πάντα τὰ δημόσια; see also Camps on Prop. 3.3.15, who compares Callim. *H.* 2.105–13, esp. 108 μέγας ῥόος [Köhnken 1981].) Probably Antimachus in some way stands for Volusius here; if the two poems are one, Hortensius has fallen out of view in the final couplet.

Leo, F. 1903. 'Coniectanea,' *Hermes* 38: 305.

Robinson, R.P. 1915. 'C. 95,' *CP* 10: 449–52.

Dunbabin R.L. 1925. (on Juvenal 3.14), *CR* 39: 112.

Paoli, U.E. 1952. 'Note di Filologia reale su C., Orazio, Marziale,' *SIFC* 10: 33–7.

Gigante, M. 1954. 'C., Cicerone ed Antimaco,' *RFIC* 32: 67–74.

Paratore, E. 1955. 'Briciole filologiche – II. Sul c. 95 di C.,' *Studi in onore di Gino Funaioli*. Rome: 322–8.

Thomson, D.F.S. 1964. 'Interpretations of C. – II: C. 95.8,' *Phoenix* 18: 30–6.

Pasoli, E. 1970–2. 'Cuochi, Convitati, Carta nella critica letteraria di Marziale,' *Museum Criticum* 5/7: 188–93.

Köhnken, A. 1981. 'Apollo's Retort to Envy's Criticism (Two Questions of Relevance in Callimachus, Hymn 2, 105ff.),' *AJP* 102: 411–22.

Noonan, J.D. 1986. 'Myth, Humor and the Sequence of Thought in C. 95,' *CJ* 81: 299–304.

Solodow, J.B. 1987. 'On C. 95,' *CP* 82: 141–5. [Read *Hatriensis in*; see esp. 143–4].

Morgan, J.D. 1991. 'The Waters of the Satrachus (C. 95.5),' *CQ* 41: 252–3 [A well-reasoned article, defending the reading *sacras* in line 5.]

96

Structure: 4 + 2; 'stiffly articulated' (Fraenkel 1956).

Propertius (2.34.89–90) informs us that Calvus composed an elegy on the death of Quintilia; the question whether she was his wife or his mistress is still debated. If she was a mistress, we have to take account of the fact that Calvus failed to replace her Roman name, in his poetry, with a Greek name, as the Augustan elegists were later to do; notwithstanding Ovid, *Tr.* 2.431–2 (just after mentioning Catullus as Lesbia's lover) *par fuit exigui similisque licentia Calvi / detexit variis qui sua furta modis*, where *sua furta* need not mean extra-marital affairs during his wedded life, and would in any case designate affairs with married women (so that Quintilia as Calvus' wife is not here ruled out). In opposition to Fraenkel's view that she was Calvus' wife, see Tränkle 1967 and Davis 1971.

A more important point is this: our poem was probably written after C. had read Calvus' elegy. Fraenkel argues cogently that Calvus' line *forsitan hoc etiam gaudeat ipsa cinis* (fr. 16 M, *FLP*), which has been plausibly attributed to this elegy, is C.'s starting-point (notice *gaudet*, answering to *gaudeat*, and also *certe*, which Fraenkel interprets as C.'s response, couched in terms of confidence and assurance, to the hesitant and uncertain *forsitan* of Calvus' own poem; in other words, C. seeks to reassure his bereaved friend).

1 *Si quicquam*: C. was fond of this rather prosaic opening; cf. poems 102, 107 (for a variant of this see poem 98). The *si*-clause (equivalent to a negative) explains *-ve*; cf. 9.11 *quid ... laetius beatiusve?*, 13.10 *seu quid suavius elegantiusve est*. *mutis*: the adj. is transferred to the tomb from the ashes it contains (κωφὰ κόνις; see on 101.4). It is really their silence that distresses the mourner. *gratum* and *acceptum* are often linked: see above, 90.5 n.

3 *dolore, quo desiderio*, 'the pain by which, in the form of longing ...' As F. says (following Haupt and E.), *desiderio* 'defines *dolore* more precisely.' The

antecedent is – by a common idiom – repeated in the subordinate clause with a
slight alteration; cf. perhaps 64.73 (but note the text there).

4 *olim*, 'formerly,' cf. 67.4 (as Kr. says, not necessarily of a *distant* past).
missas, 'abandoned' (Fraenkel 1956); 'given up' rather than = *amissas*, 'lost.'
F. quotes Plaut. *Pseud.* 685 *certa mittimus dum incerta petimus*, and compares
the expression *missum facere*. (Kr. agrees that in *mittere* the giver-up is never
completely passive.) Delz 1977 would read *iunctas*, but can hardly (see n. 7)
explain the corruption. The special poignancy of *missas* lies in the implied
self-reproach for abandonment or desertion.

5–6 *certe … gaudet*: possibly in (reassuring) answer to Calvus (fr. 16 M, *FLP*)
forsitan … gaudet (see Fraenkel); but see further the criticisms of Fraenkel's
view by Tränkle 1967: 93–9, usefully summarized by Davis 1971.

Fraenkel, E. 1956. 'C.s Trostgedicht für Calvus,' *WS* 69: 278–88.
Tränkle, H. 1967. 'Neoterische Kleinigkeiten,' *MH* 24: 87–103.
Alfonsi, A. 1971. 'Sulla "Quintilia" di Calvo,' *Athenaeum* 49: 147–51.
Davis, J.T. 1971. 'Quo desiderio. The Structure of C. 96,' *Hermes* 99: 297–302.
Bringmann, K. 1973. 'C.s Carmen 96 und die Quintilia-Elegie des Calvus,' *MH* 30:
     25–31.
Delz, J. 1977. 'C.s Konsolationsepigramm für Calvus,' *MH* 34: 74–6.

97

Structure: 8 + 4. Versified prose; hardly any attempt at poetical ordering.
Analysis in K. Quinn, *The Catullan Revolution* (1959): 36.
An exercise, above all, in richness of vocabulary; see Whatmough 1956,
who draws attention to the many 'taboo' words, and also *hapax eiremena*,
contained in the poem. (Half of all C.'s 'taboo' words are to be found here.)

The date is probably early, and the place Verona, since only a Transpadane
would understand such dialect words as *ploxenum*, which Quintilian (see
Testimonia) tells us C. found *citra Padum*. The identity of Aemilius is
uncertain: he could be either the *triumvir*, M. Aemilius Lepidus, or the poet
Aemilius Macer – from Verona – who died in 16 BC.

The language contains some prosaic expressions (*sesquipedalis, diffissus*)
as well as words and phrases elsewhere found chiefly in Comedy: *ita me di
ament; venustus; asinus* (avoided in 'serious' poetry); and *attingere*, in the
erotic sense in which it is also found at 67.20.

The first halves of the pentameters are all entirely spondaic (assuming
etiam in l. 4 to be pronounced as a dissyllable); here, at least, the effect is
comic rather than portentous. For the theme of 'personal hygiene,' cf. poems
69, 71.

1 *non ... referre putavi*, 'I should not have thought it mattered.'
  ita me di ament: a colloquial formula (note the shortening of *i* in hiatus); Plaut.
  Amph. 597 (Kr.). Cf. the 'elegant' variation at 61.189 *ita me iuvent caelites*.

2 See App. Crit. To retain *V*'s *utrum*, against *utrumne*, implies the acceptance of
  culum unelided before the diaeresis. Cf., however, for the hiatus, *V*'s reading
  at 67.44 *speret nec linguam esse* (a hiatus already observed, long ago, by A.
  Guarinus), and Politianus' autograph suggestion in Biblioteca Corsiniana Inc.
  50 F 37, *i. m.*, of *Chalybum* at 66.48 (where see n.); also notice 68.158 *primo*. See
  the preceding n. on hiatus in line 1.
  Aemilio: dative in place of genitive. C. does not use the -*ii* genitive form of
  names ending in -*ius* (*Heliconii*, essentially a Greek adjective, is another matter);
  he has *Alli, Corneli, Gelli, Meneni, Sesti, Volusi* – and of course *Favoni*. See n.
  on 113.4 (also Bailey on Lucr. 5.1006).

3 *R*²'s original correction is right in intention, but the separation at least is done
  by *m*, who also characteristically corrects the spelling of *R*'s *nichil*.
  hoc = os; illud = culus. For this order of the pronouns cf. 100.3. Lachmann's
  emendation *immundior ille* has a good deal to commend it, especially in B.'s
  amplified version *ille est* (*ille ē* would easily become *illud*, and the masc.
  immundior be changed to neuter as a result).

4 In this alliterative phrase, *melior* adds even less to the meaning than its
  equivalent often does in our 'bigger and better.'

5 Fröhlich's *os* is adopted by Lee.

5–8 A wild and fantastic enumeration of A.'s physical disadvantages.

6 *ploxenum*: said by Quint. (see Testimonia) to be a word from the region of the
  Padus (Po); usually explained, with the aid of Festus, as a kind of wicker or other
  box-cart, possibly for the removal of night-soil (e.g., in the stables, or else the
  'lines,' of transport mules – cf. ll. 7–8). See Whatmough 1956.
  m reads *ploxomio*. Observe how *m*'s carelessness goes uncorrected here.

7 *aestu*: editors seem to take this as referring to warm (summer) weather. Surely,
  however, it is more likely that it has to do with certain biological rhythms, which
  in some cases can be observed to affect even mules, though they are sterile. The
  phenomenon of mules 'on heat' may well have come within the range of C.'s
  experience in Cisalpine Gaul; he several times mentions these animals.

8 *R*²'s original correction is, as usual, followed by *m*. That *R*²'s spelling correction
  (from *mulle* to *mule*) = *O*'s reading is fortuitous.

9 *se facit*, 'makes himself out,' or more properly 'deems himself to be.' For *facere*
  = 'judge,' cf. 104.4 n.

10 *pistrino*, 'treadmill' (turned either by an ass or – sometimes as a punishment,
  cf. Plaut. *Most.* 17 – by a slave; see, further, Apul. *M.* 9.11).

11 For *attingere*, in a sexual sense, see 89.5 n.
  non ... putemus, 'must we not suppose?' Cf. 22.12 *hoc quid putemus esse?*

12 *aegroti* simply adds – rather gratuitously – one more repulsive touch.

lingere: cf. 98.4.

carnificis: a despised occupation. Juvenal, 8.174–6, lists *carnifices* in company with thieves, runaway slaves, and the emasculated priests of Cybele known as *galli* (for these last see 63.12, 34).

Whatmough, J. 1956. 'Pudicus Poeta: Words and Things,' *Poetic, Scientific and Other Forms of Discourse* [= Sather Lectures, vol. 29]. Berkeley: 29–55.

98

Structure: 4 + 2 (loosely).

The theme may again be, to some extent, personal hygiene: see the end of the intr. n. on poem 97. See however the nn. on ll. 1 and 2. As poem 97 is an exercise in vocabulary, so does this epigram appear to be an exercise in the effective use of vowel sounds. Particularly striking is the way in which *omnino*, with its wide-open long *o*'s, is deployed in lines 5 and 6 to represent a gaping mouth. Notice also the use of liquid consonants (*l* especially) in l. 4, for the licking of a tongue; and of the consonants *c* and *p*, which – as usual in C.'s epigrams – seem, when they are highly concentrated, to express disapproval. The effect of the repeated *v*'s is a good deal harder to assess.

The close relationship, just suggested, of poem 98 to 97 is confirmed by the reworking (or so it appears) of 97.12 *culum lingere carnificis* in the opening and end of 98.4 *culos et crepidas lingere carpatinas*. Moreover, two of the three pentameters are spondaic as far as the diaeresis, with the same comic effect as in poem 97 (where see the intr. n.). Nevertheless, the general impression left by poem 98 is of a great advance on poem 97 in the technique of composition.

1 *putide*: cf. *Catalepton* 12.1 *superbe Noctuine, putidum caput*; also 42.11. In both of these passages the word *putidus* is used in a transferred sense.

2 *id quod dicitur*: the formula indicates a proverb; cf. 94.2 n. For the gossiper's foul tongue, figuratively compared to a lavatory sponge (Sen. *Ep.* 70.20) or a shoe rag, see Kr.'s n. on line 3.

fatuus is glossed as ἀκριτόμυθος ('indiscreet in language'). Donat. on Ter. *Eun.* 1079 explains it as *inepta loquens*. Cf. 83.2.

3 *cum*, of a characteristic (usually as grounds for reproach); cf. Ter. *Hec.* 134 *cum istoc odio*.

si usus veniat, 'in case of need.'

4 *crepidae* were roughly made sandals (Isid. *Orig.* 19.34.3) which 'fitted' either foot.

   carpatinas: see App. Crit. (emendation by Coluccio Salutati). What is meant is, again, a crudely made and cheap kind of rustic sandal (ὑπόδημα). See the Greek definitions quoted by Kr., including that of Hesychius: μονόπελμον καὶ εὐτελὲς ὑπόδημα ἀγροικικόν.

5 *omnino*, with *perdere.* Notice the sound (open o's, for an open mouth); cf. line 6.

   perdere, 'destroy.' Cf. 29.24.

Hendrickson, G.L. 'Discas für deiscas, dehiscas bei C. 98.6,' *RhM* 59: 478.

99

Structure: cyclic narrative: 2 + (4 + 4 + 4) + 2. In slightly more detail, thus: 1–2, factual; 3–6, 7–10, 11–14, development (four-line sentences); 15–16 (*quoniam* ...), corollary and envoi.

Theme: 'Crime and Punishment.'

   D.O. Ross 1969: 24 rightly characterizes this poem, in contrast to the general tradition of C.'s epigrams, as 'an occasional experiment,' involving a 'tone of delicacy' to be found rather in the polymetrics and longer poems. Since we have already found poems 97 and 98 to be, in their differing ways, experimental also (see the intr. notes to these poems), it appears that we are confronted by a triad of studies in different kinds of technique, set out in juxtaposed epigrams. In a footnote on p. 105 of the same work, Ross, discussing the word *saviolum* and other diminutives in poem 99, remarks that 'this poem is unique among the epigrams in that 6 of its 8 pentameter lines have an adjective before the caesura, modifying the noun at the end of the line – preciosity of technique as well as of vocabulary and tone.' A contrast to its cold, meditative (cf. *memini*, l. 4) aspect may be found in poem 48. What we must remember is that C. depicts himself as having taken 'psychological hellebore' (Marshall 1971; see his good remarks), consisting in the remembrance of his miseries; hence the prosaic clarity of ll. 15–16, distinguishing them from the rest of the poem.

1 *ludis:* it is impossible to say exactly what is meant by this. Juventius, however, must have known; so perhaps the situation is one that actually occurred, despite the remarks of Kr. and others.

   mellite: cf. 48.1, and also (in another context) 3.6.

2 *dulci dulcius*, a colloquial idiom: cf. Plaut. *Asin.* 614 *melle dulci dulcior, Truc.* 371 (of an embrace) *melle dulci dulcius;* also poem 22.14 *inficeto inficetior*, 27.4

ebriosa ebriosior (where see n.; the jingling repetitiousness of the idiom lends additional support to the reading *ebriosa* against *ebria* there).

ambrosia: see App. Crit., and cf. line 13. *R*'s self-correction to *ambrosio* is of course independent of *O*.

3 Cf. 78ᵇ.3 *verum id non impune feres.*

amplius horam: exaggerating, of course, though no doubt that is what C.'s temperament *did* lead him to 'remember.'

4 *summa cruce*, 'the very worst of torture.' Cicero, *In Pis.* 42 *si te et Gabinium cruci suffixos viderem.*

5 *tibi*, 'in your eyes,' 'for your benefit.' Cicero, *Ad Fam.* 12.25.3 *quod te mihi ... purgas.*

6 *tantillum*, 'the tiniest bit': *tantum* in such usages is, as Kr. says, originally deictic, '<only> so much'; for the opposite sense, of a large amount or number, cf. 5.13 *tantum ... basiorum*, 'the sum of <all> our kisses' (and see line 11, *illa ne sciamus*, where also *illa* seems to retain something of a deictic sense).

vestrae = *tuae* (cf. 39.20 n.).

saevitiae: dative, after *demere*. Tr. 'moral disapproval'; cf. 103.4 *saevus*.

7 *nam*, in an expository sense, goes on to describe the action characterized – in C.'s eyes – by *saevitia*.

simul = *simul atque*, 'as soon as.'

id factumst (colloquial) = *saviolum surripui*; cf. 23.21, where *id* = *quod cacas*.

8 *abstersti* = *abstersisti*. On the question of hiatus (resulting here from acceptance of *O*'s reading), see n. on 3.16. Hiatus is several times indulged in by C. before the letter *o*, usually the *o* of *omnis*; e.g., at 68.158 *primo omnia* (see M. Zicàri, *Phoenix* 18 [1966]: 193–205). In poem 66, line 11 has *novo auctus*, line 48 (possibly) *Chalybum omne*. See also 97.2 n. The inversion *abstersti guttis* (*Ald.*) brings *g.* and *omnibus* into potentially misleading proximity.

mollibus: A.G. Lee's conjecture, unpublished at the time of Q.'s edition, which adopts it, has since been accepted or approved by others besides Q.: e.g., G.P. Goold, in his article 'O Patrona Virgo' (1974; see bibliography to poem 1), and P. Fedeli, reviewing Lee's edition in *Gnomon* 65 (1993): 176.

articulis, 'fingers,' for *digitis*. Cf. Cicero, *ND* 1.79, Petron. 32.3 and 96.3 (*OLD* s.v. *articulus* 2. b).

9 *contractum*, 'caught,' like an infectious disease; the transference of the image to *saliva* (line 10) is not strictly logical, but the meaning is clear enough.

10 *commictae*, etc.: cf. 78ᵇ.2 *comminxit spurca saliva tua.*

11 *praeterea*: a rather prosaic word, used by C.'s contemporary Lucretius in order to introduce a further argument, usually in passages of scientific exposition. C. employs it (in hexameters) at 64.184; also at 67.45 and 97.7, both times in contexts where the language is heavily prosaic.

13 Cf. line 2.

15–16 Notice the unhappy ring of the repeated *iam*'s (contrast poem 46 for a quite different effect); *iam* in line 16 simply emphasizes the meaning of *numquam*, but in fact it is brought in for the sake of its contribution to the sound.

15 *misero*: applied either to love (as at 91.2) or to the lover (as at 51.5, or 45.21 *misellus*).

Akbar Khan, H. 1967. 'C. 99 and the Other Kiss-Poems,' *Latomus* 26: 609–18.
Marshall, J.C.D. 1971. 'C. 99,' *CW* 65: 57–8.

100

Structure: 4 + 4.
To 'Caelius' of Verona, in gratitude for his support in the matter of Lesbia (for it is, on the whole, a reasonable assumption that she is referred to in line 7). The passion in question is, or at least appears to be (so far as C. is concerned) already extinguished, since it is described as *vesana*. C. is now able to speak of it in a detached way. For Caelius, see also poem 58, which records a very advanced stage in C.'s renunciation of Lesbia, and which, though it speaks of Lesbia's conduct in Rome, offers no proof that either Caelius or C. himself was then in Rome, but rather the contrary (the mention of *Remi nepotes* being dragged in to show where the events took place, the writer and the addressee being both at a distance – possibly, though not certainly, at Verona).

For 'Quintius' see poem 82; he is there reproached by C. for attempting to steal Lesbia away from him, but C.'s love for her is still spoken of in the present tense; it follows that poem 82 is seen as antedating poem 100.

For the spondaic first halves of the pentameters, cf. poems 97, 109, 114.

2 *flos*: cf. 64.78 *decus*.
Veronensum: the form of the gen. pl. is chosen *metri gratia*; *-ium* is the usual form. It is difficult to believe, from the evidence presented in the App. Crit., that *veronensum* was in *V*, as L. believed. More likely it was a common-sense emendation on the part of *X* or *A*. Observe that here *G* has the truth. It could be argued that this situation (where R^2 takes a reading that is otherwise known to us from *G*, and is followed by *m*) demonstrates that R^2 in his earlier recension had constant recourse to *X*, as he certainly had in his later work. But to Coluccio this correction must have been so obvious that R^2's variant is not conclusive in the sense just indicated. Notice how *m* adopts it as his text; but m^2, as often happens, feels an obligation to preserve *R*'s original reading in the form of a variant.

al. -ant: i.e., *depereant* R^2; an attempted correction of *V*'s desperate reading *depereret*.

3 *hic*, 'the former'; cf. 97.3 n.

3–4 'This is an example of the proverbial truth (a true example of the saying) that devoted friendship between brothers <and sisters> is a pleasant thing.' Here, as Q. points out, *two* pairs are involved; *sodalicium* covers both pairs, and *fraternum* has to be taken as subjective and also objective genitive.
dulce, sc. <est>. For its omission (in a proverb), cf. 113.4. Neither this word nor *vere* is mere padding (as Kr. claims). On *vere* as adding something, cf. 115.8 n.

5 *faveam*, 'wish success' (cf. line 8). Short questions, immediately answered: cf. 6.13, 22.12, 24.7, 72.7, 92.3. The idiom is colloquial.

6 Probably *X* had *est exigitur est* (the -*ex*- being expunged by himself), or else *est* (with superscript *ex*) *igitur est*, or *ē* (with superscript *ex*) *igitur ē*. See Intr. to *CE*, p. 24. In any case the R^2 reading derives from *X* a genuine attempt on someone's part to improve the text.

Palmer's emendation, approved of by F. for example, has been challenged. In 1966, M. Zicàri, in a review (*Scritti*, 1978: 265), objected to *tum* in synaloepha after the diaeresis, referring to H. Magnus, *Bursians Jb.* 51 (1887): 272. But a monosyllable in synaloepha at this position exists at 76.10 if we accept (as F. does) B.'s alternative reading there.

Forsyth, P.Y. 1977. 'The Irony of C. 100,' *CW* 70: 313–17.
– 1980–1. 'Quintius and Aufillena in C.,' *CW* 74: 220–3.
Levine, P. 1987. 'C. 100: A Potent Wish for a Friend in Need,' *Maia* 39: 33–9.
Gagliardi, D. 1989. 'Un augurio sofferto (lettura del c. 100 di C.),' *Vichiana* 18: 40–4.
Simpson, C.J. 1992. 'C. 100, Ovid, and the Patrons of the Race Track,' *SLLRH* 6. Brussels: 204–14.

101

Structure: either 4 + 6 or 6 + 4 (see below, n. on l. 5).
On a visit to the burial place of the poet's brother, in the vicinity of Troy (see 65.7 and 68.89–92). It is likely that C. made his visit in 56 BC, on his return from Bithynia, rather than (as E., Kr., and F. suggest) in 57, on his way there; according to C. himself the governor's *cohors*, of which he was a member, went out to the province together, as a body, and returned separately – and the journey to Troy would be a diversion from the normal route. This poem has been accurately described (by Wilamowitz, *HD* 1.234) as a short elegy: it is highly personal, and the emotion within it expands and develops in a way that goes far beyond the conventions of the funerary epigram (for which see poem 4 n.) or any other epigram. In antiquity it achieved a great deal of fame, and the tribute of imitation: see, for example, V. *Aen.* 6.692–3 *quas ego te terras et quanta per aequora vectum / accipio.*

On its relation to Virgil, and to the *Odyssey*, see Conte 1971 and Monteleone 1976.

The poem can be seen, in view of the triple repetition of *frater* (at four-line intervals, and always at the same place in the line), as enshrining a literary version of the ritual known as *conclamatio*, by which the relatives of the deceased called his name loudly, three times (originally no doubt as a precaution, in the belief that this might evoke a spark of recognition if any life remained). For the ritual, see *RE* s.v. *inferiae*; notice that in its full form it consisted of two parts, the *actus parentandi* (corresponding to l. 3 of the poem) and the *novissima verba* (= l. 4) (see Biondi 1976: 413 n. 22). For its other literary manifestations, see (apart from 68.19–21 and 91–3, where *frater* is thrice repeated in successive lines) V. *Aen.* 6.505–6 *tunc egomet tumulum Rhoeteo litore inanem / constitui et magna manis ter voce vocavi* (cf. R.G. Nisbet on Cicero, *De domo* 98) and Ovid, *F.* 3.563–4 *terque vale dixit, cineres ter ad ora relatos / pressit, et est illis visa subesse soror.* (See Howe 1974 on the ritual by which three handfuls of earth were also thrown.) There are archaic touches in the poem, suiting its solemn quasi-religious character: e.g., the accumulation of adverbs; the use of *more parentum* as a poetic way of saying *more maiorum*; the ritual formula *ave* (or *salve*) *atque vale.* It is however characteristic of C. that in spite of such solemnity he introduces colloquial words here and there (*alloquerer, quandoquidem*). Notice the use of sound-effects: as F. says, 'the alliteration on *m* which runs through the poem is a piece of studied technique'; also the manipulation of vowel sounds (*u, a, ae*) has been noted by Biondi, who describes the effect of *nequiquam*, with its last syllable elided at the diaeresis, as that of a sob.

2–3 *advenio ... ut ... donarem*: notice the sequence of tenses; but *advenio* is practically a formula, virtually signifying *adveni* (especially with a participle added, as here with *vectus*). As Kr. puts it, it is equivalent to *veni et adsum*; he quotes Plaut. *Most.* 440 *triennio post Aegypto advenio domum.* Or is it rather simply *vectus ... ut donarem?* (Biondi 1976: 412, q.v. for the juxtaposition *vectus / advenio*). Q. finds here an echo of Aesch. *Cho.* 3 ἥκω γὰρ ἐς γῆν τήνδε καὶ κατέρχομαι (Orestes at his father's tomb); the same line may possibly be echoed by the unknown poet quoted by Cicero, *TD* 1.37 *adsum atque advenio Acherunte.*

2 *inferiae* are 'last rites,' usually in the form of libations, offered to the *di manes* (Lucr. 3.52; see also Ovid, l. 4 n. below).

miseras, because associated with death; F. quotes Ov. *F.* 6.492 and Prop. 1.15.21.

advenio ad: *ad* with 'final' value ('for the purpose of'); possibly colloquial, as appearing only in Comedy, at Plaut. *Amph.* 669 and *Men.* 287; see Biondi 1976: 422 n. 60.

3 *munere*, 'office' as well as 'offering.'

4 *mutam*, cf. 96.1 (feminine: cf. 68.90). Kr. quotes Antipater of Sidon, *A.P.* 7.467.8 κωφὰ κόνις. Cf. Ov. *F.* 5.422 *inferias tacitis manibus illa dabunt.*
adloquerer, 'call upon.'

5 *quandoquidem*: archaic-colloquial (Biondi 1976: 421); see J.B. Hofmann, *Lat. Synt. u. Stilistik* (1965) p. 609 (quoted by Biondi), and Kr., who also points out that *quandoquidem* was in demand for versification because of its dactylic rhythm; see the passages referred to below (in the next sentence but one), both in hexameters and in hendecasyllables. Notice the strong punctuation at the end of line 6. Some editors place it at the end of line 4, with a comma at the end of line 6, as I did in *CE*; but I now regard line 6 as a climactic outburst.

Biondi's lengthy but on the whole well-argued article, defending the structure 6(4+2)+4, and hence punctuation after line 6, misses the 'adversative' force of *interea*, with its contrast to *tete ipsum.*

6 Cf. 68.20 *o misero frater adempte mihi* (and 68.92 *ei misero . . .*), here apparently reworked (Biondi 1976: 414); notice that poem 65 speaks of the brother's death as a recent event (*nuper*, line 5) which still exerts a paralysing effect on C., and the same effect is manifest in 68.19–24. The humanistic emendation *misero* here (see App. Crit.) is based on 68.20 and 92; but the elision of a long *o* at the end of a dactyl in the first foot would be awkward.
heu: colloquial.

7 *interea*, in adversative (not temporal) sense (36.18 n.); the contrast is with *ipsum*, not with anything C. proposes to do on a future occasion. C. implies that the offerings (*haec*) are a poor substitute for the reality of his brother's presence.
more parentum: a poetical variant on the formula *more maiorum.*

8 *tradita*, 'given' (as I have now done), rather than 'handed down' by tradition.
inferias: cf. line 2 n.

9 *multum* (as an adverb, modifying a participle, as here) is colloquial: see J.B. Hofmann, *Lateinische Umgangssprache* (Heidelberg, 1951): 77.

10 *ave atque vale*: a formula, found on sepulchral inscriptions (E. and Kr. cite between them *CLE* 1558.6; *ILS* 8143; *CIL* II 3490, 3506, 3512, 3519, 3686). Cf. V. *Aen.* 11.97–8 *salve aeternum . . . aeternumque vale.*

Robinson, C.E. 1965. 'Multas per gentes,' *G&R* 12: 62–3.

Conte, G.B. 1971. 'Memoria dei poeti e arte allusiva (a proposito di un verso di C. e di uno di Virgilio),' *Strumenti critici* no. 6: 325–33 (reviewed by M. Bettini, ibid. no. 29 [1976]: 172–6).

Howe, N.P. 1974. 'The "Terce Muse" of C. 101,' *CP* 69: 274–6.

Biondi, G.G. 1976. 'Il carme 101 di C.,' *L&S* 11: 409–25.

Monteleone, C. 1976. 'C. e l'Odissea dell' Eneide,' *RSC* 24: 190–210.

Gelzer, T. 1992. 'Bemerkungen zu C. c. 101,' *MH* 49: 26–32.

102

Structure: balanced, unitary (2 + 2).
An 'occasional' epigram, of a private kind ('A secret will be kept'; that is all).
The tone is generally prosaic; the repeated *me esse* is, as F. says, 'clumsy.'
Who is Cornelius? Quite possibly Nepos (poem 1); but the name is common.

1 *si quicquam*: F.'s arguments for *B.'s si quid quoi* are not quite strong enough to
overthrow the Ms reading. Cf. 96.1, 107.1. If the reading *tacito* in the Mss is
right, *tacito* is used as a noun (cf. 64.110 *saevum*, 68.154 *piis*), emphasized by
its position immediately before the caesura, and balanced by *Harpocraten* at the
end of line 4.
amico: R^2's correction is both original and sound.

2 *cuius*: related to *tacito*, rather than to *amico* (which is in a self-contained phrase,
and less emphatic).

3 *me aeque*: translate 'if ever [l. 1] . . ., then I too, just like the others (you'll find).'
If we accepted *V's meque* we should take it, not as equivalent to *me quoque* ('For
this usage . . . there is little evidence,' F.), but as being paired with *et*: 'you will
find that I have been . . . and also that I have become . . .'
iure, 'bond,' 'agreement,' or (F.) 'code,' uniting a circle of initiates.
sacratum, 'consecrated,' or better (E.) 'bound under sanction,' i.e., bound by a
lex sacrata; F. has a useful n. on *l. s.* as a technical term.
illorum = *tacitorum*, regarded as a body of devotees: cf. the reference to
Harpocrates.

3–4 Vossius, whose text omits *esse* in line 3, annotates thus: 'Me unum esse
invenies. Idem exemplar habet meque invenies. A sequenti autem versu abest
esse in veteribus quidem libris. Itaque non dubito quin Catullus sic scripserit: Me
aeque invenies illorum iure sacratum / Corneli, et factum me puta Harpocratem.'

4 *putum*, 'out-and-out' (as in *purus putus*). Though there is no other surviving
example of *putus* entirely on its own, except perhaps Cicero, *Ad Att.* 2.9.1, nevertheless the late grammarians assert that among the *antiqui* it was current as an
alternative to *purus. puta*, 'say, a H.,' would seriously weaken the force of the line.
Harpocraten: 74.4 n.

Vessey, D.W.T.C. 1982. 'A Cornelius Tacitus in Catullus?,' *LCM* 7: 59.
Edwards, M.J. 1990. 'The Secret of C. 102,' *Hermes* 118: 382–4.

103

Structure: balanced, unitary (2 + 2).
The language of this short lampoon, or pasquil, asking Silo to return some
money without making a fuss, is devoid of crudity, with one exception:

C. calls Silo a 'pimp.' Of course, he is not really a pimp; had he been, he would have been below C.'s notice, at least as far as composing a literary invective poem was concerned; the exaggeration is as palpable as in poem 58, where C. uses the equally (or even more) startling word *glubit* of Lesbia herself, as an index of his anger (cf. some of the expressions in poem 37).

1–3 *aut . . . aut*: cf. 12.10.

1 *sodes*, 'please' (= *si audes*), colloquial. C.'s politeness is, of course, ironical.
decem sestertia = 41.2 *milia . . . decem* (see context). But no conclusion need be drawn from the correspondence of these amounts.
Silo: as Kr. points out, quoting Festus, this *cognomen* occurs frequently; it may well be of Etruscan derivation.

2 *quamvis*, in its original sense, 'as much as you like' (not quite as in 12.5, despite F. and Q.).
saevus, '(unreasonably) strict'; see 4 n. and cf. 99.6 *saevitiae*.
indomitus, either (i) 'raging' (cf. 50.11), of one 'beside himself,' 'out of control' with love or anger or any violent emotion; or else (ii), perhaps more appropriately, 'unbending' (Gnilka 1975). For these expressions, cf. Plaut. *Pseud.* 1290 *saeviter*, Cic. *Part. or.* 11 *saevitia*, Juv. 2.77ff. *acer et indomitus*, etc.

3 *nummi*, 'cash' (colloquial, for 'money'); cf. Hor. *Ep.* 1.1.54 *virtus post nummos*. The merits of R^2's correction here awaken a response – very rare in this part of the book – from G^2 (who of course picked it up from m^2; he seems never to have seen *R* itself).
quaeso, 'I beg you'; for the ironical politeness cf. l.1 *sodes*.

4 *leno*, probably not to be taken literally; as Kr. points out, it would not have been worth C.'s while to attack a real pimp. F. adds that the name Silo (see n. on 1) suggests free birth, whereas a *leno* is unlikely to have been freeborn. For *leno* as a term of abuse cf. Cic. *Verr.* 2.4.71, *Sest.* 26. As Gnilka 1975 points out, the *leno* in Comedy is not depicted as having a soft and flattering address; Skinner's 1981 attempt to connect the noun *leno* with the verb *lenire* appears to be little more than guesswork.
idem, 'at the same time' (of a *contradictory* action of, or quality in, a person). We require, therefore, a meaning for *saevus* that is inherently irreconcilable with, or at least opposed to, the concept implied in the word *leno*; the simplest opposition is that between vice on the one hand and fanatical puritanism (see 2 n., and the article by Gnilka) on the other. Kr. contrasts the 'character of a *leno*, who ought to be agreeable,' with *saevitia* in the sense of harsh hostility; but see Gnilka's criticism of this view.

Lenz, F.W. 1963. 'Catulliana,' *RCCM* 5: 62–70, esp. 67–70.
de Grummond, W. 1971. 'A Note on C. 103,' *CP* 66: 188–9.

Gnilka, C. 1975. 'C.s Spottgedicht auf Silo,' *RhM* 118: 130–5.
Skinner, M.B. 1981. 'Gentlemen's Agreement: C. 103,' *CP* 76: 39–40.
Schmid, I. 1984. 'Catull c. 103 – ein politisches Epigramm?,' *RhM* 127: 317–25.

104

Structure: balanced (question and answer) 2 + 2.
Sounds: *p*, *t* (both suggesting disapproval).
Someone has taken certain words, written or spoken by C. in criticism of
Lesbia, in a far harsher sense than he intended, supposing them (wrongly)
to mean that he has fallen out with her. The poem obviously records, or
professes to record, a fairly early stage in C.'s affair.

1 *credis*: it is unlikely that the person addressed is, as Q. suggests, either Lesbia –
   inter alia, *est* in line 2 would surely be *es* – or the imaginary reader (*tu cum
   Tappone* is far too specific for this); rather, some male acquaintance is the target.
   potuisse, 'that I was capable of' (as in *potui, possem*).
   meae ... vitae (colloquial; 'my darling'), probably Lesbia, as (no doubt) at 109.1;
   cf. also 45.13 *mea vita*, 68.155 *tua vita*.
   meae dative (cf. *mi* at 83.1 and 92.1, where see notes; tr. therefore 'against,'
   not 'to').
2 *carior ... oculis*: cf. 3.5, 14.1, 82.3–4. For *ambobus*, cf. Diodor. *A.P.* 5.122.1–2
   φέρτερος. ... ὄσσων ἀμφοτέρων (Kr.).
3 *perdit(e)*: elision of a final long syllable at this place in the line is unexampled in
   the hexameter down to the time of C., so far as we can judge from Ennius and
   Lucretius, and also in Virgil after him. C. himself avoids it, though (as Kr. points
   put) he does not avoid eliding short syllables, and syllables ending in *-m*, in the
   same position.
4 *Tappo*, like Silo (poem 103), seems to be an Etruscan *cognomen*. (See W.
   Schulze, *Zur Geschichte lateinischer Eigennamen*. Berlin: 1904, s.v.) Possibly
   'Tappo' was a stock character in farcical plays; see F.'s n.
   monstra facis, 'you make everything out to be a dreadful scandal'; not containing
   'a reproach – to Tappo himself, or to the person addressed – in the sexual
   domain,' as Kr. (taking *facere* as meaning 'do,' not 'judge') believes, and perhaps
   also F., who wrongly translates 'you shrink from no enormity.'

Forsyth, P.Y. 1976. 'Tu cum Tappone: C. 104,' *CW* 70: 21–4.

105

Structure: unitary monodistich.
On 'Mentula's' literary pretensions.

1 *Mentula* = Mamurra; cf. 94.1. For Mamurra as *eruditulus*, cf. 57.7.
   Pipleium: the 'Pi(m)pleian' mountain was situated in Pieria, a district of
   Macedonia northeast of Mount Olympus; its spring, *Pipla*, was consecrated
   to the Muses. Cf. Hor. *Od.* 1.26.9 *Piplea dulcis* (of his Muse). The image of
   poetic ambition as climbing the 'hill' or 'crags' of the Muses is old; F. quotes
   Enn. *Ann.* 215 V² (= 208 Skutsch) *neque Musarum scopulos <quisquam*
   superarat>.
2 *furca* means 'pitchfork' (Hor. *Ep.* 1.10.24 *naturam expellas furca*); for the
   'colloquial' diminutive *furcilla*, the use of which at once produces a comical and
   'low' tone, cf. Cic. *Ad Att.* 16.2.4 *furcilla extrudimur*.

Boughner, R. 1983. 'Mentula in C., c. 105,' *CB* 59: 29–32.

106

Structure : unitary monodistich.
A real incident; but probably not designed to pillory anyone in particular.
Sounds: *c* deprecates (cf. poem 104); *p* is contemptuous (cf. esp. poem 81;
also poems 74 and 78 ᵇ).

1 *praeconem*, 'auctioneer.'
   esse: *R*'s deviant reading *ipse* is pure error. (Observe how *R*'s slip has been
   faithfully copied by *m*.)
2 *discupere*, 'burst with desire to …' (very rare: otherwise only Plaut. *Trin.* 932,
   and Caelius in Cic. *Ad Fam.* 8.15.2). (Kr.)
   Most readers would assume that <*puerum*> must be the subject of *discupere*,
   even though <*praeconem*> (which is the subject of *esse* in line 1) might be
   expected. But see Bushala 1981 for an interpretation which takes *praeconem* as
   the understood subject, and explains *se vendere* in the sense that the *praeco*
   trumpets or peddles his own merits (as a lover, presumably).

Bushala, E.W. 1981. 'A Note on C. 106,' *HSCP* 85: 131–2.

107

Structure: balanced (4 + 4); the two halves are joined by anaphora of the
words *restituis cupido*. Lines 1–2 contain a general statement: suddenly to
obtain what one longs for, when it is unexpected, is especially delightful. On
the the intensification of *cupido* from line 1 to line 5, see intr. n. to poem 70.
The poem celebrates a reconciliation with Lesbia, perhaps only temporary.
To attempt to date it would be guesswork. The exaggerations, and the

repetitions (which have an almost incantatory effect), serve to build up excitement. For the exclamatory ending (ll. 6–8) cf. poems 26, 43.

Notice that the words repeated (*cupido, gratum, insperanti, restituis*) are, with apparently deliberate intention, given (when repeated) in the same inflection in which they first occurred; from the point of the reader, or more properly hearer, this ties the poem together all the more tightly. It should perhaps be added that whatever form of the verb *optare* is used in the last line (see App. Crit.) certainly echoes *optanti* in l. 1, producing a 'cyclic' effect. The effect of the pattern of repetitions is to give this epigram in elegiac metre a much more 'lyric' air than such compositions normally exhibit, at least in C. Prominent among the poem's sounds are the long vowel *o*, and also *q*. It may not be wholly fanciful to suggest that taken together they convey shouts of joy.

1 See App. Crit. For *si quicquam*, the best restoration, cf. 96.1 and 102.1. *cupido optanti*: hiatus between (especially) *o* and *o* (or *au*) is favoured by C.; cf. 66.11. Against Aldus' *-que*: 'Double *-que* is a means of stressing the fact that two different things occur together, as in 76.8, and has little point when they are virtual synonyms,' L.

1–2 *optanti ... insperanti*: cf. Cic. *De or.* 1.96 *insperanti ... sed valde optanti ... cecidit.*

2 Heinsius' *insperati* is supported by Kr.; but the repetition of *insperanti* in line 5 tells heavily against it.
proprie (with *gratum*), 'quite properly,' 'in a very special way.'

3–4 However we read the text (see App. Crit. and the article in *LCM* 9.8: 119–20, where I tentatively suggest *nobis quod carius auro est*), these lines must contain the particular application of the general rule stated in lines 1–2; lines 5–8 are a meditation on this event.

3 *nobis* perhaps = *mihi*; but with my suggested reading (see previous n.) it could mean 'to both of us.'

5 *ipsa*, 'of your own accord' (F.); cf. 63.56.
refers te: cf. Prop. 1.18.11 *mihi te referas.*

6 *lucem* = 'day' (cf. 5.5.). See App. Crit.: nearby ablatives caused the change to *luce*.
candidiore nota: cf. 68.148 *quem lapide illa diem candidiore notat*, 8.3 *candidi soles*. F. adds refs. to Plin. *Ep.* 6.11.3, Mart. 9.52.5, 8.45.2, and Hor. *Od.* 1.36.10. The abl. in *nota* is 'descriptive.'

7 *quis me uno vivit felicior?* Cf. Ter. *Eun.* 1031 *ecquis me hodie vivit fortunatior?*
me uno: in such contexts, *unus* emphasizes the pronoun: F.'s n. gives references.

7–8 It is not possible to say that the textual difficulties of this passage have been satisfactorily solved. I have chosen to print, *faute de mieux*, one of the earliest conjectures. A tempting solution is ventured by Lee, who combines Kr.'s *hac re* with Statius' (and later E.'s) *optandum in vita*.

Munro, H.A.J. 1880. 'C. 107.7,' *Journal of Philology* 9: 185.
Slater, D.A. 1924. 'C. CVII,' *CR* 38: 150–1.
Conte, G.B. 1970–1. 'C. 107.7–8,' *SCO* 19–20: 338–42.
Thomson, D.F.S. 1984. 'C. 107.3–4 and 109.1–2,' *LCM* 9: 119–20.
Heyworth, S. 1984. 'C. 107.3 – A Response,' *LCM* 9: 137.
Lyne, R.O.A.M. 1985. 'The Text of C. CVII,' *Hermes* 113: 498–500.
Dettmer, H. 1987. 'C. 107.7–8,' *CW* 80: 371–3.
Ghiselli, A. 1988. 'Il c. 107 di C.,' *Filologia e forme letterarie. Studi offerti a F. Della Corte*: 2.339–48. Urbino.

108

Structure: 2 + 4. See the analysis in Gnilka 1973: 256–58.

A *diffamatio* (cf. poem 97); F. refers to Ovid, *Ibis* 165–72 for comparison. Both lines of the concluding couplet are much more regular in rhythm than the corresponding lines, whether hexameter or pentameter, of the first two couplets; an indication, perhaps, that C.'s rage (whatever its precise cause may have been) is sated by the imagined punishment of the offender.

'Cominius' may possibly be identifiable with P. Cominius, the accuser of a certain Cornelius (or with his brother Gaius): see Cicero, *Cluent.* 100; *Brut.* 270; and Ascon. *In Cornel.* 52–9. If the Cornelius of this story should happen to be the same as 'Cornelius' in poem 102, then possibly C. wrote this indignant epigram when the *populus* was angry with Cominius, as E. suggested; but the events of that year (66 BC) seem too remote to make this likely. The name Cominius is fairly common in Cisalpine Gaul; F., accordingly, thinks C.'s quarrel with Cominius may have arisen in Verona.

1 *Cominius*: see intr. n.
  populi arbitrio: i.e., if Cominius were to be put to death by lynch law, which in Rome usually involved stoning; but Gnilka 1973 contends that at least in this instance it was done by dismembering (*discerptio*).
  cana senectus: cf. 61.155 *cana anilitas*.
3 *equidem*, colloquial. When Virgil (*Aen.* 7.311) wrote *dubitem haud equidem*, was he remembering Catullus?
4 *sit data*: 'present' subjunctive for future, but perhaps – because perfect in form – with a notion, related to the events contemplated in line 5, that the punishment mentioned has already taken place.

5 *effodere* is the 'technical' (Kr.) or 'regular' (F.) word for gouging out eyes: Plaut.
   Aul. 53 *oculos ecfodiam tibi.*
6 *lupi*: cf. Hor. *Epod.* 5.99.

Gnilka, C. 1973. 'Lynchjustiz bei C.,' *RhM* 116: 256–69.

109

Structure: 2 + 4 (apostrophe to the gods). See the analysis by W.V. Clausen
in *Cambridge History of Classical Literature*, vol. 2 (1982): 203–4.
The poem reflects C.'s first doubts of Lesbia's faithfulness to him. Notice the
accumulation of synonyms – (i) for 'lifelong continuance,' in ll. 2, 5, 6 (see n.
on 5–6), and (ii) for 'sincerity,' in ll. 3–4 – an accumulation that conveys
the desperate intensity of the poet's feelings. C.'s relationship with Lesbia
was regarded by him not simply as a love affair but as having many of the
characteristics of a marriage on the one hand, and a very deep friendship on
the other; see McGushin 1967 on the implications of the vocabulary used in
the last line.

1–2 On the punctuation (colon after *proponis*) and the reading *perpetuum usque,*
   see my 1984 article, the gist of which is as follows.
   Surprisingly, a great many editors seem to have accepted it as natural that
   Catullus should be in raptures over his beloved's rather banal promise that the
   love between them 'will be pleasant.' Quinn for one perceives the strangeness of
   this: '*iucundum,* though a word Catullus is fond of, sounds odd on Lesbia's lips
   in this context, and rather an inadequate partner for *perpetuum.*' Camps 1980
   also remarks on it, and would replace *iucundum* with *continuum;* but the *ductus
   litterarum* is hostile to this change, and *continuum* is somewhat flat.
   Editors are too willing to put up with *V*'s *-que* in line 2, which they feel
   an obligation to explain, as though there were no palaeographically acceptable
   alternative. But surely there is. The text I print should be translated 'My
   beloved, I rejoice in the promise you make to me – (namely) that this love of
   ours shall last for *ever.*' B. took a small (but not the really important) step in this
   direction: '*proponis,*' promittis … *quocum artius coniunge* '*iocundum*' (= *rem
   gratam acceptamque); ad haec autem exegetice accedunt reliqua: scilicet fore
   'inter nos,' hoc est, mutuum … et in omne tempus duraturum hunc amorem.*
   But, as F. objects, '*nostrum amorem inter nos fore* is an impossible expression.'
   Yet B. is, I think, right in taking *iucundum* as equivalent in meaning to *res grata
   acceptaque;* cf., e.g., *(per)gratum mihi facies,* occurring frequently in Cicero's
   letters. Indeed, *pergratum* and *iucundum* (or *periucundum*) are often linked,
   especially in such contexts, as a pair of synonymous terms; see, e.g., Cicero,

Ad Q.F. 3.1.4 *id mihi pergratum perque iucundum erit* (cf. *De oratore* 1.205 *pergrata perque iucunda*), *Ad Fam.* 1.7.3 *litterae tuae periucundae fuerunt*, *De amic.* 16 *pergratum mihi feceris* (cf. *Ad Att.* 1.20.7), *In Cat.* 4.1 *est mihi iucunda vestra erga me voluntas*; Caesar, *BC* 1.86.1 *id vero militibus fuit pergratum et iucundum*; and, for the general meaning of *iucundum*, Juvenal 13.180 *bonum iucundius vita*, 10.349 *pro iucundis* (note the adjective here used as a noun) *aptissima quaeque dabunt di*. Finally an example, from Pliny's letters (4.15.13), where *iucundum* seems exactly equivalent to *gratum: perquam iucundum nobis erit si ... precibus meis tu potissimum adiutor accesseris.*

The important step in emending this passage lies in substituting *usque* for *-que*. The probable source of the corruption may be divined if we write *perpetuūusque* (or even *perpetuū usque* with minimal word division); three successive *u*'s were simply too many for the scribe (especially perhaps a scribe with the end of his task in sight). Did he mis-copy *perpetuūusque* as *perpetuūsque* or *perpetuusque*, and did his successor 'correct' this to the seemingly grammatical *perpetuumque*?

The rhythm of *perpetuum usque fore* is Catullan. For repeated *u*-sounds, associated with elision, in contexts suggesting long duration, cf., e.g., 5.6 *perpetua una dormienda* and perhaps 45.4 *omnes sum assidue paratus annos*; at 45.14 we have a line (*huic uni domino usque serviamus*) which both exhibits this feature and contains *usque* as it is used in our passage (and for the latter, cf. also 61.151–6 *sine serviat ... usque, dum ... anuuit* and 3.10 *usque pipiabat*). The second line of this poem has two things in common with the final line of poem 101: the word *perpetuum* and, if I am right, an elision at the same point in the second hemistich.

It is just possible that we should read *iucunde*, bearing in mind the tone of bitter irony that prevails. Yet for adj. as noun cf., e.g., 64.110 *saevum*. With *iucundum* (= *gratum*) *proponis* cf. perhaps Hor. *Od.* 1.18.3 *omnia dura deus proposuit.*

1 *mea vita* = Lesbia, as in 104.1. (Cf. *vita*, of other men's loves, at 45.13, 68.155.) *proponis*: tr. 'assert' or 'promise' (cf. line 3 *promittere*) rather than 'propose, offer.'

2 The 'strong pleonasm' detected by Kr. in *nostrum inter nos* does not occur with my reading of the text.

3 *di magni*, surely here a serious appeal to the gods, like *di* at 76.17, 26, rather than 'an outburst expressed as a prayer ... very much, therefore, as in 14.12 and 53.5' (Q.). C. hopes, perhaps against his more sober judgment, that Lesbia is capable of meaning what she promises.

5–6 *tota vita* and *aeternum* reinforce and emphasize *usque* (l. 2). *tota vita* is abl. of duration (see refs. in F., who cites this as the earliest known example).

6 The *R*[2] spelling *amicicie* (followed by *m*[2], but not by *m*) is due to medieval conservatism in spelling, not to dependence on *O*. It should perhaps be noted that the version in *m* (*amicitie*) comes down on the 'modernist' side against *R*[2] (as Poggio insisted on doing; see de la Mare and Thomson 1973: 189–91).

McGushin, P. 1967. 'C.'s "Sanctae foedus amicitiae,"' *CP* 62: 85–93.
Camps, W.A. 1980. 'Some Conjectures,' *AJP* 101: 442–6, esp. 442.
Thomson, D.F.S. 1984. 'Catullus 107.3–4 and 109.1–2.' *LCM* 9: 119–20.

110

Structure: 4 + 4. As in poem 107, the first couplet contains a general statement.
See Persson 1914 for a detailed study of the poem's linguistic aspects.
For Aufillena cf. poem 100. C. has now courted her favours with gifts; she has nevertheless rejected him, and he is angry, and is now taking out his resentment in exaggerated abuse (to be wildly intensified in the next poem). F. says only that she 'is accused of taking money for her favours, then breaking her bargain.' But there is really nothing here to say that A. takes money for her favours; she is not, in fact, called a *meretrix*. What she has done is to take C.'s presents and subsequently deny him a sexual relationship. Those who actually sell their services, whether 'call-girls' (lines 1–2) or common prostitutes (lines 7–8), are relatively honest; the real insult to A. consists not in classing her among such persons, but in comparing her unfavourably with them in the matter of honest behaviour, where she is worse than they are although she claims to be *ingenua*, which ought to imply its own code.

Notice the contrasting rhythms: smooth in ll. 1–2 (calm, level, logical); broken in 3–4 (excited, 'contradictory'). For the alternatives signalled by *aut … aut*, cf. (in a similar context) poem 103. The heavy enjambement of a sentence in l. 5 to the mid-point (diaeresis) of l. 6 is unusual in C.'s epigrams.

1, 6 Aufillena: cf. 100.1.

1 *bonae amicae* are contrasted with the *meretrix avara* of l. 7; cf. Tib. 2.4.45 *at bona quae nec avara fuit.* For *bona* = 'complaisant, obliging' cf. 89.1 n.

2 *quae*, n. pl. accus.; *eorum* (dep. on *pretium*) is suppressed; cf. the similar suppression of a pronoun at 62.60; F. gives examples of similar ellipses from Plautus (*Aul.* 605, *Curc.* 581, *Poen.* 764), adding 'but <it is> rare later.'
instituunt, 'set about (performing)' (F.); 'undertake' (Q.).

3 The punctuation adopted here seems the simplest way out of a tortuous sentence. One is tempted (as Kr. suggests) to alter *inimica* to *inimice*.

Translate: 'Inasmuch as you, in an unfriendly fashion, [contrast l. 1 *amice*], have cheated me of the thing *that* you promised, <and> inasmuch as you take without giving, you are misbehaving.'

4 *nec ... et ...,* 'both refuse to give (favours) and keep on taking (payment).' *Ferre* in this sense is colloquial. For *dare* and *ferre* together, cf. Plaut. *Most.* 614, Ov. *Tr.* 1.2.68.

saepe is doubtless, as Kr. suggests, Catullan exaggeration (in view of *mihi*, which surely implies a single incident).

facis facinus, cf. 81.6 n.

5 *ingenua* ('of free birth'), here approximately = *bona* (l. 1). The sentence is compressed: 'either you ought to perform, which would be like an *ingenua*, or you should not have promised, which would have been like a chaste woman (such as you cannot now be).'

6 Repetition of Aufillena's name serves to heighten the 'paraenetic' (admonitory) atmosphere, as Kr. points out.

fuit, 'would have been.' She can still behave as an *ingenua* should, but can no longer be considered (or be in fact) *pudica*, 'chaste'; cf. 76.24.

7 *fraudando*, equivalent in meaning to a present participle; see E. (*Commentary*²: 492).

fraudare (= *detrectare*), 'refuse.' *officiis* in effect = 'obligations.'

plus quam m. av: read as *meretricis plus-quam-avarae*, 'worse than greedy'; according to the context *plus-quam* can also mean 'better than,' or simply 'more than.' See the illustrative examples in Kr. and F.

Persson, P. 1914. 'Zur Interpretation von C. c. 110,' *Eranos* 14: 116–29.

111

Structure: 2 + 2.

Aufillena is accused of incest. For the most persuasive account of the situation, see de Grummond 1970. More recently, Watson 1985 has written as follows: 'The *vir* <Aufillena is content with> is her uncle ... She enjoys *nuptiae* ... but the marriage is incestuous.' But could its products really be called *fratres* (to her, presumably)? – see n. on l. 4.

1 Aufillena: cf. 100.1, 110.1.

For *viro contentam vivere solo*, cf. *CEL* 455.5 *solo contenta marito*, Plaut. *Merc.* 824 *uxor contentast, quae bonast, uno viro.*

1–2 The construction is loose: = *nuptarum laus est <aliquam> vivere etc.*

3 *cuivis quamvis*, 'any woman ... to any man.'

4 *fratres*, 'brothers,' not 'cousins.' See de Grummond 1970 (Aufillena bore children to her brother-in-law; this wronged her legitimate offspring – the words in 1.4, 'mother, brothers, uncle,' are those that such offspring would use in this situation).

Zicàri 1958, against Fr. and others, advances an argument for reading *parere* at the end of line 4, which may be summarized as follows:

Recent editors prefer *te parere ex patruo* because they think a long vowel is to be preferred at the end of the pentameter. But this spoils the sense: as in 110.5–8, C. says that for *any* woman it is better *succumbere cuivis viro* than *de patruo matrem fieri*; he attacks the sin, just as much as or more than the sinner. And C. does not at all avoid a short vowel at the pentameter ending; in him, one pentameter in every 14 ends thus (only one in every 100 in Ovid). How was the line corrupted? Both *par est* and *parere* were written with abbreviations; the scribe either left out one of these, or simply removed from his pentameter *par ē*, which had been wrongly repeated from the preceding line.

Zicàri, M. 1958. 'Schedae sex,' *Philologus* 102: 154–5 (= *Scritti*, 1978, 141).
de Grummond, W. 1970. 'A Note on C. 111,' *CW* 64: 120–1.
Bush, A.C. 1972. 'A Further Note on C. 111,' *CW* 65: 148–51.
Watson, L. 1985. 'Aufillena and Her Uncle: C. 111,' *LCM* 10: 80.

112

Structure: unitary monodistich.

For the text and interpretation of the poem, see Thomson 1987.

Line 1 is defective (see App. Crit.), and neither *V*'s *descendit* nor the restoration proposed by Haupt and modified by Schwabe will do. It must be borne in mind that *multus*, as an adjective denoting a quality, has to mean something like 'boring, tiresome, over-loquacious'; and that *descendit* cannot (unless such a meaning is clearly supported by the context) mean 'go down to the Forum.' I read *discumbit*: Naso is unpopular on the dinner couch, both as a bore and (a surprise at the end) also because of his sexual inclinations.

1 Naso is otherwise unknown.

   multus homo, 'a tiresome fellow' (but *neque m. h.*, 'and there aren't many').

2 *discumbit* (*tecum*), 'sit beside you at dinner.'

Sonny, A. 1900. '*Multus*, einflussreich,' *ALL* 11: 132–3.
Rosén, H. 1961. (On the text of *CIL* I² 2180). *PP* 81: 438–46, esp. 442–3.

Akbar Khan, H. 1969. 'Three Epigrams of C.,' *Renard*. Brussels: 1: 3–11. [Poems 112, 114–15].

Morgan, M. Gwyn. 1979. 'C. 112: A *pathicus* in Politics,' *AJP* 100: 377–80.

Forsyth, P.Y. 1983. 'C. 112,' *CW* 77: 65–8.

Thomson, D.F.S. 1987. 'C. 112,' *Phoenix* 41: 191–2.

113

Structure: unitary, with three enjambements.

The date (see n. on l. 1) is 55 BC; early in the year, as we can deduce from *facto ... nunc*. For Cinna, see on 10.30 and on poem 95. The target of the epigram is Maecilia: see n. on l. 2.

1–2 The references to Pompey's first (70 BC) and second (55 BC) consulship are inserted purely for dating; as L. remarked, 'Dating was not an easy matter for the Romans ... and numbers between 10 and 20 did not lend themselves to versification. So the fact that Pompey was consul in 70 and again in 55 was a gift to C. when, in the latter year, he wanted to say "a good many years ago"; the interval happened to be 15 years, which was as good a number as any.'

1 *solebant*: colloquially, some verb in the infinitive is suppressed. For this 'euphemistic ellipse' F. cites Plaut. *Cist.* 36 *viris cum suis praedicant nos solere*.

2 Maecilia is unknown. But it is an authentic Roman family name (first literary reference: Livy, 2.58); to claim that a corrupt text accidentally coincided with this form, and then to suppose that what underlies it is *Mucilla* (see App. Crit.), and further to explain that Mucilla (otherwise unattested) is a diminutive (but why use a diminutive here?) of Mucia, the name of Pompey's third wife, divorced in 62 BC – seven years before the date of this poem – strains credulity; as L. observed, a lampoon against her could hardly hurt Pompey now.

facto consule: as Q. remarks, Pompey had apparently been elected consul but had not entered upon his office; so we can date this poem at the beginning of the year 55.

3 *manserunt*: implying, not constancy on the part of the original two, but rather that the number two did not vanish; on the contrary, it increased a thousandfold.

creverunt ... singula, i.e., each of the two (l. 3) must be multiplied by 1000. (For 'distributive' *in*, F. quotes Livy 9.41.7 *binae tunicae in militem*, Suet. *Nero* 30.3 *quadringenis in punctum sestertiis*.)

4 See App. Crit. (singula > singulu > singulū).

adulterio: we might expect *-ii*; but at this period the *-ii* genitive was not yet in general use. Cf. 97.2 n. (and see C. Bailey, *Lucretius*, introduction, vol. 1, 77–8 and 92).

fecundum semen adulterio: in this proverb (whether or not it was coined *ad hoc* by Catullus, as Q. suggests), notice the omission of the copula *est*, and cf. for this 100.4 n. (*fraternum ... dulce sodalicium*).

114

Structure: 4 + 2.
On the wealth of Mamurra (= 'Mentula'; see 29.3 and 13); wealth which Cicero (*Ad Att.* 7.7.6) includes in a list of the undesirable results of the First Triumvirate and of Caesar's command in Gaul. This wealth is embodied in a huge estate at Firmum, in the Picene territory. Vast as it is, its proceeds (*fructus*, l. 4) are insufficient to keep pace with M.'s extravagance (for which again see poem 29, passim); and, says C., this is just as I should wish it, since no character could possibly be less worthy to enjoy a fortune.

1 *m* reads *firmamus* (probably a careless error rather than an attempted correction).
   Firmano: i.e., in the territory of Firmum (south of Ancona). The ablative is 'causal' = 'on the strength of.'
   saltu: this word can be applied topographically to the rough pasture and open scrub forest which lies uphill from the cultivable land in a great part of Italy (Varro. *LL* 5.36). Here, however, it is clearly used in the other sense, that of 'estate' in general. It can also be used more precisely in the sense of a measure of 800 *iugera* (Varro, *RR* 1.10).
   Mentula = Mamurra (29.3 and 13; cf. 94.1, 105.1).
2 *tot res* = 115.4 *tot bona*.
3 *aucupium*, in a concrete sense, 'fowl,' 'game-birds' (Cicero, *De fin.* 2.8.23, Cels. 2.26.2, Sen. *Dial.* 1.3.6). See App. Crit; it would be unlike *O* to attempt to correct.
   omne genus, 'of all kinds': a common idiom in the accusative (F. cites Cato *Agr.* 8.2, Varro *RR* 3.5.11, Lucr. 4.735, and Petron. 71.7). Cf. *id genus* or *hoc genus*, used in the same way.
   feras = four-footed game.
4 *nequiquam*, 'but it's no good' (Q).
   fructus, acc. pl. = 'income' (derived from produce).
5 *concedo sit dives*, 'I don't mind his being rich' (F. adds: 'i.e., being called rich').
6 See App. Crit. and also Sources, *s.v.* O.L. Richmond, p. 96 above. Lachmann's *domo* is unlikely; what has the epigram to do with a house?
   modio, 'a bushel' (of grain to feed him, the bare minimum; cf. 5 *omnia desint*).
   ipse, 'the owner' (2.9 n.); cf. 115.7.

Akbar Khan, H. 1969. 'Three Epigrams of C.' (see under poem 112).
Harvey, P.B. 1979. 'C. 114–15' (see under poem 115).

115

Structure: 2 + 4 + 2 (cyclic: notice the repetition of the name *Mentula* as *mentula*, by a kind of artificial pun [see n. on poem 94], which ties the end of the epigram to its opening line).

Clearly, this and the foregoing poem must be treated as a pair, in some sense or other. But whether they are on an equal footing as merely 'lame and laboured epigrams on the pretensions and extravagance of Mentula' (F., on poem 114) is a rather different question.

What should first be observed is the *acreage* of M.'s estate. The *saltus*, of 70 *iugera* (ll. 11–12), extends to no more than forty-seven acres of productive land (excluding *maria*). This is surprising, for two reasons: first, despite the strenuous efforts of Harvey 1979 to show that this figure exceeds the size of the *average* Italian small-holding (such as those allotted to veterans), nevertheless M. must surely be 'rich' (*dives*, 114.5) in his *saltus* in some way that is suitable for a favourite of Caesar (in Varro *RR* 1.10 the term *saltus* is reserved for estates of 800+ *iugera*); secondly, the target of poem 114 (no less than of poem 29) is surely M.'s outrageous extravagance, which cannot be matched by the revenues even of an exceptionally large estate. Apart from C.'s habitual tendency to use exaggerated language, the last three lines of poem 114 all make this point, and the poem would fall flat indeed if it were not so. Why, then, is there a sudden constriction of the estate at the beginning of poem 115? Because (it may be suggested) we, the readers, are being warned that we are to reinterpret words like *pratum* and *arvum* in a different sense from now on: a sense in which '70 *iugera*' will be a gross exaggeration in its turn; that is, a sexual sense. *Pratum* and *arvum* are well-known agricultural-sexual metaphors for the female *pudenda*, and as such may appropriately follow the opening *Mentula* (or *mentula*) *habet*. There may also be a double entendre in *maria* (taken as 'male,' from *mas*, instead of *mare*). After all, Caesar shares a bed with M. in poem 57. When M. is said to possess all this *uno in saltu*, it would sound, if the line is read aloud, as though C. had said *uno qui saltu*, 'who by a single (sexual) leap . . .' (Akbar Khan 1969; see the bibliography to poem 112).

The concluding point of the epigram comes as we turn from the *saltus* to its owner: *tamen ipsest maximus ultor* (l. 7). The element of 'threat,' *ultio*, characterized by the allusion here to the god Priapus and his *mentula*, is repeated in the closing words, a parody of Ennius' *machina magna minax* (*Annals* 620 Skutsch). As for *non homo sed mentula*, it was said of Pompey

(*GLK* 6.461.30 –463) *quem non pudet et rubet, non est homo sed sopio,*
where *sopio* = *mentula* (the only possible meaning here, as the grammarian
Sacerdos shows, and surely also the meaning intended by C. at 37.10 *frontem
tabernae sopionibus scribam*).

1 The word *instar* (*V*'s reading) has been much suspected; (i) it involves an artificial
lengthening of the short syllable of *habet* 'in arsi'; elsewhere in Catullus, this
phenomenon occurs only in the long poems, and there only before the Greek
word *Hymenaeus* (62.4, 64.20, 66.11); (ii) it almost invariably goes with the
genitive case – one would expect *iugerum* here; in some instances (e.g., Cicero,
Ad Att. 16.5.5) it may take the accusative, of a number *only* (see F.'s note on
the supporting evidence found in two exceptional passages of Columella, who
normally has the genitive); (iii) if *lustra* is read, then line 114.3 corresponds in
content with 115.1–2, and the *lustra* of *ferae* – and, more loosely, of birds –
may be said to occupy most of the estate (not surprisingly in that district, which
as Kr. pointed out is 'extremely hilly') – and it is the *silvae* that are said to be
ingentes (line 5). Cf. V. *Geo.* 2.471 *saltus ac lustra ferarum*. If *lustra* should be
read, we have to observe further that there is another correspondence, namely
with lines 5–6:
lustra = *silvae* (abode of the *ferae* mentioned at 114.3);
iugera prati = *prata*;
arvi (iugera) = *arva*;
(cetera) maria = *altas paludes usque ad mare* (Q. translates *maria* by 'swamp,'
and Kr. so interprets the word; reading *instar*, Kr. believes that 'C. has here
suppressed, for the sake of brevity, the *silvae* and *saltus*, probably also with
the malicious intention of allowing the entire residue of the estate to appear
worthless.')
2 *maria*: Killeen (1969) interprets this of land, not of sea or swamp.
3 *potis*: cf. 45.5, 65.3, 72.7, 76.24. The form is chosen on metrical grounds.
5 I have excluded Pleitner's *silvas vastasque* from the apparatus, partly on
grounds of cacophony and partly as offering insufficient advantages over other
suggestions.
6 *Hyperboreas*, a mythical people at the northern boundaries of the world. They
first appear in literature in *h. Hom. (Dion.)* 29, Pind. *Pyth.* 10.30–6.
mare Oceanum: cf. Caes. *BG* 3.7.2 *proximus mare Oceanum*. According to
Kr., Pomponius Mela is the earliest author to use *Oceanus* as an adjective
(at 2.86, where *in nostrum et Oceanum mare* suggests this, though *OLD* 2a
takes *Oceanum* to be in apposition).
7 *ipse*: 'the owner.' Cf. 2.9 n. and 114.6.
ultor: see intr. n.; there is no need to abandon *V*'s reading. For the ending
maximus ultor cf. V. *Aen.* 8.201.

8 *non homo sed*: a colloquial idiom. Cf. Cicero, *Ad Att.* 1.18.1, 7.13a.2. F. quotes
Petron. 38.15, 43.3, 44.6 (and 74.13, of *mulier*) for versions of this expression
such as *piper, non homo*.
homo: for the quantity of the final vowel, cf. 24.7; see F. on 10.27, Q. on 6.16.
vere, 'a true example of (the proverb) . . .' Cf. 100.3–4 (*quod dicitur*) and
similarly *certe* in 94 (another Mentula epigram): 'certe hoc est *quod dicunt* . . .'
   Notice, in this instance, the pun between Mentula as a 'name' and *mentula* =
membrum virile, which may well be the key to 115 (see the introductory note).
mentula magna minax: a parody of the Ennian phrase (*Annals*, fr. 620 Skutsch)
machina multa minax. (See intr. n.) Cf. *Priap.* 30.1 *minax . . . parte tui maiore
Priape*.

Killeen, J.F. 1969. 'C. 115.2,' *CP* 64: 178–9.
Harvey, P.B. 1979. 'C. 114–15: Mentula, Bonus Agricola,' *Historia* 28: 329–55.
Maselli, G. 1990. 'Un punitore incompreso: *maximus ultor* in C. (115.7),' *BStudLat*
   20: 3–9. [Read *ultor*, as in *V*, not *ultro*.]

116

Structure: 6 + 2. The threat underlying this epigram resides in the last two
lines; cf. poem 40.
Probably the earliest in date of the Gellius epigrams; poems 74, 80, 88,
89, 90 seem to constitute the new and more scathing offensive threatened
here (poem 91, where Gellius emerges as C.'s rival in love – probably that
of Lesbia, see ll. 2 and 6 – is gentler, at least in its language; see the nn.
there). Whether this poem, with its reference to 'Battiades' (Callimachus)
in l. 2 (cf. 65.16), is placed at the end of the elegiac epigrams as a sort
of counterpoise to poem 65 at the beginning, is a matter for speculation.
On the oddities of a metrical or prosodic kind in lines 3 and 8, see the
notes there; these oddities, together with the forced language and obscure
subject-matter, have inclined some editors and critics to admit the poem
only with hesitation as the genuine work of Catullus (and its position at
the end of the collection has not helped matters in this regard). There is,
however, no positive reason for doubting its authenticity. If it is by C., it
may have been composed either in violent haste, as Kr. suggested, or very
early, or (again) as an attempt to parody Gellius' unpolished style.
   For the identity of Gellius, see the intr. n. to poem 74. Valerius Maximus
(5.9.1) sheds some light on C.'s charges against him. If the other Gellius
epigrams, listed above, are not in fact the instruments of C.'s threatened
literary vengeance (see l. 8) – if, that is to say, they had already been written
– surely C. could not have regarded himself as the injured party, as he

evidently does; and (we may ask) what happened to the lampoons he *did* write in fulfilment of the threat?

1 *tibi* (for *ad te*) with *mittere*: cf. 68.1–2 *mihi … mittis*; also 14.7, 65.16, and Varro *RR* 1.1.10.
  requirens = Greek aorist, not present, participle (Kr.).
    The punctuation adopted here avoids the unlikely concatenation of adj. and participle (see the tr. in Q.'s n., indicating the difficulty). The phrases at V. *Aen.* 3.70, 5.764, *Geo.* 4.370, all cited by F., are less unnatural.
2 *uti*, either (with *requirens*) 'to see how …' (F.), or (as *ut* final) 'in order to …,' which Kr. claims to be 'the most natural way' to take it.
  Battiade: Callimachus (cf. 65.16 n.). He gave himself this nickname.
3 C.'s only entirely spondaic hexameter – indeed, the only one in Latin poetry after the time of Ennius.
  qui (the archaic form of the ablative, as in *quicum*) = *quibus*, or *ut*: 'so that thereby …' Sometimes *quo* is used, without a comparative, in the same sense (almost = *ut*); F. refers to Cicero, *Pro Cluentio* 9, *Pro Sestio* 93, and *Verr.* 2.1.17.
  nobis = *mihi*, as *nostras* 6 = *meas*.
4 *telis*, the reading of *V*, may have arisen from an inchoate attempt to make the line scan, at a period when *meum* (if Muretus' supplement is right) had already dropped out. B. prefers *mihi*, which might easily disappear before *mi(ttere)*; but cf. (e.g.) Prop. 2.8.15–16 *an usque in nostrum iacies verba superba caput?*
  in-usque, as at 4.24 *ad-usque*.
  caput: cf. 15.16 *insidiis caput lacessas*.
5 *mihi* with *sumptum*, 'by me.'
  nunc, modifying *video*.
6 *hinc*, 'on these grounds' (Fr., Kr.; the Latin is difficult, but Fr. cites Propertius 1.7.7–10). *hic* would mean 'on this point,' *huc*, 'to this end' (i.e., to prevent you from attacking me).
7 If *contra* is prepositional, *contra nos* goes with *acta*; F., however, takes *contra* as adverbial and *nos* as nominative, which seems better on the whole unless the text is to be emended radically. Camps' ingenious suggestion *contorto … amictu* has a good deal of merit, though it has been vigorously combated by Németh 1977.
  acta (*amicta GR*): see App. Crit. (Baehrens suggested that *mi-* was an intruded gloss).
8 *dabis*, with suppression of final *s*: Catullus has no other example of this. It is prevalent in the early poets (Ennius, Lucilius) and occurs fairly often in Lucretius (49 times, according to his editor, C. Bailey), where it is probably used, and regarded, by the poet as a metrically convenient archaism; the same thing may perhaps be said of its use by Cicero in his *Aratea*, where it occurs

eight times. As Kroll remarks, it was taboo to the poets of the avant garde in Rome; see Cicero, *Orator* 161, on the withdrawal of this usage from the capital to the provinces. (Cicero's text substitutes an apostrophe for the final *s*, since he is discussing pronunciation; for this reason, some editors of Catullus print the word here as *dabi'*, though there is no reason to think that the poets wrote it so.)

Stoessl, F. 1972. 'C.s Gelliusepigramme,' *Kraus*. Vienna: 410–24.
Camps, W.A. 1973. 'Critical and Exegetical Notes,' *AJP* 94: 131–46, esp. 136–7.
Macleod, C.W. 1973. 'C. 116,' *CQ* 23: 304–9.
Forsyth, P.Y. 1977. 'Comments on C. 116,' *CQ* 27: 352–3.
Németh, B. 1977. 'To the Evaluation of C. 116,' *ACD* 13: 23–31.
Gagliardi, D. 1984. 'Il carme 116 di C.,' *PP* 214: 33–8.
Kitchell, K.F. 1986. 'C. 116.7: *amitha / micta*,' *CW* 80: 1–11.

Indexes

INDEX OF METRES

Note: An asterisk indicates that the introductory note contains a section on metre.

	Poems
Dactylic hexameter	62, *64
Elegiac couplet	65–116
Phalaecian hendecasyllable	1–3, 5–7, 9, 10, 12–16, 21, 23, 24, 26–8, 32, 33, 35, *36, 38, 40–3, 45–50, 53, 54, 54^b, *55, 56–8, *58^b, frag. 3
Sapphic stanza	11, *51
Glyconic stanza	*34, *61
Priapean	*17, frags. 1–2
Galliambic	*63
Iambic trimeter	*4, *29, 52
Iambic tetrameter catalectic	25
Choliambic ('scazon')	8, *22, 31, 37, 39, 44, 59, 60
Greater Asclepiad	*30

Acmen Septimius suos amores 45
Adeste, hendecasyllabi quot estis 42
Alfene immemor atque unanimis false
    sodalibus 30
Amabo, mea dulcis ipsimilla 32
Ameana puella defututa 41
Annales Volusi, cacata carta 36
Aufillena, bonae semper laudantur
    amicae 110
Aufillena, viro contentam vivere solo
    111
Aureli, pater esuritionum 21
Aut sodes mihi redde decem sestertia,
    Silo 103
Bononiensis Rufa Rufulum fellat 59
Caeli, Lesbia nostra, Lesbia illa 58
Caelius Aufillenum et Quintius
    Aufillenam 100
Cenabis bene, mi Fabulle, apud me 13
Chommoda dicebat, si quando commoda
    vellet 84
Cinaede Thalle, mollior cuniculi capillo
    25
Collis o Heliconii 61
Commendo tibi me ac tuos amores 15
Consule Pompeio primum duo, Cinna,
    solebant 113

Credis me potuisse meae maledicere
    vitae 104
Cui dono lepidum meum libellum 1
Cum puero bello praeconem qui videt
    esse 106
Desine de quoquam quicquam bene
    velle mereri 73
Dianae sumus in fide 34
Dicebas quondam solum te nosse
    Catullum 72
Disertissime Romuli nepotum 49
Egnatius, quod candidos habet dentes
    39
Etsi me assiduo confectum cura dolore
    65
Firmano saltu non falso Mentula dives
    114
Flavi, delicias tuas Catullo 6
Furi, cui neque servus est neque arca 23
Furi et Aureli, comites Catulli 11
Furi, villula vestra non ad Austri 26
Gallus habet fratres, quorum est
    lepidissima coniunx 78
Gellius audierat patruum obiurgare
    solere 74
Gellius est tenuis: quid ni? cui tam bona
    mater 89

Hesterno, Licini, die otiosi 50

Huc est mens deducta tua, mea Lesbia, culpa 75

Hunc lucum tibi dedico consecroque, Priape Frag. 1

Iam ver egelidos refert tepores 46

Ille mi par esse deo videtur 51

In te, si in quemquam, dici pote, putide Victi 98

Irascere iterum meis iambis 54[b]

Iucundum, mea vita, mihi proponis: amorem 109

Lesbia mi dicit semper male nec tacet umquam 92

Lesbia mi praesente viro mala plurima dicit 83

Lesbius est pulcer; quid ni? quem Lesbia malit 79

Lugete, o Veneres Cupidinesque 3

Malest, Cornifici, tuo Catullo 38

Marrucine Asini, manu sinistra 12

Mellitos oculos tuos, Iuventi 48

Mentula conatur Pipleium scandere montem 105

Mentula habet †instar† triginta iugera prati 115

Mentula moechatur. moechatur mentula? certe 94

Minister vetuli puer Falerni 27

Miser Catulle, desinas ineptire 8

Multas per gentes et multa per aequora vectus 101

Multus homo es, Naso, neque tecum multus homo <est qui> 112

Nascatur magus ex Gelli matrisque nefando 90

Nemone in tanto potuit populo esse, Iuventi 81

Ni te plus oculis meis amarem 14

Nil nimium studeo, Caesar, tibi velle placere 93

Noli admirari quare tibi femina nulla 69

Non custos si fingar ille Cretum 58[b]

Non ideo, Gelli, sperabam te mihi fidum 91

Non, ita me di ament, quicquam referre putavi 97

Non possum reticere, deae, qua me Allius in re 68[b] (vv. 41–)

Nulla potest mulier tantum se dicere amatam 87

Nulli se dicit mulier mea nubere malle 70

Num te leaena montibus Libystinis 60

O Colonia, quae cupis ponte ludere longo 17

O dulci iucunda viro, iucunda parenti 67

O funde noster seu Sabine seu Tiburs 44

O furum optime balneariorum 33

O qui flosculus es Iuventiorum 24

O rem ridiculam, Cato. et iocosam 56

Odi et amo. quare id faciam, fortasse requiris 85

Omnia qui magni dispexit lumina mundi 66

Oramus, si forte non molestum est 55

Othonis caput oppido est pusillum 54

Paene insularum, Sirmio, insularumque 31

Passer, deliciae meae puellae 2

Pedicabo ego vos et irrumabo 16

Peliaco quondam prognatae vertice pinus 64

Phaselus ille, quem videtis, hospites 4

Pisonis comites, cohors inanis 28

Poetae tenero, meo sodali 35

Porci et Socration, duae sinistrae 47

Pulcre convenit improbis cinaedis 57

Quaenam te mala mens, miselle Raude 40

Quaeris quot mihi basiationes 7

Quid dicam, Gelli, quare rosea ista labella 80

Quid est, Catulle? quid moraris emori? 52

Quid facit is, Gelli, qui cum matre atque sorore 88

Quinti, si tibi vis oculos debere Catullum 82

Quintia formosa est multis. mihi candida, longa 86

Quis hoc potest videre, quis potest pati 29

Quod mihi fortuna casuque oppressus acerbo 68[a] (vv. 1–40)

Risi nescio quem modo e corona 53

Rufe mihi frustra ac nequiquam credite amice 77

Saepe tibi studiose, animo venante, requirens 116

Salax taberna vosque contubernales 37

Salve, nec minimo puella naso 43

Sed nunc id doleo, quod purae pura puellae 78[b]

Si, Comini, populi arbitrio tua cana senectus 108

Si cui iure bono sacer alarum obstitit hircus 71

Si qua recordanti benefacta priora voluptas 76

Si qui forte mearum ineptiarum 14[b]

Si quicquam cupido optantique obtigit umquam 107

Si quicquam mutis gratum acceptumve sepulcris 96

Si quicquam tacito commissum est fido ab amico 102

Suffenus iste, Vare, quem probe nosti 22

Super alta vectus Attis celeri rate maria 63

Surripui tibi, dum ludis, mellite Iuventi 99

Tam gratum est mihi quam ferunt puellae 2[b]

Varus me meus ad suos amores 10

Verani, omnibus e meis amicis 9

Vesper adest; iuvenes, consurgite; Vesper Olympo 62

Vivamus, mea Lesbia, atque amemus 5

Zmyrna mei Cinnae nonam post denique messem 95

INDEX OF NAMES IN THE TEXT OF CATULLUS

Achilles 64.338

Achivi 64.366

Acme 45.1, 2, 10, 21, 23

Adoneus 29.8

Adria, Adriaticus, *see* Hadria,
    Hadriaticus

Aeeteus 64.3

Aegeus 64.213

Aegyptus 66.36

Aemilius 97.2

Aethiops 66.52

Africus 61.199

Aganippe 61.30

Alfenus 30.1

Allius 68.41, 50, 66, 150

Alpes 11. 9

Amastris 4.13

Amathus 36.14
    Amathusia 68.51

Ameana (?) 41.1

Amor 45.8, 17

Amphitrite 64.11

Amphitryoniades 68.112

Ancon 36.13

Androgeoneus 64.77

Antimachus 95.10

Antius 44.11

Aonius 61.28

Apheliotes 26. 3

Aquinus 14.18

Arabes 11.5

Argivus 64.4; 68.87

Ariadna 64.54, 253 (*see also*
    Minois)

Arrius 84.2, 11

Arsinoe 66.54

Asia 46.6; 66.36; 68.89

    Asius 61.22

Asinius 12.1

Assyrius 66.12; 68.144

Athenae 64.81

Athos 66.46

Attis 63.1, 27, 32, 42, 45, 88

Aufillena 100.1; 110.1, 6; 111.1

Aufillenus 100.1

Aurelius 11.1; 15.2; 16.2; 21.1

Aurora 64.271

Aurunculeia 61.82 (*see also* Iunia)

Auster 26.1

Balbus 67.3

Battiades 65.16; 116.2

Battus 7.6

Bereniceus 66.8

Bithynia 10.7
    Bithynus 31.5
Bononiensis 59.1
Bootes 66.67
Boreas 26.3
Britannia 29.4; 45.22
    Britanni 11.12
    Britannicus 29.20
Brixia 67.32, 34

Caecilius (1) 35.2, 18
    (2) 67.9
Caelius 58.1; 100.1, 5, 8
Caesar 11.10; 57.2; 93.1
Caesius 14.18
Callisto 66.66
Calvus 14.2; 53.3; 96.2
Camerius 55.10; 58^b.7
Campus minor 55.3
Canopeus 66.58
Castor 4.27; 68.65
Cato 56.1, 3
Catullus 6.1; 7.10; 8.1, 12, 19; 10.25;
    11.1; 13.7; 14.13; 38.1; 44.3; 46.4;
    49.4; 51.13; 52.1, 4; 56.3; 58.2;
    68.27, 135; 72.1; 76.5; 79.2, 3; 82.1
Cecropia 64.79, 83
    Cecropius 64.172
Celtiberia 37.18; 39.17
    Celtiber 39.17
Ceres 63.36
Chalybes 66.48
Charybdis 64.156
Chiron 64.279
Cieros 64.35
Cinna 10.30; 95.1; 113.1
Circus 55.4
Cnidus 36.13
Colchi 64.5
Colonia 17.1, 7
Cominius 108.1

Comum 35.4
Conon 66.7
Cornelius (1) 1.3
    (2) 67.35
    (3) 102. 4
Cornificius 38.1
Crannon 64. 36
Creta 64. 82, 174
    Cretes 58^b.1
Croesus 115.3
Cupido 36.3; 68.133
    Cupidines 3.1; 13.12
Cybebe (Cybelle) 63.9, 20, 35, 84, 91
    Cybele 63.12, 68, 76
Cyclades 4.7
Cycneus 67.32
Cyllenaeus 68.109
Cyrenae 7.4
Cytorus 4.13
    Cytorius 4.11

Dardanius 64.367
Daulias 65.14
Delius 34.7
Delphi 64.392
Dia 64.52, 121
Diana 34.1, 3
Dindymus 35.14; 63.91
    Dindymenus 63.13
Dione 56.6
Dorus (?) 64.287
Dyrrachium 36.15

Egnatius 37.19; 39.1, 9
Emathia 64.324
Eous 11.3; 62.35
Erectheus (n.) 64. 229
    (adj.) 64.211
Erycina 64.72
Etruscus 39.11
Eumenides 64.193

Europa 68.89
Eurotas 64.89

Fabullus 12.15, 17; 13.1, 14; 28.3; 47.3
Falernum 27.1
Favonius 26.2; 64.282
Fescenninus 61.120
Fides 30.11
Firmanus 114.1
Flavius 6.1
Formianus 41.4; 43.5; 57.4
Furius 11.1; 16.2; 23.1, 24; 26.1

Gaius (Cinna) 10.30
Gallae 63.12, 34
Gallia 29.3
    Gallicanus 42.9
    Gallicus 11.11, 29.20
Gallus 78. 1, 3, 5
Gellius 74.1; 80.1; 88.1, 5; 89.1;
    90.1; 91.1; 116.6
Gnidus, *see* Cnidus
Gnosius 64.172
Golgi 36.14; 64.96
Gortynius 64.75
Graecus 68.102
Grai 68.109
    Grai(i)us 66.58

Hadria 36.15
    Hadriaticus 4.6
Haemonides (conj.) 64.287
Hamadryades 61.23
Harpocrates 74.2; 102.4
Hatriensis (?) 95.3
Hebe 68.116
Helena 68.87
Heliconius 61.1
Hellespontus 64.358
    Hellespontius Frag. 1.4
Hercules 55.13

Hesperus 62.20, 26, 32, 35; 64.329
Hiberi 9.6; 12.14
    Hiberus (adj.) 29.19; 37.20; 64.227
Hortalus 65.2, 15
Hortensius 95.3
Hydrochoos 66.94
Hymen 61 and 62, passim
Hyperborei 115.6
Hyrcani 11.5

Iacchus 64.251
Ida 63.30, 52, 70
    Idaeus 64.178
Idalium 36.12; 61.17; 64.96
Idrus 64.300
Iliacus 68.86
India 45.6
    Indi 11.2
    Indus (adj.) 64.48
Ionius 84.11, 12
Italus 1.5
Itonus 64.228
Itylus 65.14
Iunia 61.16 (*see also* Aurunculeia)
Iuno 34.14; 68.138
Iuppiter 1.7; 4.20; 7.5; 34.6; 55.5; 64.26,
    171; 66.30, 48; 67.2; 68.140; 70.2; 72.2
Iuventius 24.1; 48.1; 81.1; 99.1

Ladas 58[b].3
Lampsacus Frag. 1.2
Lanuvinus 39.12
Laodamia 68.74, 80, 105
Laris(s)aeus 64.36
Larius 35.4
Latmius 66.5
Latonius 34.5
Leo 66.65
Lesbia 5.1; 7.2; 43.7; 51.7; 58.1, 2; 72.2;
    75.1; 79.1; 83.1; 86.5; 87.2; 92.1, 2;
    107.4

Lesbius 79.1
Lethaeus 65.5
Liber 64.390 (*see also* Iacchus)
Libo 54.3
Libya 45.6
  Libyssus 7.3
  Libystinus 60.1
Licinius 50.1, 8 (*see also* Calvus)
Ligur 17.19
Locris 66.54
Lucina 34.13
Luna 34.16
Lycaonius 66.66
Lydius (?) 31.13

Maecilia 113.2
Maenas 63.23, 69
Magna Mater 35.18
Magnus 55.6 (*see also* Pompeius)
Malius 68.54
Mamurra 29.3; 57.2
Manlius 61.16, 215; 68.11, 30
Marcus 49.2
Marrucinus 12.1
Mavors 64.394
Medi 66.45
Mella 67.33
Memmius 28.9
Memnon 66.52
Menenius 59.2
Mentula (29.13); 94.1; 105.1; 114.1;
  115.1
Midas 24.4
Minos 64.85
  Minois 64.60, 247
Minotaurus 64.79
Musa 65.3; 68.7, 10; 105.2

Naso 112.1, 2
Nemesis 50.20 (*see also*
  Rhamnusius)

Neptunus 31.3; 64.2
  Neptunius 64.367
Nereine 64.28
  Nereis 64.15
Nicaea 46.5
Nilus 11.8
Noctifer 62.7
Nonius 52.2
Novum Comum 35.3
Nympha (61.29); 64.17; 88.6
Nysigena 64. 252

Oarion 66.94
Oceanus 61.85; 64.30; 66.68; 88.6;
  115.6
Oetaeus 62.7; 68.54
Olympus 62.1
Ops 64.324
Orcus 3.14
Ortalus, *see* Hortalus
Otho 54.1

Padua 95.7
Parcae 64.306, 383; 68.85
Paris 68.103
Parnasus 64.390
Parthi 11.6
Pasithea 63.43
Pegaseus 58[b].2
Peleus 64.19, 21, 26, 301, 336, 382
Pelion 64.278
  Peliacus 64.1
Pelops 64.346
Penelop(a)eus 61.223
Penios 64.285
Persae 90.4
  Persicus 90.2
Perseus 58[b].3
Phaethon 64.291
Pharsalus 64.37
  Pharsalius 64.37

Phasis 64.3

Pheneus 68.109

Phoebus 64.299

Phrygia 63.71
    Phrygius 46.4; 61.18; 63.2, 20;
       64.344
    Phryx 63.22

Pipleius 105.1

Piraeus 64.74

Pisaurum 81.3

Piso 28.1; 47.2

Pollio 12.6

Pollux 68.65 (cf. 4.27)

Polyxenius 64.368

Pompeius 113.1 (*see also* Magnus)

Ponticus 4.9, 13; 29.18

Porcius 47.1

Postumia 27.3

Postumius 67.35

Priapus 47.4; Frag. 1.1, 2

Prometheus 64.294

Propontis 4.9

Protesilaeus 68.74

Pthioticus 64.35

Quintia 86.1

Quintilia 96.6

Quintius 82.1; 100.1

Rav(i)dus 40.1

Remus 28.15; 58.5

Rhamnusius 64.395; 66.71; 68.77

Rhenus 11.11

Rhesus 58b.4

Rhodus 4.8

Rhoeteus 65.7

Roma 68.34

Romulus 28,15; 29.5, 9; 34.22;
    49.1

Rufa 59.1

Rufulus 59.1

Rufus 69.2; 77.1

Rusticus 54.2

Sabinus 39.10; 44.1, 4, 5

Saetabus 12.14; 25.7

Sagae (-cae) 11.6

Salisubsil(i)us (-salus) 17.6

Sapphicus 35.16

Satrachus 95.5

Saturnalia 14.15

Satyri 64.252

Scamander 64.357

Scylla 60.2; 64.156

Septimius 45.1, 21, 23
    Septimillus 45.13

Serapis (Sar-) 10.26

Sestius 44.19, 20
    Sestianus 44.10

Sileni 64.252

Silo 103.1

Simonideus 38.8

Sirmio 31.1, 12

Socration 47.1

Sol 63.39; 64.271

Somnus 63.42

Stymphalius 68.113

Suffenus 14.19; 22.1, 10, 19

Sufficius (?) 54.5

Sulla 14.9

Syria 45.22; 84.7
    Syrius 6.8

Syrtis 64.156

Tagus 29.19

Talasius 61.127

Tappo 104.4

Taurus 64.105

Telemachus 61.222

Tempe 64.35, 285, 286

Tethys 64.29; 66.70; 88.5

Teucrus 64.344

Thallus 25.1, 4
Themis 68.153
Thermopylae 68.54
Theseus 64.53, 69, 73, 81, 102, 110,
    120, 133, 200, 207, 239, 245, 247
Thespius 61.27
Thessalia 64.26, 33
        Thessalus 64.267, 280
Thetis 64.19, 20, 21, 28, 302, 336
Thia 66.44
Thracius 4.8
Thyiades 64.391
Thynia (Thu-) 31.5
        Thynus 25.7
Thyonianus 27.7
Tiburs 39.10; 44.1, 2, 5
Torquatus 61.209
Transpadanus 39.13
Trinacrius 68.53
Triton 64.395
Trivia 34.15; 66.5
Troia 68.88, 89, 90, 99
    Troicus 64.345
    Troiugena 64.355
    Troius 65.7
Tullius 49.2
Tyrius 61.165

Umber 39.11
Urania 61.2
Urii 36.12

Varus 10.1; 22.1
Vatinius 52.3
        Vatinianus 14.3; 53.2
Venus 36.3; (45.26); 55.20; 61.18, 44,
    61, 191, 195; 63.17; 66.15, 56, 90;
    68.5, 10 (see also Dione)
        Veneres 3.1; 13.12; (86.6)
Veranius 9.1; 12.16; 28.3
        Veraniolus 12.17; 47.3
Verona 35.3; 67.34; 68.27
        Veronensis 100.2
Vesper 62.1
Vibennius 33.2
Vibia (conj.) 61.16
Victius 98. 1, 5
Victor 80.7
Virgo 66.65
Volusius 36.1, 20; 95.7

Zephyritis 66.57
Zephyrus 46.3; 64.270
Zmyrna 95.1, 5, 6

INDEX OF RENAISSANCE AND MODERN SCHOLARS AND WRITERS MENTIONED IN THE INTRODUCTION AND COMMENTARY

Note: Frequently cited commentators, whose names are indicated by initials only, are not included; for a list of these, see the Preface. Names in bibliographies are also excepted.

Acciaiuoli, D. 35
Adams, J.N. 203
Akbar Khan, H. 368, 552
Aldus (Manutius) 48, 50, 543
Alfonsi, L. 356, 362, 368
Allen, W. 19
Aretino, P. 203
Arkins, B. 504
Arnold, M. 458
Austin, R.G. 223, 497
Avantius, H. 43, 47–9, 52, 210, 255, 261, 396, 406, 419, 453, 496, 524
Axelson, B. 401

Badian, E. 278, 281, 467
Baehrens, E. 57–8, 467, 555
Bailey, C. 267, 340, 531, 550, 555
Baker, R.J. 513
Balland, A. 396
Ballou, S. 31
Barbarus, H. 45–9, 261, 406, 420
Bardon, H. 15, 60, 196, 221, 240

Barrett, A.A. 450
Bauer, J.B. 486
Bayet, J. 514
Beavan, E. 450
Bell, A.J. 513
Benoist, E. 58, 234
Bentley, R. 362, 395, 454–6
Benzo of Alessandria 25, 294, 307
Bergk, T. 199, 211, 352–3, 378
Beroaldus, P. 46–9, 260, 311, 524
Bianco, O. 378
Bickel, E. 486
Billanovich, G. 7, 22–3, 25–8, 30, 32, 36, 294, 470
Biondi, G.G. 352, 537–8
Bishop. J.D. 202, 515
Bolton, J.D.P. 275
Bonnet, M. 30, 352
Bosco, U. 27
Bramble, J.C. 388
Bright, D.F. 486
Brink, C.O. 202

Brown, C. 209, 360
Buchanan, G. 51, 420, 501
Bücheler, F. 321, 469
Burton, R. 366
Bushala, E.W. 542
Butrica, J.L. 43–4, 46, 49, 334

Cairns, F. 199, 349
Calderinus, D. 45–6, 48
Calphurnius, J. 44, 46
Campanile, E. 523–4
Campbell, D.A. 329, 360
Campesanis, B. de 23, 26, 28–9, 32, 53
Camps, W.A. 528, 555
Carratello, U. 253–6, 470
Cataudella, Q. 368
Cazzaniga, I. 59, 240, 344
Chatelain, E. 32
Chetry, A. 366
Cipriano, P. 327
Clausen, W. 25, 199, 409, 446, 460, 520,
    545
Colaclides, P. 514
Colotius, A. 44
Comitibus, F. de 43
Connor, P.J. 226
Conte, G.B. 537
Copley, F. 195
Coppini, D. 43
Corbett, P. 261
Corradinus, J.F. 55
Couat, A. 57, 508
Coulon, V. 234
Courtney, E. 40, 303, 371, 374, 377,
    387, 447, 451, 462, 472, 479, 483
Crawford, M.H. 334
Cressy, J. 399, 405, 414, 435
Crowther, N.B. 14–15, 18–19
Curran, L.C. 388
Cyllenius, B. 45
Czwalina, J. 283

Daiches, D. 514
Davis, J.T. 494–5, 529–30
Dee, J.H. 388
de la Mare, A.C. 35–6, 359, 395, 400,
    547
Della Corte, F. 241, 366, 369, 461, 472
Delz, J. 530
Dietz, H.F. von 56
Doering, F.W. 50, 53, 55–6, 280
Dousa, J. 54, 241
Drachmann, A.B. 290–1
Dyson, M. 227

Edgeworth, R.J. 424
Edwards, M.J. 204
Eisenhut, W. 59–60, 240, 524
Elder, J.P. 226
Ellis, R. 24–5, 50, 52–9, 234, 408, 425
Engelbrecht, A. 201
Eredità, G. dalle 30

Faernus, G. 52
Fasce, S. 382
Fedeli, P. 60, 348–50, 378–80, 521, 534
Ferrero, L. 461
Fink, R.O. 408
Fletcher, G.B.A. 248
Flobert, P. 428
Fordyce, C.J. 13, 59, 449, 472
Forehand, W.E. 390
Forsyth, P.Y. 47, 60, 278, 456
Foster, J. 337
Fraenkel, E. 231, 312, 370, 444, 529–30
Frazer, J.G. 372
Friedrich, G. 59, 197
Fröhlich, J. 404, 467, 481, 527, 531

Gaisser, J.H. 9, 24, 43–7, 49–55, 60,
    197, 203, 255, 261, 278, 311, 339, 379,
    381, 384, 396, 414, 497–8, 513, 524
Gamberale, L. 260

Gebhardus, J. 55
Genovese, E.N. 203
Geymonat, M. 393
Giangrande, G. 203, 398, 405, 437, 470
Giselinus, V. 241, 498
Glasgow, P. 213
Glenn, J. 380
Gnilka, C. 540, 544
Goold, G.P. 59–60, 211, 361, 395, 457,
    459, 534, 551
Goud, T. 364–5, 368–70
Granarolo, J. 4, 352
Grant, J.N. 406, 420
Gratwick, A.S. 317, 415
Gruen, E.S. 333
Grummond, W. de 549
Gruterus, J. 54
Gryphius, S. 48
Guarinus, A. 45, 49–51, 241, 247, 254,
    334, 336, 381, 395, 397, 455, 531
Guarinus, B. 45, 49, 201, 254, 397, 412,
    458, 461, 528
Guillemin, A.M. 371, 374
Gutzwiller, K. 463

Hale, W.G. 23, 28, 31, 35, 38, 58, 303
Hallett, J.P. 465
Handford, S.A. 227
Hansen, P. 456
Harvey, P.B. 552
Haupt, M. 57, 197, 263, 274, 353, 387,
    395, 451, 529, 549
Heck, B. 6
Heesakkers, C. 241
Heinsius, N. 515, 543
Heinze, R. 426
Helm, R. 3
Henry, R.M. 500
Herescu, N.I. 447, 511
Herrmann, L. 426
Herzog, R. 4

Hofmann, J.B. 223, 538
Holleman, A.W.J. 486
Holoka, J.P. 60
Hooper, R.W. 203
Horváth, I.K. 460
Housman, A.E. 210–11, 307, 363,
    418–19, 425, 429, 456, 484, 498
Howe, N.P. 537
Hubbard, M. 7, 230–1, 255, 480, 487

Irwin, M.E. 317, 424

Jackson, C.N. 402
Jocelyn, H.D. 203, 343
Jones, D.M. 512
Jungclaussen, W.T. 57

Kenney, E.J. 515
Kidd, D.A. 215, 366, 447–8, 455, 460,
    462–3
Killeen, J.F. 553
Kilpatrick, R.S. 243
Kinsey, T.E. 226, 388, 481
Kipps, C. 203
Kitchell, K.F. 510
Knobles, C. 380
Knopp, S.E. 427
Köhnken, A. 528
Kortekaas, G. 513
Kroll, W. 59, 556

Lachmann, K. 33, 56, 229, 304, 378–9,
    384, 456, 462–3, 480, 531, 551
Lafaye, G. 59–60, 457
Lambinus, D. 260, 427
La Penna, A. 453
Latte, K. 360
Laurens, P. 492
Lee, A.G. 60, 451, 467, 527, 534, 544
Legnago, A. da 30–2
Lenchantin, M. 59, 240, 334, 455, 500

Leo, F. 525
Lesky, A. 21
Levens, R.G.C. 58, 500, 511
Levin, D.N. 513
Lieberg, G. 346
Łinderski, J. 331
Lindsay, W.M. 23, 337
Lipsius, J. 488
Livineius, J. 55
Lloyd-Jones, H. 210
Lobel, E. 447
Longford, E. 237
Lovati, L. 25
Ludwig, W. 25
Luppino. R.A. 448
Lyne, R.O.A.M. 21–2

McFarlane, I.D. 51
McGushin, P. 545
McKie, D.S. 7, 24, 26–34, 36, 41–2, 44,
    206, 210, 220, 232–3, 237, 240, 249,
    262, 277, 288, 294, 306–7, 315, 323,
    338, 401, 409, 411–13, 415, 418–19,
    421, 423–4, 431–2, 453, 455, 457, 459,
    473, 511, 518
Macleod, C.W. 7
Madvig, J.N. 298, 468
Maffei, A. 35
Magnus, H. 536
Mähly, J.A. 248–9, 306, 352
Mantero, T. 486
Manutius, P. 50
Marcilius, T. 55, 427, 483
Marinone, N. 450–3, 456, 458–60, 462
Mariotti, S. 457
Markland, J. 322, 463
Marmorale, E. 4
Marshall, B.A. 513
Marshall, J.C.D. 533
Martyn, J.R.C. 456
Matthews, V.J. 405

May, G. 401
Mayer, R. 396
Merkel, R. 501
Merrill, E.T. 58–9, 395, 511
Mette, H.J. 213
Monbrun, M. 199
Montagnone, Geremia da 25, 307
Monteleone, C. 537
Morel, W. 303, 460
Morgan, M. Gwyn 222
Morris, E.P. 226–7
Most, G.W. 387
Mowat, J. 366
Müller, K. 301
Müller, L. 57
Mulroy, D. 375–6
Munro, H.A.J. 58, 246, 261, 353, 424,
    484
Muretus, M.A. 50–3, 55, 236, 255, 257,
    344, 346, 555
Mussato, A. 25–6, 32–3
Mynors, R.A.B. 59, 228, 240, 256, 260–
    1, 263, 274, 286, 323, 350, 352–3,
    (384), 395, 445, 457, 488, 525

Németh, B. 555
Neudling, C.L. 334
Nicastri, L. 447, 460
Niccoli, Niccolò 36
Nicholson, E.W.B. 23
Nisbet, R.G. 537
Nisbet, R.G.M. 203, 230–1, 234, 255,
    260, 272, 426, 452, 459, 480–1, 487,
    494, 513
Noceto, P. da 453
Noonan, J.D. 503
Norden, E. 198, 292, 399, 403, 406, 524
Novati, F. 33–4, 220

O'Connell, M. 395
Offermann, H. 481

Oksala, P. 371
Orsinus, F. 52
Otis, B. 19
Owen, S.G. 303, 359, 435, 501, 526

Palladius (Fuscus) 47, 49
Palmer, A. 58, 237, 253, 417, 501, 536
Panormita (Beccadelli, A.) 203, 241
Parrhasius, A.J. 49
Parroni, P.G. 60
Parthenius, A. 45–9, 351, 445, 497,
    524
Pascal, C. 59
Pascucci, G. 356
Pasoli, E. 200
Pasquali, G. 360
Passerat, J. 54–5
Pastrengo, G. da 25, 28, 197
Peacock, T.L. 431
Pease, A.S. 260
Peerlkamp. P.H. 397
Peeters, C. 328
Pellegrin, É. 30
Petrarch (Petrarca), F. 7, 25, 27–9, 41,
    197, 294, 306, 323, 415, 445
Pfeiffer, R. 447, 454–5, 457–8, 460
Pighi, G.B. 59
Pleitner, C. 553
Plessis, F. 4
Poggio (Bracciolini) 35–7, 547
Polentonus, Sicco 44
Politianus, A. 44–6, 48–9, 202–3, 255,
    379, 406, 455, 498, 513, 531
Pontanus, J.J. 49, 202–3, 241, 261, 334,
    513
Pope, A. 341
Posch, S. 502, 524
Postgate, J.P. 58
Postgate, P.E. 497
Powell, J. 247
Powell, J.U. 398

Puccius, F. 49–50, 334
Puelma, M. 395, 428, 434–5, 437
Puteolanus, F. 44–5
Putnam, M.C.J. 261, 461

Quinn, K. 7, 59, 478, 500, 530

Radke, A.E. 366
Rambaud, M. 3
Rambelli, G. 470
Realinus, B. 50, 55
Rebert, H.F. 226
Reece, B.R. 23
Rehm, B. 459
Reid, J.S. 468
Reitzenstein, R. 425, 430
Reynen, H. 486
Ribbeck, O. 57, 258
Ribuoli, R. 406
Richardson, B. 24, 49
Richardson, L. 336, 414, 469–70
Richmond, J.A. 395
Richmond, O.L. 411, 551
Riese, A. 58, 270, 337–8, 360, 390, 398,
    470
Robortellus, F. 50, 55, 384, 453
Ronconi, A. 254, 356
Ronsard, P. de 50
Ross, D.O. 22, 254, 352,
    376, 533
Rossbach, A. 57
Rudd, N. 236, 247, 252–3, 269–70
Ruhnken, D. 410

Sabellicus, M.A. (Coccius) 9, 47–8, 55,
    278, 396, 414
Salutati, Coluccio 28, 32–8, 42, 206,
    220, 228, 288, 302, 361, 393, 397, 402,
    412, 420, 533
Sandbach, F.H. 267
Sannazaro, J. 24

Santen, L. van 56
Sarkissian, J. 472
Scaliger, J.J. 9, 47, 52–5, 197, 228, 255, 280, 362, 468, 470, 488, 517
Schäfer. E. 371
Schmidt, B. 3–4, 58
Schmidt, E.A. 414
Schmiel, R. 226
Schnelle, I. 226
Schrader, J. 329, 358, 424
Schulze, K.P. 57–8, 367
Schulze, W. 541
Schuster, M. 59, 226–7, 524
Schwabe, L. 30, 57, 395, 549
Scott, R.D. 379
Seneca, T. 445
Sessa, M. 50
Sillig, I. 56–7
Skiadas, A.D. 492
Skinner, M.B. 436, 506, 540
Skutsch, F. 481
Skutsch, O. 196, 234, 337, 361, 377, 422
Smith, K.F. 468
Spengel, L. 368
Spira, V. de 43–4
Stark, F. 419
Statius, A. 34–5, 51–4, 197, 236, 255, 261, 273, 279, 412, 428, 456, 544
Stoessl, F. 499
Summonte, P. 24
Sumner, G.V. 3–4
Swanson, R.A. 226
Syme, R. 229, 348, 351
Syndikus, H.P. 60, 236

Tarrant, R.J. 60, 395
Tatham, G. 402
Tchernia, A. 272
Terzaghi, N. 16
Thomas, E. 58

Thomas, R.F. 20–1, 390–1, 394, 396, 401, 482
Thompson, D'Arcy W. 203
Thompson, E. Maunde 23, 237
Thomson, D.F.S. 35–6, 58, 60, 359, 381, 387, 400, 417, 543, 545, 547, 549
Thou, J.-A. de 24
Titius, R. 54
Tortzen, C.G. 456
Townend, G.B. 387, 390
Tozzi, P. 469
Traglia, A. 451, 458
Traill, D.A. 387
Traina, A. 387, 392–4
Tränkle, H. 529–30
Tuplin, C.J. 19

Ullman, B.L. 7, 23–5, 27, 30–1, 33, 35, 38, 44, 52, 56, 197, 232, 253, 294
Usener, H. 311

Vahlen, J. 395
Valerianus, P. 49, 51, 261
van Dam, H.-J. 215–6
Van Sickle, J. 482
Verrall, A.W. 246
Viarre, S. 60
Victorius (Vettori), P. 50–3, 257
Vine, B. 329
Vitelli, G. 447, 457
Vossius, I. 55, 267, 360, 451, 454–5, 539
Vretska, K. 472, 474
Vulpius, J.A. 55

Walsh, P.G. 252
Washburn, O.M. 31
Watson, L. 548
Watt, W.S. 403, 459, 480, 483
Weber, H. 369
Webster, T.B.L. 391

Weinreich, O. 346
Whatmough, J. 530–1
Wheeler, R.L. 226
Wickham, E.C. 277
Wilamowitz-Moellendorf, U. von 352,
    373, 383, 390, 436, 536
Wilhelm, F. 317
Wilkinson, L.P. 237
Williams, G.W. 195, 211, 281, 337, 359,
    486
Wiseman, T.P. 3, 6–11, 16, 60, 197,
    200, 203, 246–7, 250, 270–1, 284, 291,
    305, 320, 336–7, 348–9, 470, 472–3,
    476–7, 488, 504, 506, 523
Wistrand, E. 368
Wohlberg, J. 472
Wolff, G. 432
Woodman, Tony (A.J.) 247

Zetzel, J.E,G. 413
Zicàri, M. 29–30, 38, 44, 60, 195–6, 199,
    201–2, 258, 265, 395, 445, 455, 470,
    480, 508–9, 534, 536
Zwierlein, O. 24

PHOENIX SUPPLEMENTARY VOLUMES

1 *Studies in Honour of Gilbert Norwood* edited by Mary E. White

2 *Arbiter of Elegance: A Study of the Life and Works of C. Petronius* Gilbert Bagnani

3 *Sophocles the Playwright* S.M. Adams

4 *A Greek Critic: Demetrius on Style* G.M.A. Grube

5 *Coastal Demes of Attika: A Study of the Policy of Kleisthenes* C.W.J. Eliot

6 *Eros and Psyche: Studies in Plato, Plotinus, and Origen* John M. Rist

7 *Pythagoras and Early Pythagoreanism* J.A. Philip

8 *Plato's Psychology* T.M. Robinson

9 *Greek Fortifications* F.E. Winter

10 *Comparative Studies in Republican Latin Imagery* Elaine Fantham

11 *The Orators in Cicero's 'Brutus': Prosopography and Chronology* G.V. Sumner

12 *'Caput' and Colonate: Towards a History of Late Roman Taxation* Walter Goffart

13 *A Concordance to the Works of Ammianus Marcellinus* Geoffrey Archbold

14 *Fallax opus: Poet and Reader in the Elegies of Propertius* John Warden

15 *Pindar's 'Olympian One': A Commentary* Douglas E. Gerber

16 *Greek and Roman Mechanical Water-Lifting Devices: The History of a Technology* John Peter Oleson

17 *The Manuscript Tradition of Propertius* James L. Butrica

18 Parmenides of Elea *Fragments: A Text and Translation with an Introduction* edited by David Gallop

19 *The Phonological Interpretation of Ancient Greek: A Pandialectal Analysis* Vít Bubeník

20 *Studies in the Textual Tradition of Terence* John N. Grant

21 *The Nature of Early Greek Lyric: Three Preliminary Studies* R.L. Fowler

22 Heraclitus *Fragments: A Text and Translation with a Commentary* edited by T.M. Robinson

23 *The Historical Method of Herodotus* Donald Lateiner

578 Phoenix Supplementary Volumes

24 *Near Eastern Royalty and Rome, 100–30 BC*   Richard D. Sullivan

25 *The Mind of Aristotle: A Study in Philosophical Growth*   John M. Rist

26 *Trials in the Late Roman Republic, 149 BC to 50 BC*   Michael Alexander

27 *Monumental Tombs of the Hellenistic Age: A Study of Selected Tombs from the Pre-Classical to the Early Imperial Era*   Janos Fedak

28 *The Local Magistrates of Roman Spain*   Leonard A. Curchin

29 Empedocles *The Poem of Empedocles: A Text and Translation with an Introduction* edited by Brad Inwood

30 Xenophanes of Colophon *Fragments: A Text and Translation with a Commentary*   J.H. Lesher

31 *Festivals and Legends: The Formation of Greek Cities in the Light of Public Ritual* Noel Robertson

32 *Reading and Variant in Petronius: Studies in the French Humanists and Their Manuscript Sources*   Wade Richardson

33 *The Excavations of San Giovanni di Ruoti, Volume 1: The Villas and Their Environment*   Alastair M. Small and Robert J. Buck

34 *Catullus Edited with a Textual and Interpretative Commentary*   D.F.S. Thomson

35 *The Excavations of San Giovanni di Ruoti, Volume 2: The Small Finds* C.J. Simpson, with contributions by R. Reece and J.J. Rossiter

36 The Atomists: Leucippus and Democritus *Fragments: A Text and Translation with a Commentary*   C.C.W. Taylor

37 *Imagination of a Monarchy: Studies in Ptolemaic Propaganda*   R.A. Hazzard

38 *Aristotle's Theory of the Unity of Science*   Malcolm Wilson

39 Empedocles *The Poem of Empedocles: A Text and Translation with an Introduction, Revised edition*   edited by Brad Inwood

40 *The Excavations of San Giovanni di Ruoti, Volume 3: The Faunal and Plant Remains*   M.R. MacKinnon, with contributions by A. Eastham, S.G. Monckton, D.S. Reese, and D.G. Steele